The Life of
William Faulkner

BLACKWELL CRITICAL BIOGRAPHIES

General Editor: Claude Rawson

The Life of
WILLIAM FAULKNER
A Critical Biography

Richard Gray

BLACKWELL
Publishers

First published 1994
First published in paperback 1996

Blackwell Publishers Ltd
108 Cowley Road
Oxford OX4 1JF, UK

Blackwell Publishers Inc.
238 Main Street
Cambridge, Massachusetts 02142, USA

British Library Cataloguing in Publication Data
A CIP catalogue record for this book is available from the British Library

Library of Congress Cataloging in Publication Data
Gray, Richard J.
The life of William Faulkner: a critical biography / Richard Gray
p. cm. – (Blackwell critical biographies; 5)
Includes bibliographical references and index.
ISBN 0–631–16415–4 (hbk) — ISBN 0–631–20316–8 (pbk)
1. Faulkner, William, 1897–1962. 2. Novelists, American – 20th century –
Biography. I. Title. II. Series.
PS3511.A.86Z784127   1994
813'.52 – dc20   94–7566
[B]   CIP

Typeset in 10 on 11 pt Baskerville
by Graphicraft Typesetters Ltd, Hong Kong
Printed and bound in Great Britain by Hartnolls Ltd, Bodmin, Cornwall

This book is printed on acid-free paper

To Sheona

Contents

List of Illustrations

Preface

We are interested in the life of William Faulkner and the place and times he inhabited because he is among America's finest novelists. Perhaps he is the finest; I certainly think so. And this book is an attempt to understand Faulkner's novels in terms of his life, his place and his times. I have tried to enter into a dialogue with the fiction set in Faulkner's apocryphal county of Yoknapatawpha or elsewhere: a dialogue that involves reinserting him in history – and, in particular, in the histories of his family and his region. In the process, I have tried to explain that fiction to myself in a way that I hope will be useful to others, anyone wanting to know more about both texts and contexts; and I have also tried to show how Faulkner's books – like anyone's, really – brim with an often undisclosed biography that is at once personal and cultural. The novels speak to us of a man, their author, living in a particular environment at a specific point in time: with, as one of Faulkner's own characters might have put it, his own personal share of the world's 'passions and hopes and skeers'. They reveal an individual whose individuality stemmed, as ours does, from occupying a special moment in history: a moment that is by definition different from each of ours but one that is vitally related, if only because we, his readers, share many of the pressures, problems and the challenges that were his. The books tell us about Faulkner and, sometimes in secretive or convoluted ways, they tell us about ourselves as well. We may not be white, male and Southern as Faulkner was, or any one or combination of these; we are certainly living at another moment in time. But, to adapt a Faulknerian image, we are caught in the web, the pattern of history just as he was; and we can, I think, come to know more about ourselves and the places we occupy by seeing how, as a man and writer, Faulkner attempted to unravel that web – to talk about the particular terms on which life came to him, to understand them, contest and even to change them.

As Faulkner shows us in his work, time and again, no explanation is ever complete, no conversation is ever properly finished; we can never stop trying to understand. So my attempt to explain Faulkner's fiction in relation to his life and times will, I hope, be taken for what it is meant to be, and must be: notes of a work in progress, a contribution to a commentary that is theoretically endless, begun by other people before me and continuing long after the completion of this study. My aim, quite simply, has been to further the dialogue: to encourage other readers to talk about Faulkner's fiction for themselves – to learn from, engage and now and then quarrel with it. My own talking about Faulkner begins, in any event, with a chapter that is intended to offer some understanding of the terms on which the writer lived his life, what made the conditions of his world peculiarly his. In the first section, 'On Privacy: Faulkner and the Human Subject', I try to show how intimately woven together were the tangled threads of his personal and public experience – the privacy he cherished and the history in which, whether he liked it or not, he was ensnared. In the second, 'History as Autobiography: The World of Faulkner', I look at the place and times Faulkner inhabited, the American South of the first half of this century: an environment that, like any situated in the past, comes to us as a haunting blend of the strange and the familiar. Then in the third section of this opening chapter, 'Autobiography as History: The Life of Faulkner', I examine the other side of the same coin: the story of the Falkner clan, and the story of William Faulkner – two tales that, besides being inseparable, both carry along with them the burden of Southern history. The emphasis in these sections, the second and the third, is on what Henry James would call the figure in the carpet, or what Faulkner himself might term (in a phrase at once more exact and more evocative, I think) the old ineradicable rhythm: that is, on the fundamental passions and obsessions that fired writer and culture into life – animating them, inspiring them sometimes and, at others, debilitating or even crippling them. The facts in the case of William Faulkner, the particulars of his story, are, I hope, clear enough from the account I have given here of how those facts affected his material and moral life and helped shape the general contours of his writing. Those facts together with relevant dates are, in any case, also set out in the Chronology at the end of this book: beginning with the birth of Faulkner's great-grandfather, 'The Old Colonel', who cast such a spell over Faulkner's imagination, and ending with the writer's own death.

After the opening chapter, this book probably needs little further explanation here. Looking at the variety of writing that preceded Faulkner's first published novel, and then dwelling on each of the novels in order of publication, I try to talk about each text in terms of that old ineradicable rhythm. I try, in other words, to attend to each book as it in turn attends to the problems and opportunities that excited its author's imagination at the time: to read, and understand, the animating impulses, the determining movements of the writer's consciousness and culture. Many of the short stories come into this review: because of their revelatory nature, it may be – the clues they offer to the habits of Faulkner's mind – or because of their seminal character – the fact that they either supplied preliminary sketches of characters or incidents used in subsequent novels, or were actually incorporated into longer fictions later. But I have made no attempt to discuss every single one of Faulkner's shorter tales, along with every one of his novels: only those tales (and there are quite a few of them) that are, in my opinion, vital to an understanding of the writer's creative practice and his imaginative inclinations. Perhaps I should add here that, as the reader will discover later, the term 'novel' is itself a contentious one in Faulkner criticism: *Go Down, Moses*, for instance, was first published as *Go Down Moses and Other Stories*, *The Unvanquished* consists of stories written and in most cases first published separately, and, besides, the very nature of Faulkner's imagination pushed him towards the clash of quite separate fictive planes – the multiplication of different narratives within the confines of a single book. I have not attempted to answer here the prickly, and probably unanswerable, question of just what is and is not a novel. I have simply concentrated my attention, after looking at that seed-bed of ideas and images that is the work of the young pre-novelist, on those books that are normally categorized as novels in the Faulkner canon – or perhaps it would be more accurate to say, those volumes that are not normally categorized as collections of disparate short stories. Some of these books I have, inevitably I suppose, found more convincing and satisfying than others: more successful in confronting the problems and exploiting the opportunities that were the given, rough terrain of Faulkner's life. I hope, though, that even when I have found more to question in particular volumes the reader will take this as part of the dialogue: a reading of Faulkner's fiction that is founded on a belief in that fiction's power not only to invite but actively to compel knowledge. I started from the conviction that Faulkner's work has more to tell us than most about ourselves as human subjects and historical agents; and that conviction has steadily grown, as I have come to understand more about both the work and the life out of which it was carved. In short, I have learned from Faulkner's books as he seems to have expected his readers would: by attending, certainly, but also by arguing – by listening to the old tales and talking that resonate through his narratives and then adding my own talking, my own measure of thought and debate.

In the course of reading and talking about Faulkner and the histories, personal and social, he was required to confront, I have had the benefit of what some literary theorists have to tell us about the relationship between writing and historical experience, language and social change. And there are many other debts besides the one to certain literary theorists: debts that go back a long way and, perhaps, go even deeper. I first became interested in the work of Faulkner over thirty years ago. An American friend encouraged me to read *The Sound and the Fury*: and, in doing so, she initiated an involvement, a fascination with both that writer and the region from which he came, the South, that has never shown signs of waning. My first visit to the South was, as it happens, two or three years after my initial reading of Faulkner when, thanks to the generosity of the Commonwealth Fund, I spent two years in the United States. The journey across the Atlantic was by boat (which may in itself be an indication of just how long ago it was!). It was early autumn, and most of my fellow passengers were Americans returning from their holidays in Europe. None of the Americans I spoke to turned out to be from the South; and, whenever I told them where I was going, the reaction hardly varied at all. 'Oh, that's a different country', most would say, or words to that effect; while a few others would simply confess ignorance of the region, perhaps adding that they *had* driven through the South while on their way to Florida. I doubt that I would get exactly the same reactions now. Thanks to the Civil Rights movement, among other things, and the economic transformation of the South (or, rather, parts of it) into the Sunbelt, the region is no longer as different, in fact or perception, as it once was. Still, regardless of whether or not any measure of difference survives (and, in my opinion, it does), the South *was* different once: it was different, not least, when the Falkner clan settled in Mississippi and while William Faulkner was growing up there. The nature of that difference, as it conditioned the writer's experience and coloured his writing, is something I have tried to explain in this book. And it was of that quality of being different that I really began to learn during my first visit to the region, and that I have been learning about ever since. '*Tell about the South*', asks a character in *Absalom, Absalom!*, the Canadian Shreve, '*What's it like there. What do they do there. Why do they live there. Why do they live at all?*' The many colleagues and friends who responded, constantly and with generosity, to my own variations on these questions are owed a particular debt of gratitude, whether I met them on that first visit to the South or later. They include Bob Brinkmeyer, Richard King, Dan Patterson, Carter Martin, Helen Taylor, Tjebbe Westendorp and Dan Young. Also to be included among those who told me about the South, whom I thank for their advice, instruction and in some cases friendship, are Tony Badger, Dan Carter, Jan Gretlund, Jack Temple Kirby, Michael O'Brien, Louis D. Rubin and Bertram Wyatt-Brown.

As far as understanding the life of Faulkner is concerned, anyone who ventures into this field owes a profound debt to Joseph Blotner, whose massive two-volume biography and later one-volume edition (abbreviated, but also with new material) offer a mine of information and critical insight. My thanks are due to him and to the many other critics and scholars who have helped me to know more about Faulkner the man, Faulkner the Southerner and Faulkner the novelist. They include several of the people just mentioned, who told me about the South, but there are many others as well. Some of them I know only from their work: David Minter, Philip Weinstein, Judith Wittenberg. Others I know both from their work and from meetings with them that have, in some instances, developed into friendship: André Bleikasten, Thadious Davis, Susan Donaldson, Richard Godden, Lothar Hönnighausen, Anne Goodwyn Jones, John T. Matthews,

Thomas McHaney, Noel Polk and Diane Roberts. To all of them a debt is owed, and warmly acknowledged, here. And in some instances there are further reasons for gratitude. Some of those people who told me about the South, about Faulkner, or both, have also commented on various drafts of all or part of this book. With them, the usual prefatory disclaimer has a very particular meaning, although it broadly applies to everyone who has helped me: what may be good or at least helpful in this study owes a lot to other people, while the faults and omissions are all my own work.

Some of the advice I have received in the course of writing this book was given during my visits to Faulkner's homeplace of Oxford, Mississippi. My initial debt here is to the British Academy, thanks to whose generosity I was able to spend a summer in Oxford, and to the University of Essex, which provided me with sufficient funds to pursue further research in Mississippi, at the University of Virginia in Charlottesville, and elsewhere. I would like to thank those institutions, and the librarians at the universities of Mississippi and Virginia, for their assistance. Other comments and criticism, as I prepared this study, came after the delivery of papers based on earlier versions of some part or other of a particular chapter. In one form or another, portions of this book were offered in this way at the annual Faulkner conference in Oxford, Mississippi, the International Conferences in Southern Studies in Genoa and Bonn, and at the universities of North Carolina (Chapel Hill), Louisiana (Baton Rouge) and Alabama (Huntsville). I wish to express my gratitude to the organizers of those conferences and my hosts at those universities for the opportunity given to me to test some of my ideas out on an informed audience. In and around Oxford, I would also like to express special thanks to all those people, academics, experts and locals, who gave me advice and information: Ann Abadie, Larry Brown, Tommy Covington, Bill Ferris, Doreen Fowler, Evans Harrington, Greg Schirmer and Charles Reagan Wilson are just a few of them.

Nearer home, I want to thank the colleagues and friends I have met over the years at Essex who have helped me towards what little I know about Faulkner and the South. They include Herbie Butterfield, George Dekker, Cherry Good, Sally Keenan, John Rabbetts, Kate Rhodes and the many students who have taken courses with me on Southern writing or Faulkner. To my older daughter and son I owe some special debts. My daughter Catharine has helped me towards an appreciation of feminist criticism; my son Ben has also been gainfully employed in stopping – or, at least, trying to stop – my intellectual arteries from hardening. The last debt of gratitude is the dearest: to my wife, Sheona. During the course of my writing this book, she has produced our two children, Jessica and Jack: which puts this product of my own labours firmly in its place. She has given me support through difficult times, listened patiently to my interminable accounts of how the book was going, and allowed me to know real peace and contentment. Towards the end of his life Faulkner declared, 'I live up to my arse in delightful family', and, thanks above all to her, I know precisely what he meant. Without her, this book could never have been embarked upon, let alone written: which is why, quite naturally, her name appears on the dedication page.

RICHARD GRAY

Wivenhoe

1

Fictions of History: An Approach to Faulkner

I ON PRIVACY: FAULKNER AND THE HUMAN SUBJECT

In 1949, when he was finally beginning to receive the kind of public recognition he deserved, William Faulkner wrote this to the critic Malcolm Cowley:

> It is my ambition to be, as a private individual, abolished and voided from history, leaving it markless, no refuse save the printed books; I wish I had had enough sense to see ahead thirty years ago and, like some of the Elizabethans, not signed them. It is my aim, and every effort bent, that the sum and history of my life, which in the same sentence is my obit and epitaph too, shall be them both: He made the books and he died.[1]

There are several ways of reading this. One, and perhaps the simplest, is to see it as a pose. Faulkner's claim that he either was or wanted to be 'the last private individual on earth' could be seen as just that: a claim, with little or no foundation in actual experience. Faulkner played many roles in his life – the effete, bohemian aristocrat, the wounded war hero, the farmer unkempt in body and mind, the red-coated, stiff-backed huntsman on horseback – and it could be argued, without much difficulty, that this obsessive, widely proclaimed pursuit of privacy was no more than another change of clothes, a further way of allowing Faulkner to enact his identity, to turn his experiencing self into a performing self. The Falkner clan, their neighbours often felt, were 'show-offs', a histrionic group of people: one had only to look at the eight-foot likeness of Faulkner's great-grandfather, Colonel William Clark Falkner, that towered above his grave – dominating its surroundings – in Ripley, Mississippi, to appreciate that. And if so many of Faulkner's family were ready to strike a pose or play a part, including Faulkner himself, then possibly they were only carrying a local tendency to extremes. An aristocratic culture, the historian J.M. Huizinga has observed, is one in which people *imitate* some idea of aristocracy, an 'illusion of heroic being, full of dignity and honour, of wisdom and, at all events, of courtesy'. The South, both before and after the Civil War, wanted desperately to see itself as aristocratic; and, to this extent, many white Southerners were ready to turn themselves into actors: to adopt the aristocratic pose and so reinvent themselves as gentlemen and ladies. Part of this pose could and did involve aloofness, a *hauteur* that at once invited admiring attention and discouraged curiosity: approval, or even wonder, was what was required rather than intimacy. 'Privacy', as invoked by the person laying claim to special, aristocratic status, became, in effect, a strategy for transmuting personality into performance; the actor was not literally to be left alone but viewed from a respectful distance, as he or she carried out a series of masterly, and mainly evasive, gestures.

To stop there, however, or to suggest, as one commentator has, that Faulkner's pursuit of inaccessibility was simply a ruse, a device for making himself more mysterious, more desirable, is hardly to do justice to the fierceness of his devotion to his own company. At his most polemical, Faulkner was even inclined to identify the entire project of America with the idea of privacy. His essay 'On Privacy', for example, is sub-titled '(The American Dream: What Happened to It?)'; and it fluctuates between fierce denunciations of institutional forces that seem bent on violating 'individualness' and simpler, but no less heartfelt, complaints about the inquisitiveness and insensitivity of journalists. Without 'individual privacy', Faulkner testily argued, there was no 'individuality', and without individuality there was 'not anything at all worth the having and keeping'; so privacy, in a sense, becomes the significant basis of life. 'The qualities of individualism whose possession we boast since they alone differ us from animals – gratitude for kindness, fidelity to friendship, chivalry toward women and the capacity for love':[2] these, he insisted, depend on a respect for distance, an absolute refusal to 'strip' the individual 'naked of the privacy' that alone saved him from degenerating into 'one more identityless integer in that identityless anonymous unprivacied mass which seems to be our goal'. The violence of the language perhaps alerts us to the extremity of the commitment: a respect for privacy becomes a ritual of deference, with sexual overtones ('chivalry toward women'), and, conversely, the lack of respect is associated with an act of violation. To preserve privacy is to keep the body of the subject intact, inviolate; to deny it is to turn subject into object, to ignore or resist the otherness of the other person in the belief that no corner of the personality is unavailable for immediate conquest and appropriation.

Faulkner's rejection of the kind of moral imperialism that, as he saw it, the failure of privacy entails carried certain significant consequences. In his life, it led to the assumption of personae, formulaic answers to interviewers, and the reinvention of his own past history. The roles, already referred to, permitted him to express specific aspects of his character and impulses but through a glass darkly, as it were, shaded by or distorted in the flamboyant details of the performance. The aristocratic dandy of his adolescence, for instance, was a convenient means of dramatizing his uneasy, ambiguous relationship to his homeplace. Like many others in Oxford, Mississippi, and in the South, he was at home and yet not at home in the modern world: compelled to inhabit a bourgeois, utilitarian culture that only minimally answered his emotional needs.[3] Unlike most of them, however, he responded to this compulsion by exaggerating his difference from *everyone*, including those who shared his uncertainties: in his clothes, the arts he favoured, and in his air of almost aggressive indolence. A pose like this at once expressed a part of his personality and kept the rest hidden: it was, simultaneously, a form of self-exposure and of conceal-ment. It allowed communication, even revelation, but it also preserved a measure of anonymity: the audience, observing such a performance, could learn something about the performer but were made aware that, in the final analysis, he remained apart, separate and private.

Similar strategies were at work in Faulkner's behaviour towards inter-viewers. Very early on in his career, he adopted what one interviewer in 1931 termed a 'barrier' to protect 'the sensitive part of him'. He was capable of what a later interviewer was to call 'the most exquisite but the most obdurate politeness' as a weapon for fending off unwelcome inquir-ies. 'That famous wall' of exquisite *politesse* was only one of many ma-noeuvres, though. Simple 'shyness and defensiveness' was another, a nervousness that, as one observer saw it, 'places an interviewer on his honour not to probe forbidden areas'.[4] Alternatively, Faulkner would fall back on obduracy and irony, claiming 'I prefer silence to sound' or that 'an artist shouldn't talk too much'. 'He is not a great talker,' one per-plexed and clearly defeated interviewer opined, 'in fact he is not a talker at all.' This comment would have surprised some of those closest to Faulkner, familiar as they were with his skill at storytelling or willingness to quote poetry at the drop of a hat. And, in any event, it sat uneasily with Faulkner's own claim that Southerners 'love to talk' because, as he put it, 'oratory is our heritage'. Sometimes, disingenuousness of the kind Faulkner reserved for certain interviewers would spin off into tall tales and comic *bravura*. In 1931, for instance, in an interview with a Memphis reporter, the writer made wry fun of his own reluctance to reveal too much about himself by offering this brief autobiographical sketch:

> I was born male and single at an early age in Mississippi. I am still alive but not single. I was born of a Negro slave and an alligator, both named Gladys Rock. I had two brothers, one Dr. Walter E. Traprock and the other Eagle Rock, an airplane.[5]

In response to persistent questioning about his books Faulkner would frequently insist that he was a farmer, not a literary man. Or he would declare that there were many things he would rather be than a profession-al writer: a tramp perhaps, the landlord of a brothel (with plenty of free time in the day and plenty of company and conversation in the evening), or even a buzzard. 'Nothing hates him or envies him or wants him or needs him', he said of the buzzard. 'He is never bothered or in danger, and he can eat everything.' Finally, if such deadpan evasiveness did not work, and the interviewer seemed determined to go home with something apparently substantial in his notebook, Faulkner would be ready to fall back on set-piece answers and formulaic phrases: about man enduring and prevailing, about a writer's responsibility to tell the truth and the difference between 'facts' and 'truth', about the books that were 'old friends' (*Don Quixote, Moby Dick, Huckleberry Finn, Madam Bovary* and *The Brothers Karamazov* were invariably included in this catalogue) and the great writers whom he believed were his 'masters'. In terms of their empirical details, none of these answers was untrue: even the weariest catalogue or the most clichéd formula was rooted, in the end, in a fiercely held opinion or commitment, just as the tallest tale or wildest *jeu d'esprit* had its ultimate source in some significant part of Faulkner's dreams, his fantasy life. It was just that, as with the role-playing, Faulkner was withholding as much as he was giving away; he was willing to surrender only on terms that enabled him to retreat with dignity – with a sense of his own privacy intact.

And then there was the lying. The legends nurtured by Faulkner about his piloting experiences are perhaps the most memorable instance of this. Anxious to be a pilot, Faulkner joined the Royal Air Force in Canada and was posted to Toronto to be trained. This was an important moment for him, since he believed in both the courage and the sexuality of flight: the pilot figured for him – as it did for many of his contemporaries – simultaneous and, to some extent, self-contradictory notions of military honour, individual daring, mastery of machinery and death, limitless freedom, and erotic conquest. Unfortunately, the dream was never realized; the war was over before he had completed his training; he may never even have had a flight in a plane, let alone served in action. Unimpeded by the facts, however, Faulkner proceeded to construct a personal myth. He wrote home about the stimulation of soloing and 'joy rides' and about crashing his plane upside down in the rafters of a hangar. Discharged as a cadet, he nevertheless purchased an officer's uniform before returning to Mississippi, complete with swagger stick; he then wore this on the train home despite the fact that, even if he had been entitled to wear it, regulations restricted the wearing of it to military occasions; and he arrived at Oxford railway station limping, having acquired a mythical war wound to complete his identity as hero of the air. By the time Faulkner moved to New Orleans, in 1925, he had even adopted a second wound, in the evident belief that no hero could have too many. His brother Jack had been injured by shrapnel while in France and severely wounded in the head; and, among his friends in New Orleans, Faulkner claimed a similar injury – some of those friends, including the writer Sherwood Anderson, even believed that the young man from Mississippi had had a steel plate inserted in his skull. As the years passed, the legend grew: he had crashed *two* planes during the war, costing the British government £4000, he had been dragged out more dead than alive from the wreck of his plane with not one but *both* legs broken. It was almost thirty years, in fact, before Faulkner felt inclined to trim the fantasy. In 1946, when Malcolm Cowley was preparing the introduction to the *Portable Faulkner*, Faulkner began to renege on his reinvention of his own history. 'If you mention military experience at all,' he told Cowley, who was planning to include some biographical notes, 'say "belonged to RAF 1918".' 'I could have invented a few failed RAF airmen', he added ominously, in parenthesis, 'as easily I did Confeds.' He would not disclose the truth, however, that he had lied consistently and magnificently. The closest he would come to candour, in response to Cowley's repeated desire to incorporate tales of military daring into the story, was this angry and desperate plea:

> You're going to bugger up a fine dignified distinguished book with that war business . . . If, because of some later reference back to it in the piece, you cant omit all European war reference, say only what Who's Who say, and no more:

> Was a member of the RAF in 1918.[6]

Faulkner, was, as usual, willing to go only so far in the name of self-revelation: even when he felt, as he evidently did in this case, that he was standing in the tribunal of history. His lies were important to him, not only because they were inseparably linked to the fictive impulse that helped him create, among other things, all the young pilots of his stories, but because they too were a means of strictly partial disclosure. In rehearsing his life as an air ace, Faulkner was telling and not telling; he was offering lies like truth in order to expose a deeper truth – about the desires and anxieties provoked in him by what he saw as the male role. 'A book is the writer's secret life', declares a character in *Mosquitoes*, 'the dark twin of a man': the terms could just as easily be reversed, under the pressure of Faulkner's tendency simultaneously to reveal and to conceal. For him, life frequently became a book on which he inscribed his secret struggle with a darker, more potent and dangerous, twin whom he both longed and feared to embrace.

'I think that a writer is a perfect case of split personality', Faulkner remarked once; and, with Faulkner himself, that split was not only demonstrable in his life but in his writing. He enacted an urge simultaneously to expose and to hide in his books as much as in his behaviour in Oxford and elsewhere. One crucial way he did this brings us right back to the issue of privacy, as he addressed that issue with reference to his characters and their voices. 'Just talk to people', Faulkner gave as his advice to the aspiring writer in one early interview. 'I listen to the voices', he said elsewhere, 'and when I put down what the voices say, it's right.' This was the initial and seminal moment in the act of creation for him: hearing the voice of another, separate if imagined, person trying to explain and, then, reproducing that speech as writing, whether that speech might be public or private, conversation or talking to oneself. An act of possession or appropriation was implicit here, of course: Faulkner was not above declaring of his characters, 'These people . . . belong to me' in the belief that, since he had given them voice and imaginative identity, he owned them, they were his. But, more often than not, he took what might seem a curiously, even naïvely, detached attitude to what, after all, were the products of his own imaginings. 'Any character that you write takes charge of his own behaviour', he declared, 'You can't make him do things once he comes alive and stands up and casts his shadow.' 'In general he has a very objective attitude toward his writings,' one commentator observed in 1932, 'and seems to take them as facts of nature, like the rain, about which one does not feel impelled to pass judgement, good or bad.'[7]

This observation is, perhaps, not quite right. Faulkner was perfectly willing to offer judgements on his books and characters. The point was not so much that he did not offer judgements but, rather, that they were offered in a decidedly unauthoritative and detached way: as if they carried no more weight than the opinions of any other 'simple private individual'. 'I don't remember the books', Faulkner insisted, 'Once I have written them they no longer belong to me.' It was the book and its characters that mattered, he argued time and again, not the author; or, as he put it, 'The artist is of no importance. Only what he creates is important.' So, if he offered opinions about characters like Jason Compson in *The Sound and the Fury* (the character he disliked most, he admitted) or Dilsey Gibson in *The Sound and the Fury* and V.K. Ratliff in *The Hamlet, The Town* and *The Mansion* (his favourites, he declared), he did so only in the same spirit as he ventured comments on other characters in other books written by other people. If he wished to pass an observation on one of his novels, he did so in the spirit of a reader who somehow possessed a separate identity from the writer: *The Sound and the Fury*, he wrote to his great-aunt, was 'the damndest book I ever read' – almost as if this came to him as a surprise. Receiving an essay from a professor of English on 'William Faulkner and the Social Conscience', Faulkner wrote back to him referring to the subject in the third person: 'I agree with it', he confided, 'I mean, re Faulkner's aim.' Asked if Charles Bon in *Absalom, Absalom!* ever suspected who his father was, he responded much more speculatively than most critics of the novel have. 'I think he knew', Faulkner said, 'I don't know whether he – his mother probably told him. I think he knew . . .'[8] In effect, Faulkner was denying the authority of authorship: once the characters 'grew up' and 'escaped the nest' (as he put it once), they assumed their own status as independent subjects.

At times, Faulkner was willing to push this insistence on the private nature and independent voice of his characters to extremes. In a very early interview, for example, he argued that the best way to keep character separate from the author was more or less to eliminate the author altogether. 'Mr. Faulkner had the very interesting idea', recalled the interviewer, centring about the thesis that Dostoevski could have written the *Brothers* in one third the space had he let the characters tell their own stories instead of filling page after page with exposition.[9]

'The character, the rhythm of the speech, compels its own dialect', Faulkner insisted elsewhere; self-revelation, with all its strange mixture of intimacy and secrecy was perhaps best left as the responsibility of each individual voice. This was, as so often with Faulkner, a partial truth, concealing as much as it revealed. In the first place, remarks about how Dostoevski might have written *The Brothers Karamazov* so as to compress and improve it sound like pure mischief, another example of Faulkner's delight in deadpan irony, when it is recalled that the book was always listed among his four or five favourites: into which, he said, he would dip again and again, 'just as you'd meet and talk to a friend for a few minutes'. In the second, a recommendation that 'characters tell their own stories' tends to play down the significance of *inner* speech for Faulkner: 'talk' for him was a matter not just of the subtle manoeuvres and rituals of everyday conversation but also of the voices a person hears within him as he struggles to emerge into identity through words. And, in the third place, nothing that Faulkner might say about the 'dead weight' of the author – and the need to eliminate him in the interests of the 'objective presentation' of something like 'play technique' – can hide the fact that the authorial voice is there in his narratives: not, usually, as an authoritative discourse but as one voice among many.

Faulkner's reference to Dostoevski, in this context, is especially and oddly relevant: because, for all his occasional, disparaging references to 'page after page' of exposition, his practice was very similar to that of the author of *The Brothers Karamazov*. Faulkner has frequently been described as 'the Dostoevski of the South': but this, more often than not, has been taken to imply a shared interest in themes of alienation and dispossession. There is another side to this connection, however, this 'spiritual kinship' (to borrow a phrase Faulkner himself used) and it has to do with the fundamentals of the two writers' imaginative projects. In his book, *Problems of Dostoevski's Poetics*, Mikhail Bakhtin argued that Dostoevski was the creator of a new form, 'the polyphonic novel'. What distinguishes this form, Bakhtin suggested, is that 'a character's word about himself and his world is just as fully weighted as the author's word usually is'. The voice or word of the character is not subordinated to the voice or word of the author; on the contrary, it 'sounds, as it were, *alongside* the author's word' combining 'both with it and with the full and equally valid voices of the other characters'.[10] 'A world of autonomous subjects, not objects' is consequently created: a dialogue of voices that engage on an equal basis with each other. There is no privileging of the author: each character, realized in terms of speech, is allowed the fundamental right of being active and apart – in Faulkner's own special terms, his privacy.

Several things need to be emphasized about Bakhtin's notion of the polyphonic novel, and its relationship to Faulkner's creative practice. A crucial one, perhaps the most crucial, is that, as Bakhtin perceives it and Faulkner practises it, dialogue does not just occur *between* voices but also *within* them. 'Our ... speech is full of other people' words', Bakhtin argued. We can therefore no more escape from dialogue, even in conversation with ourselves, than a character like Quentin Compson in *The Sound and the Fury* (or, for that matter, *Absalom, Absalom!*) can forget the voice of his father. This point about the dialogic nature of even interior discourse is another way of saying that language is social – and that, in turn, human life, which is constituted by language, is inseparable from historical life. The paradox is that we exist *apart*, as autonomous subjects and authors of our own discourse, and as *part* of what Bakhtin called 'a speaking collective' from whom our words are derived and to whom, however implicitly, they are addressed. 'Two voices are the minimum for life', to put it in Bakhtin's terms; or 'it takes two to make the book, the poem', to use Faulkner's. Even Benjy Compson in *The Sound and the Fury*, in order to 'be', has to engage in 'trying to say' (as Benjy himself puts it): he has to exist in a dialogue that he cannot literally have – because he is an idiot, with the mental age of an infant, and cannot articulate – since without words he cannot be there, not only for author and readers but for himself. As with all Faulkner's so-called 'interior monologues', the supposed monologist is actually engaged in a dialogue because (to quote Bakhtin again),

> No member of a verbal community can ever find words in the language that are neutral, exempt from the aspirations and evaluations of the other, uninhabited by the other's voice.[11]

Not only simultaneously inner and outer, personal and social, language is, according to these definitions, an open system, a 'mobile medium' that resists closure. 'Each individual utterance', Bakhtin observed, 'is a link in the chain of speech communication'; and, by its very nature, that chain is of indefinite length or duration, it can have no beginning or end. The possibility of a final, finalizing discourse is consequently excluded, along with the claims of an authoritative one. Even questions of personal identity, 'Who am I?' or 'Who are *you*?' are drawn into 'a continuous and open-ended ... dialogue': a chain of speech communication that is a process rather than a product. Even the vast sprawl of the Yoknapatawpha series is no more, and no less, than what Bakhtin would call a 'great dialogue' or 'open dialogue', in which 'the object is precisely *the passing of a theme through many and various voices*'[12] – rather, that is, than any terminal or even tentative conclusion.

The relevance in detail of all this to the fiction must be left for the moment, however; all that can be mentioned for now is the broader implications of these notions of voice both to the literature and to the life. As far as the literature is concerned, some of these implications have been hinted at already. In Faulkner's narratives, set in Yoknapatawpha or else-where, character is irrevocably private and yet implicated in history, a complex web of *social* relations: a paradox that is registered in the rhythms and inner dynamics of each individual voice. And the narratives them-selves operate within an equally complex web of *intertextual* relations: as a result of which each book or story, while constituting its own system of languages, exists in dialogic contact with other systems, other books in the series. Each of Faulkner's texts, in these respects, enacts his special notion of 'privacy', as a mode or activity of simultaneous disclosure and conceal-ment. The voices *within* the text and the voices *of* the text assert, by their very nature, both connection (I can only speak to you by inhabiting the same 'speaking collective' as you) and withdrawal (I can only speak to you by being other than you). They remind us, as Faulkner constantly re-minded his interlocutors, that 'a speaking human being' is at once situ-ated in a common verbal culture and set apart in his own verbal space: he is, as it were, a member of a club with certain tacit rules of linguistic exchange – but a member with his own private membership card, his own ticket of entry inscribing his difference.

It is perhaps worth observing, in passing, that these notions, as they inhabit Bakhtin's thought and Faulkner's practice, are inseparable from the idea of historical change. 'Language, discourse', Bakhtin observed, '. . . is almost the totality of human life', it is constitutive of human exist-ence. And 'language', he added, 'is something that is historically real': 'the entire part of human existence', as he put it once, 'does not belong to the individual but to his *social group* (his social environment)'.[13] Faulkner would have, almost certainly, resisted the particular verbal formulations Bakhtin favoured. He was, after all, a member of a quite separate 'speak-ing collective': he entered into history on radically different terms. Never-theless, it is not difficult to see how much he shares similar priorities: how much for him, too, meaning or communication is a matter of active, communal use. Communication, in Faulkner's work, implies community. Concretely, one always uses a language inhabited by the voice of another and addressed to another (actual or imagined) who does not assume a purely passive role but participates in the formation of meaning. Different voices – heard in the courthouse square perhaps or heard in the head – create identification, struggle for power, collude, collaborate and conflict in the process of understanding and explanation. They engage actively in what Bakhtin called 'the *social* dynamics' of speech; and, in doing so, they themselves and 'the whole complex *social* situation' in which this engage-ment occurs are crucially and irrevocably altered.

Faulkner was, as it happened, acutely (if intuitively) aware of the dialogic nature of his involvement with language and culture: just how much his understanding of speech and habits of behaviour were a matter of reci-procity and exchange. He was, as he never tired of saying, 'present yet detached' in his culture. This was not merely a love of paradox on his part, nor just a product of the situation of crisis that he shared with others of his generation – particularly writers, and especially Southern ones. It was related, crucially, to his sense that he was carrying on a conversation with systems of speech and value that were important to him: a conversation in which he had to play the part of double agent, a person whose collaboration was a form of subversion – who engaged with a system in a critical, even alienated, way but always, as it happened, from within. 'By Southern Rhetoric out of Solitude' was one of his formulations for explaining the nature of his style: by which he meant, he explained, that the style was 'the result of solitude, and . . . was further complicated by an inherited regional or geographical (Hawthorne would say, racial) curse'. 'You might say', he added 'studbook style: "by . . . Oratory out of Solitude".'[14] Such a formulation did two things at once: it laid claim to privacy and it also paid off a debt to his public situation. It acknowledged the fact that, as he saw it, his writing project was personal and social at the same time. And it did so, ultimately, by finding the definitive human activity in speech: the interchange between separate yet mutually involved voices.

The significance of voices for Faulkner can hardly be exaggerated. When he thought about it, in fact, he tended to associate speech with the fall into history. 'All evil and grief of this world stems from the fact that mankind talks', he declared; 'speech is mankind's curse', he added, 'just too goddam many of the human race . . . talk too much'. Remarks like this came naturally to a man who could insist, with apparently perfect candour, that he liked 'peace and quiet' or who could claim, 'I've spent almost fifty years trying to cure myself of the curse of human speech.' But they need to be set in the context of his reluctance to talk about his work to interviewers and critics: his books, he felt, did his talking for him and anything he might say about them would simply add one more, meddling and distinctly unauthoritative, voice. And they need to be set beside his admissions of his compulsive 'need to talk'. His voice, and other human voices, could perhaps produce 'evil', but that was because it was the voice that made human beings distinctively human: it was through it that men and women entered into consciousness of self and community and so into the potentiality of deliberate, moral action. 'I achieve consciousness', Bakhtin remarked,

> I am conscious of myself and become myself only while revealing myself for another, through another, and with the help of another. . . . To be means to be for another, and through the other, for oneself.[15]

As Bakhtin saw it, and as Faulkner sensed it, the Biblical Fall was a fall into speech: into the articulation of self and other, the ability to speak the words, 'I' and 'thou'. Identity, history and the need to talk became, in this context, coextensive; as long as human beings survived, they would retain their voices and therefore their capacity for doing evil and good. 'When the last ding-dong of doom has clanged and faded', Faulkner declared in his Nobel Prize acceptance speech,

from the last worthless rock hanging tideless in the last red and dying evening
then there will still be one more sound: that of his puny inexhaustible voice,
still talking.[16]

Or, as he put it in less grandiose terms elsewhere:

The last sound on the worthless earth will be two human beings trying to
launch a homemade space ship and already quarreling about where they are
going next.[17]

Voices within and voices without, talking that occurs inside human beings
and talking that happens between them: the entire process of a life history
assumes, in these terms, a special character – as a seamless pattern of
dialogue. The individual human being enters into a conversation, active
and re-active, with the whole complex web of relations that constitutes his
moment in space and time. The figure of the web, or pattern, is chosen
advisedly because it was one favoured by both Faulkner and Bakhtin when
they were trying to explain what, as they saw it, was the status of the
individual utterance within the labyrinth of conflicting voices that constitute
human history. Here, first, is Bakhtin:

The living utterance, having taken its meaning and shape at a particular
historical moment in a socially specific environment, cannot fail to brush up
against thousands of living dialogic threads . . . it cannot fail to become an
active participant in social dialogue.[18]

And here, for comparison, is a relevant passage from *Absalom, Absalom!* It
is attributed to one of the characters, Judith Sutpen, and, like all of the
voices in Faulkner's novels, it is hardly authoritative. Nevertheless, it signals one possible response to the plurality of voices that define the book's
structure; and, in that sense, it is closer to the heart of the matter, the crux
of the argument, than most remarks of this kind are:

you are born at the same time with a lot of other people, all mixed up with
them . . . all trying to make a rug on the same loom only each one wants to
weave his own pattern into the rug: and it cant matter, you know that, or the
Ones that set up the loom would have arranged things a little better, and
yet it must matter because you keep on trying or having to keep on trying.[19]

Clearly, the Faulkner passage offers us a more passionate perception, partly
because the voice that speaks here turns what Bakhtin describes as a
participative process into a devouringly destructive one, to be resisted or,
at the very least, feared. But what both voices engage with here is seen as
an historical inevitability – human experience as a kind of feverish debate
in which each participant, eagerly or otherwise, struggles to make himself
heard. The struggle is particularly difficult because the terms in which he
speaks are mediated by others. The voice that fights for a private identity

is, in sum, for all that it searches for privacy, a public one; it is inextricably interwoven with the speech that surrounds it, shaped by voices talking before and after.

Which means that, if we are ever to understand Faulkner properly, we need to situate him among the voices that circled and inhabited him. We need, in effect, to perceive his private life as part of the public life of a particular locality and moment in history. The aim of this should not be to deny his individuality, but to acknowledge that this individuality was the product of a series of intersecting, social and cultural, forces – and of Faulkner's active engagement, his entry into dialogue, with those forces. Throughout his life, he was caught up in what Bakhtin termed 'the historic, progressing body of mankind': he was involved in argument (with all that term implies by way of agreement and conflict) with a series of socio-historical positions and events, cultural traditions and allegiances, that were his peculiar destiny. On different levels, this series of pressures might have been shared with others: with other Southerners living in the twentieth century, say, with other Americans or Europeans confronted with the crisis of modernism, with other human beings faced with the irremediable problem of what Faulkner himself called 'the human heart in conflict with itself'. But on the most specific level of all, the level of the individual utterance, these pressures were uniquely and unrepeatably his, part of his own, utterly personal and particularized web of relations. 'I am telling the same story over and over', Faulkner wrote to Malcolm Cowley in 1944, 'which is myself and the world.'[20] The fact that he is telling the story of 'the world' – that he is reaching what Bakhtin termed 'the plane of consciousness of other men': this, almost certainly, is the reason we read him. However, the fact that he is telling the story of himself is inseparable from this; and it requires that we look at the 'private individual' who told the story – who made the books and died. It requires us, in short, not to void Faulkner from history as he would have liked (or, at least, claimed he would), but to restore him to it – to reinsert him in the story of his time.

II History as Autobiography: The World of Faulkner

Early on in what is perhaps his greatest novel, *Absalom, Absalom!*, Faulkner allows this observation to be made about one of its central characters and dominating voices, Quentin Compson (the 'he' referred to here):

> he would listen to two separate Quentins now – the Quentin Compson preparing for Harvard in the South, the deep South dead since 1865 and peopled with garrulous outraged baffled ghosts, listening, having to listen, to one of the ghosts which had refused to lie still even longer than most had, telling him about old ghost-times; and the Quentin Compson who was still too young to deserve yet to be a ghost, but nevertheless having to be one for all that, since he was born and bred in the deep South . . .[21]

Quentin Compson is not William Faulkner, of course, and it would be quite wrong simply to identify Quentin's own involvement with the South with that of his creator. The fact that Faulkner can actually talk about the South, whereas by the end of the novel Quentin is reduced to a series of outraged negatives (*'I don't hate it! I don't hate it!'*) is proof enough of that. But that should not prevent us from seeing that what is said here about 'two separate Quentins' owes a great deal to Faulkner's special relationship with his region – and, because of that, can help us to understand just what this relationship involved. The duality of that relationship has, in any case, already been intimated. Faulkner could talk of 'loving' his 'native land' 'even while hating some of it': it is a refrain that runs through his essay 'Mississippi' – which, as one commentator has astutely observed, 'mingles an increasingly important autobiographical element with the historical and geographical materials'. And a similar awareness of tension runs through his occasional reference to his own creative practice. Here, for instance, is a relevant passage from an introduction to *The Sound and the Fury*:

> We [Southerners] seem to try in the simple furious breathing (or writing) span of the individual to draw a savage indictment of the contemporary scene or to escape from it into a make believe region of swords and magnolias and mockingbirds which never existed anywhere. Both of the courses are rooted in sentiment. . . . Anyway, each course is a matter of violent partizanship . . . I seem to have tried both of the courses. I have tried to escape and I have tried to indict . . .[22]

Faulkner later dismissed the introduction from which this passage comes as 'smug false sentimental windy shit': which was one reason it remained unpublished during his lifetime. But the dismissal was, perhaps, a symptom of uneasiness, a pained awareness of just how much he was giving away – how little, in fact, he was fulfilling his own obsessive need for privacy. There were several problems here: he could only approach self-revelation circuitously, through (say) an essay that was then denied publication or through a fictional surrogate. And, in tiptoeing up to self-exposure, he could then only begin to explain how he felt about his native land by falling back on figures of tension, division and discontinuity. In that opening passage from *Absalom, Absalom!*, for example, there are not just two presences but four: the implied author (who invites us to look at Quentin as 'he'), and Quentin as analyst of self (who recognizes his dual attachment to his region), as well as the 'two separate Quentins' presented for our inspection. The problem was one of stance and voice: Faulkner wanted, in a sense, to be 'in' history and 'outside' it at one and the same time. He wanted to be able to participate in the processes of social and historical change (he would have to do so, anyway) *and* able to gauge and judge them from a critical vantage point, a perspective that did not imply total immersion. For him, finally, the aim was imaginative commemoration *and* analysis. He wanted, as he put it, to recreate between the covers of a book the world. . . . I was already preparing to lose and regret . . . desiring, if not the capture of that world and the feeling of it as you'd preserve a kernel or a leaf to indicate the lost forest, at least to keep the evocative skeleton of the dessicated leaf.[23]

He wanted, in short, imaginatively to return to his native land not just as a native but as an archaeologist or historian – or, to borrow a phrase from one of Faulkner's novels, 'as . . . detached as God Himself'.

Theoretically, this is not as difficult as it sounds – as long, that is, as the writer is content with something less than the omniscience and detachment of the deity. As Fredric Jameson has argued, historical epochs are not monolithically integrated social formations but, on the contrary, complex *overlays* of different methods of production which serve as the bases of different social groups and classes and, consequently, of their worldviews. It is because of this that, in any given epoch, a variety of kinds of antagonism can be discerned, conflict between different interest groups. One culture will, almost invariably, be dominant: but there will also be (to borrow Raymond Williams's useful terms) a residual culture, formed in the past but still active in the cultural process, and an emergent culture, prescribing new meanings and practices. The writer, in effect, like any other member of society, is not the victim of some totalizing structure, since (to quote Williams) 'no dominant culture ever in reality includes or exhausts all human practice, human energy, and human intention'. He is therefore able to insert himself in the space between conflicting interests and practices and dramatize the contradictions the conflict engenders. Any writer can grasp contradictions of this kind, but the novelist enjoys a privileged position because of the free mixture of voices and genres he uses. His work is, as a result, peculiarly suited to reflect the numerous 'codes' for endowing events with meaning that arise from the various classes' different functions in the multiple modes of production present in every age or social formation. The novel plays host to a plurality of consciousnesses and generic conventions: so it is more than usually capable, Bakhtin and Jameson would say, of representing a reality that is apprehended as multiple, complex and internally antagonistic. It also, through its plurality of voices, permits a realization of both synchrony and diachrony: a demonstration, on the one hand, of structural continuities between past and present and, on the other, of the processes by which those continuities are challenged, dissolved and reconstituted. So it is also more capable than other (and, by comparison, unmixed) genres of realizing what Hayden White called 'the human capacity to endow lived contradictions with intimations of their possible transcendence'.[24] It permits the possibility of getting 'into' history, to participate in its processes, and, in a perspectival sense at least, to get 'out' of it.

Which is all by way of saying that Faulkner found the solution to his problem, not in this expressed opinion or in that, but in the imaginative discovery of Yoknapatawpha county. Yoknapatawpha *became* the South, and in particular his native land of Mississippi, for him: not just an emblem for it, but his way of understanding it and its history. Faulkner was never tired of saying that he found himself living at a time of peculiar crisis and struggle: when, as he put it in one of his class conferences, his locality was experiencing the 'change from land to the town and the city'. 'It's not particularly unique to the South', he added, 'It's only that the South is a little behind the rest of the country.' But, as he was well aware, the difficulties this crisis presented were commensurate with the possibilities. For it offered a greater sense of displacement, more chance to see the discontinuities inherent in culture and to operate in the gap between those discontinuities: to apprehend the conflict between different social formations and interests rather than simply experience it. Something that Lucien Goldmann said is worth quoting here. 'All forms of consciousness', Goldmann argues,

> express a provisional and mobile balance between the individual and his social environment; when this balance can be fairly easily established and is relatively stable, . . . men tend not to think about the problems raised by their relationship to the external world. On the social as well as the individual plane, it is the sick organ which creates awareness, and it is in periods of social and political crisis that men are most aware of the origins of their presence in the world.[25]

Faulkner himself felt that he was living at just such a moment of crisis as Goldmann refers to: when the terms of his relationship with things – which included, most crucially, his language – were brought up for examination and review. He had the privilege of being born at a moment when his society, his particular locality, offered him two peculiar advantages: a complex code, a dominant culture with its own elaborate blueprint or vocabulary for mediating experience – and a sense of rupture, sufficient critical distance from that code or culture to allow him to position and explore it – to know it, one could say, even while employing it as a means of knowledge. And his narratives, or to be more accurate his gradual invention of Yoknapatawpha *for* those narratives, became his way of embracing both those advantages: his means of being both in and out of the alienating necessities of his time. Of course, Faulkner himself was not always willing to admit this. Sometimes he argued that he could not avoid writing what he called 'a pageant of my county'. 'I was simply using the quickest tools to hand', he explained,

> I was using what I knew best, which was the locale where I was born and had lived most of my life. That was just like the carpenter building the fence – he uses the nearest hammer.[26]

But this was only half the truth, or less. Yoknapatawpha was not just a convenient tool for him; nor was it invented – or, as Faulkner usually preferred to put it, discovered – in a merely intuitive way. As an apocryphal county, that grew out of the stories and yet seemed to exist above and apart from them, it supplied its 'Sole Owner & Proprietor' with a special position, a vantage point from which he could at once dramatize and investigate his 'own little postage stamp of native soil'. It enabled him, in short, to represent history as both experience and symptom, as a lived event and as an analysable process.

Faulkner once described himself as someone who had 'taken the artist in him in one hand and his milieu in the other and thrust the one into the other like a clawing and spitting cat into a croker sack'. The violent image seems an appropriate one, because the world in which he grew up, his 'milieu' to use his own word, was a place of radical tension and conflict: a 'mixed world', to adopt the euphemistic phrase of one of his biographers – or, perhaps to be more accurate, a world that combined dreams of splendour with the threat of conflict and that was experiencing a disorienting transition from one inequitable system of production to another. At the time when Faulkner was growing up, in the early years of the twentieth century, the South and in particular Mississippi was a distinctly foreign place, distanced from the mainstream of American life. It might have been becoming like the rest of the nation, or as another Southern writer Allen Tate put it, re-entering the world: but it was doing so, Tate added, 'with a backward glance'[27] – and with a distinct reluctance to relinquish those features of economic and cultural life that made it seem, to some jaundiced observers, like another country. Those features were still operative during Faulkner's boyhood, young manhood, and in some instances beyond, and they became the initial terms of culture for him. And, while there is perhaps no way of defining them that is at once convenient, adequate and concise, some sense of what was different about the world Faulkner knew can be gained by referring to four cornerstones of Southern life, four forces that helped distinguish its modes of production and structures of feeling: which is to say, agricultural monopoly, economic poverty, military defeat, and slavery/segregation.

As far as agriculture is concerned, the Deep South – and Mississippi in particular – remained wedded to a cumbersome and oppressive system of cultivation and production long after the rest of the United States had become committed to industrial change. 'King Cotton' had spread rapidly westwards after 1820, its dominance guaranteed by the invention of the cotton gin, the voracious appetite for raw cotton demonstrated by England, and the vastness and fertility of the land between Georgia and the Rio Grande. Until this date, slavery had been in decline, partly because of the contraction and degeneration of tobacco plantations. In fact, Southern planters increasingly freed their slaves between 1790 and 1820. And in 1818 the Mississippi Supreme Court actually announced that slavery was 'condemned by reason and the laws of nature'; 'it exists,' the Court added, 'and can only exist, through municipal regulations'. Within a few years, all this had changed. Cotton had gained ascendancy; slave labour was accepted as the cheapest, most effective means of producing raw cotton; and a different perception of the South's 'peculiar institution' of slavery began to develop in response to these altered historical conditions. The story of that change in perception can be left until later, though. For the moment, what is worth noting is that Faulkner himself seems to have regarded cotton cultivation, and the demands it made on the economy and ideology, as one of the most powerful influences on the development of his home state. Take this passage, for instance, from one of the prologues in *Requiem for a Nun*. The voice that speaks here is not to be simply identified with Faulkner, of course: but it does represent an attempt on Faulkner's part to capture something of the collective memory of his region. As one critic has put it, the 'narrator' here 'becomes culture itself, relating its . . . imperfectly synthesised memories of its own beginnings, memories mystical in character, compounded of fact, legend, and hope, which have been transformed into myth by the workings of . . . numerous imaginations . . . from generation to generation'. It is, therefore, worth paying unusually close attention to what is said:

> not plough and axe which had effaced the wilderness but Cotton . . . burgeoning through spring and summer into September's white surf crashing against the flanks of gin and warehouse and ringing like bells on the marble counters of the banks: altering not just the face of the land, but the complexion of the town, too, creating its own parasitic aristocracy not only behind the columned porticoes of the plantation houses but in the counting-rooms of merchants and bankers and the sanctums of lawyers . . .[28]

The ascendancy of cotton cultivation was consolidated rather than undermined by the Civil War and its aftermath. In the South generally, by 1878 the cotton yield exceeded that of 1860; and, in Mississippi, whereas in pre-Civil War times farmers grew as much corn as cotton and were largely self-sufficient in meat and vegetable production, all these other items declined steadily from 1865 until 1945. There was intense propaganda, certainly, in favour of a new South and a new industrialized ideology: what one writer at the end of the nineteenth century termed 'the mental, moral, political, and economic education and elevation of the population'. There have even been attempts made by some historians to show that this social discourse of change inhered in economic reality: that it was the symptom, or even a cause, of significant material change. But the facts tell a different story. Apart from the arrival of the cotton mills, the anticipated – and, in some quarters, devoutly desired – industrialization of the Deep South did not occur until the twentieth century. Meanwhile, at the time when Faulkner was born, the system of sharecropping had replaced the gang system of slavery in the cotton fields. An arrangement that made it possible for planters to obtain labour without paying wages and for landless farmers to obtain land without buying it or paying rent, sharecropping enabled commercial farming to function during a period when the usual commercial institutions had virtually been destroyed by the Civil War and Reconstruction. Instead of exchanging money, owner and tenant agreed to share the proceeds of the crop. And in order to meet the immediate demand of the farmer for food and appliances, the crop-lien merchant appeared, who provided credit against the prospective harvest. The merchant in turn obtained advances from a wholesale dealer or jobber, and the chain of credit ran back eventually to a Northern manufacturer or banker – with, of course, everyone making more than a little profit along the way. Once enmeshed in this chain, the farmer – who was being charged high rates of interest, obliged to obtain all his goods from the credit merchant, and buying in the highest possible market – found it difficult, if not impossible, to escape. If, as usually happened, he failed to cancel his debt with the proceeds from his crop, the contract bound him to renew his lien for the next year under the same merchant. So he was forced into a condition that one observer, in the year of Faulkner's birth, termed 'helpless peonage'.[29] The large cotton plantation survived, and even expanded; the class of independent yeoman farmers – depending on subsistence crops and livestock and owning few if any slaves – declined from a majority to a minority of the white farming population in Mississippi; and the black slave population was replaced by people, white and black, who were serfs in all but name.

Things had not significantly improved during the time when Faulkner was growing up and beginning to turn his attention to the craft of writing. 'In the 1920s', one historian has observed, 'Mississippi was a forgotten state in a forgotten region.' Nine out of ten Mississippians still lived in rural areas and six out of ten lived on farms. Cotton dominated agricultural production in the state more in 1920 than it did in 1870. More important, perhaps, 65 per cent of those on the land did not own the land they lived on, 68 per cent of all Mississippi farms in 1925 were operated by tenants, and of those tenants 60 per cent were sharecroppers. The main effect of the Great Depression that followed was simply to underline the problems in the state's economic and agricultural system and, in particular, the disproportionate role that King Cotton played – the degree, in fact, to which Mississippians were at the mercy of this single commodity. In one year, 1932, mortgages were foreclosed on one in every ten farms in the state; and on one day in April in that same year one-quarter of the land area in Mississippi was auctioned off for unpaid taxes. Dispossession was a fact of rural life: something that might be faced with stoicism, perhaps, despair or tough folk humour, but that was always there as a shared class experience and a painful personal risk. Or perhaps dispossession is not quite the right word since many of the people involved in these minor tragedies never really possessed the farms they worked. As the voice of Mink Snopes in *The Hamlet* observes,

People of his kind never had owned even temporarily the land which they believed they had rented between one New Year's and the next one. It was the land itself which owned them, and not just from a planting to its harvest but in perpetuity...[30]

In this sense, there is a representative quality to characters like Mink: they are a focus for various, often conflicting historical forces and articulate the experiences of a class in the process of living out their own, very personal hopes and problems. Mink himself seems to perceive this: for it is one of the special qualities of Faulkner's social victims that they are not *just* victims in the sense of being passive, unaware – despite their relative, political and economic, impotence, they engage in active and re-active dialogue with their condition. 'Was it any wonder', Mink asks himself as he broods on his situation,

> that a man would look at that inimical irreconcilable square of dirt to which he was bound and chained for the rest of his life and say to it: *You got me, you'll wear me out because you are stronger than me since I'm just bone and flesh.*[31]

And it is not just of himself he is thinking, Mink realizes,

> *but all my tenant and cropper kind that have immolated youth and hope on thirty or forty or fifty acres of dirt that wouldn't nobody but our kind work because you're all our kind have.*[32]

With a character such as Mink, the experience of being imprisoned by 'one worthless rental' – or, even worse, 'evacuated ... on to the public roads' each November 'to seek desperately another similar one two miles or ten miles or two counties or ten counties away' – leads to intense bitterness and frustration, feelings that eventually find expression in violence. With others, however, a kind of heroic stoicism is more evident. A family called the Griers in the story 'Shall Not Perish', for instance, respond to the death of the oldest son, in the conflict of the Second World War, by allowing themselves only one day to grieve: because, as the young narrator (and younger son) puts it,

> it was April, the hardest middle push of planting time, and there was the land, the seventy acres which were our bread and fire and keep ...[33]

For them the compulsion to 'scratch fields out of the sterile hillsides' (to borrow a phrase from one historian of Mississippi) is something to be encountered, not with anger nor even with passive acceptance, but with a courage, an active and knowing commitment to their economic situation that argues some, limited, degree of mastery over it.

That economic situation was certainly grave, in Mississippi as a whole, by the time Faulkner began writing. The South had been the poorest region of the United States ever since the Civil War, and Mississippi its most consistently disadvantaged state. In 1880, for instance, less than two decades before Faulkner was born, the per capita annual income in the South was $376, compared with $1086 in the rest of the country; the average in the nation as a whole was $876, while in Mississippi it was only $286. Things had not significantly improved by the twenties: the per capita income in Mississippi had risen by then to no more than $396, well below a third of the national average. The South was well on its way to becoming what the National Emergency Council to President Roosevelt christened it in 1938, 'the Nation's economic problem No. 1'; and Mississippi, in turn, was well on its way to establishing itself as a crucial part of that problem. Industrial development had, of course, taken place: enough, evidently, to convince Southerners with more alert social antennae, like Faulkner himself or Allen Tate, that their region was being inserted into a new economy and a new ideology. The gross wealth of the eleven former states of the Confederacy, for instance, gleaned from industrial and industrially related enterprises rose from $17,000 million in 1900 to $70,000 million in 1922. But such development, much as it elated regional boosters, unnerved traditionalists, or challenged writers like Faulkner in more complex and contradictory ways, was significant in terms of its *potential* more than anything else. As one historical commentator has put it, 'not until well after the Second World War did a majority of Southerners take industrial jobs and begin to live in places that could plausibly be described as urban'.[34] Before that – when, say, Faulkner was embarking on his literary career – the transformation from an agricultural to an industrial economy, and with it the migration from farm to town, had only just begun. The economic and cultural metamorphosis of the South was still in its earliest stages, and perhaps all the more traumatic for that.

This is, perhaps, a crucial point about a writer like Faulkner's relationship to historical change. The South and Mississippi were altering, certainly, during the earlier half of his life and career; and they would eventually be transfigured so as to become (as social scientists of the 1960s and 1970s put it) 'like the rest of American society in terms of . . . primary dimensions of living', 'urbanised, standardised, neonised'. The young Faulkner was, among others, alert enough to see this and prescient enough to anticipate future developments. In effect, he was able to read the conflicts and tensions implicit in his society and to make a reasonably educated guess (based on knowledge of earlier and similar developments in other places) as to the social formations to which those conflicts would eventually lead, and the terms in which these tensions would (however temporarily) be resolved. But the actual extent of the alterations taking place in the South between the two World Wars has sometimes been exaggerated, and not least by contemporary observers. Take this passage, for example, from a novel written by one of William Faulkner's own brothers, Jack, and published in 1941:

> The good land lay idle beneath the sun. The pale green stripes of growing corn and cotton and sorghum . . . had become solid green mats of weeds and grass. The mules stood idle in their pastures for there were no longer people to work the good land. The plows stood unused at the end of the rows and the weeds grew taller and hid all but the sweat-stained handles from sight . . . the fields became smaller and smaller. Grass grew over the furrows, covering the wheel tracks, and the ditches choked with weeds, and

filled and overflowed. And the fields lay idle beneath the sun. For the people were moving to town.[35]

The point about such funeral orations over the dead body of the agricultural economy is, not that they turned out to be wrong in the end, but that, at the time they were written, they were a little premature. People *were* moving to town between the wars, and especially after the Crash of 1929: but, even in 1940, only 35 per cent of the population were living in metropolitan areas. The emergence of the New South, epitomized by the smokestack and the sky-scraper, *was* encouraged by the First World War (with its huge demand for weaponry, and for manufactured goods no longer producible in Europe); and it continued, however erratically, in the decades that followed. But, again, even in 1940 more than a third of the population of the entire South was engaged in agriculture – and this proportion was much higher in a particularly rural state like Mississippi. Relative to their condition at the turn of the century, both region and state were more urbanized and industrialized by, say, the time Faulkner published his first novel; they were, in this sense, experiencing changes that would turn out to be radical and irrevocable. But relative to the rest of the nation they remained, in the words of one observer, 'predominantly rural areas . . . scattered here and there with cities'; only in the last decade or two of his life did Faulkner witness something like the full extent of the transformation he had anticipated – a transformation the actual *process* of which had supplied him with much of the stuff of his fiction, creative occasion and narrative substance.

Just how this process of transformation, even in its embryonic stages, fed into Faulkner's narratives can be gauged by the degree to which they concentrate on experiences of disorientation and anxieties that have a specifically social or cultural cause. His books are full of people on the move: not, as in mainstream American fiction, in search of something personally new and morally restorative but because they have been uprooted – destabilized, like Mink Snopes and his kind, by pressures they may understand but feel unable to control. To some extent, this destabilization is charted in the rise of the Snopeses. One morning, for instance, the inhabitants of Frenchman's Bend, and more particularly the customers of the blacksmith Trumbull, are confronted – and bewildered – by the appearance of a new blacksmith, I.O. Snopes. A new voice announces a new regime, one that places a primitive version of marketing cant above the more familiar virtues of craftsmanship and care:

> Well, gentlemen, off with the old and on with the new. Competition is the life of trade, and though a chain ain't no stronger than its weakest link, I don't think you'll find the boy yonder no weak reed to have to lean on once he catches onto it . . .[36]

The response of one local to this verbiage suggests a dissonant note has been struck and noted. 'What the hell's happened here?' asks Jack Houston, 'Where's Trumbull?' and receives the reply,

Oh, you mean the feller that used to be here. . . . His lease has done been
cancelled. I'm leasing the shop now. My name's Snopes, I.O. Snopes. This
here's my young cousin, Eck Snopes. But it's the old shop, the old stand; just
a new broom in it.[37]

To which Houston replies in turn: 'I don't give a damn what his name is.
Can he shoe a horse?' As it turns out, the answer is 'no', neither Eck nor
I.O. can perform this skill. And Houston thereby receives his first lesson
in the laws of credit and exchange: the 'blacksmith' is the person who can
pay the lease for the blacksmith's shop (or find someone to pay it for
him), not necessarily the person who can actually do the job. The former
blacksmith Trumbull, meanwhile, stripped of his role by the rules of the
market place, becomes one of Faulkner's many uprooted people – his
departure recorded with the kind of laconic pathos appropriate to his own
preference for quiet craft over marketing cant:

He drove through the village with his wife, in a wagon loaded with household goods. If he looked toward his old shop nearby, nobody saw him do it
– an old man still hale, morose and efficient . . . They never saw him again.[38]

One further, felicitous touch marks the change. The evicted smith has left
his successor, in place of the can of oil used to light the forge, a rusty can
of 'hog piss'; I.O. Snopes, however, cannot tell the difference.

It would be falling victim to portentousness to load too much on this
minor comic episode: but, seen in its context, it does illustrate the general
point just made – that Faulkner was absorbed in the minutiae of social
change, the gradual and almost imperceptible process by which a culture
can be 'off with the old and on with the new.' An economy founded on
a mixture of labour and exchange notions of value, where considerations
of skill and custom complicate the profit motive, is being replaced here,
however quietly and infinitesimally, by an economy based, with very little
mixing or complication, on exchange, the manipulation of money. In
terms of exchange, strictly speaking it makes little intrinsic difference
whether or not the blacksmith can do his job; it is simply a question of
what he is able to buy and sell. Equally, and comically, it makes little
difference in these terms if a can of coal oil or hog piss is on offer, a
colour print or a Rembrandt: it all depends on what the market will bear,
on the value the customer *thinks* he is acquiring. Of course, common
sense – and, more to the point, the basic needs of the customer – dictate
that a blacksmith, or in a later age a car mechanic or a car salesman, will
have to possess minimal skills in order to make a living and play the part
for which he has sold his labour. Nobody, as I.O. Snopes discovers to his
discomfiture, will be seduced for very long by a product that is *all* marketing
– all 'hype', to use a word unknown to both I.O. and Faulkner. The point
is, though, that the concept of pure marketing, and the related demotion
of every skill or artefact to the status of 'product', is the logical final stage
of strictly exchange theories of value; and of that I.O. and his incompetent

'cousin' Eck are comic illustrations. Together, I.O. and Eck augur the arrival of a new economy: a 'new broom', in a larger historical sense than I.O. can ever know, that will eventually sweep the detritus of the old system away.

Part of the old system that was being torn up by the roots had its origins in the Civil War. Unlike the rest of the nation, the South had had the stunning experience of military defeat and occupation. A whole generation of young men had been wiped out: which is perhaps why so often in Faulkner's narratives the living presences from the past, the keepers of the rites who survive, are females. The men, on the other hand, often only survive in memory and imagination: as spectres who haunt subsequent generations with dreams of impossible daring and glamour. Not only the dead survive in this form, however: the Yoknapatawpha novels and stories are also populated by men – and, to a lesser extent, women – whose experiences of war and occupation have effectively paralysed their imaginations, made it impossible for them to function as anything more than 'shadows not of flesh and blood which had lived and died but of shadows in turn of what were . . . shades too'. Time had become frozen for these people, even more emphatically and traumatically than it tends to for any generation that has suffered the experience of total war. 'Many of the men who survived that unnatural war', observed Walter Hines Page,

> unwittingly did us a greater hurt than the war itself. It gave every one of them the intensest experience of his life . . . Thus it stopped the thought of most of them as an earthquake stops a clock . . . they were dead men, most of them, moving among the living as ghosts; and yet as ghosts in a play, they held the stage.[39]

As a boy, Faulkner was growing up among people of the kind Page describes here for whom, to quote Gavin Stevens, 'There's no such thing as past'; and, significantly, he seems to have been provoked to similar associations. A subtext of Page's account, which helps him situate his feelings about the Civil War and his relationship to them, is the famous speech from *Macbeth* v. v, beginning 'Tomorrow, and tomorrow, and tomorrow': in which Macbeth compares life to 'a walking shadow' and to 'a poor player / That struts and frets his hour upon the stage / And then is heard no more'. Nobody who has read *The Sound and the Fury*, with its title (among other things) borrowed from this speech, needs to be reminded of the importance of the play for Faulkner. Not everyone, however, has noticed that his most famous vocalization of the omnipresence of the Civil War past in the Southern present is just as soaked in intertextual references to *Macbeth* as Page's brief account is. In *Intruder in the Dust*, Gavin Stevens, a lawyer of philosophical cast of mind – modelled, in part, on Faulkner himself and, in part, on his close friend and mentor, Phil Stone – observes that 'Yesterday wont be over until tomorrow and tomorrow began ten thousand years ago'; and this because 'for every Southern boy' there is the dream of altering the course of Civil War battles and therefore the course and consequences of the War itself. For them, Stevens suggests, 'it hasn't happened yet, it hasn't even begun yet'. The passage has been frequently quoted, and for good reason: it encapsulates Faulkner's sense of the interdependence and *mutually* effective nature of past and present – in short, the dialectical nature of history. What has been less often quoted, though, is the related passage that follows, of which this is just a small part and the conclusion:

> yesterday's sunset and yesterday's tea both are inextricable from the scattered indestructible uninfusable grounds blown through the endless corridors of tomorrow, into the shoes we will have to walk in and even the sheets we will have (or try) to sleep between: because you escape nothing, you flee nothing: the pursuer is what is doing the running and tomorrow night is nothing but one long sleepless wrestle with yesterday's omissions and regrets.[40]

Insomnia, flight and pursuit, the endless passage of tomorrows through which like a ghost 'you' continue to wrestle with the regrets of yesterday: the allusions to the whole imaginative fabric of *Macbeth* are, of course, specific and appropriate to the voice that speaks them. Gavin Stevens is a febrile, garrulous and yet introspective man whose sense of frustration finds a convenient avenue of expression in familiar literary texts. But a more general point is being made here too, about the way Southerners like Page and Faulkner, growing up in the region at the end of the nineteenth century, found themselves surrounded by memories of a conflict that seemed to compel imitation and reinvention. Those memories, apart from nagging them, seemed to challenge the specifics of their own lives: hence, perhaps, Faulkner's obsessive need to appropriate his own forms of military glory, by casting himself in the role of pilot. Like Macbeth, in fact, Southerners of Faulkner's generation felt themselves to be haunted by ghosts and, in effect, rendered impotent by them. In their case, those ghosts came more from the general, social and cultural past than from the personal, but the consequences were essentially the same. They felt denied the capacity for meaningful action; they sought escape from the cunning passages and contrived corridors of history but found, for the most part, no way out.

No way out, that is, except through the imagination: Faulkner's way of exorcizing the past – not just the Civil War past but the regional past as a whole – was to submit it to the powers of knowing re-creation. His solution to the sense of being encircled by voices from yesterday was to situate those voices in terms of a dialogic contact and conflict with the voices of today, and to make this engagement precisely his subject. He did not, of course, disencumber himself of past voices as a result: but, at least, he achieved the sort of imaginative liberation that could come from understanding and dramatizing them. He wrestled with his ghosts, in effect, in a way that showed he knew their measure and the nature of the wrestling match in which he was involved. For others, however, the forms of release from the past were signed in a very different way. Bakhtin has referred to authoritative discourse – that is, discourse which attempts to dictate the terms of our relation to the world and preclude dialogic engagement – as 'the word of the fathers'. 'It is a *prior* discourse', he goes on,

> It is given (it sounds) in lofty spheres, not those of familiar contact. Its language is a special (as it were, hieratic) language. It can be profaned. It is akin to taboo, i.e. a name that must not be taken in vain.[41]

'The authoritative word', Bakhtin observes, 'is located in a distanced zone, organically connected with a past that is felt to be hierarchically higher.' And, within the context of the South and Mississippi, it is easy to see that it is intimately bound up with the process of privileging memories of the Old South and the Civil War. What Bakhtin then goes on to point out, though, is that discourse of this kind depends for its power on the consent of those who hear it and affirm it: 'the word of the fathers' is only authoritative because the son accepts it as such. Whatever the initial claims of the past to privilege and obedience, it is the present that has given them currency: the son has elevated the father's word into an object of reverence by his refusal or inability to encounter it in critical debate. The relevance of all this to the Southern privileging of the past during the time when Faulkner was growing up is, perhaps, obvious: as a young man, Faulkner was surrounded by voices that not only looked back but, in the process, transformed the object of their attention, changing the nature of what they spoke about even as they spoke. Many of his contemporaries, in effect, found escape from the actual past in active collusion with the past's idealized image of itself: by collaborating in the creation of a taboo.

There were, of course, strong motives for looking back to the 'good ole times' before the war, and to the heroic conflict of war itself, particularly during the time of Faulkner's childhood. For if there was one thing that most observers of the South were agreed upon, in the last few decades of the nineteenth century, it was that the old economic and political system had broken down. One traveller, for instance, claimed to have seen 'enough woe and want and sin and ravage' during a visit of fourteen weeks to Georgia and the Carolinas, 'to satisfy the most insatiate heart'; 'enough of sore humiliation and bitter overthrow', he added, 'to appease the desire of the most vengeful spirit'. Another has left this vivid account of the Valley of Tennessee:

> It consists for the most part of plantations in a state of semi-ruin, and plantations of which the ruin is total and complete . . . The trail of war is visible throughout the valley in burnt-up gin houses, ruined bridges, mills and factories, of which latter the gable walls only are left standing, and in large traces of once cultivated land stripped of every vestige of fencing. The roads, long neglected, are in disorder . . . Borne down by losses, debts, and accumulating taxes, many who were once the richest among their fellows have disappeared from the scene, and few have risen to take their places . . .[42]

'A dead civilisation and a broken-down system' was how another traveller described the region some time after the war; and, melodramatic though this may sound, it was not without a grain of truth. The South had suffered a comprehensive military defeat. That, in itself, was bad enough. But to this was added, not only the economic deprivation that usually follows such defeat, but also a sense of moral victimization: the belief that the victors to the North were proclaiming their military success as proof positive of the superiority of their ethical case. How justified Southerners were in believing this is not the issue here – although, if Northerners did celebrate their victory in moral terms, they would not have been the first in history to have done so; it is an eminently understandable reaction and, given at least some of the issues over which the war was fought, not a wholly unwarranted one at that. What is worth noting, though, is that Southerners did believe it and were, as a result, troubled by feelings of bitterness and resentment – a nagging sense that, having been defeated, they were being humiliated as well. Their response to this was perhaps predictable: defensiveness turned gradually into defiance and a proud determination to tell *their* story, their side of things. And crucial to this was their reinvention of the past in terms that provided them with a moral defence and an emotional refuge: as a Great Good Place, the site of patriarchal virtues, which had effectively been swept away by the barbarian hordes from the North.

Other pressures encouraged the proliferation of the myth of a feudal South, in the period just before and after Faulkner was born, quite apart from the moral defensiveness of the region and the drabness of local conditions. Most notably, there was the convenient excuse offered by the war itself. Earlier generations of Southerners had promoted the idea of a feudal South, inhabited by benevolent squires, capable matriarchs, young bucks and belles and happy darkies: a family romance, in short, calculated to soften the edges of historical fact and conceal gross inequities of caste and class. But at least those earlier generations had had to confront the perceptible fissure between idea and social experience, the discomfiting sense that the romance did not fit the reality. Now, with the war and the undoubted devastation that it brought, there was no problem of explanation: the dream of a plantation family – blacks and whites together – inhabiting a sun-lit pastoral landscape could be firmly located in the past and its loss blamed on Northern invasion. Southerners were no longer hampered by any sense of contingency, any restricting concern for the ordinary details of day-to-day life. Nostalgia could run riot, distance could give a romantic blur to everything, while if any gap was noticed between ideal and reality, word and thing, it could be equated with the gap between past and present; once things were perfect, the argument went, and, if they do not seem so now, then the war is entirely to blame. In this lost world, 'peace and plenty reigned over a smiling land', as one Southern novelist wrote in 1891, the 'poorer neighbours' standing in a relation of 'part friend, part retainer' to the richer, thanks to 'an untitled manorial system'. It was a region, as the same novelist admitted seven years later, 'partly in one of the old Southern states and partly in the yet vaguer land of Memory': but it nevertheless exercised a powerful sway over the imaginations of all those in Faulkner's time – and there were very many of them – who felt dispossessed and defensive. As a focus for elegiac regret, for lamentations over dear dead days beyond recall or gone with the wind, it became the location for many of the romances Faulkner read as a boy. And perhaps the height of comic absurdity and tactlessness was achieved by the authors of these romances when, as they often did, they would place the elegy for the 'good ole times' in the mouth of an emancipated slave: as if black people had lost most when the Southern version of the pastoral had been trampled under the boots of the Union Army. Here, for instance, is one black character voicing his sense of regret for the 'laughin' times' before the war, in a very popular romance published in 1891:

> Dem was high times. We ain't neber seed no time like dat since de war. Git up in de mawnin' an' look out ober de lawn, and yer come fo'teen or fifteen couples ub de fustest quality folks, all un horseback ridin' in de gate. Den such scufflin' round. Old massa and missis out on de po'ch an' de little pickaninnies runnin' from de quarters . . . An' den sich a breakfast an' sich dancin' an' cotin'; ladies all out on de lawn in der white dresses, an' de gemmen in fair-top boots . . . Dat would go on a week or mo', an' den up day'll git an' away de'y go to der nex' plantation . . .[43]

Each of Faulkner's black characters acts as a focus for conflicting historical forces; so it would be wrong to see any one as a simple reaction to this kind of stereotyping – a stereotyping that, as a book like *Gone with the Wind* testifies, survived well into the twentieth century. Still, one source of the richness of many of them is precisely the intertextual reference: the obliquely critical relationship they have to the humble darkies, happy mammies and melodramatic mulattoes who populate conventional Southern legend.

Not only the black characters in Faulkner's narratives possess this particular intertextual dimension. There are similar forces at work in, say, his portrait of Thomas Sutpen in *Absalom, Absalom!* – a portrait which is, among other things, a slyly parodic variation on the 'from rags to riches' theme (or perhaps it would be more accurate to say, the 'from penury to aristocracy' theme) so popular with Southern romancers both before and after the Civil War. Faulkner's account, in turn, in *Knight's Gambit*, of how one brother and sister ('Their name was Harriss') arranged for 'a once-simple country house' to be 'transmogrified . . . into something a little smaller than a Before-the-War Hollywood set' offers a sly comment not only on the preoccupation with incestuous feelings so prevalent in Southern fiction (including, of course, Faulkner's own) but also on those mansions, intended to look old even when they were new, that have acted as what Bakhtin would call 'chronotopes' in so many regional stories: that is, as 'organising centres for the fundamental narrative events . . . the place where the knots of the narrative are tied and untied'. 'The chronotope', Bakhtin observed, 'serves as the primary point from which 'scenes' in a novel unfold', and so functions 'as the primary means of materialising time in space'. Faulkner frequently takes these monuments to aristocratic pretension, these icons of Southern culture that also served as objects of desire in Southern fiction, and turns them into parodic monuments: emphasizing their depthlessness, how much they were and are the products of dream and deception. The Sutpen mansion, the Harriss plantation house, the house that Flem Snopes has had embellished with (as V. K. Ratliff comments in *The Town*),

> colyums across the front ... extry big ones so even a feller that never seen colyums before wouldn't have no doubt a-tall what they was, like in the photographs where the Confedrit sweetheart in a hoop skirt and a magnolia is saying good-bye to her Confedrit beau just before he rides off to finish tending to General Grant.[44]

All these are intended as a comment not just on the substitution of surface for substance that characterizes modern culture but also on the preference of the South, Old and New, for simulacra. A simulacrum, Fredric Jameson suggests, borrowing the term from Plato, is an identical copy of something for which, in the culture in question, the original never existed. And this is precisely Faulkner's point. It is not just that people like Sutpen in the nineteenth century and Flem Snopes in the twentieth are copying some architectural grace and bravura that existed at another time or in another place in the region. It is that they are copying what never existed outside the depthless dream world of plantation legend. What they are after, in sum, is the imitation of an imitation.

The dream of an aristocratic Old South, laid waste by the ravages of civil conflict, exercised a powerful grip on the regional imagination during Faulkner's youth and early manhood; and yet it hardly accorded with the facts. In particular, it had very little to do with the economic and social facts of the immediate area in which the novelist was born and grew up. In his semi-autobiographical essay, 'Mississippi', Faulkner himself points out that the state 'might almost be said to have only ... two directions, north and south'. 'Until a few years ago', he explains, 'it was impossible to travel east or west'[45] because the main access routes did not provide the opportunity. And this problem of intra-state communication, Faulkner knew very well, was symptomatic of the topographical and, to an extent, cultural cleavage between the eastern and western sections of the state. To the west, towards the Mississippi River, were the flat, fecund cotton lands: here planters pursued conservative policies and an agricultural system based first on slavery, then on share-cropping. And in a few places in this area, around the town of Natchez for instance, it might be possible to argue that forms of baronial splendour were desired and plausibly imitated. But to the east, the area where Faulkner was born and spent most of his life, the landscape was and is characterized by red-clay hills and pine barrens. The small farmers here had little use for slaves and fostered a political radicalism and egalitarianism reflected by Jacksonian politics before the Civil War and Populism afterwards. Certainly, Faulkner's home county, Lafayette County, was situated sufficiently close to the point of intersection between these two separate cultures to accommodate them both imaginatively: there are, as a result, both cotton planters cultivating rich bottom lands and small farmers toiling away in the less fertile soil of the hills in his imaginative world of Yoknapatawpha. But that does not invalidate the fact that the *immediate* area in which Faulkner grew up was more eastern than western; and that he was therefore particularly likely to see – or, at least, intuit – the disjunction between dreams of aristocratic splendour and the historical realities of his local, rural culture. Nor does it take away from a much simpler and more general point: even setting aside this east–west cleavage, the fact was that the vast majority of Mississippians before the Civil War, let alone after, were farmers, not planters. By far the dominant class in the state in 1860, for instance, was the yeoman class: those independent small farmers who owned fewer than 200 acres of improved land and either a few slaves or none at all. Statewide, these small farmers numbered 60 to 70 per cent of Mississippi's white population. Among Mississippi farmers in 1860 rather more than half owned no slaves; another 20 per cent owned fewer than ten; fewer than 6 per cent owned more than fifty. Not more than 8 per cent of farm operators, in fact, ranked as great planters; and even those, for the most part, came from the same tough Scots-Irish stock as their less privileged neighbours. Originating from the Carolinas, Tennessee, Georgia or Virginia, the typical Mississippi planter was an adventurer like Lucius Quintus Carothers McCaslin – the ancestral figure haunting the narrative in *Go Down, Moses* – possessing pluck and luck, and a little ruthlessness, rather than a glorious lineage.

Which raises the simple question of why a dream so at odds with historical reality should have had such power: unless, that is, we are ready to operate in the crudest possible terms of false consciousness. The question may be simple to ask, but the answer is perhaps less so. One element of that answer is supplied by the historian, J.M. Huizinga, in a paragraph in his book, *The Waning of the Middle Ages*, briefly alluded to earlier. In talking about the Middle Ages and the aristocratic culture of that time, Huizinga argues that 'to be representative' then meant 'to produce by conduct, by customs, by manners . . . the illusion of heroic being, full of dignity and honour, of wisdom and . . . courtesy'. This was made possible, he goes on,

> by the . . . imitation of an ideal past. The dream of past perfection ennobles life and its forms, fills them with beauty and fashions them anew as forms of art. Life is regulated like a noble game.[46]

In effect, Huizinga claims, an aristocratic culture is one in which people *imitate* some idea of aristocracy. This is, of course, an arguable claim: and, even if it is admitted, it could and surely should be insisted that some imitations are more plausible than others. The so-called First Families of

Virginia, at the very least, offered a more convincing performance of the aristocratic role than the planters of Mississippi did, if only because the Virginians' performance was more immediately and fully coincident with economic and social realities. Nevertheless, there is an element of truth here. If the historical equivalents of Thomas Sutpen did invent themselves, then perhaps they did so, as to an extent all patriarchal cultures do, by regulating experience according to some idealized version of the past. Life, according to this prescription, is translated into heroic art: along the lines one Southern contemporary of Faulkner's, John Donald Wade, was thinking of when he observed that the aristocratic Old South was 'one of the really great abstractions of our race'.

But this is less than half the story, as perhaps that reference to 'our race' alerts us. The central fact of Southern history before the Civil War was the 'peculiar institution' of slavery, the presumption on the part of one race that it could own another; and the legend of the patriarchal South, engendered during the period before the war and then assiduously fostered in the years after, has to be seen within the context of that institution and all its cultural, political and emotional consequences. Slavery had existed in the South since the beginning, as a convenient means of working the tobacco plantations of Virginia and the rice plantations of South Carolina; and it gradually replaced the system of indenture, which at one time operated in tandem with it. So voracious was the demand for slave labour that by the end of the eighteenth century over five million black people had crossed the Atlantic, most of whom were sold into bondage in the South. Slave labour was never as widespread in the Northern states, and it was slowly abolished there. But in the South it became steadily more crucial to the economy: the slave trade was abolished in 1808, but as the cotton plantations spread over the region – and, in particular, the Deep South – breeding and trading of slaves *within* the region grew. Human reproduction became, in effect, a convenient solution to an otherwise insoluble marketing problem. As the material culture gravitated towards ever greater dependence on slave labour and exchange, so the non-material culture began to engage with these alterations and with the uneasy feelings that the traffic in human flesh necessarily provoked. A ruling of the Mississippi Supreme Court in 1818, quoted earlier, had declared slavery to be against 'the laws of nature', and such an attitude was hardly exceptional at the time: there were, for example, hundreds of anti-slavery societies in the South in the 1820s. But attitudes rapidly hardened, so as to erect an elaborate ideological scaffolding to protect what was perceived to be the basic economic interests, the material fabric of the region: by 1850, the number of anti-slavery societies (arguing, at most, for gradual manumission and wholesale expatriation of the freed) had been reduced to a mere handful. The traumatic events of 1831 perhaps acted as a catalyst here. For in that year William Lloyd Garrison began his newspaper, *Liberator*, under the masthead, 'The compact which exists between the North and the South is a covenant with death and an agreement with hell': in doing so, he helped initiate the Abolitionist movement. And in that same year, a slave named Nat Turner fomented a rebellion in Southampton County, Virginia, which, before it was put down and its leaders killed, led to the death of sixty-one whites and spread terror throughout the state and the region. Whether they had been aware of it before or not, Southerners now had to confront the fact that they constituted a separate interest, threatened by enemies without and within. Quite apart from guilt, the feelings inevitably promoted by what Faulkner called 'the old shame' of slavery, they had to deal with the defensive emotions, the desire for self-justification, aroused by organized Northern criticism and something even more elemental uncovered by the Nat Turner rebellion: the imagination of disaster – cultural anxiety and personal fear.[47]

One significant consequence of this alteration of consciousness was the gradual formulation of a 'positive good' theory of slavery. The institution was no longer defended as a necessary evil: against 'reason and the laws of nature', it might be, to be abolished in the long term, but rendered unavoidable by immediate economic contingencies. It was celebrated as a vital contribution to culture, the basic ingredient in what one apologist for slave labour termed,

> The primitive and patriarchal, which may also be called the sacred and natural system, in which the labourer is under the personal control of a fellow-being endowed with the sentiments and sympathies of humanity.[48]

As opposed to the abstract laws of capitalism, according to which the rest of the United States operated, the system of slavery promoted a feudal, patriarchal system in which the laws of the market place were supplanted by the customs and pieties of the familial group: the South was, in effect, thanks to slavery, a vastly extended family. As in a family, the argument went, 'The Negro learns each civilising art' at the knees of his 'father' and 'mother', the master of the house and wife; and he 'acquires the habit that refinement gives' in the company of his 'brothers' and 'sisters', the young white men and women of the plantation. There could be no question of exploitation, in these circumstances, because the benefits were mutual: the slave received familial care and protection in return for his labour. Slavery was translated, on these terms, from an economic arrangement into an educative one, a process of nurture – as this passage, taken from one pro-slavery book, illustrates. It is set in the future because the author is happily anticipating the day when slavery, to which he gives the euphemism, 'warranteeism', will be accepted throughout the United States:

> in the plump flush of full-feeding health, the happy warrantees shall banquet in PLANTATION-REFECTORIES: worship in PLANTATION-CHAPELS, learn in PLANTATION-SCHOOLS: or, in PLANTATION-SALOONS, at the cool of evening, or in the green and bloomy gloom of cold catalpas and magnolias, chant old songs, tell tales . . . and after slumber in PLANTATION-DORMITORIES over whose gates Health and

Rest sit smiling at the feet of Wealth and Labour, rise to begin again welcome days of jocund toil.[49]

Absurd as the portrait is, its very absurdity is perhaps symptomatic of the pressures that inspired it: only desperate states require desperate remedies. The one answer Southerners discovered to the imagination of disaster, evidently, was to dream of paternalistically authorized bliss. The family romance became a convenient means of masking fear.

The problem with any mythology that a culture organizes to explain and justify its practices is that, because it has been generated by awareness of these practices, it still bears their shape in however ghostly a fashion. The plantation romance may have been invented and promoted to act as an apology for a system that certainly required one, to defend an indefensible institution. Nevertheless, in apologizing, Southerners confessed more than they knew. On the simplest level, they were confessing their insularity: provoked by feelings of insecurity and imminent danger, the popularizers of plantation legend were seeking (as the saying goes) to keep it all in the family – to associate an entire region with what one historian has termed 'isolated family-bound plantation life'. In doing so, they were articulating otherwise inarticulable impulses of defensiveness and withdrawal, and withdrawal into a place where the word of the father was law to an extent unparalleled in other societies. Paternal authority, in these circumstances, extended far beyond its familiar boundaries into what another historian has called 'a vast metaphorical family, hierarchically organised and organically linked by (pseudo)-ties of blood'.[50] Faulkner's interest in the associated problems of genealogy and power begins to look decidedly less peculiarly personal when seen in the context of a culture that granted immense weight to the father, as head of a society that could only receive justification in *his* terms – according to the claims, that is, of paternalistic nurture and care. A shadowy patriarchal figure hovers over the action of so many of Faulkner's novels, not just for reasons of family history, but, related to this, because his society saw itself presided over by just such an admonitory absent presence: for the reason, in short, that it identified its legitimacy and authority with the law of the father. The impact of this identification on those growing up under its shadow is telling: so many of the male characters whom Faulkner identifies with his own generation are marked by feelings of impotence and inadequacy, the suspicion that they can never begin to match the stature of their predecessors. The immediate reasons for this may be personal: but behind those reasons, and intimately connected to them, lie more general, cultural factors. An impossible model of male privilege and power has been erected for these characters by their society: one that their society may require, as an explanation of its origins – but one, also, that debilitates and humiliates them. So, finding themselves unable to imitate this model, people like Quentin Compson (in both *The Sound and the Fury* and *Absalom, Absalom!*), Horace Benbow (in *Flags in the Dust/Sartoris* and *Sanctuary*) and (in a different way) Bayard Sartoris III (in *Flags in the Dust/Sartoris*) turn to the women of their own generation in the Southern family romance: only to learn that this romance has transmuted every relationship between a man and a woman into a potential version of sibling intimacy. The erotic tensions and generational conflicts generated by the South's tendency to see itself as an extended family were something that Faulkner experienced in his life and explored in his work. And, of these, not the least was the strange pattern by which, fleeing the father, the hero embraced the sister; mastered by the paternal word, he discovered refuge, and release, in incest.

But the most fundamental conflict or contradiction inherent in the Southern romance of the family had to with the people who were its unwitting authors: all those black women and men, a sense of whose enslavement and oppression had led to the construction of the romance in the first place. Southerners, and in particular, Mississippians, were surrounded by black people. In Faulkner's lifetime, Mississippi had a higher proportion of black inhabitants than any other state: three blacks for every two whites in 1900 and about numerically equal in 1940. They were, according to the master narrative of the culture, part of the family. And yet they were strangers. They were omnipresent, and yet they were unknown. 'They come into white people's lives', observes Quentin Compson in *The Sound and the Fury*,

> like that in sudden sharp black trickles that isolate white facts for an instant in unarguable truth like under a miscroscope; the rest of the time just voices that laugh when you see nothing to laugh at, tears when no reason for tears.[51]

'A nigger', reflects Quentin elsewhere, 'is not so much a person as a form of behaviour, a sort of obverse reflection of the white people he lives among.' And while such remarks suggest as much about the person who speaks them as they do anything else – his acute self-consciousness, in particular, and his need to see everything as a mirror or extension of himself – they also measure a general, cultural failure to understand the otherness of black people: to see them as anything more than minor characters in a drama written by the whites who had appropriated and tried to dominate their lives. Faulkner's position is interesting here: he never fully internalizes the consciousness of a character who is undeniably black. In the earlier work, in particular, this is often the result of inherited prejudice: he appears to be working from the assumption that black people do not *have* any internal life worth talking about. Nevertheless, there does seem to be another motive at work which increased in significance as Faulkner grew older – and more willing to analyse racial beliefs rather than just assume them. This was a suspicion, a distrust of the kind of emotional imperialism that might be involved in laying claim to a thorough knowledge of the consciousnesses of individual black people. Of course, Faulkner attempted imaginative contact; and, as we shall see later, perhaps achieved it – or certainly came near to it – from time to time. But the imagination of pain is still quite different from the actual experience of pain – the one, quite simply, does not hurt as much as the other does. And one of the more intriguing aspects of Faulkner's development is that he moved in the opposite direction from the one predicated in the family romance. Instead of pretending to understand black people, protesting that they were all part of the family, he grew more willing occasionally to admit ignorance and otherness. While adventuring sympathy or a leap of imaginative knowledge, as one critic has put it, 'he learned . . . to understand that he did not know' black people 'as much as he once thought he had'. He learned, in short, to acknowledge difference.

But to acknowledge difference is not, of course, to accept separation. Faulkner's novels are full of characters who suffer the consequences of racial division, the social and moral *apartheid* that was perpetuated and even institutionalized by the 'Jim Crow' laws, and all the other elaborate paraphernalia of segregation, long after slavery was abolished. 'Most of all he hated the intolerance and injustice', Faulkner declares of the central, semi-autobiographical character in 'Mississippi', 'the lynching of Negroes not for the crimes they committed but because their skins were black . . . the inequality . . . the bigotry.' The family romance masked all manner of fissures and inequities; and not the least of these was the gap between promise and performance as far as the question of contact between the races was concerned. The romance promised intimacy, mutual benefit and trust; what the reality it sought to explain performed every day, however, was an act of denial and subjection. Black people were only accommodated within the legend to the extent that they could be what Louis Althusser has called '(mis)recognised': that is, denied their concrete individuality in the very process of being acknowledged and identified. 'All ideology', Althusser has argued,

> represents in its necessarily imaginary distortion not the existing relations of production . . . but above all the (imaginary) relationship of individuals to the relations of production and the relations that derive from them. What is represented in ideology is therefore not the system of real relations which govern the existence of individuals, but the imaginary relation of those individuals to the real relations in which they live.[52]

In the terms of this formula, ideology is not simply a matter of conscious beliefs, nor is it a matter of 'false consciousness' – sets of false ideas imposed on individuals to persuade them there is no real conflict of class or caste interests in their society. It is, rather, a matter of imaginary versions of the real social relations that people live: imaginary versions that impose themselves not merely through consciousness nor through disembodied ideas but through systems and structures. Ideology is inscribed, Althusser insists, in the representations, the signs and the practices or rituals of everyday life. And its end result is an act of subjection, whereby 'concrete individuals' are 'hailed' or addressed as 'concrete subjects':

persuaded to see, or rather '(mis)recognise', themselves according to the terms dictated by the culture. This process of '(mis)recognition' is clearly at work in the family romance of the South, which found its most open (but not its only) expression in the writing of the region, fictional and non-fictional texts alike. And, clearly, the most radical example of this process was offered by the representation of black people as beneficiaries of the system, living in familial contact with authority – rather, that is, than what they were: victims of a fundamentally repressive and divisive social apparatus, a system designed to keep them down and apart.

Althusser uses the phrase 'Ideological State Apparatus' to describe the plurality of means by which ideology is inscribed in the codes and ceremonies of ordinary life. And, at this level, he is talking about an act of persuasion – or, as he calls it, '*interpellation* or hailing' – whereby the concrete individual is subjected without being aware of it – without realizing that the terms in which he or she lives are fundamentally ideological, the products of a specific system. Another phrase, 'Repressive State Apparatus', describes a related, parallel process, whereby a culture uses more direct means whenever necessary to prescribe and preserve its system of relations. On this level, as Althusser puts it, 'the State Apparatus in question "functions by violence" – at least ultimately (since repression, e.g. administrative repression, may take non-physical forms)'. Within the Southern context, the activities that come under this heading include the slave codes of the Old South and the segregation laws and customs of the New, designed to compel if and when persuasion failed. And at their most extreme, they include violence: the South in Faulkner's lifetime was a violent region, and Mississippi was one of its most violent states. Just a few years before Faulkner was born, for instance, in 1890, Mississippi had 106 *recorded* homicides compared to 16 in Massachusetts. Tennessee, Alabama and Texas had more, 115, 108 and 184 respectively: but that was obviated by the fact that Mississippi had a much smaller population – in 1890, there were 2,235,527 people in Texas, 1,767,508 in Tennessee, 1,513,401 in Alabama, and only 1,289,600 in Mississippi. As the history of Faulkner's own family records, violence was as Southern as sweet potato pie. His great-grandfather killed two men in duels and was himself gunned down in the street by a former political rival and personal enemy; while his father Murry nearly died from pistol and shotgun wounds resulting from a ludicrously petty quarrel in 1891. Trying to avenge the attack, Murry suffered the indignity of misfiring his pistol six times and being shot in the hand; the assailant was then, according to custom, tried and acquitted. And on the very day in 1902 when Faulkner's family moved house to Oxford, 7000 citizens gathered to watch the public hanging of two men who had murdered a federal officer investigating illegal distilling. The surfaces of Southern life might be decorous, but beneath those surfaces hovered what one social scientist has called a 'subculture of violence',[53] inextricably tied to the military and hunting traditions of the region, the partial survival of frontier habits, and, not least, to a widespread obsession with the code of honour. How white Southerners perceived themselves was, in the first instance, inscribed in their everyday practices and, in the second, in their legal and institutional codes: but last, and by no means least, it was expressed in different forms of ritualized and, in effect, legitimized force.

The extreme expression of this use of force, as far as subjection of black people was concerned, was mob violence and, in particular, lynching. Between 1882 and 1927, there are records of 4951 deaths by illegal lynching in the United States, although the real figure is doubtless higher. The majority of these lynchings took place in the Deep South, and the majority of the victims were black. It is grimly significant that Mississippi, which in 1920 had the smallest population of the states in the Deep South, had a higher number of lynchings during those years than any other state: 561 in all. And the worst period for these atrocities was during the 1890s, the decade of Faulkner's birth. Two lynchings, in particular, could be said to frame Faulkner's life: the killing of Nelse Patton in Oxford in 1906, and that of Emmett Till near Greenwood, Mississippi, in 1955. Nelse Patton was a trusty from the local jail who, while on an errand, had cut a white woman's throat with a razor. Later, after he was arrested, a mob attacked the jail, shot Patton, and castrated his dead body: after which, the body was dragged behind a car to the square and hung naked from a tree. A friend of J.W.T. Falkner, William Faulkner's grandfather, had harangued the crowd before the event, telling it to 'Shoot Patton, and shoot to kill!'; and one of William's schoolmates was the brother of the boy who fired the first shot. Inevitably, the incident fuelled the future writer's imagination, forming a basis for the final episodes of the story of Joe Christmas in *Light in August*. Equally inevitably, although most people knew who was to blame, nobody was brought to answer for this brutal incident: the coroner's jury, when convened, found that 'the said Nelse Patton came to his death from gunshot or pistol wounds inflicted by parties to us unknown'.[54] It was a perfect instance of a system of relations being underwritten by the unwritten law, popular institutionalized violence. The killers of Patton were protected, and their actions legitimated, by a code that not only condoned, but positively required, rituals of subjection.

The case of Emmett Till was even starker in its implications. Till was a black boy just fourteen years old who had come from Chicago to visit relatives in Greenwood. While there, he was accused by some white men of whistling at a white woman and making an obscene remark to her. The unwritten law of subjection again required exemplary punishment: Till was abducted, savagely beaten, and then finally murdered. Two relatives of the woman's husband were arrested: this time, at least, a court case followed. But the jury, consisting of local people, refused to convict. Even before this, on the news of the arrests and in response to a request from the United Press, Faulkner had fired off a brief dispatch expressing his horror at 'this sorry and tragic error committed in my native Mississippi by two white adults on an afflicted Negro child'. 'If we . . . have reached that point in our desperate culture that we must murder children', he added, 'we don't deserve to survive, and probably won't.' The protest was typical of Faulkner in his later years, when he felt compelled as a public figure – or, perhaps more accurately, as a private face in a public place – to make his position on issues, and particularly on the vexed issue of race, abundantly clear. Sometimes, his awareness of the racial situation, subjection and the growing resistance to it on the part of blacks after the Second World War, would drive him near to distraction. In 1956, for example, when the federal courts ordered the University of Alabama to admit a young black woman named Autherine Lucy, Faulkner became convinced that, if she set foot on the campus, she would not leave it alive. Drinking heavily to offset his growing sense of crisis, he insisted in one interview that if the problem escalated, 'The government will send its troops and we'll be back at 1860.' In terms of his expressed political opinions, Faulkner was a gradualist and a Southern moderate: that led, inevitably, to threats and vilification from white neighbours (not so much in Oxford, a relatively liberal university town, as in other parts of Mississippi) and, equally inevitably, to sharp criticism of his position from Northern liberals and black people, North and South, who suffered the daily experience of subjection. Matters were not helped by Faulkner's candour. He opposed racism, he detested in particular its more violent manifestations: but he was, he admitted, first and last a Southerner. So, he confessed,

> As long as there's a middle road, all right. I'll be on it. But if it came to fighting I'd fight for Mississippi against the United States even if it meant going out into the street and shooting Negroes . . . I will go on saying that the Southerners are wrong and that their position is untenable, but if I have to make the same choice Robert E. Lee made then I'll make it.[55]

Faulkner later disavowed the more inflammatory, and repugnant, parts of this statement; and it is clear that what he said was at least in part a function of drink. But it is not necessary to believe in the old saw of *in vino veritas* to see that, as a Southerner and a Mississippian, Faulkner felt himself torn: between identification with a region that had given him birth and helped shape his consciousness, his structure of feeling – and detestation of the daily acts of subjection and violence on which that region and consciousness were partly founded. This war within him fired his novels into life; out of it he could create genuine, dialogic conflict. But, as far as his publicly expressed opinions were concerned, it led to some hypothetical – and, in the final analysis, untenable – 'middle road': punctuated, occasionally, by the dreadful sense that his own internal contradictions would eventually be externalized, and civil war would return to the land.

As Faulkner grew older, the courage that had led him to speak out against segregation never deserted him, even if it resulted in him being labelled 'nigger-lover' and 'Weeping Willie Faulkner' by other Mississippians –

and even if it left him more or less isolated within his own family. When
Faulkner began to receive threatening letters, and anonymous callers
phoned to curse him in the middle of the night, most of his relatives were
unsympathetic: 'none of us agreed with Bill's views', his brother John
later remarked, 'we said, "It serves him right. He ought to have known
this would happen".' Nevertheless, Faulkner continued to protest, and not
just in terms of simple polemic: at times, he was capable of very sharp
impromptu social analysis. More than once, for instance, he argued that
racism was not basically a 'moral problem' but 'an economic problem', a
matter of the distribution of wealth and power: the whites, unsurprisingly,
wanted to retain a monopoly of both. And he insisted, with equal perception, that the abolition of racism was necessary for the creation of a just
society for people of *all* races: 'The question is no longer of white against
black', as he put it, '. . . it is whether or not white people shall remain
free.' The bravery and insight were undeniable, then, but so were the
occasional touches of prejudice, blindness or at least myopia: and, as the
arteries hardened, the gradualism came to sound more and more like a
form of conservatism. Faulkner's frequent use of the word 'nigger', for
instance, is disquieting. It is used in an apparently uncritical way: without,
that is, any sense of the vicious politics that engendered it and which,
in turn, it substantiates and confirms. His remark to the nuclear physicist,
J. Robert Oppenheimer, for instance, 'T.V. is for niggers', seems intended
to devalue both terms in the equation: to create guilt by association by
identifying a medium Faulkner detested in terms of a supposedly less than
intelligent racial group. Sometimes, certainly, the novelist was out to shock.
When he told a New York journalist, in 1931, that black people were
better off under slavery, it seems clear that what he said was motivated less
by conviction than by boredom, a need to conceal himself behind the
grinning mask of the good old boy – and, perhaps, a residual sense that
a benevolent patriarchy is no worse than the excesses and complacencies
of capitalism. But more often than not the prejudice, when it is expressed,
seems instinctive rather than adopted, and it fits uncomfortably well with
Faulkner's reluctance to give due credit to either African-American or
African culture: 'three hundred years ago', Faulkner observed in 1956 in
an article written for the black magazine *Ebony*, 'the Negro's naked grandfather was eating rotten elephant or hippo meat in an African rain-forest.'
By 1958, in one of his last public statements on the race issue, Faulkner
was ready to declare,

> Perhaps the Negro is not yet capable of more than second-class citizenship.
> His tragedy may be that so far he is competent for equality in the ratio of
> his white blood.[56]

Admittedly, there was a palliative here. Just as Faulkner tended to denigrate
African culture in order to point out and measure how far individual black
people had advanced, so these barbed remarks about black intellectual

attainment fuelled his demands for black education. But this hardly excused Faulkner's position. African culture was still unjustifiably denigrated; African-American culture was ignored in favour of specific blacks who had succeeded in the white world; and the language of 'blood', white and black, made Faulkner's initial premise sound crudely essentialist, an argument from unalterable 'nature' rather than 'culture' or 'nurture', and so would tend to subvert his pleas for educational reform. 'Go slow now', Faulkner was fond of saying to both Northern liberals and black activists; and, when he was asked just how slow, he would begin talking in terms of two or three centuries. His initial admission that the present system was unjust infuriated the Southern diehards: but such a prolonged time frame hardly endeared him to the other side – people who were, after all, only seeking basic civil rights. Faulkner found himself, in fact, suffering the traditional fate of the moderate, of being attacked from both directions. In the context of the immediate crisis, many took the position that those who were not for them were against them – or that clinging to the middle ground was simply another way of sitting on the fence.

All of which is to say that Faulkner found himself at the cutting edge of racial history: a corner from which he could see the road that lay behind and the road lying ahead. On occasion, especially in his discursive prose when his imagination was not thoroughly captivated by his fictive county, he would set his eyes in one direction, towards past or future. Or, alternatively, he would attempt to resolve the contradictions inherent in his position with argument – a series of embattled propositions that often conflicted with one another within the space of a single essay. The result was muddy, confused, and to many observers alienating: Faulkner would place one statement that appealed beside another that repelled and then try, desperately, to compel them into the appearance of symmetry. A resolution along these lines was impossible, because there were simply too many warring forces at work, too many disparate positions in conflict. All that Faulkner could and did do, in fact, was not resolve the tensions generated by racial conflict, in himself and in his region, but *dramatize* them – explore the actual process of conflict and the possible system of racial relations that might begin to emerge out of this process. One famous contemporary of Faulkner's, another novelist, F. Scott Fitzgerald, argued that there could be no satisfactory biography of any storyteller: 'There can't be', he insisted. 'He is too many people.'[57] Whether or not this is true as a general proposition, there were certainly 'too many people' in Faulkner as far as the racial question was concerned: the brave opponent of injustice and the cautious gradualist, the spokesman for economic equality and the instinctive racist, the articulate rebel and the good old boy, the liberal and the conservative. Too many people to be accommodated in anything other than a novel: where all their voices could be accommodated and engaged in a developing dialogue, with a sharp sense of the historical ironies involved and a nicely graduated measure of self-awareness.

The details of this dialogue are too extensive to be properly defined here: they are, after all, a product of the accumulative development of all the novels and stories. But, apart from the point made earlier about Faulkner's willingness to concede the 'otherness' and autonomy of black people, it is worth emphasizing two aspects of black identity that receive particular attention in his work. And these concern Faulkner the novelist's firm sense that such identity has to do with subjection and resistance: that the terms in which black people are known, by themselves as well as white people, are the product of social positioning, and that these terms only the strong, brave or just plain cussed among them can meet and counter. The first aspect relates to the perverse logic of guilt. 'There is a logical pattern to evil', thinks Horace Benbow in *Sanctuary*; and in Faulkner's work that pattern is intricate and interconnected. Like many writers from the South, Faulkner tended to associate the idea of evil, so potent in the region, with the black man's or black woman's shadowy figure. One of Faulkner's characters talks of a 'curse' visited upon the white race by the black; and this registers a general, regional tendency towards projection. The victims of evil become the messengers of evil and therefore the emblems of evil. In the eyes of white Southerners, including white Southern writers, black people are transmuted into vivid icons of Original Sin, simply by being there, standing on the periphery of things: reminders of a crime committed not so very long ago by some mythic, communal ancestor. Unlike most of his contemporaries, however, Faulkner went further than this. Certainly, the guilt is there, ingrained in the texture of his books: more specifically, the association of blacks and evil is part of their mythological framework, their structure of thought and feeling. But it is also the object of creative analysis: Faulkner's sense of evil, at least in his fiction, was self-aware, self-dramatizing and above all self-critical. From the legion of other possible illustrations of this, it is only necessary to cite a moment in *Go Down, Moses* when Roth Edmonds feels that he can no longer sleep beside Henry Beauchamp, the black boy who up until then has been his closest friend and constant companion. There is no specific reason why Roth feels this way, the narrator tells us. It is just that 'one day the old curse of his fathers, the old haughty ancestral pride . . . descended to him'.[58] Roth simply inherits the racial prejudice, and the guilt, of his ancestors and re-enacts their Original Sin: a Sin that is compounded by the fact that, since he and Henry share the same great-great-grandfather, he is denying his brother in a double sense. The power of this moment is extraordinary; and it issues from the fact that it encapsulates a feeling provoked by the entire narrative. For all the stories that go to make up the book present the black as a kind of Nemesis: a bringer of doom and a provoker of shame and fear. We are, in effect, invited to observe and examine evil, how it originates and expresses itself, and we are also made to feel it, to share in the sense of its presence. To be more exact, we are asked to see how black people are positioned, so as to be blamed and relegated for the very historical forces of which they were the victims; and we are drawn into participating, for a while, in the process of that positioning, the perverted logic of racial scapegoating.

'Then he was . . . enclosed . . . in that unmistakable odour of Negroes', Faulkner writes of Charles Mallison in *Intruder in the Dust*,

> – that smell which if it were not for something that was going to happen to him . . . he would have gone to his grave never once pondering . . . He had smelled it for ever, he would smell it always: it was a part of his inescapable past, it was a rich part of his heritage as a Southerner . . .[59]

Observations of this sort run through Faulkner's work: there are references, for instance, to 'the frank odour of . . . Negroes' in *Soldier's Pay*, to their 'animal odour' in *Flags in the Dust*, and to the 'smell' of the hordes of ex-slaves hurrying North in *The Unvanquished*. Repugnant though such comments may seem at first sight, they do have a positive function: which is to express, in peculiarly persuasive because sensory terms, the elusiveness and omnipresence of blacks. Odour, Jean-Paul Sartre has argued, is 'a disembodied body, vaporised, remaining complete in itself, and yet transformed into a volatile essence'. As such, it provides an extraordinarily apt way of registering the position of blacks in Faulkner's white world, who always seem to be around even when the white characters refuse to see them, creating subtle feelings of discomfort and unease. Faulkner's black characters, one could say, are there in the sense that their white neighbours have appropriated them, use them and rely on their labour, but not there to the extent that whites never grant them full reality, true identity – never acknowledge their existence as concrete individuals. They are an absent presence: just as, Sartre indicates, smell is because it is all around, quite literally part of the air one breathes, but something that must remain tantalizingly diffuse, undefined and intangible.

The second aspect of the positioning of black people in Faulkner's novels has to do, not with white perception, but with black reactions. Within the terms of the family romance of the South, black people are called upon to play parts that may appear various but are all based on presumptions of inferiority and deference. Whatever their status, Faulkner shows, they are trapped within alien vocabularies, imprisoned in rules that require more or less absolute subjection. The two most compelling examples of this predicament, and possible responses to it, are Lucas Beauchamp and Joe Christmas. In both *Go Down, Moses* and *Intruder in the Dust*, Lucas Beauchamp is presented as a man whose entire life has been consumed in fighting against his role: insisting on his rights both as a direct descendant, by the male line, of Lucius Quintus Carothers McCaslin, and as a man, an individual. In the earlier book, this takes the open, active form of actually confronting Zack Edmonds, his landlord (and relative), and attempting to kill him because Zack has taken Beauchamp's wife into his house. Beauchamp is not, it seems, content to accept the role of 'nigger' by allowing Edmonds to do with him and his family as he wishes; and he is even willing to use violence to make the point. In *Intruder in the Dust*, despite the melodramatic violence of the story, Beauchamp's resistance to the part imposed on him is quieter and perhaps more profoundly subversive, expressed in innumerable little habits and gestures. He studiously avoids addressing whites by name, so as not to have to call them 'Mister', or, if he does use 'sir' or 'Mister', he says it in such a way that it is somehow obvious that he does not mean it. He will not accept the presents of Charles Mallison, offered in a patronizing, squirearchical spirit, without responding in kind. And, having been rescued from the charge of murdering a white man, he even refuses to respond with the sort of abject humility and gratitude expected of a 'nigger', carefully paying his rescuers ('I authorised you', he tells Gavin Stevens, 'How much do I owe you?') and then, in the last breath of the book, demanding a receipt. There is clearly the implication that one reason why Beauchamp is accused of murder in the first place is that this is the only way white people can 'make a nigger out of him for once in his life'. Nor is the animosity toward him confined to whites; his behaviour irritates some black people as well. 'It's the ones like Lucas', declares Aleck Sander (Mallison's black companion), 'makes trouble for everybody.'[60] Evidently, not all those imprisoned in their roles object to it, since one person's prison may be another's safety and security. For some, like Beauchamp, the part of 'nigger' may be a source of anger and anxiety: but for others, for whom Sander appears to speak at this moment, it is just a way of avoiding trouble.

In some ways, Lucas Beauchamp continues the idea of the 'tragic mulatto' that goes back in Southern writing at least as far as the work of black novelists like Charles W. Chesnutt as well as white writers like Mark Twain and George Washington Cable. Far more than slavery, Faulkner focused on miscegenation as the repressed myth of the Southern past. And he focused on it in ways that indicated he was not just interested in what Chesnutt termed 'the problems of people of mixed blood' in and for themselves, but for the chance they offered him to explore the linked questions of social positioning, identity and knowledge. This comes out with particular force in the story of Joe Christmas in *Light in August*, whose dilemma stems not from the fact but from the *idea* of mixed blood. Neither Joe nor the reader ever knows whether he is white or part-black; Joe, however, has been convinced by his culture that he needs to know this in order to know who he is. Unable to see the issue of race as one that is incidental to the definition of self, and unable to accept wholeheartedly the role of black or that of white, he seems to be at once imprisoned and empty: imprisoned by false notions of identity that constitute the only ones he has ever been taught, and empty because, lacking the tools to create his own vocabulary of selfhood, he really ceases to exist as anything more than a cipher. It seems appropriate that his name should be no more than an arbitrary label attached to him by people who neither know who he is nor care; since, even more obviously than Beauchamp's, his problem is one of names rather than things. 'Joe Christmas' is little more than a linguistic convention, a shape to fill a lack. It is not an authentic name because Joe's is not an authentic language – which is to say, a language that relates directly to his own experience and expresses his immediate needs; and without an authentic name or language, Joe is without the agencies necessary for any understanding of himself. Extreme though his case may appear to be he is, for Faulkner, a representative instance of the tragic consequences of social positioning: an example, perhaps, of what Althusser was thinking of when he said 'a subjected being ... is ... stripped of all freedom except that of freely accepting his submission'.[61]

Submission in a different sense was required of another group who found their options painfully limited by the terms of Southern culture and, in particular, by the requirements of the family romance. The positioning of women in and by the regional culture was (and perhaps still is) peculiarly extreme: not least because of the cult of Southern Womanhood which – as W.J. Cash explains in *The Mind of the South* – made it possible to associate white women of the privileged classes with 'the very notion' of the region. The cult, Cash points out, rested on a clear division of roles. Black women, and some white women, were assigned the sexual function: which is to say, of course, not that they were the only ones ever engaged in sexual relations, but that they were those with whom the sexual dimension of experience was habitually and mythically associated. This made it possible to transform the bulk of white women into creatures of angelic perfection, stainless expressions of the ideal, whose sexuality was minimized even if it was ever acknowledged. The white woman, Cash suggests, became

the South's Palladium ... – the shield-bearing Athena gleaming whitely in the clouds, the standard for its rallying, the mystic symbol in face of the foe. She was the lily-pure maid of Astolat ... And – she was the pitiful Mother of God ... There was hardly a sermon that did not begin and end with tributes in her honour ...[62]

Despite the rather flamboyant way in which this is expressed, Cash is surely locating a significant pattern here, and one that profoundly affected Southern thought and life. By means of it, any threat to the fabric of the society could be translated into a threat to its totem: what Cash christened the 'rape complex' was powerful in the South, as the unfortunate Emmett Till discovered to his cost. While subjecting 'ladies' to protective rituals that were, in effect, forms of domination, the cult of Southern Womanhood transformed all black people who did not 'know their place' (and, of course, black men in particular) into threats to female purity, actual or potential contaminators of the Virgin shrine. Women were divided into whores or virgins to an extent unusual even in western societies, courtesans to be used or 'sisters' to be honoured (the racist question, 'Would you let your sister marry one?', had a special *generalized* force within the Southern family romance). Sexuality was acknowledged, perhaps, but only on a suppressed, subterranean level; it was contained by being compartmentalized, assigned to the lower depths of society – and to what several of Faulkner's characters term 'periodical filth'.

'The *return of the repressed*', Herbert Marcuse has suggested 'makes up the tabooed and subterranean history of civilisation.' And just such a return is a constitutive feature of many of Faulkner's narratives: the repressed facts, in particular, of sex between the races and female sexuality haunt the margins and occupy the spaces or interstices between so many of the stories that his characters try to tell. One way in which the disconcerting fact or possibility of female sexuality occurs in his work recalls the terms in which the novelist registers the peculiarly absent presence of black people: there is a remorseless emphasis on the olfactory sense, the way so many of Faulkner's young male characters smell out something they would prefer not to acknowledge, not to be aware of on a conscious level. Quentin Compson in *The Sound and the Fury*, Horace Benbow in *Sanctuary* (especially the original version), Joe Christmas in *Light in August*: all these characters feel suffocated by the odour of burgeoning honeysuckle that they associate with the sexuality, the physicality of the women they know. And not only honeysuckle: the moment when Benbow decides that he can no longer bear living with his wife Belle is worth remembering at this point, since for him the experience of married love is summed up by his weekly expeditions to collect a package of shrimps. Belle adores shrimps, Benbow explains, and every Friday he goes to collect a packet of them from the train and then carry them home. 'I still don't like to smell shrimp', he says,

> But I wouldn't mind the carrying it home so much, I could stand that. It's because the package drips. All the way home it drips and drips, until after a while I follow myself... and stand aside and watch Horace Benbow ... thinking, Here lies Horace Benbow in a fading series of small stinking spots on a Mississippi sidewalk.[63]

It does not require a particularly subtle or intensive reading of this passage to see that it involves a covert reference to female sexuality, or to be more exact, to the fact of menstruation. 'Delicate equilibrium of periodical filth between two moons balanced', Mr Compson calls it in *The Sound and the Fury*, while Joe Christmas thinks in terms of 'something liquid, deathcoloured, and foul'. The terms may vary: but the response to the menstrual cycle remains the same, and points to a set of perceptions and associations shared by many of Faulkner's white male characters. '*Women ... have an affinity for evil*', the assumption is, they are 'older in sin than men', 'not interested in morals', and 'are born already bored with what a boy approaches only at fourteen and fifteen with blundering and aghast trembling'. Mud, filth, blood are the elements that suggest this; anything 'womansmelling' supplies the appropriate, evocative imagery; and the entire complex of feeling is summed up by certain trigger words ('knowledge', 'nature', 'earth') that derive ultimately perhaps from the mythic figure of Eve.

This association of women with the idea of evil is inextricable, Faulkner suggests, from the habit his white male characters have of compartmentalizing them. Of Henry Sutpen in *Absalom, Absalom!*, for example, we are told that he had 'a simple and . . . untroubled code in which females were ladies or whores or slaves'; for him, the other sex was

> separated into three sharp divisions, separated (two of them) by a chasm which could be crossed but one time and in one direction . . . – the virgins whom gentlemen someday married, the courtesans to whom they went while on sabbaticals to the cities, the slave girls and women upon whom that first caste rested and to whom in certain cases it doubtless owed the very fact of its virginity . . .[64]

As always in Faulkner's work, it is as well to remember who is telling the tale, since this has a lot to do with what is told. In this case, it is Mr Compson speaking to Quentin; and it is not difficult to see that he is describing a complex that has profoundly affected both of them, although in rather more circuitous ways than these remarks might suggest. Henry, in Mr Compson's eyes, is (at this stage in his development, at least) an innocent: and he is regarded as such largely because he reminds Mr Compson of himself when he was young. As several commentators have pointed out, Mr Compson is a disillusioned idealist, and one of the things he has clearly become disillusioned with is women – or rather, Woman. Having subscribed once to the cult of Southern Womanhood, according to which some women at least are regarded as 'virgins', he has now come to see them all as contaminated by sexuality and 'periodical filth': as all 'whores' with *'a natural affinity for evil'*. 'No woman is to be trusted', he tells Quentin. What he means is that he 'trusted' Woman once, in other words idealized her; and that, when she turned out to be real rather than ideal, he felt humiliated and betrayed.

Some of this is hypothetical, of course: we know relatively little of Mr Compson's early life and have to draw inferences from what, in later years, he says and does. However, there is no need to fall back on hypotheses in Quentin's case, or those of Horace Benbow or Joe Christmas. Quentin, Benbow and Christmas all struggle fiercely to protect their notion of Woman as a figure of stainless perfection: dressed in white, perhaps, a temple or sanctuary for ideals, as free from the contaminations of time as Keats's Grecian Urn. But all of them find this notion challenged by events, and in particular by their own unwilling acknowledgement of the menstrual cycle, or female sexuality, or both: the dress seems muddied as a result, the sanctuary desecrated, the urn is irreparably cracked. Quentin is so shaken by this, the violation of his sister (and, by implication, of all his 'sisters' in the family romance), that he tries to evade this disabling knowledge by committing suicide. Even he, though, is tempted towards the conclusion that Benbow and Christmas reach once they feel their goddess is a false one: that Woman, if she is not the expression of a bodiless good, must be the all too fleshly embodiment of evil. '*They're all bitches*',[65] Caddy Compson's lover Dalton Ames tells Quentin: and Quentin, to his despair, feels himself seriously tempted to agree. If Caddy his sister is not a virgin, then she must be a whore: that is the devastating logic that is beginning to go to work in his mind before he puts a stop to it – terminates it in the most drastic possible way, by suicide.

The matter does not stop there, however, as a problem of Quentin's or Benbow's or Christmas's: as something to do simply with Faulkner's characters. Here again it is worth emphasizing that what Faulkner is doing is dramatizing and exploring a complex of feeling he shares, a code that was his as a white, male Southerner. Several attempts have been made to label Faulkner a misogynist – which is surely wrong. His attitude towards women is far too intricate to be described in such terms. Apart from anything else, one of his purposes in presenting us with people like Mr Compson or Quentin is to help us to place them: to understand, certainly, the motives behind the equation 'woman = evil' but also to criticize it, to see it as a symptom rather than an explanation. One does not have to subscribe to the wound and the bow theory, however, to realize that one reason why Faulkner describes this particular obsession so powerfully is that it was his, part of his own experience and psychological make-up. *Sanctuary* is the classic instance here. It is a disturbing book, and not simply because it dwells on various incidents of violence and perversion. It is also because the author appears to be implicated himself, involved however circuitously in those incidents. The way in which Faulkner observes Temple Drake, for instance, is disconcertingly close to the voyeuristic ('long-legged, thin-armed, with high small buttocks . . . she moved swiftly . . . writhing into her scant, narrow dress'); while he even seems to participate, to be involved in her rape in a distanced, vicarious way (like Popeye, he cannot perform the act himself, and so he recruits someone else to do it for him while he watches). Moreover, he is often painfully close, embarrassingly sympathetic to Horace Benbow, sharing in his protagonist's sense of betrayal – and in his related suspicion that woman is evil, 'older in sin than he would ever be'. Admittedly, the eventual published version of *Sanctuary* is much less introspective and narcissistic than the original, less preoccupied with Benbow, his Prufrockian postures, and what his wife mockingly terms his 'complex' about his sister. But even here the opulent and crushing inwardness of the prose, its febrile intensity and scarcely suppressed hysteria, provide the best possible proof that Faulkner understands that 'complex' because he was the man, he suffered, he was there:

> he . . . plunged forward and struck the lavatory and leaned upon his braced arms while the shucks set up a terrific uproar beneath her thighs. Lying with her head lifted slightly, her chin depressed like a figure lifted down from a crucifix, she watched something black and furious go roaring out of her

pale body. She was bound naked on her back on a flat car moving at speed through a black tunnel, the blackness streaming in rigid threads overhead, a roar of iron wheels in her ears . . . Far beneath her she could hear the faint, furious uproar of the shucks.[66]

With the loss of his sanctuary, Benbow, like many a disillusioned idealist, becomes prey to the belief that the world is broken, pointless. And it is precisely this sense of a broken world that comes through the narrative, with its apparently wilful refusal to explain things, to link character and motive to events, or to connect one event, one moment in time, to another. *Sanctuary* has often been called Faulkner's 'vision of evil'. It would probably be more accurate to describe it as the book of his that most clearly illustrates his relationship to his region's cult of Woman: a relationship that was characteristically balanced between love – or, at least, identification – and hate. More generally, it provides another example of how, in drawing a map of the regional code, he was also charting his consciousness of himself, his own spiritual geography.

Geography of a more material kind is also worth noting here: for many observers, anyway, there is a close connection between the weather and the physical world that were Faulkner's familiars and his habits of mind, the landscape of his imagination. W.J. Cash is among those who push this argument still further, by insisting on a *general* relation between Southern climate and character. Extravagant colours, lush fertility, perpetual heat-haze, and a prevailing mood of 'drunken reverie' disrupted by violent thunderstorms: all of these, Cash argues, contributed to a 'physical world' that was 'a sort of cosmic conspiracy against reality', and helped predispose the regional character towards dreamlike animation and emotional excess. As a climatic and cultural generalization this seems highly arguable: not even the single state of Mississippi has a uniform landscape and weather, let alone the South as a whole. Nevertheless, a peculiar pattern of indolence punctuated by violence is noticeable in Southern narratives at least as far back as *The Adventures of Huckleberry Finn* and, before that (if we accept Poe as a Southern author), *The Narrative of Arthur Gordon Pym*. And, as one of the best of Faulkner's critics has rightly pointed out, nature often tends to 'generate . . . mood' in the Yoknapatawpha stories: in 'Dry September', for instance, a lynching seems to issue from the 'sixty-two rainless days' that precede it – from a claustrophobic, combustible physical environment that only requires one spark, one small occasion, to set it alight. 'That's the trouble with this country' a character declares in *As I Lay Dying*,

everything, weather, all, hangs on too long. Like our rivers, our land's opaque, slow, violent: shaping and creating the life of man in its implacable and brooding image.[67]

Such feelings are, of course, partly a matter of attribution. Faulkner was well aware that we make a landscape in the process of perceiving it: that we attempt to give our lives a geographical location, a local habitation and a name and then, having done this, are inclined to confuse effect with cause. But Faulkner was no more a solipsist than he was a positivist. His characters may be keen to leave some 'fragile and indelible' evidence of themselves on the surface of the earth, like the girl in *Requiem for a Nun* who scratches her name on a window-pane in the town jail: something that says, *'Listen, stranger; this was myself: this was I.'* The activity, however, is not a matter of simple imposition. For all that Shreve, in *Absalom, Absalom!*, may describe the South as 'a kind of vacuum', it has its own indelible contours, its own harsh weather patterns and brute materiality. So the relationship between it, and character, has to be one of collaboration, participation not projection. Mind does not dominate world, any more than world merely dictates the terms of the mind: between life and landscape, character and climate, there is active dialogue, created out of habit it may be, or simple need.

Something of this dialogue is registered in that moment in *The Hamlet* when Flem Snopes has just sold his wild Texas ponies to the gullible locals of Frenchman's Bend. As the untameable beasts scatter in all directions, causing havoc, V. K. Ratliff and his companions fetch Will Varner to help the injured Henry Armstid. 'They went up the road in a body', the narrator observes,

> treading the moon-blanched dust in the tremulous April night murmurous with the moving of sap and the wet bursting of burgeoning leaf and bud and constant with the thin and urgent cries and the brief and fading burst of galloping horses . . .
>
> . . .
>
> . . . The moon was new high overhead, a pealed and mazy yawn in the soft sky, the ultimate ends of which rolled onward, whorl on whorl, beyond the pale stars and by pale stars surrounded . . . Then the pear tree came in sight. It rose in mazed and silver immobility like exploding snow; the mockingbird still sang in it. 'Look at that tree,' Varner said. 'It ought to make this year, sho.'
>
> 'Corn'll make this year too,' one said.
>
> 'A moon like this is good for every growing thing outen earth,' Varner said. 'I mind when me and Mrs. Varner was expecting Eula. Already had a mess of children and maybe ought to quit then. But I wanted some more gals . . . there was an old woman told my mammy once that if a woman showed her belly to the full moon after she had done caught, it would be a gal. So Mrs. Varner taken and laid every night with the moon on her nekid belly, until it fulled and after. I could lay my ear to her belly and hear Eula kicking and scrouging like all get-out, feeling the moon.'
>
> 'You mean it actually worked sho enough, Uncle Will?' the other said. 'Hah,' Varner said. 'You might try it. You get enough women showing their nekid bellies to the moon or the sun either . . . and more than likely after a while there will be something you can lay your ear and listen to . . .'
>
> . . .
>
> . . . there was a brief rapid thunder of hooves on wooden planking.

'There's another one on the creek bridge,' one said. 'They are going to come out even on them things, after all,' Varner said. 'They'll get the money back in exercise and relaxation. You take a man that aint got no other relaxation all year long except dodging mule-dung up and down a field furrow. And a night like this . . . is good for him. It'll make him sleep tomorrow night anyhow, provided he gets back home by then.'[68]

At first, it may seem that the conversation and activities of the characters are in awkward contrast to the disconcerting beauty of their surroundings, but, as one Faulkner critic has commented, despite their distance from the ornate splendour of the narrator's language, they are clearly not unaffected by what they see. Varner's ready deployment of folklore is itself a dialogic reading of nature: a communal attempt to interpret the perceived rhythms of day, month and year that is given a sharply personal edge by his bawdy humour. The voice of his culture, registered in the inherited folk wisdom ('A moon like this is good for every growing thing'), engages with the extravagant voice of the narrator ('the moon . . . a pearled and mazy yawn'), and with a more personal voice compounded of memory and comedy. All of these, in turn, engage with the fluid voices of the countryside – the song of the mockingbird, the galloping hooves, 'the tremulous April night murmurous with the moving of sap' – so as to produce a feeling – not of unity, still less of the imposition of one voice on another – but of a complex, fertile engagement of opposites. 'The novel', observes Bakhtin, 'is . . . multiform in style and variform in speech and voice.' And here the multiplicity of style and variety of voice extend from nature through culture to the individual to project a creative interrelationship: in which each element possesses its own identity while being involved in contact with the other elements, and in mutual shaping. Varner himself seems shrewdly aware that the anarchic energy of the 'almost musical' cries and hoof-beats is somehow in keeping with the tremblings and murmurings of the night: the rueful pursuers of the ponies will at least have an adventure to talk about for years to come. And the reader, taking a cue from him, may intuit a further, underlying relation between the fecundity of nature, represented by the spring night, the ponies, the story of Eula's conception and after, and the ravishing sexuality of Eula herself – who appears, shortly before the passage just quoted, looking through a window, 'full in the moon . . . the strong faint lift of breasts beneath marblelike fall of the garment'.[69] Faulkner brings these things together, just as he does the voices of the episode, but he never collapses them into some spurious notion of harmony. Nature, culture and human nature are separated out and endowed with their different languages, so that the reader can all the more easily see the moments of sympathy and connection between them, and take the measure of their difference.

It is worth observing, in passing, that the entire episode of the Texas ponies from which this passage comes illustrates Faulkner's easy commerce with the tradition of frontier humour and, in particular, with the group of writers known as the Southwestern humorists: people like Augustus

Baldwin Longstreet, author of *Georgia Scenes* (1835), and George Washington Harris, who was responsible for *Sut Lovingood's Yarns* (1867). Faulkner,
like Mark Twain, knew that tradition intimately, just as he was familiar
with the whole habit of 'old tales and talking':[70] folk stories, gossip, tall
tales, and anecdote – all the transactions of an oral culture that might
occur around the fireside, on the front porch, in the general store or
barbershop, or (and this was particularly relevant for Faulkner) on a
hunting trip. And the intimacy bred a sophisticated, critical use of the
genre. The story of the Texas ponies is, in fact, a variation on one of the
favourite themes of the storyteller and humorist: the cunning trader who
outwits his neighbours in some apparently fair exchange of goods. The
theme is a common enough one, dating back to the time of the ancient
Greeks, with their legends of Odysseus and trickster gods, and finding
expression nowadays in the slightly bastardized form of jokes about commercial travellers and used-car salesmen. It was particularly popular with
the humorists of the Old Southwestern frontier: one of the stories in
Georgia Scenes is actually called 'The Horse-Swap', and describes in detail
how a horse-trader who does not attempt to conceal his delight in his own
cunning is outwitted by another member of his fraternity who poses as a
simpleton. And any comparison of the humorists' treatment of this theme
with that of Faulkner tends to show just how much Faulkner took from the
folkloric tradition and just how much he added to it: in particular, just
how far his subtle deployment of voice turned a static social event into a
dynamic one.

In Longstreet's tale 'The Horse-Swap', for instance, the narrator emphasizes, just as Faulkner was to do later, the communal nature of the
event: its status as a ritual, a contest of skill that attracts the interest of the
community because the skills being tested are held in general esteem. At
the close of the horse-trading, we are told,

> The prevailing feeling ... was that of mirth. The laugh became loud and
> general at the old man's [the worsted trader's] expense, and rustic wittic-
> isms were liberally bestowed upon him and his late purchases.[71]

Even this brief passage suggests, however, how the narrative voice acts to
distance event from reader: polite, genteel, intent on placing the subject,
it opens up an unbridgeable gap between them, the 'folk' acting as a
cohesive group, and 'us', the literate and probably town-dwelling outsiders. Not all Southwestern humorists used a narrative voice of this kind: but
even the best of them tended to imprison their subject in a language that
acted like a time capsule. Dialect or intrusive commentary, a moralizing
framework or a precious, mandarin vocabulary: various devices were seized
on to prise horse-swapping community and book-reading audience apart
and then seal them off – define them both, implicitly, as self-contained
units.

Faulkner's answer to this was an intelligent mixture of imaginative adventure and historical analysis. In the first place, he sought and gained a

greater sense of engagement in peasant life: its raw energy and the excitement that could occasionally spill over into violence. For this his models
were the people at the beginning of the humorist tradition rather than
those at the end, whose undeclared purpose it was to honour the gusty
pleasures of the life they described: they included all those anonymous
balladeers and amateur storytellers, firmly allied with the folk, on whom
Longstreet and his successors depended for much of their material. And
in the second place he sought and also acquired something that would
displace both the distanced perspective of a Longstreet and the unselfconscious involvement of a balladeer: a technique that, in promoting a multiplicity of voices, would allow not only for a variety of perspectives but for
a perception of the event being narrated as a dynamic, interactive process.
In the episode of the Texas ponies, Faulkner permits different voices to
engage with the event of barter: among them, as we have seen, the voice
of Will Varner, the voice of folkloric wisdom, the voice of a more sophisticated narrator, and the 'voice' of nature. As a result, that event is no
longer perceived as stable, a scene from provincial life recollected in tranquillity by a cosmopolitan narrator for the benefit of an audience just as
cosmopolitan as himself. It is seen, rather, as a collision: a conflict of
certain, specific forces that are themselves unstable and variable – subject
not only to interaction but to change. Trader and victims, individual and
culture, interloper and insiders, community and nature, narrator and
character, reader and character/narrator: none of these relationships is
fixed, there is continuous flux and reflux, as the different narrative voices
shift between different systems of exchange, economic and verbal. The
voices, the languages remain distinct, of course, but they engage with each
other: since Faulkner's simple, fundamental point is that different ways of
trading and talking *do* meet and interact in the general process we call
history – and in the particular moments of contact inscribed in the text.

The instability that distinguishes Faulkner's representation of relationships extends to his presentation of what is commonly accepted as the
most stable of all relations: that between a human being and the earth.
Some of the reasons for this particular instability have already been intimated: most notably, the collaborative nature of the creation of landscape, a sense of place, and the fluctuating nature of the intimacies between
man and land. Mind and the brute materiality of earth conflict and collude in most of Faulkner's narratives, and the intimacies range from the
protective to the outraged – from a sense of community felt by Will Varner
and his companions on a mild April night to the cold, bitter outrage of
the tenant farmer Mink Snopes. A further and deeper cause, however,
stems from the novelist's feeling for the history of the land. Faulkner
thinks historically even when it comes to his encounter with the earth and,
for him, that history is marked in particular by the assumptions of possession and dispossession. Nobody owns the land, that is Faulkner's initial
premise: to think so is a snare and a delusion. The point is made insistently throughout his work, for example in the story of the 'education' of

Ike McCaslin in *Go Down, Moses* or the tragic narrative of Thomas Sutpen in *Absalom, Absalom!*, a man who is destroyed by his assumption of power over nature. And it is summed up very neatly in a brief passage in *The Unvanquished*, describing two members of the McCaslin family, 'Uncle Buck' and 'Uncle Buddy'. The two men, the narrator informs us,

> believed that the land did not belong to people but that people belonged to land and that the earth would permit them to live on and out of it and use it only so long as they behaved and that if they did not behave right, it would shake them off just like a dog getting rid of fleas.[72]

The ironies implicit in all this are explored in Faulkner's accounts of whole generations who believe they have thoroughly possessed and permanently named the places they inhabit: rather, that is, than passed over them and given them passing identification. And they lie only just below the surface of the novelist's own claim to be 'Sole Owner & Proprietor' of Yoknapatawpha County. Faulkner might have cherished his postage stamp of native soil, he might have tilled it in his imagination and reaped the appropriate rewards: but, as he evidently realized, he could never exercise complete dominion over it. To this extent, his relationship to Yoknapatawpha was analogous to that of his characters: claiming to possess it he was in fact possessed by it, wishing to appropriate it he could do no more than inhabit it temporarily. Like the land to which the label 'Sutpen's Hundred' is attached in *Absalom, Absalom!*, it existed apart from any specific acts of naming, all pretensions to ownership and control; it was inertly, continually resistant to fixed signs.

The assumption of power over nature links up closely, in Faulkner's work, with the assumption of power and proprietorial control over human nature, witnessed in historical injustices towards the members of two races. As a Mississippian, Faulkner had particular reasons for linking the fact of the land to the idea of betrayal: because massive land claims, the dispossession of Native Americans and the claim to possession of African-Americans were all marked and related features of the state's history. Between 1820 and 1832, huge land cessions amounting to two-thirds of the state were wrung from the Choctaws and Chickasaws by what one historian has called a combination of 'bribery and drink', and 'threats and promises . . . of only two alternatives – extinction or forcible removal'.[73] These transactions set Mississippi on a different road that led not only to secession and civil war but, afterwards, to an insularity remarkable for its extent and persistence. In the short term, there was a massive explosion of cheap public land and the speculative farming population. During the 'flush times' between 1830 and 1840, the state population as a whole increased 175 per cent while the slave population grew 197 per cent: by 1840, for the first time, black people outnumbered white in Mississippi. And, in the long term, towns failed to develop, industry was stifled, education remained dormant: in short, a pattern was set that for a century after 1830 would keep Mississippi one of the most rural states in the nation. Of course, other states seized land from the Indians and experienced booms in land speculation and slavery. But the speed, scale and consequences of the flush times in Mississippi were unusually dramatic. So it is hardly surprising that, as a native son of Mississippi and an unusually alert one, Faulkner should have registered the tangled, tentacular nature of the relationship between man and land. The vicissitudes of history were something written into his surroundings, promoting instabilities that seemed to be as much a matter of place, really, as of time.

Something of the way history was inscribed in geography for Faulkner is registered in two of his stories that deal with the complex, ironic relationship between red, white and black people in Yoknapatawpha, 'Red Leaves' and 'A Justice'. 'Red Leaves' concentrates on the autumn of the Old Days, the time of the Indians in the county. Issetibbeha, the Man, has just died and his black body-servant has fled, in order to escape the traditional burial of the slave with the dead chief. With this story of escape and pursuit acting as the narrative spine, the anonymous narrator then comes back into earlier times to recall the arrival of black slaves among the Chickasaws. To the Chickasaw Indians, we are told, their newly acquired human property seemed

> remote, inscrutable. They [the slaves] were like a single octopus. They were like the roots of a huge tree uncovered, the earth broken momentarily upon the writhen, thick fetid tangle of its lightless and outraged life.[74]

The intensely poetic conceit hardly seems out of place. This is partly because of the ritualistic quality of the narrative: Faulkner may be intent on establishing the past as something vitally connected to the present, but he also wishes to respect its specificity and radical difference; and one convenient way of doing this is through an oracular, shaman-like style of storytelling. The conceit has a more particular relevance here, however, since it expresses the sense of violation, natural forces disrupted and disturbed, that characterizes this era of exploration, enslavement and conquest. The reader is continually reminded of the frontier as a site of struggle and confusion, where trophies and status have become blurred, unpredictable and faintly ominous. Issetibbeha, for instance, owns 'ten thousand acres of matchless parklike forest where deer grazed like domestic cattle', a 'herd of blacks for which he had no use at all', 'a gilt bed, a pair of girandoles . . . and a pair of slippers with red heels' brought back from a trip to Paris; and he lives in the rotting shell of a steamboat which slaves have hauled twelve miles overland, its 'carving glinting momentarily and fading through the mould in figures cabalistic and profound'. A similar mixture, or conflict, of cultural icons is notable in the representation of the escaped slave: who, we are told, wears

> a pair of dungaree pants bought by Indians from white men, and an amulet slung on a thong about his hips. The amulet consisted of one half of a

mother-of-pearl lorgnon which Issetibbeha had brought back from Paris
and the skull of a cottomouth mocassin. He had killed the snake himself
and eaten it, save the poison head.[75]

The tensions between the residual culture of the Chickasaws, and the
emergent one of the whites, is neatly caught here and then expanded in
the larger terms of the story. Most of 'the People' (as the tribe is called)
observe the rituals of the hunt. However, Moketubbe, Issetibbeha's son,
prefers wearing the red slippers to engagement in strenuous, ritualistic
practices; and, in any event, *this* rite is contaminated by the simple fact
that the hunt is for a commodity, a human being reduced to a property.
As the useless trinkets Issetibbeha brings back from Paris indicate, the
tribe has already surrendered to the white man's world of exchange value;
and it has virtually abandoned hunting as a source of physical and spiritual sustenance in favour of the white man's ideology of ownership and
trade. The escaped slave, we learn, had once eaten a rat, which he had
caught easily since it had been 'civilised, by association with man reft of
its inherent cunning of limb and eye'; and the People have come to
resemble that rat, corrupted by association with a culture that will, in any
case, supplant them. The lesson of possession, of land and slaves, is one
they have learned without, it seems, much deliberation or even desire; and
it will lead, eventually, to their dispossession by the men who have been
their teachers – distant, enigmatic creatures who seem to have won the
struggle between cultures even before it has begun.

One of the triumphs of a story like 'Red Leaves' is that, implicitly, it
takes cognizance of a crucial problem in the representation of history:
which Fredric Jameson has called the 'unacceptable option, or ideological
double bind, between antiquarianism and modernising "relevance" or
projection'. If we assume the radical difference of the alien object we shall
be faced with the prospect of being shut off from its otherness by all the
intervening accumulations of history that have made us what we are. On
the other hand, if we choose to affirm the identity of the alien object with
ourselves, we shall miss 'the essential *mystery* of the cultural past' and will
inevitably fail to touch the strangeness of a genuinely different reality.
Only a genuine philosophy of history, Jameson argues, is capable of acknowledging that the past does constitute an alien reality, while recognizing that there are continuities of consciousness that help forge links between
past and present: continuities that constitute an 'uninterrupted narrative'
and that can therefore form the basis of an interpretative mastercode.
Only a genuinely historical understanding can give us an adequate account of an earlier culture 'which [as Jameson puts it] like Tiresias drinking the blood, is momentarily returned to life and warmth and allowed
once more to speak, and to deliver its long-forgotten message in surroundings utterly alien to it'. Just such an account occurs in the story of
Issetibbeha and his slave precisely because, while honouring the particularity
and even the peculiarity of the People, Faulkner discloses the solidarity of

its passions and polemics with those of the present day, the structural connections that exist between then and now. In 'Red Leaves', the past speaks with its own voice, its strangeness registered among other things in the strangeness *it* perceives in the figure of the white man, a scarcely decipherable source of trinkets, whisky and odd new customs like finance and ownership. But it speaks in a language not unrelated to our own, uncovering traces of a struggle that was and is the grounds of our own existence. It speaks to us, in short, in terms that reconstitute it as what Jameson would call a vital episode 'in a single vast unfinished plot'[76] – and as the necessary, and bloody, prehistory of the present.

In 'A Justice', the sense of the Native American past as separate and yet a precondition of the present is closer to the surface of the narrative because, as so often in Faulkner's work, the act of telling, 'old tales and talking', becomes a paradigm of the way we reconstitute history and situate ourselves as historical beings. The levels of the telling are several: Quentin Compson is the narrator and he tells a story that he heard, as a boy, from Sam Fathers who, in turn, had heard it from Herman Basket, one of the People. It is set in the last, corrupted era of Choctaw (in later stories, Chickasaw) life as it began to be disrupted by contact with white culture; and it is a tale of origins, concerning Sam's birth and naming. The situation may have an autobiographical source, since the young Faulkner and his brothers frequently visited their grandfather's farm a few miles north of Oxford, where John Faulkner remembered William habitually spending his time listening to a Negro blacksmith: 'he would be the last one back', John recalled, 'when Grandfather rounded us up to go home.' Be that as it may, it unobtrusively links a tangled tale of lineage to the plight and problems of one of Faulkner's most autobiographical characters, whose relationship to the South, as was observed earlier, divided him into 'two separate people': one living 'then', in some disinterred regional past, and another one living 'now'. The genealogy of which the tale tells is a radically mixed one: as Sam himself, Quentin and the reader all learn, Sam was born of a black slave woman by a Choctaw warrior named Crawfish-ford, much to the chagrin of the slave woman's black husband. The rivalry between Crawfish-ford and the husband supplies much of the narrative substance: a rivalry that is given an ingenious resolution by the then chief of the tribe, Ikkemotubbe – or Doom, as he came to be called. His solution to the problem is to require Crawfish-ford to build a palisade fence around the slave woman's house to keep its young builder out, and, apparently, this makeshift 'justice' works. Sam's complexion may be suspiciously copper-coloured and his origins dubious – hence his initial name, Had-Two-Fathers – but the next child born to the woman is as black as could be wished, and clearly begotten by the woman's husband. Quentin's response to this narrative, when he first hears it, is uncertain to the point of incomprehension: 'I was just twelve then', he recalls, 'and to me the story did not seem to have got anywhere, to have had point or end.' But, as he re-tells it, the older Quentin remembers his

conviction that he would one day understand the significance of what he
had heard: that he would not always have the experience but miss the
meaning. 'Grandfather called me again', he informs us,

> This time I got up. The sun was already beyond the peach orchard . . .
>
> . . .
>
> 'What were you and Sam talking about?' Grandfather said. We went on,
> in that strange, faintly sinister suspension of twilight in which I believed I
> could still see Sam Fathers back there, sitting on his wooden block, definite,
> immobile, and complete, like something looked upon after a long time in
> a preservative bath in a museum. That was it. I was just twelve then, and I
> would have to wait until I had passed on and through and beyond the
> suspension of twilight. Then I knew that I would know. But then Sam Fathers
> would be dead.
>
> 'Nothing, sir,' I said. 'We were just talking.'[77]

Whether Quentin, at any age, begins to *know* the significance of what
has been said remains dubious: he seems trapped in the voices and stories
of the past, mastered by them rather than mastering them. The famous
description of him in *Absalom, Absalom!*, as an 'empty hall echoing with
sonorous defeated names', comes to mind here; and, of course, on 2 June
1910, the assault of the 'loud world' of *The Sound and the Fury* finally
overwhelms him and he takes his own life. There are odd foreshadowings
of the outraged negatives and sense of impotence with which Quentin's
whole attempt to 'tell about the South' ends in *Absalom, Absalom!* ('Nothing,
sir': '*I don't hate it! I don't hate it!*');[78] and the haunting deployment of the
arrival of evening, always a time of uncertainty and unease in Faulkner's
work, reminds us that his 1929 novel about the Compson family began as
a short story called 'Twilight'. But if this story of origins seems strangely
opaque to the twelve-year-old Quentin, and even to the older Quentin
who remembers him, the lines of meaning are clearer to us the readers,
while by no means transparent: the different tellings are locked in, at
some point, to an uninterrupted narrative, a repressed history of conflict
and division. The first and most evident conflict is that between youth and
age, innocence and experience: reflected not only in the contrast between
the young Quentin Compson and the venerable Sam Fathers but between
the younger Quentin and the older. When offered a glimpse of the authentic, and ugly, realities of frontier life, the young boy's initial response
is one of incomprehension and denial. The older Quentin, the one whose
telling frames the tale, never gets beyond this into conscious knowing, still
less into understanding of the *historical* dimensions of what he has been
told. But there is a quality of recognition, however internalized, a repressed acknowledgement of the forces of disruption and death, that leaves
its surface traces in, for instance, the closing image of Sam Fathers immobile 'like something . . . in a museum'. The penultimate sentence, 'But
then Sam Fathers would be dead', may come as a shock, but it has been
subtly prepared for in this tale of 'the old days' that reaches its conclusion

at the moment of twilight. This may be a tale of origins but it is also a tale of endings, and the one thing that Quentin certainly learns – even if this is an intuition rather than an acknowledged thought – is that in his beginning is his end – the one too closely tied into the other, really, for his comfort.

A more radical division than this, in the sense that Quentin himself can neither resolve it nor ever manages to understand it, is the sexual one: which carries with it bitter intimations of the dual role of woman as taboo and commodity. The offence Crawfish-ford commits is not just that he crosses the colour line but that he violates the property rights of another man; since in this irredeemably patriarchal society one person is deemed to 'belong' to another – even if both, in turn, belong to a third party – because one is a woman and the wife of the other. These rights are eventually protected by the fence men are accustomed to build around their property to mark out their territorial rights; and the fence is built sufficiently high to prevent trespass. With his rights confirmed, the husband can then set about his proper, male business of securing a successor, and this time there can be no problems of paternity. The sanctity of the woman has been affirmed for the fundamental reason that the integrity of the line of succession, the *male* line, would otherwise be in doubt. In a matriarchal culture, tangible proof of legitimacy is possible: but, in a patriarchal one, that proof must always remain abstract and symbolic, based on 'a justice' that positions woman as temple and chattel – denied access to all but one, particular man. The ironic implications of this spill over in several directions. There is, first, the analogous presumption of possession of one race over another: the two slaves are, after all, the property of the chief who administers justice. Quite apart from adding to the judicial confusion (Is the woman primarily in the ownership of her husband or her master?), this serves to situate the whole business of justice itself as an historical phenomenon. Doom, the chief, is resolving a problem he has helped to create. By bringing slaves into his tribe, including the two at the centre of the dispute, he has helped introduce (or, at least, reinforce) the concept of a human being as a securible property on which the case against Crawfish-ford rests. The law, in this sense, serves to buttress and perpetuate a system that commodifies relations, turning them into a matter of contract; and the principal agent of the law not only supports that system, he is also one of its authors and main beneficiaries.

Beyond this specific range of textual implication, there is the dimension of intertextual reference: the way the notion of woman as sanctuary and commodity links up with the story of Quentin Compson and the history of his region. The connection with the cultural history of the South is, perhaps, evident from the earlier discussion of the regional culture and the family romance: the story of 'A Justice' offers one vital episode in a vast unfinished plot that marginalizes women while making claims to protect and reverence them. The link with the tale of Quentin, in turn, will be clear to anyone who has read *The Sound and the Fury* and *Absalom, Absalom!*

'Between the psyche and ideology there exists . . . a continuous dialectical interplay', observes Bakhtin, 'the psyche effaces itself . . . in the process of becoming ideology, the ideology effaces itself in the process of becoming the psyche.' This complex interplay between psyche and ideology is particularly notable in Quentin's response to women – and to one woman, his sister, in particular. For him, Caddie Compson is a sacred object who must be rendered inviolable, for reasons that show he has incorporated the regional cult of womanhood into his own biography: female honour has become a part of what Jameson might call his 'mapping fantasy', overlapping with the individual fantasies of others and with regional myths but not precisely coextensive with any of them. 'The champion of dames', his friend Spoade calls him in *The Sound and the Fury*; 'Bud', he adds, 'you excite not only admiration but horror.'[79] And, although Quentin hardly realizes it, he deserves this response. For his obsession with the honour of his sister is a derivative of that same structure of feeling that makes it possible for the characters in 'A Justice' to privilege questions of paternity and then translate these questions, in turn, into a dispute over purity and property.

The third and final division or conflict in the story is, unsurprisingly perhaps, the racial one. Sam Fathers's problematic racial origins and identity supply the occasion of the narrative. 'He lived with the Negroes', we are told,

> and they – the white people; the Negroes called him a blue-gum – called him a Negro. But he wasn't a negro. That's what I'm going to tell about.[80]

Quentin tells about this in telling the story Sam told him and was told in turn. Sam tells of the problem, too, in the very act of telling anything: 'he talked like a nigger', Quentin says,

> But his skin wasn't quite the colour of a light nigger and his nose and his mouth and his chin were not nigger nose and mouth and chin.[81]

In a superficial sense, this problem is solved when we learn who Sam's father was. But this hardly makes the younger Quentin feel more comfortable or knowledgeable; and the older Quentin still remembers Sam as an enigmatic, hieratic figure – 'like something . . . in a museum', representing secrets from the past shrouded in mystery. Not everything in the past is mysterious of course. Sam has a remarkably frank way of dealing with some subjects that makes those subjects painfully clear: 'a Choctaw chief', he instructs the young Quentin, 'sold my mammy to your great-grandpappy'. The facts of bondage, possession and dispossession, and the corruption of one culture by another: these are all indisputable facts of early Mississippi life that have contaminated relations ever since. There is, however, a difference between the raw, originary state of relations between people and between people and land and their subsequent state; if for no other reason than because those were the old times before (as it is put in another story) 'Issetibbeha and General Jackson met and buried sticks and signed a paper, and ... ran a line through the woods.' Intervening accumulations of history, measured here by cumulative layers of old tales and talking, mark off the gap between that time when Had-Two-Fathers was born and the moment when the older Quentin looks back at his younger self travelling home in twilight. The past is another country, then ... and yet, and yet: it shares its borders with the present. As the 'two fathers' of Sam and the two selves of Quentin indicate, the tragic divisions of yesterday are structurally related to those of today; the fissures between races that scar the very identity of the narrators and the land that situates them – these are part of one, developing story of conflict, one unending history of internecine struggle. No wonder, then, that the words with which 'A Justice' ends set a claim to knowledge ('I would know') in tension with an admission of ignorance ('Nothing, sir'), since it is precisely this, Faulkner intimates, that the simultaneous identity and difference of the past demands. We *can* know the past and can imaginatively participate in it, because its processes form a continuity with our own. But what we know, among other things, is its otherness: it is not the present, not least because it has shaped the present and helped to determine what we are.

One of the difficulties involved in understanding Faulkner is that he was born and lived in an exceptional place: a region, and more specifically a state and locality, that formed a kind of colonial economy in which the national alterations in production and consumption had been delayed or radically qualified. This is not to say that he participated in historical processes that were different in kind from those experienced in other industrialized cultures. But it is to state what is, perhaps, the obvious: that history is not a monolith and changes that occur in one particular part of the world do not act in precise synchrony with changes in another. Faulkner's protagonists, most of whom are roughly of their creator's generation, suffer a feeling of radical cleavage that fictional characters situated in other cultures share, as one form of social production and cultural perception yields to another. The cleavage is marked in the case of Faulkner's characters, however, by peculiar differences of timing and detail: differences that issue directly from the special nature of the Southern present and past. Faulkner had been born and brought up in a place where slavery, and after it the system of sharecropping had resisted the change to a *laissez-faire* economy, helping to generate social forms quite different from those which that economy fostered, with its stress on individual autonomy. And he began writing just before a flood of federal funding, encouraged by the programmes of the New Deal, began to transform the social order of the New South. His best work, in fact, from *The Sound and the Fury* (1929) to *The Hamlet* (1940) spans the revolution in the

Southern economy associated with what was, in effect, a movement away from low-wage, labour-intensive agricultural production (what some historians have called the second Reconstruction); and, inevitably, the changes in culture and consciousness that accompanied this revolution gave rise to new fictional imperatives, fresh imaginative forms. Quite simply, Faulkner's writing was forced out of specific social and cultural developments; and it is in terms of those specifics that, at some point, it deserves and needs to be known. 'History is what hurts,' observed Fredric Jameson,

> it is what refuses desire and sets inexorable limits to individual as well as collective praxis, which its 'ruses' turn into grisly and ironic reversals of their overt intention.[82]

For Faulkner, that history was a regional and local one, even if at some juncture it locked into other histories: it was this, what happened to him in his own immediate environment, that he had, in the first instance, to countenance and confront. 'You know,' Faulkner said once in one of his typically casual asides,

> sometimes I think there must be a sort of pollen of ideas floating in the air, which fertilises similarly minds here and there which have not had direct contact.[83]

In his case, that 'pollen of ideas' was mainly Southern and Mississippian in origin, part of the matter of Oxford. With its help, he managed to produce fiction that was historical in the best sense: something that could speak from the conflicts of his hometown, and the land he loved and hated, to anyone anywhere willing to learn.

III AUTOBIOGRAPHY AS HISTORY: THE LIFE OF FAULKNER

The problems of autobiography vexed Faulkner. On the one hand, as we have seen, he actively discouraged investigation of his private life, let alone any idea that there might be some significant connection between that life and the work. 'You seem to be spending too much time thinking about Bill Faulkner',[84] he testily observed to one interviewer, inviting him to leave this dull, profitless practice immediately and turn from the man to the texts. On the other hand, as we have also seen, he was prone to interpret any writing, including his own, as a revelation of the writer's secret life, as his or her dark twin. 'I am telling the same story over and over', he admitted once, 'which is myself and the world.' Repetition was rediscovery, or perhaps even reinvention, of the life he had lived but missed. In Eliot's famous phrase, he had had the experience but missed the meaning; and telling became an almost compulsive reaction to this, a way of responding to the hope that perhaps by the indirections of the fictive impulse he could find directions out. That the hope was partial was implicit in the activity of telling the story 'over and over': Faulkner, like so many of his protagonists and/or narrators kept coming back, and then coming back again, to events that seemed to resist understanding, to brim with undisclosed biography. There would always be blockage between the commemorating writer and the commemorated experience, as Faulkner's habitual use of the window metaphor indicated: the window on which a name is inscribed in *Requiem for a Nun*, for instance, or through which Quentin Compson gazes at the South as he travels home from Cambridge, Massachusetts. Writing, for Faulkner, was consequently defined as a transparency and an obstacle: offering communication and discovery to the inquiring gaze of writer and reader but also impeding him, sealing him off from full sensory contact.

But, at least, the chance of revelation was there, in the process of telling or writing. By these activities, Faulkner seems to have believed, he was at least entering into dialogue with event. To gaze through a window implied blockage and frustration but not so much of either as that other, habitual activity of the Faulkner character: listening, passively, through a wall to a drama from which that character is excluded – a conversation on which he or she can only eavesdrop and which is reduced, much of the time, to incoherent whispers and murmurs. To tell and to write is, in this respect, to engage and, in the first instance, to engage with the writer himself as subject. 'It is himself that the Southerner is writing about, not about his environment', Faulkner insisted,

> He's got to tell the story in the only terms he knows, the familiar terms, which would be coloured, shaped, by his environment. He's not really writing about his environment, he's simply telling a story about human beings in the terms of environment, and I agree that any work of art, any book, reflects its social background; but I doubt if that were the primary consideration of that writer. That reflection or that background was simply the story told in the terms of its own environment.[85]

The distinction between writer and environment, work of art and background, is perhaps an exaggerated or even false one: since a writer, like any human subject, exists as a point of intersection between conflicting forces and those forces, in turn, are constituted by his environment. For Faulkner, as for everyone, life is ultimately inseparable from situation, historical time and place. But, as a rhetorical gesture, what Faulkner says here makes a point: that his experience of time and place was *his* and nobody else's. And, to this extent, his work could not help being autobiographical: as one of Faulkner's critics has observed, in the chronicles of Yoknapatawpha 'every exploration of family becomes an exploration of region and every exploration of either becomes an exploration of self'.

The broad lineaments of the life of Faulkner and his family reveal just how closely the story of self was wedded to the story of region: playing

intimate personal variations on the family romance of the South – a romance that, in turn, locks into (although it was and is not precisely coextensive with) other dramas of genealogy, maternal love and paternal law.
'No man is himself', Faulkner once observed, 'he is the sum of his past.'[86]
And, for Faulkner, the significant past of which he was the 'sum' began
with the arrival of a penniless runaway in the hill country of Mississippi,
east of the delta and about fifty miles north-east of Oxford. This was
William Clark Faulkner, born in 1825 and Faulkner's great-grandfather;
and he soon made his mark in his adoptive hometown of Ripley, Mississippi, and beyond. At the age of twenty, William Clark earned his first
money from his pen by writing up in pamphlet form the life story of an
axe murderer whom he had helped to capture, and then selling it to the
assembled onlookers on the day of the execution. Only a few years later,
while reading law, he became a murderer himself, when he stabbed to
death one Robert Hindman, who had pulled a gun on him. At the subsequent trial, William Clark pleaded self-defence and was acquitted. But
this did not stop the Hindman family from erecting a gravestone for their
dead kinsman which read, 'Murdered at Ripley, Miss. by Wm. C. Falkner'.
The bereaved kinsfolk of Robert Hindman had not mis-spelled William
Clark's surname in some obscure act of revenge. At some point, William
Clark himself dropped the 'u' from the family name. Just when this occurred is unclear. Certainly, when he was discharged from the army in
1847, having lost the first joints of three fingers and acquired a military
reputation during the Mexican War, his name was still spelled the way he
inherited it. But then, for some reason that can only remain the subject
of guesswork, he made the small but significant change from 'Faulkner'
to 'Falkner'.

Other changes, equally significant, occurred over the forty or so years
of William Clark's life. Married twice, he had become a slaveowner since
his first marriage, bought and sold slaves, practised law, invested in land,
and by 1859 was worth $50,000. Dabbling in politics, he ran unsuccessfully
for the state legislature; before this, in 1851, he had killed another man
in a quarrel, this time with a pistol, and was again acquitted. Ironically, the
prosecutor at this second trial was Thomas C. Hindman Jr, the brother of
his first victim; and, after the acquittal, Hindman's father tried to shoot
William Clark, but missed. Violence on a much larger scale became a part
of William Clark's life with the entry of Mississippi into the Civil War. As
a colonel, he led his own 2nd Mississippi Infantry Regiment, the 'Magnolia Rifles', in the first battle of Manassas. He lost two horses from under
him during the battle: and, when he seized a third mount in order to
continue, the Louisianian General Beauregard was reported to have shouted
out to him, in admiration of his courage, 'Go ahead, you hero with the
black plume: *history shall never forget you!*'[87] Another general, Joseph E.
Johnston, commended him: but this did him little good with his men.
They saw his gallantry as recklessness, causing unnecessary risks to them,
and in the regimental elections of 1862 voted him out of office.

Undiscouraged, 'The Old Colonel' returned home and raised a new unit, The First Mississippi Partisan Rangers, who fought a guerrilla-style campaign in north-east Mississippi and southern Tennessee. The Rangers lasted less than a year, being outnumbered, defeated and ravaged by a regiment of Wisconsin cavalry in 1863. But although this was the end of 'The Old Colonel''s military career, it seems likely that he continued clandestine military activities, including running the blockade around Memphis in order to bring back vital supplies – and, also, some profitable commodities.

That peculiar combination of gallantry and guile which enabled 'The Old Colonel' both to help his community and line his own pockets, towards the end of the Civil War, did not desert him when the conflict was ended. He returned to his law practice, found time for political activities including the harassment of black voters, and was instrumental in the building of a railroad through the Mississippi hill country. He also wrote a serialized novel, *The White Rose of Memphis*, first published in 1881, which went to thirty-five printings, and operated a large plantation and a saw mill. Nor did the violence that had characterized his earlier life entirely disappear. By the autumn of 1889, when he was purchasing other lines to link with his railroad, he was also running for the state legislature. His opponent for office was Richard J. Thurmond, a former partner in the railroad business whom 'The Old Colonel' had forced out. The campaign was a bitter one; and, when William Clark was elected with a large majority, Thurmond sought him out and shot him dead in the street. 'Why did you do it, Dick?', 'The Old Colonel' was reported to have asked as he lay dying. For whatever specific reason 'Dick' did it, like his victim before him he was tried for murder by a local jury and acquitted. His great-grandson was later to say of him that Colonel William Clark Falkner 'rode through the country like a living force'.[88] To the rest of his family who came after, he seemed a gigantic authoritative figure: an impression compounded by the monument raised over his grave in due course – a pediment six feet square and fourteen feet high, with an eight-foot statue of 'The Old Colonel' rising above it.

Given the power of this figure from his past, it is hardly surprising that William Faulkner was haunted by his great-grandfather, to the point of finding in his own life repetitions of his forebear's experience: his frequently announced ambition as a schoolboy was, 'I want to be a writer like my great-grandaddy.'[89] But the character of that stated ambition also suggests the ambiguity of his response, the complex and even devious nature of the young William's attitude to the man who was clearly, for him, the image of the father. 'The Old Colonel' was a person who managed to incorporate many regional legends. He was the Cavalier, an adventurer, whose heroic journey into a new world had initiated an heroic line; he was the Planter, who had presided over a patriarchal idyll; he was the Knight of the Black Plume, who had fought with bravery and even recklessness before going down to inevitable defeat; he was the Redeemer who had brought back life to the dead land, the world that the Yankees had laid waste. For that matter, he was also the New Man who had helped introduce the machine into the garden in his small corner of the world, and so prepared the way for all the forces that were to make his own style of life an anomaly. In short, he was an inexhaustible supply of imaginative sustenance, a vividly personal equivalent for the larger public myths as well as an unusually powerful focus for the intersecting forces of history. What his great-grandson chose to emphasize, however, when it came to saying how precisely he was going to imitate him, was one of the least significant areas of his experience, his life as a writer. And, in doing so, William Faulkner was slyly – if, no doubt, intuitively – measuring a distance between himself and the man who incorporated so much of the regional story: inscribing likeness, certainly, but also difference.

The issue of the relationship with this surrogate father-figure goes further than that, however. 'The Old Colonel' might have been, in fact, the same height in maturity as his great-grandson, with features and carriage like him: but, recalled in the stories of several generations, he seemed to William a much taller, more heroic and much more *masculine* figure. At times, Faulkner seems to have been able to live with this. After all, in choosing to become a writer rather than, like 'The Old Colonel', dabble in writing, he was going against the grain of conventional masculine roles in the region. The South, before and after the Civil War, was not alone among cultures in regarding writing as a rather feminine occupation. As one historian has put it, in the Southern states until recently, 'To write was respectable. *Only* to write was less so.'[90] And in deciding, if he was able, *only* to write, the young William Faulkner was placing in question his culture's ideas of masculinity and respectability in a way that 'The Old Colonel', for all his (socially approved) violence, never did. He was taking his stand against his father-figure – and the regional law that figure enshrined – even while he protested that he wanted to be 'like' him. Such protestations were not, however, mere disingenuousness or double agentry. In a way, Faulkner did want to be like his great-grandfather. At times, he did try to live up to the image of mastery, masculine control and local heroism, that 'The Old Colonel''s story seemed to enact. He drank, as they say, 'heroically' – in a way that signified, in the regional culture, that he was 'a real man', able to hold his alcohol. He took to flying at a time when – as the fate of his brother, Dean, was to indicate – it was still a risky pastime. He was wedded to the mythology of the hunt to the point of obsession, determined to be the man with the rifle and then, later, the man on horseback up to a stage in his life when he was quite clearly not capable of pursuing those roles physically. And, of course, when the facts failed him, there was always fabrication: unlike his great-grandfather, he had missed the great war of his generation but, thanks to the fertility of his imagination, there was, he sometimes felt, no reason on earth for others to know this.

Estelle Oldham Faulkner, William's wife, was of the opinion that there were 'two Bills'. 'He is so definitely dual', she added. Meta Carpenter, his lover for many years, took the notion one stage further, when she ventured the idea that Faulkner had 'many selves'. This duality, or even multiplicity, of character perhaps explains why, as a writer, Faulkner was driven to create what one critic has called ' "linked" characters . . . who represent closely interrelated ego fragments': Benjy and Quentin Compson in *The Sound and the Fury*, for instance, Cash, Jewel and Darl Bundren in *As I Lay Dying*, maybe even Popeye and Horace Benbow in *Sanctuary*. Certainly, it offers a reason for his constant pairing of figures of heroic action and adventure with ones of contemplative inertia and impotence: Bayard Sartois III and Benbow in *Flags in the Dust/Sartoris* and Thomas Sutpen and Quentin Compson in *Absalom, Absalom!* are only the most obvious examples. Just as certainly, it helps solve the problem of Faulkner's re-naming of himself. Faulkner's later explanation of his addition of a 'u' to the family name was as follows:

> My first recollection of the family name was, no outsider seemed able to pronounce it from reading it, and when he did pronounce it, he always wrote the 'u' into it. So it seemed to me that the whole outside world was trying to change it, and usually did. Maybe when I began to write . . . I secretly was ambitious and did not want to ride on grandfather's coat-tails, and so accepted the 'u', was glad of such an easy way to strike out for myself.[91]

Plausible though this may sound, there is a significant omission: the family name, as we have seen, *was* 'Faulkner' and 'The Old Colonel' set the example of name changing by dropping the 'u'. So William was at once imitating his great-grandfather, by initiating a small but significant alteration in the family title, and defying him, by reinventing the vowel which that great-grandfather had dropped. He was asserting his independence, in a way, from the romance of the family and the pressures of genealogy: but, in another, more covert and subterranean fashion, he was restoring himself to a place in that romance, taking on those pressures, by reverting to an earlier naming. Identifying himself as unique in the familial group, he was announcing his belonging as a kind of prodigal son. Dropping out of history, he was also returning to it: in the sense that he was recollecting a name and story that, he knew, could be traced back to well before the settlement of Mississippi. By this simple act of the word, the father figure had been resisted and copied. And by other, much more complex acts of the word, this dual process of defiance and imitation was to go on. For, in the end, the struggle with the father *is* one of the stories of the novels and tales, and that one of the most telling ones; the loving war with history, and genealogy, is embedded in nearly everything he ever wrote.

Ironically, Faulkner was to confirm his own patriarchal status even while he seemed to be putting patriarchy in doubt by his act of re-naming himself: two of his younger brothers eventually added the 'u' to the family name in deference to his fame, and gradually acquired status as head of the family. With quite as much irony, Faulkner never thought of his actual father as his father figure. The story of the two generations after 'The Old Colonel' is, in fact, one of slow decline, paralleling or rather focusing a regional process. Faulkner's grandfather, John Wesley Thompson Falkner, was physically an imposing figure, tall and dignified in his linen suits and Panama hats and generally sporting a cigar. He also achieved some success as a railroad president, criminal lawyer, state senator and banker. Despite all this, however, there was an underlying unease, even disturbance to his life. He was, one grandson said, 'the loneliest man I've ever known'; and, like the creator of Yoknapatawpha Country, he was given to bouts of solitary drinking that often ended in his being sent off to a local clinic to be dried out. Perhaps his energy, his desire for glamour and adventure, never found adequate expression. At all events, the daring that led 'The Old Colonel' to an almost suicidal charge against the enemy at Manassas issued in less romantic, more obviously self-destructive exploits in his son: such as a drunken car ride around Oxford town square that ended in his throwing a brick through the window of the bank of which he happened to be president. Asked why he did this, he replied simply, 'It was my Buick, my brick, my bank':[92] an explanation that combined a sullen refusal to explain with almost child-like assumptions of proprietorial control. He was called 'The Young Colonel', but as a matter of courtesy and inheritance, not, as his father had been termed 'The Old Colonel', in recognition of achievement. And that, the different reasons for the naming, seems to sum up the difference between the two generations.

Murry Falkner, William's father, was if anything an even sadder figure that 'The Young Colonel'. He was 'a dull man', his novelist son opined. Another son, John, spoke more charitably and more accurately of Murry's failures and thwarted hopes when he said, 'The only things Dad ever loved were [the] railroad and horses and dogs and the Ole Miss football and baseball teams.'[93] An enthusiastic horseman, and an avid reader of pulp Westerns, Murry nurtured a desire to go West and become a cowboy long after the responsibilities of a family had effectively imprisoned him in Mississippi. It was a project to which his wife, Maud Butler Falkner, was adamantly opposed: something for which, according to William Faulkner's biographer, Murry 'never forgave her'. So, a helpless, hopeless, lackadaisical man, generally withdrawn but given to outbursts of irrational anger, he drifted from one occupation to another, sinking finally and with some relief into the post of business manager at the University of Mississippi in Oxford, known familiarly as 'Ole Miss'. This might have been pleasant enough, certainly there were no arduous duties involved, and it allowed Murry more opportunities for what he enjoyed most, spending time with male companions. But unfortunately the state of Mississippi paid its public servants as little as it possibly could for their labours. So the life Murry offered his children continued to be what it had always been, one of more or less genteel poverty. It could give them little shelter from their surroundings; in a sense, because it was so fluid and uncertain, it even seemed to reflect those surroundings. There was no chance of that fairly cloistered upbringing that, say, other Southern writers like Thomas Wolfe or – at another point in the social scale – Katherine Anne Porter were experiencing at about the same time. While he was growing up, Faulkner found himself exposed to all the forces and changes operative in his neighbourhood; of necessity, he knew both rich and poor, as well as those in between, both black and white; he was, in effect, in painfully immediate touch with history.

Just how the weakness of his actual father affected Faulkner, apart from forcing him to rub shoulders with social change, is perhaps suggested by the meditation of Gail Hightower in *Light in August*. Hightower, like his creator, is haunted by the male hero of an earlier generation: in his case, his grandfather. And, as the ghost of his grandfather becomes ever more real to him, so the figure of the father 'he knew and feared' fades until it becomes 'a phantom'. 'So it's no wonder', Hightower realizes, 'that I skipped a generation. It's no wonder that I had no father.' Faulkner's protagonists may be haunted by patriarchal ghosts and burdened by issues of genealogy: but so many of them are like Hightower in having 'no father', since their literal, biological father is conspicuous only by his absence from the scene, his psychological distance or emotional impotence. They are weighed down by the past, certainly: that past, however, is a distant one, while the immediate past registers only as confusion and disappointment. A notable illustration of this dilemma is the story of the Sartoris family in what was Faulkner's first fictional exploration of his 'apocryphal' county, *Flags in the Dust*, initially revised and published as *Sartoris*. Drawing extensively on family lore, Faulkner makes sure that the generation of his great-grandfather is clearly there in the stories of Colonel John Sartoris and Colonel Bayard Sartoris I, two revered heroes of the Civil War. The next generation is also represented by Colonel Bayard II, an old man when the story begins but still a vivid, visible presence. But then Faulkner skips a generation to Bayard II's grandson, Bayard Sartoris III and his twin brother John. Bayard II's son and his wife are hardly mentioned, except for a few words on their death in an epidemic when the twins were eight. Asked once why this generation was omitted, Faulkner replied,

> The twins' father didn't have a story. He came at a period in history which, in this country, people thought of and think of now as a peaceful one . . . This John Sartoris, the father, lived in that time when there was nothing that brought the issue to him to be brave and strong or dramatic.[94]

This, however, is disingenuous. Bayard II, after all, is also without a war in which to perform glorious deeds: in fact, there is even a reference during the course of the novel to his 'having been born too late for one war and too soon for the next'. As Faulkner well knew, to be denied the possibility of heroic action is not to be denied a story; and so Bayard II is allowed *his* place in the novel. The real reason for the omission of the twin's father is much more fundamental. Dispensing with the actual father enabled Faulkner to concentrate on the image of the father, the spectral figures of patriarchal authority that haunt and debilitate Bayard III; it allowed him to focus on issues of genealogy, authoritative discourse and law, and to separate these from questions of biology. Later – by the time of writing *Light in August*, for instance – Faulkner was prepared to turn this problem of having 'no father' into a subject of investigation and not just part of the structure of assumptions, a premise from which the narrative tacitly begins. He was to attend to it, in effect, as a chapter in the family romance of the South as he and others of his generation had experienced it: situated, as they were, in a region that accorded special status not to recent memories but to distant ones. At the moment of *Flags in the Dust/Sartoris*, though, he was not ready for this; all he could do was react to the dilemma, not dramatize it. The absence of the literal father is registered in the first Yoknapatawpha novel as just that: an absence not to be analysed, and barely acknowledged.

As Faulkner himself knew, absences and prevarications are often more revelatory than confession; and not the least symptomatic of his statements, in this respect, is the novelist's claim that 'being the oldest of four boys' he 'escaped' his 'mother's influence pretty easy' – so, as he put it, 'it was fine for me to apprentice to the business'. This was so far from being the truth as to be a downright lie. All the facts from his early life indicate that, on the contrary, he was deeply under the influence of his mother. Maud Faulkner was a shy, insecure woman: as one of her granddaughters saw it, she was 'often afraid of strange people and situations. She masked her vulnerability with a cold hard manner.' Outwardly, she could appear brusque, or even tart in her behaviour: she placed a sign in her kitchen that read simply, 'DON'T COMPLAIN – DON'T EXPLAIN'. Evidently, she was dissatisfied with her marriage: when told, for instance, shortly before her death that she would not see Murry in the after-life if she did not want to, she replied simply, 'That's good. I never did like him.' As an old lady, she was cantankerous, spunky and suspicious, but when it came to her oldest son, the 'light of my life' as she called him, she was first and last adoring and tender. And William Faulkner responded in kind. Even after his marriage, at almost thirty-two, William visited his mother every day when he was in Oxford; and, when he was away, his letters addressed to 'Dear Moms' would arrive regularly and faithfully at her door. 'I think that probably Pappy's idea of women – ladies – always revolved a great deal around Granny', Faulkner's daughter Jill once remarked,

> She was just a very determined, tiny old lady that Pappy adored. Pappy admired that so much in Granny and didn't find it in my mother and I don't think he ever found it in anybody. I think that maybe all of those [women] were just second place.[95]

Deny it as he might occasionally, his mother haunted the novelist just as his great-grandfather did. To the image of the man on horseback, presiding over a dream of patriarchal order, could be added that of the woman as nurturer, the quiet and capable sustainer and provider.

The role of Maud in this particular version of family romance was far more ambiguous than these remarks might suggest, however. At a certain point in Faulkner's early life, it has been suggested by several biographers, when his youngest brother Dean Swift Faulkner was born, young William felt displaced in his mother's affections. This was in 1907, when William was not far off puberty, and not long after the death of both his grand-mothers, and so needed particular care and attention. Instead, because Dean suffered from a severe case of cradle cap and required to be watched and carefully attended to, William was shuffled off to the sidelines of the family for a while, left emotionally to fend for himself – or, as he perhaps melodramatically saw it, abandoned. This may be so: certainly it would help to account for his interest in the theme of emotionally betrayed children. But it is not necessary to accept this reading of a particular moment in Faulkner's youth in order to see that, as he grew up, the future novelist encountered a primal drama. Nor is it difficult to see that, in his case, that drama was additionally coloured by two things: the fact that he was male and the fact that he was a Southerner. The primal drama in question is the one Jacques Lacan has famously described, drawing upon and developing the ideas of Freud. According to this drama, the child – any child – begins in union with the mother: but as he or she realizes its split from the mother's body (the trauma of the 'primal gap') this pleni-tude or wholeness is lost. And this split or loss is inextricably connected to the structure of language and narrative, since language both reveals and conceals the fracture. For Lacan, as one commentator expresses it,

> narrative is the attempt to catch up retrospectively on this traumatic separa-tion, to tell this happening again and again, to re-count it: the narrative caught in the net of signifiers . . . the story of the repetition compulsion.[96]

The trauma of loss was, in effect, something that Faulkner shared with others as part of a necessary process, as he entered into what Lacan calls the symbolic order or state of full subjectivity through the acquisition of language. Perhaps he experienced it a little more fiercely than most, but it was something that was inevitable. Less inevitable, though, is what he did with it. For the 'repetition compulsion' that drives the human subject to keep going back, and going back again, to a lost wholeness, the absent figure of the mother, supplies a telling gloss on Faulkner's fiction as a whole. Not only do his narrators/protagonists demonstrate a compulsive and repetitive reflection on the subjects of their narration: what one critic has termed the 'empty centre',[97] the absent figure of the mother (*As I Lay Dying*) or the sister (*The Sound and the Fury*). His fiction as a whole reveals his own compulsion to return to the same subjects, replayed again and again in a variety of forms and texts, and frequently centred around some-thing that, despite this compulsive attention, remains elusive. In novels

like *As I Lay Dying* and *The Sound and the Fury*, the re-enactment of traumatic separation is played out explicitly by the male protagonists who
search along a chain of signifiers, 'supplements' for their loss which inevitably only reinforce this loss by inscribing the absence of the object of
desire. And in other work, too, less explicitly but no less obsessively, the
text itself seems to chase after an elusive, ever-vanishing object, the sign
of which is also the woman, whose name (Temple Drake, Charlotte
Rittenmeyer, Laverne Shumann, Eula Varner) is always at the centre of
the text, but who is represented within it only in marginalized and shadowy or slippery form, as an obscure object of desire.

Observing his daughter at the age of eleven, Faulkner observed with
melancholy, 'It's over very soon. This is the end of it. She'll grow into a
woman.' Such sad reflections give a particularly male orientation to the
drama of growing up as Faulkner experienced and saw it; and, besides,
they link up with some comments made earlier about the way the novelist's responses to women were significantly connected to regional obsessions. Faulkner's relationships with women were troubled. Besides his
intimate but vexed and life-long love affair with his mother, there was, for
instance, his relation with the woman he married, Estelle Oldham. Faulkner
grew up with Estelle, she was a neighbour and a kind of sister. He had
fallen in love with her, but she married someone else. The marriage was
not a happy one, however. After bearing two children, she was divorced,
returned to Oxford, and in 1929 was married to Faulkner. The novelist
would seem, then, to have captured his elusive object of desire. The evidence of the time, however, hardly suggested it. 'Women are completely
impervious to evil', he wrote to a friend in the year of his marriage. And,
then, to another friend, just before he was married, he wrote this:

> I am going to be married. Both want to and have to. THIS PART IS CONFI-
> DENTIAL, UTTERLY. For my honour and the sanity – I believe life – of a woman.
> This is not bunk; neither am I being sucked in. We grew up together and
> I don't think she could fool me in this way; that is, make me believe that her
> mental condition, her nerves are this far gone. And no question of
> pregna[n]cy: that would hardly move me: no one can face his own bastard
> with more equanimity than I . . . Neither is it a matter of a promise on my
> part: we have known one another long enough to pay no attention to our
> promises. It's a situation which I engendered and permitted to ripen which
> has become unbearable, and I am tired of running from the devilment I
> bring about. This sounds a little insane . . .[98]

'Insane' or not, the sense of doom that runs through this letter soon
found its fulfilment on the honeymoon, when Estelle tried to commit
suicide after an evening of heavy drinking. And the marriage, as a whole,
gravitated between periods of equanimity and estrangement punctuated
by the occasional consideration of divorce. Eventually, towards the end of
their life together, the couple seem to have reached some accommodation
– or, as their daughter Jill romantically saw it, to have fallen in love with

each other all over again. Before that, however, there was a history of unease and even rupture brought on by their shared liking for alcohol (Estelle was to join Alcoholics Anonymous in the end), by what Faulkner saw as his wife's extravagance (he once put a notice in the local newspaper announcing that he would not honour her cheques), by their physical incompatibility (Faulkner claimed that they had not had 'male–female sex' since the birth of Jill) – and, not least, by the novelist's own preference for work, solitude or male company.

Symptomatic of the reasons why Faulkner and Estelle were so often at odds were his relations with young women. Faulkner had fallen in love with Estelle when she was young and virginal: an intimate playmate or sister. However, he had married her when she had already been married once and was a mother of two: even more than most victims of the romantic imagination, then, Faulkner was presented painfully with the lesson that to touch the object of desire is to lose it. The virgin is no longer a virgin once desire has been consummated; the lover, simultaneously fulfilled and disappointed, must go on to pursue some other pure, enchanted object. In Faulkner's case, this replay of a singularly male pattern of behaviour involved him with women increasingly younger than himself whom he would often fantasize as being even younger than they were. 'It's a dull life here', he wrote from Oxford in 1946, 'I need some new people, above all probably a new young woman.' For part of his life, this need was filled by Meta Carpenter, a young woman whom he had met in 1935 while working as a scriptwriter in Hollywood. Meta Carpenter was canny enough to realize that, as she put it, 'Bill ... saw me as being far younger than I was. A girl-child.' 'With one flourish of his mental blue pencil', she added, 'he would edit out all the facts of my life since Memphis [she was born in Tennessee] – my birthdays, my marriage, my work – and behave toward me as if I were just out of high school.' She felt confounded sometimes by Faulkner's need to turn her into 'a sweet, tremulous girl' when she was, after all, an independent woman; and she could be simultaneously amused and annoyed by his occasional gifts to her, such as ribbons, which implied that she was much younger than her actual age. Nevertheless, she recognized and accepted that the 'sexual key' to him was (in her words) 'the image of a young woman, fresh and fragrant of skin beneath her summer cotton dress, tremblingly responsive to his desire'. 'Bill feels some sort of compulsion to be attached to a young woman at all times',[99] Estelle observed sadly in 1956. Estelle herself met this compulsion for a while, although she hardly knew it when it happened; then Meta Carpenter, who clearly did know it; and, before and after that, other young women like Helen Baird, Joan Williams and Jean Stein.

Several things could be said about these habits of belief and behaviour: this pattern of attachment and abandonment of which, in his relations with women (mother, daughter, lovers) Faulkner was both the perpetrator and the victim. In the first place, and most obviously, it links up with the virgin/whore complex commented on earlier: that split in the perception of women so common to the male imagination and so particularly acute in the family romance of the South. Like most males, and most Southern males especially, Faulkner was capable of idealizing women out of existence. 'He was obsessed with keeping from me the grossness of his physical self', Meta Carpenter remembered,

> running the water in the bathroom to cover the evidence of his animality, bathing each time we made love . . .
> It was . . . another manifestation of the romantic in him compounded of the Southern gentleman's need to pedestal the female, to spare her the indelicacies and harshnesses . . . I would have loved him profane, but he didn't know it and it would have shocked him had he guessed.[100]

Like most males, however, and again like most Southern men in particular, he was just as capable of dismissing women as earthy to the point of grossness: incapable of appreciating the higher things of life. 'Ah, women', Faulkner wrote in an early review,

> with their hungry snatching little souls! With a man it is – quite often – art for art's sake; with a woman it is always art for the artist's sake.[101]

Demanding and threatening, seen in this mood the entire female sex was demoted to the level of appetite – or, as Faulkner would sometimes put it, 'physical spittoons'.

In the same review from which the dismissal of women was taken, the young Faulkner goes on to suggest that two of the services writing performs are 'to temporarily blind the spirit to the ungraceful posturings of the flesh' and to further 'philanderings', 'to speed onward the whole affair' a man may be having with a woman. Puerile and posturing as this may seem, it does help to unpack a second, significant consequence of Faulkner's uneasy relation with women: significant, that is, to his writing. For the triumph and failure of art for Faulkner seems to have resided precisely in this: that it enshrined the paradox of attachment/abandonment, consummation/substitution on which, for him, the male–female relationship rested. A telling piece of evidence, in this respect, is the Introduction to *The Sound and the Fury*, 'There is a story somewhere', Faulkner concludes after giving an account of how he came to write the book,

> about an old Roman who kept at his bedside a Tyrrhenian vase which he loved and the rim of which he wore slowly away with kissing it. I had made myself a vase, but I suppose I knew all the time that I could not live forever inside of it, that perhaps to have it so that I could lie in bed and look at it would be better.[102]

A remark like this illustrates just how paradoxical Faulkner's attitude toward language could be. The image of the 'old Roman' carries reverberations of impotence, certainly, but it also manages to suggest consummation, a denial of life but something of an apotheosis as well; there may not be a body there with the old man, but what he does have brings its own compensations and is a not entirely unwelcome substitute. More to the point, it shows just how prone Faulkner was to using particular, genderized terms for describing the act of substitution: the process whereby experience is turned into language, the 'thing or the deed' into art. A woman and an urn: these are the terms of the act. 'I who never had a sister', Faulkner says in another version of the Introduction, 'and was fated to lose my daughter in infancy, set out to make myself a beautiful and tragic little girl': that is, he set out to turn a female who was simultaneously there (to the extent that she was sensed and desired) and not there (because she was never reached or embraced) into a palpable presence, a tangible shape – to capture her essence in a fragile web of ink and paper. In this context, it is perhaps worth noting that Faulkner very often attributed his own distrust of artifice in general and the artificial structures of language in particular to a woman. 'Women', we are told in his first novel, 'know more about words than men ever will. And they know how little they can ever possibly mean.' This is a sentiment echoed in *Mosquitoes* ('They don't care anything about words except as little things to pass the time with'), and either illustrated or expressed by such otherwise diverse figures as Laverne Shumann in *Pylon*, Charlotte Rittenmeyer in *The Wild Palms*, Eula Varner and her daughter Linda (Linda, because she is deaf, is actually said to live 'immured, inviolate in silence', 'outside human sound . . . outside human time too').[103] There is more to this than just a fairly commonplace belief in 'feminine intuition'; although Faulkner was not averse to the idea that a woman's intelligence was different from a man's, more concrete, less interested in abstraction. For behind it lay something mentioned earlier: Faulkner's impulse, his fundamental inclination, to associate women with otherness, the world outside the ego. Small wonder, then, that his women tended to distrust words, since what they distrusted was, as he saw it, the machinery devised to capture and contain them. Small wonder, either, that they despised words, or were indifferent to their claims, for what they were despising or dismissing were the pale shadows of them, the reflections that pretended to be them, the substitutive object that dared to challenge comparison with the subject.

Of course, in conceiving of women in these terms Faulkner was not being particularly original. But he was unusual, if not original, in the persistence with which he pursued this image and explored its different manifestations: in the way in which he kept coming back to what he referred to, in a story written early in 1925, as 'that imminent . . . that troubling Presence'. The story, 'Nympholepsy', as itself derived from two earlier works, 'L'Apres-Midi d'un Faune' published in 1919 and 'The Hill' published in 1922; and it shows just how early and deeply embedded in Faulkner's mind the image of the seductive, elusive, ineffable female was. Briefly, it describes how a young man returning from work just before sunset suddenly sees 'a golden light among dark pines'. The light turns out to be a girl, a nymph-like figure who seems to partake of the sun's brilliance and who makes the boy feel hopelessly 'swinish' by comparison. He pursues this 'ghostly' vision, 'not knowing whether it was copulation or companionship that he wanted'; and, for a moment, as he sinks into a woodland stream, where 'the water murmured in a dark and sinister dream', he seems to reach out and touch her, to make contact with 'something more than water'. 'Beneath his hand', we are told,

> a startled thigh slid like a snake, among dark bubbles he felt a swift leg; and, sinking, the point of a breast scraped his back. Amid a slow commotion of disturbed water he saw death like a woman shining and drowned and waiting, saw a flashing body tortured by water . . .[104]

But then he loses her. 'Like a match flame', she appears for a moment against the darkness of the trees and then disappears, leaving her pursuer with the rather cold comfort that maybe he did achieve some strange sort of consummation – that perhaps, for a moment, 'I touched her!'

'Nympholepsy' is saturated in the kind of *fin-de-siècle* romanticism that Faulkner was later to control and criticize. Nevertheless, it is of vital interest because it is packed with so many anticipations of its author's later work, prophetic guides to the country of his imagination. A woman like a spirit or a twilight dream, a woman offering the otherness of love or death, a woman associated with the primal element of water – a woman, too, to whom the man who pursues her reaches out like the lover on Keats's Urn and who may, or may not be, touched for a moment: no reader of Faulkner needs to be reminded just how much of the fabric of his novels is woven out of these ideas, with their deployment of the male as the poet, lover, maker of words and the female as his beloved, tantalizingly ungovernable object. Nor, probably, does he need to be told what the animating conception, the primary belief is behind all such ideas: that, like Eula Varner as she is described in *The Town*, woman/reality is 'too much' for any man, that there never will be 'enough of any one male to match and hold and deserve her'.[105]

Mention of Eula Varner is a useful reminder that by no means all the women in Faulkner's work possess the teasing bodilessness of the girl in 'Nympholepsy'. Quite the contrary, for every nymph, every woman whose epicene figure, shimmering clothes and rapid movements express her elusive, uncontrollable otherness, there is someone like Eula or Lena Grove who is other in a quite different sense: because she is of the earth, earthy, clinging to its curves and rounds – while man seeks to climb up, further and further away from the concrete surfaces of things. The two versions of woman, which appear so different and yet issue from the same equation, are both sketched out in Faulkner's first novel. Here, the part of nymph is taken by the boyish, irritatingly unpredictable Cecily Saunders, whose body is compared by her lover to 'a narrow pool, flowing away like two silver streams from a single source'.[106] In turn, a warmer, maternal, and yet still elusive presence is supplied by Margaret Powers. Married twice, to men who never even begin to know her, pursued by others whose passion is matched only by their sense of impotence, her unreachability is summed up in the last moment when we see her: as she departs on a train one of her admirers runs wildly and desperately after her vanishing image, like the 'bold lover' who can never quite catch his beloved in 'Ode on a Grecian Urn'.

A similarly double image of the female is projected in *Mosquitoes*; and here – not surprisingly, given the more discursive nature of Faulkner's second novel – it is more openly explored, even explained. Pat Robyn suggests that aspect of 'the feminine nature' which, we are told, makes it 'impalpable as moonlight': a slim, boyish figure with a 'clean, young odour . . . , like that of trees', she is so light and bodiless that she seems to make no sound as she walks. Like the girl in 'Nympholepsy' (or, for that matter, Temple Drake or Laverne Schumann), she is all activity: possessed of a 'childish delight in strenuous physical motion' that comes out especially in the descriptions of her swimming by night, moving fluently and 'naked and silver as a ghost'. Likewise, her admirers are reminiscent of the young man in that early – and, for a long time, unpublished – short story: pursuing her 'with . . . unutterable longing', or simply gazing at her, and objects associated with her, with 'passive abjectness', 'an utter longing, like that of a dog'. Paired with Pat is her friend of a day, Jenny Steinbauer. Her appeal is equally powerful but quite different: stemming, as one of the other characters observes, from 'an utterly mindless rifeness of young pink flesh, a supine potential fecundity lovely to look upon'. One of Jenny's many admirers, Dawson Fairchild, seems to have her in mind – or, rather, the particular image of woman she suggests – when he declares, 'Women can do . . . without art – old biology takes care of that . . . Creation, reproduction from within . . . [is] the dominating impulse in the world feminine.'[107] Woman is, man does, it seems; woman is a creator, a part or function of reality, while all man can do is attempt to *re*-create.

Just what man re-creates is implied by that image of the vase or urn; 'I had made myself a vase', said Faulkner of *The Sound and the Fury*, and as he said it he must have realized the multiple ironies packed into that phrase. After all, it could hardly have been mere coincidence that the woman/urn comparison (or contrast) occurred to him so often, or that he felt compelled to allude time and again to 'Ode on a Grecian Urn'. Lena Grove, in *Light in August*, is compared to something moving interminably across an urn, while when Joe Christman learns about menstruation he has a vision of urns cracked and bleeding. Later, in *Go Down, Moses*, Ike McCaslin reads the Keats poem and then, to the suggestion that the lines 'She cannot fade, though thou hast not thy bliss, / For ever wilt thou love and she be fair' refer to a girl, retorts that the poet was also 'talking about truth': an observation that suggests not only the permanence of 'truth' but just how teasingly elusive it can be. Linda Snopes is described in *The Mansion* as 'the bride of quietude and silence'; and in a much earlier book, *Flags in the Dust*, we are twice told that Horace Benbow addresses his sister as 'Thou still unravished bride of quietude'. The first time we are told this is well worth quoting – and not least because it bears such a striking resemblance to the passage quoted earlier from the Introduction to *The Sound and the Fury*. Horace, we learn, took to blowing glass as a hobby,

> and produced one almost perfect vase of clear amber . . . chastely serene and which he kept always on his night table and called by his sister's name in the intervals of apostrophising both of them impartially in his moments of rhapsody over the realization of the meaning of peace and the unblemished attainment of it, as Thou still unravished bride of quietude.[108]

Again, the suggestiveness and serviceability of this image is striking. The act of creation as an act of substitution; the ambiguous relationship between art and narcissism; the notion that any attempt to translate things into other terms can be seen as both a consummation and a gesture of impotence; the belief that the world's body remains immune to the raids made on it by the plundering mind. All these ideas and possibilities are contained within a passage that perceives making and encoding in a paradoxical way, as both a triumph and a failure: a marriage that apparently keeps the bride 'unravished', and an escape from the self into language that seems to leave otherness unrevealed, intact and quiet. Another way of putting all this would be in terms of the obvious. The vase is not Horace's sister; nor, for that matter, could *The Sound and The Fury* ever begin to compensate for the absence of a sister in Faulkner's own life, or his loss of an infant daughter. Nevertheless, both artifacts, the urn and the book, were cherished, both had their substitutive use and expressive value: as Horace's behaviour here and Faulkner's habitual, loving references to the story of the Compson family – and Caddy Compson in particular – clearly indicate.

A third and final point needs to be made, briefly, about the complex issue of Faulkner's response to the women who inhabited his life and the images of womanhood they engendered. Women inhabited that life, certainly, but most of the time they inhabited its edges: nothing was more important to Faulkner than his work. In this respect, a famous remark he made about 'the writer's . . . responsibility to his art' is worth remembering. Everything else 'goes by the board' for the writer in the name of his writing, Faulkner insisted,

> If a writer has to rob his mother, he will not hesitate: the 'Ode on a Grecian Urn' is worth any number of old ladies.[109]

A questionable distinction, perhaps, a piece of bravura, undoubtedly: but, just as undoubtedly, Faulkner was making a point about where, as he saw it, his priorities lay – and making it by consigning women to the periphery. On one level, Faulkner might see the process of writing as something indelibly associated with his vexed, contentious and paradoxical relationships with women. On another level, however, when it came to the actual details of these relations – even those with his mother – he could dismiss them, as he does here, relegate them without hesitation so as to concentrate on what he saw as the real business of life.

All of which is to say that Faulkner was inclined towards the familiar male habit of marginalizing the other sex. And in his best work – in a way that should be familiar by now – he made this act of marginalization not just an assumption but an object of attention: a focus for creative analysis in the text as well as part of the structure of assumptions that underpins it. As Julia Kristeva has suggested, it is a tendency of the socially dominant male imagination to position women at the limits of culture, no matter how that culture may be defined. There, they can be invested with the traditional ambiguity of a borderline or frontier: seen as both a line or limit of control (a lady, perhaps, situated on a pedestal) and a point of access to the unlimited, uncontrolled, and therefore dangerous (a hungry, snatching little soul). Faulkner absorbed this tendency from his culture and upbringing and enacted it in his life: but he also pressed it into imaginative debate. Like so much else in his major writing, the social positioning of women, their construction as marginal figures is a subject of dialogue: part of what Bakhtin has termed the 'relativised, Galilean linguistic consciousness'[110] of the text.

There is one woman crucial to Faulkner's life who has not been mentioned up until now, and that is Caroline Barr ('Mammy Callie'), the black nanny to whom the novelist dedicated *Go Down, Moses* and on whom Dilsey Gibson in *The Sound and the Fury* is largely modelled. 'She was born in bondage', Faulkner observed of her when he gave her funeral oration,

> and with a dark skin and most of her early maturity was passed in a dark and tragic time for the land of her birth. She went through vicissitudes which she had not caused: she assumed cares and griefs which were not even her cares and griefs. She was paid wages for this, but pay is still just money. And she never received very much of that . . . Yet she accepted that too without cavil or calculation or complaint . . .[111]

Like many Southerners of his time and before, Faulkner had both a white mother and a black mother; and from the black mother in particular he took in knowledge of the oppression that he and his kin had visited upon a race, and some understanding of the courage with which that oppression had been faced. Born in slavery, Mammy Callie was a direct link with the old shame of region and family. Steeped in the family history and ghost stories of the Tallahatchie bottom, she nurtured in her 'white children' (as Faulkner termed himself and his brothers) a sense of the past and, however unintentionally, a sense of guilt – and, perhaps above all, a love of storytelling. Caroline Barr was not, by any means, the only person

from whom the young Faulkner heard stories. He listened, and he listened. He listened to his maternal grandmother, for instance, Leila Butler
(nicknamed 'Damuddy'), a fierce spirit who believed her daughter had
married beneath her and wrote letters to 'Miss Maud Butler in the care
of Mr. Murry Falkner'. He listened to his beloved great-aunt 'Bama, Alabama Leroy Falkner, after whom he was to name his first daughter who
died only a few days old: born before William, and dying five-and-a-half
years after him, great-aunt 'Bama's span of ninety-four years covered the
period from 'The Old Colonel''s successes to his great-grandson's Nobel
Prize and made her the keeper of the family story. He listened, also, to his
grandfather's accounts of the past, to his father's friends on hunting trips,
to gossip around the courthouse square. Caroline Barr was not unique,
then, as a source of stories and storytelling. She was, however, the most
significant, intimate line of contact he had to the mixed history of his
family and region, the tangled relations of black and white – and she
offered the most immediate access possible to the oral tradition, the ingrained Southern preference for old tales and talking.

If Caroline Barr acted as an alternative mother-figure to Faulkner, reminding him of the peculiar, painful and peripheral role played by black
people in the family romance of the region, then a diminished, surrogate
father was supplied to the budding writer by Phil Stone. More to the
point, perhaps, Stone helped introduce Faulkner to literary modernism:
as he would recall later, he gave his young friend Keats and Swinburne to
read but also 'a number of the then moderns, such as Conrad Aiken and
the Imagists'.[112] And in doing so he was supplying the future novelist with
a necessary counterweight to the oral tradition inherited from Caroline
Barr, great-aunt 'Bama and others. Faulkner's literary project grew out of
the tension between the tradition of old tales and talking he took from his
region and the disruptive techniques of modernism: just as his historical
project (in so far as the two can be distinguished) issued out of his involvement with a traditional society in transit. Phil Stone was not alone in
bringing the news of the modernist writers to Faulkner. Others, such as
the novelist Sherwood Anderson (whom Faulkner met in New Orleans),
were to help; the impact of modernist techniques was, in any event, being
felt by most young Southern writers at the time, connected as those techniques were with contemporary economic and social changes. Nevertheless, Stone did more than anyone else to help the young Faulkner
understand how other novelists and poets of the period, mostly outside
the region, were finding the means to articulate social disruption and
cultural tension: how they were struggling, as he would later, to turn a
world in crisis into words.

Actually, Phil Stone was only four years older than William Faulkner.
What made him seem older, and enabled him to act as a mentor, was his
education and experience. Educated at Yale, where in 1904 he added
another degree to his Mississippi BA, he was an example of the bright
young man who travels north for his cultural development and professional

training but then returns to his homeplace to practise his trade – in this case law – and to act as the resident intellectual. A compulsive talker (the character of Gavin Stevens was, in part, based on him), and a person who loved to teach and tell stories, he was driven by impulses toward literary creation but lacked the energy or commitment to realize them. 'I'm like an elaborate, intricate piece of machinery which doesn't quite work', he once said of himself. And, in a way, he was helped by William Faulkner – who offered him a means of satisfying his creative impulses vicariously – just as, for a time, Faulkner was helped by him – towards an appropriate, literary education. Certainly, education in the formal sense was something the young Faulkner conspicuously lacked: he played the truant often while at school, dropped out at the eleventh grade, and entered the University of Mississippi only briefly in 1919–20 as a special student. His private reading was the thing. And, it has to be said, he had been reading widely for several years before he came under the tutelage of Stone; he had even begun to write, in particular imitating certain *fin-de-siècle* poets. 'It was Phil who educated Bill', someone who knew both men declared; and Stone himself would sometimes later make large claims for his influence. 'There was no one but me with whom William Faulkner could discuss his literary plans and hopes and his technical trials and aspirations', he once said. Faulkner himself was inclined to contest such claims, as he grew more famous: 'I don't hold with the mute inglorious Miltons', he insisted, 'I think if you're going to write, you're going to write and nothing will stop you.' Faulkner's brother Jack put it more plainly and personally, 'I'm certain he had such friends', Jack declared of literary mentors such as Stone,

> and I'm certain he would not have disdained any suggestions they might have had, but he was perfectly capable of making his own selections, and I'm certain that, to a large extent, [that] is what he did.[113]

The truth seems to have been, not that Stone shaped Faulkner into the writer he was (as Stone himself sometimes suggested) nor that he was entirely irrelevant (as Faulkner, when older, occasionally tended to claim), but that he acted as a catalyst – that he offered the emerging writer a guiding, paternal hand. Stone himself put it nicely in one of his less self-aggrandizing moments: 'I just carried water to the elephant.' As he was growing up and into the situation of writer, Faulkner needed objective confirmation of his subjective commitment. He needed dialogue, some-one with whom to engage in the development of his ideas about writers and writing. He needed a figure he could trust to assure him that his pose of 'Count No 'Count' (as the locals called him), the literary dandy, was not totally absurd: that it had some basis in a potentially fruitful stance towards reality – that it expressed, in however odd a form, a valid alle-giance to art. Above all, perhaps, Faulkner needed someone to supplement his reading, particularly in late nineteenth- and early twentieth-century

literature: to lend him books, and to confirm that – in his anxieties as well
as his interests – he was not alone. Stone helped more than anyone else
to satisfy those needs. He would send his younger friend off in the Stone
family's Studebaker car stacked with books to read for the day. He would
introduce him to other, helpful people such as the critic and novelist
Stark Young, who lived part of the year in Oxford. He would also talk and
talk to him: about such things, Stone later said, as 'the idea of avoiding
the contemporary literary cliques', 'the dread of the easy bottomless pit of
surface technical cleverness' and 'the idea of literature growing from its
own natural soil'.[114] There is no doubt that Faulkner would have got what
he needed for himself, if Stone had not been around to help him. But
Stone *was* there, to listen, lend books and offer advice; and that, quite
simply, made a difference. In later years, relations between the two men
were generally uneasy: something not helped by Stone's need to borrow
money from Faulkner or his occasional resentful or patronizing remarks
about Faulkner's success. But the friendship came at a crucial time for the
apprentice writer. And, despite all his reservations about his old, garrulous
friend, Faulkner himself testified to this: not least, by dedicating the three
Snopes novels 'To Phil Stone' – with the added comment, in *The Town*, 'He
did half of the laughing for thirty years.'

Last, but by no means least, in the extended family romance of Faulkner's
life there were his younger brothers: Murry Charles Falkner Jr (nicknamed
'Jack') born in 1899, John Wesley Thompson Falkner ('Johncy') born in
1901, and Dean Swift Falkner. William Faulkner, as he pointed out with
some pain more than once, 'never had a sister'. That part was played for
him, in an imaginative sense, by the girl who became his wife and, in a
more literal sense, by his cousin Sallie Murry Wilkins, the daughter of
Murry's sister. Born in 1899, Sallie was a lively, tomboyish girl who accompanied the three older Falkner brothers on many of their escapades and
often spent time playing with William alone. Both Jack and Johncy later
recalled the close, brother-and-sister relationship they enjoyed with her:
Jack called her 'sister', while Johncy said 'the four of us were together like
we were one family'. The boys' father seems to have been equally fond of
her. 'Holdy,' he said to his sister on one occasion, 'I'll give you any
two of my boys for your girl.' Relations within the family, and the general
tenor of William's life, seem to have been relatively unproblematic at this
stage: with William dividing his time between playing with his two younger
brothers and Sallie Murry, enjoying quieter pastimes with Estelle (one day
he began to write for her, stories and sketches and bits of poetry), and
engaging in more solitary pursuits such as reading, writing, drawing or
simply daydreaming. There were, inevitably, moments of tension: both
mother and father tended to punish William more severely than the others
(in his mother's case, perhaps, because he was the favourite and more
was expected of him), and Murry could occasionally reveal a streak of
indifference or even cruelty – by, for instance, referring to his oldest son
as 'Snake-Lips'. But, on the whole, there were no actue anxieties, no real

signs of trauma. Trauma came, though, in 1907. After Murry's mother died at the end of 1906, Damuddy followed her a few months later. More to the point, in August of 1907, just short of eleven years after William's birth, his youngest brother Dean was born. 'He's the best birthday present I ever had',[115] Murry Falkner said of his new child, who arrived two days before his own birthday. From the beginning, Dean was his father's favourite, with Murry accepting from him the sort of behaviour he would never have tolerated from William. Far closer to home, however, was the reaction of Maud Falkner: Dean required special treatment during the first few months of his life, and Maud was kept busy and preoccupied by the preparation of special treatments along with the normal requirements of baby care. Reference was made earlier to the thesis, favoured by several biographers, that this turn in events was crucial for the future novelist: because the apparent 'treachery' of Maud's devotion to the newly born child, and her consequent withdrawal from her oldest, persuaded William into an altered perception of women. Whatever the merits of this thesis – and, as has been said, it is neither demonstrable nor necessary as an explanation of the writer's imaging of the other sex – one thing is clear: that the birth of Dean initiated a change in Faulkner's life. It made him more solitary and withdrawn; it pushed him closer towards the emotional compensations of books and writing. Above all, it brought into existence a brotherly relationship that was intimate, passionate even, and mixed violent extremes of emotion, and that Faulkner could only begin to cope with in his fiction – where he could see it, as it were, through a glass, darkly.

On the surface, at least, the relationship between William and Dean was one of unqualified affection. William was loving and protective towards Dean, almost paternal in his feelings towards his youngest brother. He played games with Dean and his friends, served for a while as scoutmaster of Dean's troop, and sent him affectionate letters whenever he was away. Dean, in turn, worshipped William. He grew a moustache just like Bill's and changed his name to Faulkner. And, when William suffered from bouts of alcoholism and depression, it was always Dean – much more open, easygoing, and gregarious in his nature than his oldest brother – that Maud Falkner would send to talk to and take care of him. Shortly after his marriage, Dean even warned his new wife, 'Mother and Bill will always come first'; and his wife, Louise, seems to have accepted this. Certainly, most of the family appears to have understood that there was a special intimacy between oldest and youngest brother. So it was no surprise, when Dean died suddenly in a plane he was piloting in 1935, that William took it especially hard. William had, in any case, particular reasons for taking it this way. It was his encouragement and example that had promoted Dean's interest in flying; it was his plane that Dean had trained in and finally bought. 'I've ruined your life', he told Dean's wife, 'It's my fault'; and, when Louise told him she had dreamed of the fatal accident one night, he replied, 'You're lucky to have dreamed it only once. I dream it every night.' Faulkner moved into the house with Louise and his mother for a time, in order to share and help them with their grief; later, he assumed financial responsibility for Dean's widow and, after she was born in 1936, Dean's daughter, named after her father. Resorting to drink even more than usual at certain times after the tragic accident ('He had to have some relief', Maud said sympathetically), he saw to the preparation of his youngest brother's hideously scarred body for burial, to the details of the funeral, and to the preparation of a marker over the grave. Dean's epitaph was also William's choice. After the name and dates of birth and death, it said simply: 'I bare him on eagles' wings and brought him unto me.' Some might have taken this as a borrowing from the Bible, adapted from Exodus 19: 4. Others, however, including Maud Faulkner, recognized a different origin. It was the epitaph Faulkner had given another ill-fated pilot, John Sartoris in *Flags in the Dust/Sartoris*. Maud did not like it at all. She regarded it, another member of the family said, as 'a monument to William's grief and guilt'[116] rather than to Dean himself. It was almost as if Faulkner was taking on himself the burden of the seer: as if he had prophesied his brother's death in his first Yoknapatawpha novel and was now assuming moral responsibility for the prophecy.

Which brings us to the darker side of the relationship between the two brothers. There is no doubt that William loved his youngest brother. But he had, after all, been displaced for a while in his mother's affections by the arrival of Dean; and as Faulkner himself has reminded us – along with many other novelists – love and hatred, tenderness and resentment, can easily coexist. There must have been times after Dean was born when his oldest brother, suddenly abandoned as he perceived it, wished the new arrival out of existence: blamed him, in effect, for what was in any case inevitable, the 'primal gap' or loss of union with the mother. Such feelings could hardly be acknowledged openly: indeed, Faulkner's very solicitude for Dean, his adoption of a protective, paternal role, may have been in part a means of actively supressing them. Having 'lost' his mother, and sensed that the eruption of his youngest brother into their shared life was responsible for this loss, William may very well have played the part of father as a way of concealing hostile feelings (not least, from himself) and as a substitutive, self-compensatory gesture. Be that as it may, acknowledgement of these feelings could only come from him in his fiction: where they could be externalized and, to an extent, exorcized. And in Faulkner's first published Yoknapatawpha fiction, in particular: the twin brothers, Bayard Sartoris III and John, are hauntingly like William and Dean – in their respective characters, their tangled relationship, and not least in the way John's death and Bayard's reaction to it anticipate what was to happen to the author and his youngest brother some six years after the novel was published.

John Sartoris has died, while piloting a plane in the First World War, before *Flags in the Dust/Sartoris* opens, but he is recalled by those who knew him as someone 'merry and bold and wild'. He is, memorably, like Dean

Falkner in a number of ways: generous, exuberant, with a 'frank sponta-
neity, warm and ready and generous', fondly recollected and rehearsed by
friends and family alike. So close was the connection, evidently, between
Dean and John Sartoris that, later, when Dean's daughter sought to describe her father in a biographical study she turned to the fictional portrait of John for help: Dean was, his daughter said, just like that doomed
member of the Sartoris clan, with his 'warm radiance', and his possession
of a character (as she put it) 'sweet and merry and wild'. Bayard Sartoris
III, in turn, is just the opposite of this. Like his creator, he is an insomniac
and uses alcohol to relieve physical pain; there is, others feel, a quality of
aloofness, even 'bleak arrogance' about him; and he seeks refuge from
others and from his own thoughts in solitary pursuits, forays into nature
and hunting. More to the point, perhaps, Bayard remembers his dead
brother as someone braver, more attractive and glamorous than him; and,
despite the fact that he had nothing to do with John's death, he wrestles
constantly with a sense of guilt. Sometimes, he accuses himself directly of
responsibility: '*You did it!*', he tells himself on one occasion, '*You caused it
all; you killed Johnny!*' At others, he goes to the other extreme: protesting,
too much, that he has nothing for which to blame himself. 'I tried to keep
him from going up there on that goddam little popgun', are Bayard's very
first words to his grandfather on his return from the war – a piece of
gratuitous self-exoneration that anticipates Faulkner's own, later words to
Meta Carpenter, 'I grounded Dean. I told him not to fly.'[117] Nearly all
Bayard's actions in the time present of the novel seem rooted in a desire
to punish himself for some guilt he can hardly articulate and, in effect, to
liberate himself from his brother's death by repeating it: he dies, eventually, flying a crackpot experimental plane. It is not necessary to dip down
very far into the regions of Bayard's subconscious to see that his morbid
preoccupation with what happened to John, his sense of guilt and impulse
towards repetition of his brother's death, spring from a sense that he
willed the crucial event: he dreamed it, he believes, the disappearance of
his twin, he desired it and then it was so. Nor is it necessary, either, to
reach down far into the impulses that fired Faulkner into creative life to
see that, in imagining Bayard and John and their fates, he is sublimating
his own desires and enacting his own anxieties: freeing himself, for a
moment, from his darker feelings about Dean by enacting them, projecting them into fiction.

The only problem for Faulkner was that, like Bayard, he then saw his
scarcely acknowledged desires realized: the brother he loved and resented
was destroyed in a plane crash. In his own way, like his fictional *alter ego*,
he had tried to liberate himself by repetition: which, in his case, meant an
imitation of some of the more destructive aspects of his life in his art.
Tragically, life then imitated art. And Faulkner, in his own way, inscribed
his recognition of this in the epitaph he chose for his brother: which, as
his mother sensed, said more about the commemorator than it did about
the commemorated. The recognition was devastating, certainly, so was the

grief and anxiety that precipitated it: but it was also, somehow, purgative. For Faulkner, the death of his brother was a terrible, traumatic event that, like many such events, initiated radical, emotional change by acting as a rite of passage. This was notable, not least, in his fiction. The theme of sibling intimacy and rivalry had been a recurring one in the fiction up until 1935, and in particular the idea of the dead brother-rival. After that, it largely disappeared from Faulkner's work, except for *Intruder in the Dust* where it played a minor role. 'A book is ... the dark twin of a man', Faulkner had had a character say in *Mosquitoes*; and Faulkner himself had struggled with his own 'dark twin' in story after story. But now he did no more: the death of his youngest and evidently dearest brother had shaken him to his foundations, but also released him. Ironically, the last significant appearance of this theme of a deadly struggle between brothers is in the book Faulkner was writing at the time Dean died and completed after his burial: in *Absalom, Absalom!*, published in 1936, Henry Sutpen comes home from the Civil War and, at the entrance to his father's house, actually kills his half-brother, Charles Bon.

With the death of Dean, Faulkner was confirmed, in any event, as the head of his own family romance: son, lover, brother he might have been and continue to be, but he was more and more compelled into the role of father. His own father had died in 1932 and, along with the titular leadership of the clan this implied, came increased financial responsibility. 'Dad left Mother solvent for only about 1 year', he reported shortly after his fathers' funeral, 'Then it is me'; and, within a year indeed, Faulkner was writing about the responsibility of having 'two families to support now'. His daughter Jill was born in June 1933; there was, of course, the widowed Louise and her daughter to care for only a short while later; and by 1938 Faulkner was complaining, 'last spring I inherited another indigent brother with his wife and children' – by which Faulkner meant his brother John and his family whom he had installed on a farm, just a few miles outside of Oxford, purchased with money received from the sale of a novel to Hollywood. Faulkner was capable of feeling resentful about his role as patriarch. In 1940, for example, he wrote this:

> Every so often ... I take these fits of sort of raging and impotent exaspera-
> tion at this really quite alarming paradox which my life reveals: Beginning
> at the age of thirty, I, an artist, a sincere one and of the first class, who
> should be free even of his own economic responsibilities and with no moral
> conscience at all, began to become the sole, principal and partial support –
> food, shelter, heat, clothes, medicine, Kotex, school fees, toilet paper, and
> picture shows – of my mother, ... my brother and his wife and two sons,
> another brother's widow and child, a wife of my own and two step children,
> my own child; I inherited my father's debts and dependents, white and black
> without inheriting yet from anyone one inch of land or one stick of furniture

or one cent of money . . . I am 42 years old and I have already paid for four funerals and will certainly pay for one more and in all likelihood two more beside that, provided none of the people in mine or my wife's family my superior in age outlive me, before I ever come to my own.[118]

It is a magnificent tirade, and some of the anger and frustration it express-es encouraged its author to seek refuge from the family over which he presided. Men like war, Faulkner sardonically remarked, because it gives them an excuse to get away from their kinfolk without guilt or recrimi-nation; and, in the absence of a good war, Faulkner sought other boltholes – in work perhaps, in drink, walking, flying and riding, and in passionate liaisons with women like Meta Carpenter. However, it would be an act of supererogation to point out that Faulkner had taken these burdens upon himself, and that his so-called 'dependants' were hardly enjoying a condi-tion of privilege – on the contrary, his black and female 'dependants', in particular, were even more the victims of the situation he described than he was. He had worries and responsibilities, certainly, but he also had some mastery over his condition, now that he was head of the clan: he was in a position where he was able, more than most, to say what he wanted to say and do what he wanted to do. The mastery was not unlimited, of course; it was hedged about with conditions inextricable from that elabo-rate circuitry of passion and power we call the family. But, then, no mas-tery ever is. And it is surely better – which is to say, more comfortable and desirable – to be the patriarch in a patriarchal structure than to be any-thing else: some power and mobility is preferable to hardly any or, it may be, none at all. All of which is by way of saying that Faulkner's engagement with the issue of fatherhood, and in particular with the experience of the son who becomes a father, is as subject to the pressures of debate and dialogue as his imaginative encounter with other details of the family romance is. And this is the case, not least, because he approached that issue, and the whole, vexed problem of patriarchy, from extreme, oppos-ing positions, as one of the victims and one of the privileged. 'I am telling the same story over and over, which is myself and the world', Faulkner had said; and with him, perhaps in an even more acute sense than with most people, the stories of self and world *were* one and the same. Autobiogra-phy *was* history, he recognized, the material conditions and moral ro-mances of his world were woven into the fabric of his life: which is why, when he wrote out of his own tensions, he wrote out of those of his place and time.

2

Faulkner the Apprentice

I TRYING OUT DIFFERENT VOICES: THE EARLY PROSE AND POETRY

Writing to his mother from Royal Air Force training camp in Canada in 1918, Faulkner observed, 'Isn't it queer that the ones whose home life has been everything . . . are the ones who when the time comes . . . do everything possible to go?' But then he added, it was not so 'queer' after all. 'Only he whose heart and soul is wrapped about his home', the apprentice airman declared,

> can see beyond the utterly worthless but human emotions such as selfishness, and know that home is the thing worth having above everything, and it is well known that what is not worth fighting for is not worth having.[1]

The sentiments are bathed in the kind of *fin-de-siècle* romanticism that characterizes Faulkner's earliest excursions into literature, mixed here with that reverential attitude towards war and warriors that had provoked a young Southerner to enlist as a British pilot. Nevertheless, they point to a fundamental impulse that animates much of his writing: an impulse that set him adrift in Oxford, even while he tried to anchor his life there, but that, equally, pierced his heart with a sense of exile when he was elsewhere. Later, it was to enable Faulkner to weave his major novels around a sense of place (particularly homeplace) and past (particularly personal and familial past) experienced as much as a significant absence as anything else. Yesterday, in books like *The Sound and the Fury* and *Absalom, Absalom!*, becomes the golden mirror in which today is perceived; today is consequently given an additional magical dimension of meaning, and yet somehow deprived of intrinsic significance and even substance. Like their creator, the protagonists of these novels are caught re-inventing their homeplace, and the precious associations it engenders, even while they perceive or remember it. But that was later: at the time of writing this letter, Faulkner was incapable of fictionalizing this predicament – partly because he was too busy experiencing it. Clearly, he needed to get away from home, in fact or imagination, for many of the reasons that any young person does: in order to take risks, savour new and possibly dangerous experiences, escape material and emotional confinement, and take the first, faltering steps towards a new life and vocation. Equally clearly, however, he felt even more urgently and painfully than most young people do the tearing of the umbilical cord, the emotional consequences of rupture with the homeplace.

The letters Faulkner posted home, principally to his mother, in the period before the publication of *Soldier's Pay* were, in fact, one of his principal *written* means of coming to terms with the place where he was born: a place that was as much an invention of memory and imaginative need as an actual, historical situation. 'I'm waiting for a letter', he admitted in his earliest extant letter, characteristically addressed to Maud Faulkner. 'I'm cold all the time', he complained whenever he moved out of the deep, torrid South. 'I'm homesick'; 'I'd give anything in the world for a horse to ride now'; 'golly, I miss the hills and fruit trees and things now'. Remarks such as these ring like a plaintive anthem through the early correspondence, given added flavour – sometimes of a rancid kind – by his attempts to remind the recipients of his letters just how much he belonged to the South even when he was away. 'Well, sir, I could live in this country a hundred years and never get used to the niggers', he wrote to his father in 1921,

> The whites and niggers are always antagonistic, hate each other, and yet go to the same shows and same restaurants, and call each other by first names . . . You cant tell me these niggers are as happy and contented as ours are, all this freedom does is to make them miserable because they are not white, so that they hate the white people more than ever, and the whites are afraid of them. There's only one sensible way to treat them, like we treat Brad Farmer and Calvin and Uncle George.[2]

It is not enough, really, to defend remarks like this, as some commentators have, by suggesting that Faulkner was simply seeking the approval of his elders. This begs the question of why he should seek such approval or seek it in this particular way. The references to 'niggers' and 'yids' and so on that occasionally scar the earlier letters are surely more accurately seen as further symptoms of the deep ambivalence of the young Faulkner's response to his homeplace. He could leave it, and needed to leave it sometimes: but in leaving it he was like that most autobiographical of his later characters, Quentin Compson. For like Quentin he could not do otherwise than see and measure himself in that golden mirror: he was still thinking of home and still thinking *in terms of home* even when he was in New York, Toronto or Paris. He was still caught, irresistibly, in the idioms and masks of his birthplace even when he was a thousand or more miles away.

The spellbinding figure of the young pre-novelist is not just caught in letters home, however. There is also the wealth of material, mostly poetry, poetic drama, sketches and short fictions that Faulkner produced in the period roughly from 1919, when his first published piece the poem 'L'Apres-midi d'un Faune' appeared in the *New Republic*, to 1926, when Faulkner presented a hand-lettered gift book of poems, *Helen: A Courtship*, to the young woman with whom he had fallen in love, Helen Baird. Much of the very earliest material, prose, poetry and sketches, appeared in the newspaper of the University of Mississippi, *The Mississippian*. 'Naiad's Song', which was published in that paper in 1920, captures much of the flavour of these early, faltering attempts at verse:

> Come ye sorrowful and keep
> Tryst with us here in wedded sleep
> The silent moon lies over us
> And shaken ripples cover us,
> Our arms are soft as is the stream.
>
> . . .
>
> Our eyes are soft as twilit streams,
> Our breasts are soft as silken dreams
> And white at dusk; our breasts the beds
> On which we soothe all aching heads,
> Binding each in a scented tress
> Till he glides in forgetfulness,
> While the night sighs and whispers by
> Sowing stars across the sky.
> Come ye sorrowful and keep
> Here in unmeasured dream and sleep.[3]

Dreams of fair women: fleeting, ethereal presences associated with streams, dreams, and half-heard voices that lure the male protagonist away from the noisy, sweaty business of everyday life and into forgetfulness. In part, this is a later Romantic cliché, of a piece with the young Faulkner's 'Count No 'Count' pose and, as such, a way of distancing himself from his surroundings: the verse, like the bohemian pose in other words, enabled its creator firmly to establish his credentials as resident alien in Oxford, at home and yet somehow not at home. In part, though, it is also a recollection of the dualistic terms in which the young Faulkner had been raised and an anticipation, however feeble, of the predicament that fires his later protagonists into agonized life. There is art, according to these terms, and there is the real business of work (one of these early poems, 'Study', makes this opposition explicit); there are dreams and there are heroics; there is female fluidity and there is male fixity. To listen to, and eventually drown in, the voices of the naiads is, as a consequence, clearly a calculated risk: it is to achieve fulfilment of a kind ('wedded sleep') but also oblivion ('unmeasured sleep'). The lover/artist listens to these voices, forsaking 'bitter science' and, in doing so, he consummates a marriage with faery creatures, and with a subterranean realm of dreams and desires, that is, by its very nature, a gesture of impotence, an act of substitution: a motion of worship from – to quote one of Faulkner's earliest portraits of the artist – 'an emasculate priest'.

Just how intimately the young Faulkner's notions of art were bound up with his ideas of women and sexuality is suggested by some of his reviews and essays of this period as well as by his poetry. In an essay entitled 'Verse Old and Nascent: a Pilgrimage', for instance, first published in the New Orleans periodical *The Double Dealer,* Faulkner jettisoned the pose of the romantic dreamer in favour of one that came just as easily to him at times, that of the knowing, and slightly world-weary, cynic: the nexus woman/ art/sexual satisfaction/sexual compensation was retained but in a different, more sardonic way. Part of the essay has been alluded to and quoted already. Nevertheless, it is worth recalling here and quoting in a little more detail, since it unravels so many of the convolutions of attitude lurking behind this particular mask. 'I read and employed verse, firstly', Faulkner breezily declared,

> for the purpose of furthering various philanderings in which I was engaged, secondly to complete a youthful gesture I was then making of being 'different' in a small town. Later, my concupiscence waning, I turned inevitably to verse, finding therein an emotional counterpart far more satisfactory for two reasons (1) No partner was required (2) It was much simpler to close a book, and take a walk.[4]

Art is seen, then, both as an access to sex and as an alternative to it. This is contradiction enough, perhaps, but the contradictions proceed to multiply. For following this – in a passage quoted earlier – Faulkner goes on to express a sentiment he was to repeat in his fiction: that, while men are usually concerned with 'art for art's sake', women are *always* directed towards 'art for the artist's sake'. So, working from the assumption that the artistic subject is normally masculine and the artistic object normally feminine, Faulkner forces the argumentative wheel to come full circle, with the woman/object finding sexual access to the male/subject via the artifact. What began as male seduction, and moved into substitution, ends (for the moment, at least) with the woman turning sexual aggressor. The beliefs and contradictions at work here help explain a number of things: why, for instance, Faulkner the apprentice writer chose to weave such an ambivalent portrait of fair women, why he chose to associate language with the male gaze and the female voice responding to that gaze – above all perhaps, why for the most part he allows romantic sentimentalism to replace sexuality. There is nothing in this early writing of what, in theory, the young Faulkner asked for in poetry and claimed that he found in, say, the work of Keats: 'a still water strong and potent, quiet with its own strength, and satisfying as bread'. On the contrary, there is a febrile emotionalism springing from the fact that, as a writer, Faulkner cannot make up his mind whether he is fulfilling the male role or failing it. The sex is there in a shifting, suppressed and uncertain fashion because he cannot, with any degree of assurance, place either himself or his art in relation to it. This is his predicament here; later, in the major novels, it was to become one of his abiding subjects.

With art perceived, at least some of the time, as absence, an inverse image of life, it is perhaps not so surprising that the homeplace so persistently invoked in the letters should be mostly missing from the verse. Even the essays rarely allude to the South; and, when they do, it is usually in terms that ignore or reject its historical dimension, presenting it as uncultivated 'nature'. 'The beauty – spiritual and physical – of the South', Faulkner the apprentice essayist observed, 'lies in the fact that God has done so much for it and man so little.' 'I have this for which to thank whatever gods may be', he added, 'that having fixed my roots in this soil all contact, saving by the printed word, with contemporary poets is impossible.' Freed from a network of entangling literary alliances, the young Faulkner saw himself separated as well from *culture*: because, at this time, he could perceive things only in terms of another familiar dualism, that of nature versus culture, and because (again, at this time) he could think of 'culture' only as everything that was other than his homeplace. Everything, but not quite: the Faulkner of these years was nothing if not self-contradictory, and there was one element of culture that he was willing to attribute to the South. 'America has no drama or literature worth the name', he loftily declared in one review, 'and hence no tradition'. However, he suggested, 'perhaps in time' writers 'will make something of the wealth of natural dramatic material in this country, the greatest resource being our language'. 'Nowhere today', he went on,

> saving in parts of Ireland, is the English language spoken with the same earthy strength as it is in the United States; though we are, as a nation, still inarticulate.[5]

This was something, a possible resource: 'the lustiest language of modern times', as the young Faulkner put it elsewhere. And what made it even more exciting, from his perspective, was that an 'inexhaustible fund of dramatic material' springing from an idiom in comparison with which British speech was merely 'a Sunday night affair of bread and milk – melodious but slightly tiresome nightingales in a formal clipped hedge': this was all to be found flourishing with especial vigour in the South, in such eras as 'the old Mississippi river days'. True, Faulkner hardly seemed willing to take advantage of this resource in most of his poetry. Equally true, he seemed unwilling to acknowledge that other writers before him had fashioned Southern voices into an imaginative weapon, a flexible instrument of exchange: Mark Twain, he declared in the same review that invoked old times on the Mississippi, was no more than 'a hack writer who would not have been considered fourth rate in Europe'. Nevertheless, his willingness even at this juncture to qualify his strictures on the Southern absence of culture and, more specifically, to greet language as 'our logical saviour', the true coinage of the region and a potentially valuable currency for the aspiring writer: this was evidence that he sensed where his true strengths and direction lay – and at what point he could enter into his Southern inheritance.

That Faulkner, even in his early work, was beginning to confront the problems and possibilities of voice, if not specifically Southern voice, is suggested by two works that he produced special copies of in the early 1920s: the play *The Marionettes*, six hand-lettered copies of which were completed in 1920, and the verse sequence, *Vision in Spring*, a gift copy of which Faulkner presented to Estelle Oldham Franklin in 1921. As the editor of the 1977 published version indicates, *The Marionettes* looks both backwards and forwards. Behind it may be sensed many of the literary figures who shadowed the young Faulkner: Oscar Wilde, the T.S. Eliot of 'The Love Song of J. Alfred Prufrock' (a poem that is paraphrased several times in the play), and above all the French Symbolists Verlaine, Mallarmé, Laforgue, Baudelaire, Valéry and Gautier. And after it lie the mature fictions, many of which it anticipates in terms of technique. There is the structural frame: the entire action is presented as the dream of one character, Pierrot, who then weaves his way in and out of the dream he is dreaming. There is the counterpointed plot: the tale of Pierrot and the dreamy figure whom he loves, named Marietta, is placed in equilibrium with the story of another love, involving a personified Summer and a garden nymph, who have parted for no other reason than the irrevocable passage of time. Above all, there are the multiple voices of Pierrot and the figures in his dream: his own and those of Marietta and various choric figures, including the Spirit of Autumn. A word of caution is necessary here, however. As far as counterpointed plot and multiple voices are concerned, *The Marionettes* anticipates the later work only in the feeblest sense: it traces the lineaments of these designs rather than fully realizing them. The story of Summer and the garden nymph, for instance, is a counterpoint only to a minimal degree, since it does little more than repeat the themes of the major tale – time and change, thwarted desire, and the elusive nature of the loved one – in the same muted and melancholy key. And the different voices that dramatize, duplicate or dispute the narrative of Pierrot and Marietta are, in the end, only one voice – sad, softly swooning, delicately voluptuous, as in these lines attributed to Marietta:

> How still it is! and cool, but my face and my body are not cool: my hands are hot like magnolia petals at noon, my body is hot like the earth of a moon drenched garden. How cool the pool looks! It is like a naked girl lying on her back among the roses, it is so cool that I shall cool my face and my hot hands in it. There is no one here, dare I bathe in this pool?[6]

The structural frame is another matter. The figure of Pierrot initiates the action: lover, dreamer, even poet of a kind, he recalls the persona that haunts many of the early poems and anticipates many of the pale, ineffectual and Quixotic creatures that inhabit the later fiction. Within a few moments of entering the exotic garden scene that circumscribes the play, he has fallen into 'a drunken sleep';[7] and we are then invited to observe what happens as the offspring of his imagination, his dreams woven out of desire. After two other, choric figures have spoken, Marietta enters: a creature who – as the passage just quoted indicates – is associated in her own words with images of imaginative longing (the moon), desire (heat, magnolia, roses), and a Narcissus-like world of self-reflection (the pool, the naked girl). All this is *dreamed* by Pierrot. He dreams the elusive object of desire: she, in turn, expresses her own longing for that elusive object. In effect, Marietta is at once object and subject, desired and desiring: an ambivalent status expressed, during the course of the action, by her stepping into the pool to unite with her own image. Following this gesture of immersion, Pierrot himself appears in his dream, pursuing the now curiously doubled figure of his beloved. And the suggestion clearly is that Pierrot appears as an incarnation of Marietta's desires, expressed prior to her stepping into the pool. So, even as Pierrot desires his own creation, the dreamy projection of his desires, Marietta desires *her* own creation, the invention of what she terms her 'strange desires' for 'vague unnamed things'. In this hall of mirrors, in fact, everyone is falling in love with his or her own reflection: the 'I' longs to merge with a 'not-I' that is no more and no less than a repeated image of the 'I'.

After the insertion of Pierrot into his own dream, *The Marionettes* offers us an ever more shifting, metamorphic world, a dimension where the one law is change. Marietta leaves, haunted by memories of her mother whose story she feels she is repeating ('my mother went this way / Slipped from her bed at break o' day');[8] 'like a sleepwalker', she is seduced by song into 'the garden of forgetting' where perhaps the mixture of memory and desire that confuses her may temporarily disappear. Choric figures comment on what has passed; the story of Summer and a garden nymph echoes that same story; and the Spirit of Autumn reminds us, time and again, that all stories have an end with the seasonal death of nature and the death of the body. Marietta then reappears. 'How the garden has changed!' she observes, adding 'Am I changed very much, I wonder?' And to this plaintive query two voices respond by describing her for us: one seeing her as a consummate work of art ('her hands are . . . little pieces of silver for which lives have been bartered'), the other preferring on the contrary to present her as a pristine, almost prelapsarian figure ('her hands are like little fluttering birds'). One critic has attributed this double vision of Marietta to the ambivalence of the character herself: which is to forget the framing figure of Pierrot, the poet/dreamer. What is caught here, surely, is not the ambivalence of this or any other female figure *per se* but, rather, the ambivalence of Pierrot's, and Faulkner's, feelings about her. Quite simply, through the device of the dreaming narrator, Faulkner is allowing himself for the first time to investigate questions about woman, nature and otherness that exist only as assumptions in other early work. Is 'woman', as object of male desire, actually 'there' in the field of vision and longing or 'not there', the projection of that longing, the invention of – and coextensive with – that field of vision? Is 'nature', for that matter tamed or redeemed by 'culture'? And is otherness to be grasped in all its rawness, or is it transformed in the process of perception – turned, by that process, into a 'made' thing? There are no answers, even tentative ones, to these questions here. All we have, at the end, is the refrain, 'I desire – what do I desire?', reminding us of the conditions that frame such questions: human existence as an always deferred fulfilment, an experience of longing, an imagination of the absent. *The Marionettes* is no masterpiece, certainly. But its basic conceit, of a protagonist telling himself a story of which, eventually, he is the absent centre: this was to enable masterpieces in the future – which is to say, works in which the enigma of desire, in all its personal and social ramifications, was vividly rehearsed if never resolved.

The figure of Pierrot reappears in *Vision in Spring*. Even more than in *The Marionettes*, he is seen here as a creature reluctant to move or act. 'You, the silver bow on which the arrow of your life is set', observes a third-person narrator of Pierrot while addressing him,

> The shaft is tipped with jade desire, and feathered with your illusions,
> The bow is drawn, yet unreleased
> For you are not sure, you are still afraid
> That you will miss the mark on which the dart is laid.[9]

Desiring, isolated, volitionless, this Pierrot seems to be incapable of speech much of the time ('I am dumb / I am dumb and huge in starlight'), or of self-definition. His identity in fact, like that of Eliot's Prufrock, seems to be dissipated, scattered amongst the components of the scene:

> Who am I, thinks Pierrot, who am I
> To stretch my soul out rigid across the sky?[10]

The result is a figure whose voice, or accompanying voices, may fluctuate between romantic fantasy and sardonic knowingness but whose personality must always be refracted through a fragmented persona, dissolved into a series of objective correlatives. At its most obvious, as in these lines that embarrassingly echo the famous opening of the Eliot poem, the 'I' becomes 'you and I' to dramatize the narcissism of isolation, and the narcissistic ego translates the blank stare of reality into, alternatively, a mirror of its own concerns or a threat to its purity, and even its existence:

> Let us go then; you and I, while evening grows
> And a delicate violet thins the rose
> That stains the sky;
> We will go alone there, you and I,
> And watch the trees step naked from the shadow
> Like women shrugging upward from their gowns.[11]

'Life is not a passing: it is an endless repeating', observes the poet elsewhere; and the repetitions, together with the constantly shifting voices
and identities, trace out a world of masks and mirrors in which nothing
is certain or stable – least of all, the self. Pronouns and perspectives alter
without warning: as in the lines just quoted, 'I' quickly becomes 'you and
I' or just 'you' and then, perhaps 'we' or 'he'. Further displacement is
offered by the frequent adoption of an ironic or parodic voice, so that
identity is further split by self-deprecation, a distancing of self from self:

> I smoothe my mental hair
> With an oft changed phrase that I revise again
> Until I have forgotten what it was at first;
> Settle my tie with: I have brought a book
> Then seat myself with: We have passed the worst.[12]

Certainly, at the close of the poem sequence, an impersonal and apparently authoritative voice does appear for a moment to announce that
Pierrot and his dreams are dead, 'the lidless blaze / Of sunlight' having,
we are told, burned away all moonlit dreams of 'shortening[-]breasted'
nymphs. However, the terms in which this is announced curiously recall
the imagery of the opening poem in the sequence: *Vision in Spring* begins
and ends, as its title intimates, in April and, despite all protestations to
the contrary, Pierrot's voice and visions do not appear entirely to have
disappeared.

What are we to make of all this? One commentator has claimed that
Vision in Spring is 'the pivotal work in Faulkner's self-apprenticeship':[13]
because, borrowing ideas and strategies from Conrad Aiken, the young
writer here models himself an instrument for dramatizing his own fragmented state. The character of Pierrot, so the argument goes, supplied
Faulkner in this instance with a character type possessed of multiple and
often contradictory voices through which problems of identity could be
creatively explored. In turn, the poem sequence offered a formal structure by means of which the young pre-novelist could begin to explore
multilinear, noncausal, disjunctive forms of narration. In short, the major
novels are there in embryo in *Vision in Spring*, from the isolated, fragmented narrator who talks to himself in different voices to the ending that
is as much a beginning as an end. There is an element of truth in such
a claim: to the extent that this poem sequence does rehearse styles and
structures that characterize the major novels. The problem is, the re-
hearsal is a very rudimentary and ramshackle one. The style, when not
queasily romantic, is embarrassingly derivative; the persona of Pierrot is
not so much fragmented as lost at several moments in the sequence; while
the structure is only rarely disjunctive to a purpose – more often than not,
voices switch, idioms alter and perspectives change, not in a fashion that
fruitfully subverts and exposes (as in, say, *As I Lay Dying*) but in a way that
simply confuses. There is no need to break a butterfly on a wheel: as a very
early work, *Vision in Spring* offered Faulkner a further step towards the

designs and obsessions of his mature fiction and proper attention should consequently be paid to it. But it *was* an early work and, in this capacity, no more significant than, say, *The Marionettes* – perhaps rather less so. It was, in short, only one among many avenues the young Faulkner explored during the period of apprenticeship to his craft.

For all his prolific poetic output during these early years, and the several gift volumes of verse he presented to friends and loved ones, Faulkner was in fact to publish only two volumes of poetry. The first of these, *The Marble Faun*, was published in 1924 by the Four Seas Company in Boston, after Phil Stone had submitted the volume and agreed to pay the $400 required by the company for publication. The opening poem in the book, 'Prologue', swiftly establishes the world this collection inhabits – a world already familiar to any reader of Faulkner's early verse:

> The poplar trees sway to and fro
> That through this gray old garden go
> Like slender girls with nodding heads,
> Whispering above the beds
> Of tall tufted hollyhocks
> . . .
> And clouds glide down the western sky
> To watch this sun-drenched revery,
> While the poplars' shining crests
> Lightly brush their silvered breasts,
> Dreaming not of winter snows
> That soon will shake their maiden rows.
> . . .
> The days dream by . . .[14]

This is the shifting, metamorphic garden world of *The Marionettes*, where trees are like girls whispering, and girls or rather nymphs assume the shape of trees; and where trees, girls, clouds, flowers all in turn are possessed of the fluidity and fluency of water. All are possessed of this fluidity, that is, except for one: the marble faun of the title, who is saddened at once by the transience of the world about him ('winter snows') and by his own imprisonment in 'marble bonds'. 'The sky warms me', the marble faun admits,

> and yet I cannot break
> My marble bonds. That quick keen snake
> Is free to come and go, while I
> Am prisoner to dream and sigh
> For things I know, yet cannot know
> . . .
> The whole world breathes and calls to me
> Who marble-bound must ever be.[15]

The faun is another dreamer, like Pierrot. But in his intense stillness, set on a pedestal as an ornament for a garden, he is a reminder too of another, ancient theme: that art kills in order to create. As an artifact, the marble faun is released from the transience of nature: but he is released only into the imprisonment of form, the 'marble bonds' that are, in their way, only another kind of death.

'If I were free', the marble faun declares plaintively in the second poem in the collection, 'then I would go / where the first chill spring winds blow': he would follow Pan, the leader of the dance of nature, where 'Pan's sharp hoofed feet have pressed / His message on the chilly crest'. But he cannot: because, as the faun and his creator intimate throughout this volume, the paradox of art is that the artist is both a liberator – since he is freeing his subject from time – and a jailer – since he is reducing the bewildering variety of experience to a system, or prison-house of signs. Registering the irresistible otherness of things, he must take them out of their living context and insert them, and their lovely transmutations, within another, essentially still frame. What these poems do for the most part, in fact, is describe and dramatize their own impotence – and in more ways than, perhaps, their creator realizes. There is, of course, the figurative impotence of the faun, imprisoned in 'marble bonds'. But there is also, in most of the volume, the verbal impotence of the poet, imprisoned in the marmoreal structures of his poems. For the most part, this is a verse that commemorates rather than dramatizes, that rehearses familiar idioms rather than reinvents:

> Away
> To brilliant pines upon the sea
> Where waves linger silkenly
> Upon the shelving sand, and sedge
> Rustling gray along the edge
> Of dunes that rise against the sky
> Where painted sea-gulls wheel and fly.[16]

There is little activity in lines like these. The plangent rhythms, the sonorous word-music, the imagery drawn it seems from some late Romantic lexicon: everything has an air of predictability, dreadful inevitability, about it. There is no sense here that language can be a process, since all *this* language does really is offer us a series of fixed gestures – and, as a consequence, remind us that words are a sign of absence, of substitution and 'no-thing'.

To leave it there, however, would be unfair to these poems. In his mature work, Faulkner could register language as a substitution *and* a kind of fulfilment, a gesture of impotence *and* an act of consummation; and, just occasionally in *The Marble Faun*, he ceases to be 'marble-bound' and catches that same duality. In the process, he intimates that the traditional dichotomy of art/fixity versus life/fluidity is, like the many other dichotomies inhabiting his early work, a false – which is to say, an unnecessarily exclusive – one. In these lines, for instance, the young Faulkner manages to re-create in the stillness of language the vibrancy, the vitality and the susceptibility to change that characterize the natural world:

> Swallows dart and skimming fly
> Like arrows painted on the sky,
> And the twanging of the string
> Is the faint high quick crying
> That they, downward shooting, spin
> Through the soundless swelling din
>
>   . . .
>
> A sudden brook hurries along
> Singing its reverted song,
> Flashing in white frothèd shocks
> About upstanding polished rocks . . .[17]

'The aim of the artist', an older, maturer Faulkner was to say,

> is to arrest motion, which is life, by artificial means and hold it fixed so that a hundred years later when a stranger looks at it, it moves again since it is life.[18]

For a moment or two, in these poems, the younger Faulkner does just that.

The one other collection of poetry Faulkner saw published during his lifetime, *A Green Bough*, did not appear until 1933. However, most of the poems in this collection had been written, in some form or other, considerably earlier: several of them, for instance, appear in earlier versions, in the gift booklet *Mississippi Poems* that Faulkner presented to a woman friend, Myrtle Ramey, in 1924. Poem XLIV in *A Green Bough* is an interesting illustration of this, since it is an abbreviated version of the seventh piece in *Mississippi Poems*: a piece that, as the title, 'Mississippi Hills: My Epitaph', intimates, represents one of Faulkner's few attempts to encounter his homeplace openly in his poetry. 'Far blue hills, where I have pleasured me', begins the original version,

> Where on silver feet in dogwood cover
> Spring follows . . .
>
>   . . .
>
> Return I will! Where is the death
> While in these blue hills slumbrous overhead
> I'm rooted like a tree? Though I be dead,
> This soil that holds me fast will find me breath.[19]

The note of exile that sounds in this earlier version, tempering the declaration of rootedness and loyalty, was toned down for *A Green Bough*. Nevertheless, in both versions, the most remarkable feature of the poem remains: this is a song to Mississippi that owes more to literature – specifically, British literature and, more specifically, A.E. Housman – than to life.

The hills of Faulkner's northern Mississippi are transmuted into the 'blue remembered hills' of *A Shropshire Lad*, accompanied by the appropriate tone of melancholy and the required intimations of death. In this context, the poet's claim that he is 'rooted like a tree' is neatly subverted by his unwillingness or inability to speak in the language of the 'soil that holds' him, or even to see that soil for what it is. The poem may appear, at first sight, to be a portrait of the place where the poet was born and where he expects to die: but it is hardly *of* that place and, apart from a passing reference to dogwood, it is not really *about* that place either.

There are echoes of other poets throughout *A Green Bough*: including writers as otherwise different as Thomas Gray ('The sun lies long upon the hills, / The plowman slowly homeward wends') and, inevitably, T.S. Eliot ('We sit drinking tea / Beneath the lilacs on a summer afternoon'). The elusive, ethereal woman-figure reappears, associated with twilight and memory ('I see your face through the twilight of my mind, / A dusk of forgotten things, remembered things'). So, too, do the imagery of nymphs, fauns, and voyeuristic satyrs ('The old satyr, leafed and hidden, dreams her kiss . . . / Dreams her body in a moony night / Shortening and shudder-ing into his') and the familiar, metamorphic elisions of girls, trees and streams ('forty poplars like the breasts of girls / taut with running'). Faulkner the poet is at his worst here, as he usually is when he is trying to be 'poetic': which is to say, adopting the marmoreal diction, plangent rhythms, and above all the monolithic voice that overshadow so many of the poems in *The Marble Faun*. Conversely, he is at his best when he approaches closest to the condition of the novel or, to be more exact, of the novel as he was later to practise it. Several of the earlier poems in this volume, in particular, are written in an unbuttoned, flowing form of free verse, something that enables the poet to go some way towards capturing the random movements of thought and the oblique, chancey rhythms of ordinary speech:

> – Are you quite all right, sir? she stops to ask.
> – You are a bit lonely, I fear.
> Will you have more tea? cigarettes? No? –
> I thank her, waiting for her to go.[20]

These lines are taken from a poem originally titled 'The Lilacs', which attempts to dramatize the living death in which some badly wounded pilots of the First World War, like the narrator, found themselves trapped. Surrounded by strange voices, the central figure in this poem sits in ap-parent silence, talking only to himself while he listens and observes. The anticipation of Faulkner's first novel, *Soldier's Pay*, and in particular of its central, catalysing figure Donald Mahon, is perhaps obvious. What is less so, however, is that poems like this one also anticipate the later, mature fiction: in which the consciousness of the narrator becomes a battlefield – an area of debate in which different voices argue, complain, interrogate and struggle for control. 'I hear their voices as from a great distance –', admits the narrator at the end of this poem, 'Not dead / He's not dead, poor chap; he didn't die–'. Cut off from the murmurs and whispers by which he is nevertheless haunted, torn between a bleak present and 'the quiet darkness' of the past when he received his wound, this anonymous, crippled aviator anticipates several of Faulkner's major protagonists: people who, like him, may insist 'I – I am not dead' but, in a sense, already are – save for the voices within and around them that fight to make themselves heard.

This use of the poem as a site of verbal struggle is characteristic of all the best pieces in *A Green Bough*. Another piece, for example, presents that struggle in a comic light: a young man finds himself caught between his polite words addressed to the mother of his beloved ('madam I love your daughter') and his far from polite, in fact ragingly lustful, thoughts ('these slender moons' unsunder I would break / so soft I'd break that hushed virginity'). A third poem, in turn, takes a story from the newspapers to enact its debates. Originally titled 'The Cave' and then 'Floyd Collins', it recalls the ordeal of a young man of that name who was trapped in a cave in Kentucky early in 1925 and died there despite the best efforts of others to rescue him. Other writers, notably Robert Penn Warren in his novel *The Cave* (1956), have exploited the specifically public dimension of this event, the media circus that developed around the rescue bid. The young Faulkner, however, chose to focus on something quite different – the prisoner in the cave struggling to survive, and the warring voices he hears in his head as he does so:

> Now comes the dark again, he thinks, but finds
> A wave of gold breaking a jewelled crest
> And he is walled with gold. About him snored
> Kings and mitred bishops tired of sin
> Who dreamed themselves of heaven wearied
> And now may sleep, hear rain, and snore again.[21]

There is a foretaste here of the closing paragraphs of *The Mansion* when Mink Snopes, lying on the ground, feels all his 'passions and hopes and skeers' begin to seep away into 'the little grass blades and tiny roots', and senses that he and all 'the folks' are 'all mixed and jumbled up comfortable and easy' now together in the earth – all at one with

> the beautiful, the splendid, the proud and the brave, right on up to the very top itself among the shining phantoms and dreams which are the milestones of the long human recording – Helen and the bishops, the kings and the unhorsed angels, the scornful and graceless seraphim.[22]

More significant than any specific connections between the two passages, however, is the clash of idioms poem and novel share. Floyd Collins is caught just as Mink Snopes is, by a vocabulary that registers both the pungent actualities of his life and the plaintive nobility of his dreams: moving suddenly and without warning from the demotic to the grandiloquent – from the voice, we might say, of Huckleberry Finn to that of Poe's Roderick Usher. This was one way, and not the least important, that Faulkner turned the confusions of his culture to his advantage: by seeing the war between different Southern idioms not just as a class war but, integrally related to that, as a war of consciousness – occurring not only in obviously public arenas but also inside each Southerner's head.

At the time when Floyd Collins was lying in his cave waiting to be rescued, Faulkner was in New Orleans beginning to discover his vocation. He had gone there in order to sail for Europe: but, invited by Elizabeth Anderson (whom he had met in New York) to lodge in the apartment she shared with her husband Sherwood Anderson, he decided to stay there for a while. Sherwood Anderson was then a novelist with a considerable reputation; and it was he, in particular, who encouraged the young Faulkner to turn from poetry to prose and helped to get Faulkner's first novel published. Working on *Soldier's Pay*, and enjoying the cosmopolitan atmosphere of New Orleans, Faulkner also found time to write a series of prose sketches for *The Double Dealer* and, more notably, for the local newspaper the *Times-Picayune*. These *New Orleans Sketches*, as they eventually became known when they were published in volume form, were all written in 1925. In many ways, they prepare the ground for later fictions: in their subjects, occasional themes, and most notably of all in their experiments with language. Again and again, Faulkner tries out different vocabularies here, discovers or even becomes a character in a way that grew to be standard practice with him, by assuming his or her voice. This experimenting with voices is perhaps most obvious in the group of short sketches Faulkner wrote for *The Double Dealer*, entitled simply 'New Orleans'. Briefly, the young writer tries to re-create eleven different New Orleans characters, among them a 'Wealthy Jew', 'The Priest', 'The Sailor', 'The Longshoreman', 'The Cop', 'The Artist' and 'The Tourist', by making them speak for themselves. There is sometimes an air of contrivance about the speech attributed to these people. 'Evening like a nun shod with silence', begins 'The Priest',

> evening like a girl slipping along the wall to meet her lover . . . The twilight like the breath of contented kine, stirring among the lilacs and shaking spikes of bloom . . .[23]

The predictable sonorities of expression here find their analogy in some equally predictable patterns of conception: the Priest, as this passage indicates, is spellbound in a fairly standard Faulknerian way, by the linked visions of twilight, blossoms and an elusive girl. Similarly, the Sailor is an outcast and a wanderer ('Ah, lads, only fools go to sea . . .'), the Cop is torn between the dreams of his youth and the disillusionment of his maturity ('man does not ever get exactly what he wants in this world'), the Artist is inspired and consumed by 'a dream and a fire' that he 'cannot control' ... and so on. Beneath the clichés of language and thought, however, there is a sense of a writer not merely in love with words but trying to deploy those words to unearth personality. He makes his people speak in different tongues – sometimes sonorous, sometimes streetwise, and some-times both – not just to rehearse a familiar litany of preoccupations but so as to capture what it must be like to *be* them and think and feel like them: in short, as an act of imaginative empathy.

This strategy of excavating character via speech is illustrated in two quite different ways by two of the pieces Faulkner wrote for the *Times-Picayune*, 'Mirrors of Chartres Street' and 'The Cobbler'. In the first of these, Faulkner uses a technique borrowed from Mark Twain and the Southwestern humorists: a genteel narrator describes, with fascination, disgust, amusement and just a touch of bemused admiration, an example of local low life – in this case, a beggar seen wandering around the streets of the French Quarter and eventually arrested. The comic tension issues here from the encounter between two quite different idioms. 'His voice had the hoarseness of vocal chords long dried with alcohol', the narrator observes of the beggar; and when the beggar speaks, as he does at length, Faulkner clearly revels in the opportunity this gives him to create a char-acter that looks back to Twain's Pap Finn and forward to some of the Snopes family. This is a vivid, vocal portrait of an individual that swiftly blossoms into a satirical account of Southern white populism, and an old regional tradition of rabble-rousing:

> Arrest me! Where's laws and justice? Ain't I a member of greatest republic on earth? Ain't every laborer got his own home, and ain't this mine? Beat it, you damn Republican. Got a gov'ment job; thinks he can do whatever he wants ... Listen, man. I was born American citizen and I been a good citizen all my life. When America needs men, who's first to say 'America, take me?' I am, until railroad cut off my legs ... I been laboring man, and ain't every laboring man got his room, and ain't this mine? Now ... can damn Repub-lican come in laboring man's room and arrest him?[24]

Despite his attempts to tarnish his arresting officer as a Republican and to convince an inquisitive crowd of bystanders that the street is his 'room', the beggar *is* arrested. And as he is taken away the narrator's speech, not for the first time, assumes a comic magniloquence. 'One thought of Caesar mounting his chariot', he says of the beggar disappearing into the police-wagon, 'among cast roses and shouts of the rabble ... while ... centurions clashed their shields in the light of golden pennons flapping across the dawn.' The comparison with Caesar is no more absurd than an earlier one, with 'the young Jesus of Nazareth' ('his was an untrammelled spirit: his the same heaven-sent attribute for finding life good ...') or, for that matter, than the narrator's general capacity for turning hard facts into overdressed phrases. Clearly, the two voices of the sketch are being delivered with the same astringent wit: this is a portrait of the two extremes of white Southern culture that casts a cold eye on, and lends a coolly amused ear to, both. Unlike many of the Southwestern humorists in effect, the author of this piece keeps his allegiances to himself: preferring, simply, to record with dispassionate humour the discordances between 'high' and 'low'.

'The Cobbler' takes a different tack. A development of one of the twelve brief character-sketches for *The Double Dealer*, it offers us two idioms again: but this time the idioms belong to the same person. The piece opens with the cobbler's earthy speech rhythms as he goes about his business: 'You wan' getta thees shoe today? Si, si, Yes, I coma from – tella in my tongue? Buono signor.' Then as the voice continues, telling its tale of migration from Tuscany to Louisiana, it modulates gradually into a more lyrical idiom as the speaker remembers his youth and the girl with whom he fell in love, but lost:

> After the fiddles were silent and the sun had dropped beyond the dreaming purple hills and the bells chimed across the dusk like the last golden ray of the sun broken and fallen echoed among the rocks, we often walked. The belled flocks were stilled and candles guttered about the supper tables and we walked hand in hand while the stars came out so big, so near...[25]

As the voice ends its story, we are returned to a refrain that punctuates the narrative and to the original, earthy dialect: 'I am very old: I have forgotten much. You getta thees shoe today. Si, si.' The strategy is not a complicated or particularly sophisticated one, certainly. But it is a reminder of how even the young Faulkner could duplicate class conflicts of voice in vocalized conflicts of consciousness. And it is another anticipation of Faulkner's multivocal narrative technique – and, more precisely, of how he could register the multiple planes of an individual personality through the multiplicity of voices granted to that personality by the specifics of a history and a culture.

In July 1925, Faulkner finally set sail for Europe; and he spent the next six months travelling in Italy, Switzerland, France and (for a short while) England. Foreign travel did not halt his productivity, however, any more than had his movements immediately prior to this, between Oxford, New Orleans and the Mississippi coastal resort of Pascagoula. This was a period of immense promise, in fact: when his work not only began to bear fruit but also offered signs of ever more abundant harvests to come. 1926, of course, witnessed the publication of his first novel, *Soldier's Pay*. But, quite apart from that and the prose sketches for *The Double Dealer* and the *Times-Picayune*, the years 1925 and 1926 together saw an immense flurry of activity. It was towards the end of 1926, for example, that Faulkner worked for a time on an abortive project, a novel *Father Abraham*, that introduced the character of Flem Snopes, 'ruminant and unwinking and timeless', sitting behind 'the new plate glass window of his recently remodelled bank' in a town called Jefferson. Before the novel breaks off, after twenty-four manuscript pages, we have also met many of the inhabitants of a place known as Frenchman's Bend situated 'in the hill cradled cane and cypress jungles of Yocona river'. 'Of Scottish and Irish and English blood', these people, the narrator tells us,

> make whiskey out of corn and sell what they do not drink. County officers do not annoy them save at election time, and they support their own churches and schools, and sow the land and reap it and kill each other occasionally and commit adultery and fear God and hate republicans and niggers.[26]

They include 'Uncle' Billy Varner, 'beat supervisor, politician, farmer, usurer', and Eula Varner, the 'softly ample daughter' of Billy, a girl 'with eyes like cloudy hothouse grapes and a mouth always slightly open in a kind of moist unalarmed surprise'. The story of her marriage to Flem is duly told, as is the tale of the horses that, under the unacknowledged supervision of Flem, a stranger from Texas 'in a clay coloured Stetson hat' sells to the gullible people of Frenchman's Bend. Mrs Littlejohn, a voluble sewing machine agent at present named V.K. Suratt, the other members of the Snopes family who arrive in the wake of Flem, 'cunning and dull and clannish': they are all there. And so too is the sense of a community that seems to exist in language: that confirms and develops its collective identity through the subtle rituals of conversation.

Quite apart from *Father Abraham* and the New Orleans sketches, Faulkner was also trying his hand with short stories about this time. Two written around the turn of the years 1925 and 1926 are especially full of promise: 'Mistral' and 'The Big Shot'. 'Mistral' is the first of the so-called 'Don and I' stories in which two young Americans, Don and an unnamed narrator, construct stories as an act of collaboration, unravelling the mysteries of the past by devising hypotheses, making guesses and telling tales to each other. A later 'Don and I' story, 'Evangeline', was to be one of the germs of *Absalom, Absalom!*; and already, in this very early piece, the basic narrative device of that novel is in place. 'The Big Shot' also uses the framing device of 'Don and I'. However, it is more notable for introducing us to a gangster called Popeye, 'a slight man with a dead face and dead black hair and eyes and a delicate hooked little nose and no chin':[27] someone who is clearly the prototype for the character of the same name in *Sanctuary*. In addition, the story tells us about Popeye's protector, Dal Martin. The son of a Mississippi tenant farmer, the determining experience of Martin's life was apparently the time when he was told by his father's landlord – to whom he was delivering a message – not to come to the front door but to use the back. Since then, his main aim in life has been to acquire the same wealth and power, and therefore the same capacity to humiliate, as the man and class that humiliated him. If Martin supplies a blueprint for Thomas Sutpen in *Absalom, Absalom!*, then Martin's daughter in 'The Big Shot' offers a preliminary sketch for Temple Drake in *Sanctuary* – she is, we are informed, a 'thin creature, a little overdressed', a spoilt woman-child with a face like a 'little painted mask' – while yet another character in the same story, a Dr Blount, prepares the ground for Gail Hightower in *Light in August* – like Hightower, Blount is haunted by his grandfather, a Confederate cavalryman killed during the Civil War, and so obsessed with 'the old blood, the old sense of honour' of the past that he cannot really cope with the present. Everywhere in the sketches, stories and other pieces of this time, Faulkner seems, however unknowingly, to be laying down markers for the future. The poet Rilke once remarked that all writers are assaulted in childhood by the images that they will then spend the remainder of their lives trying to digest. If that is so, then these years could perhaps be called a kind of second childhood for Faulkner: a time when he was confronting himself, again and again, with the images, the enigmatic figures and characters, that it would take him the rest of his career even to start to explain.

Other work of this period tends to confirm the suspicion that the young Faulkner was trying things out, somehow defining the figurative parameters of his art. Especially notable here, perhaps, is the novel he began in 1925 and then worked on intermittently during his trip to Europe, writing more than 30,000 words before abandoning it. Many years later Faulkner was asked why he never finished this book, initially entitled 'Growing Pains' and then *Elmer*. His reply was that it was 'funny, but not funny enough'. This seems, at best, a half-truth: a more plausible explanation might be both technical and personal. *Elmer* begins as a portrait of the artist, Elmer Hodge, as a young man. As the story opens, Elmer, a painter, is travelling to Europe. Then, in a long flashback, we learn about his insecure childhood, born into a poor migrant family, and the one redeeming feature of that childhood, his intimate relationship with his sister Jo-Addie, 'with whom he slept, with whom he didn't mind being naked'.[28] Lying in bed with her in the dark, Elmer longs to touch her unseen body. Occasionally and grudgingly Jo-Addie lets him; yet, even when he touches her, we are told, she seems to be 'somewhere else', as elusive and untameable as the trees amd wild mares with which she is constantly associated. When together, their sexual roles seem to be reversed: she is 'Jo' and he is addressed as 'Ellie'. But all intimacy of any kind comes to an end when Jo-Addie leaves home at the age of sixteen. Elmer, now eleven, crawls into the womb-like space beneath the family house for comfort. Then comfort of a different kind arrives when Jo-Addie posts him a gift of crayons, initiating Elmer's life as an artist. Art, in effect, becomes a substitute for his lost sister, and for his mother who dies suddenly not long after Jo-Addie disappears. Jo-Addie is only, possibly, glimpsed once more after this: when, years later, Elmer catches sight of an apparently familiar 'slight taut figure fiercely straight as ever . . . proud . . . and beautiful as a tree' across a crowded street in New Orleans.

After a brief return to Elmer sailing on a freighter to Europe, the narrative dips back into the past again: this time telling disconnected tales of an older boy and young man. We learn about Elmer's youthful admiration for 'a college man' named Joe who seemed to possess the sexual confidence

Elmer lacked. We hear about Elmer being wounded during the war, fathering a 'bastard son' in Texas, and about his falling in love with one Myrtle Monson – a woman who scornfully rejects his offer of marriage and promptly sets off with her snobbish mother on a trip to Europe. Further back in time during his schooldays, we are told, Elmer worshipped 'an older boy, tall and beautiful as a young man' who, like most of the people Elmer loves, rejects and abandons him. At school, Elmer also learns about sex. 'Things . . . now had a terrible soiled significance for him', the narrator observes: 'that night he undressed in the dark' and, listening to the cries of the wild geese 'lonely and high over thin maples', he swore 'he was through with women. He'd just be Elmer and paint pictures.' As if to emphasize the onanistic nature of art for Elmer, the next few episodes of this unfinished novel are replete with phallic imagery. 'When he was little Elmer had a passion for cigar stubs', we are told, and 'he would stand in a dull trance staring at a factory smokestack'. Imagery like this gathers in particular about Elmer's response to the tools of his trade. Right at the beginning of the narrative, for instance, comes this densely suggestive passage:

> Then he would rise, and in his cabin draw forth his new unstained box of paints. To finger lasciviously smooth dull silver tubes virgin yet at the same time pregnant, comfortably heavy to the palm – such an immaculate mating of bulk and weight . . . Elmer hovered over them with a brooding maternity, taking up one at a time those fat portentous tubes in which was yet wombed his heart's desire . . . thick-bodied and female and at the same time phallic: hermaphroditic. He closed his eyes the better to savour its feel . . .[29]

Elmer is seen here as mother ('brooding maternity') and father ('phallic') to his art, the androgynous source of a 'portentous' substitute for a living organism. And he is also seen as a callow virgin brooding in masturbatory fantasy over an immaculate vision that enables him to close his eyes to the world. The uncertainty of tone here is radical. The author is, by turns, embarrassingly confessional and wilfully satirical because he does not really know what to make of his protagonist. Part of Faulkner wants to make condescending fun of him: but another part, recognizing that many of Elmer's feelings and experiences replicate his (the lost girl, art and abandonment, the problematical sexuality of the artist), feels more inclined to identify with him.

This uncertainty continues in the later pages of the story. It attaches itself at several moments, for instance, to the portraits of women. The mother of Elmer's child, called Ethel, is one narrative victim: presented in a callow, dismissive way whenever she is there on the scene but recalled, whenever she is gone, with dreamy romanticism. So too is Myrtle Monson. Her most notable characteristic when she first appears is her brute vanity – she seems, in effect, to be a shallow tease: 'Myrtle', we are informed, 'believed you could control' men 'better if you didn't kiss them so often'. Yet when she sails away to Europe and away from Elmer she leaves behind

her the image of 'a Dianalike girl ... arrogant and virginal and proud'.[30]
This curiously Romantic ambivalence is not, it should be emphasized,
simply a characteristic of the protagonist, it is a feature of the text: Elmer
may be imprisoned in a sort of sub-Keatsian attitude towards women (which,
simply and crudely put, suggests that women are better dreamed about
than possessed) but so, too, is the narrator and the narrative. Later,
Faulkner was to investigate the causes and consequences of the disease
(although he was never, as a white, Southern male ever quite free of it):
in this narrative, however, he can do little more than rehearse its symptoms with enthusiasm sometimes and sometimes embarrassment.

As the narrative continues, other uncertainties eat away at the confidence
of the narrative voice. In the later portions of the story, for instance, concerned with Elmer's experiences on arrival in Europe, Faulkner tries
his hand at satire. The satirical darts are aimed broadly at pretentious
Europeans, Americans abroad, and the artist as romantic egotist. They are
for the most part, however, woefully blunt (there are, in particular, some
dreadful attempts at comic English accents) and the satire is constantly
disrupted by passages of lyricism. So, a penniless English 'milord', burdened
with the unsubtle comic eponym Lord Wysbroke, steps from the train and
the prose suddenly stands on stilts:

> Dusk preceeded [*sic*] the train and dusk followed it ... Fog and smoke and
> dust evenly and grayly blended ... Perhaps his lordship remembered other
> dusks ... when he was young and passionate with belief in a waiting magnifi-
> cent future lying somewhere in the fog, this mist troubled with colored
> lights and a hushed imminence of traffic: people and movement like a
> music.[31]

Moments after this, we are returned to sub-Jamesian comedy: impover-
ished English aristocrats like Lord Wysbroke pursuing American money,
crass Americans seeking to buy up European style. While in the middle of
Elmer in the summer of 1925, Faulkner had written to his mother that this
new book would be 'a grand one ... new altogether'. The trouble is that
it is, if anything, too 'grand': which is to say, too many things at once. As
he ploughs on, Faulkner seems to be writing not one novel but four or
five: a *Bildungsroman*, a novel of ideas, a satirical novel, an international
novel, and a story of war and postwar disillusionment. By turns lyrical and
satirical, romantic and comic, the story sits uneasily between genres never
quite managing either to be one or other of them or, alternatively, to
bring them into a fruitful tension.

The technical problems are, of course, closely connected to the personal ones here: Faulkner is not so much using autobiography in *Elmer* as
allowing himself to be swamped by it. There are, clearly, a plethora of
factual connections between Faulkner's life and the life of Elmer Hodge:
the sojourn in New Orleans, the trip to Europe, romantic loss (Faulkner
felt himself rejected at this time, not only by Estelle Oldham, but also by
Helen Baird, a woman he had met in Pascagoula), and so on. Far more

important than these factual links, however, is the pattern that shapes the narrative and that responds to some of the deepest rhythms of the author's experience: a pattern of attachment and abandonment leading to art. Substitution is rehearsed here with a profound ambivalence. On the one hand, sex is 'dirty'; confident sexual beings are other, variously called 'Jo' and 'Joe'; woman, even when she is present, seems to be 'somewhere else' or, less fortunately, has 'that unmistakable scent of female flesh no longer fresh' about her. So perhaps art is a substitution devoutly to be wished: Elmer should continue to brood over his 'portentous tubes' of paint. On the other hand, there is the central agony, the longing for a 'Dianalike girl' who is sister, mother and lover. So perhaps the substitutive object is no more than a shape to fill a lack: Elmer may continue to brood, but his activity is really no more than self-abuse masquerading as self-protection. If the contradictions that scar this narrative articulate any satisfactory compensatory fantasy, it is of the woman just out of reach: Jo-Addie reluctantly allowing herself to be touched in the dark for a moment, a figure hauntingly like Jo-Addie seen for a few seconds across a crowded street. But this too is a familiar late Romantic dream: art as constantly deferred satisfaction, the artist always on the brink of orgasmic fulfilment, desire indefinitely prolonged. Which is not to devalue the centrality of that dream for Faulkner: he dreamed it with a ferocious passion and it helped mould his finest work – in particular, his attitudes to his own creativity and to women. All that can be said is that, at this stage in his career, Faulkner could neither find any way out of his impasse nor imaginatively investigate it: the dream, and the contradictions that generated it, controlled him with his hardly being aware of it. Quite simply, *Elmer* was too close to the autobiographical bone. Faulkner must have sensed this, and wisely decided to abandon his manuscript. He would return to many of the problems that plague his portrait of the artist: but later, when he could see those problems as something to be interrogated, not assumed – as symptoms, that is, rather than evidence.

Many of the obsessions that at once animate and subvert *Elmer* are to be found in the two works that Faulkner presented as gifts to Helen Baird, in January and June of 1926 respectively, the tale *Mayday* and *Helen: A Courtship*. One commentator has described *Mayday* as 'an allegory of the author's disappointed love'. In it, the hero, a young knight called Sir Galwyn, looks in the stream of time, asking 'what does this signify?' and sees 'a face all young and white, and with long shining hair like a column of fair sunny water'. He than sets out on a quest, with the allegorical figures of Hunger and Pain, in search of this vision. On the way, he encounters three princesses, all of whom fail his ideal, partly because of their eagerness to seduce him and partly because Sir Galwyn senses that 'it is not the thing itself man wants, so much as the wanting of it'. Returning to the original scene, marked by 'a dark hurrying stream' and 'a tree covered with leaves of a thousand different colours', Sir Galwyn feels that 'he need never have left'. There, he chooses to immerse himself in the stream where his 'memory will be as a smooth surface after rain' and he 'will remember nothing at all'. And, as he sinks into the water, he is granted another vision of the woman 'all young and white', while being instructed by St Francis, who appears at this moment, that this vision only exists as 'Little sister Death'.[32] There are echoes here of one of the New Orleans sketches, 'The Kid Learns', in which the protagonist, as he dies, is taken by the hand by a 'shining' female figure who announces herself as 'Little sister Death'. More to the point, though, is Faulkner's recovery here of the notion of an obscure object of desire that has linked connotations of Eros and Thanatos. Since what we see is what we create, the suggestion is, then the self can never be united with the not-self: the pursuit must be circular and end in annihilation. Desire as anxiety and absence must be the constant accompaniment of life because the hungering human creature, whether he is called Sir Galwyn or Quentin Compson, can only find fulfilment by stepping into the mirror: there to realize a fate like that of Poe's Roderick Usher with *his* sister Madeline, in a consummation that is also oblivion. Clearly, Faulkner's recent disappointment in love may have pushed him towards a rehearsal of this theme; the choice of recipient of the gift copy, in particular, shows a nicely acid touch. But, equally clearly, there is more to it than that. Incest, desire, death, ends that circle back to beginnings, reflective surfaces that offer a vision that is simultaneously subjective and objective: this is a constellation of images that antedates the romantic involvements of Faulkner's youth and that was to stay with him, too, long after he had forgotten specific moments of rejection.

Helen: A Courtship is a sequence of sixteen poems developing several of the themes of *Mayday* and earlier works. The introductory piece, 'To Helen, Swimming', offers the reader the vision of a woman with 'boy's breast and the plain flanks of a boy': the familiar, angular and epicene, figure that complements and contrasts with the ample curves of a Eula Varner. Then, in the sonnets that follow, some new and some of them written long before this sequence was ever thought of, Faulkner rehearses such topics as the impotence of words in the face of life ('Words can break no bonds, while life is green'), the games that fauns and dryads play amidst 'the moist flanks of spring', the poet/satyr as voyeur observing a burgeoning sensuality in which he cannot participate, the nagging, persistent nature of sexual desire and the fragility of dreams ('the dream once touched must fade'). The dominant tone is a sort of glassy-eyed formality, as in these lines from an autobiographical sonnet called 'Bill':

> Son of earth was he, and first and last
> His heart's whole dream was his, had he been wise,
> With space and light to feed it through his eyes
> But with the gift of tongues he was accursed.[33]

In fact, such power as these poems possess comes precisely from the tension between, on the one hand, their formal structures and stiff diction and, on the other, the raging ferment of sexual desire to which they try to give voice. The result is frequently strained: an opaque or tortuous style that, as one critic has commented, issues not so much from any innate difficulties of conception as from the difficulty the poet seems to be having matching impulses to forms.

Nevertheless, through the opacity of much of the phrasing, an image of a woman can be glimpsed that is characteristically double-edged. In 'Bill', for instance, she is all silence and peace, a mothering or perhaps sisterly figure in whose bosom the poet can find repose and rest:

> Then he found that silence held a Name,
> That starlight held a face for him to see
> ... and She
> Like silver ceaseless wings that breathe and stir
> More grave and true than music, or a flame
> Of starlight, and he's quiet, being with her.[34]

Immediately afterwards, however, in the next poem, we are offered a quite different figure, woman as temptation, all breathing human passion and trouble:

> Beneath the apple tree Eve's tortured shape
> Glittered in the snake's, her riven breast
> Sloped his coils and took the sun's escape
> To augur black her sin from east to west.[35]

Woman in effect inhabits two domains in these poems: the world outside history, where she offers the possibility of quiet, and the world inside history, where the power of sexuality she embodies seems to antedate and imply all cultural forms, 'Nazarene and Roman and Virginian'. The last line in the eighth sonnet in the sequence, 'Virginity', offers a telling gloss on all this: 'But sown cold years the stolen bread you reap / By all the Eves unsistered since the Snake'. In the Southern family romance, all women may be sisters, but that depends upon the presumption of (or, as Quentin Compson might have put it, the need for) their virginity. Sisterhood is lost with sexuality; romance fades into the sound and fury of time and change (that is, if the timeless state is not preserved as it is in *Mayday* by an incestuous consummation that is also death); the timeless peace of myth is supplanted by the untimely turmoil of history. The sense of betrayal felt by the white male, as he sees his 'sister' transformed into a sexual being and consequently 'unsistered': this was part of a peculiarly regional structure of feeling that, in his work, Faulkner both inherited and exploited. 'Do you know what the trouble is with me?', Faulkner asked once when talking about sexuality, 'I'm a puritan.' Puritan he might have been, but he was a puritan of a peculiarly Southern kind: in his best writing too – which, unfortunately, does not include *Helen: A Courtship* – he was also an unusually knowing one.

II   OF LOSS AND LONGING: *SOLDIER'S PAY* AND *MOSQUITOES*

Even before he had returned from his trip to Europe, or presented *Helen: A Courtship* to Helen Baird, Faulkner learned that his first novel, written in New Orleans, had been accepted for publication. Entitled *Mayday* for a while, it was renamed *Soldier's Pay* and as such published in February 1926. Faulkner's procedure for composing the book had been the same as it would be for much of his subsequent longer fiction. He had begun with two separate stories: one about a satyr-like young man called Januarius Jones in conversation with an Episcopalian minister whose son had been killed in the First World War, the other concerning a group of drunken American soldiers disrupting a train on their way home south. The character who offered a link between these two stories, the minister's dead aviator son David (David, incidentally but significantly, was a name the novelist used for many of his most autobiographical characters), was soon dropped as Faulkner struggled to weld these and other stories and ideas into a novel. David was, however, replaced by a more haunting figure: Donald Mahon, a pilot so severely wounded in the war that, as one character says, he is 'practically a dead man already' – and yet sufficiently alive to act as dramatic catalyst and a vividly absent/present narrative centre. Writing in longhand, adding and cutting, and then typing for further revisions, Faulkner gradually wove together what was in one sense his own novel of postwar disillusionment, as the sardonic title he finally chose implies. His reading helped him in filling out some of the details of the story: unsurprisingly, there are echoes here of Housman, Eliot and the French Symbolists as well as novelists like James Branch Cabell – whose most famous novel, *Jurgen*, is alluded to during the course of the story. Personal experience played its part, too, in helping him to conceive of and come to terms with his characters. Reverend Mahon, for instance, big and bulky and awkward, resembles Murry Falkner in his physique and his ineffectuality; while Cecily Saunders, Mahon's fiancée, Estelle Oldham later felt, was a portrait of her penned in the bitterness of rejection – 'it hurt my feelings terribly',[36] she once told an interviewer.

Above all, as far as this autobiographical dimension is concerned, there is the wounded war hero, Donald Mahon, and Cadet Julian Lowe who can only dream of heroism. Mahon was given many of Faulkner's own physical characteristics. He has small hands, a 'thin face', a 'delicate pointed chin and wild soft eyes'; he also wears a British officer's uniform, just as his creator did, and carries a copy of *A Shropshire Lad* with him. Lowe, in turn, is endowed with Faulkner's aggrieved sense that, to quote from the opening page of the novel, 'they had stopped the war on him', so denying him the opportunity to prove himself as a male. 'To have been him!', Lowe muses to himself when he first sees Mahon, 'Let him take this sound body of mine! ... To have got wings on my breast ... and to have got his scar, too, I would take death tomorrow.'[37] Not for the only time in *Soldier's Pay*, the author seems to be using a character as a mouthpiece here: in this case to express his envy of those who had received their wings, emblems of male prowess and conquest. There is a sexual dimension to this, of course: the mythical and psychological links between the dream of flight and sexual activity have been well documented, and such links would have been forged with particular strength during the 1920s when the figure of the lonely aviator (battling in Europe, perhaps, or like Lindbergh crossing the Atlantic) seemed to dominate the popular imagination. So it is worth noting that this particular hero of flight is rescued from the possibility of sex by his living death: an object of envy or desire for so many (even Lowe thinks that 'if he were a woman' he would love Mahon), he is without desire himself. 'He doesn't seem to care where he is or what he does', one doctor declares of Mahon: his 'detachment' makes him seem like a 'foreigner' in his own land. In short, in this strange, spectral figure Faulkner appeared able to unite two apparently irreconcilable longings: the dream of male power, the fulfilment of desire, and the pursuit of privacy, distance and silence.

The general critical response to *Soldier's Pay* was favourable: a reviewer in the *New York Times*, for example, praised it for showing 'hard intelligence as well as consummate pity'. The local reaction, however, was quite different. Murry Falkner refused to read the book, the University of Mississippi in Oxford rejected Phil Stone's offer of a free copy for the library, while one older female relative wrote to inform Faulkner that leaving the country was just about the best thing he could do. One possible reason for the hostile reaction of people in the writer's home state to his first major publication was probably to do with his treatment of sex: like other writers of the era, Faulkner took advantage of more relaxed attitudes after the war to talk openly about sexual desire and disease. There are still nymphs and fauns here, the familiars of Faulkner's earlier writing. Januarius Jones, for instance, is repeatedly caught in the posture of the poet-satyr: with his eyes 'obscene and old in sin as a goat's' busily observing 'fauns and nymphs', the gilded youth of his locality, at play. But, for every moment given over to 'a chaste . . . nympholepsy', there are many others devoted to flappers and seductions, to young girls 'in pale satin knickers . . . with . . . slim legs elevated' or enjoying the 'physical freedom' of a 'young, uncorseted body . . . pleasuring in freedom and motion, as though freedom and motion were water, pleasuring . . . flesh to the intermittent teasing of silk'. There are many other moments still that itemize male sexual hunger (and, as the passages just quoted indicate, the sexual hunger in this book is usually male), that allow talk of unwanted pregnancies or syphilis, or that refer us to 'the rhythmic troubling obscenities of saxophones' accompanying and encouraging this masquerade. There are visions here, certainly, of a girl 'with . . . the passionate serene alertness of a faun' and of a woman 'that Beardsley might have sickened for': but there are also more openly erotic dreams, say of a 'narrow body sweetly dividing naked'. More to the point, perhaps, there are, too, several occasions like the one when a female character responds to a proposal of marriage from the man who loves her by suggesting that they should simply take off together for a while. That way, she explains, 'when we get fed up all we need do is wish each other luck and go our ways'.[38]

Another possible reason for the mainly negative response of local people to *Soldier's Pay* was the author's determined attempts to appear 'modern'. The dominant narrative tone is often obtrusively cynical and knowing, as if the author is deliberately setting out to shock his more conservative readers ('Sex and death: the front door and the back door. How indissolubly they are united in us!'). Conservatism of a different kind, formal rather than social, would also have found much to offend it in Faulkner's constant fluctuations of narrative style. The novel moves from conversation to dramatized thought-processes to baroque commentary with a flamboyant ease and bravura that recalls the early writings of F. Scott Fitzgerald or John Dos Passos. Public occasions in particular – a dance, say, or a funeral or the local, communal reaction to the arrival home of Donald Mahon – are presented in jazzy, disjunctive idioms that would certainly have unnerved any reader expecting another *White Rose of Memphis*. It is not, really, that there are many voices in *Soldier's Pay*. Most of the voices in the novel tend to melt into one: something most clearly indicated, perhaps, by the way ideas or associations sounded by the narrator are often then taken up and discussed in the dialogue. A female character, for instance, is described in the narrative commentary as coming 'suddenly from out her Cinderella dream'; then, moments later, she is addressed by Januarius Jones, 'Well, Cinderella' – to which she responds icily, to the narrator it seems as well as to Jones, 'My name is Emmy.' As this peculiar habit of narrative transforming itself into conversation, or vice versa, indicates, there may seem to be a plethora of speech idioms here, but they tend for the most part to be mastered by just one idiom: which belongs to the brooding, monolithic voice of the narrator. That voice, in turn, is one familiar to us from other sources: that is, from the earlier work, in verse as well as prose, of the young pre-novelist. Sometimes the voice may startle the reader with its daring: 'There was something frozen in her chest, like a dish-cloth in winter.' On other occasions, it may surprise with its frenetic impressionism:

> 'Clo-hoverrrrr blarrrr – sums, clooverblarrr-summmzzz,' sang a nasal voice
> terribly, the melody ticked off at spaced intervals by a small monotonous
> sound, like a clock-bomb, going off like this: Clo(tick)ver(tick)rrr(tick)bl(tick)
> rrs(tick)sss(tick)umm(tick)zzz.[39]

Alternatively, it may simply irritate with its flamboyant 'poeticisms': 'The intermittent shadows of young leaves were bird cries made visible and sparrows in ivy were flecks of sunlight made vocal.' Whatever its manifestations, though, that voice is constantly there monopolizing the narrative and swamping the reader's attention; and in its studied avoidance of the conventional and respectable – in other words, of anything that middle-class Oxford would have expected or wanted – it was bound to cause aggravation and even offence.

Less offensive to local people, perhaps, but still disturbing was the way the young Faulkner played in his first novel with some of the Southern pieties. Certainly few of the more conservative of his white, male readers would have been likely to object to the narrator's easy generalizations about black people and women. One black character, for instance, is said not to exhibit the emotion of surprise 'as is the custom of his race', while a female character, we are told, 'was going to make the best of' the serious difficulties in which she found herself 'as women will'.[40] Such remarks are typical. For the most part, black and female characters function as *objects* in the narrative: perceived, with admiration, envy or even resentment, by the gaze of the white, male subject. The internalized life, in all its turmoil, is the subject's; the black or female object, by contrast, is rarely permitted more than a surface, a smooth membrane of exteriority that is never penetrated. And the narrator then proceeds to turn this exteriority into a dimension of character, evidence of stoicism and imperturbability, or just carelessness and superficiality (women and blacks, we are advised repeatedly, have a 'vast tolerance' and are free 'of all impulsions of time or . . . learning'), rather than see it for what it is, a measure of his own limitations: a symptom of his unwillingness or inability to escape from the confines of his own voice. The *detailed* positioning of black and women characters is, admittedly, different. Black people hover on the choric edges of the action, as they do in so much Southern writing: until the final chapter when – in an anticipation of *The Sound and the Fury* – the 'pure quivering chord' of their song 'wordless and far away' supplies the narrative with a notably sonorous conclusion. Women, on the other hand, are more observed than (notionally) observing: victims of a voyeuristic stare – narrator's as well as white, male characters' – that finds its most extreme, parodic expression in the figure of Januarius Jones. In either case, however, it is the basic strategy of positioning that matters: since the effect is to measure out the boundaries of the text. Black characters and women characters, in their various ways, are on the margins, like border-guards patrolling the territory of the known: as such, they can seem reasssuring and protective or dangerous and unnerving. Either way, as protectors of the familiar or routes of access to the unfamiliar, they are irredeemably other: the narative can go so far, up to the appearances of them, and no further.

Which is to say, really, that Faulkner is writing from within the prevailing (white, male, Southern) ideologies here. When it comes to his investigation of place and past, however, the situation is a little more problematical and interesting. Like their creator, Donald Mahon and the other veterans return to a home that, they find when they get there, they never really had. In the simplest possible sense, they are homeless, placeless. And the portrait Faulkner offers the reader of Charlestown, the setting for most of *Soldier's Pay*, serves as an ironic counterpoint, a reminder of the cosy securities and sense of belonging that are not really available to them:

> Charlestown, like numberless other towns throughout the South, had been built around a circle of tethered horses and mules. In the middle of the square was the courthouse – a simple utilitarian edifice of brick and sixteen beautiful Ionic columns stained with generations of casual tobacco. Elms surrounded the courthouse and beneath these trees, on scarred and carved wood benches and chairs the city fathers, progenitors of solid laws and solid citizens who believed in Tom Watson and feared only God and drouth, in . . . the faded brushed grey and bronze meaningless medals of the Confederate States of America . . . slept or whittled away the long drowsy days while their juniors of all ages . . . played checkers or chewed tobacco and talked.[41]

The anticipations of Jefferson here are perhaps too obvious to be remarked on: one almost expects to see Benjy Compson appear in a carriage rattling from left to right. What is certainly worthy of remark, though, is the way that Faulkner, while drawing on a tradition of portraits of sleepy Southern towns that goes back at least as far as the writings of Mark Twain, manages to give it an additional dimension, an extra edge. This he does simply by setting his portrait within a context of loss: a narrative framework that is defined chiefly by characters who do not belong to their surroundings, who are at best only loosely attached to the imagined places in which they are set. 'You can go home', says Joe Gilligan; 'I've got to go home', declares Donald Mahon. Once 'home', however, they find themselves even more 'puzzled and lost' than before, 'the hang-over of warfare in a society tired of warfare'. In this respect, they stand at the beginning of a long and distinguished line. One thinks, for example, of Bayard Sartoris III in *Flags in the Dust*, watching 'the noon throng' and noting a painful contrast between their easy 'murmuring and laughing' and his own nervous agitation and restlessness. Or one thinks, perhaps, of Horace Benbow in *Sanctuary*, whose agony and sense of displacement are quietly mocked by the people he sees around him on the courthouse square: 'slow as sheep', possessed of the 'mild inscrutability of cattle', revealing the same patience, impassiveness and even mystery as the 'imponderable land' they inhabit. It was not just that, through the use of the context of loss, Faulkner found a way of expressing those feelings of crisis and exile he shared with many other Southern writers of the time, and that had helped lead him so often in pursuit of privacy. It was also that, in this fashion, he managed to inject a special – and, to many of his Southern readers, probably discomfiting – tension into his work; since in their relationship to place protagonists like Mahon or Gilligan – or, for that matter, Bayard Sartoris III or Benbow – frequently act as masks, a means of fictionalizing their creator's peculiar status in Oxford, his role of double agent.

There is a similarly uneasy relationship between characters such as Mahon and Gilligan and the burden of the past. 'In wartime', the narrator observes, 'one lives in today. Yesterday is gone and tomorrow may never come': but, in fact, it is much more equivocal than that. With several of the characters, veterans of the war and others, the Faulknerian strategy of using the past to explain the present is anticipated here: one voice tells the tale of yesterday, in collaboration with a second, sympathetic voice – questioning, goading, or even offering its own hypotheses – and, via this process, today is, if not understood, at least placed in a clearer, brighter light. With Donald Mahon it goes even further than that. He is certainly living in today throughout most of the novel, since he is cut off from the past by the loss of memory. A dangling man, he appears to be waiting for something, as another character observes: 'Something he has begun, but not completed, something he has carried from his former life that he does not remember consciously.'[42] The nature of that 'something' eventually becomes apparent: towards the end of *Soldier's Pay* he remembers the day on which he was wounded, when he was reduced to a living corpse and, having done so, he then dies. His past has been reimagined, the clear implication is; and because it has he can have a present; the story has been recovered, retold, and can now be given the sense of an ending.

Ironically, given his state of uneasy suspension between present and past, Mahon is described as 'motionless . . . as Time': which is perhaps intended as a way of suggesting, not his immersion in temporality, but his separation from it – like the allegorical figure of Old Father Time, for most of the novel he sits apart from all the sound and fury of the other characters, in stillness and virtual silence. As a singularly absent centre, he soon becomes the site of fantasies, personal or collective, the focus of other people's projections. For Cadet Julian Lowe, for instance, as we have seen, he represents the challenge of war, the linked heroics of adventure and sex. For Margaret Powers, on the other hand, who fears that she cannot feel ('Can nothing at all move me again? . . . Nothing to stir me, to move me . . . ?'),[43] he represents precisely the challenge of feeling: it is in this spirit that she decides to marry him. For Cecily Saunders, he represents a challenge to personal sacrifice that she cannot accept; for Joe Gilligan, a challenge to responsibility and care that he believes he can; for the Reverend Mahon, Donald's father, he represents the challenge of death, a challenge which, for most of the novel, the minister cannot even begin to cope with – he tries to pretend that his son is as sound in body and mind as ever and, when that seems impossible, he talks and behaves as if Mahon is not there. These are not, it should be repeated, qualities that other people find in Mahon but ones they simply superimpose on him. In his quietness, the young lieutenant becomes a means by which those who meet him can talk to themselves; in his blankness, he is a white space on which they can inscribe their obsessions. 'Division and death', we are told, is the *donné*, the situation all these characters inhabit, 'longing and despair' their habitual response. And in their longing – their need, as the narrator puts it, for 'oneness with something, somewhere' – they turn to the figure of the wounded soldier for understanding and perhaps relief: he becomes, some of the time, the mirror in which they see reflected their own needs and dreams.

Some of the time, but by no means all of it: a feeling of absence haunts all the characters, a longing for 'something you want and can't get' (as one of them puts it), and that feeling seeps into areas of the narrative that have little or nothing to do with Mahon. Voices of desire, plaintive or eager, punctuate the novel. 'Cecily, Cecily', implores one voice, '. . . Is this death?'; 'Dewey, my boy', mourns another, '. . . so brave, so young'; 'Ah, come to me Donald', begs a third and then adds, 'But he is dead.'[44] In addition to this, a sense of abandonment and need actually feeds into two recurrent dramatic situations, those of the voyeur and the eavesdropper. The voyeur greedily observing bodies he cannot have or events in which he cannot participate, the eavesdropper listening to 'hushed talk and sweet broken laughter', 'hushed night sounds' and 'muffled footfalls' the source of which he cannot comprehend: positionings of character like these are brimming over with undisclosed anxiety, the regret and pain that issue from the irrepressible suspicion that the real thing, life, is elsewhere. Other voices, other rooms, bodies momentarily glimpsed but not touched – and letters sent but never answered or even perhaps received. The novel is full of messages that seem not to reach their destination or that fall on deaf ears: communications that do not communicate, from Julian Lowe to Margaret Powers, then from Powers to Lowe, from Margaret Powers to her husband 'dear dead Dick' and from her husband to her, and from Emmy during wartime to Donald Mahon. There could hardly be a more powerful image of unfulfilment than the dead letter: it reeks of frustrated purpose and truncated desire. It also suggests the impotence of the word: the writer tries to inscribe his or her story, to reach out and explain, but the audience is not listening or is incapable of understanding or, it may be, is just not there. We are back here with a deep-rooted pattern: in which language both hides and exposes the primal gap or fracture, the loss of plenitude or absent figure of the mother. And in this novel that pattern gathers as it so often does in Faulkner's writing: about an 'empty centre', certainly, in the form of the living corpse of Mahon, but also about the teasing, multiple figure of woman.

Something of the elusive, metamorphic nature of female character in *Soldier's Pay* has been suggested already. The linked images of the epicene Cecily Saunders and the earthy Margaret Powers, alike in their irrevocable otherness and unreachability; the familiar comparisons of these and other women to trees, water, the fluid rhythms and fluent movement of the earth; the conviction, subtly communicated, that women are pure, reflective surfaces giving back to 'us' (that is, white, male author, narrator, character and reader) no more than a mirror image of 'our' needs and dreams; even the positioning of the woman at the borders of the text where she can assume the traditional ambivalence of borderlines: all this and more finds its originating impulse in the primal, traumatic experience of fracture – or, to use Faulkner's own phrase in this book, 'division and death'. With 'her body created for all men to dream', the woman of this novel – and it is, finally, one woman, one focus of desire – is as she is when George Farr sees her in the shape of Cecily Saunders:

> Her white dress in the sun was an unbearable shimmer sloping to the body's motion and she passed from sunlight to shadow, mounting the steps. At the door she turned, flashed him a smile, and waved her hand. Then her white dress faded beyond a fanlight of muted colour . . . , leaving George to stare at the empty maw of the house in hope and despair and baffled youthful lust.[45]

The one thing George learns during the course of the novel is that it is *not* lust that drives him: even after he has, as he sees it, 'possessed' Cecily the same bewilderment and longing gnaw away at him. As in the early story, 'Nympholepsy', there is a sexual element at work here but it is overshadowed by a more fundamental desire, issuing out of the aboriginal experience of separation: a desire that, by its very nature, can never be satisfied. 'I don't want your body', Januarius Jones testily insists to one of the several women he pursues. 'If it was just your body I wanted', Joe Gilligan confides with puzzled candour to Margaret Powers, 'But I want – I want –'. 'What do you want, Joe?', Powers asks: a question to which Gilligan can give no answer. Like the other men in the book, he cannot say what he wants: he can only see that want reflected, or projected, in a woman. In this, he is like his creator: for whom the female characters of *Soldier's Pay* are, eventually, no more and no less than vessels of male desire and the text that incorporates them is, in turn, no more than a sublimation of similar feelings – a revelation of, and possible compensation for, loss. The novel ends with an elaborate series of gestures of abandonment and its aftermath: Joe 'stretching his arms out' to the train carrying Margaret away from him, Joe telling himself 'I'll go to Atlanta tomorrow and find her, catch her', Joe coming across a parodic doubling of his own predicament in the grotesque, sweaty figure of Januarius Jones – whom he catches trying to scramble up to the window of the latest object of his affections. The series concludes with Joe and the Reverend Mahon discovering release and consolation of a kind in overheard song: the hymns of black people from a ' shabby church', 'beautiful with mellow longing, passionate and sad'. Outside the church, there is an 'occasional group of Negroes', Joe notes, 'bearing lighted lanterns that jetted vain little flames futilely into the moonlight'. 'No one knows why they do that',[46] the minister replies when Joe asks for an explanation of this curious ritual. In a way that could stand as an epigraph to Faulkner's first novel – and not just because it characteristically places black people in the position of 'them', the inscrutable object of 'our' attention. It also reminds us that, ultimately, nobody in *Soldier's Pay*, including the narrator and the implied author Faulkner, seems to know why they do what they do, to understand the impulses that drive them. The impulses are simply there to be acted upon and returned to; 'division and death' are present, it seems, merely to be rehearsed again and again in an automatic, almost dreamlike fashion. There is no interrogation in this book of the sources of division: the trauma of loss that impels the human subject to keep coming back to a subject the actual departure from which is implicit in the use of language. There is simply the fact, or feeling, of division; the sense that 'song' exposes absence but also consoles; and the belief, or more accurately the assumption, that the act of repetition may itself have a point – that it may, in effect, *be* the point.

In the same year as *Soldier's Pay* was published, Faulkner began work on his second novel, *Mosquitoes,* set in and around New Orleans. As usual, his choice of sources was eclectic. One of the characters, Ernest Talliaferro, is reminiscent of Eliot's J. Alfred Prufrock, not least in his prim appearance and behaviour, his femininity and preoccupation with sexual failure. At certain moments, the prose style indicates that Faulkner had been reading Joyce recently ('yes yes Jenny her breath Yes yes her red soft mouth where little teeth but showed parted blondeness . . . her breath yes yes');[47] while the novel as a whole, with its obsessive 'talk, talk, talk' and preference for ideas over action, also suggests a fairly close study of Aldous Huxley. The impact of autobiography is also, and often painfully, felt. The book was dedicated to Helen Baird, despite the fact that she had rejected its author (she was to reject the book too, telling a friend, 'Don't read it, it's no good'); and the portrait of Pat Robyn, 'almost breastless and with the fleeting hips of a boy', is clearly a fictional recovery of her in all her elusiveness and delight in motion. Helen's brother was called Josh just as Pat's is, and once worked assiduously at making a pipe just as Josh Baird does, and to this constellation of associations with a woman he had loved and lost Faulkner adds a touch from his dream life, and also an inverted echo of *Elmer*: Pat is devoted to her brother to the extent of wanting to get into bed with him. Josh is reluctant to let her do so ('get out and stay out') but, when she manages to slip between his bedsheets for a moment, she begins to pet and stroke him, meanwhile 'making a kind of meaningless maternal sound' and nibbling his ear. There may be an element of sweet revenge involved in the author's suggestion that the only people Pat Robyn is erotically interested in are her brother and another woman: Pat also slips into bed with Jenny Steinbauer, who is sleeping naked, in order to kiss and caress her. Just the same, Pat's behaviour finds its complement in the design of *Mosquitoes* as a whole, which links its major preoccupation, art, to 'emotional bisexuality', 'hermaphroditism' and sexual inversion. And any element of bitterness that may be implicit in the portrait of this slim, epicene and ruthlessly evasive figure is more than counterbalanced by the 'doglike devotion' shown to her by characters like Gordon and

David West and by the omniscient narrator – the narrator, in particular, never misses an opportunity to linger adoringly over her figure, 'naked and silent as a ghost', in the moonlight. To this extent, there is a curiously personal edge to one of the many remarks about writers and writing made by the garrulous Dawson Fairchild: 'You don't commit suicide when you are disappointed in love. You write a book.'

Fairchild is, of course, one of the several artists populating this novel: one of the many people who prompt Mrs Maurier to tell herself 'with helpless despondence', 'It's being an artist . . . You simply cannot tell what they're going to do', as her planned river excursion goes from bad to worse. In a sense, some of these artist figures are modelled on people Faulkner knew. The poet Mark Frost, for instance, 'a tall ghostly young man' who thinks himself a genius and produces 'an occasional cerebral and obscure poem . . . reminding one somehow of the function of evacuation excruciatingly and incompletely performed', resembles Samuel Gilmore, an acquaintance in New Orleans and a regular contributor to *The Double Dealer*. Gordon the sculptor, with his 'hawk's face . . . remote and insufferable with arrogance', his silence, detachment and utter devotion to his craft, recalls Bill Spratling, the friend with whom Faulkner had travelled to Europe. Most notable of all, Fairchild himself brings to mind Sherwood Anderson. A 'benevolent walrus' of a man, like Anderson Fairchild is talkative, the conversational centre of the group and a spinner of tall tales (the Al Jackson stories that enliven *Mosquitoes* are, in fact, drawn from the correspondence between Faulkner and Anderson). He is also, like Anderson, a firm believer that 'the function of creating art depends on geography', the spirit of a specific locality, and a writer whose work seems 'fumbling, not because life is unclear to him, but because of his innate humourless belief that though it bewilders him at times, life at bottom is sound and admirable and fine'.[48] Anderson might not have entirely appreciated these comments any more than, if he had taken the personal connection, he would have liked Fairchild's confessed feeling that the 'sheer infatuation with and marvelling over the beauty and power of words' had 'gone out of' him now and that as a poetic writer at least, he was 'used up'. On the other hand, he might have seen what is clearer now: that, despite a number of resemblances between the artist figures in *Mosquitoes* and people Faulkner had known, the ultimate source and reference was autobiographical – that over them all, in their arrogance and impotence, their desire for mastery and their sense of failure, lies the uncertain shadow of their creator.

In some ways, this autobiographical dimension is hinted at by clues scattered through the text. Fairchild's dogged persistence in 'clinging spiritually to one little spot of the earth's surface' (as Mrs Maurier sniffily puts it) recollects that sense of place that was always there in Faulkner, gathering power the older he grew. In turn, Ernest Talliaferro is dressed in the straw hat and given the cane that the young 'Count No 'Count' affected in Oxford, while his spiritual demeanour, earnest, comically romantic and ineffectual, recalls Quixotic autobiographical figures from Pierrot to Elmer and Sir Galwyn. Mark Frost writes poems that are, in effect, parodies of Faulkner's own earlier verse, as if the author were using this character as a means of exorcising his older, more uncritically aesthetic self, sloughing off an artistic skin he has outgrown. Gordon not only shows the same dumb devotion to Pat Robyn as Faulkner had to the objects of his affection: he even repeats to himself a phrase, 'your name is like a little golden bell hung in my heart', borrowed from a rejected lover with whom Faulkner felt special affinity, Cyrano de Bergerac, and actually used in a passionate letter to Helen Baird that the young novelist wrote but then never sent. As if to emphasize the way the ghostly figure of the author weaves in and out of the action, he even allows himself a brief entrance on stage without any disguise: during the course of a long conversation, Jenny Steinbauer reveals that she met a man in New Orleans, 'awful sunburned and kind of shabby dressd' who 'said he was a liar by profession' and seemed 'crazy. Not dangerous: just crazy.' His name, she eventually remembers, was Faulkner. 'Faulkner?', Pat Robyn responds, 'Never heard of him.'[49] There is, Fairchild suggests, 'a kind of voraciousness' in a writer 'that makes him stand beside himself with a notebook in his hand always', 'killing' 'all . . . the things that ever happen to him' for the sake of his work. And this notion of art, the book as a sort of devouring of the self, an act of self-consumption, seems peculiarly appropriate to *Mosquitoes*: where, for all the elaborate social comedy or play of conversation, Faulkner seems to be looking principally in a mirror, absorbing, replicating and talking to versions of his own identity.

This act of self-replication is not merely a matter, it should be emphasized, of certain, specific autobiographical connections. Nor is it just to do with Faulkner's interest in this novel in forms of sexual inversion: 'women too masculine to conceive, men too feminine to beget', as Fairchild puts it, an emotional bisexuality or incestuous desire that seeks satisfaction only in its mirror image or 'dark twin'. It has to do, as well, with the way *Mosquitoes* folds back on itself, in a peculiarly self-reflexive process that offers the reader multiple versions of the author and his response to authorship and authority – the impulses that, among other things, went into the making of *this* particular book. It is no accident that it is from this novel that the famous remark, 'a book is the writer's secret life', comes. Of general application perhaps, it nevertheless seems to apply with especial ferocity to a narrative in which the author himself turns up to comment on his characters ('he said if the straps of my dress was to break I'd devastate the country', Jenny Steinbauer observes of 'Faulkner'), and the characters, in turn, comment on the author, while also comparing themselves to 'people . . . in books' in terms of their consistency of behaviour and credibility. This is a fiction that trumpets aloud its own fictiveness: the language is persistently transforming characters into objects (Jenny is a green dress, Pat is a bathing-suit, Pete Ginotta is a 'slanted stiff straw hat', and so on), and the fluidity of nature into the solidity of an artifact:

the moon was still undimmed ... affable and bloodless as a successful procuress, bathing the yacht in quiet silver; and across the southern sky went a procession of small clouds, like silver dolphins on a rigid ultramarine wave, like an ancient geographical woodcut.[50]

At one point, a character tells the story of a girl loved by an artist who, in order to possess her, 'locked her up. In a book': which is one symptom of just how strong the association is in *Mosquitoes* between art and imprisonment. The principal artifact alluded to in the course of the narrative is, in fact, a statue that truncates and contains, '*the headless, armless, legless torso of a girl, motionless and virginal*'. Everyone Faulkner creates here seems, to an extent, to be like that girl. Caught in 'terrific, arrested' motion ('They are not going anywhere and they don't do anything', one character observes of her companions), they approximate more to frozen images of personal fantasy or shadowy reflections of personal need: rather, that is, than to the fluctuating and contingent – to the status of even minimally independent subjects.

It is a measure of just how self-consciously self-referential this novel is that it includes a character looking for his own body. During the course of the action, Gordon the sculptor goes missing from the boat on which the rest of the characters are staying. While away from the boat, he receives the garbled news that someone called *Dawson* has gone missing. And so, before returning to the others, he joins the search party. On hearing about this, Fairchild can scarcely contain his delight, spluttering with half-repressed laughter, 'And so – he comes back and sp-spends ... half a day looking – looking for his own bububod –'. What Gordon seeks, however, others have no trouble in finding. Other characters not only spend much of their time looking at the people around them as if they were objects, they look on themselves as objects as well. Jenny Steinbauer, for instance, is perceived by Dorothy Jameson as 'a doll'; Ernest Talliaferro, meanwhile, sees her as something 'blonde and pink and soft' to be fondled, furtively, through 'the sagging embrace of a canvas chair'. More disturbingly, Jenny sees herself in the same way, with or without the help of a mirror:

Jenny yawned, frankly, then she did something to the front of her dress, drawing it away from her to peer down into her bosom. It seemed to be all right, and she settled her dress again ...[51]

In *Mosquitoes*, there is little or no contact or mutuality, no '*touch of flesh with flesh*' to borrow a phrase from *Absalom, Absalom!*. Characters look for or look at their own bodies, or look at the bodies of others, all in the way their creator looks at them: as still reflexes of desire. The main emotions generated, consequently, are ones of curiosity and fascination. With sheer curiosity, the characters inspect each other as if they were actual or potential works of art; with fascination, they examine themselves as if they were 'people ... in a book'. With mixed curiosity and fascination, in turn, Faulkner seems to gaze at them: like the voyeur/narcissist of his earlier writings, he turns his 'puppets' around, watches them carefully, tries out their voices – in an intricate and obsessive investigation of his own secret life.

The two characters who carry the main burden in this process of authorial self-examination are the two confused in the search for the missing body, the main artists of the piece, Gordon and Dawson Fairchild. Fairchild has to shoulder the burden of his creator's obsessive and ambivalent attitude towards language. 'It is a kind of sterility – words', Fairchild observes at one point, and then goes on with one of Faulkner's own favourite analogies:

> You begin to substitute words for things and deeds, like the withered cuckold husband that took the Decameron to bed with him every night, and pretty soon the thing or the deed becomes just a kind of shadow of a certain sound you make by shaping your mouth in a certain way . . .[52]

Taking art to bed instead of a body was an image that haunted Faulkner: among many other locations, it had appeared already in an early review of Joseph Hergesheimer and in *Elmer* and was to find a place in *Flags in the Dust* as well as the 'Introduction' to *The Sound and the Fury*. Having made the comparison, however, Fairchild then backtracks more than a little by claiming that, while words do not 'have life in themselves', nevertheless, 'brought into happy conjunction', they can 'produce something that lives, just as soil and climate and an acorn in proper conjunction will produce a tree'. Despite the appearance of reasoned argument, this is flat contradiction; the second half of Fairchild's statement simply denies the first. Does language consume life or complete it? Is art perversion or a kind of procreation? The questions are not answered; nor is any credible alternative discovered, a route out of the impasse to which such questions lead. In his later work, Faulkner was to use his radical uncertainty about the tools of his trade to his advantage. In *Mosquitoes*, however, we have the queer sight of a man using words to deride words, trying to employ language to interrogate or at least subvert itself; and, in the process, saying one thing – and then something else completely different.

If Fairchild helps Faulkner to map out some of his conflicting ideas at this time about speech, then Gordon helps him to consider the possibilities of silence. Taciturn, detached, it is Gordon who is given the chance to deliver the most damning verdict on the buzz of conversation that more or less monopolizes the book: 'talk, talk, talk', the sculptor thinks,

> the utter and heartbreaking stupidity of words. It seemed endless, as though it might go on forever. Ideas, thoughts, became mere sounds to be bandied about until they were dead.[53]

Gordon is wedded to the world of 'doing': in this, he bears comparison with Cash Bundren in *As I Lay Dying* and with the hypothetical figure of the carpenter that Faulkner often used, in conversation, when he was

trying to explain his own attitude to his craft. He rarely utters a word –
and, when he does, unlike the other characters his words are normally
closely aligned to actions, they usually have a specific, pragmatic purpose:

> Gordon stood against the wall, aloof, not listening to them hardly, watching
> within the bitter and arrogant loneliness of his heart, a shape strange and
> new as fire swirling, headless, armless, legless, but when his name was spo-
> ken he stirred, 'Let's have a drink,' he said.[54]

As this passage indicates, the figure of the lonely sculptor absorbed in
either (as here) the conception or (as elsewhere) the execution of his art
– the statue of a 'headless, armless, legless' girl – also enabled Faulkner to
continue his examination of privacy. In his own way, Gordon is as apart
and impenetrable as Donald Mahon is. The difference is fairly obvious,
however: Gordon is separate from the other characters, but he is not so
nearly separate from the reader. We are invited to share his obsessions
(which are, of course, some of his creator's) to a degree that we are never
asked to share Mahon's. We are also alerted to the fact that, to the extent
that any of the characters in *Mosquitoes* is, Gordon is reactive: caught in a
web of desire for the pale, virginal figure of a girl that he associates with
Pat Robyn and then tries to capture in his statue. In other words, Gordon's
privacy is far more a form of enclosure than Mahon's is: it seems to
express far more fiercely than the lieutenant's strange detachment does
the suspicion that being apart can be a kind of imprisonment. Keeping
himself to himself, the sculptor does complete the work that obsesses him
but, even 'locked' in stone, the figure he has pursued seems to escape
him. When the reader last encounters him, in fact, Gordon is embracing
and kissing a prostitute while remaining haunted by his vision of a '*motionless and virginal*' girl: life, it seems, never ceases to disappoint while art
offers no adequate compensation. The only person locked in the artifact,
really, turns out to be the artist himself: caught in a jail of his own making,
constructed not so much of bars as of mirrors.

Speech and silence: the contrast sounded in the pairing of Fairchild
and Gordon reverberates through *Mosquitoes*, helping to determine its
structure. On the one hand, there is a chorus of voices, arguing, thinking,
spinning tall tales, trying out street idiom or aspiring to poetry; on the
other hand, there is the slippage towards dumbness or incoherence. At
times, the slippage seems to take place openly in the text. Which is to say
that, at several moments in the narrative, words and objects seem to dissolve
under the pressure of desire – as when Ernest Talliaferro pants for the
touch of Steinbauer – or fear – as in this passage in which David West
tramps down 'an endless blistering ribbon' of road in a swamp, wondering
if he will even find civilization:

> Three steps. All right. One. Two. Three. Gone. gone. gone. It's a red sound.
> Not behind your eyes. Sea. See. Sea. See. You're in a cave, you're in a cave

of dark sound, the sound of the sea is outside the cave. Sea. See. See. See. Not when they keep stepping in front of the door.[55]

Always, on the river or in the swamp, there is the buzz of the mosquitoes, mocking the chattering human voice, or reducing the human animal to 'thin whimpering sound[s]' of discomfort and pain. And when they attack in earnest, as they do several times in the novel, they invariably force the characters to shut their mouths, stop their talking, and retreat from their 'foetid and timeless, sombre and hushed and dreadful' natural surroundings to the comfort and safety of some protective structure: a room, a ship, any enclosure.

The structures of language, in effect, find their visual and metaphorical equivalents here in cultural constructs: closely linked to the opposition between talk and silence/incoherence – and, indeed, overlapping with it often – is the contrast between the fixity of human objects (bodies, technological structures, artifacts) and the fluidity of natural processes (the river, the swamp). A constant, signifying motif here is the object surrounded by shapelessness and emptiness, the human body in the dark, the yacht stranded in the river, the ribbon of road running through the swamp. Within this metaphorical series, the human voice that elsewhere announces its presence so loudly and confidently seems not only mocked but also dwarfed, reduced by the amorphousness of its surroundings to minimal, reactive and almost meaningless sounds:

> Trees heavy and ancient with moss loomed out of it hugely and greyly: the mist might have been a sluggish growth among them. No, this mist might have been the first prehistoric morning of time itself: it might have been the very substance in which the seed of the beginning of things fecundated; and these huge and silent trees might have been the first of living things, too recently born to know either fear or astonishment, dragging their sluggish umbilical cords from out the old miasmic womb of nothingness latent and dreadful. She crowded against him, suddenly quiet and subdued, trembling a little like a puppy against the reassurance of his arm. 'Gee,' she said in a small voice.[56]

There is, as the voices in the novel argue remorselessly, culture and there is nature, 'literature' and 'biology', the constructs of language on the one hand and on the other silence or a booming, buzzing confusion. It would come as no surprise, really, to readers of the earlier writing that in *Mosquitoes* the first series of terms is associated with the male principle and the second with the female. Nor would it come as a surprise to anyone acquainted with the *Elmer* manuscript that *Mosquitoes* ends with a mocking allegorical confrontation between male language and female biology: believing that he now knows 'the magic Word' required to get himself a woman, Ernest Talliaferro takes Jenny Steinbauer dancing only to find himself not only deserted but, in the process, made to look a fool. The mosquitoes mock human articulation, the swamp dwarfs human artifacts, the female principle eludes male structures; and Talliaferro is left, in the last lines of the novel, to survey his own isolation and impotence – with the sounds of 'a remote buzzing' and a mocking, disembodied female voice on the telephone ringing in his ears.

There are several things wrong with *Mosquitoes*, notably its radical solipsism. And there are several things about the early writing in general that, if not wrong exactly, nevertheless require interrogation. The most notable of these is the model or paradigm at the back of all the earliest work that Faulkner learned from his culture: a version of the drama of the 'primal gap' that acquired its particular intonations from the fact that Faulkner was a Southerner, male and white. Something of the nature of this model has been suggested already: but it is perhaps worth spelling out some of its starker implications here, not least because they helped to polarize and (to some extent) paralyse the younger Faulkner's thinking. The model is predicated on the idea that the realm of the male, the father, is the realm of all that constitutes culture and that is articulated in language: language itself being innately binary, an endless series of oppositions. The realm of the female, the mother, in turn, is, according to this model, that of the unseparated, prelinguistic body: the mother's role being to nourish the human subject so that he (since the model is male, the human subject is also inevitably conceived of as male) becomes prepared for alienation, the sense of fissure that accompanies entry into the realm of the father. A subtext of all this is the idea of woman as sanctuary (supplying an aboriginal experience of plenitude) and/or betrayer (when that experience is not in place) and/or lost girl (reminding the male subject of his fall into the broken world); and a consequence of it is that dualism coextensive with meaning, the figures of division that underpin Faulkner's work, tending to dictate the terms in which it (re)constructs the world.

Faulkner was never to escape this model. In fact, he could hardly do so, since in all its intonations it was an integral part of the place and time into which he was born; he could no more get outside of it than he could get outside of history. It was what Althusser would have called his 'script' or Pierre Bourdieu would have glossed as his 'habitus': an 'immanent law' laid down to Faulkner, as to each human agent, by his upbringing, 'inscribed in the body schema and in schemes of thought'.[57] But just as the notion of the script or habitus allows for what Bourdieu calls 'conditioned and conditional freedom' – the chance, that is, to read the script in one's own way – so Faulkner did have the opportunity, like anyone else, to investigate the model he had learned, critically to place it and, in the process, intimate alternative strategies. It was an opportunity he would seize in his later and best work. There, he not only conducts such an investigation through the lives of his characters or permits them, at least occasionally, to anticipate what one figure in *Absalom, Absalom!* calls *'the fall of all the eggshell shibboleth[s]'*; he also gravitates towards a style that flows between, and insinuates itself behind, rigid, dualistic structures. It is a style that stands comparison with Julia Kristeva's notion of the 'semiotic': which, for Kristeva, is a fragmented, impulsive, errant language, originating in the experiences of childbirth or breast-feeding, that inserts itself between and subverts oppositional models. In its own way, Faulkner's mature style – the style, in other words, of the major fiction roughly from 1929 to 1940 – moves in a direction similar to the 'semiotic'. Its slipperiness permits it to seep through conceptual boundaries; its random, discontinuous nature enables it to expose gaps in, or actively puncture, seamless figures of division; while its random fluency, its disjunctive pressures work towards a shattering of *'all the eggshell shibboleth[s]'*, the thin carapace of dualistic ideology. The earlier style, however, is quite different. In his earliest writing, Faulkner rarely seems inclined to interrogate the model he has learned, let alone deploy the kind of idiom that would allow for slippage or even subvert. For the most part, the barriers stay firmly in place; character, persona and narrator remain imprisoned within terms that freeze life into intolerable contraries. That, perhaps, is the source of the fascination of the early work and its attendant feelings of melancholy, longing and loss; it is certainly the source of its failure. Ironically, for all his apparent gestures of rebellion, Faulkner is still mostly writing at this stage within the authoritative discourses of his region; like the young man who emerges from his earliest letters to his mother and father, he is still thinking of home and thinking in terms of home even when he may be a long way away.

3

Rewriting the Homeplace

I ANCESTOR WORSHIP, PATRICIDE AND THE EPIC PAST:
FLAGS IN THE DUST AND *SARTORIS*

It was while Faulkner was living in New Orleans that he began work first
on *Father Abraham* and then, around the end of 1926, on a book he would
later call *Flags in the Dust*. Only two years later, Faulkner would admit the
profoundly autobiographical basis of this narrative. 'I began to write without much purpose', he declared, 'until I realised that to make it truly
evocative it must be personal.' The characters he now created, he explained, were 'composed partly from what they were in actual life and
partly, from what they should have been and were not: thus I improved on
God'. Working both in New Orleans and in Oxford, Faulkner applied
himself with genuine passion to an enterprise that seemed to involve not
only recovery and reinvention but also resistance to the pressures of time:
'nothing served', he explained, 'but that I try by main strength to recreate
between the covers of a book the world . . . I was already preparing to lose
and regret.' It was as if Faulkner believed that, in writing about his
homeplace and his past he was simultaneously exorcizing it and embalm-
ing it: liberating himself, perhaps, through the sheer acting of telling
himself about the South but at the same time endowing his 'own little
postage stamp of native soil' with a sort of permanence, the fixity that
came from translating a world into words. 'All you know is that little patch
up there in Mississippi where your started from',[1] Faulkner remembered
Sherwood Anderson had told him, advising him imaginatively to return to
it. Faulkner not only returned to it in imagination, he returned to it in
fact: more and more of his time was to be spent in Oxford and its environs, less and less in New Orleans, New York or elsewhere, as if Faulkner
needed to be in the place where he was born in order to sort out his
attitudes to it. Distance lent enchantment: he was never likelier to talk
lovingly of Mississippi than when he was, say, working as a scriptwriter in

Hollywood or revising a manuscript in Manhattan. Proximity, being there, lent, if not clarity, then at least the rewards of confrontation: the intensity of focus acquired from encountering his ghosts head on.

'Thus I improved on God': this was a sardonic joke in one way but, in another, it measured the scope of his ambitions. Faulkner often used the comparison with an omnipotent creator or talked of 'a cosmos of my own'. Equally often, he expressed a longing to 'crowd and cram' all experience into one, all-embracing sentence. Circumscribing all that needed to be said, 'all the recaptured light rays' of an event, in one statement; moving his 'people ... around like God, not only in space but in time too'; these were both, for Faulkner, unambiguous signs of mastery and control – or, rather, symptoms of his *need* for such control, his desire for total imaginative possession. And one other symptom was evident very early on: as early as 1926, he seemed to be trying to lay down the parameters of Yoknapatawpha (although he was not actually to name his invented county until a few years later). Between them, *Father Abraham* and *Flags in the Dust* establish the two poles in the white social structure of Jefferson and its environs as well as what one critic has termed 'the two poles of history' – which is to say, the two events that act as major historical catalysts in the story of Faulkner's South – the Civil War and the First World War. As even Faulkner's first attempts at prose and verse had shown, however, the need for mastery is one thing and actual mastery quite another; a shadow seems to fall inevitably between desire and possession. Faulkner might pursue imaginative containment, as if he could lay down the tracks for all that was to come; he might even declare, in moments of self-congratulation, 'all the people of the imaginary county, black and white, townsmen, farmers and housewives, have played their part in one connected story'.[2] But, as he evidently sensed at the outset, he would never live long enough to exhaust all the possibilities of the 'gold mine' he had discovered.

Nevertheless, Faulkner was full of confidence when he completed the nearly 600 manuscript pages of *Flags in the Dust*. 'I have written THE book of which those other things are but foals', he told his publisher, 'I believe it is the damdest book you'll look at this year.' And when the publisher flatly rejected the manuscript, complaining that it did not 'get anywhere' and had 'a thousand loose ends' – and, still worse, was 'so diffuse' that no cutting or revising could save it – his feelings were equally extreme. 'I was shocked,' Faulkner later remembered,

> my first emotion was blind protest, then I become objective for a moment, like a parent who is told that its child is a thief or an idiot or a leper; for a dreadful moment I contemplated it with consternation and despair, then like the parent I hid my own eyes in the fury of denial.[3]

Eventually, the manuscript was placed with another publisher, who stipulated extensive cuts before publishing it with the new title *Sartoris*. Most of the cuts were made by Faulkner's friend Ben Wasson – although the critical consensus is that, after washing his hands of the process at first, Faulkner did provide some assistance; and most of those cuts, as the altered title implies, tended further to foreground the story of the Sartoris family at the expense of Buddy MacCallum, Byron Snopes, and above all Horace Benbow. As the remarks quoted here indicate, however, the emotional trauma of rejection was at least as significant for Faulkner as the logistical difficulties of finding another publisher that it posed. The practical difficulties were soon solved, although not without Wasson's active intervention, while the trauma lingered on: a measure not only of Faulkner's protectiveness towards his work in general but also of his particular parental love for this book – even in its altered form. 'William Faulkner cared deeply about *Sartoris*', a friend of this period observed. Which is not surprising: it is, after all, the sourcebook for Yoknapatawpha, 'the germ of my apocrypha' as Faulkner put it later, in which he introduced his readers to people like the Sartoris clan, the Snopes clan, and Horace Benbow and his sister. And it is, too, the book in which he confronted the story of his family most openly: where the ghosts of the Faulkners, past and present, hover closest to the surface.

Some of the ways in which Faulkner confronted his own story here – or, more interestingly still, failed to confront it – have been considered already. Faulkner's great-grandfather, 'The Old Colonel', clearly lurks behind both Bayard Sartoris I and John Sartoris: with his reckless behaviour during the Civil War being shadowed in Bayard, and much of the rest of his life – his killing of two men, his building of a railroad, and his death at the hands of a former business partner and political rival – finding its echo in the tale of that first John. Old Bayard, in turn, recollects the author's grandfather the banker, not least in his deafness and loneliness; Aunt Jenny recalls Faulkner's straight-talking great-aunt Alabama; Simon, Old Bayard's coachman, owes something to the Falkner family servant Ned Barnett. And so on. Apart from the absences and repressed impulses of the family romance mentioned earlier, however, the most significant autobiographical dimension of *Flags in the Dust/ Sartoris* is the 'twinning' of Bayard III and Horace Benbow. Bayard III is another fated aviator, a recapitulation of Donald Mahon in a different key. Kissing him, Narcissa Benbow tastes 'fatality and doom': a taste that seems to be there for the reader from the first time he appears – 'a tall shape' in the darkness, 'with the moonlight bringing the hawklike planes of his face into high relief'[4] – until the moment he is killed flying a crackpot experimental plane. Inhabiting silence, he also inhabits the past: haunted, not like Mahon by the forgetting of his own wounding, but by the obsessive, passionately resisted remembering of the killing of another, for which he feels responsible. He tries to escape the past but it insistently pursues him: even his death is a form of repetition, recalling not only the air crash in which his brother died but also the foolhardy, semi-suicidal exploits of his namesake and great-grandfather during the Civil War.

A haunted figure, suffering from the same strange malaise as many of Edgar Allan Poe's heroes, Bayard III sketches out one set of possibilities for his creator: not least, in the way his obsession with privacy and silence leads eventually, and somehow inevitably, to his annihilation. Horace Benbow, especially in *Flags in the Dust*, sketches out quite another set. Denied the possibility of heroism (he has spent the war working for the YMCA), he is 'a poet' in the contemptuous eyes of his neighbours: a man whose forms of fulfilment and escape are the (for Faulkner) linked activities of art and incest. 'I have exchanged you for Belle', he tells his sister shortly after he marries Belle Mitchell. In his life as well as his art, Horace seems to figure his creator's suspicion that sexual and aesthetic pursuits are crucially linked, since both act as forms of restitution and/or replacement for a lost wholeness. If Bayard hardly ever speaks unless spoken to (and not always then), Horace never stops talking: 'I have always been ordered by words',[5] he admits. And if Bayard rejects the past only to imitate it, then Horace capitulates to all his yesterdays – he becomes a lawyer, we are told, because that is the family tradition – only to find himself rootless, adrift, gazing from his rented house across 'his rented lawn where his rented garage stared its empty door at him like an accusing eye'. They are dark twins of each other, in sum, as each is in turn of his creator. And they are shadowy reflections, each of them of two conventional Southern character types: the plantation Hotspur, embodiment of the regional preoccupation with chivalry, heroism and glamorous adventure, and the plantation Hamlet, image of the South's pretensions to aristocratic status – to delicacy, manners, in short all that might be the opposite of Northern crassness and utilitarianism. Bayard III is, of course, Faulkner's own dark version of the Hotspur figure, the chivalric impulse translated in him into febrile intensity, and the sense of adventure into a death wish. While Horace is a pale descendant of the regional Hamlet, in whom delicacy and aristocratic grace have degenerated into a failure of nerve and related feelings of drift, impotence and surrender. How far this parodic dimension, this shadowing of traditional regional figures, is intentional it is difficult to say, although most likely Faulkner was drawing on a regional typology by instinct. What is more to the point, however, is that it enabled him to bring together several, related impulses at the back of the novel: the sense of regional decline, a feeling of bitter personal loss – and the suspicion, issuing from this, that the present is overpowered by a past that it cannot tap as a living source, and of which, as a consequence, it can only be a dim shadow.

The kind of relationship between past and present that masters most of this narrative is, in fact, succinctly described in Bakhtin's essay on 'Epic and the Novel'. Here, Bakhtin makes a distinction between that historicizing of time that turns it into a process in which 'there is no first word (no ideal word), and the final word has not yet been spoken', and what he calls the 'epic past'. 'Absolute conclusiveness and closedness is the outstanding feature' of the epic past, he claims. 'Walled off from all subsequent times

by an impenetrable boundary', it is 'inaccessible to personal experience and
does not permit an individual, personal point of view'; 'an utterly finished
thing', one cannot 'glimpse it, grope for it, touch it', it is 'impossible to
experience' and is 'given solely as tradition, sacred and sacramental'. This
epic past is, of course, what most of the characters in *Flags in the Dust/
Sartoris* have. Drawn back continually towards something that, like a half-
remembered dream, at once obsesses them and eludes them, they are as
Sartre once famously described the characters in *The Sound and the Fury*:
like 'a man sitting in a convertible looking back' for whom the future is
unknown, the present a blur, and the outline of the past 'hard, clear, and
immutable'. People like the Sartorises and the Benbows find themselves
dealing with a ghostly, confusing world, so close to them that it seems to
control their thoughts and dominate their actions and yet so distant from
them – because it *is* the past and they *are* 'walled off' from their inheritance
– that they cannot understand it, or objectify their feelings about it. Their
lives become a sort of dialogue with spectres, conducted in a language
they hardly know. This, for example, is how 'Colonel' Bayard Sartoris is
introduced to us at the beginning of *Sartoris*, as a man haunted:

> Feed as he was of time and flesh . . . John Sartoris seemed to loom . . . above
> and about his son . . . so that as old Bayard sat with his crossed feet propped
> against the corner of the cold hearth, holding the pipe in his hand, it
> seemed to him that he could hear his father's breathing even, as though
> that other were so much more palpable than transiently articulated clay as
> to even penetrate into the uttermost citadel of silence in which his son lived.
>
> The bowl of the pipe was ornately carved, and . . . on the bit were the
> prints of his father's teeth, where he had left the very print of his ineradi-
> cable bones . . . like the creatures of that prehistoric day that were too grandly
> conceived . . . either to exist very long or to vanish utterly when dead.[6]

In his original manuscript of *Flags in the Dust*, Faulkner began with
'Colonel' Bayard meditating in the attic over relics untouched for twenty
years: a Toledo blade, some lace, two pipes, a cavalry sabre and a family
Bible containing the names of the Sartoris clan 'growing fainter and fainter
where time had lain upon them'. The detailed positioning of character is
different here but the fundamentals are the same as in the book eventually published in 1929: in both cases, the past seems to be more alive than
the living. More specifically, Colonel John (whose voice is remembered,
roaring 'genealogy is poppycock', as Old Bayard fingers the relics) seems
to be more alive than his son and great-grandson, and yet he is a wraith
– an insubstantial nothing, whose nothingness nevertheless manages to
dominate their being. Clearly, he represents a force to be reckoned with,
a memory that his descendants must come to terms with before they can
ever hope to be free. But all Old Bayard can do, apparently, is try to lose
himself in memory, seal himself off from his surroundings behind his own
personal smoke screen, while Bayard Sartoris III makes the equally desperate mistake of thinking that he can deny it, even though its influence is

to be traced in almost every step he ever makes. To embrace a ghost or to flee from it, neither really constitutes an act of exorcism. Yet these are the only routes most members of the Sartoris family appear capable of following, or for that matter most of their neighbours: a dilemma that is, ultimately, a product of the situation in which they find themselves – where (to quote Bakhtin again) the past is conceived of as 'completed, conclusive and immutable', 'beyond the realm of human activity, the realm in which everything humans touch is altered and re-thought'.

Conceived of by the characters, that is, and by the author/narrator: it is important to emphasize this – that the absence of any genuinely historicizing sense is a function not merely of the Sartorises but of the texts they inhabit. The notion of a relativized past, and so of a living, changing relation between it and the present, is, for the most part, conspicuous only by its absence. As far as the characters are concerned, this problem is caught not just in the kinds of contrasts already mentioned, but in an elaborate figurative pattern that tends to associate each individual with either theatrical performance or the rituals of somnambulism. References to a character 'performing his past' or someone in 'a self-imposed . . . role' are reinforced by the tendency of many people in *Flags in the Dust/Sartoris* to assume personae and scripts for which they are peculiarly unfitted. There is Horace, of course, trying to learn the lines of the gentleman lawyer, and Old Bayard framed by his relics and repetitive rituals; there is Narcissa Benbow acting out the part of genteel Southern lady, while hoarding the letters sent to her by Byron Snopes. In a more comic vein, there is even Simon who, with 'his race's fine feeling for potential theatrics'[7] (a typically generalizing remark in this novel, which, like *Soldier's Pay*, reduces black people to objects), plays the part of 'majestical' guardian of Sartoris lore and, more inappropriately still, banker to the local black community. With the epic past, Bakhtin observed, only two manoeuvres are possible: reverential imitation or iconoclastic rejection, both of them founded on the premise of distance, the belief that no genuine interaction between past and present is possible. To this could be added two corollaries: in this novel, the imitation is always imperfect precisely because of that distance – the failure to observe that changed times require changed practices – while the gesture of rejection inevitably fails because the past inheres in mind and body. To reject the past, in such circumstances, is simply to reject or rather suppress a part of the self; and the repressed then has its revenge as it does in the case of Bayard Sartoris III by condemning the human agent to a cycle of repetition. Like a sleepwalker, Bayard is driven to actions imitative of the past of which he is hardly aware; he takes flight from his ghosts, not realizing at first that those ghosts are inside him – then, when does realize it, he deals with them in the only way he knows how, destroying them by destroying himself.

The degree of complicity of the author/narrator in all this is implicit in its profoundly autobiographical nature. Faulkner traced out the intolerable alternatives of imitative repetition or rejection in the twinned characters of Horace Benbow and Bayard Sartoris III, certainly: but they are also inscribed in the making and functioning of the book. In both versions, *Flags in the Dust* and *Sartoris*, the imitation of – or, to be more exact, capitulation to – the past is traceable in the author's almost obsessive recapitulation of family lore: there is the father figure, Colonel William Clark Falkner, dominating the proceedings even in his absence – dictating the shape of the narrative and forcing those in the novelistic present into the roles of imitators and/or recorders. The opening chapter is exemplary in this respect. Beginning in the 'now' of the novel, after the First World War, the pressures exerted by the shadowy figure of the Old Colonel push character, narrator and reader further and further back in time with compulsive re-tellings of the past. Aunt Jenny, who tells the story of Colonel John Sartoris and his brother here over and over again – from the first recorded occasion in 1869 to the most recent in 1919 – is really only an extreme instance of a function all the characters and the narrator share, that of keeper of the flame, commemorator of the family legend. Like Old Bayard musing over the Sartoris relics in the attic, they are all drawn into the role of antiquary or memorialist: their sole purpose being, it seems, not to act but to record – not to add new stories but to remember and rehearse old ones.

Or almost their sole purpose: Faulkner's first novel set in Jefferson is full of commemorative gestures but, on a more submerged level, it is also packed with murderous impulses. And not unrelated to this is the fact that while Bayard III and Horace Benbow are certainly perceived as sons of the fathers they also manage to be orphans. They may be overshadowed by their ancestors: however, both lose their parents when they are young and, like Bayard's father, Horace's is only mentioned by the way, in terms of a passing reference to his death. The implications of Faulkner's omission of the generation between Bayard II and Bayard III have already been discussed, as has the novelist's disingenuous attempt to explain why he omitted all but the most cursory reference to Bayard III's father. All that needs to be done here, perhaps, is note the duplication with the orphaning of Benbow, and to point out that the death of John Sartoris in the First World War assumes an additional dimension when seen, as it can be, as a mode of displacement. Fratricidal impulses, in both myth and psychological theory, are often perceived to have their origins in an impulse even more intolerable because unacknowledgeable: the longing for the death of the father.[8] There is no need to labour the point that Dean was the Falkner son most closely identified with his father Murry to see what is going on at a subterranean level. Nor, possibly, is it necessary to remind ourselves that John Sartoris is named after his patriarchal great-grandfather and shares his heroic stature. If one tendency of the narrative is to commemorate the past, another is to bury it, to suppress it. If, on one level, the characters in the narrative present in *Flags in the Dust/Sartoris* surrender to their predecessors, on another they resist and defy them. Finally, if one shaping motive of the book is reverential then another, quite the opposite, is rebellious; the desire to worship the father is twinned, in the male protagonists and their creator alike, with the desire – however concealed – to kill him.

The extremes of motive between which the novel swings – from ancestor worship to patricide and back – may help account for some of its more problematical areas. Most obviously, they may help explain a radical uncertainty of tone epitomized by the famous concluding remarks when the narrator is saying goodbye for a while to the Sartoris lengend:

> the dusk was peopled with ghosts of glamorous and old disastrous things. And if they were just glamorous enough, there was sure to be a Sartoris in them, and then they were sure to be disastrous. Pawns. But the Player, and the game He plays . . . He must have a name for His pawns, though. But perhaps Sartoris is the game itself – a game outmoded and played with pawns shaped too late and to an old dead pattern . . . For there is death in the sound of it, and a glamorous fatality, like silver pennons downrushing at sunset, or a dying fall of horns along the road to Roncevaux . . .[9]

The passage bears traces of the *fin-de-siècle* writers whom the young Faulkner admired so much – in the obvious, world-weary elegance of certain phrases, for instance, and the tired, semiphilosophical references to a 'Player' God. More interesting than this, however, is the divided response towards the subject that lurks behind and within the fluencies of phrasing: signalled in part by the narrator's rapid and scarcely acknowledged shift from 'ghosts' to 'pawns' – from the perception of the Sartoris ancestors as haunting, controlling subjects, that is, to the suspicion that they are powerless objects. At one point, it may look as if the narrative voice is gravitating towards a gesture of rejection: when the Sartorises are dismissed, with bitter wit and apparently monosyllabic finality, as functionaries in an 'old, dead game'. This does not last for long, though. Feelings of commemorative reverence soon return: with the result that, while we are not allowed to forget the skull beneath the skin of the Sartoris family, any reference to death and the waiting grave is radically qualified by an opulently nostalgic evocation of old, forgotten, far-off things and battles long ago. Of course, this could be seen as a matter of balance, as if Faulkner were trying to separate the different strands woven together in his feelings for the Sartoris past and measure them, weigh them out. The problem is that to read the passage in this way is to ignore the extent to which the language used seems intended precisely to mask differences. The coupling of 'glamorous' and 'disastrous', for instance, may in principle acknowledge a gap or fissure but in practice it acts to conceal it: the sonorities of phrasing serve only to suppress the dissonances of motive. Even while the narrator labours with his divided feelings he seems, in fact, to be aiming for coherence and closure: deploying figures of sunset and dying falls, as well as elegant diminuendos of cadence, in the hope that they may engineer the sense of an ending. Darkness and light, despair and glamour jostle for supremacy in the sentence that concludes this passage; reverence and rejection are not so much balanced here as blurred, because the narrator does not know finally whether to salute his flags in the dust or bury them.

The few moments in the narrative that do not possess these disconcerting but fascinating elisions of language and motive occur when the past is not simply recalled but resurrected. At times, protagonist and/or narrator seem to step outside the rigid temporalities, the wall between yesterday and today that imprisons them, and to step back into the security of a past, not simply remembered, but experienced as if it were the present. The most notable instance of this is when Bayard Sartoris III, in flight from the killing of another father-figure, his grandfather Old Bayard, takes refuge at the home of the MacCallum family. As he approaches the house, the intimations of pastoral peace, idyllic retreat, are unavoidable: 'at last a pale and windless plume of smoke stood above the trees ahead', we are told, 'and in the rambling wall of the house a window glowed with ruddy invitation across the twilight'. There is no knowledge here of the death for which Bayard III is responsible: the MacCallums are cut off from the world by geographical distance, a broken axle tree on their wagon, and above all by their utter self-containment. To call them a family is misleading. The only female surviving in the place is the cook Mandy, otherwise there are five young men and the patriarchal figure of their father Virginius: the temptations of women are evidently not to be encountered in this mythic, prelapsarian haven. Neither are the depredations of time and history a worry, as the portrait of Virginius makes clear:

> In 1861 he was sixteen and he had walked to Lexington, Virginia, and enlisted, served four years in the Stonewall brigade and walked back to Mississippi . . . he sat now before the fireplace . . . , beneath the roof he had built in '66, and on the mantel above him the clock sat, deriding that time whose servant it had once been.[10]

The narrative voice here is comfortable with its own assurance that time has been denied, even derided. The dissonances of motive that characterize most of the book have been jettisoned in favour of a different, more sweetly simple key: sounded in the belief that, somehow and miraculously, Bayard, narrator and reader have been carried back and liberated from the burden of memory. In this mythic space, the therapeutic rituals of hunting can be conducted and the pressures of history can be simply ignored ('pappy and Stonewall Jackson ain't never surrendered', one MacCallum son observes); the epic past can be experienced as if it never went away. It is a comforting moment for Bayard, and a moment of singular calm for the narrator; it is, however, deeply sentimental, a dreamlike evasion of all that elsewhere in the book drives both of them to vexation and despair.

Flags in the Dust and *Sartoris* have both been called confused books: a confusion that has usually been attributed to the episodic structure of both. The publisher to whom Faulkner first sent the manuscript of *Flags in the Dust* did, after all, reject it on the grounds that it was 'diffuse and non-integral'; while one critic has called *Sartoris* 'structurally . . . one of Faulkner's weakest novels'.[11] This is certainly true, both books do have a disconnected structure; simply to lay the blame there, however, is to fall back on a fairly crude kind of formalism, ignoring the point that forms do have meanings. For that matter, it is to forget that, as Faulkner's own best work shows, disconnectedness is not necessarily a bad thing: it may be a way of stopping the intellectual arteries from hardening, a strategy for slipping between and even releasing blocked channels of thought. The structural incoherences of *Flags in the Dust* and *Sartoris* must, in effect, be seen for what they are – as symptoms of a deeper confusion, issuing out of Faulkner's evident reluctance at the time to think in terms of anything other than an absolute past. The authoritative discourses of the past must be accepted without question or rejected wholesale, the father must either be worshipped or destroyed: these are the contraries between which both versions of the Sartoris legend vacillate – generating and aggravating confusions, creating the sense that, as that first publisher who read Faulkner's story put it, it just does not 'get anywhere'. Faulkner's way out of this impasse would be to 'think in voices': to use speech, within both what is conventionally called dialogue and what is usually considered outside it, to create a world of autonomous subjects. The sense of a past that is hopelessly finished would then be supplanted by a sense of the past as part of a process. Ideas would then be encountered as lived events, played out between different consciousnesses at different moments in time; and the historical community, under the impact of these events, would be seen as something susceptible to change, condemned neither to sink back into its roots nor to break with them. There are occasions when this thinking in voices begins to occur in *Flags in the Dust* and *Sartoris*. They include those times when the inhabitants of Jefferson are allowed to debate and collaborate in the creation of communal memories; more strangely effective still, they include the time that Bayard Sartoris III and Narcissa Benbow come together via an elaborate interplay between sounds and their absence, their love for each other woven apparently out of the fabrics of language and silence. But these moments are few and far between. For true thinking in voices, Faulkner had to wait; he did not, however, have to wait very long. The publication dates tell the story: *Sartoris* was published on 31 January 1929, *The Sound and the Fury* a little more than eight months later, on 7 October.

II VOICES, ABSENCE AND CULTURAL AUTOBIOGRAPHY: *THE SOUND AND THE FURY*

The Sound and the Fury began as a story, 'Twilight'. Faulkner had written short stories about the Compson family before: 'A Justice', and a piece called 'Never Done No Weeping When You Wanted to Laugh' – which in later, revised versions was to be titled 'That Evening Sun Go Down' then 'That Evening Sun'. This time, however, the story soon began to grow into a narrative: a novel into which, as Faulkner later put it, 'I had written my guts'. Faulkner often contradicted himself in his comments about his work, but in one respect at least he was remarkably consistent: when asked what his personal favourite was among his books, he never tired of saying it was *The Sound and the Fury*, 'the one that failed the most tragically and the most splendidly'. 'I like the one which caused me the most trouble', he declared in an interview. 'That is *The Sound and the Fury*.' And elsewhere, in his class conferences at Virginia, he continued this line of thought: *The Sound and the Fury*, he insisted,

> was the best failure. It was the one I anguished the most over, that I worked the hardest at, that even when I knew I couldn't bring it off, I still worked at it ... The others that have been easier to write ... I don't have the feeling toward any of them that I do toward that one ...[12]

The trouble and anguish that Faulkner was talking about was more emotional than mechanical – the manuscript shows, in fact, that he made relatively few radical alterations as he went along. And this may be one of the reasons why the book held such a special place in Faulkner's affection: that it came at a particularly critical moment in his life and was wound intimately into his own experience. In a way, it had had a long gestation period: characters, situations, and images recur here from most of Faulkner's earlier writing. Behind the figure of Quentin alone, for instance, hover all the pale, impotent narrators and protagonists of so much of the previous prose and verse: among many others, the marble faun, Pierrot in *The Marionettes* and *Vision in Spring*, Sir Galwyn in *Mayday*, and Elmer Hodge. 'I am Quentin in *The Sound and the Fury*', Faulkner once admitted. And while the Quixotic figure of Quentin Compson is the most obviously autobiographical figure in the novel, he is not the only one: in the other Compson brothers traces of their creator can be found. Benjy, for instance, recollects Faulkner's preoccupation with privacy and silence; Jason parodically recalls the young novelist's hunger for success, his feelings of insecurity and capacity for rage; while both share their older brother's, and their creator's, obsession with the experience of loss.

Faulkner himself admitted that 1928, the year when he wrote *The Sound and the Fury*, was a time of particular crisis for him. As he later explained it, he was suffering from 'severe strain' then, brought on by 'difficulties of an intimate kind'.[13] His intense privacy stopped him, as it usually did, from venturing any further into self-revelation: but a reasonable guess might be that the difficulties to which he referred stemmed from radical anxieties about his role. Faulkner had recently been shattered by the rejection of *Flags in the Dust*. He was, he must have felt, failing as a writer. At the same, he seemed to be failing in a more conventional male role: for he was, after all, still living at home – in the house of a father he depised – while his younger brothers had married and were producing offspring. Certainly, the role of lover was one that appeared to be available: Estelle Oldham had returned to Oxford and was in the process of getting a divorce. But, quite apart from the fact that Faulkner, like all his romantic protagonists, feared consummation as much as he desired it, there was the brutal truth that Estelle herself was no longer the young virgin he had originally pursued – she was a mature woman with two children of her own. Writer, patriarch, lover: these possibilities must have teased him with particular force at this time. He had passed his thirtieth birthday a short while ago: but he was still not secure in his vocation, he was still not his own householder (a crucial consideration in the patriarchal culture into which he had been born), and he was confronted with the probability of marriage to a woman who, at one and the same time, was and was not the lost girl of his dreams, the childhood playmate with whom he had fallen in love.

Not unconnected to all this, as an explanation of why Faulkner loved *The Sound and the Fury* above all his other novels, was the intensely personal strategy of displacement and compensation at work here: 'I who never had a sister', as he was to put it, '. . . set out to make myself a beautiful and tragic little girl.' The other reasons for the special status enjoyed by *The Sound and the Fury*, in fact, gather around this one: its author's utter devotion to the figure of Caddy Compson. Explaining why a short story grew into a novel, Faulkner spoke with an open, autobiographical candour that was unusual for him – *except*, that is, when he was talking about the sister the Compson brothers had loved and lost. 'I loved her so much', he said,

> I couldn't decide to give her life just for the duration of a short story. She deserved more than that. So my novel was created, almost in spite of myself.[14]

To an extent that was to be unmatched in any of his other work, Faulkner made a woman the abiding, guiding presence of his fourth novel; and, in doing so, he raised the whole problem of otherness with a fierceness and intensity that could hardly have been anticipated from a reading of *Soldier's Pay*, *Mosquitoes*, or *Flags in the Dust/Sartoris*. The question of just how, if at all, the shimmering light of reality is related to the artifacts we make, the words we use, the myths we devise: that question hovers behind every section of the book. The voices that debate here not only rehearse the experiences of abandonment and substitution that went into their making; they invite us, through their debate, critically to investigate those experiences themselves. Through a complex and constantly fluctuating series of relations between those speaking, those being spoken to, and those being spoken of, Faulkner obliges the reader (who is, of course, one of those being spoken to) to see the language that is the medium of the novel also as its subject: to recognize how we constitute our reality, personal and social, with the words we use.

Just how seminal the figure of Caddy was in the making of *The Sound and the Fury* is suggested by Faulkner's famous account of how he came to write the book. She was, he claimed, the novel's source and inspiration. 'It began with a mental picture', he said,

> I didn't realize at the time it was symbolical. The picture was of the muddy seat of a little girl's drawers in a pear tree where she could see through a window where her grandmother's funeral was taking place and report what was happening to her brothers on the ground below.[15]

Not only its source, she was also the book's subject. 'To me she was the beautiful one', Faulkner admitted,

> she was my heart's darling. That's what I wrote the book about and I used the tools which seemed to me the proper tools to try to tell, try to draw the picture of Caddy.[16]

And not only *that*, she could also be seen as its ideal audience: that is, if Dawson Fairchild in *Mosquitoes* is to be believed. 'Every word a writing man writes', Fairchild declares, 'is put down with the intention of impressing some woman.' This is pretty arguable as a general proposition, perhaps, but it seems to have had some personal force: Faulkner had said as much about himself, and his motives as a writer, in the 1925 essay, 'Verse Old and Nascent'. And, even if it is rejected as pure mischief, two further points can hardly be denied: that it was from Caddy's story that Faulkner tried to 'extract some ultimate distillation' by telling it four or five times, and that it was while trying to extract this distillation, to capture this essence, that he seems to have experienced certain quite extraordinary feelings. As he put it later, what was absent in the preparation of *As I Lay Dying* was precisely what made the writing of *The Sound and the Fury* such a painful pleasure:

> that emotion definite and physical and yet nebulous to describe; that ecstasy, that eager and joyous faith and anticipation of surprise which the yet unmarred sheet beneath my hand held inviolate and unfailing, waiting for release.[17]

At the very least, such feelings matched in intensity the ones he attributed to the Compson brothers, Quentin and Benjy: in their intensity, that is, their ephemerality, and also in their sexual connotations.

So Caddy Compson was and is the novel's beginning, middle and end, its *raison d'être* just as, we are told in *Flags in the Dust*, Narcissa Benbow was the reason why her brother Horace's 'chastely serene' vase was brought into existence. Both book and vase, we could say, represent an attempt to imitate the shape of the beloved object, the curves of her being, and a possible way of commemorating, containing her. Imitation and containment are not so easy, however. Faulkner may well 'try to tell, try to draw the picture of Caddy' in words, but she seems somehow to resist his efforts; she seems to exist apart from or beyond the narrative frame, and so escape the clutches of Faulkner and all the other storytellers. To some extent, this is because she is the absent presence familiar from many of Faulkner's other novels. Far more important, though, is the related but separate fact that she is a woman – and a peculiarly haunting woman even by her creator's own standards. She is Eve and Lilith, virgin and whore, mother, sister, daughter and lover, and she is these with an unmatched passion, a ferocious intensity. She is also a nymph and a maternal figure, combining many of the teasing qualities of Cecily Saunders with the soft receptiveness and warm protectiveness of Margaret Powers: a slim, boyish, active figure like Pat Robyn who yet also, to her brothers' despair, has some of the 'mindless rifeness', the 'supine potential fecundity' of Jenny Steinbauer. In short, Caddy is compounded of paradox to a degree that is rare even among Faulkner's female characters. So it is hardly surprising that, while she is there in the sense that she is the focal point, the eventual object of each narrator's meditations, she is not there to the extent that she remains elusive, intangible – as transparent as the water, and as invisible and disconcerting as the odours of trees and honeysuckle, with which she is constantly associated. More than any of Faulkner's women – more even than Eula Varner – she is 'too much' for her men, too various and unpredictable for them to handle. As each of them, including the author, tries to focus her in his camera lens she seems to slip away, leaving little more than the memory of her name and image.[18]

Not that Faulkner ever stops trying to bring her into focus – for himself, his narrators, and of course for us. Each section of the book, in fact, represents a different series of strategies, another attempt to know her. Not only that, each asks us to consider what 'knowing' means: how the human subject uses voices, and is used by voices, as he tries to position himself in the world. Essentially, the difference in each section is a matter of code and rhetoric: in the sense that each time the tale is told another language, an alternative model is devised and a different set of relationships occurs between author, narrator, subject and reader. The opening section, for instance, is marked by an attempt to melt language and experience down into a series of separate, all equally egocentric, units, and to obliterate the distance between narrator, subject and reader. Benjy wants to ignore the otherness of his sister; and for him, unlike his older brother Quentin, this seems to involve very few immediate problems since, according to his own radically limited perception of things, otherness simply does not exist. There is nothing 'out there', as he sees it, everything is merely an extension, an adjunct of his own being. A major purpose of Benjy's discourse is, in fact, to deny the irreducible reality and particularity of the objective world and to absorb every experience, each person or thing that confronts him, into a strictly closed system. There are other denials, too. The reader, for instance, is simply ignored; there is no attempt made to address him or explain things to him, because his otherness is never acknowledged any more than Caddy's is. Even the gap between thing and word, Caddy as she is and Caddy as she is perceived and named, is extinguished in Benjy's consciousness; for him, the signified and the signifier are one and the same. This emerges on the very first page of the book, when the punning cry of golfers, 'caddie', is enough to make Caddy present for her idiot brother: she is there for him, it seems, because her name is there.

'I was trying to say', says Benjy at point, when he recalls the time he chased some schoolgirls, confusing them with his lost sister,

> and I caught her, trying to say, and she screamed and I was trying to say and trying and the bright shapes began to stop and I tried to get out. I tried to get off of my face, but the bright shapes were going again. They were going up the hill to where it fell away . . . and I tried to keep from falling off the hill and I fell off the hill into the bright whirling shapes.[19]

This passage is fairly typical of Benjy's habits of language and perception, and it shows how rigidly constricted they are. Vocabulary is kept to a minimum; the sentences are simple, declarative and repetitive; and the distinction between predicate (once again, a girl) and subject (Benjy, who does not even see her, realize who she is) is almost completely flattened out. Benjy's 'trying to say' involves little more than an attempt to simplify by identifying knowing with being – an attempt, not to understand and communicate, but to reduce everything to a private code; and, in response to it, the reader is likely to fluctuate much of the time between feelings of strangeness and defamiliarization and a more radical, less pleasurable sense of alienation.

Another way of putting all this is to say that Benjy's response to division is noise. Faced with the loss of anything, from Caddy to a condom tin, he howls. Of course, he is told to 'hush' (the word runs like a refrain through the section), but the noises he makes do either get him what he wants or, if what he wants is Caddy herself, allow him to labour under the delusion that he has got it. Benjy's section almost seems to parody the idea that language at once reveals and conceals absence: except of course, that as the author constantly reminds us he does not actually employ language. 'He can't talk', observes one character: 'he deef and dumb', declares another. 'Surrounded by words he cannot use', as one recent commentary on Benjy puts it, 'he is used by words':[20] different voices occupy his consciousness, fight for attention and supremacy, while he himself inhabits silence. The devastating corollary of this is that, if 'to be means to communicate', then the youngest Compson brother does not properly exist: he may identify knowing with being but, strictly speaking, there is no being there – which is to say, no speaking consciousness, no human agent. From one point of view, Benjy's project – or, to be more exact, the project that Faulkner gives voice to in this section – is, certainly, egocentric to an extreme: an absorption of otherness in self. From another point of view, however – and it is the one determined by the section as a whole rather than just Benjy's vocal activities within it – that project is ultimately ego-less: since the figure called 'Benjy' flattens out into a series of mute com-munications, failed interactions, an arena for other people's words. This helps to explain a third response the reader is likely to have when reading the opening pages of *The Sound and the Fury*: pleasure issuing from trans-gression, the kinds of freedom offered by a vocal field without a determinate subject. Defamiliarization and alienation there certainly is, as the reader struggles to 'make sense' of what is being said: but there is also the sense of play that comes from sharing the punning associations, enjoying the liberty of verbal and mental processes without anchorage and, indeed, without any evident boundaries. Benjy invades otherness appropriating it to himself, otherness invades him obliterating his subjective space: these are really only different ways of making the point that the subject/object distinction is effectively collapsed because there is no sense of speech struggling towards identification here. A remark made about Benjy in the first chapter now needs qualifying. As a character, of course, Benjy does exist because of his voices, the dialogues that he cannot literally have: as a human subject, however, he does not, and for precisely the same reason.

Undoubtedly, there is something of Faulkner in Benjy: not least because Faulkner occasionally seemed to share the feeling generated by the first section that words have a talismanic power, and can summon into being the things they describe. But as he himself intimated, there was consider-ably more of him in Caddy's oldest brother. Faulkner tends to identify with Quentin to the point where the second section can become almost impenetrably private – or, alternatively, can gravitate towards familiar Faulknerian cadences, as if protagonist and narrator were able to speak with one voice. On his way home by train, for instance, Quentin sees a black man with a mule and, as he leans out the window, looking back at them – 'the two of them shabby and motionless and unimpatient . . . with the quality of shabby and timeless patience, of static serenity . . .' – it is difficult to tell whether it is he or his creator who is doing the talking. For his part, Quentin tries to abolish the distance between Caddy and himself – although, of course, not being insane he is less successful at this than Benjy; and he tends sometimes to address the reader or, at least, try to address him and, sometimes, like his idiot brother, to forget him. Whether addressing the reader or not, however, his language remains intensely claustrophobic: based not on a logic of the senses as Benjy's is, nor on the appearance of rational logic as is Jason's, but on a tortuous and convo-luted series of personal associations. The style is intense and disjointed, ranging between attempts at orderly narration and uncontrolled stream-of-consciousness. Quentin, it is clear, is continually attempting to place things within conventional linguistic structures only to find those struc-tures slide away or dissolve:

The three-quarters began. The first note sounded, measured and tranquil . . .
and that's if people could only change one another for ever that way merge

like a flame swirling up for an instant then blown cleanly out along the cool
eternal dark . . . it seemed to me that I could hear whispers secret surges
smell the beating of hot blood under wild unsecret flesh watching against
red eyelids the swine untethered in pairs rushing coupled into the sea . . .[21]

The disintegration of syntax in passages like this one finds its analogue, in
the second section as a whole, in Quentin's failure to tell his story in an
orderly manner. Quentin cannot quite subdue the object to the word,
painfully though he wants to; equally, he cannot quite construct a coherent narrative for himself because, in losing Caddy, he has lost what Henry
James would call its 'germ' – the person, that is, who made sense of all the
disparate elements of his life by supplying them with an emotional centre.

Throughout the second section, in both the time present and the times
past of the narrative, Quentin is struggling like Benjy to find the words
that will summon Caddy into being: as if, like the boys he hears discussing
how they will spend the money they will receive for the fish they have not
caught, his mere speaking will make 'of unreality a possibility, then a
probability, then an incontrovertible fact'.[22] He cannot speak to Caddy,
however, any more than he can speak to her parodic equivalent, the little
Italian girl who follows him on the last day of his life. He cannot get her
or get to her, nor even like Benjy persuade himself that he has done so:
even his memories recall his inability to take Caddy when she offers herself
to him in the linked unions of love ('come here Quentin') and death
('push it are you going to'). The portrait of Quentin is an incisive examination of the self-destructive paradoxes of romantic desire: the oldest
Compson brother, like the narrator of Faulkner's earliest poems, pursues
a phantom that is simultaneously Eros and Thanatos – a 'Little sister
Death' figuring his own instinctive equation of desire with language and
living and consummation with silence and death. He moves towards a
healing of division that is also annihilation; and, as he does so, he reminds
the reader that to an extent this is another 'impossible dialogue' – in this
case not because the speaker is speaking out of the silence of insanity, as
in Benjy's case, but because, like the persona in some of Emily Dickinson's
poems, he is speaking out of the silence of the grave. He speaks too in a
speech that, like his youngest brother's, is not just full of other people's
words but overpowered by them: voices from the narrative present and the
past colonize Quentin's mind, mastering him even while he is trying to
achieve mastery. The voices are multiple: Faulkner uses his control of
different idioms here to dramatize the sheer variety as well as the weight
of the talk that burdens Quentin. One voice in particular, however, tends
to drown out the others, and it is what Bakhtin would call 'the voice of the
fathers': that is, an authoritative discourse issuing out of some epic past,
which requires not active collaboration but passive repetition – resignation
and obedience.

Most obviously, the voice of the fathers is heard in the voice of the
father: the plangent, melancholy voice of Mr Compson is there right from

the first page of the section, reminding Quentin that 'women are never virgins', that 'no battle is ever won' and that 'man is conceived by accident . . . with dice already loaded against him'. Like Faulkner's own voice, Mr Compson's tends sometimes to blend into Quentin's, dyeing it with the colours of his own corrosive cynicism in a process that is so subtle it is scarcely observed. The voice of the fathers works in another, more radical way, however: not in this particular voice or in that but in the model, the series of assumptions that Quentin uses to mediate between himself and the world. Unlike his brother Benjy, Quentin has an instinctive sense of how life should be, which derives most of its force from notions of gentility and *noblesse oblige* traditionally attached, in the South, to the plantation aristocracy. Much of the comedy in this section, in fact, derives from Quentin's absurdly misplaced idea of himself as 'a half-baked Galahad' (to quote Caddy's husband, Herbert Head), 'a champion of dames' (to cite Quentin's friend at Harvard, Spoade): in short, a gentleman of the old school. For example, at one point he tries rather disingenuously to dissuade Caddy from marriage by telling her that her prospective husband 'was dropped from his club for cheating at cards': a remark that draws the gloriously sardonic reply, '*I'm not going to play cards with* [him].' The comedy always has a serious thrust, though: as Quentin's relationship with blacks memorably illustrates. Not surprisingly, given that he sees himself as a young Southern gentleman, Quentin tries to adopt a paternalist role with black people: throwing quarters to grateful darkies ('Thanky, young master. Thanky'), and making arrangements for Deacon, his black factotum at Harvard, to inherit one of his suits of clothes after he commits suicide. Black people, in turn, play the role of Uncle Tom with him: for convenience's sake, it may be, in order to survive – and in Deacon's case for the purpose of exploiting the 'young master', making him 'completely subjugated' and dependent. 'A nigger', reflects Quentin, 'is not so much a person as a form of behaviour, a sort of obverse reflection of the white people he lives among';[23] and while, as this remark indicates, Quentin knows he is being exploited by his black 'guide mentor and friend' he can never do anything about it. The reason is simple. The role Deacon plays fits perfectly into the idealized version of things that Quentin has constructed – or, rather, has had constructed for him: a version that has himself as gentleman at its centre, and the purity of white womanhood (and of one white woman in particular) as its emblem and apotheosis. In this case, Faulkner is not as he was in *Flags in the Dust/Sartoris* being mastered by an epic past: he is offering a powerful analysis of the whole process of mastery, the way the 'voice of the fathers' exercises control. In the process, he is also offering a slyly subversive comment on the patriarchal model of his region, with its assumptions about paternalist responsibility, its allegiance to fixed standards of refinement, and its careful deployment of male and female roles, white and black.

If the second section of the novel draws some of its power from Faulkner's anatomizing of the patriarchal model, then the third involves among other

1. Faulkner's great-grandfather, William Clark Falkner, 'The Old Colonel', near the time of his death, in 1889. (Brodsky Collection, copy supplied by Center for Faulkner Studies, Southeast Missouri State University)

2. Faulkner's grandfather, John Wesley Thompson Falkner, 'The Young Colonel', in his Masonic uniform. (Courtesy Dean Faulkner Wells)

3. Faulkner's mother, Maud Falkner, when she was a young woman. (Courtesy of Dean Faulkner Wells)

4. The courthouse, with Confederate monument, centre of Oxford, Mississippi, where Faulkner spent most of his life. (Courtesy of UPI/Bettman Archive)

5. Faulkner at the age of eleven (second from the left, middle row), with schoolmates at Oxford Graded School, 1908. (Courtesy Brodsky Collection, copy supplied by Center for Faulkner Studies, Southeast Missouri State University)

6. Caroline Barr, 'Mammie Callie', the African-American woman who helped to raise Faulkner and his brothers. (Courtesy Brodsky Collection, copy supplied by Center for Faulkner Studies, Southeast Missouri State University)

7. Estelle Oldham, later to become Faulkner's wife, in 1913 when she was seventeen.

8. Faulkner posing in the uniform of an R.A.F. flying officer, probably in December, 1918. (Courtesy Brodsky Collection, copy supplied by Center for Faulkner Studies, Southeast Missouri State University)

a colonnade, and the nine white column of the colonnade are nine muses standing like votive candles before a blue mountain, they are nine candles flaming quiet circles on the ceiling of a marble pavilion where a young man, surrounded by slaves, lies sleeping, and the sky behind the pavilion is a curtain of purple velvet painted with stars in heavy gold. Do you not see how the sky sags with the weight of the

7

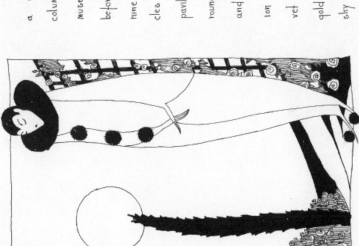

9. 'Pierrot Standing', drawn by Faulkner for his play *The Marionettes*, 1920. (Courtesy William Faulkner Collection [#6271-aj] Special Collections Department, Manuscript Division. University of Virginia Library)

10. Helen Baird, whom Faulkner met and fell in love with in 1925. (Courtesy of William B Wilson Collection of William Faulkner Manuscript Department, Howard-Tilton Memorial Library, Tulane University)

things an even more ruthlessly critical look at the residues of Southern populism. Jason Compson has been compared by several critics to some of the protagonists of Southwestern humour, such as Sut Lovingood, the protagonist and narrator of *Sut Lovingood's Yarns* (1867) by George Washington Harris: because of his racy colloquial speech, his brutal wit, and brutally sensible – not to say, selfish and opportunistic – approach to things. A more appropriate comparison, however, would be with Twain's Pap Finn or one of Faulkner's own earlier creations, the anonymous vagrant in 'Mirrors of Chartres Street'. Like Pap Finn and, to a lesser extent, that unnamed beggar, Jason Compson offers a comic portrait of white populist bigotry, a man whose verbal energy is matched only by his detestation of blacks, women, Jews, intellectuals, Yankees, bankers or anyone else who appears to threaten his self-esteem. Not only that, like Mark Twain, Faulkner does what he did – admittedly, with far less conviction and dramatic bite – in his New Orleans sketch: he combines a satirical dissection of his character's greed, hypocrisy and egotism with evident delight in him – not, that is, in his opinions and prejudices but in him as an imaginative creation, provoking humour and horror and condemning himself out of his own, forever open mouth. Which is to say that Faulkner is evidently fascinated by this figure he has brought into existence, even while he is disgusted by him, not that he feels in any way close or affectionate; on the contrary, the Jason section is masked by a much greater sense of distance than the others – a much larger gap, not only between author and narrator, but between narrator, subject and reader. Faulkner is clearly out of sympathy with this Compson brother, even if he is amused by him. His admission that he disliked Jason most of all his characters was mentioned earlier; and maybe it is not irrelevant to add that, according to Maud Falkner at least, Jason speaks just like William's father Murry did – the voice of the fathers is being mocked and subverted here with a vengeance! Jason, in turn, while obviously obsessed with his sister never claims any intimacy with her: even his struggle to get at her – which, in his case, means to get revenge on her – is mostly transacted at secondhand, by way of the figure of Caddy's daughter Quentin. And the reader too is denied intimacy, kept at a remove by the specifically public mode of speech Jason uses – which is full of swagger, exaggeration, saloon-bar bigotry and desperate attempts to bolster his image of himself:

Once a bitch always a bitch, what I say . . .

. . .

I never promise a woman anything nor let her know what I'm going to give her. That's the only way to manage them. Always keep them guessing. If you can't think of any other way to surprise them, give them a bust on the jaw . . .[24]

The rhetoric in the Jason section is insistent and declamatory: 'what I say', 'like I say', 'I say' are phrases that constantly recur, as the speaker unknowingly exposes his attempt to use words as weapons, to get on and to get back at the world. Its key is self-justification and its aim is normalcy: Jason longs to attach himself to one of life's normal plots,[25] no longer to be a part of the insane incoherences of the Compson story. Critics have sometimes been disappointed that, after the disjunctive modernist poetry of the first two sections, the reader is returned to something that sounds more conventional – as if, say, James Joyce had suddenly been transmogrified into Arnold Bennett – but to be disappointed by this is to mistake what is going on here. Like his brothers, Jason Compson doubts the integrity of his own identity. The only, but crucial, difference is that he interprets this doubt in strictly materialist terms: when he panics, it is time to go to his cash box. His main revenge on the other members of his family is to steal from them: to trick them out of their substance so as to aggrandize himself, to fill the gap where his subjectivity should be. Money = identity = plot: the equation links the idea of self-identity, of which Jason fiercely feels the lack, to the substantial items of hard cash and straight stories. It is in this spirit, surely, that the more conventionally linear narrative and demotic speech of the third section should be viewed, not as a surrender to mainstream novelistic norms but as a critique of them: which is to say, as an analysis of the empiricist, utilitarian values to which they allude – and to which, however perversely, Jason would like to lay claim. Jason hungers to be the man of sense: the person who, in conspicuous contrast to the rest of the family, does something useful, deals with the facts and makes something out of them. One irony of this section, however, is that his 'realistic' strategies are no less of an artifice, a construct predicated on certain assumptions about how things are and how they should be, than those of his brothers are. And a further irony is that such strategies serve only to aggravate Jason's dilemma: in the last analysis, he is not only distanced from author, subject and reader, he is distanced from himself, since his pretensions to normalcy *are* an absurd mask. A vividly self-contradictory character, he conceals his irrationality behind vociferous appeals to common sense and reason, invokes principles he never practises, and tries to suppress his precarious sense of his own subjectivity by adopting the role of a straight-talking, hard-working hell-of-a-fellow. Quite as much as his two brothers, Jason uses an idiom that hardly begins to bridge the gap between himself and the world, or to heal his divisions; and in his case otherness is not only resisted, it is blamed.

The final section of the novel never fails to come as a surprise: not least because the reader is suddenly addressed directly and with consideration, in an attempt to communicate that scrupulously avoids the self-conscious swaggering of Jason's monologue. Caddy, in turn, is recalled with warmth, but with the acknowledgement, at least, that she is a separate person whose separateness needs to be remembered and respected. And Faulkner himself, or to be more exact the implied author, appears as a distinct voice and distinctive presence, ready to engage with the characters and their points of view while describing them strictly from the outside. In effect, all the relationships here between author, narrator, subject and reader are characterized by a combination of intimacy and detachment; while the language carries us into a world where significant contact between quite separate individuals does at least appear to be possible. This brief passage, taken from the account of the Easter Day service, measures something of the alteration:

> The preacher . . . tramped steadily back and forth . . . hunched, his hands clasped behind him. He was like a worn small rock whelmed by the successive waves of his voice. With this body he seemed to feed the voice that, succubus like, had fleshed its teeth in him. And the congregation seemed to watch with its own eyes while the voice consumed him, until he was nothing and they were nothing and there was not even a voice but instead their hearts were speaking to one another in chanting measures beyond the need for words . . .[26]

For once the closed circle of interiority is broken, the sense of the concrete world is firm, the sensory outlines of things finely and even harshly etched, the rhythms exact, evocative and sure. And yet, and yet . . . despite all that, the language is emphatically figurative, obsessively artificial; and the stress throughout is on appearance and impression, what *seems* to be the case rather than what is. We are still not being told the whole truth, the implication is, there remain limits to what we know; despite every effort, in fact, even this last section of the novel does not entirely succeed in naming Caddy. So it is not wholly surprising that, like the three Compson brothers, the congregation described here is eventually tempted to discard language altogether. In this respect, Benjy's howling, Quentin's suicide and Jason's moments of impotent, speechless fury find their equivalent in 'chanting measures beyond the need for words': in all four instances, the characters place a question mark over their attempts to turn experience into speech by turning aside from naming, to seek deliverance and redress in a non-verbal world.

The fourth section of *The Sound and the Fury* is sometimes termed 'the Dilsey section': which is to forget that Dilsey Gibson hardly monopolizes the reader's attention here. On the contrary, almost as much space is devoted to Jason and Benjy as is directed at her. In other words, even if the conventional wisdom is accepted, that Dilsey – in the words of one critic – 'is the symbol of resurrection and life' in whom 'the moral light rays emanating from Jesus . . . burn brightly': then we have to remind ourselves that even here almost as many pages are given over to shadow, something that casts a further pall over things. The feverish haste of Jason, bent on pursuit of his niece, offers an unmistakable contrast to the deliberate rituals of Dilsey and the Easter Day congregation; his pride, rage and isolation clearly set themselves against their sense of collective voice and movement; above all, his experience of blockage and frustration, of not getting what he wants in any respect, provides a brutal response to their evident feelings of spiritual consummation – the belief, put in the mouth of Dilsey, that they have 'seed de first en de last . . . seed de beginnin, en de endin'. With Benjy, who takes over the very last pages of the novel, matters are slightly more complicated because the sense of an ending appears to be at once underlined and denied by his actions: things seem at once complete and incomplete. To an extent, the very reintroduction of the youngest Compson brother carries us back to the beginning of the book, as if the author were making a desperate attempt to have the wheel come full circle. And the feeling of circularity is reinforced by the reappearance of certain familiar motifs, including the fence, the golfers, and Benjy's habit of whimpering and moaning. Even the famous last lines of the novel seem at first sight intended to round things off, and put everything in its appropriate place. The objects of this world have now been arranged, the initial impression is, the artifact has been completed and can stand there in its own right, entire and 'chastely serene'.

> The broken flower drooped over Ben's fist and his eyes were empty and blue and serene again as cornice and facade flowed smoothly once more from left to right; post and tree, window and doorway, and signboard, each in its ordered place.[27]

The problem is, of course, that this is the order of an idiot, dependent on certain radical acts of exclusion. It is as if Faulkner were reminding us that the ending of *The Sound and the Fury* is no ending at all: that it represents, at most, a continuation of the process of speech – the process, that is, of trying to put things 'each in its ordered place' – and an invitation to us, the readers, to continue that process too. Benjy's 'empty' eyes are poignant reminders that no system is ever complete or completely adequate. Something is always missed out it seems, some aspect of reality must invariably remain unseen; and, since this is so, no book, not even one like this that uses a multiplicity of speech systems, can ever truly be said to be finished. Language can be a necessary tool for understanding and dealing with the world, the only way we can hope to know Caddy; yet perversely, Faulkner suggests, it is as much a function of ignorance, idiocy, as of knowledge. It implies absence, loss, as well as fulfilment.

'The best failure': the triumph of *The Sound and the Fury* issues from Faulkner's recognition that we make our identities, personal and communal, out of a process of speech that is continuous and open-ended – an active, historically situated exchange of words that, as far as literature is concerned, involves author, narrator, character *and* reader. Its failure, if that is the right word, is inseparable from this recognition. No human experience is ever complete; there is no last word to be spoken; absence and unfinality are inevitable, even – or, rather, especially – in a book like this one that accepts absence and unfinality as the preconditions of its existence. Absence in *The Sound and the Fury* is not, however, just a matter of the 'empty centre' Caddy: the denial of whose subjectivity it is, after all, precisely the purpose of the novel to investigate. It reaches beyond this, to an extent of which Faulkner – and, quite probably, the white reader – is hardly aware. Along with Caddy Compson, there is one other main character, one major human subject whose subjectivity is denied; and that is the figure who is constantly offering commentary on what she calls 'Compson devilment', Dilsey Gibson. Like all the black characters in the book – for instance, the anonymous black man Quentin sees from the train – Dilsey is presented as an object, from the outside. The presentation is powerfully eloquent, certainly, but it never goes beyond appearances: Dilsey is always separated from narrator and reader by a thin membrane of descriptive detail and dialect speech. More to the point, she and her family are never permitted their own history. What little we know about them or hear from them normally functions as marginalia:

> 'That's what I tell you,' Roskus said. 'They ain't no luck going to be on no place where one of they own chillen's name ain't never spoke.'
> 'Hush,' Dilsey said, 'Do you want to get him started.'
> 'Raising a child not to know its own mammy's name,' Roskus said.[28]

This choric role extends beyond what the black characters say or do to what they are. Dilsey's main characteristic is the one she shares with the anonymous black man with a mule whom Quentin encounters, or for that matter with the black people in *Soldier's Pay* and *Sartoris*: 'unimpatience', a serenity or imperturbability that renders her immune to 'Compson devilment'. The sound and the fury of time, change and separation are things she perceives, apparently, but, along with other black people in the book, never has to share.

This is not simply to equate the narrative stance towards Dilsey and other black characters with that of, say, Quentin Compson; although it is noticeable that the voices of the narrator and Quentin do seem to blend at exactly those moments when black people become the object of attention. But it is to suggest that, as far as black characters are concerned at least, Faulkner is carrying over a habit from his earlier work: the character is denied his or her subjective status, and then is either mocked or admired for the actual consequences of that denial. Perceived as an object, Dilsey is then praised for being an object: that is, a character emphatically *not* drowning in the processes of her own subjectivity. Dramatized in terms of her 'indomitable' physical presence, the warmth of her household routines and the comforting familiarity of her talk, she is circumscribed by the very details of that dramatization. By definition, she can be no more than a rock-like figure of endurance, an emblem of the pieties of home and domestic ritual: she cannot, in effect, be afforded her own privacy. The white characters live in history, a world where identity is constructed out of verbal and social exchanges; they are seen as human subjects either struggling with their subjectivity or struggling against its denial. The black characters, however, dwell in a realm of timeless myth: here, character is not constructed, it is given – someone like Dilsey is mythicized, monumentalized into an embodiment of 'naturalness', while as a human agent she remains invisible.[29] What persuaded Faulkner in this direction is not difficult to guess. Dilsey, a character modelled in part on 'Mammy Callie', enshrines the brighter side of childhood memories: the comforts of kitchen, a warm bed and a secure maternal presence. *The Sound and the Fury* may be obsessed with the agonies of children, most of which Faulkner saw as stemming from the tyrannies of adults, but it has time too for their pleasures; and the memories of those pleasures – all that once prompted Faulkner to declare wistfully, 'It's over very soon' – tend to gather around the abiding figure of the black housekeeper, the one person who keeps the home fires burning. The personal nostalgia is compounded by a regional impulse, equally nostalgic, that would locate the security of natural rhythms and ancient rituals in the 'timeless' figure of the black man toiling in the fields or the black woman calmly going about her business in the kitchen. Behind the figure of Dilsey as earth mother and keeper of the rites, in other words, lies a powerfully pastoralizing tendency to which Faulkner was not the only white Southerner to be drawn. 'A nigger', Quentin had said, 'is not so much a person as . . . a sort of obverse reflection' of the white people who observe him; and, ironically, that is precisely the problem here – Dilsey is a reverse image of the white characters around her, and perhaps of her white creator into the bargain. She does not suffer the agonies of inwardness; her desire for completeness and closure 'de beginnin, en . . . de endin', has evidently been met; she is, we are asked to believe, exempt from desire and division. Hers is the human absence we are not asked to investigate, the loss of whose subjectivity measures, much more fiercely than the loss of Caddy's does, just how much knowledge can be a form of ignorance. *The Sound and the Fury* may be among Faulkner's finest novels: but, as Faulkner understood, even the finest books have their gaps and enact their own kinds of repression. Even here, to an extent that Faulkner could hardly suspect or most white readers even notice, language is accompanied by a certain silence.

III   A SOUTHERN CARNIVAL: *As I Lay Dying*

Faulkner's next published novel after *The Sound and the Fury* was not the next manuscript he worked upon: that was *Sanctuary*, written as Faulkner claimed later because he 'liked the sound of dough rising'. 'I got married', he explained, and in order to meet the expense of being a married man, 'I thought of the most horrific idea that I could think of and wrote it.' The empirical details are not quite right here: Faulkner was told of a grisly incident of sexual outrage similar to the one on which *Sanctuary* rests, and so was remembering as well as inventing. And the first version of the book was, in fact, written just before he was married, in the first few months of 1929. Nevertheless, the curious psychological process that Faulkner intimated remains intact, unaltered by these slight deviations from the literal truth: marriage – or, to be exact, the immediate prospect of marriage – led him into writing a book, as he put it, 'about a girl who gets raped with a corn cob'. Quite why this happened must be left for consideration until later, when the eventual published novel is discussed. All that needs to be mentioned here is the brutal irony that, if *Sanctuary* began life as a way of making money and an emotional safety-valve for a man suddenly realizing he was about to lose his bachelor status, then, as far as the first purpose was concerned at least, the immediate result was a dismal failure. Not only was Faulkner's new wife shocked when she was allowed to read the manuscript ('It's horrible', Estelle declared), his publishers were too: 'Good God', Faulkner invariably recalled his publisher telling him, 'I can't publish this. We'd both be in jail.' 'So I told Faulkner, "You're damned"', the novelist remembered (referring to himself, not for the first time, in the third person), 'You'll have to work now and then for the rest of your life.'[30] He took a night job and tried to write something quite different from both *Sanctuary* and *The Sound and the Fury* in his spare time. The title of the new book, *As I Lay Dying*, was taken from two different versions of the 'spotted horses' story that would eventually find a place for itself in *The Hamlet*; its social situation was that of *Father Abraham*, the world of the tenant farmers and poor whites of Mississippi; and its main characters, the Bundrens, were a group invented specifically for this novel, although as usual they carried traces of earlier, often autobiographical figures. Perhaps Faulkner's sense that he was for once fulfilling the conventional male roles of husband and provider made it easier for him to write, when he had the time. Whatever the reason, he worked with unusual ease and speed, so that the book was completed in just forty-seven days. Faulkner later described *As I Lay Dying* as 'a tour-de-force', which was perhaps a reference to its highly wrought nature: the narrative offers us fifteen different speakers and no less than fifty-nine sections ranging in length from several pages to one line. Certainly the description captures something of the sheer bravura of the book, its dizzying capacity to shift between not only different voices but different genres without allowing the reader time to adjust. Subversion is a characteristic of all Faulkner's best work, issuing out of his use of discontinuity, slipperiness of idiom and sudden gaps in the narrative. The subversive character of this particular book, however, is more confident, even cheekier, than most. The art of discomposing the reader is carried to an extreme: something measured by the fact that what is, arguably, the pivotal section of the novel is spoken by a corpse – a character mainly present in the narrative, up until the moment of her speaking, as a putrefying corpse persistently delayed on the way to a distant burial ground.

One reason why *As I Lay Dying* is such a disconcerting story is because we, the readers, are never allowed to be sure what we are reading. There is, certainly, a vein of knockabout comedy at work here, derived ultimately from the traditions of Southwestern humour: inviting us into a world of henpecked husbands and bossy wives (the Tulls), people falling victim to cruel practical jokes (Dewey Dell and the chemist), or suffering bizarre forms of physical pain (Cash and the cement cast on his broken leg). Even the basic premise of the story, involving the transportation of a corpse, growing smellier by the minute, past a gallery of variously shocked and amused spectators, is like a graveyard joke out of one of the cruder Southern folk tales – or, for that matter, like those versions of 'grotesque' humour that Poe enjoyed so much and tried to imitate in some of his work. Co-existing with this, however, is a vein of feeling tapped from elsewhere in Faulkner's regional tradition, inviting us to see the characters in a quite different, heroic mould. The Bundren's stoicism, the sheer tenacity they show in fulfilling their promise to Addie in defiance of fate, fire and flood, invites a comparison with those folk heroes who embodied Southerners' sense (and especially Southern poor folks' sense) of the troubles they had to face and the courage they needed to face them. The journey itself that forms the spine of the narrative, macabre though its physical consequences may be, is a trial of a kind, a way of testing strength and endurance; and the qualities the different members of the family reveal during the course of it seem intended to invite our respect along with our laughter. We are pained, impressed and amused – occasionally even at one and the same time. 'But I ain't so sho that ere a man has the right to say what is crazy and what ain't', observes Cash Bundren,

> It's like there was a fellow in every man that's done a-past the sanity or the insanity, that watches the sane and the insane doings of that man with the same horror and the same astonishment.[31]

Horror, astonishment, and more fundamentally the sense that we do not know how to feel or whether we can gauge a situation accurately: all this is likely to be incorporated into our response to a moment like that one, say, in which Cash himself has the cement cast removed from his leg. It is the doctor, Peabody, removing the cast, who is describing the incident:

> 'Don't you lie there and try to tell me you rode six days on a wagon without springs, with a broken leg and it never bothered you.'
> 'It never bothered me much,' he [Cash] said.
> '. . . And don't tell me it ain't going to bother you to lose sixty-odd square inches of skin to get that concrete off. And don't tell me it ain't going to bother you to have to limp around on one short leg for the balance of your life – if you walk at all again.
> 'Concrete,' I said, 'God Almighty . . . Does that hurt?'
> 'Not to speak of ,' he said, and the sweat big as marbles running down his face about the colour of blotting paper.
> 'Course not,' I said. '. . . If you had anything you could call luck, you might say it was lucky it was the same leg you broke before. . . .'
> 'Hit's what paw says,' he said.[32]

A further complicating factor at work here, contributing to readerly dis-composure, is the balladic quality of many of the sections. This is especially true of those moments when relatively minor characters like Vernon Tull or Samson take over the telling of the tale. They tell the story of the Bundren family and their journey to Jefferson – at least, as far as they encounter and know it – but, at the same time, they tell us about their own domestic rituals and how they and their neighbours pass the day in talk, rehearsing and recapitulating old tales, creating folk memory. It is surely no accident that Yoknapatawpha County is named in *As I Lay Dying*, since this is the first time in a completed novel that Faulkner shows how his characters 'name' their surroundings: which is to say, give them cultural identity by placing them within a communal story. The Bundren family are not only observed by their neighbours: they are situated within an accumulating store of legend, linked up in an apparently casual way to other people and other stories that are sometimes told, sometimes half-told, and sometimes simply referred to. The strategy is similar to that of a folksong or ballad, in which a particular story being remembered (and it does always seem that it is being remembered rather than invented) is given an additional depth and significance by the sense of the numerous other tales that lie behind it:

> It was just before sundown. We were sitting on the porch when the wagon came up the road . . . 'What's that?' MacCallum says: I can't think of his name: Rafe's twin: that one it was. 'It's Bundren from down beyond New Hope,' Quick says. 'There's one of them Snopes' horses Jewel's riding.'
> 'I didn't know there was ere a one of them horses left,' MacCallum says, 'I thought you folks down there finally contrived to give them all away.'[33]

In effect, no work of Faulkner's comes as close as *As I Lay Dying* does to illustrating the idea that the novel is an intentional and conscious hybrid. Faulkner presents us here with a narrative that, to the extent it draws on folk tale, folk epic, folk comedy and the ballad is recognizably embedded in the traditional cultures of the South. Where it appears to part company with those cultures, however, is in Faulkner's evident willingness to mix genres: to move between them, and sometimes collate them, in a way that openly invites 'horror and . . . astonishment'. Voices join to tell us about their lives, to agree, to present evidence or just to argue. No one voice can be regarded as authoritative but equally no voice can be discounted either; consequently, the narrative assumes a character that is even more frankly relativistic than most of Faulkner's major narratives are. All this is normally attributed to Faulkner's participation in modernism, with the gloss that *As I Lay Dying* is a comic novel. To call the story of the Bundrens comic, though, is hardly to do justice to its radical shifts of tone, the extent to which utterly contradictory emotions can be aroused even by the rendering of one incident – such as the episode of Cash and his cement cast. And while much of Faulkner's major fiction certainly invites the modernist comparison, it seems less apt here: the disjunctions in *As I Lay Dying* are far more unnerving, at least to readers unfamiliar with folk culture, than they are in, say, *The Sound and the Fury*. Instead of comic or modernist, perhaps this novel could more usefully be seen in terms of carnival: those rituals of subversion, barely organized riot and release, that every society – and every hierarchical society, in particular – seems to require. What takes place in carnival, according to Bakhtin, is 'a comical operation of dismemberment'. The audience is invited into a celebration of 'the social consciousness of the people' and the body as process: to witness the linked realities of an unruly folk culture and 'the grotesque body' – which is to say, 'the body in the act of becoming . . . never finished, never completed'.[34] The key to the forms of the carnival is that they are open, requiring participation: the audience is not so much apart from as a part of the proceedings, required to 'walk round' and take in events from all sides. Carnival offers the opposite of all those pieties on which the official culture rests: fixed rituals, the prerogatives of power and status, the respect and the closure that comes from distance. And its effect is not just to unsettle, it is to offer an alternative view of life, as human subjects are forced into riotous proximity with other, grotesque human subjects – and all are immersed in a dizzying process of change.

All of this means that, as we read *As I Lay Dying*, we are unable to pin down the Bundrens, to be sure about them even to the extent that we are 'sure' about, say, the Compsons. Each member of the family becomes as edgy, protean, and occasionally as baffling and grotesque – that is, as contrary to our expectations – as people that we know from our own intimate experience sometimes are. Take Dewey Dell, the one girl in the family group, who is young, unmarried and pregnant: she is presented differently by every voice that talks about or for her. Her youngest brother Vardaman, for instance, tries to locate her as a replacement for Addie and so practically worships her. What she says must be right, he feels, because *she* says it:

> The hill goes off into the sky . . . In Jefferson it is red on the track behind the glass. The track goes shining round and round. Dewey Dell says so.[35]

Anse Bundren on the other hand, the head of the family, describes Dewey Dell more as a thankless child – someone who will never allow anything he does, however slight, to pass without criticism. She is the guardian of the law for him as well, perhaps, but it is a law seen more as a nuisance than a need – the law, in a way, as understood by the congenital lawbreaker.

For all their differences, there is a clear connection between the assessments of father and brother; the woman, the reader may feel, remains the same in principle – only the judgement passed on that principle, the perspective from which it is seen, is altered. This is hardly true, however, of a third version of Dewey Dell, voiced by a boy who seduces her during the course of the journey. The story of his seduction sounds as if it could have come straight out of folk comedy, although folk comedy of a coarser, more robust kind than anything we are likely to come across in the *written* culture of nineteenth-century America. As assistant to the chemist in

Jefferson, and so someone who has gained a bogus medical status from his surroundings, the boy – called MacGowan – persuades Dewey Dell that the only way she can terminate her unwanted pregnancy is with 'a hair of the dog' that bit her. One act of intercourse, he advises, will cancel out another and he is ready to perform the service free of change when the shop is closed. He obviously has no misgivings about this, no sense of guilt over the trick he plays, and the reason is simple: he never thinks of Dewey Dell as a person. She is merely a type for him, a nice, juicy country girl who almost deservers to be duped as a punishment for her gullibility and seductive good looks:

> She looked pretty good. One of them black-eyed ones that look like she'd as soon put a knife in you as not if you two-timed her. She looked pretty good.[36]

From the moment when Dewey Dell walks into the chemist's store, she enters a world utterly different from the ones in which we have seen her up until then, a world where a different set of relations apply effectively turning her into a different person. It is like meeting an old friend unexpectedly in a strange place, perhaps, or with a new group of companions. A side of him or her we had never noticed before is suddenly exposed, and we are forced to reassess our assumptions of intimacy.

To talk simply about the characters who describe Dewey Dell from the sidelines is, of course, to leave one, crucial series of voices unaccounted for: those that belong to Dewey Dell herself, as she debates her situation in the world. The entire structure of *As I Lay Dying* is restlessly dialectical, involving a continual and rapid movement between character as object and character as subject – which means that someone like Dewey Dell can bring her own expressions of identity into the argument. She can tell us about dimensions of her personalty that no outside observer can properly know. Of course, her voices do not always operate at a submerged level. Very often all Faulkner does when he allows her to speak is remind us, in and through the use of the vernacular, that she is a country girl, a being defined on one level by her geographical and social surroundings. At such times, she comes closest to the kind of person others describe – as in this moment, when she talks about working in the fields with the man who then impregnated her:

> The first time me and Lafe picked on down the row . . . We picked on, . . . the woods getting closer . . . and the secret shade . . . with my sack and Lafe's sack. Because I said . . . if the sack is full when we get to the woods it won't be me. I said if it don't mean for me to do it the sack will not be full . . . but if the sack is full, I cannot help it . . . And we picked on toward the secret shade and our eyes would drown together . . .[37]

This is not simply colloquialism, though: that last phrase, 'our eyes would drown together', hardly belongs with the ordinary, everyday idioms of country speech. With its help, the reader is being shifted into a different dimension of voice, and of Dewey Dell's personality, and a more purely inward one at that. Here, words act as signs for the unarticulated and otherwise inarticulable impulses running through the character's consciousness: they are used as symbolic gestures rather than naturalistically – to chart, in Dewey Dell's case and others, how an apparently impassive character is actually drowning in his or her own subjectivity.

This is one of the main strategies Faulkner uses for disconcerting the reader: he pulls the verbal ground from beneath our feet, as it were, and from beneath the feet of the characters, forcing them and us to tumble down below the level of demotic speech into other, more dreamlike and dissociated, areas of language. Just when we think we have a clear picture of somebody like Dewey Dell, and can place her as an attractive, emotionally generous but rather simple-minded country girl, our assumptions are suddenly undermined – our snobbish detachment shown up for what it is – by the revelation of her inner fears and even despair. We move in under the equable surfaces of her behaviour to something else, a terror or sense of disaster by no means simple or simple-minded, that can only be expressed in the sort of language that works as much by rhythm and repetition as it does by any attempt at representation:

> I heard that my mother is dead. I wish I had time to let her die. I wish I had time to wish I had. It is because in the wild and outraged earth too soon too soon too soon. It is not that I wouldn't and will not it's that it is too soon too soon too soon.[38]

And that is not all. In case we now start to feel secure, when Dewey Dell's conscious fears have been expressed, Faulkner will occasionally offer us another jolt. Without any warning, he will take an abrupt step down beyond this towards an even more incantatory and imagistic level of speech that is intended to recover Dewey Dell's subconscious for us – the secret, subliminal impulses that help make her what she is or prompt her to do what she does. Here her dimly realized fear of losing her identity, which includes her fear of death but goes beyond it, becomes a controlling factor:

> The dead air shapes the dead earth in the dead darkness, farther away than seeing shapes the dead earth. It lies dead and warm upon me, touching me naked through my clothes. I said You don't know what worry is. I don't know what it is. I don't know whether I am worrying or not. Whether I can or not. I don't know whether I can cry or not. I don't know whether I have tried or not.[39]

Thanks to all this, character is transformed into process rather than product, seen as a state of perpetual becoming: there is no possibility of closure, no bedrock certainty here. A grotesque denial of any claims we might make for completeness, Dewey Dell – like the other major characters in *As I Lay Dying* – exists in the clash of voices, *between* the different consciousnesses that continually debate her. She, and they, offer the revelation that identity is made through activities of speech that can never be terminated or contained.

It is not always easy to live with the acceptance of this, the idea of identity as an intersubjective phenomenon realized through speech. Or, to put it more simply, we are generally happier with certainty: living with people we can pin down, and with a life that seems to have a settled meaning. The temptation to fix things is, consequently, always there: not only for the reader, as he or she struggles to 'know' the Bundrens, but for the characters themselves as Faulkner deploys them. In *As I Lay Dying*, people are constantly watching one another closely, as if the act of quiet, concentrated observation will put the observed in his or her place. As Addie Bundren dies, for instance, and 'all her failing life appears to drain into her eyes', she looks with simple ferocity at her family around her bed; they, in turn, look at each other or at her. The act of gazing seems intended to halt the processes of living, and dying, but it does not work here or anywhere else in the narrative. For the moment, under the pressure of the gaze, the subject may be translated into an object, apparently as solid and immobile as wood. But the figure frozen in time then moves again; the character that seemed 'made out of wood', 'with the rigid gravity of a cigar-store Indian', assumes a different, more fluid shape; the caravan, or carnival, passes on. This temptation to watch rather than participate, and so become incarcerated in one's own private world of observation, is shared by many of the characters. It is, however, Darl Bundren who carries it to an extreme. 'That's ever living thing the matter with Darl', comments Vernon Tull, 'he just thinks by himself too much.' He thinks; and he gazes. This permits him a special access to information at times, apparently. He seems to know, for example, when Addie is about to die, and to sense that Jewel is illegitimate and Dewey Dell pregnant. But it also deprives him of any sense of self-definition. Other members of his family feel the temptation simply to watch just as he does, and accordingly experience a slippage of identity; the temptation is embraced much more fiercely in his case, though, with the result that the slippage becomes complete disintegration, an utter lapse of being into nothingness. The extent of his slide can be measured: from those moments when he seems to see things hidden from others thanks to the sheer ferocity of his stare, through the weary nihilism to which his detached observations seem inevitably to lead ('how do our lives ravel out into . . . dead gestures of dolls'), to eventual dislocation of voice and consciousness. The last time this lonely watcher speaks, in fact, his voice seems to come from anywhere and nowhere: he is at once 'I', 'you', and 'he' as speech and mind slide into terminal division.

> Darl has gone to Jackson. They put him on the train, laughing, down the long car laughing, the heads turning like the heads of owls when he passed. 'What are you laughing at?' I said.

'Yes yes yes yes yes'
Two men put him on the train . . .[40]

To some extent, Darl enables his creator to investigate both the lure and the perils of privacy: like Faulkner, the second son of Addie and Anse Bundren is on the outside looking in at the other characters, trying to work out what it is that makes them tick. He is the author as observer, or even voyeur. Cash, in turn, is the author as craftsman, quietly devoting himself to the job just as Gordon in *Mosquitoes* does; while Jewel, 'his whole body earth-free' as he strains to tame and control his mount, summons up more primitive ideas of the author as horseman, fighting to overcome and direct instinctual energies. The dispersal of the author's sense of himself through three different but related consciousnesses is symptomatic of something else besides autobiography: which is the shifting, metamorphic nature of *As I Lay Dying* – language and identity are constantly slithering and blending in this novel. Vardaman, for example, speaks of a sense of personal identity that seems to *depend* upon intersubjectivity, identification with the other: 'Jewel is my brother . . . Darl is my brother . . . I am. Darl is my brother.' And, at another moment in the book, he talks of a fish that *is* his mother that *is* his father that *is* Cash and *is* Dewey Dell:

> And now it's all chopped up. I chopped it up. It's laying in the kitchen in the bleeding pan, waiting to be cooked and et. Then it wasn't and she was, and now it is and she wasn't. And tomorrow it will be cooked and et and she will be him and pa and Cash and Dewey Dell and there won't be anything in the box and so she can breathe.[41]

In this fluid verbal environment, there is not so much intimacy as identification – people and things *become* one another: 'My mother is a fish.' 'Jewel's mother is a horse.' Which makes naming intolerably difficult: nowhere else in Faulkner's work do characters have quite as many problems finding or inventing the right sign, speaking things into being, achieving even tentative, temporary articulation. In the more obviously public areas of speech, these problems encourage the habit of interpellation. Characters are constantly hailing one another, trying to summon the other into a particular, fixed identification, a definite, subject(ed) status: 'You, Cash!', 'You, Vardaman', 'You, Jewel!', The corollary of this is that, when they cannot name, they feel they cannot know. In a passage quoted earlier, for instance, Samson confesses in passing that he cannot remember the name of Rafe MacCallum's twin. The failure of naming dogs him so that, several pages after this, it comes to occupy the foreground of his attention. Not to know the name is not to know the man – to fail to identify and, to that extent, to lose control of the story:

> That MacCallum. He's been trading with me off and on for twelve years. I have known him from a boy up; I know his name as well as I do my own. But be durn if I can say it.[42]

In the more private arena, as far as voices in the mind are concerned, a similar failure to name usually provokes even more anxiety. There is real pain or panic felt nearly every time a character senses the forms of identification slipping away from him. To listen to Darl Bundren, for instance, talking about emptying himself for sleep, is the nearest verbal equivalent there is to watching a man trying to cling on to a greasy rock so as to save himself from drowning. The words slide and slither, and elide, even as he tries to pin them down, with the result that what begins as an attempt at self-identification – a struggle to fix and name the subject – ends in dizzying confusion, accompanied by desperate feelings of exile and loss:

> In a strange room you must empty yourself for sleep. And before you are emptied for sleep, what are you. And when you are emptied for sleep, you are not. And when you are filled with sleep, you never were. I don't know what I am. I don't know if I am or not ... I can hear the rain shaping the wagon ... And since sleep is is-not and rain and wind are *was*, it is not. Yet the wagon *is*, because when the wagon is *was*, Addie Bundren will not be. And Jewel *is*, so Addie Bundren must be ... How often have I lain beneath rain on a strange roof, thinking of home.[43]

The failure to name that Darl is confronted with in this passage may hit him with particular force, but it is an experience that is by no means unique to him. On the contrary, not only do the other characters share it at times, the reader of *As I Lay Dying* is likely to do so as well, as he or she becomes immersed in a text that seems to delight in transgression: in the carnival world of this novel, the familiar boundaries of explanation are there it seems only to be breached, the rules exist only to be broken. Even motivation defies closure. 'God's will be done', says Anse Bundren when his wife dies, 'Now I can get them teeth.' And critics ever since have been struggling gamely to construct coherent motives for Anse: to offer a consistent interpretation of this and other statements, and the journey that follows them. This usually involves wagging a moralistic finger at this clearly failed father-figure: telling him off for his apparent weakness, selfishness and cant. To treat Anse in this way, however, is to fall victim to some fairly banal notions about character, and to forget the intersubjective space in which he, like all the other characters, lives. Character in *As I Lay Dying* is existence not essence: Anse is caught in the stream of his actions, not in some monolith of fixed motive. He is present in the flux of different discourses, the riot of voices that constitute the narrative; and, as a result, he resists any attempt the reader may make to insert him in a set framework of interpretation, a stable and finished world. So, he goes to Jefferson to honour a promise he made to Addie to have her buried there. *And* he goes there to buy a new set of false teeth and, with the help of his improved appearance, to acquire a second wife. In marrying once again, he finds the sort of helpmeet, or rather drudge, he requires. And he also obtains by way of a dowry the gramophone for which his oldest son has always pined. Anse's motives for travelling to Jefferson are no more the one or

the other of these, than Anse himself is simply as one or the other voices
in the novel describes him. 'Anse. Why Anse. Why are you Anse',[44] asks
Addie. And we never have a complete answer; since, like all the other
characters in *As I Lay Dying*, he exists in constant metamorphosis, a climate of change. Thanks to the multiple voices of the narrative, we are
invited to walk around him and take in his identity, what choices compel
him, as a shifting, unfinalizable process. He offers, in short, a 'grotesque
body' that resists closure: and we must accept that offer – not, like Darl,
try to stand back, observe, then lower down on the observed some fixed
explanatory grid.

The resistance to closure, the opposition to stable forms of explanation,
is expressed most openly in the one section that is spoken by Addie
Bundren, when she is already dead. Addie rehearses her past life – her
childhood, her experience as a teacher, her marriage to Anse – and then
tries to explain what it has all taught her, the lesson that somehow she
now wants to pass on. 'I learned that words are no good', she says,

> that words don't ever fit even what they are trying to say at. When he [Cash]
> was born I knew that motherhood was invented by someone who never had
> to have a word for it because the ones that had the children didn't care
> whether there was a word for it or not. I knew that fear was invented by
> someone that had never had the fear; pride, who never had the pride ... so
> when Cora Tull would tell me I was not a true mother, I would think how
> words go up in a thin line, quick and harmless, and how terribly doing goes
> along the earth, clinging to it ...[45]

This, it seems, is a devastating assault on the harmful effects of language:
the way that speech systems – like any system devised to organize experience and enable knowledge – can castrate the personality and paralyse
experience, substituting for living a frozen series of signs. We talk, Addie
suggests, and as we do so we impoverish and distort what we are talking
about. Life, instead of being multidimensional, a various and constantly
altering process, is turned into a fixed quantity, something made up out
of the patterns of our syntax, the distinctions implicit in our vocabulary –
in short, out of our own painfully restricted and restricting stock of 'words'.

To say all this, however, is to miss out the obvious. Addie is talking,
telling us this. She herself is using words, and she is not just using them
as, say, a postmodernist writer might do – in a negative way, that is, so as
to locate their essential futility. She is actually trying to explain; she is
struggling to forge an adequate style, even while she argues that a style
adequate to any human occasion is impossible – including, it must be
inferred, this one. The circularity here is dizzying. Addie is deriding words;
she is using words; she is deriding her own use of them; she is, therefore,
simultaneously demonstrating and denying her own point. She is saying
and not saying: using language because she must (what else does she
have?), but intimating that language conceals even more than it reveals
and, in the process, calling into question her own use of language. It is

difficult to think of a more subversive strategy, a more radical way of shifting the ground beneath the reader's feet. What at first sight looks like the 'message' of the book denies the viability of 'messages' from anyone, let alone 'messages' from a decaying corpse. There is no need to labour the point to see what is going on here: to add, for instance, that any woman who denies one child (Darl) and, by her own admission, 'gave'[46] two others away emotionally (Dewey Dell and Vardaman) is hard to describe as 'a true mother' – which further casts into doubt Addie's claims to have 'learned'. What is clear from all this is that even the authority of an apparently authoritative statement about the unauthoritativeness of words is seen to be unauthoritative: the terms in which it is communicated at once support and subvert the communication. To this extent, the section devoted to Addie is true to the carnival spirit of the book as a whole, it can even be regarded as a kind of paradigm: here as elsewhere, one voice speaks but even in its speaking its silences and exclusions are noted – its truth, the reader can sense, is also a form lying.

All of which is to say that meaning is to be found in *As I Lay Dying* where character is: in the warring space between voices, the process of debate. True to the discomfiting rituals of the carnival, the reader learns by being seduced by a particular voice, a certain way of looking at personality and behaviour, and then being quietly mocked or chided for permitting the seduction. Expectations are raised only to be reversed, so that a lesson can be carried to us on the back of our own shattered preconceptions. Do we think the Bundrens are involved in a heroic quest, like something out of Homeric legend? One remark by an observer, comparing the Bundren wagon as it comes into town to 'a piece of rotten cheese coming into an ant-hill', appears to persuade us that we are wrong. So can we assume the observer is right? Hardly, because no sooner has he spoken than we are back with the family again, sharing in their journey and in the agony that seems to give it epic proportions. One vocabulary is suddenly jettisoned for another one quite different and then, almost as soon as we have come to accept *that* as accurate, it too is discarded in favour of something else. The process is the thing: the ever unfinished passing of one form into another, the continual battling and eliding of voices. Even when we think we have reached journey's end, we are reminded how mistaken we are ever to believe that the process is ever finished, that closure is ever possible:

> 'It's Cash and Jewel and Vardaman and Dewey Dell,' pa says, kind of hang-dog and proud too, with his teeth and all, even if he wouldn't look at us. 'Meet Mrs. Bundren,' he says.[47]

In comes another Mrs Bundren, trailing a fresh set of possibilities behind her – inviting the journey, and the story, to continue.

Writing to a friend in New Haven in 1919, Faulkner insisted that he had 'had enough of' his ' "God forsaken" home town' to last him the rest of his life; he sometimes feared, he added, that some unkind power would force him after his death to be 'returned to Oxford from Hell'. But Faulkner, as it turned out, was to spend most of his life in this 'God forsaken' town: it was only ten years after saying this that he settled down there, as a married man with a job, to write *As I Lay Dying*. He found Oxford and Mississippi and the South claustrophobic certainly; it was, however, where he felt he belonged. Even when he contemplated moving from his home state, it was only to somewhere else in his home region: to Charlottesville, Virginia, where he bought a house in 1959. The South held him, and for the major part of his time Mississippi held him, for all that they often stifled him with their pieties and rituals. The elaborately mannered, enclosed culture of his region was something he complained of constantly, but he was reluctant to leave it for more than a short while. Not the least important reason why he was so reluctant to leave was that, as he sensed, the South was not, after all, a feudal monolith – even as far as its own versions of itself were concerned. Coexisting with the repressive patriarchal model that was the novelist's inheritance via 'The Old Colonel' was another, populist one: a folk tradition that put a question mark over Southern paternalism, and the elaborate edifice of assumptions on which it rested. Faulkner could be just as fiercely critical of Southern populism as he was of its paternalist equivalent, as the portrait of Jason Compson in *The Sound and the Fury* makes only too clear. But one thing in particular he did cherish about the folk/populist tradition: and that was talk, habits of debate the sheer energy and inexhaustibility of which seemed to mock the paternalist tendency – and, not least, the paternalist inclination towards flamboyant rhetoric and gentility, more refined manners of speech. 'I like these people', Faulkner said once in a class conference,

> I like to listen to them, the way they talk or the things they talk about. I spent a lot of time with my uncle . . . I would go around with him and listen on the front galleries of country stores and listen to the talk that would go on . . . and I remembered most of it, and I have known them in farming and in dealing with horses and hunting, things like that, but without carrying a notebook at all, just to remember.[48]

That listening pays one of its first major dividends in *As I Lay Dying*, where Faulkner makes the talk of 'these people', the dispossessed whites of northern Mississippi, both his occasion and his subject: showing how they construct identities for themselves, personal and communal, out of the activities and the flux of speech. The feudal model of the South was predicated on a vision of the lower white orders that saw them as, at best, stout supporters of the system that repressed them or, at worst, a lesser breed without the law. The carnival impetus of this book, however, drawing on populist resources and the novelist's remembering of folk speech, describes something quite different: the ordinary white people of the South weaving an alternative reality together out of a continuous succession of vocal acts – a reality that, in its degradation as well as its energy, reminds us of the vital, grotesque underbelly of official culture. There are exclusions here too, of course. Black people are conspicuous by their absence: even as objects they hardly appear, and their voices take no part in the debate. But the achievement of *As I Lay Dying* is still considerable: in the war of their words, the clash of their voices, the poor white people of Yoknapatawpha make a place for themselves in this novel, into which they invite the reader to enter. They create their own transgressive space, an assertion of vulgar power and possibility, that mocks claims to authoritativeness and authority of any kind – including, quite clearly, our own.

IV AND WOMAN WAS INVENTED: *SANCTUARY*

About a month after *As I Lay Dying* was published, in the middle of November 1930, Faulkner received the galley proofs of the book he had previously been told was unpublishable. Whether a genuine change of heart or just a simple desire for profits had prompted this volte-face on the part of his publisher is not clear. Whatever the reason, when Faulkner read the galleys of *Sanctuary* it was, he later claimed, his turn to be shocked. The story was 'badly written' and 'cheaply approached', he declared; 'the very impulse that caused me to write the book was so apparent ... and ... I said I cannot let this go'. He insisted on radically revising and rewriting the novel, agreeing to share in the consequent costs; it took him something less than a month and, by the end, he pronounced himself reasonably pleased with the result. 'I made a fair job', he concluded, in shaping the original manuscript into 'something which would not shame *The Sound and the Fury* and *As I Lay Dying* too much'.[49] Faulkner's alterations were numerous and some of them quite major. Events were rearranged so as to make the narrative structure more strictly chronological; the role and story of Popeye were given fuller and clearer articulation; above all, perhaps, the part played by Horace Benbow was reduced and, along with this, the details of his relationships – particularly, with his sister – were considerably pruned. Any idea that Faulkner toned down potentially objectionable material during the course of revision has, however, to be resisted. Certainly, some of the more explicit details Temple gives of the rape are excluded: but, on the other hand, more episodes of violence are added to the original material – relating to Goodwin's death and Popeye's life – while no attempt is made to moderate the accounts of the Memphis underworld and backcountry low life according to contemporary canons of taste. A lot of the narrative substance of the original version of *Sanctuary* was drawn from Faulkner's own experience of the dark underbelly of Southern life: his acquaintance with local moonshiners, his visits to the bars and brothels of Clarksdale and Memphis, his knowledge of notorious gangsters like 'Popeye' Pumphrey – a wealthy bootlegger who was supposed to be cripplingly shy with women. None of this was omitted or even

minimized in the course of rewriting. On the contrary, one result of reducing the importance of Benbow was actually to foreground the violence
of the central action: deprived of the atmosphere of brooding melancholy
with which the Prufrockian lawyer surrounds them, the events at the Old
Frenchman place, and in Memphis, take on a starker outline, a more
jagged edge.

The nature of that outline can, perhaps, be traced by first recalling the
moment when the original text was written: when Faulkner was about
finally to marry the women he had loved and lost. His feelings at the time
can be gauged by that extraordinary letter he wrote to a friend just before
his marriage, which was quoted in the first chapter: what is shadowed here
is not so much triumph but genuine fear, a sense of doom and even despair. Perhaps it was this that evidently led him to delay for as long as
possible: Estelle was divorced in April 1929, Faulkner then dragged his
feet for two months until Estelle's sister telephoned him to tell him that
it was time he and Estelle were married – following this up by accompanying
them to the church and then organizing their honeymoon. Certainly,
Faulkner's own deep unease seems to be echoed by a remark he gives to
Horace Benbow. In flight from his wife Belle Mitchell, a divorcée, and his
stepdaughter Little Belle, Benbow observes bitterly,

> When you marry your own wife, you start off from scratch . . . maybe scratch-
> ing. When you marry somebody else's wife, you start off maybe ten years
> behind, from somebody else's scratch and scratching.[50]

'Somebody else's wife': the childhood companion, the sisterly nymph whom
he had cherished was seen, even before they were married, as a sort of
fallen woman, someone else's property that he was getting at second-
hand. There was fear at the prospect of intimacy in Faulkner's feelings
about the impending union; there was nervousness about the responsibilities he was assuming as, he felt, the man of the house; there was anxiety
about whether he could measure up to his predecessor, the handsome,
successful Cornell Franklin; and there was a whole complex of feelings,
about woman as property – and pretty dangerous property at that – as a
passive instrument of male designs, an object or medium of exchange,
that he had not even begun to negotiate. In effect, marriage confronted
Faulkner with his feelings, his often unacknowledged impulses about women
in the most urgent way imaginable: without his fully knowing what was
going on, it forced him to encounter the terms in which the female had
been constructed for him. It was probably the very urgency of this exercise
that kept the negotiations one-sided: Faulkner did not begin, really, to ask
what women wanted, only what he wanted from them. There is, in other
words, little sense of women as subjects in *Sanctuary*: they are objects in
whom the male gaze situates its fears and desires. At its most fundamental,
women in *Sanctuary* are as Luce Irigiray describes the virginal story in male
discourse: as 'pure exchange value . . . nothing except . . . the place, the

sign of relations between men'. Faulkner pursues the sign with a feverish intensity, an obsessive ferocity here, however: so as to make this novel, not just a painful personal fragment but a passionate cultural fragment – revealing the curious parts women play in the tales told by men.

The place to begin here, perhaps, is with Julia Kristeva's notion of femininity mentioned earlier: according to which femininity is seen as a position, 'that which is marginalised by the patriarchal symbolic order'. Women are placed on the margins, or the borderline of the culture, and there assume the shifting, disconcerting properties of all boundaries or borderlines: neither outside nor inside, neither precisely known nor unknown. More to the point, they acquire an ambivalent character, simply because they *are* both within and without, on the edges of the male order. To the extent that they are within that order, protecting and shielding it from an imagined chaos, they can be seen as precious guardians of the law; to the extent that they are outside, however, in contact with that chaos and even perhaps offering glimpses of it, they can be perceived as creatures of turbulence and darkness – not preventing chaos but partaking of it, even encouraging it to come again. 'If the feminine *exists*', argues Kristeva,

> it only exists in the order of significance or signifying process, and it is only in relation to meaning and signification, positioned as their excessive or transgressive other that it is *exists, voices, thinks* (itself) and *writes* (itself) for both sexes.[51]

It is in these terms, in fact, that it exists in a book like *Sanctuary*: what it offers the males here, narrator and characters, is a mirror and a measure – a series of positionings or situatings of themselves and their own culturally ordained dreams and nightmares.

The nature of these dreams or nightmares is perhaps clearest when we look at the two main female characters in the book: Temple Drake and someone crucial to the original version of *Sanctuary* and still important in the revised text, Horace Benbow's sister Narcissa. The first time we and Horace see Narcissa in the revised version, she is dressed in white and has, we are told, 'that serene and stupid impregnability of heroic statuary'. Within a short while of brother and sister meeting again, sister is lecturing brother for his errors of judgement: his leaving his wife to come back to his childhood home in Jefferson, his decision to represent a man accused of murder, and, still worse, the assistance he has given to the accused's common-law wife and child. In terms of appearance and attitude, Narcissa looks at first sight like a variation on the guardian figure: the heroic lady on the pedestal, the pale virgin, offering both example and advice. The Southern belle, the sister Faulkner never had and whose purity Quentin Compson was obsessed with: all this constellation of associations is there, suggesting that, if this is a marginal creature, it is the marginal creature as would-be protector and shield. The problem is, however, that there is at once less and more to Narcissa than meets the eye. What she is interested in, it is clear from her advice, is not morality but respectability: not that Horace should do the right thing, merely that he should not be *seen* to do the wrong one. This is the point of an apparently irrelevant episode, involving a member of the Snopes family: Byron Snopes writes anonymous love letters to Narcissa that, far from destroying, she keeps and hides in her bedroom drawer. The virginal façade conceals a far from virginal secret inner life: the controller, the guardian, is in effect unable to control herself. When Byron eventually steals the letters back, characteristically Narcissa's feelings centre around the fear of exposure or the mere suspicion that she might be caught out by the knowing gaze of others: as the original text of *Sanctuary* puts it, she momentarily loses 'her poise . . . at the idea of having letters addressed to her read by someone she did not know'.[52]

'Dont talk to me about love', Horace's wife tells him, 'You're in love with your sister. What do books call it? What sort of complex?'[53] The remark was dropped from the eventual, published version of *Sanctuary*, as was Horace's desperate attempt, reminiscent of Quentin Compson's, to dissuade his sister from marriage. The latently incestuous feelings survive, however: caught, not least, in the way Horace tends to see Narcissa both as a refuge from his wife and a replication of her. Narcissa writes to Belle – in Horace's bitter view, colludes with her; still worse, she works actively against Horace as far as his defence of the accused murderer, Goodwin, is concerned, because of the damage that, as she sees it, that defence is doing to the family reputation and, in particular, to her good name. In the small, dry world of *Sanctuary* the idea of woman as protector is, in effect, present as little more than that: an idea, a hypothesis that is offered to us briefly only to be whisked away. Narcissa is not only a statue who fouls her own pedestal; she is an idol who betrays those who worship her, a virginal sister who seems actively to promote incestuous desires. She offers a minor key, perhaps, in comparison with Temple Drake, but the tune played is unnervingly similar to the one heard in the main story: woman as apparent protector and stay against confusion is suddenly transformed into the agent of degradation, the guard who opens the gates wide to let chaos in. Interestingly, the same word is used to describe Narcissa and Temple: Narcissa has a 'stupid impregnability' while Temple, we are told, behaves 'stupidly', with the automatic gestures of a doll. It is verbal gestures such as this that help to measure just how implicated the narrator is in the book's portrait of women: the female characters, the reader is being advised, are possessed of only a minimal inner life. They are unthinking creatures, responding merely to impulse (fear, sex) or to superficial triggers (respectability, authority). To be more exact, they are human subjects denied their subjectivity and then blamed for the absence: characters dismissed to the edge of things and then treated as if the dismissal were somehow their fault.

The first time we see Temple Drake she is running: the reader is invited to watch her disappear 'in a swirling glitter', catching glimpses of 'her high delicate head and her bold painted mouth and soft chin, her eyes blankly right and left looking, cool, predatory, and discreet'. That first sight of her not only registers the voyeuristic note that invariably creeps into descriptions of her: it also suggests something of the aggression the narrative voice seems to feel toward her, and the quality of elusiveness, even evasiveness, that surrounds her at almost every turn. Apart from the obvious implications of her name and the way that, as a college girl and the daughter of a judge, she is tapped in to the sources of social respectability, there is, in fact, very little of the guardian element attributed to Temple even at the beginning of the novel. She is pure mobility, a creature who may sometimes seem like an automaton and sometimes like a trapped animal but who, whatever the details of her associations, never manages to stay still. At certain points in the story, particularly after Horace has heard from Temple's lips the details of the rape and begins to vomit, Temple Drake becomes confused with Narcissa Benbow and Little Belle: a complex pattern of incestuous feelings is used, in other words, to underwrite the primary emotional pattern of the story – from assumptions of intimacy and worship to a sense of betrayal. Even without this pattern, however, which suggests that the 'sister' has become 'unsistered' by her violation of the family romance, it is clear what trajectory Faulkner is making Temple follow. As the protector who eventually colludes in the collapse of the protective barriers, the guardian who not only welcomes chaos but enacts it, she illustrates just how closely woven together are feelings of desire and degradation in the male psyche: just how close – in terms of objectivizing and marginalizing the human subject – are the apparently opposing tendencies to reverence and rape. Towards the end, not only does Temple seem to take actual pride in what has happened to her; as Horace sees it and Faulkner describes it, she assumes the character of lust in action – desire perceived as a deathly, degrading impulse.

> Her eyes began to grow darker and darker, lifting into her skull above a half-moon of white, without focus, with the blank rigidity of a statue's eyes. She began to say Ah-ah-ah-ah in an expiring voice, her body arching slowly backward as though faced by an exquisite torture. When he [Red] touched her, she sprang like a bow, hurling herself upon him, her mouth gaped and ugly like that of a dying fish.[54]

The intimations of death and dead, stinking creatures from a subterranean underworld, the clinical detailing of the bodily spasms of sexual hunger, even the sardonic transmogrification of the imagery of statuary and virginal white moonlight: it is difficult to see all this as anything other than the narrative's act of revenge. Temple's last two appearances after this, in court and in the Luxembourg gardens with her mask restored and 'her blank face rigid', only serve to confirm the fear and anger that went into her making. She is a character who seems, in the last analysis, to have been invented to prove the equation: woman = nature = chaos/evil.

'That's why nature is "she" and Progress is "he"', observes Horace Benbow early on in the novel, 'nature made the grape arbour, but Progress invented the mirror.' The immediate occasion of this remark is the memory of a time when Horace discovered, via a fortuitous pairing of reflections, that his stepdaughter was deceiving him while she was embracing him: watching herself over Benbow's shoulder in one mirror, 'with pure dissimulation', and forgetting about another mirror behind her in which her stepfather could see her doubly reflected face. That moment brings together many of the primary impulses of *Sanctuary*: not least, its tendency to generalize or even parody the feelings that went into the making of the major female characters. One aspect of this generalizing tendency is, quite simply, the multiplication of often anonymous female figures who function either as totems or taboos or as both. There are the 'church ladies' of Jefferson, for instance, who insist that the common-law wife of a murderer cannot stay in the local hotel, and whose sanctimonious postures seem to satirize Narcissa's pretensions to respectability even while they imitate them. And there are the innumerable unnamed college girls whom Horace meets on his travels: 'their blonde legs monotonous, their bodies moving continually inside their scant garments with that awkward and voluptuous purposelessness of the young'. In their mobility, their remorseless seductiveness and superficiality, they multiply Temple Drake a hundredfold; just as the terms in which they are presented to us repeat and extend those feelings of resentful lust, angry and impotent sexual need, with which Temple is invariably described. What complicates matters, however, is that Faulkner does not simply broaden the picture in this way, nor merely depend on a characteristic (for him) series of associations of women with grape arbours, the odour of honeysuckle, face-painting and filth. He pushes things further by offering the reader male characters whose gestures of adoration and/or appetite reflect and repeat the verbal gestures of the narrative. Sometimes, it is a grotesque form of adoration that is foregrounded: as when, for example, the district attorney at the trial of Goodwin invokes 'the most sacred affairs of that most sacred thing in life: womanhood' – or, even more obviously, when a drunken Gowan Stevens mumbles, 'Got proteck . . . girl. 'Ginia gem . . . gemman got proteck . . .' At other times, appetite is more the object of attention: every white male in Jefferson, for instance, seems to hunger after Temple Drake (' "College girl. Good looker. Didn't you see her?" "I saw her. She was some baby." '). More often than not, however, the gestures are mixed, the signals are ingeniously confused, as in that bizarre moment when a taxi-driver tries to explain why it was necessary to take Goodwin out of jail and kill him: ' "Served him right," the driver said. "We got to protect our girls. Might need them ourselves." '[55]

What are we to make of all this? At times, Faulkner genuinely seems to be on top of his material: demonstrating the ludicrous, self-serving nature of male deference and protectiveness ('Got proteck . . . girl'), showing how forms of deference are really only forms of oppression – or how protectiveness is just a mask for appropriation, the need to prevent damaged goods ('Might need them ourselves'). Not all the sex war in *Sanctuary* is waged in favour of the male. For a brief moment, at least, the woman = evil equation looks the absurdity it is when it is put in the mouth of Clarence Snopes: 'Half the trouble in this world is caused by women, I always say.' More to the point, perhaps, one of the prostitutes at the Memphis brothel where Temple is sent is actually allowed to voice the conviction that the problem lies not in female nature but male culture, the notions of women constructed by men:

> 'It's us girls,' Miss Myrtle said. 'Men just cant seem to take us and leave us for what are. They make us what we are, then they expect us to be different. Expect us not to never look at another man, while they come and go as they please.'[56]

The problem is, none of this lasts for long or inheres very deeply in the narrative: the power of *Sanctuary* lies, ultimately, not in its criticism but its replication of the impulses Miss Myrtle describes. The symptoms of this are numerous, and many of them have been referred to already: but perhaps the crucial one, and the most worrying, is the repeated suggestion that Temple herself is to blame for being raped. This is not just a matter of the emphasis on Temple's seductive looks and behaviour, or the hints that her constant running and jumpiness act as a provocation. It also has to do with what another woman, Ruby, Lee Goodwin's wife, says of her.

Ruby is a curious figure, in some ways more man than woman – when she is introduced to us, for instance, she is wearing 'a worn pair of man's brogans' – and in others more the sort of passive, enduring personality that Faulkner tended to associate with black women. She is not unambiguously admired, but she is not nearly as weak or evil as most of the other characters in the novel; and her remarks are given the kind of weight and authoritativeness that is denied to those of, say, Horace Benbow or his family. What is notable with Ruby is how deep-rooted is her mistrust of Temple, and how remorseless she is in her criticism of someone she sees as an interloper. 'Oh, I know your sort', she tells Temple, '. . . You'll slip out at night with the kids, but just let a man come along . . . You've never seen a real man.' 'It's not Lee I'm afraid of', she adds later,

> Do you think he plays the dog after every hot little bitch that comes along? It's you . . . I know your sort . . . All running, but not too fast. Not so fast you cant tell a real man when you see him. Do you think you've got the only one in the world?[57]

Extraordinarily enough, some critics have taken remarks like this at face value, effectively saying that, to use the standard cant, Temple 'asked for it'. It is surely superfluous to say that this is wrong, dangerous nonsense. What is more useful is to see how it happens; since it is, after all, a logical outcome of the assumptions, the moral economy of the narrative. Woman is seen as the agent of the evil of which she is, in fact, the victim; while man, who has in reality constructed the story and controls it, is seen as an essentially passive instrument, in terms of impotence and (often bewildered) innocence. Innocent men, experienced women: the formula is repeated even in an apparently irrelevant comic episode, when the Snopes brothers stay in a brothel believing it to be a hotel. It is a powerful strategy of displacement, either suppressing or deflecting any accurate sense of the origins of male/female relations; and, apart from one or two more rebarbative remarks, it dictates the terms in which the tale is told.

Closely related to this figuring of male/female relations, although not precisely identifiable with it, is the experience of watching: 'nature made the grape arbour, but Progress invented the mirror'. The revised version of *Sanctuary* opens with two men, Horace and Popeye, watching each other 'for two hours'; characters are constantly peering at each other, through windows or keyholes or around open doors; and, of course, Popeye turns Temple into what Miss Reba, who runs the Memphis brothel, sardonically calls 'a peep-show'. This is a novel of the eye far more than the ear, in which character is seen and spied upon rather more than attended to and heard. The peculiar effect of this is suggested by the following, brief passage, which comes from a much longer description of Tommy, the eventual, feeble-minded victim of Popeye's violence, observing Temple through a window:

> Temple's head began to move. It turned slowly . . . on to an excruciating degree, though no other muscle moved, like one of those papier-mâché Easter toys filled with candy, and became motionless in that reverted position. Then it turned back slowly. . . . She unfastened her dress . . . In a single motion she was out of it, crouching a little, match-thin in her scant undergarments . . .[58]

Tommy is unseen, Temple is seen; and the author/narrator and reader are unseen watching with Tommy. As in the central events of the novel, we can look but not properly touch; and, under the inspection of our unseen eyes, the character is reduced to an object that fluctuates between the mechanical and the pornographic. The levels of voyeurism in *Sanctuary* are frequently multiplied: at one point, for instance, we watch Minnie, a maid at the brothel, watching Popeye watching Clarence Snopes watching Temple through a keyhole. And, just as frequently, voyeurism is transmuted into narcissism. In the moments before Benbow and Popeye start watching each other at the beginning of the novel, Benbow is leaning his face 'to the broken and myriad reflection of his own drinking' in a pool; Popeye's last words, 'Fix my hair, Jack', reflect his own preoccupation with his image, his own tendency to gaze in a figurative mirror; while even Temple, when she is not being watched, often watches herself in a curiously dissociated fashion – as if she were somehow her own object of desire ('She . . . saw within her fallen coat naked flesh between brassiere and knickers and knickers and stockings'). 'There's a corruption about even looking upon evil', Horace observes; and it is precisely with looking that this novel is concerned. Voices in Faulkner notably take us in, to the feverish subjectivities of inner dialogue or the collaborative intimacies of talk. Vision, however, takes us out, to the predicament of author, narrator, reader and character dependent on the alienating detachments of the eye. There are voices, of course, in *Sanctuary* but they are for the most part overwhelmed by the desire to see: to get pleasure, such as it is, from solitary staring at something that, preferably, is unable to stare back.

Two points, in particular, need to be made about this constant habit of watching. The first is that, while the watcher/watched opposition is not exactly coextensive with that of male/female, they do often coincide. As in the passage just quoted, concerning Tommy and Temple, the watcher tends to be male and the watched female. 'Nature is "she" and Progress is "he" ': feminine nature, according to the terms of this book, is normally the object of sight, while the male 'mirror' is usually the medium of seeing. The second point is more crucial. What the entire emphasis on the visual field in *Sanctuary* does, ultimately, is to forestall the kinds of critical interrogation, those investigations of cultural forms that characterize *The Sound and the Fury* and *As I Lay Dying*. The reason is simple. The sense of being in history as process, involved in its past and possible changes, is so much a matter of the vocal field in Faulkner, a complex interplay of voices; and what the emphasis on sight *Sanctuary* does, in effect, is to deny that process.[59] Far from being involved in something that is fluid, enigmatic, unfinished, character and reader are asked mainly to stand back and observe a product, a model evidently based on a series of fixed polarities. Experience, according to the voyeuristic tableaux that characterize this novel, is something 'out there': quite separate from the perceiver and, consequently, leaving the perceiver's illusion of innocence intact. Change is impossible, because there is no possibility of involvement; to be more exact, a chance for the cultural negotiation of change does not exist, because there is no sense that the culture has previously had to be negotiated. The dualities male/female, progress/nature, innocence/evil and so on were there from the beginning, it seems, constituting the way things are, always have been, and always will be. We see the world around us, but we are not complicit with it; history is something that happens to us, that we watch but do not make.

Watching: the revised version of *Sanctuary* opens with Benbow looking at himself, then looking at Popeye who is looking at him. The original began in a different way: with the description of the prison in which Goodwin is being held, along with an unnamed 'negro murderer' who has slashed his wife's throat with a razor. Quite apart from startling the reader immediately into an awareness of the sex war, the sexual enmity and violence that is to be one of the novel's dominant ideas, that earlier manuscript introduces what is, along with watching and its accompaniments, the presiding image or obsession of *Sanctuary*: entrapment, enclosure in

what is literally or figuratively a prison. When, late in both versions of the
novel, Benbow hears the story of Temple Drake and is violently sick, he
has a nightmare vision of Temple, 'Popeye, the woman, the child, Goodwin
all put into a single chamber, bare, lethal, immediate and profound':[60] all
confined in the same closed space. Most of the time, that vision seems to
be true. Temple is trapped, first at the Old Frenchman place then in the
brothel; Goodwin is trapped in prison, as is Popeye eventually; Goodwin's
child is trapped in a box; and his wife is trapped in the Old Frenchman
place, then in a series of temporary living spaces not her own while she
visits her husband in jail. These enclosures are all, to an extent, literal: but
far more powerful is that feeling of psychic entrapment that, for instance,
Benbow is in flight from at the beginning of the novel – and from which
he never fully escapes. 'You can't stop me like this', says Horace to Popeye
after they have been staring at each other for two hours, 'Suppose I break
and run.' 'Do you want to run?' asks Popeye sardonically: to which the
answer is a simple, 'No.' Benbow does not want to run, because he cannot
really run and some part of him senses that: the only place his frantic
activity gets him, by the end of the novel, is the place from which he was
trying to flee. When we last see him, in fact, he is back with Belle Mitchell,
in a home that seems more than ever a prison, and the last conversation
between husband and wife is a straightforward, wifely command: ' "Lock
the back door," she said.'

The prison into which Benbow eventually locks himself is the one that
entraps, not only the other characters, but the reader and presumably the
author as well: that of the solitary, perceiving consciousness, frozen out of
history and condemned not to do but to look. Enclosure in *Sanctuary* is,
in fact, closely linked with watching: the characters can only gaze at one
another because some barrier, literal or invisible, seems to block and
frustrate them, to deter them from intimacy. Or, like Temple, they gaze
at themselves in a curiously dissociated, detached way, as if their own
bodies constituted their prisons. The sense of entrapment is similarly felt
by the reader: the airless environment of the novel is at once gripping and
alienating, a place – like the one where Horace and Popeye meet – of
silence and surface.

> From beyond the screen of bushes which surrounded the spring, Popeye
> watched . . . a tall, thin man, hatless, in worn grey flannel trousers and car-
> rying a tweed coat over his arm . . .
>   . . . the drinking man [Benbow] saw . . . the shattered reflection of Popeye's
> straw hat, though he had heard no sound . . .
>   He saw, facing him . . . , a man of under size, his hands in his coat
> pockets . . . he had that vicious depthless quality of stamped tin.[61]

We are not drowned in the subjectivities of the characters as we are in, say,
The Sound and the Fury; nor are we dragged into a carnival of debate and
dialogue as we are in *As I Lay Dying.* On the contrary, we are asked to

inspect these 'dolls' (the term of comparison is constantly used in *Sanctuary*) as they move towards an apparently irreversible doom ('Something is going to happen to me', Temple repeats). The notation of physical detail may fluctuate between the empiricism of the detective story – as in the passage just quoted – and the bleakly surreal – as in the moment when Horace vomits after listening to Temple – but, invariably, the net effect is to keep the characters at a distance from the reader: they are like commodities, exclusive properties of a closed fiction, at which we can look but which we had better not touch.

Another way of putting all this is to borrow an idea from Barthes and to say that, of the novels of this period, *Sanctuary* is the least 'writerly', the least calculated to make the reader feel like a producer rather than a consumer of the text. In *The Sound and the Fury* and *As I Lay Dying*, the narrative requires us much of the time to establish priorities and distribute emphases and so participate in the job of 'making' it; we collaborate in the creation of meaning. We are not entirely exempt from that task in *Sanctuary*, of course: but there is, surely, far more sense of a closed world here, moving on tramlines already set down to an established destination. There is little sense that we can significantly alter the implications of what is happening (once, at least, we accept the initial premises of the narrative), that we are involved in a system of debate and conflict that invites constant, painful reinterpretation. All we can do really is what the characters do: watch, while the prison doors close.

Those prison doors are additionally powerful for the characters because they seem to have reflective surfaces: in *Sanctuary* – to pick up a point made earlier – voyeurism and narcissism frequently elide, because what the solitary seer sees is a reflection of himself, the imperatives of his own gaze. There is a constant pattern of doubling, replication of the perceiver in the perceived, which helps to confirm the suspicion that what we, the readers are being invited into is an enclosure erected out of mirrors. Even the agent and the victim of the rape, for example, are curiously doubled. Both are compared to children: Popeye is 'like a sullen and sick child', while Temple wears the 'round, hopeless expression of a child'. Both are possessed of a strange, unfleshly quality: Popeye is like 'stamped tin' and has a 'waxy lifelessness of shape and size', whereas Temple has a 'little putty face' like a mask. Both, also, are defined in terms of their absence, or at least their marginal presence. When Popeye is there, it is usually in the form of a few, random physical notations: smoke from a cigarette, the flicker of a match, the smell of brilliantine. Equally, when Temple appears it is in the act of disappearing: all we normally catch sight of are the diminishing ripples of her departure – a flicker of legs, perhaps, a 'swirling glitter' of clothes. Partly inhuman, partly pure surface, partly an absence: the gangster and the college girl are peculiarly perverse mirrors of each other, drawn into a game that seems to involve mutual humiliation. The humiliation inflicted on Temple is infinitely more violent and terrible, of course: but Temple, with her taunt, 'You're not even a man!'[62]

seems to know at least one way to get some revenge. 'Cool, predatory': the terms are applied to Temple Drake, but they could just as easily be attached to the man who violates and imprisons her. Even their eventual situations, juxtaposed in the revised version, are unnervingly reflective of each other: Popeye at his execution asking for his hair to be fixed, Temple in the Luxembourg Gardens yawning and gazing at her 'face in miniature' in her compact mirror. It is as if, in these final gestures, the two characters confirm their apathy, their moral indifference, and above all their narcissism – their tendency to perceive in the other merely an extension, or projection, of themselves.

The odd way in which Popeye and Temple appear to look like each other, even in the process of looking at themselves, is duplicated with Temple and Benbow. Gazing at the self is one link between the judge's daughter and the lawyer; fear is another. 'I lack courage', Horace admits; and there is a curious repetition noticeable in his and Temple's behaviour at the Old Frenchman place – jumpy, anxious, clearly sensing that they are interlopers and threatened, they seek reassurance in memories of home. In this respect, Temple's talking to Ruby Goodwin about her father, and thinking about him 'in a linen suit, palm-leaf in his hand, watching the Negro mow the lawn', has the same comforting, ritualistic function as Benbow's attempts to tell Ruby about his Jefferson homeplace. Both characters are attempting to ward off evil spirits as if, in an odd reversal of exorcism, it were possible to liberate the past by suppressing the energies of the present. Not only that, if Horace nurtures 'some sort of complex' about his sister back at home, then Temple clearly harbours similar impulses towards her father. 'My father's a judge, my father's a judge', she repeats as she feels danger gathering around her at the Old Frenchman place. And the reverse image of this reverence comes after the rape, when Temple starts to call Popeye, 'Daddy'. The incestuous pattern that enmeshes Temple Drake is, in fact, a shadowy replication of the one that enfolds Horace: the father as refuge is translated into the father as violator and then into the father as jailer. The description of Temple, as her father leads her from the courtroom after she has obediently given false witness, weaves the final threads in the pattern: 'the old man . . . bent toward her, speaking; she moved again, in that shrinking and rapt abasement . . . her body arched again . . . and disappeared'.[63] Mirroring Benbow as he locks the back door, Temple resigns herself, simultaneously surrenders and withdraws; the sexually authoritative figure is translated into an agent of regression, offering a sanctuary that is also a prison.

Popeye and Temple, Temple and Horace – and Horace and Popeye: the doubling is sustained and the circle of replication completed by the mirroring of gangster and lawyer. Watching each other from the opening pages of the revised version of the novel, they are also watching themselves. In his own way, for instance, Popeye is just as frightened as Benbow is. 'I be a dog if he aint the skeeriest durn *white* man I ever see', says Tommy, referring to the gangster's fear of nature – a fear that, as it turns out,

Horace shares. He is just as incapable, it seems, of pleasure of any kind; and just as capable, as far as women are concerned, of fluctuating between iconoclasm and worship – as his treatment of Temple and his attitude to his mother make only too clear. As voyeuristic and narcissistic as Benbow is, Popeye is impotent physically just as Benbow is psychologically: 'I cant help it', says Benbow when trying to explain his actions, 'Sometimes, when I think of all the time I have spent not learning to do things ...' – characteristically, the admission of ineffectuality trials off into an ineffectual silence. And the impotence, in both cases, leads inevitably into failure: defeated by the law (that engine of a society to which neither really belongs), both men end up turning the key on themselves, since Horace's obedience to his wife's command to lock himself in is repeated in Popeye's refusal to defend himself against a false change of murder. The last twist of the knife, perhaps, is that Popeye is arrested 'while on his way to Pensacola to visit his mother'.[64] The woman is there too, it seems, involved in the entrapment of an only too willing victim, helping to bait the trap just before it is sprung.

There is no point in trying to 'make sense' out of *Sanctuary*, if that means trying to resolve its contradictions. The contradictions are, quite simply, irresolvable. Temple, for instance, is the betrayer, to the extent that she is observed negotiating with chaos, and the betrayed, in the sense that she replicates the voyeuristic imprisonment of people like Popeye and Horace Benbow.[65] 'There is a logical pattern to evil', Horace remarks to himself at one point. Perhaps: but the logic of *Sanctuary* is the logic of crisis. Faulkner wrote the book at a time when he felt obliged, not really to investigate his ideas about women, but to spill them out, to unravel them in all their often conflicting implications. So it is all, or nearly all, there: woman as guardian and as enemy agent, woman as sanctuary and as seducer, woman as security and as entrapment, woman as observed object and reflected subject, woman as totem and as taboo. Admittedly, there is a certain frigid coherence at work in all of this. The circularity, the repetitions of character, the centripetal pattern of watcher and watched all press the novel towards closure, a kind of claustrophobic, self-reflexive autonomy. But there are some pretty radical disturbances at work here too. Just to take one example: the sense of outrage that surrounds the account of the rape of Temple Drake is contradicted not only by the narrator's voyeuristic attitude towards her – even when she is defecating – but by the violence of the language marshalled to describe her at times, which performs its own cool act of violation. Clearly, the closure as well as the contradictions of *Sanctuary* issue from its urgently autobiographical nature: it has not gone unnoticed that the two major male characters replicate not only each other but Faulkner himself – Horace Benbow psychologically and Popeye, 'the little black man', physically.[66] *Sanctuary* is not just an excerpt from autobiography, however, it is a complex register of the terms on which male/female relations were predicated in the author's culture, and, for that matter, are in our own. 'The dungeon was Mother herself', thinks Quentin Compson in *The Sound and the Fury*. That remark could be inscribed as an epigraph to the story of Temple Drake, Horace Benbow and Popeye, with the rider that it is the male script that makes 'her' so. In other scripts, written by Faulkner at other times and even alluded to at moments in this novel, 'she' is not the dungeon but its inhabitant – not the prison, in fact, so much as the prisoner.

4

Of Past and Present Conflicts

I LANGUAGE, POWER AND THE VERBAL COMMUNITY:
LIGHT IN AUGUST

The year in which Faulkner began work on *Light in August* was a peculiarly traumatic one for him. On 11 January 1931, his daughter Alabama was born. Only nine days later, the baby died without her mother ever having seen her. The acute grief this death caused was hardly assuaged by the problems Faulkner was having at the time in his professional life. *Sanctuary* was published in February, to be greeted with consternation or downright hostility by neighbours in Oxford, and even friends and relatives. 'Do you think of that material when you're drunk?' his cousin Sallie Murry asked Faulkner; while Murry Falkner was reputed to have told a female student whom he saw with a copy of the novel, 'It isn't fit for a nice girl to read.' Shortage of money continued to be a problem: Faulkner was selling so little of his own work that, in March, he was obliged to defer mortgage payments on his house for six months. Despite all that, however (or, perhaps, even because of it), he threw himself back into his writing: working first on a story, 'Evangeline', that was to become a prototype for *Absalom, Absalom!* and then turning to a novel provisionally entitled 'Dark House'. At the centre of 'Dark House' was Gail Hightower, a character modelled upon the Gavin Blount who had appeared in two earlier stories, 'The Big Shot' and 'Rose of Lebanon': a man just as obsessed with the heroics of his grandfather as Faulkner was with those of 'The Old Colonel'. Not far into the writing of the manuscript, though, 'Dark House' became *Light in August*: so named, Faulkner explained, 'because in my country there's a peculiar quality to the light . . . a lambence, a luminous quality, as though it came not from today but from back in old classic times'. As the title changed, two other characters entered the frame. First, there was Lena Grove: 'I began Light in August', he wrote a short while after completing the book, 'knowing no more about it than a young woman, walking along a strange country road.'[1] But Lena did not offer the kind of narrative catalyst her creator clearly required. That came only with Joe Christmas: a figure whose fate was reminiscent of that of Nelse Patton and other victims of the lynch mob of whom Faulkner knew, and whose personality in some ways recalled that most autobiographical of the novelist's creations, Quentin Compson. With Joe came a whole cast of other characters with whose story his was involved – among them, the McEacherns, Percy Grimm and Joanna Burden – and a fierce new emphasis on the tangled vocabularies of sex and race. The process of writing was in this case relatively complicated: *Light in August* was to prove one of Faulkner's most heavily reworked manuscripts, in part because it interwove so many different narrative threads. Nevertheless, by early in 1932 the book was completed; and in September of that year, when the galleys arrived, Faulkner could pronounce himself well satisfied with his own work in a characteristically laconic, apparently self-deprecating way – 'I dont see anything wrong with it', he declared.

Looking at *Light in August* within the framework of the novelist's preoccupations at the time, certain patterns and connections achieve a sharper focus, and sometimes a bitterly ironic one. This is, after all, a novel that has as one of its nodal points the birth of a child. There is, for instance, a familiar triad of figures carried over from *As I Lay Dying* – the detached intellectual (in this case, Hightower), the quiet and conscientious worker (Byron Bunch), and the lonely man of violence (Joe Christmas) – all of whom seem to be exploring, in their different ways, the uses and abuses of privacy. There is the character who has missed out on the chance of heroic action, this time perceived in sharply parodic terms: Percy Grimm, whose fascistic love of military hardware and violence can at least be partly explained by the fact that (as the narrator puts it) 'he was too young to have been in the European War . . . born too late but not late enough to have escaped first hand knowledge of the lost time when he should have been a man instead of a child'. There is also the character who, by his own admission, has 'skipped a generation'. 'It's no wonder that I had no father', thinks Gail Hightower musing over that substitution of an earlier, epic, grandfatherly figure for his actual, biological father which has pushed him towards the status of an alienated spectator of life. Traces of autobiography can, in fact, be detected in nearly all the male characters, becoming particularly powerful in the adolescent sexual preoccupations of Joe Christmas: Joe loses an intimate 'sister' figure when he is still young, a girl named Alice, and swings just as radically between reverence and rejection, woman as urn and woman as 'womanfilth', as any of Faulkner's angry young idealists do. There is even the by now familiar, bitter warning not to marry 'a woman who has chosen once and now wishes to renege that choice': as if Faulkner could not let a story go by without harping on his own, scarcely suppressed suspicion that he had bought damaged goods. Yet despite all that, *Light in August* does not have the sometimes claustrophobic personal focus that, on the one hand, fires *The Sound and the Fury* into life and, on the other, twists *Sanctuary* into potent confusion. So it is perhaps not surprising that, when he was writing it, Faulkner declared that he did not experience the rapture he felt when composing his story of the Compson family. What he was feeling instead, he said, was an awareness 'before each word was written down' of 'just what people would do'; he was 'deliberately choosing among possibilities and probabilities of behaviour' and 'measuring each choice by the scale of the Jameses and Conrads and Balzacs'. [2] In other words, he was writing in a peculiarly knowing, self-conscious way, the way of the painstaking artisan; and, all the while, he was comparing himself with those of his immediate predecessors who saw themselves as the chroniclers of a culture – the great novelists of *social* exchange.

Two points need to be made here. The first is that perhaps Faulkner was predisposed towards a more immediate confrontation with social dynamics by the particular crisis of his times: between 1929, the year of the Wall Street Crash, and the year *Light in August* was published per capita income dropped 100 per cent, unemployment rose from 500,000 to 13 million, and the average income of working Americans dropped back to what it had been at the beginning of three decades of technological revolution. The South was especially badly hit – the Roosevelt Administration was, after all, later to see the region as its most pressing economic problem[3] – and, for all his pursuit of privacy, Faulkner could hardly have sheltered himself from the economic whirlwind. On the contrary, in his own small way, he was one of its victims. The second point follows from this. In becoming more openly interested in how a society defines itself and its members through its rituals, allocates power and distributes rewards and punishments, Faulkner was only continuing an interest or obsession that had been there from the first, in the sense that he had always been concerned with the inter-subjective nature of reality: the way we as individuals live both as part of and apart from society via speech. The gravitation towards a more social mode that is witnessed by this novel is undeniable: but it is indelibly attached to Faulkner's earlier exploration of the way people and communities identify themselves through language – and it is predicated on the belief that the terms 'social' and 'personal' are matters of emphasis and perspective only. Faulkner's characters are arguing with their predecessors and neighbours even when they are arguing with themselves; equally, they are talking to themselves even while they are talking to others.

'The novel is for the ear', Faulkner said once, when he was trying to explain the difference between fiction and other forms of cultural expression. True of any novel perhaps – true of most of Faulkner's novels, certainly – it is particularly true of *Light in August*. The book is full of what is referred to, at one point, as 'voices, murmurs, whispers': veranda-talk, street-corner conversation, courthouse-square gossip, all that goes to make up a verbal community – which is to say, a community that defines itself through the developing rituals of speech. And it is equally packed with dialogues and fluctuating speech levels of an apparently more interior kind, which go to show just how notions of status and identity are a matter of the voices a person sometimes hears in his or her head. In this novel, people do not, as some critics have claimed, know who they are and where they belong, what they and their community are, as if such knowledge were a timeless and unquestionable right. They know because they engage in social exchanges that substantiate or complicate their sense of belonging. They know because they *talk*: the speech of Yoknapatawpha County, here as elsewhere, is the link between external and internal worlds. Vocal exchanges embody and then re-embody the changing relations between classes, sexes and races, help to shape beliefs and behaviour – and, in general, exist in a genuinely dialectical relation with the developing rituals of the community. 'As a social animal, man is a ritual animal', observes the anthropologist Mary Douglas,

> ritual focusses attention by framing; it enlivens the memory and links the present with the relevant past. In all this, it aids perception. Or rather, it changes perception because it changes the selective principles . . . It does not merely externalise experience . . . it modifies experience in so expressing it.[4]

'Rituals and beliefs change', Douglas insists, 'they are extremely plastic'; and their plasticity, as she sees it, derives above all from their being voiced and energetically debated. They can be argued over in what Fredric Jameson has termed 'the privileged meeting places of collective life', which in Yoknapatawpha include the front porch, the timber yard, the barbershop or the courthouse square. They can be argued over inside the head. Either way – or, rather, both ways, since the two are inseparable – rituals become a site of struggle, as different groups, classes and individuals seek to appropriate and use them. And language, in turn, becomes a field of ideological contention, as those same groups, classes and individuals seek to control the sign and imbue it with their own meanings.

Another way of putting all this is to say that Faulkner had an unusually sensitive ear for talk, and that this sensitivity is especially apparent in his seventh novel. Talk, as he instinctively recognized, was not just a medium of communication; it was a means of revelation and transformation. Situated in communal use, the language of a society or group contains those commonplaces which that group has accepted as common; it quietly announces that system of assumptions, or shared beliefs, without which that society would cease to operate. What is called, at several points, a 'myriad voices' populate *Light in August*; and, much of the time, they demonstrate a vocabulary, accepted habits of idiom and expression, that are by no means innocent nor inevitably correct or true, but simply the means by which a culture seeks to impose and perpetuate its sense of how things are. Take this passage, for instance, where talk takes on a distinctive, active and malleable, personality of its own:

> Through the long afternoon they clotted about the square and before the jail – the clerks, the countrymen in overalls; the talk. It went here and there

about the town, dying and borning again like a wind or fire . . . Then the talk flared again, momentarily revived, to wives and family about supper tables . . . And on the next day, the slow, pleasant country Sunday while they squatted . . . with peaceful pipes about country churches or about the shady dooryards of houses . . . they told it again: 'He dont look any more like a nigger than I do. But it must have been the nigger blood in him.'[5]

The distinction of a passage like this, and what follows it, is that it shows a community trying to come to terms with an unexpected event by absorbing it within a familiar – and, in this case, racist – vocabulary: reports of Joe Christmas's murder of Joanna Burden are to be defined and determined, it seems, in terms of what is called 'the nigger blood in him'. Two points need to be emphasized about this. In the first place, Faulkner's interest here clearly lies in the process by which different groups come together to try to explain what is for them the inexplicable: to accommodate an awkward historical reality to the language that supports and authenticates their way of life – that serves to confirm their own interests. And, in the second, Faulkner's concern in the book as a whole, or at least one of his major concerns, is to show how that language – and, with it, social relationships and systems of belief – can begin to change when faced with the assault of history, the particular stories *Light in August* has to tell.

In the passage just quoted, talk is personified. More often than not, however, Faulkner shows a sharp ear for the way intimate and communal levels of language interact. There is a constant shifting of speech levels: the opening account of Lena Grove, for instance, moves rapidly and without warning between the different if related voices of Lena thinking almost aloud ('I have come from Alabama: a fur piece'), Lena talking to herself on a less tangible if nevertheless demotic level ('*I am now further from Doane's Mill than I have been since I was twelve years old*'), the narrator talking and trying to explain ('She had never even been to Doane's Mill until after her father and mother died . . .'), and others talking and issuing instructions ('Then one day her father said, "You go to Doane's Mill . . ."'). What links these different levels is their slippery, speculative nature. 'Man knows so little about his fellows', observes the narrator early on in the novel, 'In his eyes all men or women act upon what he believes would motivate him if he were mad enough to do what that other man or woman is doing.' And, as if to prove the point, the narration is alive with hypotheses and guess-work: 'perhaps', 'possibly', 'maybe', 'if', 'very likely' are part of the book's staple idiom. The characters, anonymous townsfolk and others, share in this constant hypothesizing. Gavin Stevens, for instance, speculates about the behaviour of Joe Christmas: 'there were many reasons, opinions as to why he [Christmas] fled to Hightower's house at the last', we are told, and Stevens had his own, characteristically 'different theory'. Byron Bunch, meanwhile, tells his own stories, littered with 'I reckon's and other marks of uncertainty, about both Joe Christmas and Lena Grove. And the townspeople sometimes tell tales, about for example Gail Hightower, that they do not even believe while they are telling them: 'there were some who said that he [Hightower] had insured his wife's life and then paid someone to murder her', the narrator confides, 'but everyone knew that this was not so, including the ones who told and repeated it and the ones who listened when it was told'.[6] Rumours abound; stories circulate, becoming ever more recessively third-hand or fourth-hand or fifth-hand; interior dialogue spirals down into hints, haphazard guesses and the bewildered pursuit of clues. The common denominator in all this is the sheer relativity of what is usually identified as fact. Clearly, it matters what stories are told, not least because those stories distribute responsibility and privilege: but by watching the storytellers in action – and often strained action, at that – we become aware that storytelling is, in the end, a matter of power. Struggling to organize fluid events into fixed and credible meanings, arguing or agreeing or just plain guessing, the characters in *Light in August* along with the narrator show just how much the community is a system of naturalized conflict and collusion – and just how much, as Mary Douglas suggests, we make (and can alter) the terms by which we live.

A crucial variant on this exploration of the relationship between language and power comes at that moment when Joanna Burden learns from her father about the so-called 'curse' visited by the black race on the white, and then tries to explain how this changed her attitude towards black people. It is crucial because it demonstrates in terms basic to the novel how words can act as a personal *and* a social agent: to manipulate, to exclude and to suppress. 'I had seen and known negroes since I could remember', Joanna says,

> I just looked at them as I did at rain, or furniture, or food or sleep. But after that I seemed to see them for the first time not as people, but as a thing, a shadow in which I lived, we lived, all white people, all other people.[7]

The irony of this passage stems from the fact that Joanna does not really see or know the black people around her at any moment in her life. Far from progressing from simple seeing to deeper vision – which, of course, is her notion of the change effected by her father's lesson – all she does is move from one form of blindness to another. Like so many of Faulkner's characters, in fact (like, for instance, the deputy in the story, 'Pantaloon in Black'), she uses her eyes and idiom to perform an act of exclusion. To be more exact, she begins by regarding black people as an unremarkable part of life's furniture, something not to be noticed or noted; and then subsequently she turns them into an object of fear – a tactic that seems to dematerialize them, in a way, and certainly serves to dehumanize them. A further irony lies in the relationship this speech implies between Joanna and the people of Jefferson, and between their respective vocabularies. Joanna may feel distanced from the community by her Abolitionist forebears and her supposedly progressive views about what she terms 'a shadow'. The community, in turn, may feel distanced from, and suspicious of, her.

The significant point, however, is that both use speech to deny substance. Joanna may appear to be talking about black people and so by implication acknowledging their existence: understanding them by bringing them within the confines of speech. But what she is really doing is what the townsfolk do: relegating individual black men and women, and the black race as a whole, to silence – a shadowy area (circumscribed by words like 'thing' or 'nigger') where they must remain anonymous and unknown.

'The speech of the book', observes Pierre Macherey, 'comes from a certain silence, a matter which it endows with form, a ground on which it traces a figure.' When 'speech . . . has nothing more to tell us', he goes on, then 'we investigate the silence, for it is the silence that is doing the talking';[8] and what that silence speaks of, above all, is the buried land of the subconscious – personal, or cultural or, more likely, both. The relevance of this to *Light in August* is perhaps obvious: the silences, the interstices or gaps between the speeches and conversations of the people in this novel are just as important as their actual talk. What their vocabularies omit or suppress is just as significant and revelatory as what they get around to saying. Joanna Burden's speech illustrates a paradoxical situation, in which an apparent acknowledgement of presence is actually a revelation of absence. And the speech of many of the other white inhabitants of Yoknapatawpha also places the black on the margins of language: denies him or her the dignity of an adequate definition. Constitutive absence – that is, absence that helps to define meaning – may assume one of several forms in the narrative. A screen of words may provide a means of concealment, perhaps, as it does in Joanna Burden's case. Or the gap between word and object may be widened to the point at which it becomes an unbridgeable abyss. Whatever the form it assumes, though, language acts in such cases to exclude and conceal: to 'unsay', as it were, what is 'unsayable'. It serves to deny the personally unacceptable and the socially unmanageable or intolerable. And in *Light in August* one of the primary acts of exclusion is performed by that one word, 'nigger'.

'Nigger', according to the Oxford English Dictionary, is 'A negro (colloquial and usually contemptuous)'; 'negro', in turn, is defined as 'An individual (especially a male) belonging to the African race of mankind, which is distinguished by a black skin, black woolly hair, flat nose and thick protruding lips.' The terms, and in fact the definitions, are clearly pejorative: so much so that they now circulate in only the most restricted and bigoted corners of society. 'Nigger', in particular, has become the equivalent of a four-letter word: recent black critics have even suggested that it should be excised from mainstream classic texts such as *The Adventures of Huckleberry Finn*. At the time when *Light in August* was written, however, the use of 'nigger' was commonplace. Malcolm X, for example, in his *Autobiography*, recalls the constant repetition of the word even in the mouths of apparently kindly white liberals, like the couple who supervised the juvenile detention home to which he was sent in 1937. 'One of their favourite parlour topics was "niggers"', he explains,

> They would even talk about me, or about 'niggers' as though I wasn't there, as if I wouldn't understand what the word meant. A hundred times a day, they used the word 'nigger'. I suppose that in their own minds, they meant no harm; in fact, they probably meant well.[9]

Whatever intentions might lurk about the use of the word, though, its dehumanizing and divisive effects are clear. As Malcolm X claimed he saw even then, at the age of thirteen, the term 'nigger' turned him into 'a pet': a creature, or object, existing on the other side of some impenetrable emotional barrier, denied 'sensitivity, intellect, and understanding' – or even ordinary human awareness. 'What I am trying to say', he concludes, is that,

> it has historically been the case with white people, in their regard for black people, that even though we might be *with* them, we weren't considered *of* them. Even though they appeared to have opened the door, it was still closed. Thus they never did really see *me*.[10]

The term 'nigger', as Malcolm X saw it and defines it, shuts the door on the visibility of black people. It articulates, it puts in one word, that denial of black humanity – the simple, human presence of black people – on which white society seems often to depend for its survival, its self-justifying image of itself.

If the word 'nigger' is freighted with an elaborate system of ideas concerning racial superiority and social status, then racial demarcation in turn can be seen to support and be supported by a whole range of social divisions. In *Light in August*, 'nigger' becomes part of a network of linguistic divisions – black/white, female/male, damned/elect, poor/rich, and so on – through which the system manages to define and perpetuate itself. What is more to the point, the vital clues to the fate of Joe Christmas can be found in the use of that keyword, and for a very simple reason: in Joe's case, the black/white opposition, which gives the word its substance and turns black people into a peculiarly absent presence, is non-operative. Faulkner has made sure that the question of Joe's racial status can never be answered. 'How do you know that?' asks Joanna Burden when Joe tells her he is 'part nigger'; 'I dont know it', he replies. All we have really, to assign him a possible status, is the story of a decamped circus owner, the ravings of a crazy grandfather, the willingness of various white people (the dietician, Bobbie Allen, Lucas Burch/Joe Brown, the sheriff, Gail Hightower, Gavin Stevens) to fall back on the idea that Joe is black when it suits their purposes – and, perhaps above all, Joe's evident willingness to seize on the word 'nigger' as *his* word. The inhabitants of Jefferson would have accepted him as a Mexican or, more vaguely, a foreigner. But *he* chooses to inform Burch/Brown about his supposed black blood. The information leads eventually to Joe's death. And, in offering it, Joe includes Burch/Brown in a long line of people to whom he has revealed his black identity – or, to be more exact, at whom he has thrust this self-identification: in order, it seems, to challenge them, to disorient and confront. In this sense, surely, Joe is not the archetypal victim he is commonly assumed to be. Nor is he, as one critic has put it, 'a kind of modern Ishmael, who believes that every man's hand is against him'. He is, in a way, more like the figure that tends to occupy centre stage in what Georg Lukács has called 'the classical form of the historical novel'. For it is the task of such a figure, Lukács argues,

> to bring the extremes whose struggle fills the novel, whose clash expresses artistically a great crisis in society, into contact with one another. Through the plot, at whose centre stands this hero, a neutral ground is sought and found upon which the extreme, opposing social forces can be brought into a human relationship with one another.[11]

Joe can be this, a catalyst for conflicting social forces, because he is neither white nor black. Or, rather, he can be either; the choice is his. And, by manipulating a white appearance and a black word, he can challenge the linguistic divisions of the people of Yoknapatawpha; he can subvert their confidence in the allocation of meanings. Joe's presence on his own kind of neutral ground throws the dualistic categories of his society against one another. Standing between extremes, between divisive definitions or terms, he casts doubts on *all* such terms. 'You are worse than that [a 'nigger']', one black man tells him, 'You don't know what you are. And . . . you won't never know. You'll live and die and you won't never know.' Not knowing, though, becomes a weapon for Joe as well as a wound: a way of exposing, to himself and others, the irrevocable connection between the distribution of meaning and the allocation of status – the link, in short, between naming and power.

Voices surround Joe. From fairly early on in *Light in August*, for example, comes this passage:

> Then it seemed to him, sitting on the cot in the dark room, that he was hearing a myriad sounds of no greater volume – voices, murmurs, whispers: of trees, darkness, earth; people; his own voice; other voices evocative of names and times and places – which he had been conscious of all his life without knowing it, which *were* his life . . .[12]

Voices surround him but, almost from the first, he attempts to defy them. There is a constant struggle in the book between the verbal community Joe inhabits – and which demands that a man should act 'like a nigger or a white man' – and the sheer indeterminacy of Joe himself, the fact that he is, as one critic has put it, 'the sign of resistance to fixed signs': a shadowy figure, hiding behind borrowed masks, faked gestures, laconic speech and, whenever necessary, acts of violence. The struggle is complicated, of course, because it occurs *in* Joe as well. Of necessity, his speech and thoughts are full of other people's words. He cannot escape from the

terms of his verbal culture, or the word 'nigger', even in conversations
with himself. So the dialogue, the debate (or, to be more accurate, the
fight for survival), occurs not just *between* but *within*: its arena is not just the
courthouse square, 'about country churches or the shady dooryards of
houses', it is also in Joe's interior speech, inside his head.

Much of the indeterminacy of Joe Christmas comes in effect from this:
that he cannot, even in his mind, step outside the terms of moral and
social self-definition predicated in the word 'nigger', even though he instinctively knows them to be wrong. Much also stems from the way Joe's
story often comes to us, via oral conjecture. The account of his flight after
the death of Joanna Burden, for instance, and his subsequent capture, is
heavily mediated: more often than not, it is the product of communal
debate and tale-telling. More positively, however, at least some of the
mystery, the strangeness of this 'stranger' (as Joe is termed on his first
appearance in the novel) issues out of his violent refusal to play by the
rules. He may set himself up to be called a 'nigger' for his apparent crime,
the murder of a white woman, but he then subverts all the expectations
of the white people around him by failing to run far or fast enough, laying
false trails in such a way as to make fun of his pursuers, and then finally
allowing himself to be captured in Mottstown in a fashion that violates all
the known rules of escape and surrender. 'He never did anything', the
locals observe, talking about Joe's flight and capture: that is, he never
performed in the way expected of him in his newly acquired role of fugitive from justice. 'He never acted like a nigger or a white man', the talk
goes on,

> That was it. That was what made folks so mad. For him to be a murderer and
> all dressed up and walking the town like he dared them to touch him, when
> he ought to have been skulking, and hiding in the woods, muddy and dirty
> and running. It was like he never even knew he was a murderer, let alone
> a nigger too.[13]

Once Joe is captured, a fresh attempt is made to pin the label of 'nigger' on him, to tie him down to a particular – and particularly demeaning
– name and identity. This comes out, in the first instance, among the
people of Mottstown, many of whom demand that Joe should be lynched.
The demand is a horrifying one, certainly, but it may not be so unexpected, given its source. For lynching, too, can be seen as part of the
communal language: a tribal ritual accepted, it seems, even beyond the
borders of Yoknapatawpha. Not just an act of violence, it is an act of
collaboration: meant to underpin a whole series of categories, and so
reassure the community, by putting a so-called 'nigger murderer' in his
place. This time the language fails, however; the collaborative ritual is
botched. What happens to Joe, when he is taken back to Jefferson, cannot
be accommodated within the traditional vocabulary of crime and punishment. Admittedly, Joe's eventual death has a grimly ritualistic quality to it,

that seems to relate to primitive notions of scapegoating and sacrifice: as the killer and, so the rumour goes, possible violator of a white woman, he is killed and also castrated. Admittedly, too, Joe's killer, Percy Grimm, while an aberrant figure, could be said to be responding to the hidden impulses of his community: like so many of Faulkner's outsiders, in fact, Grimm seems to be alienated from the group by the very ferocity with which he embraces its beliefs. Having admitted all that, though, it has to be added that what Grimm does is perceived by the people around him, his white neighbours in Jefferson, as nothing other than a 'murder': that is, an act of violence deprived of even unofficial communal sanction. And for this perception it is surely right to say that it is Grimm's victim, Joe Christmas, who is primarily responsible. For Joe – as it has been suggested already – is a subversive agent: an indeterminate figure whose indeterminacy, and whose willingness to bring that indeterminacy into issue, calls into question the fixities and definites, and the exclusions, of the communal language. Confronting everyone he meets with the inadequate, arbitrary nature of the black/white division, he above all ensures that what happens to him is, in the end, something to which the language of rough justice does not apply. 'It is human history', argues Roland Barthes, 'which converts reality into speech, and it alone rules the life and death of a language'. And the description of Joe's death makes it sound like one of those moments when history is beginning, specifically, to rule the *death* of a language, when the vocabularies evolved by a group to enable them to conceive of and manage the world begin to disintegrate, dissolve into irrelevance:

> When the others reached the kitchen . . . they saw that the man was not dead, and when they saw what Grimm was doing one of them gave a choked cry . . . and began to vomit . . . the man on the floor . . . looked up at them with peaceful and unfathomable and unbearable eyes. Then . . . from out the slashed garments about his hips and loins the pent black blood seemed to rush like a released breath . . . upon that black blast the man seemed to rise soaring into their memories forever and ever. They are not to lose it, in whatever peaceful valleys, beside whatever placid and reassuring streams of old age, in the mirroring faces of whatever children they will contemplate old disasters and new hopes. It will be there . . .[14]

'It' – the memory of Joe Christmas killed and castrated – 'will be there', we are told, suggesting a very different reading of experience from the one predicated in the word 'nigger'. The choked cry that one of the observers utters here is one of those moments of absolute inarticulacy that punctuate Faulkner's narratives – like, say, Benjy's howling in *The Sound and the Fury* – and that seem to define the limits of vocal acts, any attempt to turn experience into a communal language, by seeking refuge beyond or beneath coherent speech. In turn, the vomiting that follows this cry, as a clear gesture of horror and denial, is one of the things that helps us to take the measure of this act of violence: that helps us to locate it, in fact, as a possible act of transformation. As the image of Joe Christmas solidifies in memory, the suggestion is, then perhaps the verbal and moral *apartheid* practised in the use of the word 'nigger' will begin to be dismantled: the linguistic and ideological divisions between black and white will be called into question and subverted. The reference to 'peaceful valleys' and 'placid and reassuring streams' is, in this context of violence, sharply ironic. Yoknapatawpha is not Arcadia, a world of pastoral certitude, despite what some critics of this novel may try to intimate; nor, for that matter, can anywhere situated in history ever be. But the reference to 'old disasters and new hopes' does surely prevent a response of horror freezing into a reflex of despair – does allow, in effect, for the chance of improvement. More to the point, the passage as a whole and the story of Joe Christmas that it concludes do anticipate the possibility that history may generate new directions in language, fresh habits of voice and meaning.

Joe Christmas is not just a being conceived of and defined in racial terms, of course. He is a man, and a body. And that reference which concludes the account of his struggle, to his 'pent black blood' rushing from his violated body 'like a released breath', offers one, significant link in the elaborate chain of references to blood, bodily fluids and emissions, that sometimes appears to dominate the novel. If the verbal divisions of black and white, signalled by the compulsive, repetitive use of the word 'nigger', are of primary interest in the story of Joe, then they are only just so. Close behind those divisions, in terms of the demands made on our attention in this story and elsewhere, are the different if related fissures between female and male. Joe experiences these fissures for himself. His first sexual confrontation, for instance, is with a figure described as 'womanshenegro': which effectively connects the disadvantaged term in the binary opposition female/male to its similarly disenfranchised counterpart in the duality black/white. And Joe's story carries the opposition forward. 'Why in hell do I want to smell horses?' he asks himself at one point, when he flees into a stable, and then answers his own question: 'It's because they are not women.' Women appear to plague him throughout his life, to unnerve him and even (in his eyes, at least) to betray him – from the dietician who 'names' him ('You little nigger bastard!'), through the foster-mother, Mrs McEachern, who, with her 'woman's affinity and instinct for secrecy', seems to frustrate his desire for confrontation, to the 'slight, almost childlike' figure of his first lover, Bobbie Allen, whose reference to being 'sick' (in other words, having a period) brings on this violent vision:

> he seemed to see a diminishing row of suavely shaped urns in moonlight, blanched. Each one was cracked and from each crack there issued something liquid, deathcoloured, and foul. He touched a tree . . . seeing the ranked and moonlit urns. He vomited.[15]

'Womanfilth', 'womanevil', 'God's abomination of womanflesh': remarks like these run through *Light in August* with disturbing frequency. At their most powerful, as here, they are linked with imagery of menstrual blood. This is different from 'black blood' and yet it is connected: as a mark of origin, it too helps to define its possessor as someone who is imprisoned in the messy, muddy origins of things, the base, biological facts of consumption, gestation and expulsion ('woman's muck', says Joe at one point, rejecting some food). If woman is not an urn, to repeat the devastating equation, then she is 'hot wet primogenitive Female' flesh: she, too, seems to belong to the margins of the body and of society.

The association of woman and menstrual blood in *Light in August*, besides being linked with the series black = 'nigger' = 'black blood' = animal/object, is in fact part of an elaborate narrative equation that locates the sources of male domination of women. 'All margins are dangerous', Mary Douglas has observed; and, in this novel, women, like blacks, are identified with the dangerous margins of the body biological and the body politic. Soft, fluid creatures, they present an unnerving challenge to the rigidities of male law; they seem to offer the seductions, and the perils, of dissolution, letting go. They are associated with bodily emissions or bodily absorption – the first time Joe meets Joanna Burden, for instance, he is caught by her in the dark eating her 'invisible food' – with the body as open process, in exchange with other bodies, rather than with the body as closed, tightly controlled system. Male resistance to this, in *Light in August*, is sustained and intensive. If dirt is 'matter out of place', to cite Douglas's famous definition, then most of the male rituals of Yoknapatawpha seem designed to keep 'womanfilth' firmly *in* its proper place: the narrative enacts an ancient male gesture whereby (to quote Douglas again) 'to express female uncleanness is to express female inferiority'.[16] Most of the major male characters of the novel are engaged, at some time or another, in gestures of purification, attempts at rejection or domination. The most obvious in this respect are Joe Christmas and Doc Hines, Joe's grandfather: but Gail Hightower, too, denies his wife in a fairly radical way (driving her, as a result, into promiscuity and suicide), while even Byron Bunch has to learn how his 'words' 'protected' him from any human acknowledgement of Lena Grove. And the gestures are usually successful. The normative position for women in *Light in August* is as adjuncts or observers of men – that is, when they themselves are not being observed, on the dangerous margins: 'womenvoices', like 'the summer voices of invisible negroes', supply for the most part a steady ground-bass or hum, a backdrop against which the activities of the real, male world can be displayed. Even the names of many of the female characters declare their adjunct status: Mrs Armstid, Mrs Beard, Mrs McEachern, Mrs Hines. The text follows the town here: these women are so peripheral, apparently, so much an extension of their men, that they have ceased to have separate names. Even a demeaning individual label, such as 'nigger', is unavailable to them.

The obvious question to ask here is how much the narrative colludes in all this: how far this particular linguistic division is a subject, and how far it is a symptom, of the text. The answer has to be an equivocal one. Much of *Light in August* is devoted to an imaginative dissection of male discourse as a site of male power; almost as much of it, however, participates in that discourse. There is, in the first place, the somewhat ambiguous evidence supplied by the slippery narrative voice of the novel. Many of the references to 'womanevil', or suggestions such as the one that 'women made marriage', can perhaps be explained by saying that, at such points, the narrative is recollecting the voices of the town – as those voices struggle to subdue event to ideology, what they know to what they can say and believe. But there is an insistence and occasional intensity about such remarks that suggest there is more to it than that: that the vocabulary of male domination is not just a matter of investigation, it is at least residually there in the narrative approach. The fact that it is there is most obvious when we look at the figure of Lena Grove, who supposedly was the original inspiration for the novel. Original inspiration she might have been, but she is consistently denied her own subjective space; she is seen through an elaborate screen of male stories, the reports of the men who react to her and discuss her fate. There is no attempt made at an interiorizing approach; nor any suggestion that men make her up, reinvent her as they perceive her. Instead, following a route that is worn down with familiarity by now, the author/narrator looks at Lena as an object and then celebrates her for the apparent possession of qualities that have, in fact, more to do with his exteriorizing approach than with any genuine discovery of her: the qualities, that is, of serenity or placidity, unimpatience and a supposed freedom from anxiety. It is as if Dewey Dell Bundren (a very similar character, in some preliminary ways) had been denied most of her voices, most of the dimensions of speech that make her so unpredictable. What we are left with is what others, and more specifically what male others, see, or what they profess to see: a nurturing, motherly figure, a white equivalent of Dilsey Gibson in a sense, the key to whose life is its utter absence of surprise. It is one of the profound if unintended ironies of the novel that Byron Bunch is meant to be released from the confines of his rigid, male-centred vision and vocabulary by sudden exposure to the otherness of Lena. Byron may achieve this liberation, if we are to believe what we are told. However, the narrative never really does. From the moment Lena Grove appears, observed and discussed by Armstid and Winterbottom, to the last time we see her, captured in the chuckling, generalizing speech of a man talking to his wife in bed ('I was pulling for the little cuss',[17] the man says of Byron's sad attempts to seduce Lena): through all this, she remains a prisoner of male discourse. In a way, she is an even lonelier figure than any of the other, more obviously tragic characters in the book: because she exists apart, not only from the inhabitants of Jefferson, but from us. We are separated from her by an invisible wall of male words.

To leave it there, however, is to do *Light in August* an injustice. Two further points need to be made: one relating to the specifics of male discourse, the other to do with the novel's general investigation of the relationship between language and power. The specific point concerns Joanna Burden. Like Joe Christmas and Gail Hightower, she has been a victim of the family and the family romance: the network of entangling alliances in which one generation enmeshes the next. Like Joe, in particular, she is confronted by the dualisms black/white, female/male and, for that matter, damned/elect; and, unlike him, she seems almost powerless to resist them. The law has been passed down to her by her father, a law given additional weight by being announced beside the graves of her brother and grandfather; and by this exclusively male *fiat* she is obliged to live – a series of injunctions that require her, in effect, to be a man. White = male = elect, black = female = damned: these are the equations implicit in what her father says to her, and they form the cross to which her life is nailed. Told to deny the female part of her – the part which, in turn, is associated with everything in her that is construed as weak or pliable – she is given the equally impossible task of raising 'the black race' to the level of the race that enslaved it. Woman must become man, black must become white, in order that damned can become elect: the binary oppositions can only be abolished, it seems, by the absorption of the 'inferior' term into the 'superior' one. The demand is as impossible as it is absurd; nevertheless, it dictates the terms by which Joanna is supposed to live. As far as her status as a human subject is concerned, it leaves her hopelessly divided, 'two creatures' struggling in one body, a 'dual personality' that can never be properly either female or male. The fissure, or split, in her is caught in one crucial stage in her relationship with Joe. By day, we learn, she sits 'manlike' at her desk going about her self-appointed task as racial saviour: by night, however, she goes through 'every avatar of a woman in love', embracing sex as degradation – whispering 'Negro! Negro! Negro!' in Joe's ear as she sinks down, as she sees it, 'into a bottomless morass'.[18] Perhaps the sheer ambiguity of Joanna's sexual identity made it easier for Faulkner to investigate the destructive nature of male discourse in her case, just as the ambivalence of Joe's racial status enabled a similarly incisive examination of the vocabulary of race. Whatever the reason, an investigation *is* made here. In the story of Joanna, and at many other points in *Light in August*, the verbal and social dynamics of male voices are as carefully and critically analysed as the dynamics of white voices are.

Faulkner's sense that language, speech is involved in a specific, changing network of social relations – that it constitutes an arena in which a continuing debate reallocates meaning: this is something that is registered not only in the speech acts of the community, or the stories of Joe Christmas, Lena Grove or Joanna Burden, but also in the entire structure and texture of the book. Which brings us to the second and final general point to be made about *Light in August*: that, like so many of the novelist's major works, it is insistently figurative, reminding us (if reminder is needed) of the 'made', created nature of language and knowledge. The scene towards the beginning of the novel is a case in point, describing Lena Grove travelling across the Mississippi countryside towards Jefferson and encountering

Henry Armstid in a wagon. Within the space of a few sentences, for instance, we are invited to consider Lena herself in terms of 'something moving forever and without progress across an urn' – caught in frozen mobility, in fact, like the figures in the Keats Ode; to compare motion to stasis in the description of the 'steady and unflagging . . . progress' of Armstid's mules and waggons; to connect hearing and vision (and, to an extent, sound and silence), in the account of the wagon's creaking wheels, the noise of which the narrator compares to 'a ghost travelling a half mile ahead of its own shape'; and to think of all the country wagons that have carried Lena on her journey, together with the mules that have drawn them, as 'a succession of creak-wheeled and limpeared avatars'.[19] This is not just verbal bravado; nor is Faulkner simply intent on violently yoking the most heterogeneous particulars together. The calculated 'high profile' vocabulary used here, the elaborate conceits and patent fictiveness, are just another way of making the point that the scene in question – that this place, like any other – is a product of human creativity: fashioned out of words, grammar, syntax – or, it may be, out of codes, conventions and rituals.

This foregrounding of the speculative, tentative and essentially creative nature of speech and knowledge is carried into every area of the book. The slippage between different narrative voices and styles, mentioned earlier, is matched by a constant and often confusing slippage of names: Joe/Joanna, Bunch/Burch/Burden/Brown. And the feeling of guesswork, uncertainty that attaches to nearly every story in *Light in August* is compounded by Faulkner's use, unusually persistent even for him, of the strategy of partial disclosure: the burning house, for example, that Lena sees in the opening pages of the novel is only 'explained' a long time later – while it takes almost the entire book to find out who 'they' are who 'have thundered past and crashed silently on into the dusk' in the recesses of Gail Hightower's imagination. All this is not wilful mystification, any more than the 'high profile' idiom is. Nor is Faulkner merely intent on presenting language as an endless process of difference and absence: trying to show that, as Lacan puts it, 'language is what hollows being into desire'. On the contrary, what the novelist is trying to do here is to show how language *works*; or, to be more exact, how it is susceptible to use and change. In a book quoted from already, *Mythologies*, Roland Barthes observes that 'the world enters language as a dialectical relation between activities, between human actions', and then comes out of it 'as a harmonious display of essences'. In and through the speech habits of a community, Barthes goes on, elaborating this point, 'things lose their memory that they once were made'.[20] What Barthes is saying, in effect, is that, once any historical reality is converted into a communal language, the process of conversion is quickly and conveniently forgotten. And so what is, after all, only one particular and provisional vocabulary – one very limited and highly debatable version of things – comes to be accepted as a direct transcription of the real. By this process, for instance, the word 'nigger' is taken as a statement of essence, a reflection of the actual nature or historical

character of black people, rather than what it is: a temporary verbal construct, a statement of value – and, it hardly needs to be said, pretty ugly
value at that. By foregrounding language in the way he does in *Light in
August*, Faulkner in fact *reverses* this process for us. He recovers for us the
memory that 'things . . . once were made'. He reminds us of the means,
the procedures by which experience becomes speech; he actually dramatizes
the process of making. And he invites us to consider, too, that what is
made can be unmade and then re-made: not only can be, but must. The
voices that are heard in the streets of Jefferson, in the courthouse square
and the timber yard, have little time at first for moral uncertainties. They
tell the stories of Joe Christmas and Joanna Burden, at least to begin with,
with a shared conviction that words immediately and irreversibly reflect
things. Faulkner recognizes the necessity that lies behind this. A degree
of unanimity, collective assumption, is essential to communication, he
intimates, because communities depend on shared meanings; without them,
nothing would get said or done. However, he also recognizes the necessity
that lies *beyond* this: to accept the partial, provisional character of any
verbal community – and to acknowledge the inevitability, and in some
ways the moral imperative, of change. Much of the excitement of a book
like *Light in August* comes precisely from this: the author's experience of
language, which he then communicates to us, as a field of contention, an
area of debate where different voices dispute meanings and distribute
power. But just as much of it comes from the sense that, since it *is* a field
of contention, language can alter: that different, less polarized and less
exclusive, systems of speech and habits of social exchange are not only
necessary but perfectly possible.

II THE VIRILE PILOT AND THE SEDUCTIONS OF THE AIR: *PYLON*

Well over two years were to elapse after the publication of *Light in August*
before Faulkner's next novel came into print. Faulkner was far from inac-
tive during this time, however. When he had the opportunity, moments of
release from other duties, he began work on a number of projects that
were later to become full-scale fictions. At different moments during this
period, in fact, he worked on the story of the Snopes family that was later
to form part of *The Hamlet*, a book already entitled *Requiem for a Nun* that,
Faulkner explained to his editor, would 'be about a nigger woman' and
'a little on the esoteric side', and on several of the stories that would
eventually be collected together in *The Unvanquished*. Nor was the lapse of
time between October 1932, when *Light in August* appeared to largely
enthusiastic reviews, and March 1935, when *Pylon* emerged to be given a
rather more lukewarm reception, without publications of any kind. Faulkner
continued to place some of his short stories in periodicals, *A Green Bough*
was published in 1933 and *Dr. Martino and Other Stories* in 1934. This may
have been a time when Faulkner found it difficult to concentrate on one

single, sustained project for very long: but it was nevertheless one of immense activity, not only in his professional but also in his personal life. On the personal side, Faulkner found himself the head of the family. Murry Falkner died in 1932. 'He just gave up', Murry's oldest son dryly observed, 'he got tired of living':[21] which indicates how, even at the end, relations remained cool between them. Faulkner now had, as he put it, 'two families to support': with his mother and his youngest brother Dean, in particular, emotionally dependent upon him. He also now had the child he longed for: his daughter Jill was born in 1933. And, given the intimate connection between Faulkner's sense of himself as man and as writer, it is perhaps not so surprising that he chose around this time to begin composing what he entitled 'The Golden Book of Jefferson & Yoknapatawpha County in Mississippi as compiled by William Faulkner of Rowanoak'. Becoming a father, at last, excited him into considering his fatherly relation to his apocryphal county; paternity fired him into imagining himself in the role of patriarch, the paternalist source of authority. Losing a father and gaining a daughter brought the whole, thorny issue of patriarchal law into the foreground of Faulkner's imagination: at first in a fairly simple way, maybe, but eventually, as *Absalom, Absalom!* was to show, as a subject of radical interrogation.

One of the main reasons why Faulkner could not concentrate on any lengthy project at this time was because financial need compelled him to work in Hollywood, as a scriptwriter for Metro-Goldwyn-Mayer. None of the treatments or scripts Faulkner wrote there were actually produced. Nevertheless, they bear powerful testimony to his preoccupations. In particular, they betray an obsession with triangular relationships and, not unrelated to this, with the world of flight – not only the the pilots of the First World War, but also the daredevils and barnstormers who toured the country entering air races and participating in what were known as air circuses. A relationship involving one woman and two men is not uncommon in Faulkner's work generally: issuing, almost certainly, out of his scarcely suppressed sense of rivalry with his father and with Estelle's first husband, Cornell Franklin. Still, it recurs with a frequency that is unusual even for Faulkner in his treatments of the experience of piloting: in scripts like 'Turn About/Today We Live' and 'War Birds/A Ghost Story'. 'Bless you sir', says a character of the *ménage à trois* involving brother, sister and fiancé in 'Turn About/Today We Live', 'they was like one family. You couldn't hardly have knowed which was the brother and which the fiancey.'[22] It was as if Faulkner found it easier to examine sexual transgression in a world that appeared to transgress other norms of bourgeois behaviour. 'Those frantic little aeroplanes which dashed around the country', Faulkner said of the life of the barnstormers, '. . . people wanted just enough money to live, to get to the next place to race again.' There was 'something frenetic and in a way almost immoral' about that life, he added, as if the air aces and their companions 'were outside the range of God, not only of respectability, of love, but of God too'.

The tone of this remark, from someone who appears to be on the edge of what he observes, feeling both a collusive sense of excitement and some unease: this can be explained, in part, by the fact that it reflects just where Faulkner was at the time, as far as the life of the pilot was concerned. At long last, he had learned to fly: characteristically, he had told his instructor that he was a First World War pilot who had lost his nerve! By the end of 1933, he had earned his pilot's licence, later he was to buy a plane: so to some extent he entered into that exclusive male domain of solitary adventure that he had always envied. Only to some extent, however: Faulkner never became as involved in piloting, let alone the excitements of air races and circuses, as his youngest brother Dean, who also learned to fly about this time. He remained just on the margins of things: knowing enough now to share in the adventure, to experience vicariously the thrill of transgression, but unwilling to push things further, to venture beyond the role of weekend pilot in order to become, as Dean did, a part of this incurably restless, mobile world. This was the immediate personal reason for Faulkner's curiously double focus on the experience of flight: but, as his earlier writing had revealed, before he ever learned to fly that duality had been there – even in his first published novel. There were, perhaps, many reasons for this: but two, in particular, shine out because they show how very much Faulkner participated in his culture: how far the autobiography unique to him was wedded to history. 'The air is female. Or so the ancients thought',[23] begins a recent study of the dream of flying entitled *The Prehistory of Flight*. To adventure into the air was therefore to venture into a soft, transparent, unnervingly fluid and unstable world, the world of woman: 'the air's fickleness, variability of mood, and liability to sudden storms seemed especially female' to the ancients, according to this study, 'while its mixed nature, ranging from brilliant clarity to dark and unpleasant fog, suggested the troubling duality of virgin and whore'. At whatever distance, Faulkner participated in this male, Western imagining of the air; and, as a result, he was even more likely to see the pilot as a vexed, dualistic figure – someone who ventures to the precipice, up to and even beyond the boundaries of the male realm, to confront or even immerse himself in the female element.

The first, broadly based reason why Faulkner was always attracted to the experience of flight, and yet nervous of it, begins to generate contradictions in his idea of the pilot. The pilot is male, according to this formula, a paradigm of masculine discipline, intelligence and courage, but also a venturer beyond the borders inscribed by the male principle: someone who has crossed over, for a time, into a more amorphous, instinctive and uncontrollable area associated with woman. A second reason why, from the moment he began to dream about flying, he found himself torn between different feelings, defines Faulkner as very much a person of his times: which is to say, an American living in the first half of the twentieth century. 'In 1927', Faulkner's contemporary F. Scott Fitzgerald declared, something bright and alien flashed across the sky. A young Minnesotan who seemed to have nothing to do with his generation did a heroic thing, and for a moment people set down their glasses in country clubs and speakeasies and thought of their best dreams.[24]

Fitzgerald was referring to the solo flight of Charles Lindbergh across the Atlantic: an event that stirred the imaginations of many Americans – among them, unsurprisingly, Faulkner. The trouble is, when one asks just what it was about Lindbergh that stirred their imaginations, and more generally just what it was about the 'best dreams' of flight that excited them, then the answer has to be deeply contradictory. On the one hand, Lindbergh became in the minds of his contemporaries a living embodiment of the pioneer spirit, the 'spirit of St Louis', the young, independent individual, unaffected by public institutions and pressures. Yet, on the other, his achievement was also seen as a witness to the miracle of technology, what was possible with the help of teamwork, organization and commitment to a production economy. Lindbergh had done it alone, it was pointed out. 'No kingly plane for him', one very minor American poet proclaimed, 'No endless data, comrades, moneyed chums; / No boards, no councils . . . / he plans Alone . . . and takes luck as it comes.' As such, his heroic flight could be seen as a gesture of defiance to the anonymity of the urban, mechanical present, a recovery of true pioneer values, the self-sufficiency of the frontier. Lindbergh himself, however, gave at least equal credit to the plane, 'that wonderful motor', and to team spirit: something clearly acknowledged in the title he chose for the book describing his flight, *We*. President Coolidge chose to point out that Lindbergh's plane was his 'silent partner', that 'in every particular represented American genius and industry'. And, despite their odes to individualism, Americans in general could never really ignore the fact that Lindbergh had been borne to success in a product of the city, industry and technology. 'All day I felt the pull / Of the Steel Miracle', another minor American poet confessed while celebrating Lindbergh's flight: in some; fairly crucial, respects, this was a triumph of modernity.

The dual response to Lindbergh is significant in a general sense because it indicates just how much, in the first few decades of this century, Americans were torn between conflicting notions of their experience. The same groups or individuals could and did respond to Lindbergh's achievement as an anticipation of future technological miracles and as an affirmation of the values of the past. Committed to the power, leisure and wealth of the new, urban world, people nevertheless felt themselves irresistibly drawn towards what they saw as the simpler, purer and more individualistic values of the old. At the end of the 1920s, two American sociologists commented, 'we today are probably living in one of the eras of greatest rapidity of change in the history of human institutions'; 'any people are in a process of change',[25] they added, but the change of pace was now radical and unique. This was a feeling widely shared by other

Americans. As one contemporary politician put it, 'We live in a new creation. Literally, the old things have passed away and all things have become
new.' The conviction of newness and uniqueness mattered to Americans
at the time, profoundly affecting their thought and language; and while,
as their reaction to Lindbergh showed, part of them was inspired by it,
another part was clearly frightened. Compelled towards the horizons of
tomorrow, they were also drawn to the golden landscapes of yesterday.

That was the general emotional climate of the times: an oppressive
mixture of desire and memory, or what one historian has called progress
and nostalgia, that found expression for many Americans in the troubling
dualities of flight – or, to be more exact, in the *idea* of flight. Faulkner's
participation in all this was simple. He felt and responded to that climate
to a peculiarly intense degree. And he did so, not only because he was
emotionally involved with the figure of the pilot in any case – to an extent
undreamed of even by most of his contemporaries – but because of his
location, his geographical situation. The point about location has been
made already, really, in the first chapter of this book: if the United States
in general was caught between progress and nostalgia during this period,
then the South was caught even more painfully than other regions. The
South was witnessing change – economic, social and cultural transformation – at a pace that was unusual even by contemporary American standards; and it was entering the modern world with profoundly mixed feelings,
looking both before and after. Both as an individual human subject, then,
and as a Southerner, Faulkner offered an extreme version of a typical
case. He was experiencing a general, or at least widely shared, trauma in
an exceptional and almost intolerable way. The symptoms of all this,
Faulkner's participation in his generation's ambiguous response to progress
and change, are not, of course, confined to his imaginative readings of the
life of the airman. They do, however, achieve unusually powerful focus
there: just as similarly mixed emotions do in his generation's readings of
the stories of Lindbergh and his kind. It is, above all, in the novel Faulkner
wrote about this time and published early in 1935, *Pylon*, that the dualities
circulating around the idea of cultural alteration begin to spin out of
control: as Faulkner struggles to make sense of what he termed 'a fantastic
and bizarre phenomenon on the face of a contemporary scene, of our
culture at a particular time'[26] – the barnstormers, the people of the air
who travelled around the country in search of adventure. *Pylon* has often
been called Faulkner's least satisfactory novel. That may be so, although
it has to be said that there are some other contestants for that title. What
is surely indisputable, though, is that it is a novel grounded in anxiety.
The nervous textures of the narrative speak of a deeper unease, of unre-
solved uncertainties about male and female, past and future, pastoralism
and technology, stability and change – all of which narrow down on the
ménage à trois at the centre of the story: the pilot, the parachutist and the
woman they share.

To some extent, the fractiously syncopated nature of *Pylon* is due to the fact that it represents Faulkner's first real attempt to register the voices of the city. Influenced, perhaps, by his recent encounters with the cinema and, in particular, with cinematic effects of montage, Faulkner seems to be pursuing a verbal equivalent of what Marshall McLuhan has termed the discontinuous landscapes of urban life: a fractured, disjunctive mixing of disparate media and messages, alive with implication and rumour. The narrator of the novel refers, at one point, to 'the garblement that was the city'; and, by bringing into collision the roar of advertisement hoardings, newspaper headlines, the scattered sense impressions of the streets, and a great deal of the verbal detritus of modern times, Faulkner works in the same direction as John Dos Passos, it seems: towards a sense of mobility and energetic dissolution – the experience of a cultural system that is a series of unanchored signs, fragments without even the illusion of coherence. The narrative alludes, now and then, to the 'fragile web of ink and paper' stringing this world very loosely together: the verbal and aural signature of accelerated social change. More interestingly, it links this to the 'fragile web of flesh and nerves' in which the inhabitants of the city streets reside. In this place, and time, character is translated into a receptacle for sense impressions, a medium through which various words, sounds and experiences pass. People do not act; they do not really react; all that happens is that things happen to them. Even here, however, in its verbal imitations of city life, the book is not without its contradictions. Every so often, the narrator falls back on the lush pleasures of a more exotic, far more conventional, *fin-de-siècle* rhetoric:

> Now they could cross Grandlieu Street. There was traffic in it now; to clash and clang of light and bell, trolley and automobile crashed and glared across the intersection, rushing in a light kerb-channelled spindrift of tortured and draggled serpentine and trodden confetti pending the dawn's white wings – spent tinsel dung of Momus' Nile barge clatterfalque.[27]

It is as if Faulkner were trying to compensate for the radical innovations of some of the idiom of *Pylon* by falling back, occasionally, on a more familiar voice, evoking old, forgotten, far-off things and battles long ago – the voice that, for instance, concludes *Sartoris*. To be more exact, it is as though the actual verbal textures of the novel speak of both progress and nostalgia: the jumpy, anxious sounds of tomorrow and a more plangent series of sounds, recollecting all the author's yesterdays.

It is in the portraits of the major characters, however, that the contradictions multiply and syncopation begins to accelerate into discord. The story gathers around a character called simply the Reporter, another version of the writer as voyeur and parasite (he is several times compared to a bird of prey), and the barnstormers with whom he becomes infatuated: above all, Roger Shumann, the pilot, Jack Holmes, the parachutist, and Laverne Shumann – who evidently married Roger on a spin of the dice, when she found out that she was pregnant but, unfortunately, could not be certain whether the child was Roger's or Jack's. Some of the constellations of motive and relationship here are familiar from Faulkner's earlier novels. The Reporter, the man of words, is drawn to Roger, who is emphatically not a man of words or a 'man of thought' but a man of action. Drawn to him, that is, in love and hate: he sees Shumann as a brother but, as Shumann himself jokingly intimates, a brother whom he would quite like to see dead. This replication of the relationship of Bayard Sartoris III and his brother Johnny is accompanied by other echoes of earlier narratives. The main reason, it turns out, why the Reporter sometimes longs for and even seems to connive in the death of Shumann (after all, he helps to validate the purchase of the dangerous plane in which Shumann is eventually killed) is that he desires Laverne: a woman like so many of Faulkner's women – slim, boyish, but tough, a 'bright, plain shape of love' who seems to disappear as she is pursued. Like the objects the pilots ride and the air through which they fly, she is a troublingly plural creature. When the Reporter first meets her, she looks 'almost like a man' in her 'greasy coverall'. However, the story of her making love to Shumann in a plane and then falling to earth with her sexual parts exposed, 'in the very traditional symbology – the mired dress with which she was trying wildly to cover her loins, and the parachute harness – of female bondage': this indicates how unnervingly like a woman she is, for both character and narrator. 'I would believe you even if I knew you had lied',[28] says the Reporter to her at one point: which suggests just how much his longing for her is entangled in familiar dualisms. She is, it seems, and has to be, both truthful 'virgin' and lying 'whore': a mother whose last recorded actions are as mysterious as her first – since it is not clear whether her surrender of her son to his grandfather, after Roger's death, is an act of sacrifice or a gesture of irresponsibility, a way of giving the boy a better chance or, more simply, a means of cutting herself loose.

Here already, however, with the role of Laverne as mother, we are moving into less familiar territory. 'Who's your old man, kid?' the mechanic Jiggs tauntingly asks Laverne's child, Jackie (the name itself emphasizes the uncertain nature of any answer since it recalls Jack Holmes, the man Laverne did *not* marry). This is not so much a family as an anti-family, a grouping that defies the familiar patterns and apparently does so without friction: the sense of sexual rivalry in the novel, such as it is, comes from outside the group, from people like the Reporter, not from any serious conflict between Roger and Jack. And the oddity of this is that, like so many of the other aspects of these people of the air, neither the narrator nor his surrogate – that is, the Reporter – know what to make of it. Is this evident transgression of the established laws of sexual bonding and ownership a function of their liberty or of their inhumanity? Are they oblivious to the principles of paternity – principles that carry along with them the whole freight of ideas about property, possession and inheritance on which civil society rests – because they are as free as air, instinctive individualists, or because they are unthinking, uncaring machines? We do not know, since we are not told. Or, to be more accurate, we are told different things at different times. The pilots are huntsmen of the air, we are advised. They are nature's gentlemen, like the pioneer: capable not only of disinterested teamwork, quiet professionalism and laconic commitment to their own code of living, but also of genuine heroism. The way Roger Shumann manoeuvres his plane, in the last moments of his life, so as to avoid death or injury to others is only one of many particular cases in point. But they are also described as 'mechanical', giving off the 'illusion of tautly sprung steel', 'creatures imbued with motion but not with life'. They have no home, apparently, except like Jiggs a home to stay away from – Jiggs, in fact, claims that he comes from anywhere. In the words of the Reporter, they have 'no ties; no place where you were born and have to go back to it now and then even if it's just only to hate the damn place good and comfortable'.[29] And this absence of place and past is like everything else that is crucial to their depiction. It implies mobility, of course: but it is never clear whether this is the adventurous mobility of the frontiersman or the restless mobility of urban life – a sign that they are free of the city, or in thrall to it.

'They ain't human', the Reporter observes at one moment of Roger, Jack and Laverne, 'It ain't adultery; you can't any more imagine two of them making love than you can imagine two of them aeroplanes back in the corner of the hangar, coupled.' The trouble is, this attempt to establish the pilots as a collective other, a generalized 'they' outside the boundaries of normalcy, is itself flawed. 'You will see a living man, a man like yourselves . . . hurl himself into space', declares the announcer at the air circus. And this remark alerts us to another contradiction at work in the novel of which Faulkner himself seems hardly aware. At times the generalizing tendency of *Pylon* pushes the reader towards an acknowledgement of the strangeness of the barnstormers, their peculiar otherness. At others, in an equally generalizing way, the narrative voice intimates or admits a connection, or likeness: whether because everyone is now seen to be implicated in the machine (thanks to the car, we are told, we are all becoming 'a new and legless kind'), or because we are all drawn to adventure and 'crazy' risks, depends on the mood of the narrator or the Reporter or the occasion. Are the pilots like 'us' or unlike 'us'? Are they pioneers or machines? Is the air they penetrate an inviting virginal space or a seductively dangerous element? The sheer uncertainty of Faulkner's answers to these questions can perhaps be measured in his opening description of the site these people of the air have chosen as their own, the airport that – along with the city of New Valois, a thinly disguised fictional version of New Orleans – supplies *Pylon* with whatever sense of place it possesses:

Now the bus, the road, ran out of the swamp . . . it ran now upon a flat plain of saw-grass . . . a pocked desolation of some terrific and apparently purposeless reclamation across which the shell road ran ribbon-blanched towards something low and dead ahead of it – something low, unnatural: a chimera quality which for the moment prevented one from comprehending that it had been built by man and for a purpose. The thick heavy air was full now of a smell thicker, heavier, though there was yet no water in sight; there was only the the soft pale sharp chimera-shape above which pennons floated against a drowsy immensity which the mind knew must be water, apparently separated from the flat earth by a mirage line so that, taking shape now as a double-winged building, it seemed to float lightly like the apocryphal turreted and battlemented cities in the coloured Sunday sections, where beneath sill-less and floorless arches people with yellow and blue flesh pass and repass: myriad, purposeless, and free from gravity.[30]

This is only part of a descriptive sequence that then goes on to talk about the 'air both aerial and aquatic' of the airport terminal, and about the 'plaza of beautiful and incredible grass labyrinthed by concrete driveways' across which can be seen 'a mathematic monogram of two capital F's' celebrating the name of Feinman, the airport's founder and financer. What is remarkable about all this is how the sheer confidence, even bravura, of the tone conceals radical incoherences of mood. The passage just quoted begins with implications of a waste land, tying in with the profusion of Eliotic references inhabiting this novel: one chapter is even titled 'Love-song of J.A. Prufrock'.[31] Intimations of sterility, futility and waste suddenly slip away, however; the reference to 'a chimera quality' marks the turning-point. The waste land then transmogrifies into a dream landscape – like, say, something out of the poems of Poe – which exists in, and indeed seems to be a part of, a fluent, magical atmosphere, to float above (in the air) and below (in the water) the earthy commonplace. To complicate matters further, the turn is neither unambiguous nor complete: the reference to 'the coloured Sunday sections', after all, carries with it suggestions of vulgarity and the market place, while the later description of the 'capital F's' reverberates with implications of power and control – locating the airport, in effect, as a product and producer of hard cash rather than the site of dreams. What the reader is left with, at the end of all this, is simple confusion. Just as the status or identity of the barnstormers tends to fluctuate, so does the character of the place they mostly inhabit, where they seek their adventures and ply their trade. As Faulkner describes it, here and elsewhere, Feinman Airport is constantly shifting focus: at one moment the habitation of romance and magic, at another just one more modernist factory – sometimes, the site of battlements and pennons, like the dreamscapes in which Colonel John Sartoris and his generation are remembered, and sometimes a world of greed and destruction, like the cityscape in some dystopic nightmare.

Eating into almost every area of *Pylon*, the contradictions on which Faulkner's idea of the pilot – and, more generally, the world of the air – were founded make even some of the more familiar patterns of the author's rhetoric problematical. For instance, when Colonel Feinman is confronted with the question of whether Roger Shumann can be permitted to fly the plane he claims to have bought from another pilot, he falls back on the kind of anti-government, individualistic idiom that Faulkner himself favoured in many of his speeches and letters. 'Let me get this straight', Feinman says to the government agent who wants to invalidate the sale,

> We've had our crops regimented and our fisheries regimented and even our money in the bank regimented. All right . . . But do you mean to tell me that Washington can come in and regiment a man that's trying to make his living out of the air? Is there a crop reduction in the air too?[32]

The crop analogy, in particular, seems to reinforce this diatribe against those institutional forces that would seek to suppress freedom – and, above all, the freedom of the air. It is as if Faulkner the farmer were adding the weight of his own personal anger to the alarm voiced here by his character. The only problem is that, as usual in *Pylon*, things are neither as clear nor as clearly thought out as the fluency of the rhetoric would suggest. Quite apart from the fact that Feinman is, on the whole, an unsympathetic character – a paradigm of mercantile power rather than a torch-bearer for freedom – there is the unsettling point that he is really only saying what he says so as to manoeuvre others into doing what he wants: not actually respecting their opinions but imposing his will. And what he wants – in this instance, a good race with plenty of controversy and danger – will lead to Shumann's death, something that nearly everyone else in the novel correctly anticipates and fears apart from Shumann himself. In other words, this is a *corruption* of the rhetoric of freedom; the idiom of individual liberty and choice is being used as an instrument of manipulation and power. It would be pleasing if this could be interpreted as Faulkner's intention: if we could say, in fact, that the author's deployment of an individualistic language here is critical, a way of interrogating its uses – and its uses, especially, in a complex, urban world like that of *Pylon*, where it may not be entirely or immediately applicable. The truth, however, is at once simpler and more troubling than that. Like so much else in the novel, Feinman's attack on regimentation is riven with conflict because Faulkner himself cannot make up his mind whether the belief in individualism in which that attack is grounded is appropriate or an anomaly. He cannot decide whether the airport (which is, after all, the world Feinman has helped create, and on which he has inscribed his name) is a place where the language of freedom has a meaning – or one where it has become at best irrelevant and at worst a mask for, or even an extension of, the real machinery of power.

Pylon ends with a pair of discarded documents, written by the Reporter after the death of Roger Shumann and found by the copy-boy in the newspaper office after the Reporter has left. One document, carefully 'salvaged and restored to order and coherence' by the copy-boy, is a kind of prose elegy for the dead pilot, so composed as to seem 'not only news but the beginnings of literature'. 'On Thursday Roger Shumann flew a race against four competitors, and won', it begins. 'On Saturday', it goes on, 'he flew against one competitor. But that competitor was Death.' The piece continues in the same romantic vein, right down to a closing reference to the 'simple wreath' that 'two friends' dropped for Shumann to 'mark his Last Pylon'. The other document, left lying on the editor's desk, is quite different. It starts with what purports to be simple fact; the futile and eventually abandoned search for Shumann's body lost with his plane in the lake near the airport, and the departure of Laverne Shumann 'with her husband and children for Ohio where it is understood that their six-year-old son will spend an indefinite time with some of his grandparents'. Added to this, 'savagely in pencil', the copy-boy discovers, is a note from the Reporter to the editor beginning, '*I guess this is what you want, you bastard*', and telling the editor to get down to Amboise Street in New Valois where the Reporter is planning, not for the first time, to get drunk. '*When you come bring some jack with you*', he concludes, '*because I am on credit.*'[33] The passage that these recovered, and in one case reconstituted, fragments trace is the erratic journey of the novel: incorporating, at different times, admiration, flat documentation of apparent fact, distortion, bewilderment and anger. The knightly figure whose heroic corpse is lost in the waters jostles for our attention with intimations of futility, waste and loss; a sense of deep confusion, nausea and frustrated rage finds an escape-route in willed oblivion. It would be wrong to identify the Reporter with the narrator, let alone the author, even if all three share the same rhetoric at times, and the same capacity for oscillating violently between wordy idealism and laconic cynicism. It would equally be stretching a point to say that Faulkner goes no further than his hard-talking, soft-centred journalist character in the attempt to articulate his uncertain feelings for someone like Roger Shumann. Just the same, there is a connection to be made here. The Reporter, after all, attempts on a small scale what his creator seeks for on a much larger one: he tries to write the life of piloting, to turn the experience of flying into words. And he ends as Faulkner does: with fragments, however colourful, that simply replicate the impasse in which their author is caught. Piloting exercised a special fascination for Faulkner for most of his life: it was, among other things, the source of some of his very best lies. But although it was so fascinating to him – despite the fact that it bore the signature of many conflicts and convictions that were partly his, and partly those of his generation and culture – he could never properly get to grips with or make sense of it; he could never sort out just what he felt about piloting and why. He could not, in short, turn the dream of flight into a convincing fiction, although he tried to do so more than once. He could only report his confusions and leave it at that; after which, it was not the bar he sought, by way of compensation, but other stories nearer the earth.

III   History is What Hurts: *Absalom, Absalom!*

Faulkner later explained that he wrote *Pylon* because, as he put it, 'I'd got in trouble with *Absalom, Absalom!* and I had to get away from it for a while.'

What he had to get away from was a story the different elements of which had haunted him since at least as far back as 1928. Some time in that year, Faulkner completed 'Mistral', the paired narrators of which anticipate the narrative relationship of Quentin Compson and Shreve. Not long after that, in 1929, he wrote another short piece, 'The Big Shot', which includes a character whose life broadly parallels the early career of Thomas Sutpen. Then two other tales, 'Evangeline' written in 1931 and 'Wash' devised in 1933, took Faulkner into the deeper recesses of the Sutpen story: on the one hand, into the triangular relationship of Henry and Judith Sutpen and Charles Bon and, on the other, into the death of Thomas Sutpen at the hands of Wash Jones. The process by which *Absalom, Absalom!* took shape – gradual, accumulative, circuitous and sometimes even repetitive – foreshadowed both the structure and the preoccupations of the finished novel. And that process continued through the early months of 1934, as Faulkner made several tentative and false starts on a manuscript titled 'Dark House'. 'A plantation in the South in 1858', begins one of these manuscript fragments, 'Col. Sutpen, his daughter Judith, his son Henry. Henry attends college about 50 miles away.'[34] Slowly, the fragments began to gather around a story: a story that, by August of 1934, Faulkner was calling *Absalom, Absalom!* – 'of a man', the novelist explained to his editor, 'who wanted a son through pride, and got too many of them and they destroyed him'. However, Faulkner went on, the material was 'not quite ripe yet'; he had a 'mass of stuff, but only one chapter' that satisfied him. So he turned to *Pylon* for a few months, writing it quickly between October and December; and, by March of the following year, when *Pylon* was published, he was ready to go back to the story of Sutpen and his family again. The interlude spent on his novel about piloting had worked, it seemed, releasing his mental block just as he had hoped it would.

Returning to *Absalom, Absalom!*, Faulkner 'almost rewrote the whole thing', he claimed. The work was intensive, but it was also interrupted. Between March 1935 and October 1936, when the book was eventually published, the novelist took three extended trips to Hollywood, where he worked for Twentieth Century-Fox. Closer to the emotional bone, his brother Dean was killed in November 1935; and in Hollywood, shortly after this, he met and began a serious relationship with Meta Carpenter. Despite the extraordinary demands on his time and the even more extraordinary drain on his emotions, Faulkner managed to complete the manuscript by January 1936 – written at Rowan Oak, in Hollywood, and at his mother's house in Oxford – and the typescript, with an added chronology, genealogy and map of Yoknapatawpha County, by May of the same year. 'I think it's the best novel yet written by an American', Faulkner proudly declared before publication: a claim that was probably reinforced by his awareness of the long gestation period *Absalom, Absalom!* had undergone, the complexly layered, slowly accreted character of the narrative, and the emotional traumas he had experienced during the process of writing – and which he had somehow managed to channel into one or other layer of the text. The book had been written, in part, in the house of his dead father. It had been disrupted by the death of a brother, for which he felt responsible ('I've ruined your life', he had told Dean's widow, 'It's my fault'). And, in the closing stages of writing and revision, it had been accompanied by the beginnings of a genuinely passionate relationship. 'I've always been afraid of going out of control', Faulkner confided to Meta Carpenter, 'I get so carried away';[35] and with Meta, perhaps for the first time in his life, he allowed himself to let go – he enjoyed the sheer uncontrol of prolonged sexual abandon. *Absalom, Absalom!* is Faulkner's greatest historical novel, in the sense that it investigates the meanings of history: just what it is to be born, as Judith Sutpen puts it, 'with a lot of other people, all mixed up with them', from the past, present and future. It is also an extreme instance of the narrative as process: in which an elaborate network of coinciding and conflicting voices and genres replicate historical experience – and register being in time as a fluid, inconclusive movement, a matter of collective debate and continuing revision. Because of all this, it is easy to forget just how powerful the stories of *Absalom, Absalom!* are on a simple human level: stories of incest, miscegenation, fratricide, patriarchal power and filial obsession, the fatally linked encounters of sex and death – all of which, and more, give the arguments of the narrative their living tissue, remind us forcefully what Fredric Jameson's phrase, 'history is what hurts', really means. Faulkner was capable of writing with this degree of power at many times in his life. Just the same, it is surely right to say that one reason why he wrote so powerfully of such things on this occasion was because he was confronted with similarly primal events in his own life: the loss of a father and a dearly beloved brother and the gain of a lover that, in its own way, reminded him of yet another loss – of the 'sisterly' companionship of Estelle Oldham, the childhood friend and intimate with whom he had once been in love.

'History is what hurts.' One reason it hurts so much in *Absalom, Absalom!* is that, as so many commentators have observed, everything is open to debate: anything said in or about the novel can be convincingly disputed and denied. Experience becomes a field of contention where different voices continually argue out meanings. This is a process similar to the one we find in, say, *The Sound and the Fury, As I Lay Dying* and *Light in August.* The difference, if there is one, is that in this book the field of contention is a much more openly and specifically historicized one, as the following famous and frequently quoted passage testifies:

> *Maybe nothing ever happens once and is finished. Maybe happens is never once but like ripples maybe on water after the pebble sinks, the ripples moving on spreading, the pool attached by a narrow umbilical water-cord to the next pool which the first pool feeds, has fed, did feed, let this second pool . . . reflect in a different tone the infinite unchanging sky, it doesn't matter: that pebble's watery echo whose fall it did not even see moves across its surface too at the original ripple-space, to the old ineradicable rhythm . . .*[36]

This intuition is attributed to Quentin Compson. And what Quentin appears to be intimating here is what Judith Sutpen suggests in that passage, referring to the figure of a pattern in a rug, which was quoted in the first chapter: that history is a complex series, a continuum out of which the individual being emerges and to which, irrevocably, he or she belongs. A multiplicity of cords – or, as it is put elsewhere, a set of invisible but unbreakable 'strings' – bind him or her to all other beings, all other people before and after who function both as influencers and influenced. This sense of history inevitably transforms historical experience into a process of repetition and replication. Things happen, events occur, but the meaning of those events is subject to continual revision; the present is constantly 'rewriting' the past and future and, in its turn, being 'rewritten' by them. And this is not just a matter of debate – of experience being passed through many voices – it is also a matter of connection and context. One moment in time, one ripple in the pool, shifts character as it links up with other, different moments: those occasions when Quentin and Shreve seem to 'become' Henry Sutpen and Charles Bon, and so alter the character of both narrative present and past, are only the most obvious examples of this. Not only that, that moment or ripple assumes new dimensions every time it is placed in another context: with every repetition, for instance, the moment when the young Thomas Sutpen knocked at a plantation house door, only to be told to go round to the back, is changed because of the changed framework in which it is lodged – the continually altering and *expanding* narrative structure in which it is reinserted.

To an extent, what we are being offered here in the view of history predicated in *Absalom, Absalom!* is a version of Einstein's theory of relativity or Heisenberg's formulation of the indeterminacy principle. There is no absolute view of historical events in the novel, no 'God's view'. The relationships of before and after, and simultaneous with, depend on the observer's position in relation to those events. Or, to put it another way, the object of investigation (in this case, the past) is altered by the actual process of being investigated; and the outcome of the investigation depends on the standpoint that was originally taken. Quite a few critics have seized on this to argue that *Absalom, Absalom!* is consequently founded on, or rather floating in, indeterminacy: that what it offers us is no more than verbal play, a potentially infinite series of signifiers. There is an element of truth in this. In this book, as in all Faulkner's major fictions, no voice speaks the simple truth and every voice is remorselessly speculative: 'maybe', 'perhaps', 'probably' and their equivalents are the standard currency of narration, while the narrative itself is an elaborate and often bewildering network of 'old tales and talking' – conversations overheard, stories recounted at several removes, partial disclosure, imaginative hypotheses and sheer guessing. Most of the story comes to us mediated by not one but several narrators, and is punctuated by such remarks as 'I was not there', 'All I have heard', 'I have this from something your grandfather let drop', 'the tale came through the negroes', 'That was how he told it'. The account of Sutpen's experiences in Haiti, for example, is offered by Quentin to Shreve; Quentin, in turn, learned it from his father, who learned it from *his* father General Compson, who learned it from Sutpen. The reader is presented with a series of receding pictures – Quentin and Shreve at Harvard, Quentin and his father in Oxford, Quentin's father listening to General Compson, General Compson listening by the campfire to Sutpen – all of which revolve around the act of storytelling, constructing a version of things. Nor do these pictures end with the version Sutpen supplies, since he seems to be quite as distanced from the story as anyone else. 'It was not absolutely clear to him', we are informed,

> – the how and why he was there and what he was – since he was not talking about himself. He was telling a story... he was just telling a story about something a man named Thomas Sutpen had experienced.[37]

In this context, something that Mary McCarthy said about Vladimir Nabokov's novel *Pale Fire* seems relevant. When we read *Pale Fire*, she explained,

> a novel on several levels is revealed, and those 'levels' are not the 'levels of meaning' of modernist criticism but planes in fictive space... Each plane or level in its shadow box proves to be a false bottom; there is an infinite regression, for the book is a book of mirrors...[38]

'The book is a book of mirrors.' Certainly, *Absalom, Absalom!* is like this in many respects. The several narrators of the book offer versions of the past that tell us as much about their creators as they do about their apparent subject; in doing so, they dramatize the notion of the historical process as an active re-creation, a reinvention of the past by the present. People such as Quentin and Shreve, in particular, are like detectives who try to construct out of 'the rag-tag and bob-ends' of recollected voices and gestures a coherent and plausible account of yesterday's events: who did what, and why. 'The hero of the detective novel', argues R.G. Collingwood in *The Idea of History*,

> is thinking exactly like an historian when, from indications of the most varied kinds, he constructs an imaginary picture of how a crime was committed and by whom.[39]

Which suggests a further and more telling analogy: the narrators of *Absalom, Absalom!* could also be compared to Collingwood's ideal historian, who weaves together 'a web of imaginative construction' (as Collingwood puts it) 'stretched between certain fixed points provided by the statements of his authorities'. History, Collingwood insists, is a re-enactment of past experience. 'The history of thought, and therefore all history, is the re-enactment of past thought in the historian's mind.' 'This does not involve a passive surrender to the spell of another's mind', he goes on, but rather,

> a labour of active and therefore critical thinking. The historian not only re-
> enacts past thought, he re-enacts it in the context of his own knowledge and
> therefore, in re-enacting it, criticises it . . . This criticism of the thought whose
> history he traces is not something secondary to tracing the history of it. It
> is an indispensable condition of historical knowledge itself.[40]

It is not difficult to see the parallel here. The activity Collingwood describes is not that far removed, after all, from (for example) Quentin's
and Shreve's attempts to reinterpret the Sutpen story by relating it to their
own experience and the broader historical experience of the South: to
recover the past by resurrecting its inhabitants and to 'become' them –
trying to imagine how they thought and what they believed. In turn, that
activity is not so very different from the one the narrative of *Absalom,
Absalom!* imposes on us. Like the narrators, we are compelled to compare
versions, fill in gaps and discover inconsistencies: 'we have a few old mouth-
to-mouth tales', as Mr Compson puts it at one point in the novel, and by
attending to these we may hope to 'see dimly people, the people in whose
living blood we ourselves lay dormant and waiting'. *Absalom, Absalom!* is
'about' the making of history and enforces just such a making not only on
its characters but also on its audience, each member of which consequently becomes a part of what Mary McCarthy termed 'an infinite regression'. With its recurring characters, its constant repetition and revision of
familiar stories, and its slow, circuitous accumulation of argument and
incident, it ends up by offering us a paradigm of history and historical
knowledge: a model in which 'nothing ever happens once and is finished'
either for the characters or for the reader.

There is, however, a possible difference between Collingwood's notion
of the historian and the situation in which Faulkner places his characters
and readers – or, for that matter, himself – and it takes us back to those
critics who would see *Absalom, Absalom!* as little more than a lexical playing
field. In constructing his imaginative web, Collingwood suggests, the historian tries to use 'nothing that is not necessitated by the evidence', but
nevertheless to provide sufficient 'points' (in the form of documents,
artifacts and other data) for only one 'thread' or hypothesis to fill the
space between. And 'if these points are frequent enough', Collingwood
argues, 'and the threads spun from each to the next are constructed with
due care . . . the whole picture . . . runs little risk of losing touch with the
reality it represents.' The trouble with something like the Sutpen story,
though, is that the 'points' are not necessarily frequent enough. One critic
has put it this way: 'there are too many holes in it [the story] and no
possible access to factual filler for the holes. At best, it is a series of
dramatically potent pictures.' That may be arguable. What is unarguable,
however, is that, while a narrative that links yesterday to today is something that Quentin and Shreve clearly yearn for, all that they *feel* they
weave out of the clues given them, most of the time, is something
disconcertingly artificial, evidently fictive: a world inhabited by

people who perhaps had never existed at all anywhere, who, shadows, were
shadows not of flesh and blood which had lived and died but of shadows in
turn of what were . . . shades too, quiet as the visible murmur of their vapour-
ising breaths . . .[41]

The past, in this view, seems to be 'a kind of vacuum' (as Shreve the
Canadian describes the South itself, at one point), which the observer
must populate with his or her imagined inhabitants. Or, if not that exactly, it does appear at any rate to be uncharted territory containing a few
traces, one or two stray points of reference, calculated to tease even the
least curious and speculative of minds.

Are Quentin and Shreve right here? For that matter, are those critics
right who claim to find undiluted relativism in *Absalom, Absalom!*: an
elaborate network of language that manages both to conceal and to expose a total absence of meaning – and, in the strict sense, an equally total
absence of subject? Does the connection with Collingwood's idea of historical knowledge in effect stop here, because *all* the evidence is untrust-
worthy – for the simple reason that what both narrator and reader are left
with, by the end of the novel, is no more than the slipperiness, the eva-
sions and opacities, of words? In response to these kinds of questions, it
might be useful to recall what someone other than Collingwood, Fredric
Jameson, has said about knowledge of history. 'History is *not* a text, not a
narrative', Jameson argues. Although 'it is inaccessible to us except in
textual form', history – which is to say, an account of the past – has a
referent that is real, not imagined. Admittedly, the past has to be approached by 'passing through its prior textualisations' to a recognition of
its function as the 'absent cause' of the present social effects that we
experience as 'Necessity'. But to those who draw the currently fashionable
inference that, because history is a 'text, the "referent" does not exist',
Jameson simply proposes the theoretical irrelevance of such a position.
'History as ground and untranslatable horizon needs no particular theoretical justification', he insists, 'we may be sure its alienating necessities
will not forget us, however much we might prefer to ignore them.'[42] For
Jameson, the question is not whether history exists but whether (and to
what extent) we can make sense of that 'Necessity' which our present
experience compels us to recognize, not as a product of our own making,
but as a consequence of the actions of past human agents: to see the past
as a necessary precondition of the present in all its identity and difference
– its significant links with, and its equally significant separation from, our
own times. History is what hurts, and it will hurt regardless of whether or
not we acknowledge its presence, admit that it is in fact there. If we fail
to make sense of it, to locate ourselves in terms of it, then we become its
unknowing, powerless victims. Not only that, if we fail to see those people
'in whose living blood we ourselves lay dormant and waiting' (to recall
that phrase of Mr Compson's), then we fail to see a crucial determining
factor in our lives – and, to that extent, fail to see and understand ourselves.

Another way of putting all this, and relating it more directly to *Absalom, Absalom!*, is to say (picking up a point touched upon earlier) that Faulkner's tale of Thomas Sutpen presents us with a paradigm of history at work. In his versions of the Sutpen story, Faulkner apprehends – and requires us, the readers, to appreciate – a historical reality that is complex, multiple and internally antagonistic, forever in dispute and in the process of revision. The different voices and mixed genres of the narrative register the various codes present in any age or social formation: the conflicting languages that, in turn, reflect and represent conflicts of class and interest group – the antagonistic cultures existing within even what might seem the most monolithic 'culture'. And, as they quarrel and collide, those voices and genres allow a realization both of the continuities between past and present – how yesterday shadows today and today reconstitutes yesterday – and also of the process by which those continuities are disrupted, dismantled and rebuilt. It is not really a question of asking whether there was a man called Thomas Sutpen who did what, it is said, he did in Virginia, Haiti and then in Mississippi. It is not a matter, in other words, of inert facts, to be collected and compiled as if they were somehow separable from the processes of time and then constructed into some unalterable, contextless 'truth'. It is, rather, a question of relating the lived contradictions of Sutpen's life, as they are recollected, to the equally lived contradictions of those who engage in the process of recollection – which means author, narrators and readers – so as to establish the significant pattern, of resemblance and difference, that exists between a pluralistic past and a changing present. 'The breakdown of narrativity in a culture, group, or a social class', Hayden White has observed, 'is a symptom of its having entered into a state of crisis': because, he goes on, 'with any slackening of narrativising capacity' a group 'loses its power to locate itself in history, to come to grips with the Necessity that the past represents for it'.[43] This is the problem that cripples the individual narrators of *Absalom, Absalom!* – how to construct a viable story relating yesterday to today, one that unearths the past in all its pastness and also in its ties, the umbilical cord, to the present. It is not, however, one that cripples or even debilitates the book that acts as host to these individual narrators and the narratives they devise. Far from it, the thrust of *Absalom, Absalom!* as a whole (or, to be more exact, a complex series) is to show how we, as human agents, can get into history, in the sense of being immersed in its processes, and out of it too, to the extent of seeing how the narratives of history are made, contested and then made again. Working both with and against the grain of the different stories that comprise the novel, Faulkner aims precisely to show that we *can* 'narrativize' the past: which is to say, come to terms with it as a force both controversial and innate – something open to argument and yet also inward, an understanding or impulse latent within us.

The first story of Thomas Sutpen is, of course, told by Sutpen himself: as he attempts both to enact meaning in his life and later, particularly in the hearing of General Compson, to recollect what happened and why.

Told at one, two, three or more removes, through the filter of conflicting voices and guesses, most of the details of what happened are open to debate. Nevertheless, a fundamental and funadamentally 'male' narrative of union, division, alienation and conquest shines through all the different versions: as if, somehow, this were the *ur*-text of history, the past as it has been constructed for us by the dominant (white, male) ideology – yesterday as it is received by most of us in the first instance. The model, or narrative, is by now a familiar one. The hero begins in a state of instinctive union with his surroundings, where 'the land belonged to anybody and everybody' and there is no suspicion of 'I' and 'you', 'mine' and 'yours'. He then experiences the traumatic fall into an utterly different condition, in which union is replaced by division; a new world, 'all divided and fixed and neat', confronts him with his own ignorance and alienation. He wants to cross the threshold – a crucial act of passage in this novel – but he cannot: the warm world where, he believes, power over nature will compensate for loss of unity with it is closed to him. And, dispossessed, he passes through a feeling of radical disintegration: 'he seemed to kind of dissolve', we are told, as his sense of identification with the Other – and, for the time being, his identity – melt away. By way of resistance to this, Sutpen begins to construct a narrative, a story – which he first acts out and then tells – that requires him to learn new languages: not only the 'strange' tongues of Haiti, it turns out, but words that will enable him to fill the vacuum of his loss, to replace absence with a sense of presence. 'You see', Sutpen confides to General Compson, 'I had a design in my mind.' 'Whether it was a good or a bad design is beside the point', he adds, 'The question is, Where did I make the mistake in it.'[44] The two, opposed terms, 'design' and 'mistake', measure the parameters of Sutpen's narrative. Struggling to fulfil his 'design', to direct all his words and actions towards one overwhelming purpose and exclude everything that does not fit (his first wife, a 'nigger' child, a female child, and so on), Sutpen unknowingly outlines the centripetal tendencies of his story: the way he would use his newly minted vocabulary to conceal fracture. But the 'design' is also rife with 'mistake'. Gaps in the narrative abound ('he never told whether the voyage was hard or not, how much he must have had to endure to make it'; 'he not telling ... what had happened during the six years between the day when he decided to go to the West Indies and become rich and this night ...'). Information is withheld or even false ('the old man's wife had been a Spaniard'). The story is alive with incoherences and inconsistencies. In 'telling' and 'not telling', Sutpen uses language both to conceal and, however unintentionally, to reveal the dissonances by which he is haunted. Oscillating constantly between the extremes of 'design' and 'mistake', his story speaks of the use of words both to suppress and to expose division: the traumatic moment of separation and dispossession 'the boy-symbol at the door' experiences when he is told by a 'balloon-face ... nigger' to use the back entrance.

Sutpen's story also speaks, in more detail, of power and possession: his belief that, if he cannot be at one with the world, he can overpower and control it – that, in place of Eden, he can have Empire. The dominating impression when it comes to describing him is of a man on horseback: 'man-horse-demon', according to Rosa Coldfield, 'the fine proud image of the man', as Mr Compson puts it, 'on the fine proud image of the stallion'. The associations of mastery over nature that this image carries with it are developed in a narrative that has, as a recurring theme, the conquest of the wilderness. Having made a fortune in 'a little island . . . which was the halfway point between what we call the jungle and what we call civilization', Sutpen returned to the South, we are informed, and there 'dragged house and gardens out of a virgin swamp'. In this virile tale of adventure and empire, women and black people are marginalized. At best, they are seen as commodities: Sutpen brought two women slaves from Haiti, we learn, 'deliberately . . . he probably chose them with the same care and shrewdness with which he chose the other livestock'.[45] And, at worst, they are perceived with 'dread and fear' precisely because they are situated on the dangerous margins of the 'design'. Either way, their voices are hardly heard. Combining with this tale of power, and supplanting it at times, is a tale of patriarchy. What Sutpen is doing, it seems, is trying not only to tame a 'wilderness' but to found a dynasty: to replace 'nature' with 'culture', the 'jungle' with 'civilization', not just for the present but for the foreseeable future. Notionally a separate strand in the narrative pattern, this 'family romance' element in the Sutpen story coincides with the 'conquest of the wilderness' dimension, not just because it sustains the culture/nature duality but because it further identifies this as a distinctly male tale. 'We in the South made our women into ladies', comments Mr Compson. 'Then the War came and made our women into ghosts.' To which it can only be added that women in this story seem to be ghosts from the very beginning. Like the black characters, they are sometimes not even given a name: we only learn that Sutpen's first wife was called Eulalia from the genealogy at the end of the novel. They wait and hover, listening outside doors (both Rosa Coldfield and Judith Sutpen do this), perceived at a distance 'as though . . . through glass', neatly divided into 'ladies, women, females': the second and third categories being those, white and black respectively, on whom the white male discharges his sexual needs, the first incorporating the figures onto whom he projects his dreams of mastery, his fantasies of founding a civilization and a dynasty.

At the core of the family romance, of course, constituting its crisis point, are the linked threats of miscegenation and incest. '*You are my brother*', Quentin and Shreve imagine Henry Sutpen saying to Charles Bon. '*No, I'm not*', they fancy Charles replying, '*I'm the nigger that's going to sleep with your sister. Unless you stop me, Henry.*' '*It's the miscegenation, not the incest, which you cant bear*',[46] Charles is imagined observing. In fact, incest and miscegenation are inseparable in this and other family romances. The story of the Sutpens involves a supposed violation of the family biological *and* cultural, behind which hovers the old racist question, 'Would you let your sister marry one?' 'Tell about the South', Shreve demands in one of the most famous moments in the novel; and the fundamental narrative of Sutpen, the *ur*-text that supplies the field of debate, is just such a telling. As Sutpen lives and recollects it, his story identifies the story of the region as one in which the dualities of culture/nature, male/female, white/black (with, in each case, the first term being given priority over the second) buttress assumptions of conquest of place and person – domination not only of nature but of other human natures. The tale of empire and the family romance coincide not least in this: that they tell how the South resisted history with myth – imposing a distinctively male pattern of power and primogeniture on what were seen as the dismal, divisive processes of time.

'Is it any wonder that Heaven saw fit to let us lose?' asks Rosa Coldfield, shortly after she has begun telling Quentin Compson her version of the Sutpen story. There is a strongly moralistic streak at work in Rosa's narrative, those passages in *Absalom, Absalom!* when the tale of the Sutpen 'design' enters into what Bakhtin would call her 'character zone' – which is to say, the field of action circumscribed by her voice and vocabulary. This can, perhaps, be accounted for by two things: the 'grim mausoleum air of Puritan righteousness' in which she was raised, and 'an outraged female vindictiveness' that has its grounds in the realization that Sutpen not only humiliated her (when he demanded that she should bear him a son before they were married) he denied her humanity, her status as anything other than chattel or breeding stock. The outrage is particularly understandable because Rosa's early life, as she recalls it, is painfully marginal: even more on the edge of things, it seems, than the lives of most women in the Southern family romance. She acts as a housekeeper to others – among them, her father – and as a passive observer: she had never been taught anything, we are told, 'save listen through closed doors'. Marginal and invisible: Mr Compson sardonically refers to Rosa being raised in a 'closed masonry of females', apart from and unseen by the 'real', male world. Until, one day, Sutpen had seemed to offer her an entry into visibility: '*And then one afternoon*', Rosa remembers, '*I looked up and saw him looking at me. He had seen me for twenty years, but now he was looking at me.*'[47] Sutpen appears to give her the chance of being something other than an appendage or a commodity. So it is a particularly cruel shock when she realizes that, as she puts it, 'he did not even see me': that she means no more to him than 'a bitch dog or a cow or mare' or any other piece of potentially useful property would. The shock propels her into a revisionary view of Sutpen's career that seems to be determined by one motive above all: revenge, for the fact that he had held out his hand, Rosa remembers, 'and said "Come" as you might say it to a dog' – and for a while at least, as she admits, 'I came.' Whenever the story enters into Rosa's character zone, in fact, it assumes not just moralistic but also gothic dimensions. Sutpen is still an emblem of male power but the power is overwhelmingly malevolent: that of a 'fiend blackguard and devil', rather than a noble conqueror or a benevolent patriarch – a destroyer rather than a redeemer of the land.

It is important to see the different elements at work here, in Rosa's account, and to measure the relationships they establish between past and present. This is a revision of the past predicated on hindsight and on the assumption, shared with the other narrators, that the personal dimensions of the Sutpen story are inseparable from the public ones. Sutpen fell, it is insisted, because he was doomed from the start and deserved to fall; and the 'fatality and curse' he carried with him was a paradigm of the 'fatality and curse on the South' – 'a land primed for fatality', Rosa declares, 'and already cursed with it'. It is also a version of Southern myth that seems calculated not only to call the image of Faulkner's own great-grandfather, as conqueror and redeemer, into question, but to cast a cold eye on the entire notion of patriarchy. It is not the fact of patriarchal power that is questioned, of course; Rosa is in no doubt that it was Sutpen, and people like him, who were in charge – and, perhaps, still are. It is, instead, the moral implications and consequences of that power that are not just interrogated but unremittingly attacked: as Rosa draws a portrait of Sutpen that gravitates between jeremiad and nightmare. Thomas Sutpen, as Rosa describes him, is by turns an antichrist carrying a 'faint sulphur-reek still in clothes and beard', a mad knight with a 'lust for vain magnificence', a febrile, destructive aristocrat who seals himself and his family off in a grim 'ogre-bourn' that is an extension of his own flesh – and, more generally, a 'light-blinded, bat-like being', 'from abysmal and chaotic dark to eternal and abysmal dark completing his descending' into absolute degeneracy. 'The South is the thirteenth and fourteenth centuries', the Abolitionist Wendell Phillips asserted, and there can be little doubt that the story Rosa tells draws much of its energy from her use, however instinctive and unknowing, of the verbal armoury of Abolitionism: that version of the Old South that accepted the region's own feudal image of itself but then turned the moral implications of that image on their heads – translating a pastoral idyll into a gothic horror story. And this dimension of the tale correlates with the attack on patriarchal power; since it was precisely the 'masculine'/'feminine' opposition that both Southern and Northern spokesmen deployed before the Civil War. As one writer of the Old South put it, the North was a culture dominated by 'female' notions and, sometimes even more literally, by the sort of women who 'write books, patronise abolitionist societies; or keep a boarding-school'.[48] Sentimental, hypocritical and self-righteous: the North as perceived by the Old South was a misogynist's nightmare, a world filtered through and distorted by a mixture of humour, hatred and fear. Sensual, cold and overpowering: in turn, the Old South as perceived by the North was a nightmare of patriarchy, a world of male power *in extremis* in which cruel parodies of the family were presided over by perverse versions of the father figure.

All the different elements that feed into Rosa's story are, of course, not so much a matter of specific influences as of a common stock of assumptions and language: an interrelated series of idioms that reveal the intimate connection between personal feeling and public argument, and the degree to which the past and present mutually inform each other as a tale is told. Quite simply, her version of Thomas Sutpen and his fate is historically situated, in the sense that she would not describe events in the way she does were she not willing to link critical moments in her own life to equally crucial moments in the life of her region – and were she not looking back on both with the benefit of retrospective wisdom, and with some awareness (or, at least, absorption) of the wider debates about the South. The narrative she offers is undeniably gothic. There is the familiar, grim castle of gothic stories, a 'private hell' apparently reserved for 'some desolation more profound than ruin'. There also is the traditional villain, Sutpen, a perpetrator of horrible deeds on innocent victims: a man who, we are told, carried his second wife off to his 'ogre-djin' and subsequently permitted her, by means of infrequent visits to church, 'to return, through the dispensation of one day only, to the world she had quitted'. Even the narrator as she recalls herself , and the rest of the family as she portrays them, are sucked into the atmosphere of gothic nightmare. Rosa, by her own account, becomes like one of Ann Radcliffe's heroines: a feverish eavesdropper, haunted by disembodied 'faces', 'voices' or 'hands', and experiencing a numb 'terror' at the mere suspicion that there is 'something hidden' at the top of a 'nightmare flight of stairs'. And the 'two half phantom children' born in the dark house, together with the black maid Clytemnestra who – by virtue of being fathered by 'fell darkness' – has become its 'cold Cerberus': they seal the fate of the family in this version of the tale of the fall of the house of Sutpen – helping to assure its 'doom' as the Sutpen 'name and lineage' are finally 'effaced . . . from the earth'. Undeniably gothic, the gothicism of Rosa's account must, however, be seen for what it is: the product of certain, very specific emotional and historical pressures. Sutpen is perceived as a gothic villain, and the story in which that villain is inserted becomes an assault on patriarchal power, precisely because of what Rosa sees as her own betrayal and the betrayal of the South – a land marked for retribution, according to her, by 'men with valour and strength but without pity or honour'.[49] 'Our father's progenitors' and the father-figure of Sutpen let 'us' down, she believes. So, 'Is it any wonder that Heaven saw fit to let us lose?'

'Sutpen was acting his role', Mr Compson insists, as he tries to describe to his son how Thomas Sutpen gradually gained ascendancy in Yoknapatawpha, 'he was the biggest single landowner and cotton-planter in the county now.' However, Mr Compson goes on,

> he was unaware that his flowering was a forced blooming too and that while he was still playing a scene to the audience, behind him Fate, destiny, retribution, irony – the stage manager, call him what you will – was already striking the set and dragging on the synthetic and spurious shadows and shapes of the next one.[50]

This captures something of the difference between Mr Compson's narrative and Rosa Coldfield's. The feverish, often hallucinatory idiom of Rosa's version of things is replaced by a willed pursuit of verbal decorum, with touches of delicate irony and self-consciously felicitous imagery. More to the point, the dry dispassion of the style registers the terms in which Mr Compson would seek to perceive Sutpen: not as the villain of a gothic tale but, rather, as the hero of a decadent tragedy, in which the noblest possible 'dream' is destroyed by the 'illogical machinations of fatality'. Like Rosa, Mr Compson is in part seeking an explanation of his own failure, as he recalls what happened to Sutpen: in his case, his failure to play the part of father adequately and to sustain the Compson family fortune and name. And, like Rosa too, that explanation of personal misfortune becomes inextricable from an account of public disaster: the story of the South and its decline, perceived through the filters of time. The difference arises from the simple fact of identification with the subject: Mr Compson is inclined to identify, or at least link, his story with those of Thomas Sutpen and the South – to see in the personal and cultural downfalls he describes a mirror image, a mocking reflection of his own. Sutpen, the man who would be patriarch but whose efforts are demolished by 'destiny . . . the stage manager', is not a surrogate for the narrator here: but he does offer Mr Compson what he perceives as an ironic anticipation of his own life, as seen through a glass darkly, as well as a sad recollection of the fate of their common homeplace. As a result, the telling of his tale does tempt Mr Compson into a late romantic, simultaneously sardonic and elegiac, vein.

In short, every time the story of Thomas Sutpen enters the character zone of Mr Compson it takes on a peculiarly Southern colour; it begins to read like a deliberate, mannered version of plantation romance. Sutpen assumes the dimensions of a visionary, and his vision is one of patriarchal power and *politesse*. He actively struggles to become a perfect gentle knight and, in the process, to turn life into dream. 'He was like John L. Sullivan having taught himself painfully and tediously to do the schottische', Mr Compson suggests, 'having drilled himself and drilled himself in secret until he now believed it no longer necessary to count the music's beat.' Sutpen is willing to learn a new language, apparently, and to submit himself to a discipline so 'painful and tedious' that it looks sometimes as if he is pitting 'his own fallible judgement against not only human but natural forces'. He attempts, quite deliberately, to live up to an heroic version of himself. If Sutpen seems to be playing a part then, nearly every time Mr Compson describes them, the people around Sutpen appear to be playing parts too – and parts drawn, just as much as his is, from the Southern version of its own past. Ellen Coldfield, for example, is said 'to rise to actual stardom in the role of matriarch' with her 'carriage a little regal', her manner 'gracious and assured' – just as soon, that is, as she becomes Mrs Thomas Sutpen. Ellen as matriarch – the good woman, keeper of the house and mother to the plantation 'family' – is complemented in this version of things by two other traditional icons in the regional variation on the pastoral: the plantation Hotspur and the plantation Hamlet. Henry

Sutpen is the Hotspur figure here, an ideological descendant of the gay young Confederate officer of military lore (or, for that matter, Bayard Sartoris I). 'Given to instinctive and violent action rather than thinking', we are told,

> his entire worldly experience consisted of sojourns at other plantations almost interchangeable with his own, where he followed the same routine which he did at home – the same hunting and cockfighting, the same amateur racing of horses.[51]

The Hamlet role in turn, sketching out the more intellectual and aesthetic possibilities of patriarchy, is played here by Charles Bon. Bon is described by Mr Compson as a 'cerebral Don Juan', a man 'handsome and elegant and . . . catlike' who meets Henry for the first time 'in a flowered, almost feminised gown', reclining 'in a sunny window in his chambers' and carrying about him 'some tangible effluvium of knowledge, surfeit: of actions done and satiations plumbed and pleasures exhausted and even forgotten'. Given the fragile dilettantism of his nature – he seems, as Mr Compson portrays him, like some of Poe's more precious, dandified heroes (Dupin, say, in *The Murders in the Rue Morgue*) – it is appropriate that Bon's final resting place should belong to the world of artifice. He is buried, we are told, in a spot that resembles a 'garden scene by the Irish poet, Wilde', so redolent of the 'hothouse' that people lose their ordinary personalities when visiting it and are translated into beings 'Beardsley might have dressed'.

The references to artists of the late romantic period suggest just how much Faulkner is interrogating his own youthful allegiances here. We are not, after all, being asked to share in Mr Compson's aestheticism but to see it as a clue to his feelings and his re-enactment of the past. This narrator is clearly someone intent on giving the story of Thomas Sutpen an emotionally pleasing and intellectually manageable form. Like the Southerners who retreated into what W.J. Cash termed 'Cloud Cuckoo Land' after the Civil War, he is forging a myth – one that distances the spectres of guilt and defeat by exonerating the defeated and identifying 'fateful mischance' rather than some moral law as the force guiding the destinies of nations. The dominant tone is one of irony – an uncertain irony, perhaps, coupled with a rather desperate imitation of Wildean detachment – because, in fact, Mr Compson is claiming that Sutpen did not deserve to fail at all. He rose to momentary realization of his patriarchal vision, and deserves some credit for having done so, and then fell prey to 'the stage manager, call him what you will'; he was a blameless, and within the limits of human possibility even heroic, victim of events beyond his control. In *this* reading of history, an intricate play between private feeling and public meaning, past actions and present revisions, leads not to an assault on patriarchy but, on the contrary, to a defence and even celebration of it: as an admirable social arrangement or, at the very least, a noble project. So the belief that 'Heaven saw fit to let us lose' slips away, supplanted by the conviction that all that happened was 'a horrible and bloody mischancing of human affairs'.[52] Sutpen was 'innocent' (so General Compson tells his son, and Mr Compson believes him); the Old South was innocent; both are now, unfortunately and irrevocably, gone with the wind.

'*I have heard too much*', thinks Quentin Compson about midway through the novel, '*I have been told too much; I have had to listen to too much, too long.*' In a way, it is not just a matter of being told about the Sutpen story. As Quentin admits to himself elsewhere,

> *you knew it already, had learned it, absorbed it already without the medium of speech somehow from having been born and living beside it, with it, as children will and do: so that what your father was saying did not tell you anything so much as it struck, word by word, the resonant strings of remembering.*[53]

The story seems to be a part of the climate, inherent in the fabric of his surroundings, and it seems to be something in himself as well, an element in his own consciousness and flesh. Not that this makes it easier for Quentin to cope with the Sutpen story. Far from it: the pattern of re-enactment becomes particularly tangled and difficult to handle in his case. For Quentin is drawn in several different directions at once. He is, in the first instance, torn between different versions of the past, the parameters of which are marked by the opposing narratives of Rosa Coldfield and Mr Compson. And, in the second, he suffers an extreme case of the temptations confronting anyone who attempts to recall and represent earlier times: the temptations, that is, of identity or difference – the urge either blankly to identify with the people and events of yesterday or, alternatively, to see the intervening accumulations of history as an impenetrable barrier walling one off from an age now gone. Quentin has '*heard too much*' and absorbed too much because of what seems sometimes like an infinite process of documentation: a sea of voices – 'mouth-to-mouth tales', letters and rumours – over which the story of Thomas Sutpen has had to pass to reach him. These previous textualizations, which effectively constitute the story for him, have to be engaged with if he is ever to understand that story in its historical specificity and strangeness. And yet they also threaten him with intellectual impotence: the failure to see and achieve contact with people who are his precursors and determinants – in whom, as his father would put it, he lay dormant and waiting – and the consequent failure to see and understand his own times and himself, his present conditions and his subjectivity.

Quentin, of course, receives assistance of a kind and accompanying comment from Shreve. The voice of Shreve is particularly noticeable during the 'account book' moments of their re-enactment of the past: when, for instance, between them Quentin and Shreve construct the hypothetical figure of a New Orleans lawyer who kept track of Thomas Sutpen – a cool, calculating person who perhaps helped manipulate events and wrote down potential plot manoeuvres in a ledger, as part of a scheme for turning Sutpen's 'mistakes' into profit. '*Query: bigamy threat, Yes or No,*' the lawyer is imagined writing, '*Possible No. Incest threat: Credible Yes.*' The detached terms in which the lawyer writes and is written here tend to lock into those moments of bizarre comedy or mock-heroic that punctuate this joint re-enactment. At one point, for instance, Sutpen and Rosa Coldfield are jokily described as 'an ancient stiff-jointed Pyramus' and an 'eager though untried Thisbe' 'betrayed by the old meat'. For that matter, this detachment finds its ultimate, dour expression in the mathematical formula with which Shreve's voice concludes. 'So it takes two niggers to get rid of one Sutpen, dont it?' he says,

> Which is all right, it's fine; it clears the whole ledger, you can tear all the pages and burn them, except for one thing . . . You've got one nigger left. One nigger Sutpen left.[54]

The detachment here is such that Shreve seems to be mocking the rigidity of his own conclusions. He is so much the distanced spectator, it seems, that he can stand back not only from the story of Sutpen and the South but from his attitude towards them as well – smiling at his stance and suggesting its possible limitations. Shreve's comments mark the limits of strangeness. It is as if suddenly one of Nabokov's heroes had been asked to pass judgement on the Sutpen tale and had succeeded in reducing this, along with everything else in the past, to the status of an exercise – anthropologically interesting, perhaps, but totally alien and 'other'. At best, the tale consequently becomes theatre, exciting amazement and applause ('Jesus, the South's fine, isn't it', Shreve says at one point in the book, 'It's better than the theatre, isnt it'); and, at worst, it represents a shabby piece of self-deception. Either way, it is not something to be taken too seriously, if only because it can never properly be known. All we have, finally, are a few, indeterminate scratchings in a ledger.

If Shreve seems especially to be foregrounded when the past is seen as an account book or 'the lawyer's design' is debated, then in turn Quentin plays a particularly prominent role when it comes to re-enacting the story of Henry Sutpen. As several critics have pointed out, Quentin sometimes sees both Henry and Charles Bon as dark reflections of himself, since the two are remembered as respectively the self-proclaimed protector and the would-be violator of a sister's 'honour'. This helps to explain those moments of identification that mark Quentin's and Shreve's versions of the story: when Quentin, Shreve, Henry and Charles become 'first, two . . . then four; now two again'. 'They were both in Carolina and the time was forty-six years ago', begins a passage rehearsing one such moment,

> and it was not even four now but compounded still further, since now both of them were Henry Sutpen and both of them were Bon, compounded each

of both yet either neither, smelling the very smoke which had blown and faded away forty-six years ago from the *bivouac fires burning in a pine grove, the gaunt and ragged men sitting or lying about them, talking not about the war yet all curiously enough . . . facing the South where further on into the darkness the pickets stood . . .*[55]

The activity of re-enactment, at such times, becomes a process of total immersion. Under the pressure of heightened speculation (marked here by italics), the intervening passages of history are abruptly wiped out, and the present is simply merged with the past. It is important to note, however, that even these experiences of identification are surrounded by times when the pendulum swings back again, to feelings of strangeness and difference that border, occasionally, on bewilderment. A measure of this is that, not long before Quentin and Shreve are transported back to Carolina during the Civil War, they speculate about a letter that their New Orleans lawyer might have had written. The letter they imagine is a fake one, meant to convince Eulalia that 'they' – the people the lawyer has supposedly employed to track Sutpen down – are close to Sutpen and know that he is still alive. And it is written in English, a tongue foreign and unknown to Eulalia: 'maybe', Quentin and his friend hypothesize, 'the only word in it she could even recognise would be the word, "Sutpen"'. An imaginary letter written by a character who is himself imagined by an imaginary character, and offered as documentary evidence to someone who herself just might possibly be imaginary and is certainly anonymous for the duration of the narrative. A document only one word of which, 'Sutpen', appears to be decipherable before it is set fire to 'and so would not be perused but consumed' – leaving the frustrated reader 'sitting there with a black crumbling blank carbon ash in her hand'. There could hardly be a more haunting image than this for the elusive nature of the past and the fragmentary, fugitive nature of the terms in which it comes mediated to us. 'Nothing matters but breath', thinks Quentin at one point; and sometimes it seems that breath is all he has, despite his strenuous attempts to immerse himself in the Sutpen story. Sometimes, in fact, that story bears a remarkable resemblance to the state of virginity as Mr Compson wryly defines it: something that somehow 'must depend upon its loss, absence, to have existed at all'.

Mr Compson has a powerful impact on his son – it is, in fact, the only way in which he even begins to play the role of patriarch, even if his patriarchal influence is malign: which is perhaps why much of what Quentin – with the help of Shreve – recollects and re-creates concerning Henry Sutpen seems to bear the imprint of the stories of his father. As Quentin rehearses the story of Henry, it is as if he is engaged in a dual act of repetition: imitating and even exaggerating the idealizing tendencies of his father and, at the same time, repeating, in his account of the young squire of 'bucolic Mississippi', his own romanticized image of himself as the Southern gentleman exposed to a cosmopolitan education. Henry, as Quentin imagines him, is the squire in the process of becoming knight:

which is an extension of how Mr Compson reconstructs him, and also maps out a rite of passage that Quentin would dearly like to experience for himself. It is Charles Bon, Mr Compson's plantation Hamlet and Quentin's own darker self-reflection, who acts as Henry's tutor: for Henry, as for Quentin, the journey 'out' of his homeplace, in this version of the tale, is also the journey 'in' to the deeper, darker recesses of identity. Henry, Quentin supposes, learns some tricks of the gentlemanly trade from Charles: 'how to lounge about a bedroom in a gown and slippers such as women wore', for instance, '. . . yet withal such an air of indolent and lethal assurance that only the most reckless man would have gratuitously drawn the comparison'. But the most significant thing that he learns from his dark twin is evidently much closer to home than this: how to condone incest, between Charles and their sister Judith. The feelings Henry is imagined harbouring towards Charles are, in fact, like nothing so much as courtly love: like the knight with his lady, Henry ends, we are told, by attributing all possible graces of mind and body to Charles and then offering him 'the humility which surrenders no pride – the entire proffering of the spirit'. So, when it comes to the possibility of incest, he is recalled in the traditional posture of the courtly lover, describing various historical precedents for the liaison as a way of making 'his conscience . . . come to terms with his will'. 'Kings have done it!' Quentin has Henry declare,

> Even dukes! There was that Lorraine duke named John something that married his sister. The Pope excommunicated him but it didn't hurt! It didn't hurt! They were still husband and wife. They were still alive.[56]

This imagined speech is nominally addressed to Charles: but it is not difficult to see that it is really directed at Henry, the speaker, and Quentin, the narrator. The pressure of identification works here, mainly via the 'mouth-to-mouth tales' told by Quentin's father, to expose and exorcize some of the darker impulses of both past and present. Incest, one of the most powerful threats latent in the Southern family romance, is actively confronted: but it is so only as part of a strategy of special pleading – in an attempt to turn even this repressed impulse into a mark of aristocratic exclusiveness, an integral element in the closed, self-contained world of the feudal dream.

The stumbling-block, as Quentin and Shreve rehearse the story, is miscegenation: '*it's the miscegenation, not the incest, which you can't bear*' is, after all, how they have Charles put it to Henry. In Quentin's imagination, at least, the threat of sexual intercourse across the racial boundaries is not linked to the perils of sexual relations within the family. The reason is simple. Linked they may be at the general level of the Old South's notion of itself as a patriarchal 'family', incorporating both black and white. In Quentin's own mind, however, they have to be scrupulously separated, because incestuous impulses are buried deep within himself in a way that the drive to inter-racial sex is clearly not. In extenuating incest, consequently, or rather having Henry extenuate it, Quentin is (however unknowingly) defending his own position. To be more exact, he is nervously assuaging his own incipient guilt and so making it possible for him, for a while, to live with himself. And, almost as an act of over-compensation, miscegenation becomes by his reckoning the determining factor in the destruction of the house of Sutpen: not linked to the general idea of use, the denial of human subjectivity, nor more specifically connected to the issues of patriarchal power and family tyranny and desire but, on the contrary, pictured as the one forbidden apple in this feudal Eden – the original and the ultimate taboo. This is undoubtedly why, whenever the fact or suspicion of inter-racial sex enters Quentin's version of the tale, the genre alters from pastoral romance to gothic melodrama. The visit that Quentin pays to Sutpen's Hundred, for instance, in Rosa Coldfield's company the day after she has given him her account of the Sutpen history, is recalled in terms that replicate Rosa's own feverish tendencies – and that bear down, with particular obsessiveness, on the ideas of darkness and transgression. Night enveloped Quentin and Rosa, Quentin remembers, as they approached the house – which seems, as he recalls it, to be as surreal as the House of Usher and even more terrifying than the 'ogre-bourn' that Rosa herself described:

> It loomed, bulked, square and enormous, with jagged half-toppled chimneys, its roofline sagging . . . beneath it, the dead furnace-breath of air . . . seemed to reek in slow and protracted violence with a smell of desolation and decay as if the wood of which it was built were flesh.[57]

Inside this dark corpse of a house, Quentin and Rosa find three people, all of whom – as Quentin recollects them – tend to take on the grim coloration of their surroundings. They are Clytemnestra the housekeeper, a 'tiny gnomelike creature' with a 'worn coffee-coloured face'; Jim Bond, 'a saddle-coloured and slack-mouthed idiot' who by virtue of two generations of illegitimacy has become 'the scion, the heir-apparent' to the estate; and a third figure lying on a filthy bed in a 'bare, stale room' whose 'wasted yellow face with closed, almost transparent eyelids' and 'wasted hands crossed on his breast' make him look 'as if he were already a corpse'.[58] The third figure is Henry Sutpen, returned from self-imposed exile and apparently still haunted by his murder of his half-brother. It seems almost superfluous to say that this version of him utterly contradicts the earlier, bucolic image of a squire being educated to become a knight. What perhaps require more emphasis here – when it comes to this portrait of Henry and the house in which he has imprisoned himself – are two, not totally unrelated, points. The first is how much, in this world shadowed by the memory of miscegenation, even Henry is coloured by what he has known and experienced. He is not 'coffee-coloured', certainly, nor 'saddle-coloured': but his 'yellow face' does, at the very least, remind us of the grotesque refinements and anxieties that the South's secret history of sex across the colour line tended to promote. The second point is, quite simply, the degree to which all this serves to compound Quentin's confusion: to make him feel, like his father, that, 'It's just incredible. It just does not explain'. It is not only that the gothicism of this account, set as it must be against the earlier tendencies towards pastoral romance, registers just how sorely torn he is between the different terms in which, for him, the past comes mediated. It is, on top of this, that Quentin seems even more adrift, further away from the past than ever. Recollecting Henry and Charles in Carolina during the Civil War, Quentin somehow drowned in the past, making himself victim to the illusion that he could totally identify with yesterday. Now, confronted with what remains of Henry Sutpen and the Sutpen estate, he feels only alienated from it: all the past tends to excite in him is dumb astonishment – bewilderment closely followed by a sense of exile.

Certainly, in the final pages of *Absalom, Absalom!*, Quentin does appear to cross the threshold, if not by the front entrance or the back, then at least through the smashed glass of a window. 'If we can just get to the house', he tells himself, 'get inside the house': as if to get inside the Sutpen house will be to get inside the past, to gain entry to its inner truth and meaning. He gets inside. What he acquires access to, however, is not a vital organism but a relic, a living corpse that is both Henry and the mansion: leaving him thinking, 'Nevermore of peace. Nevermore of peace. Nevermore Nevermore Nevermore.'[59] Like the protagonist in Poe's poem 'The Raven', Quentin is left merely rehearsing, over and over again, the memory of what he has desired and missed. After this, the house is burned to the ground, its fleshlike wood consumed by fire: recollecting that imaginary letter – written by a character imagined by a character who is himself imaginary – that was reduced to 'a black crumbling blank carbon ash' even before it could be properly read. With the house that seemed constructed out of sweat and flesh goes the 'yellow' flesh of Henry and the 'coffee-coloured' flesh of Clytie: house, flesh, documents – all the structures of the past, and by which the past is transmitted to the present, seem to dissolve, to disintegrate, bequeathing Quentin little more than the recollection of their loss. Not literally stopped at the threshold like Sutpen, Quentin is nevertheless denied entry into a genuinely interior knowledge of the house Sutpen built. The belief that he could not only know his ancestors but be them has been shifted aside for the conviction that they must remain behind closed doors for him – isolated as he is in the 'cold air', the vacuum of the present.

It is tempting to suggest that there are moments in *Absalom, Absalom!* when the problems involved in knowing the past are conquered: when, to recall a remark of Fredric Jameson's quoted much earlier in this book, the essential mystery of the past is momentarily restored to life – so that, 'like Tiresias drinking the blood', the past is permitted to speak its long-forgotten message in surroundings utterly strange to it. Certainly, the idea

of a dialogue that overpowers the boundaries between past and present –
honouring the past in all its 'pastness' while acknowledging its vital, determining connection to the present – is something that seems to be ventured
in this passage, in which Rosa Coldfield meditates on what she has wanted
in her life and missed:

> *there is something in the touch of flesh with flesh which abrogates, cuts sharp across
> the devious intricate channels of decorous ordering . . . touch and touch of that which
> is the citadel of the central I-Am's private own . . . let flesh touch with flesh and watch
> the fall of all the eggshell shibboleth of caste and colour too . . .*[60]

The problem is that, if we look for such an occasion in the novel, in which
the the past seems to cut '*sharp and straight across the devious intricate channels of decorous ordering*' and to speak to the present in a tongue both
intimate and strange: then, we are likely to be disappointed. Quentin
Compson, to take only the strongest possible example, remains doubly
trapped: in the dichotomies of identity and difference, and in the conflicts
generated by prior textualizations of the Sutpen story – the voices, documents and guesses that *are* the story for him. When Henry, the mesmer-
ising paradigm of the past for Quentin, does speak to him, it is like a
conversation between ghosts:

> *And you are – ?*
> *Henry Sutpen.*
> *And you have been here – ?*
> *Four years.*
> *And you came home – ?*
> *To die. Yes.*
> *To die?*
> *Yes. To die.*
> *And you have been here – ?*
> *Four years.*
> *And you are – ?*
> *Henry Sutpen.*[61]

This is not so much a dialogue as the failure of one. Henry is a 'wasted'
relic, a residual memory made flesh, while Quentin is the awe-struck
novitiate, unable to venture more than the most rudimentary of questions.
In a way, the gaps between the speech are more eloquent than the speech
itself, since they speak of the silence, the emptiness across which the two
characters cannot reach – the plain fact that, here at least, the past cannot
talk to the present.

'*Maybe nothing ever happens once and is finished.*' That remark from *Absalom,
Absalom!*, and the passage already quoted from which it comes, indicate
just where the dialogue between past and present occurs in the novel:
which is not in the novel at all, but in the reading of the novel. The point
has been made, but it is perhaps worth recalling: the complex narrative

structure, with its gaps and repetitions, imposes on us, the readers, the task of careful attention and re-enactment. It makes the voices of the past talk to us; in turn, it requires us to 'talk to' them – in the sense of responding critically to what we hear, selecting, interpreting and shaping. What we emerge with from this is, ideally, not some nugget of absolute truth but the knowledge of truth as process: an understanding of history in the making. Faulkner presents us with an open field of lived relations – between past and present, public and private – and he invites, almost compels, us to participate in that field, to share in an experience in which the idea of yesterday is constantly being reconstituted in terms of the unfinished business of today. The separateness and autonomy of the past have to be respected in all this; we have to accept that it speaks to us in a different, unfamiliar tongue. But its vital connection to ourselves must be acknowledged as well: the fact of a mutually determining relationship between the voices that address us and the 'voice' with which we respond – which is to say, the language and experiences that each of us brings to the novel. The tempting impulse to retreat into some kind of atemporal solipsism must be resisted – the past, after all, is real, it is there: so too, though, must the equal temptation of assuming that history is no more than a series of vacuum-packed empirical facts, sealed off from the grimy impact of change. The narrative asks us to recognize the otherness of the past and to recognize, too, how it is tied irrevocably to the present; then, out of these twin recognitions, to construct our dialogue. Inevitably, this means that we must redraw the map every time we read the story of Thomas Sutpen; the terms of our conversation with it must alter, in response to our own altering idiom and conditions. To read *Absalom, Absalom!* properly – in other words, actively and critically – is to know what knowing the past entails, but it is also to know that such knowing is never ended: that we are not doomed but, on the contrary, challenged to think and think again every time we open the book – because the activity of reading it *is* its meaning.

IV   THE PLANTATION ROMANCE AND THE MADWOMAN IN THE
ATTIC: *THE UNVANQUISHED*

The book that Faulkner published next – in 1938, some fifteen months after the appearance of *Absalom, Absalom!* – was one of what he liked to call his 'hybrid' works: not quite a novel, as he saw it, but more than just a collection of short stories. Most of what eventually appeared in *The Unvanquished* certainly first saw life in separate, short-story form. All but the final section, 'An Odour of Verbena', was originally written before *Absalom, Absalom!* had been completed, and published in the *Saturday Evening Post* and *Scribner's Magazine* between 1934 and 1936. Then, looking for a marketable volume following the publication of *Absalom, Absalom!*,

Faulkner wrote to his editor, 'I have a series of six stories about a white boy and a black boy during the civil war. What do you think about getting them out as a book?'[62] Meeting with encouragement, Faulkner revised the six stories. Some of the alterations and additions he made emphasized the autobiographical dimension. In what became the first section of the book, 'Ambuscade', for example, Faulkner inserted details about John Sartoris that were borrowed from his knowledge of his own great-grandfather. Some revisions were clearly intended to lock *The Unvanquished* more firmly into the accumulating legends of Yoknapatawpha County: to 'Retreat', for instance, the second section, Faulkner added half-a-dozen passages that expand the story of the McCaslins, the family central to a later, equally 'hybrid' work. And still other changes seem to have had the broader purpose of translating the narrative as a whole into a kind of initiation ritual – a story about the moral evolution of Bayard Sartoris. 'Retreat', for instance, was padded out with some general reflections on the way a child alters and matures; while in 'Raid' – which was to become the third section – Faulkner developed some comments on the way a young boy can be fascinated with the perils of a war that he has never actually experienced for himself. The third aim, of welding the stories together into a sort of *Bildungsroman*, also helps to explain the one story or section that Faulkner wrote specifically for the volume: the final one in which Bayard refuses to avenge the death of his father in the way previous generations would have done, choosing instead to confront his father's killer unarmed. Even here, Faulkner was drawing on family lore, since the episode recollects and revises the time when, Colonel William C. Falkner having been murdered by his former business partner and political rival, his son John Wesley Thompson Falkner decided not to seek revenge. With this gesture, we are perhaps invited to believe, Bayard has shuffled off the influence of the patriarchal figure overshadowing his life – together with the code of kinship and vengeance to which that figure would tie him – and managed finally to assert his independence, his status as an individual moral agent.

'As far as I am concerned', Faulkner wrote to his agent while he was working on the original version of one of these stories, 'while I have to write trash, I dont care who buys it, as long as they pay the best price I can get.'[63] Faulkner was to have a higher opinion of *The Unvanquished* once it was finished: but it is clear that one motive that lay behind both the stories and the volume was the simply desire to make money. In this respect, what could be better, he may have thought, than the kind of writing that comes into most people's minds whenever the South is mentioned – rousing tales of tricks and adventures, gallantry, suffering and violence during the Civil War? As far as this understandably venal ambition was concerned, Faulkner was for once reasonably well rewarded: the film rights to *The Unvanquished* were quickly sold, the reviews were far more favourable than the ones *Absalom, Absalom!* had received, even people in Oxford seemed to like it. Despite attempts by several recent commentators to rehabilitate the book, however, as either a trenchant narrative of maturing or, more personally, the work in which Faulkner finally came to terms with his father figure – exorcizing 'The Old Colonel' just as Bayard rids himself of the ghostly influence of John Sartoris – it is difficult to accept any large claims for its achievement, as either a series of tales or a connected narrative. It repeats situations that haunt *Absalom, Absalom!*: but it repeats them in radically diminished terms – in such a way as to make them emotionally controllable and so defuse them. The conflict between father and son, woman as the site of a struggle between different forces in a culture, the Civil War as the explosive focus for divisions that are at once social and psychological, black people as intimate strangers with whom white Southerners spend their lives without ever knowing them: all these obsessions, which also grip *Absalom, Absalom!*, are here. Here, however, they are contained in narratives that rely on conventional solutions and familiar pieties: that not only offer those preoccupations to the reader in predigested form, as it were, but also circumscribe them and make them safe. Dangerous ideas are played with only to be dismissed; disruptive energies are released for a moment only to be corralled and controlled; what seems, at first, calculated to subvert the ceremonies of society turns out, in the end, to have reaffirmed them. Perhaps the inertia of the romance and adventure form is to blame for this; perhaps (and more likely) Faulkner was using *The Unvanquished* as a kind of safety-valve, a means of indulging in forms of closure and feelings of, among other things, nostalgia that he simply could not and would not entertain in *Absalom, Absalom!*. Whatever the reason, the fascination of *The Unvanquished* lies in Faulkner's evidently unknowing use of a classic comic pattern: in which normalcy is turned upside down for a while as a way of ensuring its permanence – in which, in other words, the whole function of disturbance is not to dislodge the accepted order of things but to make that order easier to accept, to use crisis as a strategy for consensus.

Just how this strategy works is illustrated by the first story, 'Ambuscade'. It begins in design and ceremony: Bayard remembers how he and his black companion, Ringo, made 'a living map' of the Civil War, out of 'a handful of chips from the woodpile', packed earth and some water – all used to represent the battlegrounds to which, they believe, Colonel John Sartoris has gone. This opening, which transforms war into game, a childishly abstract plan, and that reminds us, all the while, of another 'game' – the ritualized relations between white and black – is abruptly disturbed by a 'nigger in the woodpile' (the allusion to the familiar racist phrase is subliminal, perhaps, but clear). Ringo's uncle Loosh, standing between the boys and the woodpile from which they have gathered the handful of chips for their rudimentary map, mocks them for not really knowing what is going on in the war or where Bayard's father now is. Although Bayard and Ringo do not yet know it, Vicksburg and Corinth have fallen, opening Mississippi to the Union army; and that major disruption, unacknowledged on their map, initiates a series of more personal ones. Colonel John suddenly and surprisingly returns home, in the anomaly of Yankee trousers

(captured, of course, from the advancing army), to supervise the hiding
of the family silver before the Yankee troops arrive. Doubts are sown in
Bayard's mind; and, all at once, nothing seems to be going according to
the accepted rituals or plan. At dinner, table is set 'with the kitchen knives
and forks' because the silver ones have been hidden; and the sideboard
– 'on which', Bayard says, 'the silver service had been sitting when I began
to remember' – is utterly and disconcertingly bare. There are none of the
expected thrilling war stories from Colonel John, before he leaves; nor
does Louvinia, the black maid, go through the normal, nightly ritual of
following the two boys up to their bedroom and scolding them until they
are in bed – 'I in the bed itself', Bayard points out, 'Ringo in the pallet
beside it'.[64] Worse still, the exciting game of war threatens to become a
frightening reality when the boys come across a Union soldier and shoot
at him. Discovering that there is a whole regiment with the soldier, Bayard
and Ringo have to race back to the house to escape capture; and, having
told Bayard's grandmother 'We shot the bastard!', are made to hide under
her skirts while the Yankees search the house for them. This very literal
step beyond the borders of normalcy seems to subvert both the maleness,
the virility of Bayard and Ringo ('hiding behind a woman's skirts') and
the traditional Southern notion of the woman as sacrosanct. And the disturbance it creates is compounded when Bayard and his companion hear
Granny Millard – who had never, Bayard recalls, 'whipped us for anything
in our lives except lying' – firmly and consistently lie to a Union sergeant,
and then his colonel, about the presence of boys in the house.

It is about now, however, that the disruptive movement in the story
ceases and the forces of closure and consensus begin to reassert themselves. The Yankee colonel shows himself to be a gentleman, ready to
accept a lady's word even if he does not believe her – and to acknowledge,
implicitly, that she cannot be searched because she is inviolable. The
hiding of the two boys underneath her skirt may have seemed a curiously
disturbing and disorienting gesture on Granny Millard's part at first, a
breach of the conventional walls of female privacy. It turns out, though,
to be only a way of affirming the security, the ultimate impenetrability of
those walls. Nobody, least of all a man and a gentleman, would ever dare
violate the sanctuary Granny Millard offers the two boys: so what she has
done is no more, and no less, than perform a small act of sacrifice. In its
own modest way, the grandmother's behaviour here confirms her status as
a true lady of the Confederacy: someone like, say, those women who were
celebrated by numerous apologists for the South for their eager sacrifice
of womanly modesty (their willingness, for instance, to tear up their pet-
ticoats to bathe and dress the wounded) in the service of the heroic Lost
Cause. As Southern writers from Thomas Nelson Page to Margaret Mitchell
have intimated, a lady may occasionally transgress the traditional boundaries of male/female relations: but only so as to ensure that, in the long
term, those boundaries survive. Decorum may be challenged at times, but
only as a tactic – as part of a strategy for securing the safety of the culture

on which that decorum rests for its continuance. In this story, in any event, there is no real need to think in the long term: the proper order of things is restored by Granny Millard, just as soon as the Union troops depart. After leading a prayer for forgiveness of the lie she has told, she makes Bayard and Ringo wash their mouths out with soap and water as a punishment for their use of the 'obscene word', 'bastard'. For a while, Bayard recalls, 'just by breathing we could blow soap bubbles',[65] and the 'glassy weightless iridescent' objects they create every time they exhale suggest that, for them at least, the bubble has not burst: the ritual of cleansing has restored lost innocence and stability. Everything is once more in its place in this fragile world of games and ritual. Even 'Father' returns, from the mountains of Tennessee, a place that Ringo tends to confuse with a cloudbank: an appropriate location, the reader might think, for such a godlike figure who only occasionally erupts on to the scene. The familiar dispensation, the pieties of the plantation and the playfulness of childhood, have survived the invasion, and the narrative circle has been closed.

The impression of closure created by this story, and for that matter by the other pieces in *The Unvanquished*, is underlined by the narrative treatment of both authority and marginal figures. As far as authority is concerned, some critics have attempted to argue that the book accomplishes a demythologizing of John Sartoris, the 'Father' in these tales. He is, so the argument goes, less demonic than Thomas Sutpen in *Absalom, Absalom!* and more frail and vulnerable than the John Sartoris of *Flags in the Dust/Sartoris*; and he consequently represents a form of catharsis for the author, a coming-to-terms with the dominant male figure in Faulkner's life. The argument is seductive, certainly, and it has some truth as far as 'An Odour of Verbena' is concerned: for reasons that will be looked at in a moment, Colonel Sartoris *is* a relatively diminished figure in that last story. Up until then, however, the general thrust of the narrative presentation is to celebrate him as a hero: a 'little man' in stature, perhaps (as so many of the Falkners were), but made to seem 'big' by 'the things he did' – and on his horse, Jupiter, in his cocked hat 'beneath the arcy and myriad glitter' of his sabre appearing 'exactly the right size . . . bigger than most folks could hope to look'. 'The odour in his clothes and beard and flesh too', Bayard recalls, 'which I believed was the smell of power and glory, the elected victorious but know better: know now to have been only the will to endure.'[66] The way Bayard formulates his perception here may make it sound like a diminishment, the realistic assessment of the mature, even disillusioned: 'I believed . . . know now . . . only'. Looked at closely, however, it is clear that what Bayard is doing is not substituting mature realism for childish romance, but jettisoning an obviously fake brand of romanticism (Sartoris was not, after all, one of 'the elected victorious', he was on the side that lost) for romanticism of a more typically Southern and Faulknerian kind – that celebrates stoic nobility, trials and failures heroically endured. Endurance was one of the cardinal virtues in Faulkner's eyes: attributed most often to black people, like Caroline Barr, who had to suffer the almost intolerable burdens of victimization, prejudice and peonage. And when ascribed, as here, to a white person – or, to be more exact, a white person of the ruling class – it tended to lock in neatly with the whole Southern mythology of heroic defeat, a cause that seems all the more glorious and irretrievably chivalrous once it is lost. Caught in the golden glow of recollection and apparently measured reflection, John Sartoris is a figure who is not larger than life literally, but in a more important sense: in terms of the authority he represents and imposes. Whenever he appears – and it is, more than once, towards the end of the tale – it is to certify the restoration of some sort of security and stability: to set *his* seal on the strategy of closure.

As far as the representation of marginal figures in *The Unvanquished* is concerned, the portraits of black people are relatively less interesting – although they, too, underwrite the general impetus towards narrative closure. There are, as 'Ambuscade' makes apparent, 'good' blacks and 'bad' blacks: on the one hand, Ringo, Bayard's constant companion and 'brother', and , on the other, Loosh, who tries to subvert childish games and triumphantly cries out, at one point, 'Gin'ral Sherman gonter sweep the earth and the race gonter be free!' Loosh's cry is 'placed' for us by the young Bayard's echoing it without understanding what it means ('Loosh saw them! They're just down the road. It's General Sherman and he's going to make us free!'): which is clearly intended to make that cry appear nonsensical by being reduced to childish nonsense. Even more telling, perhaps, it is 'placed' by Louvinia, who informs Loosh: 'You black fool! Do you think there's enough Yankees in the whole world to whip the white folks?'[67] The confusions implicit in this remark (us/them = family/Yankees = white/black) are not criticized or investigated. On the contrary, they are accepted with a quietly approving, only slightly ironic smile: seen as part of a homely, human and cosily illogical world in which most black characters – like Louvinia or 'Father's body servant' Joby, who accompanies his master to war – are evidently comfortable with their peripheral, property-driven status, at ease with their role as appendages. Ringo is a case in point here. The reader is told that he is more intelligent than Bayard. However, that does not stop fun being made at the expense of his 'ignorance': in the manner of any 'dumb-fool' black character out of plantation romance, Ringo confuses states with cloudbanks and infers, when he sees a railroad track torn up and wound round a tree by the Yankee invaders, that trains must go up and around trees. It is somehow symptomatic of the diminished terms in which black people are represented in *The Unvanquished* that there is nothing like that moment in *Go Down, Moses* when the white boy begins to take on the 'old curse of his fathers' by denying his 'brother'. There is no equivalent, in other words, of the famous episode in the later book in which the white character, Roth Edmonds, asserts his difference from the black boy who has been the companion of his childhood and (replicating 'the old haughty ancestral pride') tries to establish his distance – among other things, by insisting they sleep separately. The reason is simple. Bayard does not have to do this, because the narrative has done it for him. Distance has already been inscribed, as part of the order of things, in the very first story: Bayard is already in the bed by himself while Ringo is there, but apart from and below him, lying in his proper place on a pallet. The elaborate pattern of deference on which this culture depends for the illusion of intimacy between the races is assumed without even being looked at, let alone critically interrogated. Ringo accepts his subordinate status, without even thinking about it, just as Bayard simply assumes his privileges. There consequently appears to be no problem: the system 'works' because it is never questioned.

'Who are you going to mind from now on?' Granny Millard asks a band of escaped slaves. 'You, Missy', one of them replies. That brief interchange takes the measure of another way in which black characters appear in *The Unvanquished*: as an anonymous tide flowing northwards in what is perceived as inexplicable and futile pursuit of 'Jordan', a nonexistent promised land. It also suggests the authoritative status of Granny, Rosa Millard herself: who, in the earlier stories in the volume, acts as the keeper of the plantation. Granny represents a different kind of subordination to that figured in the black characters, but one that is no less automatically accepted – no less necessary to narrative closure: the subordination of women to the constraints, and demands, of the plantation idyll. Her adventures are the conventional tall tales of Civil War: outwitting the Yankees, hiding the family treasure. More to the point, she herself is a character straight out of plantation romance: the 'Ole Miss' who acts as regent while the master is away, keeping the family pieties alive and the home fires burning. This necessarily involves her in a number of ordinarily 'masculine' activities, but she remains nevertheless the preserver of 'feminine' standards of behaviour: as the prayers and mouthwashing ceremony at the end of 'Ambuscade' amply testify. At her most effective, as in 'Raid' where she successfully demands the return of stolen mules and silver from the Yankee invaders, she openly invokes the assumptions on which she depends and which, to an extent, she enshrines: her privileges of race and class, her borrowed male authority, and her status as lady. 'I want my silver!' she announces, 'I'm John Sartoris's mother-in-law!' There is an acute irony at work in the details of her death. The careful balancing of conventional 'masculine' and 'feminine' activities on which her role as steward of the plantation relies seems to wobble for a moment. 'Even Yankees do not harm old women', she insists and, believing that her age and gender make her sacrosanct, she rides off into an outlaw male world where she is murdered. Her death is a comment both on the perils of the life that ebbs and flows outside the boundaries of the plantation, and on Granny Millard's temporary aberration – the momentary lapse of concentration that makes her forget that the war has turned her from plantation matriarch into Confederate lady. However, the narrative is clearly not criticizing the role of 'Ole Miss' itself, only Granny's brief forgetfulness of that role – and, more acerbically still, the dreadful violence that infects the wilderness beyond the plantation fences. What her killing initiates, in other words, is not a reappraisal of all that she represents and defends, but a reassertion of its value. The closed feudal world for which Granny Millard worked and died rises up to take revenge, carried out by its novitiates Bayard and Ringo; while Granny herself is commemorated, in death as in life, not as a woman but a lady. When Bayard gazes at her dead body, what he sees is 'a lot of little thin dry sticks notched together and braced with a cord' with 'a clean and faded calico dress over them'.[68] Like all true ladies of the South, evidently, Granny Millard is possessed of a body that is not really a body at all, since it is closed off from observation – an absence.

Drusilla Hawk, who takes over from Granny Millard as the main female character in the later stories, is a different, and in many ways more interesting, matter. Drusilla loses her sweetheart during the Civil War, and so finds herself reserved for what her mother, at least, regards as 'the highest destiny of a Southern woman – to be the bride-widow of a lost cause'. However, she rejects the part and tries instead to adopt a male role, leaving her home in Alabama to spend the last years of the war fighting in Colonel John Sartoris's troop. In pursuit of her ambition, she even has her hair cut short and assumes the garments (as her mother puts it, with a palpable shudder) *'not alone of a man but of a common private soldier'*. Even when she comes back to Jefferson with Sartoris after the war, she continues to work and dress like a man: until her mother arrives from Alabama, forces her daughter into a dress, and insists that in order to regularize things – that is, place the relationship on a conventional footing – Drusilla and the Colonel should get married. There is more than a touch of comedy in Faulkner's presentation of these events; and not least in the account of the horror with which most other Southern ladies regard this aberrant sister. 'It is not myself I am thinking of', says Mrs Hawk a little disingenuously,

> I think of my husband who laid down his life to protect a heritage of courageous men and spotless women looking down from heaven upon a daughter who . . . deliberately cast away that for which he died, and . . . I think of my half-orphan son who will one day ask of me why his martyred father's sacrifice was not enough to protect his sister's good name . . .[69]

Drusilla is, in fact, regarded with evident dissatisfaction by her fellow prisoners, those who have managed to accept the role she rejects. This is one of the few points in *The Unvanquished* when the subordinations on which the plantation idyll relies for its continuance are submitted to interrogation, however circuitous: in which a marginal figure is allowed seriously to question, and resist, her marginality.

Of course, the mere fact that Drusilla dresses in male clothes is not enough to give her this occasionally subversive status. The tomboy heroine has a long and distinguished history, she even makes an appearance in one of Colonel William C. Falkner's novels, *The Spanish Heroine*, published in 1851; and, in the setting of the Civil War, she became the Confederate girl-soldier, who stepped outside the prescribed boundaries of the plantation idyll on behalf of the South. The point about these conventional character types is that they *were* conventional, that they did not disrupt accepted norms: the heroine was assumed to have kept her 'essential femininity' even when she took on the disguise of the opposite sex. Although she risked the sacred vessel of her body, she was not changed into a man, nor did she become sexually ambiguous. On the contrary, the male clothing tended simply to emphasize her womanliness: to offer an expression of 'femininity' that was – as in the case of, say, several of Shakespeare's comic heroines (most notably, Rosalind in *As You Like It* and Olivia in *Twelfth Night*) – all the more piquant for being oblique. The fact that the girl-soldier very often went to war following the man she loved underwrote the idea that her adoption of a male exterior was at once a temporary measure and an indirect statement of her 'true', female self. After the crisis was over, she returned to the plantation she had fought to protect, usually in the arms of her man, and slipped quietly back into her skirts.[70]

Drusilla also enters the theatre of war in the company of the man who eventually becomes her husband. In her case, though, as her mother's horrified comments indicate, her actions and her dress have genuinely subversive tendencies. 'Dress, as a highly regulated semiotic system', one commentator on the habit of cross-dressing has argued, can become 'a primary site where a struggle over the mutability of the social order [is] conducted'; 'when rules of apparel are violated', he goes on, 'class distinctions break down'. And, although it is difficult to see Drusilla Hawk's cross-dressing as a calculated act of rebellion, it is clear that it expresses a challenge to a 'dull', 'stupid' social economy that would reduce women to just two roles, those of wife and mother. Not only that, it is equally clear that at times she senses just how challenging her behaviour is. 'Living used to be dull, you see', she tells Bayard in 'Raid',

> Stupid. You lived in the same house your father was born in, and your father's sons and daughters had the sons and daughters of the same Negro slaves to nurse and coddle; and then you grew up and you fell in love with your acceptable young man, and in time you would marry him, in your mother's wedding gown, perhaps, and with the same silver for presents she received . . . But now . . . it's fine now; you don't have to worry about the house and silver because they get burned up and carried away . . . and you don't have to worry about getting children . . . because the young men can ride away and get killed in the fine battles; and you don't have to sleep alone, you don't have to sleep at all . . .[71]

For a while, as these remarks illustrate, Drusilla revels in what she sees as the demolition of the past and the uninvestigated traditions it enshrines. The war, as she understands it, offers her freedom just as much as it does the slaves: allowing her the chance to escape from the subordinate positions in which the Old South threatened to imprison her, along with all the other white women of her class.

The problems arise for Drusilla when she returns from the 'fine' theatre of war: to be suspected, variously, of having 'tried to unsex herself' or of carrying an illegitimate child. In the eyes of her female peers, she is suffering the common fate of the woman who transgresses the prescribed boundaries of male/female relations: she is either a monstrous aberration from the natural, they assume, like Lady Macbeth ('tried to unsex herself'/'unsex me here': the echo of a famous phrase from Faulkner's favourite Shakespeare play is surely unmistakeable) – or she is sexually incontinent, a libertine and a whore. Standing accused – by her mother, among many others – of having stepped into some unspeakable realm, beyond the narratives of her race, class and gender, she has to be compelled back into the domain of the spoken; she has to be dressed, and addressed, as a woman and then tied to a man. The dress that her mother makes her wear and her marriage to John Sartoris do certainly reinsert her in the culture she once dismissed as 'dull' and 'stupid'; they do reinscribe her as a lady, the wife and keeper of the house. However, the reinsertion is precarious. Her dress does not suit her. And, at the first attempt, Drusilla claims that she 'forgot' to get married, because she and her intended husband were too caught up in the male world of politics and violence: involved in killing the Burdens, two 'carpetbaggers' who were encouraging freed slaves to vote. Under duress, and at the second attempt, Drusilla does finally get married – in a 'torn wedding dress' that is a relic of the day's adventures: but her position remains not only ambiguous but precarious. The last few times the reader encounters her, she wavers vertiginously between male and female roles. These occur in 'An Odour of Verbena', when she speaks for the traditional Southern code of honour, trying to persuade Bayard to seek vengeance by killing the man who killed Colonel John. Continuing her pursuit of the male prerogative, in fact, Drusilla tries to assume the mantle of Duty. She attempts to turn herself into a spokesman for those stern martial virtues that once drew her into war, requiring a life to be taken for a life. 'There are worse things than killing men, Bayard', she proudly declares a few weeks before her husband dies,

> There are worse things than being killed. Sometimes I think the finest thing that can happen to a man is to love something . . . hard hard hard, then to die young because he believed what he could not help but believe . . .[72]

Her position is embarrassingly compromised, however, by her demand, following shortly upon this declaration, that Bayard should kiss her. In other words, she tries to use her sexual attractiveness to support her case: she speaks 'as a man' and then acts 'as a woman'.

A similar discontinuity is even more noticeable later on in this final story in *The Unvanquished*, in the scene where Drusilla tries to prepare Bayard for vengeance by handing him two duelling pistols:

'Take them, Bayard,' she said in the same tone in which she had said 'Kiss me' . . . , already pressing them into my hands . . . speaking in a voice fainting and passionate with promise: 'Take them. I have kept them for you . . . Do you feel them? the long true barrels, the triggers . . . quick as retribution, the two of them slender and invincible and fatal as the physical shape of love?'[73]

The sexual dimension is even more obvious here, as is the 'passionate and voracious' nature of Drusilla'a approach; again, she seems to be oscillating violently between two quite disparate roles. At one moment assuming the male, martial position and at another that of seductress, her behaviour is equivocal to the point of incoherence: something that is registered in her description of the pistols, instruments of death that are temporarily trans-figured in her eyes into instruments of love. Drusilla's dissatisfaction with the Southern versions of womanhood has been enough to drive a wedge between her and the conventional, even though she now dresses as a woman. However, it has not enabled her either to repress her sexuality, that force which makes her imitation of a man less than convincing, or, alternatively, to express her sexual drives in terms that are adequate for her. What we are confronted with in Drusilla, finally, is neither a marginal nor a transgressive figure but a confusingly multiple one: who desires both sex and death, the restoration of the patriarchal code and demolition of the roles it prescribes. The last we see of her she exits 'screaming with laughter, trying to deaden the sound by putting her hand over her mouth, the laughter spilling between her fingers like vomit'; the last we hear of her, she is on her way out of the plantation, on a train to the city of Montgomery. She has become the 'hysterical' woman, whose position as the site of competing constructions of the male and female has become intolerable – for her and for others, the people around her; her danger-ous energies can no longer be contained, and so her place in the narrative has disappeared.

Her place in the narrative of the plantation economy, that is, and in the narrative of the story: the point about Drusilla Hawk is that, by the end of 'An Odour of Verbena', she has to be dismissed, consigned to the danger-ous edges of the tale. The story has often been misread. Even critics who are uneasy about the complacencies and closures of the other six sections of *The Unvanquished* often make a case for what they see as the more adventurous, more critically rebarbative character of the final piece: in which, so the argument goes, by refusing to kill Colonel John Sartoris's killer, Bayard is denying patriarchal authority and defying the traditional Southern code. In fact, 'An Odour of Verbena' is just as closed as the tales it follows: even if that closure assumes more sophisticated, less easily dis-cernible forms here. Part of the seductiveness of the story for commenta-tors is, in any event, that it tends to comment upon, and explain, itself. In the first few pages, for instance, the nature of the choice that confronts Bayard is clearly announced (*'this will be my chance to find out if I am what I think I am'*), as is the decision he will eventually make ('Thou shalt not kill'). This is the one tale in which John Sartoris appears in a less than glowing light: the reader learns, among other things, about his inexcusable behaviour towards Redmond, the man who shoots him, and about his previous acts of violence – including his murder of a hillman who he only thought was about to rob him. This necessarily makes the Colonel's position less than authoritative; and in any case the paternal authority that he previously monopolized now has to be shared with another father-figure, Professor Wilkins at Bayard's college, who, we learn, has helped his young pupil understand the value of non-violence. A sadly contracted character here, even John Sartoris seems to be edging away from his violent past: 'I am tired of killing men, no matter what the necessity or end', he is recalled admitting the evening before his death, 'Tomorrow, when I go to town and meet Ben Redmond, I shall be unarmed.'[74] To the extent that the Colonel still offers Bayard a model then, it is a curiously ambiguous one: since he himself seems finally to have reneged on a code of honour that prescribes vigorous self-defence and vengeance – fighting your corner, and the taking of a life for a life.

All this makes the decision that Bayard has already made that much easier. It is as if people and events are conspiring to ensure that he does not kill. What is more, Aunt Jenny, who is the real source of female authority in this story, actually tells Bayard, 'You are not going to try to kill him. All right'; then, having said this, dismisses Drusilla as 'a poor hysterical young woman'. Drusilla Hawk is, in effect, positioned as the false priestess: driven by her own neuroses to direct the novitiate towards destruction and death. The true priestess is Aunt Jenny – here, as in *Flags in the Dust/Sartoris*, the keeper of the flame and guardian of the family legend; and her matriarchal authority confirms what the patriarchs of the story, the Professor and the Colonel, respectively advise and admit – '*Thou shalt not kill.*' Once embarked on his course of non-violence, Bayard also finds that just about everyone approves: unlike, say, Quentin Compson and Horace Benbow, his idea of doing the right thing does not lead him into collision with the rest of the community. Even the Colonel's killer, Ben Redmond, appears to collaborate with Bayard: shooting to miss and then leaving town – so preserving not only Bayard's life but also his reputation, confirming that his choice was in every respect the correct one. 'You ain't done anything to be ashamed of', declares George Wyatt, one of the more bloodthirsty of Colonel John's followers, 'I wouldn't have done it that way myself. I'd a shot him once, anyway. But that's your way or you wouldn't have done it.'[75] This is the closest the men of the town come to criticizing Bayard's actions; and what it amounts to is an expression of respect that is only slightly puzzled and not at all grudging.

The town approves; the sources of authority, male and female, approve; and Redmond shows his approval, to the extent that he reacts to Bayard's non-violent behaviour in a way that mirrors that non-violence, while admitting defeat. There is just about no pressure on Bayard actually to kill Redmond: except, that is, from Drusilla Hawk. And even she, in the last moments of the tale, leaves a sprig of verbena on Bayard's pillow: an evident admission that what he has done is what, not only he, but also the consensus of the community now define as courage, even if she herself cannot share in that definition.[76] So what appears, at first sight, to be an act of defiance of the community and its standards turns out to be a reassertion of them – which is to say, a reworking and a reinscription – a defence of communal value, made in necessarily altered terms. Bayard rejects, not the code of honour as such, but the ossified relics of that code; and that is something that nearly all the characters in the story are prepared to acknowledge. The traditional Southern ethic is sustained by a sly procedure of metamorphosis: it is quietly adjusted to an altered historical reality – a mental and material landscape devastated by the mass violence of war. Bayard has not resisted the beliefs of his fathers. Instead, he has learned how to perpetuate them – and in a way that *his* father was already beginning to anticipate: through a process of assimilation and adaptation – by ensuring survival through change. Honour is satisfied: but this is done in terms responsive to recent memories of wholesale slaughter – and to the fact that even the most violently inclined are now, as they admit, 'tired of killing men'.

The one thing that does not fit into this restatement of the old pieties is, of course, the lonely figure of Drusilla Hawk. She is marginalized: excluded from the communal consensus and the closure of the tale. No longer openly criticizing the Southern ethic but, in her own eyes, subscribing to it, her presence nevertheless renders that ethic problematic: her confusions, in other words, register just how much it distorts and suppresses – whether in its 'old' form of preserving honour by killing, or in its 'new' form of preserving it by ritualized confrontation, being (in this respect) neither here nor there. As a result, she has to be despatched to the other side of the plantation wall and the borders of the narrative; she has to be dismissed as a neurotic, whose opinions no longer count. 'An Odour of Verbena' may be a more sophisticated story than those it follows. It is so, however, not because it interrogates the forces of patriarchy (or, still less, subverts them) but because it allows those forces to regroup and be redefined. With Bayard as the main agent of change, but assisted by others, the social and emotional transformations initiated by war are assimilated; then, and only then, the code of honour is confirmed and narrative closure secured. In this scheme of things, the positioning of Drusilla is vital, as is her eventual expulsion from the story, since both gestures give the appearance of legitimacy to a new order that is not so much new as craftily reconstituted. Drusilla momentarily raised problems about male power and female subordination that have not been solved, nor even properly addressed: still, by placing her as unstable and anachronistic and then condemning her to exile, the narrative invites the reader to dismiss those problems – or, to be more exact, to infer that they are as irrelevant now as Drusilla appears to be herself. The design or pattern that haunts the other pieces in *The Unvanquished*, of ceremony/disruption/

restoration of ceremony, is not dropped for this tale. On the contrary, it is simply replicated in a more convoluted and cunning form. The power of patriarchy, and the pieties of plantation life, have been quietly reaffirmed; the circle is closed yet again, the plantation gate is shut; and only a madwoman, or rather 'a poor hysterical young woman', has been left outside.

5

Public Faces and Private Places

I NOW ABOUT THESE WOMEN: *THE WILD PALMS*

In April 1938, Faulkner wrote to his publishers to explain that his new novel had been delayed because, as he put it, he had been 'a little mad . . . nerves frayed from three months' pretty constant pain and inability to sleep'. Then in July he wrote to his publishers again, in even franker terms. 'I have lived for six months in such a peculiar state of family complications and back complications', he said,

> that I am not able to tell if the novel is all right or absolute drivel. To me, it was written just as if I had sat on the one side of a wall and the paper was on the other and my hand with the pen thrust through the wall and writing not only on invisible paper but in pitch darkness too, so that I could not even know if the pen still wrote on paper or not.[1]

The novel he was referring to was eventually to be published as *The Wild Palms*; and the 'complications' that had made him sleepless and 'a little mad' all circulated around the evident end of his affair with Meta Carpenter. That affair had been probably the most passionate sexual experience of Faulkner's life; and in its closing stages especially it had exposed, like a series of raw nerves, the deep ambiguities inherent in his feelings about women, sexuality and love. Meta later admitted that she was both confused and disturbed by the ambivalence of Faulkner's behaviour towards her. At one moment, he would treat her as if they were equal partners, secret sharers in a world of absolute erotic abandon. He would write letters and poems to her that were notable for their sexual candour; he gave her his unexpurgated copy of *Lady Chatterley's Lover* to read and then, in imitation of the lovers in that novel, gave names to his and Meta's sexual parts – 'Mr. and Mrs. Bowen', names that indicated that, on this special level at least, they were 'married'. At the next moment, however, he would insist on behaving towards her as if she were, in Meta's own words, 'a girl-child . . . just out of high-school': a 'maiden' for whom gifts of ribbons and little puppy dogs were appropriate.

The contradictions went further: biting more deeply and, as Meta sensed, more seriously. Much of the time, Faulkner seemed to want to keep the two of them in what Meta saw as 'self-isolation', in 'a bubble' in which, so she feared, 'one day we would not be able to breathe'. He did not want to go out; he did not want to visit friends, or be visited; he seemed, Meta felt, not to need others besides herself 'to relate to'. However, when his work consumed him, he could be unnervingly quick to abandon her. As he embarked on the early stages of *The Wild Palms*, for instance, he started to spend less and less time with the woman he supposedly adored. 'He became obsessed with the novel', Meta recalled, and began to leave her earlier at night so that he could get back to his writing desk. Unsurprisingly, she felt unclear about just where she stood with a man who claimed to be overwhelmed with passion for her but who, apparently, would prefer to write about rather than make love. And her uncertainty was compounded by the fact that, while Faulkner talked about divorcing Estelle to both Meta herself and at least one close friend, Ben Wasson, he made no moves in that direction – eventually saying that he could not get a divorce for many years because he would then lose his daughter Jill. A slightly sinister charade that Faulkner devised, when Estelle and Jill came to stay with him in Hollywood, is perhaps significant here. Faulkner arranged for his wife and mistress to meet, through the device of having Ben Wasson bring Meta to the Hollywood home that he and Estelle had rented. The pretence was that it was Ben and Meta who were lovers. In the event, the plan backfired: Estelle was not fooled, although she only revealed this to Wasson after the meeting, and Meta found herself feeling only pity for a woman she had expected to hate. What is interesting about this bizarre event, though, is not how it turned out but Faulkner's possible motives for organizing it. Later commentators have tended to assume that it was all done to humiliate Estelle. Meta was probably nearer to the truth, however, when she guessed that the whole 'mindless imposture' was thought up by Faulkner as a scheme for comparing his 'two women', as a means of experiencing 'a sexual thrill by playing a dangerous game' – and, above all, as a way of feeding 'a morbidity in his nature that even he could not fully understand'.[2] In other words, if the wife was being humiliated, then so too was the mistress, even if she did not fully appreciate this at first. Faulkner was toying with the possibilities in his life – on the one hand, home, respectability and family and, on the other, erotic adventure – by bringing them into embarrassing collision. He was comparing the different routes his future might follow, playing a secret game of choice – without regard for the feelings of the women drawn into that game and, quite probably, without being fully aware of what he was doing.

Not long after this charade, Meta Carpenter gave up hope of Faulkner ever leaving his wife and became engaged, then subsequently married, to another man. During the period of the engagement, Faulkner tried to persuade Meta to continue sleeping with him: 'he's off somewhere', he said of Meta's fiancé, 'a thousand miles or more away' – and so, he implied, infidelity did not matter. Meta refused, however, and Faulkner turned to drink for comfort. It was during a particularly ferocious drinking bout that he incurred the 'back complications' that he complained of to his publisher: injuries that, along with the mental and emotional torture he was enduring as a result of the end of his affair, made it difficult for him to continue with *The Wild Palms*. 'You don't think I'm going to let you out of my life?' he asked Meta, shortly before she was married. As he must have sensed, however, he *had* let her out, as much by failing to commit himself as by making an active decision: the affair was over, to be replaced by an intermittently renewed loving friendship. The fact that he realized this, reluctantly, is indicated by Meta's account of a brief meeting that she and Faulkner had in Central Park in New York City, after she was married. 'Meta', she recalled him saying, 'one of my characters has said, "Between grief and nothing I will take grief".' Then, she went on, 'he studied my face as he would a map that confused him with its dim, indistinct iconography'.[3] The implication was plain enough, although Meta herself did not grasp it until later, when Faulkner sent her a copy of *The Wild Palms*: somehow, he saw a connection between his own desperate attempts to map out his relations with the women he loved and the emotional geography of his eleventh novel – the passionate manoeuvres of at least some of its male characters.

The connection between Faulkner's problems with women and, at the very least, the genesis of *The Wild Palms* is underscored by the fact that many years later, in 1952, Faulkner wrote to Joan Williams, a young woman with whom he had become infatuated, saying that he had written the stories of Harry Wilbourne, Charlotte Rittenmeyer and the tall convict 'to stave off what I thought was heartbreak'. His heart 'didn't break then', he recalled, 'so maybe it won't now'.[4] It was as if the author felt that there was a fragile thread of potential 'heartbreak', tying together his past and his present, and maybe his future, which his eleventh novel in particular might help to unravel. The feeling was clearly there, even at the time Faulkner wrote *The Wild Palms*, since that novel not only reverberates with suggestions of the woman he had recently loved and lost, Meta Carpenter, it also recollects a lost lady of much earlier times, Helen Baird: the trauma of breakup with Meta seems to have carried him back to an earlier erotic trauma, his frustrated longing for another woman who had married someone else. Charlotte Rittenmeyer, the principal female character in *The Wild Palms*, may carry traces of Meta Carpenter with her but many of the more striking parallels are with the woman to whom Faulkner dedicated much of his earliest writing: most notably, Charlotte has the same colour eyes as Helen Baird, the same complexion and epicene figure, the same childhood injury, the same directness and vivacity. Nor are the parallels just with the woman to whom Faulkner had proposed in 1925, they are also with an older Helen whom he had known in the years after her marriage: Helen, for instance, was an artist as well as a wife and a mother of two children, just as Charlotte Rittenmeyer is – although, unlike Charlotte, she was quite unwilling to give her family up for someone else. What fired Charlotte into fictional life, in fact, seems to have been not so much one specific woman or one particular moment in Faulkner's life but something that had occurred to him more than once before he had written *The Wild Palms*, and was to occur to him again after he had written it: the idea of woman as challenge and adventure – a being whose seductive otherness invites man to take risks and let go, to drown in potentially dangerous but liberating experiences.

There is a lot more to *The Wild Palms* than this, of course, and even to the character of Charlotte Rittenmeyer. Faulkner suggested as much when, many years later, he said of the stories of Harry Wilbourne and the tall convict that 'one man gave up everything for love of a woman, the other gave up everything to get away from love',[5] There is a curious replication in the novel, in effect, of the two routes that Faulkner saw mapped out for himself and that he had brought together for a moment, via the 'dangerous game' of that dinner party involving both wife and mistress. On the one hand, there was the the route marked 'all for love'; on the other, there was the one inscribed with the pieties of home, marked 'security and responsibility' ('Why does all the responsibility have to fall on you?' Meta Carpenter had asked Faulkner once when, yet again, he had invoked the impediments posed by his family. 'It just does', he replied). In his life Faulkner committed himself to erotic escape but then held back, he accepted the discipline of family duty but then constantly chafed at the bit: he wavered between the two paths in a way that was painful for him and cruel to others. And in a novel like *The Wild Palms* he brought the two into often startling juxtaposition: routine and revolt, the prisonhouse of quiet desperation that people make for themselves and the full flood of adventure in which, quite possibly, they drown.

In the past, attempts have been made to treat the two stories that comprise *The Wild Palms* as totally distinct. The New American Library published the work as two separate fictions in 1948; then, in 1954, the same publishers published the two narratives in one volume but as discrete units rather than in alternating chapters. In 1946, *The Portable Faulkner* included 'Old Man' without 'Wild Palms', and in 1950 the Modern Library published *Three Famous Short Novels: Spotted Horses, Old Man, The Bear*. The manuscript of *The Wild Palms*, however, bears out Faulkner's own descriptions of how he wrote the book, by cutting constantly between the two stories to create 'a contrapuntal quality like music'. What these descriptions leave unclear, though, is the matter of priorities. Sometimes, Faulkner would claim that 'the story I was trying to tell was the story of Charlotte and Harry' and that 'Old Man' 'wasn't too important', it was there 'simply to underline' the tale of the two lovers. At other times, he would insist that 'Old Man' was absolutely integral, that he wrote it because 'something was missing' from 'Wild Palms' and that 'they are only two stories by chance, perhaps necessity'.[6] The contradiction implicit in these accounts in fact only adds to the intimacy that clearly exists between the two tales: since the inference must be that 'Old Man' performs two tasks at once. It underlines something already in place and it also supplies a shape to fill a lack, in response to the suspicion that something is missing. By Faulkner's own account, the tale of the tall convict pursues the story of the lovers in the same way language pursues its object in his fictions, and the male gaze searches out the female object of desire: by emphasizing presence while admitting absence – inscribing something that is somehow 'there' and 'not there'.

Having accepted that 'Wild Palms' and 'Old Man' must be read together, that there *is* an intimate connection between them, then another problem arises. In what sense, in terms of narrative detail, are they connected? Apart from the general notion of 'contrapuntal form', and setting aside even the idea that the one story pursues the other both as a presence and an absence, what specific strategies link them together? Most of the commentators who have confronted this problem have tended to concentrate on questions of content and theme. Anything from the broadly shared narrative rhythms of imprisonment, escape and reimprisonment to far more specific connections – the fact, for instance, that both Harry and the tall convict are arrested adolescents, products of rural backgrounds and institutions – has been excavated and closely discussed. What has come in for less attention, however, is the way the problem in itself exposes what is arguably the most significant result of juxtaposing the two narratives. We ask these questions about the specific connections, and differences, between 'Wild Palms' and 'Old Man' because we are continually pressed to ask them in the act of reading the book. Every time we move from one story to the other, we are required to renegotiate our relationship with the text: to reconstruct our position, our reading of the narrative, and to redefine the possible points of elision and separation between one part of the narrative and the other. The opening of 'Wild Palms', for instance, raises expectations of a tale set firmly within the naturalistic mode ('The knocking sounded again, at once discreet and peremptory, while the doctor was descending the stairs . . .'): expectations that are hardly disappointed by the 'hard-boiled' dialogue ('I can smell a husband'; 'Jesus, there I went again'), and the characters that seem to come straight out of a novel by James M. Cain or Horace McCoy (the depressed middle-aged professional man, his tough irascible wife, the streetwise estate agent, the penniless fugitive lovers). However, just as we are about to settle into this narrative mode and wait to be taken in to 'see' the immediate cause of crisis in this first section – Charlotte Rittenmeyer bleeding on a bed from a botched abortion – the narrative suddenly stops short. 'You can come in', Harry Wilbourne says; and the reader enters, not the room where Charlotte is lying, but the story of the tall convict. With a jolt, we are ironically reminded of our position as voyeurs, waiting to 'see' the body, and confronted with a quite different narrative strategy. 'Once', 'Old Man' begins, '(it was Mississippi, in May, in the flood year 1927) there were two convicts';[7] and that sentence initiates us into a dimension somewhere between myth and folktale, where anonymous figures do battle with elemental forces. Exactly what are the particular comparisons and connections that we will make between this story and its predecessor (later its successor, then its predecessor again) will depend upon our singular activities as individual readers: what we choose to concentrate upon and remember and what, in one way or another, we suppress. What is common to all of us, however, is the activities themselves, forced upon us by the shifts and interruptions in the narrative. Walter Benjamin said of Brecht that his theatrical practice was better 'the more consumers' it was able 'to turn into producers, that is, readers or spectators into collaborators'. Similarly, the practice of *The Wild Palms* is better – which is to say, the more effective – the more we realize that Faulkner is foregrounding the textuality of the text, making us aware of what we are doing while we read and why, perhaps, we are doing it.

It is not just the narrative shifts that compel us to attend to our position as readers and to the status of the text as construct. A lot of the criticism of *The Wild Palms* has been devoted to its intertextuality: the extent to which its two stories invoke not only generally recognizable narrative conventions (the dime novel, the tall tale, and so on) but an elaborate network of other specific texts from the *Odyssey* and the Bible to the fictions of Sherwood Anderson and Ernest Hemingway. To search for meaning, as some have done, in the interstices between Faulkner's text and the plurality of texts to which it alludes is surely mistaken, though. There may, for instance, be a number of detailed connections between Charlotte and Harry and the lovers in *A Farewell to Arms*: but so convoluted are the terms in which those connections are made, that critics are just about equally divided between those who see Charlotte and Harry as heroic avatars of Hemingway's couple and those who describe their function as ironic and parodic. Faulkner's narrative sets up an elaborate circuit of allusion, not however to illuminate some argument – some idea or theme carried to us by the momentum of intertextual reference – but to rearticulate the book's concern with textuality: the fact that we are confronted here with a sophisticated construct that requires our active attention, renegotiation not just consumption. The kinds of pleasures of the text that we are denied are precisely those Harry offers his unsuspecting readers in the cheap novels he scribbles to make money: books beginning, 'I had the body and desires of a woman, yet in knowledge and experience of the world I was but a child' or 'If I had only had a mother's love to guard me on the fatal day.'[8]

The relationship between *this* text and the texts Harry churns out is not quite as simple as that, however. The way Harry's writing is described – not least, by him – is clearly ironic, but the irony is by no means one-way: some of it circles back on *The Wild Palms* itself. After all, the fact that what Harry writes about is mostly, as he puts it, 'on the theme of female sex troubles' makes it sound disquietingly similar to the romantic melodrama that is at the heart of 'Wild Palms'. The story of Charlotte and Harry is marked by an extraordinary – and what at first sight might seem rather heavy-handed – use of the narrative mechanisms of popular fiction: including, most notoriously, the casual use of accident. Faulkner makes no effort to hide it. Harry first goes to the party where he meets Charlotte as the result of pure chance: a friend opens a telegram addressed to Harry by mistake, discovers that it is Harry's birthday, and invites him along to celebrate. Then, just when it seems that, the lovers having met, they will have to separate because they are strapped for cash, Harry makes a lucky find: a wallet containing $1278 lying in a rubbish bin. Critics have been bemused by this *deus ex machina*, falling back on calling it a 'minor miracle' or citing examples from real life to show that such things do happen. But the whole point about it surely is what is, equally, the whole point about some of the tall convict's tall tales: that it *is* implausible, patently fictive – the fact that it reminds us, in no uncertain fashion, that we are reading (and reconstructing) a text. '*It's all exactly backward*', Harry thinks when he finds the wallet,

It should be the books, the people in the books inventing and reading about us – the Does and Res and Wilbournes and Smiths – males and females but without their sex.[9]

The effect of a remark like this is like the effect of the episode in which it occurs: to collapse the distinction between fictions that make no claim to be 'real' (such as 'the people in the books' Harry reads and writes) and the fictions that, for a moment at least, might tempt us into forgetting their fictiveness (most immediately, the one in which a character named 'Harry' appears). They are all levelled into one, flat landscape of fiction: all the more so here because the syntax of this passage makes it uncertain at times just who Harry is talking about – 'the people in the books' or 'us', the people in a book called *The Wild Palms*.

It is important at this point to establish what Faulkner is *not* doing as much as what he is. He is not trying to construct a prisonhouse of language, multiple layers of artifice that demonstrate nothing except their own falsity. Nor is he saying that a novel like *The Wild Palms* is no different at all from the kind of novel Harry writes: they are both fictive, but the measure of the authenticity of Faulkner's book is precisely that it insists on its own fictiveness, then invites us to investigate the consequences of that insistence. There is, here as elsewhere in Faulkner's work, a space left for distinguishing between the actual and the artificial, historical experience and experience that has been transformed into a commodity – a predigested product, artifice masquerading as the real. And in *The Wild Palms* that space is signposted, among other ways, by the central characters' failure to find it: the fact that all three are placed for us within the novel by their inability to circumvent fiction and engage with the real. Two notable examples of this spring to mind. The first is the more obvious. The tall convict is where he is, at the beginning and end of his story, because of what he has read. His anger at being imprisoned is in effect reserved not for the police, the lawyers and judges, but for those who, as he perceives it, really put him there, because he believed them: 'the writers, the uncorporeal names attached to the stories, the paper novels' who convinced him that he could manage to rob a train. His plan of action was constructed out of his passive acceptance of the lies like truth told in the tales of 'the Diamond Dicks and Jesse Jameses and such'; his plans for life, involving a 'fast car filled with authentic coloured glass and machine guns',[10] had a similarly fictive source. Writing has been his prisonhouse, and it has literally consigned him to prison, where he is left to rage against what he sees as his betrayal.

Charlotte Rittenmeyer is a more complicated illustration of the same dilemma; her entire affair with Harry Wilbourne is, in fact, circumscribed by her belief in stories. 'The second time I saw you', she tells Harry,

> I learned what I had read in books but never actually believed: that love and suffering are the same thing and that the value of love is the sum of what you have to pay for it and any time you get it cheap you have cheated yourself.[11]

This is a seductive formula, certainly, not least because it is uttered with such passion, but that does not make it inherently or automatically true. Charlotte has read this formula in books; she subsequently allows it to dictate her life. The ultimate course of her destruction is her faith in a romantic equation that sets love in opposition to pleasure, or even survival: that measures the value of love in terms of the suffering she or anyone is willing to incur for it, the price one is willing to pay – the highest price being, of course, death. If this is the ultimate cause, however, there is a more immediate, bloodier one: the abortion that Harry performs on her, which goes wrong. This is sometimes interpreted as fate taking a hand in the affairs of the lovers: but what this ignores is Charlotte's explanation of how and why she came to be pregnant in the first place. 'I should have known better. I always did take it easy', she says, referring to her failure to take precautions,

> Too easy. I remember somebody telling me once, I was young then, that when people loved, hard, really loved each other, they didn't have children. Maybe I believed it. Wanted to believe it. Or maybe I just hoped. Anyway, it's done.[12]

The story is an oral one, this time: but its romantic implications are similar to those of the stories she had 'read in books'. Love is divided off from the mundane activities of procreation and survival, the ordinary business of life. 'Drowning' in love (the image is used several times in 'Wild Palms'), the lover shuffles off the constrictions of the commonplace: in a romantic apotheosis that is figuratively, and then literally in Charlotte's case, a dying away from the world.

Love and death, drowning, a consummation that is somehow sealed off from the squalid manoeuvres of the everyday . . . and incest. 'Maybe I was mixed up with incest', observes Charlotte ruefully almost immediately before the passage just quoted. Much earlier on in the story, she explains that she had married Francis 'Rat' Rittenmeyer, the man she leaves for Harry, because, as she puts it, 'I liked my oldest brother the best but you can't sleep with your brother and he and Rat roomed together at school.' Similarly, when the tall convict sees the woman who then accompanies him on his journey, she is perched, like the young Caddy Compson, in a tree. She 'was very probably somebody's sister', the narrator points out, and her first words, although they have a more mundane literal explanation, carry intimations of *déjà vu*: 'I thought for a minute you wasn't aiming to come back.' What the reader is being confronted with at such moments is a constellation of images and ideas familiar from some of Faulkner's earlier work – and, in particular, the work freighted with the most intimate, autobiographical associations. In one sense, *The Wild Palms* is a model analysis of what Fredric Jameson has called 'the commodity age' and what Faulkner himself preferred to term 'the Kotex age': a culture, that is, in which people's mental and emotional lives, along with their material existences, are shaped and distorted by their failure to distinguish between the artificial and the authentic – by their inability, to use the terms implicit in this book, to recognize the textuality of the text. The narrative comment on this is powerful, motivated in part perhaps by Faulkner's recent encounters with Hollywood, the paradigm of a culture intent on packaging experience. 'Hollywood which is no longer in Hollywood', the narrator of *The Wild Palms* observes, 'but is stippled by a billion feet of burning coloured gas across the face of the American earth.'[13] And his observation is fired into imaginative life, not only by the numerous, anonymous characters whom Charlotte, Harry and the tall convict meet on their travels ('broad strong Western girls', for example, 'got up out of Hollywood magazines . . . to resemble Joan Crawford'), but by the evident willingness of all three main characters to arrange their lives according to the books. Powerful though the narrative comment is, however, it is complicated – and the model analysis of cultural determination it supports is, to an extent, subverted – by one simple but radical fact: the cultural determinants Faulkner analyses were also, many of them, his. The dreams that Charlotte and Harry and the tall convict imbibe were ones in which Faulkner himself was implicated – and with particular intensity at exactly the time he was trying to write *The Wild Palms*.

Critics have been confused by Faulkner's eleventh novel, and especially by the character of Charlotte Rittenmeyer: uncertain about how to take her intense romanticism – wanting, for the most part, to see Faulkner as an ironic critic of the kind of romantic love she embraces but feeling uneasily that, as one commentator has put it, 'Faulkner's attitude toward Harry and Charlotte is . . . perhaps too complex for the good of the novel.' The confusion stems, though, from the dilemma in which Faulkner found himself while he was working on *The Wild Palms*, and at which he was hinting when he admitted to his publisher that he 'not able to tell' if it was 'all right or absolute drivel'. As he thrust his hands through the 'wall', the miasmal mist of intense, mixed and mostly painful emotions that accompanied the end of his affair with Meta Carpenter, he was engaging with a task that was just about impossible. He was trying to chart mental and emotional processes, forms of belief – especially about love – which he could see came heavily mediated, via the complex machinery of his culture, but which, precisely because they were a part of his own cultural experience, he could not entirely escape – least of all, at a time when his own romantic affairs had made him, as he felt, 'a little mad'. The opposition between love and responsibility, for instance, the tendency to link erotic experience to suffering, and the assumption that love must seal lovers off from the everyday world: these are all aspects of the romanticism of Charlotte and Harry, their failure to get outside the cultural texts they have read. However, they were also functions of Faulkner's own 'learned' experience, facets of his own understanding of possible relations between the sexes. Neither Charlotte nor Harry can think of anything worse than treating each other as if they were conventionally married. 'I had turned into a husband', Harry says of himself at one point with undisguised disgust,

> I have even caught myself twice . . . thinking 'I want my wife to have the best' exactly like any husband with his Saturday pay-envelope and his suburban bungalow full of electric wife-saving gadgets and his tablecloth of lawn to sprinkle on a Sunday morning . . . the doomed worm blind to all passion and dead to all hope and not even knowing it, oblivious and unaware in the face of all darkness, all unknown the underlying All-Derisive biding to blast him.[14]

There may be an element of placing here, as Harry persuades himself that he and Charlotte must move on to avoid being ground in the mill of the conventional. The narrative may, at moments, seem to be edging towards locating Harry as another victim of the romantic formula, love = suffering versus marriage = survival. However, as the unmistakably Faulknerian cadences and idiom of the latter half of this passage intimate, the author is more than a little in sympathy with what his character is saying; he could at times – as in the period just before and after his breakup with Meta Carpenter – be just as addicted to that formula as Harry is. So if the reader is often confused about Harry and Charlotte and their affair, then this should come as no surprise, since Faulkner was just as confused himself. He was, after all, writing out, and out of, his agony: mapping out territory the 'dim, indistinct iconography' of which he could never fully trace or understand.

The degree to which Faulkner is implicated in a dilemma that, at least at times, he is trying to analyse helps account for some of the more puzzling or apparently intractable aspects of *The Wild Palms*. For example, it helps to explain why even those critics who insist that Faulkner is formulating a trenchant critique of romanticism find themselves occasionally seduced by the intensity of the romantic affair: because Charlotte and Harry are not as tightly contained in critical ironies or strategies of alienation as, perhaps, we would like to think. The formula of 'all for love' is, now and then, allowed free play, given the full blast of the mature Faulknerian rhetoric – as in that passage just quoted. The circuit of emotional involvement, in such cases, runs from author through narrator through character to reader, momentarily abolishing the narrative distance, the sense of displacement required to remind us that this is, after all, a text. More fundamentally, perhaps, Faulkner's involvement in the imaginative constructs that imprison Charlotte, Harry and the tall convict helps to determine what might be called the deep structure of the novel, the series of assumptions and oppositions on which narrative representation in *The Wild Palms* finally rests. This structure recalls the idea that, in male discourse, woman is not only the other but specifically man's other: a figure defined by the gaze of the male and marking out the borderline between 'culture' and 'nature'.[15] As such, she assumes a dual role. Marking the limits of culture, she is a guardian of cultural authority; hovering on the edges of culture, however, she is a reminder of what lies beyond that authority, the seductive if unnerving possibilities that stretch outside the cultural domain. She is an arbiter of respectability and responsibility, and an instigator of revolt. She is, we might say, Estelle Oldham Faulkner and Meta Carpenter, as Faulkner chose to see them while (for instance) playing that 'dangerous game' at a dinner party: the one defining the comforts and constrictions of routine, a home that is also a prison, the other offering the delights and dangers of release, a flood in which it is possible to drown.

Another way of putting all this is to say that at the back of *The Wild Palms* is a series of dualisms that help determine the narrative development: dualisms with either term of which woman can be associated, thanks to the sheer ambiguity of her role as 'other'. The series includes culture (law, 'the grim Moses' Harry offends when he goes to the party where he meets Charlotte) and nature (where chance holds sway, and both Harry and the tall convict can be compared to Adam); prison (literal or metaphorical: for instance, the hospital and the mine in 'Wild Palms') and space (the wilderness the lovers flee to; the flood the tall convict negotiates); stasis (the small coastal resort in which the middle-aged doctor has 'lived . . . all his life'; the unexamined existence to which the tall convict longs to return) and mobility (the train on which Charlotte and Harry first make love; the boat on which the tall convict travels with the woman); routine (the 'peace' of a 'middleaged eunuch' that Harry enjoys before he meets Charlotte; the daily rituals of the prisonhouse) and escape (dangerous adventures on the road or the river); language (the naming practices of court, hospital, prison) and silence (the social anonymity of the lovers; the non-verbal communication that the tall convict and the Cajun share);

institution (the rules that regulate both the bourgeois family and the prison) and dissolution (the sense of '*getting out of timing*' that Harry has when he first becomes involved with Charlotte; the dissolving of the known contours of the world that accompanies the flood); fixity (the structures of society where everyone has 'official sanction in the form of a registered Social Security number'; the firm surfaces of the earth where the tall convict can enjoy the comforting rituals of the plough) and fluidity (the falling away of Charlotte's body in death 'as undammed water collapses'; the 'running backward' of the flooded river, 'travelling at dizzy and inexplicable speed above the largest cottonfield in the world').[16] In his life, Faulkner tended to associate different women with the opposing terms in these equations; or, if not always different women, then, as in the case of Estelle, the same woman at very different times. In *The Wild Palms*, however, the same woman may keep oscillating between those terms as the gaze of the narrator/character alters: so she can be, in quick succession, both respectability *and* release, control *and* abandonment, or – to use the terms current in Faulkner's own experience at the time – Estelle *and* Meta.

Charlotte Rittenmeyer is, unsurprisingly, *the* woman here: the character most affected by the erratic habits of the male gaze. Of course, she enables Harry to break away: that is her initial and primary function. 'I had rather drown in the ocean', she declares, 'than be urped up on a strip of dead beach . . . with . . . just *This was* for an epitaph.' Inviting him to surrender himself to a life of motion and risk, she takes him outside the limits of the known: 'either heaven or hell', she insists, 'no comfortable safe peaceful purgatory between'. All this talk of liberation, however, does not stop Faulkner from also assigning to her the marks of authority. Showing what is termed 'the ability of women to adapt the illicit, even the criminal, to a bourgeois standard of respectability', she turns even the hotel room they rent for one night into a home that is also a prison. 'Now he mused indeed on that efficiency of women in the mechanics, the domiciling, of cohabitation', the narrator says of Harry as Charlotte goes about her self-appointed task of domesticating their temporary bolt-holes,

> he thought, *It's not the romance of illicit love which draws them, not the passionate idea of two damned and doomed and isolated forever against the world and God and the irrevocable which draws men; it's because the idea of illicit love is a challenge to them, because they have an irresistible desire to . . . take the illicit love and make it respectable, take Lothario himself and trim the very incorrigible bachelor's ringlets . . . into the seemly decorum of Monday's hash and suburban trains . . .*[17]

The echoes of *The Sound and the Fury* here ('*two damned and doomed and isolated forever . . .*') merely give this passage an additional force, an edge of scarcely subdued, autobiographical intensity. Not for the only time in the novel, by any means, the Charlotte who wants to be 'a good whore' is transmogrified into a Charlotte with a frightening 'skill in the practical affairs of love', whose 'unwinking yellow stare' makes Harry 'blunder . . . like . . . a rabbit caught in the glare of a torch'. Just as the woman the tall convict meets and rescues fluctuates disconcertingly between an Eve figure, the sister in the tree, and a parodic wife who requires constant support for herself and her child, so Charlotte continually moves between two vocabularies, two roles: at one moment, the idiom of abandonment, at the next that of regulation – at one time, the voice of escape, then at the next the agent of control. The conception, needless to say, is profoundly contradictory, helping to account for the problems many readers have when trying to interpret Charlotte's character. Once it is seen that the contradictions issue from the deep structure of the novel, rather than anything specific to the representation of Charlotte herself, those problems do not disappear: but they are, at least, supplied with an explanation. Charlotte is as she is because that is how Faulkner has learned to read 'woman'. In this instance, just like his characters in *The Wild Palms*, he remains trapped in the cultural text.

It is, it has to be said, a fairly radical form of entrapment: not least, because the reading of woman is so fundamental to the book. And it leads inevitably to the feelings of emotional paralysis with which both 'Wild Palms' and 'Old Man' end. For Harry, there is no way out. You cannot, he believes, stay outside or break away for very long. You let go, he says, you,

> surrender volition, hope, all – the darkness, the falling . . . you feel all your life rush out of you into the pervading immemorial blind receptive matrix, the hot fluid blind foundation – grave-womb or womb-grave, it's all one . . .[18]

But then, sooner or later, 'you return'. 'Maybe', he suggests,

> you knew all the time, but you return, maybe you even live out your three score and ten or whatever it is, but forever afterward you will know that for ever more you have lost some of it . . .[19]

After the passionate abandonments of sex come the routines of survival: routines by which life is measured, as it is whenever Charlotte and Harry settle down for a moment, by a shrinking store of cash or a 'diminishing row of cans'. And at such junctures, woman as 'grave-womb or womb-grave', inviting a consummation that is also a dissolution, shifts into woman as little wife threatening to make 'chiropracters and clerks and bill-posters and motormen and pulp writers of us'. Sandwiched between these intolerable alternatives, perhaps the conclusion to be reached is the one towards which Harry gravitates: that 'love . . . can't last' and so 'we are doomed'. Certainly, both Harry and the tall convict end in isolation; the journey for the two of them concludes in 'little monastic cells'. The tall convict's conclusions are the less ambiguous: 'Women, shit' is his final remark, an evident gesture not only of retirement from the battle between woman as release and woman as regulator but also of disgust with 'woman' in either capacity. The company of men is, it seems, safer.

The last words of Harry Wilbourne in the book are much less dismissive than this, and famous: '*between grief and nothing I will take grief*'. Perhaps, however, we should remind ourselves that what Harry is committing himself to is not love or emotional entanglement of any kind but, rather, the recollection of love – emotion safely distanced in time, packaged like a little piece of private property to be fondled while he is all by himself. The reminder seems to be there, anyway, in the closing description of him, since, as that description intimates, Harry is masturbating. Memory becomes in his hands a gesture of self-absorption and self-abuse: 'so long as there was flesh to titillate', 'it would stand to when the moment came', 'thinking of, remembering the body, the broad thighs', 'and now it did stand to in his hand'.[20] Onanism, retreat from the perplexing otherness of woman, marks the completion of his narrative just as it does that of the tall convict; the fact that Harry wraps it up in romantic rhetoric is merely a symptom of the peculiar terms in which *his* problems with the other sex are addressed. In the end, Faulkner's account of the relationship between 'Wild Palms' and 'Old Man' turns out to be less than completely accurate. 'One man gave up everything for love of a woman, the other gave up everything to get away from love': that is how the two male characters see themselves, it may also be how Faulkner preferred to see them – but Harry, having made the gesture of erotic abandonment, finishes by getting away from love too. Despite the romantic momentum of the language, and the sexual energy of his relationship with Charlotte, his story has the same fundamental trajectory as that of the tall convict, deriving from the same highly charged, deeply contradictory notions of woman. He may not say 'Women, shit', but he winds up equally in withdrawal; he retires to a private space where, quite literally, he can embrace and enjoy himself.

Faulkner had pronounced himself confused about *The Wild Palms*, to the extent of suspecting that it might be 'pure drivel'. That tentative judgement is, of course, unfair. The book is, at the very least, a startlingly economical examination of the way a culture can determine not only the material fabric of experience but also the terms in which that fabric is understood, the emotional co-ordinates of our lives. Where the problems occur is where they often do in Faulkner's work: in the mapping out of relationships between the sexes, when the the writer and his male characters try to define just what 'woman' is and wants. This does not make *The Wild Palms* any the less intriguing. On the contrary, it means that the reader can measure just how deep the culture reaches: so deep, in fact, that the model of woman as 'other', and specifically male 'other', becomes an engine of the narrative, as well as an object of examination, helping to shape its conceptual framework and development. Faulkner was aware, acutely and painfully, of the divided terms in which he saw women and the erratic behaviour to which that could lead: but that awareness, while it enabled him to trace many of the mistakes his male characters made, did not give him absolute immunity. It did not, in other words, permit permanent release from the reading of woman he had learned; at most, it allowed the occasional moment of parole. Charlotte and Harry are the clearest testaments to this, since they oscillate between being examples of the way a culture can entrap people in its text and projections of Faulkner's own entrapment; the narrative alerts us to the lovers' failure to distinguish between the artificial and the authentic, but then falls prey to its own, related forms of inauthenticity.

One analogy here might be with *Sanctuary*, where similar problems lead to a similarly rich and confused brew: with Horace Benbow in that earlier book, instead of Harry Wilbourne, acting as both subject and surrogate for the author. Or a more immediate and pressing analogy might be with that dinner party at which Faulkner contrived to have his wife play hostess to his mistress. The fact that he devised the event suggests, after all, that he was capable of standing aside from his own emotional difficulties so as to turn them into a dark game, a polite occasion with a sinister subtext. But it indicates something else as well: that Faulkner could not get outside those difficulties enough to realize that what was needed was not so much play as change: a fundamental alteration in the terms in which he 'read' women, and more especially the women in his own life. Admittedly, it would be wrong to go far in comparing a cruel social joke with a potent, if deeply flawed, novel: there is infinitely more understanding at work in *The Wild Palms*, even concerning the peculiar habits of the male gaze. Still, Faulkner was right to suspect a connection between the complications in his life at the time and the confusions of his eleventh novel. The stories of Charlotte, Harry and the tall convict are not 'a little mad' but they do involve collusion in a kind of madness: the kind that prevents us, so often, from recognizing that what we see is what we have learned to see. What might have begun as diagnosis ends up by revealing certain specific symptoms of the very disease it set out to examine. In this way – and not for the only time in Faulkner's work, by any means – the text assumes a double-edged character. In failing to acknowledge its own textuality, when it comes to the fundamentals of its representation of women, it becomes both the agent and the victim of cultural determination – not only the doctor, we could say, but also the patient.

II LET'S MAKE A DEAL: *THE HAMLET*

The Wild Palms was published in the middle of January 1939. A little more than a month before this, Faulkner wrote to his publishers to tell them that he was 'working on the Snopes book'. The letter was an unusually detailed one, in which he outlined a plan for three volumes, to be called 'The Peasants', 'Rus in Urbe' and 'Ilium Falling'.[21] One reason why it could be so detailed was because Faulkner was excavating, rediscovering and revising material that reached back as far as *Father Abraham*. That unfinished story had already anticipated Flem Snopes's remorseless ascent to the presidency of a Jefferson bank. And, since he had written it in 1926, Faulkner had been working with the material of Frenchman's Bend and the Snopes clan, off and on, in several short stories as well as in books like *Flags in the Dust/Sartoris* and *The Unvanquished*. Incorporating much of the narrative matter of *Father Abraham*, borrowing and rewriting stories in which, in some cases, the Snopeses themselves had never originally appeared, Faulkner wrote steadily on, with the occasional interruption forced on him by the need to produce a more immediately saleable product ('Maybe what I need is a bankruptcy', he declared ruefully in May 1939, 'like a soldier needs delousing'). As he wrote, his experiments with voice prompted him to devote more attention and time to a character whom Faulkner later admitted he 'fell in love with': the itinerant sewing-machine salesman named V.K. Suratt in *Father Abraham* who had been rechristened V.K. Ratliff. The special attention paid to Ratliff was symptomatic of the importance of talk in this new book: as he crafted his stories together with fresh material, Faulkner used voices talking and trading as a dominant framing device – a variation on the strategy of 'old tales and talking' previously most extensively exploited in *Light in August* and *Absalom, Absalom!*. There is a narrative plenitude to Faulkner's twelfth novel, a rich overplus of stories rehearsed and repeated, that derives its major rhythms and sense of lively continuity from the rituals of conversation and communal storytelling. Weaving in and out of his voices, using Ratliff as the closest thing to a master storyteller, Faulkner was ready to send the last chapter of his new book to his publishers in October 1939. By this time, the projected trilogy had been renamed. The volume Faulkner had just finished should be called *The Hamlet*, he now suggested; the other two, to be written some time in the future, were to have the titles *The Town* and *The Mansion*.

'You fellows dont know how good a man's voice feels running betwixt his teeth',[22] Ratliff says to some of his friends in Frenchman's Bend. The thing is, though, they do. Like Ratliff, they have two principal forms of exchange: one of them is speech, the other is goods and cash. They spend their lives in talk and trade: a plurality of transactions that are all, at basis, verbal and economic. The two forms of exchange are, of course, related because they enable the group to enact its sense of itself. Frenchman's Bend, like any society, talks itself into being – it develops identity through speech – and it certifies its existence through the activities of bargaining and barter. It defines an environment in which people are who they are as a result of what they say and what they sell: what they sell being, as it happens, themselves and the products of their labours. Some readers have been tempted to interpret *The Hamlet* as the tale of a peaceful and bucolic community disrupted by an agent of capitalism, in the cool, quiet shape of Flem Snopes. More recent commentators, turning that interpretation on its head, have found a kind of structural anti-Semitism at work in the narrative: by which Flem Snopes becomes the scapegoat, the object of blame for the callous indifference of an economic system that he did not introduce, and still less controls, because it was already in place when he arrived. But perhaps it would be more useful to see *The Hamlet* as a novel that brings myth into collision with history: since it shows how a culture uses talking and trading as forms of accommodation – ways of constructing a group identity that seems authorized and natural, and a convenient defence against the challenge of change.

Even before the arrival of Flem Snopes, Frenchman's Bend is not set and stable, a bucolic idyll immune to disruption. It is made up of people who are engaged in a constant struggle to make their voices and value heard, trying to turn the fluidities of personality and history into the fixities of custom and ritual. In this respect, something that Mary Douglas has said is worth recalling. People in a group may get 'the feeling of being controlled by an external, fixed environment of ideas', she admits, 'but the feeling is an illusion'. They are not 'set somewhere below and apart from their cosmological ideas': on the contrary, they are 'living in the middle of their cosmology', she suggests, 'energetically manipulating it, evading its implications in their own lives if they can, but using it for hitting each other'.[23] So, Ratliff and his companions do not inhabit some uniquely stable world, authorized by a collaboration between nature and legend. They live in a cultural environment that is going through a process of constant alteration, generated by verbal and economic exchange. The challenges this environment faces can sometimes come from dimensions of experience that appear to exist outside the systems of exchange: in *The Hamlet*, such challenges issue from the silence of a woman like Eula Varner, who seems 'to be not a living integer of her contemporary scene', and from the brooding imperturbability of nature. But they can also come from inside: in this case, from someone like Flem Snopes who helps introduce to Frenchman's Bend the surprise and perturbations of a substantially altered, 'rationalized' system. Seen from this perspective, Flem is neither the outsider, the stranger who brings an alien virus into an otherwise whole and stable body politic; nor is he the victim, the symptom of an established disease who is mistaken somehow for the cause. He is, quite simply, another if radical step in the continually unfolding history of the community: an agent of a transformation that comes from within. He represents change of a substantive kind, certainly, but change that is evolved out of the established practices of Frenchman's Bend: by which both trading and talking are stripped down to a functional minimum. What we are left with, via this process of what would now be called rationalization, are the bare, utilitarian bones of verbal and economic exchange: the flat message, the hard sell and the quick deal.

Not that the inhabitants of Frenchman's Bend see it that way. Like any community, they tend to regard the status quo as something authorized by time immemorial. They do not appreciate, in other words, what is established in the opening pages of *The Hamlet*: that they inhabit a very particular place that also, and not by coincidence, happens to be a very specific moment in historical time. Frenchman's Bend, we are told, 'had been the original grant and site of a tremendous pre-Civil War plantation, the ruins of which . . . were still known as the Old Frenchman's place'. The broad acres of the estate have been 'parcelled out now into small shiftless mortgaged farms for the directors of Jefferson banks to squabble over before selling finally to Will Varner'. Varner, as this implies, is 'the chief man' of this society in transition: the largest landholder, 'beat super-visor in one county and Justice of Peace in the next and election commis-sioner in both', owner of the local store, the cotton gin, and 'the combined grist mill and blacksmith shop'. Faulkner could be a little uncertain about dates. When he wrote to his editor about the new titles for the trilogy, for instance, he declared in a mild fit of panic, 'Book Four [of *The Hamlet*] happens in 1890, approximately. Hence Civil War ended 25 years ago. Have recollection of dating War somewhere in script as 40 years ago. Please watch for it.'[24] However, he was much more certain and clear when it came to the processes of historical change. Neither a patriarch nor a capitalist in the modern sense, Varner occupies that special moment in Southern history, at and around the meeting of the nineteenth and twen-tieth centuries, when the great plantations had been broken up into small farms which were sometimes rented, sometimes mortgaged up to the hilt, and sometimes operated on the sharecropping system. He represents, because in this small world at least he controls, a system that is moving slowly and, it seems, inexorably from a semi-feudal economy to a *laissez-faire* one. As *The Hamlet* opens, Frenchman's Bend has already shrugged off the paternalist assumptions of the pre-Civil War system but it has not yet invested completely in notions of individual autonomy: habits of social deference, among other things, complicate the profit motive even if they do not contradict it. It is a place on the brink of alteration, waiting for the logic of its prior economic and social alterations to be continued; it is, in this sense, waiting for the arrival of Flem Snopes.

Like so much else in the novel, the arrival of Flem in Varner's store and his gradual ascent to power is filtered through the voices of Ratliff and his companions: observing, recollecting, arguing over the possible implica-tions of events. This is not merely a device of the narrative, it is a strategy of the community, as it struggles to accommodate the disruptive presence to known patterns of behaviour. In effect, the talking about Flem is an equivalent of Jody Varner's hiring of Flem; it represents an attempt to deal with a potential threat by inserting it in familiar structures – the social economy of the store, the verbal economies of old tales and yarn-spinning. The motive, however unacknowledged, is clear enough. Flem will be ren-dered safe by being linked up with stories of clever dealing – good tricks played with bad horseflesh – just as he will be, Jody hopes, by being put behind the counter with a job. Neither strategy works, though. Flem remains a destabilizing narrative presence. The communal space is undermined by his habitual silences: so unnerving is his refusal to go beyond flat matter-of-fact, the minimalist verbal gesture, that Ratliff even tries to accommodate *this* into a tall tale about Flem not out-talking but out-silencing the Devil. At the same time, the illusion of peace, a cyclical dream-time of repeated practices and recurrent rituals, that sustains the community in its sense of itself and its immunity from change, is undermined by Flem's quiet mobility. His steady social ascent in the first book of *The Hamlet*, for instance, is matched by his introduction of the restlessness of event into the narrative: 'then something happened' is a key phrase associated with him. As Flem destabilizes the narratives in which the locals of Frenchman's Bend seek to imprison him, so he resists and revises the customary methods of economic exchange. Will Varner now has to pay for the tobacco he takes from his own shop, just to keep the books straight. No mistakes are made any more when it comes to counting out change, not even in the shop-keeper's favour. No credit is given to anyone: not even, we are told, 'to a man who had been into and out of the store's debt at least once a year for the last fifteen'.[25]

Some commentators have argued that Flem's alteration of shopkeeping practices signals a shift from the benign rituals of a traditionalist com-munity to the less attractive habits of undiluted *petit bourgeois* capitalism. But this is to ignore the fact that a concern with property, the possession of it and the dealing in it, is obsessive in *The Hamlet*. We are told many tales, by the people of Frenchman's Bend, by Ratliff in particular, and by an anonymous narrative voice that weaves in and out of the voices of the community, sharing its inclinations and idiom; and what all these tales have in common is a preoccupation with the minutiae of exchange – goods bought and sold, notes transferred, the hiring of labour, the precise paying for what you get whether it involves a poundage fee or some bor-rowed feed. It is worth noting that when Henry Armstid is persuaded into parting with the only cash he has to buy one of the spotted horses, Ratliff refuses to replace the money, even though he could and even though Armstid's family may suffer. A trade is a trade; others, according to this code, can only stand by, 'sober, and attentive, and neat', while it is con-ducted; it is up to those individuals involved in the trading to make a profit or, if necessary, live with the loss. Even when a minor character like the schoolteacher Labove is introduced, he is absorbed into the domi-nant, trading ethos of the narrative. As soon as he is 'hired' by Varner, as a result of a fairly complex deal that allows him to continue playing foot-ball and studying at the state university, he carries the keys to the school-house, we are told, 'as a merchant carries the keys to his store'. And, as so often in the novel, his possessions are catalogued in detail: 'he owned', the narrator explains,

> a razor, the unmatching coat and trousers he stood in, two shirts, the [uni-versity football] coach's coat, a Coke, a Blackstone, a volume of Mississippi Reports, an original Horace and a Thucydides which the classics professor, in whose house he had built the morning fires, had given him at Christmas, and the brightest lamp the village had ever seen.[26]

In this environment, in which what you are is intimately related to what you say and what you own, the figure of Will Varner assumes particular importance. He owns most, and he owns it because he is quite as ruthless in his pursuit of profit and property as Flem is. Not only that, far from being a traditionalist icon, he is rather more interested in the standard bourgeois comforts than any member of the Snopes family ever appears to be. The difference between Flem Snopes on the one hand and, on the other, Varner, the locals of Frenchman's Bend or even Ratliff is, in fact, not a difference in kind – between, in other words, capitalism and traditionalism – but, crucially, a difference in degree. Flem adds a new intonation to the rituals of talking and trading through the simple expedient of narrowing things down to minimal conversation and stark event, so trading is focused down into a transaction in which there is no delight in the actual process of bargaining and swapping, since *all* that matters is the result of the deal. Flem follows the logic of the trading ethos of *The Hamlet* through to the point where 'the pleasure of the shrewd dealing'[27] that, for instance, Ratliff enjoys simply vanishes, is pared away: so that what is left is just the original aim and ultimate end of such dealing – profit and accumulation. It seems appropriate that, even as early as halfway through Book One, the reader is told where Flem will end up his career: in finance, as president of a bank in Jefferson. For all their preoccupation with trading, most of the inhabitants of Frenchman's Bend do find time to be interested in the nature of what they are buying and selling (good or bad horseflesh, for instance) and in the performative details of the deal. To Flem, however, that matters not at all: all that counts is the bottom line, the figure at the end of the balance-sheet that is the abstract sign of a successful exchange.

The silence of Flem Snopes is one thing, the silence of Eula Varner quite another. However, both forms of silence testify to flaws in the communal fabric, its version of itself; both, in their different ways, expose the gaps in the talking and the omissions inherent in the trading. Eula speaks only nine sentences in *The Hamlet*. We, the readers, never share in her subjectivity any more than the other characters do. What we are offered, instead of the language of consciousness or conversation, is an account of male reactions to her. These reactions can vary from one man to the next in terms of their details, but they have in common a mixture of awe, desire and resentment: awe at her sheer otherness, desire aroused by the spectacle and smell of her body, resentment about the hopeless longings she creates, her 'silent resistance' to the impulse to possess her. The portrait of her at the beginning of Book Two covers most of the language used to describe this creature who is evidently beyond the scope of language. 'Her entire appearance', the reader is told,

> suggested some symbology out of the old Dionysic times – honey in sunlight and bursting grapes, the writhen bleeding of the crushed fecundated vine beneath the hard rapacious trampling goat-hoof.[28]

Later, within the next few pages, we learn that,

even at nine and ten and eleven, there was too much – too much of leg, too much of breast, too much of buttock, too much of mammalian female meat.[29]

The language of nymphs and satyrs borrowed from Faulkner's earliest writings collides with the language of the flesh: woman is a daughter of the gods, a creature of legend, 'one blind seed of the spendthrift Olympian ejaculation', and she is also something far more carnal and fundamental, 'the supreme primal uterus'. The common factor here is Eula's strangeness, her positioning outside the normal systems of exchange. She is not, after all, the agent but the object of talk. Men see her and speak of her not as a human subject like themselves but as myth or meat: something superhuman, a seed of the deity transmitted to their village, or subhuman – 'a blooded and contrary filly', say, or the earth in all its 'mammalian maturity'.

The figure of the earth, in particular, suggests the double-edged nature of the way Eula is perceived by the other, male characters and, for that matter, the narrator. The feverish, excited idiom that is constantly deployed to register her being links her as woman with 'the ardour-wearied earth, ancient Lilith'. Earth as woman, a virgin in spring but revealing an 'old invincible courtesan's' splendour in autumn, elides with woman as earth, simultaneously innocent and carnal – a young girl with the 'mammalian female meat' of a seductive adult. At the age of eleven, we are told, Eula, 'sitting with veiled eyes against the sun like a cat', carries with her 'that ungirdled quality of the very goddesses in Homer', of being 'corrupt and immaculate, at once virgins and the mothers of warriors and grown men'. Virgin and whore, goddess and animal, myth and flesh, Eula has the same mystery as the land the men plough. Both she and the land are seen as fecund and fickle, rich and strange. Both arouse love and hatred, desire and despair: Eula, the narrator observes, has the face of 'another mortal natural enemy of the masculine race', while the 'piece of earth' the poor farmer works, requiring a 'constant and unflagging round of repetitive nerve-and-flesh wearing labour', is his 'mortal enemy' until he drops dead. Above all, both Eula and the land are possessed of a curiously dual role when it comes to the world of dealing and exchange. Of course, they exist outside that world to the extent that they inhabit silence and a seasonal cycle that cannot be brought under the realm of law. But, at the same time, both are sucked into that world in the sense that they are treated as commodities to be traded: Eula, like the land the men till, is not an agent but an object of exchange in terms of trading as well as talking. Even Ratliff is inclined to think of women as property – 'Yes', he thinks at one point, 'A man takes your wife and all you got to do to ease your feelings is to shoot him. But your horse';[30] and, as if to prove this association, Eula herself has her 'exchange value' assessed during the course of the book. Not only that, she is bought and sold.

Much of the peculiar quality and status of Eula stems, in effect, from this: that she registers Faulkner's own uncertainties about ownership, that claim to being 'Sole Owner & Proprietor' of something that he could fiercely dissect but, just as fiercely sometimes, embrace. Eula is certainly said, upon occasion, to be priceless: with an 'exchange value' that goes beyond 'the puny asking-price of any one man's reserve of so-called love'. No man will be able to 'possess her', the schoolteacher Labove observes. All any male will be able to do is to 'own her by the single strength which power gave, the dead power of money': own her, that is, 'as he might own, not a picture, statue: a field, say'. 'He saw it', says the narrator of Labove, as the land/woman analogy is continued,

> the fine land rich and fecund and foul and eternal and impervious to him who claimed title to it, oblivious, drawing to itself tenfold the quantity of living seed its owner's whole life could have secreted and compounded, producing a thousandfold the harvest he could ever hope to gather and save.[31]

Eula is impervious to possession, according to this estimation of her value. All that is possible is the illusion of ownership, which can be shrugged off just as easily as the land shrugs off each generation that attempts to till it and control its moods. It is this that generates the sheer resentment felt towards Will Varner's daughter, just as it provokes anger at the earth among those who must 'fight' it to earn a living. What the men of Frenchman's Bend want and claim can never really be theirs: woman and the land remain outside the reach of cash, as well as words.

Still, that does not prevent the male characters in *The Hamlet* from claiming that they own the fields and, along with them, 'their' females. The land is bargained over, bought and sold: treated, in fact, as a commodity. Possession of it may be described as an illusion, *sub specie aeternitatis*: but it becomes the determining element in the systems of exchange, the original and ultimate form of property. Similarly, Eula may be said to exist apart from talk and trading: she is, however, the object of talk and a tool of trade, almost from the moment she appears in the novel. The local youths treat her as their property: which is why they so resent, and even attack, Hoake McCarron, the man who goes out with and eventually impregnates her. Her brother Jody, in turn, is just as preoccupied as Quentin Compson ever was with the honour of his sister: not, though, for any deeply personal, psychological or sexual, reason but for the sake of the family reputation, the Varners's *value* within the community. Will Varner is even more openly concerned with exchange value than his son is. Will, we are told, 'declined to accept any such theory as female chastity other than as a myth to hoodwink young husbands with just as some men believe in free tariff'.[32] So when Eula loses her virginity, what needs to be done as he sees it is not to make a fuss but to make a deal: a deal by which his daughter, slightly damaged goods by now, can be married off with her credit rating (and, just as important, the credit of her family) carefully protected. Her market value has declined, Varner believes, so it is necessary to use money, another form of property, to close the deal. And Flem

Snopes is the best person to bargain with because he needs what Eula brings with her – connections and cash – while, being impotent as we learn later, he is uninterested in the particular marketable asset she has lost. Flem resists the existing systems of exchange to the extent that he successfully rewrites the terms in which exchange is conducted. Eula's position is more ambiguous and less fortunate. A mythic creature, perhaps, for the other, male characters and her creator, she resists to that extent the forms, verbal and economic, in which her neighbours deal. Nevertheless, those neighbours manage to accommodate her within their forms: as a piece of female flesh which, like a piece of earth, can be marketed. She is a woman and so, according to the terms of her historical environment, up for sale.

The degree of narrative collusion in all this is difficult to measure. Certainly, as far as the treatment of Eula as an object of talk is concerned, the voice of the narrator collaborates with the voice of the community, and the voice of the author, however implied, seems to be in there co-operating as well. The lip-smacking, tumescent prose used to describe her indicates that author and narrator, just as much as the male characters, are talking about Eula rather than talking with her; and so too does the inclination of the narrative, whenever Eula appears, to fall into the familiar Faulknerian equation woman = mystery/meat = the passive victim of speech. When it comes to trading, however – the transformation of Eula, and other women in *The Hamlet*, into objects of exchange – things become more problematical. Faulkner was sometimes tempted to consider the women in his life as property, just as he was susceptible to prevailing illusions about the ownership of land: his tendency to think of Estelle as 'somebody else's wife', second-hand goods, was eloquent testimony to that. But just as the fantasy of land ownership could be ferociously criticized in his work, even while he shared that fantasy, so could the idea of owning women. There are several ways in which a clearer critical purchase on the equating of women with commodity is acquired in *The Hamlet*. One has been intimated already: the sheer duality of Eula Varner – the fact that her position outside the normal parameters of dialogue and dealing casts a coolly ironic light on any attempt to treat her as simply something to be possessed. Two others take us into two quite different forms of narrative: different from each other, that is, as well as from the narrative styles that enclose Eula. One is ironic romance. The other is less easily defined because it is an inimitable mixture of historical realism, Southwestern humour, folklore and rural melodrama. The second permits Faulkner to chart differences between men and women, as he perceives them, when it comes to the law of necessity, the mechanisms governing social life. The first, in turn, enables him to introduce us to the idiot, Ike Snopes, and his beloved, the object of Ike's dreams and attentions: who is, it turns out, not a woman but a cow.

What is remarkable about the love story of Ike and his cow is the sheer diversity of the language in which it comes to us. Of course, much of the idiom is mock-heroic, archly romantic, like the style of his own short story, 'Afternoon of a Cow', from which Faulkner borrowed some of the material for this episode. There are even sly parodies of Faulkner's own earlier excursions into romance. 'He cannot make one with her', says the narrator of Ike, as the idiot pursues the elusive object of his desire through 'the motionless fronds of water-heavy grasses' and the morning mists; and, reading remarks like this, we are likely to be reminded of the frustrated longings and futile pursuits that characterize pieces like 'Nympholepsy' and 'L'Apres-Midi d'un Faune'. However, at times the language Faulkner deploys assumes an intensity, a fervour that leaves behind, not only the folkloric origins of the story – the tall tales of bestiality that circulate in most rural communities – but also his own earlier stab at the love story of a man and a cow. Mock-heroic then takes on more straightforwardly heroic dimensions; and the romantic idiom no longer tends towards making fun of its own pretensions. In a passage like the following, for instance, the reference to forequarters and hindquarters is just about the only element that does not seem calculated to make the reader forget that this is, after all, about a mentally retarded man and an animal:

> But she is there, solid amid the abstract earth. He walks lightly upon it, returning, treading lightly that frail inextricable canopy of the subterranean slumber – Helen and the bishops, the kings and the graceless seraphim. When he reaches her, she has already begun to lie down – first the forequarters, then the hinder ones, lowering herself in two distinct stages into the spent ebb of evening, nestling back into the nest-form of sleep, the mammalian attar. They lie down together.[33]

At times like this, the narrative dips down below normative prescriptions of behaviour to achieve a kind of experiential purity. By showing how Ike's devotion is, in its own terms, genuine, Faulkner shifts away from the social and cultural categories that would define this occasion as perverse and so require any intimations of romance to be parodic. Faulkner was always testing the margins; and as his portrait of another idiot, Benjy Compson, shows, he was fascinated by the way the pathological impulse can collapse the boundaries on which ethical articulations rest. He is testing them with particular intensity here, by moving towards what might perhaps be called the poetry of pure process, the phenomenological moment.

Poetry or parody, however, it hardly matters to the inhabitants of Frenchman's Bend, since they are uninterested in the possibly romantic elements in the liaison. Apart from the opportunities that Ike and his cow offer for the occasional bit of voyeurism, they are not even very interested in the sex. What matters, for them, is the business side of things. The laws of property and credit have been violated, because Ike has stolen someone else's goods and brought the family name into disrepute. Worse still, as the locals see it, having taken the cow, Ike has had the temerity to break into someone's barn to obtain some feed for it. So he extends what is adjudged a 'crass violation of private property'[34] by invading property to steal property to feed the property he has stolen. His offence is triple. First and last, though, it is an offence against the law of possession: he has stolen goods and good name, reputation being an important family asset (one thing, at least, on which the Snopeses and Varners can agree). The problem having been defined in economic terms, it is then solved in economic terms as well. The feed is paid for. The cow is bought by those who have an investment in preserving the credit of the Snopes family name (there is some haggling over the percentage of individual investments – reputation is evidently a quantifiable asset). It is then slaughtered and, by way of compensation, Ike is offered a reproduction, the crude wooden effigy of a cow. The gift of the wooden cow is kindly meant, it comes from Eck Snopes – easily the most guileless of the Snopeses: nevertheless, it cannot help but emphasize just how circumscribed the terms of the debate are in Frenchman's Bend. The object of love has been turned into an object; the 'flowing immemorial female' flesh of the cow has been paralysed into a fixed structure. A series of deals have been struck that more or less ignore the erotic implications of the problem, the baffling currencies of desire, and that settle instead for a much simpler currency of dollars and cents and goods.

The issue is complicated by the fact that the episode of Ike Snopes and the cow sets up a circuit of connections with other episodes in *The Hamlet*, along which meanings run both ways. The cow is like a woman – she is even described, at one point, within the conventional parameters of virgin and whore: she is, we are told, 'maiden meditant, shame-free'. In turn, Eula Varner is several times compared to a cow. Ike enters the cowbarn, 'breathing in the reek, the odour of cows', the narrator confides, 'as the successful lover does that of a room full of women'. In similar fashion, the men of Frenchman's Bend take in the odour of Eula, as she passes, as if she were an animal in heat: 'You can smell it!' one of them shouts, 'You can smell it ten feet away!'[35] Clearly, this breaks into our understanding of Eula to some extent. Among other things, it makes her seem more like a creature that exists outside the confines of language; and it helps to give a rougher edge, an ironic twist, to the mythical associations she trails with her wherever she goes – not only the daughter of a god, apparently, she is also a sacrificial beast. But the connections cut both ways. Ike exists beyond language too: all he can do is moan and repeat his name, 'Ike H-mope, Ike H-mope'. The cow is also a creature of legend: a Juno, at one point, and then later compared to Helen of Troy. Their story, illuminated by the circuit linking it to Eula Varner and her admirers, assumes a more powerfully sensual quality: it becomes even less easy to take it as simply *mock*-heroic. More to the point, perhaps, the currents running between these two narratives of erotic longing and its objects cast a further light on the failure of Frenchman's Bend – or, at least, its male inhabitants – to read either of them properly. We are reminded by these links, if reminder is needed, that the way the community handles the problem of Ike is like the way Will Varner, his family and neighbours handle the problem of

Eula – and, for that matter, the way it tries to cope with everything. Moral value is computed into cash; notions of property and possession are paramount; nothing can be accounted serious outside the currency of conversation and the 'currency of coin'. Connected up with stories of women as it is, and in particular with the story of Eula, the odd tale of Ike and his cow registers just how the talking and trading of the community manage to supplant love with the law, to transform the subject of passion into a commodity – and to assume that, somehow, the claims of desire can be met with a deal.

Imprisonment within a world of commodities is registered in different ways in the three major episodes that conclude *The Hamlet*: the story of the conflict between Houston and Mink Snopes, the episode of the spotted horses, and the tale of how Flem Snopes outwits Ratliff, Bookwright and Henry Armstid, tricking them into buying the Old Frenchman's place. Different as they are from each other, all three nevertheless involve the mixing of folk humour, and other elements of folklore, with the kind of raw naturalism, and historical specificity, characteristic of some of the major writing about rural life during the period between the two World Wars. What is remarkable about these three episodes, in fact, is something that is remarkable about many of Faulkner's representations of the poor, white South: the way he engages different genres, conflicting voices, to register his version of things. Faulkner stretches a particular genre to the limits, and brings it into collision with other genres, for the same reason that he stretches other categories: so as to squeeze new meanings, fresh possibilities out of the conflicts between the rules and the occasions which those rules are meant to (but do not quite) circumscribe. So, as mentioned much earlier, there is a strong element of folk humour at work in the episode of the spotted horses – or, for that matter, the macabre tale of how Mink Snopes tries to rid himself of the decaying body of the man he has killed. But there is also the kind of telescopic particularity, devoted attention to the details of the 'nerve-and-flesh wearing labour' of country people, that is to be found in, say, some of the novels of Ellen Glasgow – like *Barren Ground* (1925) or *Vein of Iron* (1935) – and in the documentary writing of the 1930s like Erskine Caldwell's *Some American People* (1935) and the Federal Writers' Project's *These Are Our Lives* (1939).[36] Beyond that, there is too an attentiveness to the stoicism of poor farming folk – a willingness to take many of their reactions to material necessity as heroic in effect if not in intention – that recollects aspects of another Southern version of rural life: the romance of the plain man, also to be found in the work of Ellen Glasgow (and some of the documentaries, at times) and of other, popular writers of the region like Elizabeth Madox Roberts. This is not simply a matter of the mixing of influences (although Faulkner did know both Ellen Glasgow and the Southwestern humorists well). It is also a case of Faulkner responding to the changes and conflicts of his times by taking the languages that were available to him, part of the verbal currency, and then making sure that no language remained undisturbed by its opposite:

that, in effect, the versions of rural life his novels confront us with are fluid, challenging and unstable. Folk comedy, historic naturalism and a more heroic idiom, they are all clearly there in these stories. But they are there just as every received genre is in his best work: to be quickened into life by a particular voice – and to acquire power in the same way the rib of a Gothic arch does, from the counter-thrust of its opposite.

'I dont understand it', one rural character, Houston, habitually thinks to himself, 'I dont know why. I wont ever know why. But You cant beat me. I am as strong as You are. You cant beat me.' Like so many of the male characters in *The Hamlet*, Houston is caught in the grip of a necessity which he tends to identify with some elusive metaphysical force ('You') – but which, when we look at it closely, comes down to the material conditions that define and contain his life. A powerful passage, alluded to already, describing the existence of another – and, in this case, anonymous – rural character, applies equally to Houston, the man who murders him, Mink Snopes, and many of the other men of Frenchman's Bend:

> at home there was that work waiting, the constant and unflagging round of repetitive nerve-and-flesh wearing labour by which alone that piece of earth which was his mortal enemy could fight him with, which he had performed yesterday and must perform again tomorrow and tomorrow, alone and unassisted or else knock under . . . – this until the day came when (he knew this too) he would stumble and plunge, his eyes still open and his empty hands stiffening into the shape of the plow-handles, into the furrow behind the plow, or topple into a weedy ditch . . .[37]

The sheer sense of effort generated here, among other things by the contorted syntax and the repetitive, polysyllabic vocabulary, is complicated by the intimations of a radically qualified awareness ('he knew this too'): this character, like Houston, is trapped in circumstances only the effects of which, not the causes, he can begin to understand. This simply makes his plight seem the more intolerable, and his reaction to it all the more absurdly heroic: just as the echo from Faulkner's favourite Shakespearean speech ('tomorrow and tomorrow') only aggravates the sense of despair, and impotent rage, that boils beneath the surface of the prose here and elsewhere in *The Hamlet*'s portrait of rural life. This character is not tragic in the traditional sense, because he is caught, like the other poor farmers in the book, in a specifically economic nightmare: but, like Macbeth, he is forced to confront every day (as is said of Mink Snopes) 'the impasse his life had reached' without ever being able to contemplate the possibility of significant change. As Houston falls to the ground shot by Mink, he sees two things: 'the orderly sequence' of the 'thirty-three years' of his life running 'inverted' into a 'blank gap', a 'chasm' before him, and the face of his killer 'which with his own was wedded and twinned forever now by the explosion of [a] ten-gauge shell'. The experience effectively sums up the entrapment of his life. More to the point, it links his imprisonment to that of Mink: killed and killer, the sacrificed and the sacrificer ('thirty-three years': the Christ/scapegoat analogies are inescapable) are shut up in the prisonhouse, along with all the other victims of necessity in the book.

The relation of the women characters to these stories of necessity is peculiarly subtle; and it brings us back to the complex variations Faulkner plays in *The Hamlet* on the notion of the female as a commodity. In the eyes of their men, at least, women do help to define the terms that dictate male life: they are that which is to be exchanged, like Eula Varner, and sometimes the prisonhouse of exchange itself. So, the woman Houston eventually married, we are told, was someone from whom he fled for much of his life: because, as he saw it, she represented 'true slavery', a circumscription that was simultaneously sexual and economic. She would condemn him, Houston believed, to flesh and to work, the lure of 'the olden Snake' and the pursuit of security. Moving away westwards, he 'fled, not from his past', the narrator observes, 'but to escape his future. It took him twelve years to learn that you cannot escape either of them.' Announcing one day, 'I'm going home', he returns to meet what he sees as his doom. His marriage is, in fact, described just as Mink Snopes's is: as an inevitability and an imprisonment, requiring very little more than the flat statement, 'They were married in January.' ('Five months later they married', the narrator says in a similar vein of Mink and his wife, 'They did not plan it.') And the image that sums up what Houston feels is the change in his life announced by his wedding is that of a horse that has been bitted:

> He was bitted now . . . the beast, prime solitary and sufficient out of the wild fields, drawn to the trap and knowing it to be a trap, not comprehending why it was doomed but knowing it was, and not afraid now – and not quite wild.[38]

Whatever Houston's reasons for feeling this way, that image acquires particular resonance because he gives his new wife, as a wedding present, a stallion that seems to represent – on a repressed and unacknowledged level – 'that polygamous and bitless masculinity which he had relinquished'. For her part, the bride brings gifts to the marriage that are no less significant for our understanding of what is being offered, and what is being taken, here. She brought with her, the narrator confides, nothing except,

> the domestic skill of her country heritage and blood and training and a small trunk of neat, plain, dove-colored clothes and the hand-stitched sheets and towels and table-linen which she had made herself and an infinite capacity for constancy and devotion . . .[39]

The itemizing of the property the woman brings with her to the union is characteristic of *The Hamlet* – for a moment, she seems to be no more than one commodity among others – and it aligns the narrative with the community's rules of exchange. But equally characteristic of the book is something rarely acknowledged in communal talk, and certainly beyond Houston's own terms of reference at this point: the gifts of emotion that she brings to the 'trade'. It is this, an 'infinite', unstinting generosity of feeling that exists outside the parameters of bargaining, which Houston evidently did not notice: not only when he fled from his future wife, but when he married her as well. And, ironically, it is this that he misses (in a profoundly different sense) once she is dead. Only six months after the marriage, we learn, the stallion killed Houston's wife. At once, Houston killed the stallion and then embraced a bitter seclusion, a life of scarcely controlled grief and rage, from which only the gun of Mink Snopes releases him.

Houston never articulates his loss in so many words: but that, of course, is part of the point. What his wife offered him, and what he loses by her death, is beyond the reach of his talk just as it stretches beyond the scope of trade: a 'constancy and devotion' that is without condition or measure. All he could read in the marriage contract was the denial of masculine freedom and the assertion of feminine control; and it is this failure to recognize just how much his wife exists outside the rules of bargaining that leads directly to her death, since the stallion is clearly an expression of his resentment at being 'caught'. Death for one is also despair for the other: when recognition comes, it is powerfully felt if never properly spoken, let alone clearly understood. The unbending male adherence to laws of contract and exchange is made to seem wildly destructive here. Elsewhere in *The Hamlet*, it often seems just absurd. For instance, towards the end of the novel there are two trials at Frenchman's Bend at which women clearly speak for fundamental justice against the comic myopia that male commitment to the letter of the law can produce. The second of these trials involves Mrs Tull trying to get compensation for the damage caused by one of the spotted horses: the one that the Texan auctioneer gave to Eck Snopes just to get the auction started. Eck is perfectly willing to pay compensation ('How much do I have to p—', he says before he is interrupted by the majesty of the court). However, the Justice of the Peace stops him from doing so, on the technical grounds that the horse never became Eck's property 'either by recorded or authentic document, or by possession or occupation': there was no bill of sale or exchange, nor was the horse formally handed over to Eck, nor did Eck manage to get a rope on it before it bolted. The Justice then goes on magnanimously to explain that all Mrs Tull can expect for her losses is the horse that did the damage: which has, of course, completely disappeared. The collision of styles here, between the circumlocutions and abstractions of the Justice, and the flat statements of fact and feeling coming from Mrs Tull, is at once radical and comic:

> 'Yes, ma'am,' the Justice said. 'Your damages are fixed by statute. The law says that when a suit for damages is brought against the owner of an animal which has committed damage or injury, if the owner of the animal either

cant or wont assume liability, the injured or damaged party shall find re-
compense in the body of the animal. . . .'

. . .

'The horse!' Mrs. Tull shouted. 'We see it for five seconds, while it is climb-
ing into the wagon with us and then out again. Then it's gone, God dont
know where and thank the Lord he dont! And the mules gone with it and
the wagon wrecked and you [Mr. Tull] laying there on the bridge with your
face full of kindling-wood and bleeding like a hog and dead for all we know.
And he gives us the horse!'[40]

This collision of styles in turn signals a clash of positions as violent, and
extreme, as anything in the tradition of Southwestern humour, up to and
including *The Adventures of Huckleberry Finn*. There is the truth-telling vernacular voice: in *Huckleberry Finn*, this is, famously, Huck's voice, while in
this passage it is Mrs Tull's. And there, set in opposition to it, is the voice
of a system trapped in its own self-delusions, unable to measure its own
absurdity: a voice which, in this instance, is that of male law. A more
succinct expression of female resistance to the lies male society tells is Mrs
Littlejohn's reaction when she surveys the wreckage caused by the spotted
horses: ' "I'll declare," she said, "You men!" '[41] In both cases, it is the
woman who speaks for recognition of the actual, the man who remains
trapped inside the vocabulary of contract – who apparently cannot see the
way things are, or how they should be. Such comic dissonances measure
the degree to which, on occasion at least, Faulkner could represent women
as better materialists, able to perceive matters of fact and justice to which
men's habits of exchange tended to blind them. That did not prevent
Faulkner himself from sharing those habits and suffering similar blindness
at times, even in *The Hamlet*: but it did and does make the story of male/
female relations in his twelfth novel more complicated than it might appear to be at first. There is collusion with male posturing here, perhaps,
but there is also subversion.

To mention the voices of Mrs Tull and Mrs Littlejohn, reacting to the
sale of the Texas ponies, is to be reminded of the rich plurality of styles
on which the entire episode of the spotted horses rests. That plurality has
received enough attention already, in the first chapter of this study. All
that needs to be pointed out here is just how much Faulkner uses voice
both to re-create and to place an historical community. The talking of the
people of Frenchman's Bend – and, especially, its male inhabitants – is
one thing: a system of verbal collusion that implies its own gaps and
omissions, such as the failure to think of women in terms other than those
of 'exchange value'. The talking that incorporates and surrounds these
people – that is, the talking of *The Hamlet* as a whole – is something quite
different: an exchange of voices which challenges the idea that any relationship is fixed and stable, and invites us to see all relationships – between, say, character and narrator and reader, or personality and
environment – as existing in a medium of change. The problem with the
inhabitants of Frenchman's Bend is precisely that they see their world as

set firm and authorized. This prevents them from appreciating that Flem Snopes, involved in the processes of history just as they are, is both like and unlike them.[42] They cannot cope with the linked facts of similarity and difference; and so they cannot understand that Flem (like so many of Faulkner's outsiders) is distinct from the community because he pushes communal practices a little further and more fiercely than others. In his case, this involves exploiting laws of exchange that are already present in Frenchman's Bend, however ameliorated they might have been up until that time by other habits. Of course, the way Flem conducts the auction of the spotted horses is different from the way horsetrading has been done in the community before: most significantly, he distances himself from any personal involvement by using an agent to close the deal. But it is different in the way that any stage in historical development is, surely, different: because it represents a reaction to and revision of an existing logic, not an absolute denial of it. Flem tricks his victims by extending the systems of trickery favoured by other horsetraders celebrated in Frenchman's Bend. He makes a ruthless new move in the game: but he does not try to alter the basic rules, nor does he have to.

The difficulties in which the locals find themselves with Flem are acute. Sometimes they see him as a stranger; sometimes they try to accommodate him within their own terms of reference. Both strategies involve an assumption that their own culture is somehow innocent, an historical vacuum capable of repelling or absorbing invaders, and so neither strategy works. Flem, in turn, does not have to think about change because he *is* change. In his own deadpan way, wearing his 'tiny machine-made black bow'[43] and chewing his wad of tobacco, he represents the logic of history. The peculiar relationship that builds up between him and the community that, more and more, he comes to dominate reaches its climax when, in his final sharp deal, Flem tricks the character who, more than anyone, tends to speak for that community, V.K. Ratliff. Some commentators have been uneasy about this episode, arguing that it shows Ratliff in a poor light, greedy for profit, or that the trick Flem plays is too puerile to fool the sewing-machine salesman, or both. But this is to ignore the fact that Ratliff is no less interested in a smart trade than any of his neighbours are, and – as his account of the horsetrading duel between Pat Stamper and Ab Snopes shows – actively enjoys a piece of trickery. It is also to miss the point that what Flem plays on, in tricking Ratliff, Armstid and Bookwright into buying the Old Frenchman's place, is their belief in *him*. Their assumption is that stories about treasure hidden on the estate must be true if Flem believes in them enough to go out and dig. All that Flem then has to do is to ensure the deal goes through with the help of a little planted evidence. Once again, it is a case, not of innocent victim and experienced trickster, but of a victim and trickster who, at least in some ways, resemble each other too much.

Admittedly, Ratliff and his partners – the collective 'victim' in this episode – are not exactly the same as Flem. For one thing, they want to plunder the land; whereas Flem it turns out, plans to plunder them. For another, they are hoping to live off the past, in the shape of the riches it has left behind, while Flem has his eyes set firmly on the future. And, for a third thing, they are still carrying over habits and beliefs from an older world of folk superstition that lead them to think that Uncle Dick, an expert in nostrums and charms, will be able to help them locate the treasure. Flem, on the other hand, has already jettisoned such beliefs: a seamless capitalist, he depends entirely on his own quickness of wit, his individual power to control the terms of an exchange. Still, trickster and victim are sufficiently entwined for the trick to work. The aim of Ratliff and his friends is profit, just as Flem's is; their actions are based, just as his are, on the premise that greed is good; and their assumption is that the greediest of them all knows best how to get rich quick – Flem, they believe, has the secret and, if they watch him carefully and use him craftily, they can get rich quick as well.

What we have to return to, in fact, is the recognition that, here as elsewhere (in, for instance, the tale of the spotted horses), the locals of Frenchman's Bend are disabled in any contest with Flem Snopes, not by their utter separation from his practices nor by their total immersion in them, but by the linked facts of distance and connection. They want what he wants but they lack his logic: that unswerving ability to strip things down to their essentials that enables Flem always to get what he wants. His strength, in effect, is that he is a little further on down the path of history than they are; their weakness, in turn, is that precisely because of this they are in awe of him – 'Couldn't no other man have done it', marvels one local, 'Anybody might have fooled Henry Armstid. But couldn't nobody but Flem Snopes have fooled Ratliff.'[44] The scene with which *The Hamlet* ends sums up the relationship between Flem and the culture into which he has, for a while, erupted. Flem is now leaving Frenchman's Bend, in search of fresh accumulations of capital; with him is Eula, the subject of one of his deals with Will Varner. The locals watch him go, interrupting for a while their watching of Henry Armstid: who continues to dig away on the Old Frenchman's place, in the belief that, despite all the evidence to the contrary, it must contain some buried treasure. Armstid, at least, continues to be convinced that a coming man like Flem would never have been interested in the estate unless there were something there: pathetically missing the point that this something was its value as a tool of exchange, which Flem has already exploited. The locals, meanwhile, watch passively – in this case, with 'grave' passivity – as they always do: entranced by the spectacle of trading and trickery but never daring to question the assumptions on which that spectacle is based, let alone intervene, because in the end a deal is a deal. And Flem, having acquired all he wants from Frenchman's Bend, sets out in search of more property and profit, a theoretically endless chain of exchange stretching before him. 'Come up', are his last words: an appropriate command from someone who has turned upward mobility into an art-form. The command is not, of course, addressed to the people who witness his departure: but there can be little doubt that, if they could, they would be 'up' there with him. After all, he is only acting out their desires: devoting himself to what they value above everything, a good trade – even if they have not worked out, as yet, the most cost-efficient way of making it.

III THINGS FALL APART: *GO DOWN, MOSES*

At the time when *The Hamlet* was published, early in 1940, Faulkner was preoccupied even more than usual with money. His financial position had been precarious for some time but, over the past year or so he felt, it had approached the calamitous. 'I need $1000.00 now, to pay debts and current bills', he wrote to his editor in April 1940, 'I want $9000.00 more, say $400.00 per month over two years.' So serious was his position, he added, that he had spent the previous month 'mortgaging my mare and colts one at a time to pay food and electricity and washing and such, and watching each mail train in hopes of a check'. Quite probably, this preoccupation with his own household bills helps explain the openly economic bias of the first novel in the Snopes trilogy: the extent of its concern – unusual even for Faulkner – with the details of trade. Certainly, Faulkner believed that it was preventing him from getting on with his real work. He was having to spend his time writing 'trash stories' which were 'not selling even fifty percent', he complained, when he should be engaged with more serious projects. Two projects, in particular, attracted him, he explained to his editor, in that same letter in which he detailed his financial plight. One was 'a blood-and-thunder mystery novel' which he felt would sell – 'they usually do', he insisted – but which, he confessed, 'I dont dare devote six months to writing'. The other was a book 'in method similar to THE UNVANQUISHED' but again, he went on mournfully, 'since the chapters I have written and tried to sell as short stories have not sold, I haven't the time to continue with it'.[45]

The 'blood-and-thunder mystery novel' was probably an early reference to *Intruder in the Dust*; the second, and more immediately realizable, project was to become *Go Down, Moses. Intruder in the Dust*, however, was not to appear for another eight years. As for *Go Down, Moses*, even that had to wait another year before Faulkner found time to formulate a more detailed plan. It was not, in fact, until May 1941 that he wrote to his publishers outlining 'a volume, collected short stories, general theme being relationship between white and black races here'. And it was not until a year after that, in turn, that the volume was published. Economics played their part here, certainly. Faulkner was constantly having his time consumed and his attention diverted by the need for cash. 'I am broke' is a constant theme of the letters of this period, along with all its miserable variations: 'for a month now I have had no cash whatever', 'I have been buried here for three years for lack of money', 'I must have something somewhere, quick'.[46] But ambition was responsible for the delay as well. Faulkner worked hard to rewrite and reshape stories, to organize material into something that would, as he put it, 'scratch the face of the supreme Obliteration and leave a decipherable scar of some sort'. 'I haven't said at 42', he had declared early in 1940, 'all that is in the cards for me to say.'

In some cases, Faulkner felt that he had to make very few revisions to the stories he had written: the versions of 'Pantaloon in Black' and 'Go Down, Moses' that appeared in the final, published volume are virtually identical with the ones that first appeared in, respectively, *Harper's* in 1940 and *Collier's* magazine in 1941. In others, the alterations, although significant, were made mainly to relate the stories to the volume as a whole. So, with three pieces, 'Was', 'The Old People' and 'Delta Autumn', Faulkner altered the names of characters in the originals, and other details, so as to make each narrative more clearly and more closely a part of the saga of the McCaslin clan. The most serious and radical alterations came with the two stories that are the most substantial in the book, and that contribute most to its overriding concerns: 'The Fire and the Hearth' and 'The Bear'. With 'The Fire and the Hearth', Faulkner began with three stories, two of them already published. One was a comic tale about moonshiners, another equally comic concerned the search for hidden treasure with a divining machine, the third told the story of the time when Molly Beauchamp demanded a divorce from her husband. Lucas Beauchamp is important to all three of these stories. But, in all three, he is an essentially stereotypical character: the wily 'nigger', whose tricks and cunning recall the tales about Brer Rabbit. He is referred to, more often than not, as 'Luke' and he is separated from the genteel, white reader (who nevertheless is supposed to find him endearingly mischievous) by a thick dialect. Faulkner's changes here were extensive but they were all made, really, to promote a deeper examination of the relationship between the black and white races and, related to this, to explore the tangled genealogy of the McCaslins. One immediate result of this was to transform 'Luke' into Lucas Quintus Carothers McCaslin Beauchamp: the character had come into the patrimony of his full name – a name that, in itself, registered Faulkner's vastly increased intensity of focus on Southern history and the Southern family romance. If Lucas Beauchamp came into his own now, in 'The Fire and the Hearth', then a similar metamorphosis was granted Ike McCaslin in 'The Bear'. In this case, Faulkner took some already existing material, namely a short story called 'Lion' which had Quentin Compson as its protagonist, and used that as the beginnings of his tale: one just as embedded as 'The Fire and the Hearth' was in the rich confusions of region, family and race. Faulkner hoped that 'The Bear' would centre *Go Down, Moses* just as he believed 'An Odour of Verbena' had *The Unvanquished*. And its fourth section, in particular, in which Ike discovers that his ancestor had fathered a child on his own daughter by a slave woman – an act of incest and miscegenation that provokes him into relinquishing his inheritance – was something that cost Faulkner particular effort. It was something he was going to be proud of, he told his publishers: so, he explained, it required 'careful writing and rewriting to get it exactly right'.[47]

There were several problems inherent in the genesis of this project. Some were specific to certain stories. For instance, in 'The Fire and the Hearth', Faulkner was using comic narratives dependent on stereotypical characters and situations – what he himself referred to as 'stories about niggers' – as, at least, the basis for a serious examination of race. Others had to do with the volume as a whole. Faulkner began, for example, by using the mixed vocabulary of 'chapters' and 'stories' to describe the several components that went to make up *Go Down, Moses*; and, as the writing continued, he tended to waver uncertainly between the conflicting implications of those terms. The book would be variously described, before its completion, as 'a novel, new original materials not a collection of short stories', 'a mss. based on short stories', and as 'collected short stories'. In retrospect, Faulkner was to pronounce himself mildly shocked when he received the first copies of the book, and found that the publishers had added 'and other stories' to the title; 'Moses is indeed a novel', he insisted. But that did not stop him from telling some students, in 1947, *Go Down, Moses* . . . is simply a collection of short stories.' Nor did *that* prevent him, in turn, from informing some other students, ten years later, that 'the *Bear* was just a part . . . of a novel'.[48] This was not simply a matter of abstract classification. The novel and the collection of short stories are, after all, different if significantly related forms of representation; Faulkner recognized this – which was why he worried away at just what to call *Go Down, Moses*, even after its publication.

The worries went deeper than that, however. The preparation and publication of the book coincided with the entry of the United States into the Second World War. Even before the attack on Pearl Harbor – during the period when the United States was acting as what was known as 'the arsenal of democracy' – Faulkner was complaining that the world was 'bitched' and 'destruction-bent', with 'Saxon fighting against Saxon, Latin against Latin . . . nigger fighting nigger at the behest of white men'. He was desperate to help the Allied cause in any way he could. Once the United States was in the war, this included trying to get a commission and involving himself in local defence work. And some time even before that, Faulkner was keen to have his say about the implications of global conflict: that is , if he could find enough time left over from producing, as he put it, 'pot-boilers . . . just enough of them to keep my head above water'. *Go Down, Moses* must be seen as part of this plan to resist the creeping tide of fascism, and to assert what Faulkner believed were the genuine strengths of his people and his country. The trouble was, the method he had chosen for saying something was, in this instance, not necessarily the best one. Salvaging material from, among other places, the very pot-boilers he blamed for wasting his time, rewriting old material and snatching any spare moment to pursue new aims: all this was perhaps not the ideal way to make his mark on the times, or to leave his trace on 'the face of the supreme Oblivion'. Moments of extraordinary self-confidence could be followed by attacks of profound uncertainty about his own work and abilities, or the whole point of writing. 'I have become so frantic trying to make a living', he wrote while waiting for reviews of *Go Down, Moses* to appear, '... that nothing I or any body else ever wrote seems worth anything to me anymore.'[49] Confusion about what to label his new book could be seen, in this context, as a symptom, a function of a deeper anxiety: the suspicion that what he had said was not quite what he had wanted to say – that the whole of the volume did not add up to any more than the sum of its parts.

The notion of saying something, making a statement is, in any event, a problematical one: not least, because in Faulkner's best work meaning is inseparable from the activities of the narrative. It occurs in the clash between positions, the collision between different voices: it is not the prerogative of one voice, nor is it available for flat announcement – articulation in terms of some universal, and implicitly unalterable, 'truth'. From fairly early on in his career, Faulkner had been tempted towards the declamatory, the big statement: but in the major fiction, at least, that temptation is resisted and overcome – among other things, by the transformation of narrative into a field of verbal conflict, and the translation of style into styles, a subversive mixing of different genres and forms. For example, Gavin Stevens is allowed to spout forth his theories about 'white' and 'black' blood in *Light in August* – and about the impact of the clash between these supposedly different blood-groups on the last moments of Joe Christmas. But those theories are clearly placed for us as one, highly tendentious set among many: interrupted as they are by other stories, interrogated by other versions of events, overwhelmed finally by our experience of the novel as a whole. In *Go Down, Moses*, several characters spout forth their ideas in a similar way. And, this time, there is not always the same resistance. Even when two characters are involved in conversation, they often seem to be talking with the same voice. This voice may talk of immediate issues, such as how 'this country ... will cope with one Austrian paper-hanger' named Adolf Hitler. Or it may invoke large abstractions: '*courage and honour and pride, and pity and love of justice and of liberty*', and '*truth*' that '*doesn't change*'. Or, as in this passage, it may employ a kind of *faux naïf* rhetoric, as a sugar coating for what is after all a not-so-bitter pill of truth:

> He said on the way here ... that does and fawns – I believe he said women and children – are two things this world aint ever lacked. But that aint all of it ... That's just the mind's reason a man has to give himself because the heart dont always have time to bother with thinking up words that fit together. God created man and He created the kind of world He would have wanted to live in if He had been a man – the ground to walk on, the big woods, the trees and the water, and the game to live in it. And maybe He didn't put the desire to hunt and kill game in man but I reckin He knew

it was going to be there, that man was going to teach it to himself, since he wasn't quite God yet –[50]

The voice may be attributed to a character (if so, it usually involves Ike McCaslin, as here), or it may belong to the narrator. But, time and again, it remains resonantly monolithic. It is, we could say, the voice of Faulkner, already preparing for his Nobel Prize acceptance speech.

It is important to see what is at stake here, since *Go Down, Moses* marks a significant moment in the development of Faulknerian language. The trouble with a passage like the one just quoted (which comes, incidentally, from 'Delta Autumn', the sixth story in the volume) is not that what it says might be wrong, but that it never entertains that possibility: it never really permits antagonism, confrontation with an alternative opinion. So it never admits the chance of change, and it is never likely to offer the opportunity for change either. If those reading it agree with what is said in the first place, there is no problem. And, if they disagree, there is no problem either, since there is no space left open for debate. This is not all there is to *Go Down, Moses* by any means. But, too often, a declamatory idiom or sentimental rhetoric alerts us to the fact that the authorial voice is intervening and insisting on its authority: requiring us to listen and attend. Dialogue is refused; a contest between different forms of speech, conflicting movements in the narrative, is jettisoned in favour of something dangerously close to a public address system. Exactly what drove Faulkner in this direction at this time can only be guessed at: although most likely it had to do with matters both public and personal – the sense that the urgencies of world war, and the seriousness of his vocation, required such declarations. This was a critical moment in history, Faulkner may well have felt, needing firm declarations of principle. Besides, he may also have believed, he had to establish as fully as possible the difference between this kind of writing and the 'pot-boilers' on which he depended to keep the debt-collectors from the door. And what could be a better way of doing this than affirming, loudly and clearly, what he took to be the eternal truths?

Whatever the reason Faulkner moved towards the declamatory now, though, it was a direction he was to pursue with ever greater devotion over the years, as the sense of his public status was promoted by growing public recognition. And he was aided and abetted in all this because, as it turned out, his direction was a shared one. His evident need to announce universal truths, uncontaminated by the pressures of history, was precisely the source of his appeal to the culture that emerged in the United States, and elsewhere in the West, after the Second World War, which boldly proclaimed an end to ideology. As the global conflict drew to a close, and disengagement from historical commitment became a dominating impulse, Faulkner's celebrations of what he saw as the old verities struck a responsive chord. A story like the one that forms the centrepiece of *Go Down, Moses*, 'The Bear', could be elevated into a cultural icon. It could be, and was, interpreted as a justification for a withdrawal from history, and the blood and guilt of the past, in pursuit of a world elsewhere, a space circumscribed by the solitary, brooding consciousness. This is not, of course, to suggest that Faulkner anticipated the way things were going. Nor is it to agree with some people who have argued that Faulkner owed the promotion of his work during the fifties to a sort of conspiracy between a-historical New Critics and others prompted by the anti-ideological leanings of the times.[51] It is simply to say what is, perhaps, obvious: that much of the later writing from *Go Down, Moses* on is vitiated by Faulkner's apparent need to strike the public pose and make the public statement, that this often diverted him from where the real strengths of his fiction lay (that is, in the transformation of historical conflict into the processes, the enacted debates of fiction), and that, ironically, it was this diversion and its consequences that attracted many of his first critics. Faulkner's work tended towards the monologic and monolithic in the last twenty years of his career, even if it could sometimes recover its earlier capacity to surprise and startle – to interrogate its own assumptions and to require similar interrogations on the part of the reader. It was precisely this tendency, however, that permitted many of those who first brought Faulkner to public attention to see in him, not only a major novelist, but a sage, a cultural spokesman: someone, too, who spoke of transcendence, the denial of the worrying contingencies of the times, in the name of some specious notion of the universal – and the absolute autonomy of the subject.

The particular strengths and weaknesses of *Go Down, Moses* circulate around Faulkner's representation of its two major themes: which are, as almost every critic of the book has observed, the themes of wilderness and race. The wilderness theme is powerfully rendered in those stories that concentrate on Isaac McCaslin: revealing Ike's initiation into the values of the hunt and, by extension, into the secret, subliminal forces that govern experience. The theme of the developing relationship between the races is also examined in the Ike McCaslin tales, and in the pieces concerning Lucas and Molly Beauchamp. More memorably still, it is at the centre of what is arguably the single most successful story in the volume, 'Pantaloon in Black'. In the first tale in *Go Down, Moses*, 'Was', the racial theme predominates. Set in 1859, it describes a highly stylized series of relationships: the idea of human experience as play, or ritual, is basic both to the narrative and to the society it portrays. Human problems are solved by hunts and games, relationships are strictly codified, patterns of behaviour are carefully prescribed – as, indeed, are patterns of speech. Some of the humour derives from the transgression of these codes. For instance, the moment when Uncle Buck McCaslin creeps all unawares into Sophonsiba Beauchamp's bed is a key one in the story. He has entered a lady's sanctuary, her sacred, private space, however innocently, and he must therefore pay the price. Some of it, in turn, issues from the conflict of styles that both the highly stratified culture and the elaborately stylized narrative initiate. A great deal of the comedy, for example, is of a kind familiar to any reader of Southwestern humour, depending on the clash of different speech idioms. When the genteel Miss Sophonsiba talks coyly of 'a bee sipping from flower to flower and not staying long anywhere and all that stored sweetness to be wasted on Uncle Buddy's desert air', all that the rough-and-ready Uncle Buck can come back with by way of a response to these soft blandishments is a simple, bemused, 'Ma'am?'.[52]

Most of the activity of the story, however, goes neither into transgression nor into conflict but into absorbing these and other potentially dangerous energies. Uncle Buck's transgression is resolved in play; conflicts of style and speech are eventually reconciled in the ritual of marriage. In this respect, the comic strategies of 'Was' are on a par with the games-playing of its characters. Both are devices for defusing trouble. The narrator and the *dramatis personae* collude in tactics that drain the events of ordinary, everyday human anxieties: what remains, after all this, is a tall tale. This certainly makes 'Was' entertaining, but it also renders it anomalous. It is difficult, for instance, to see the Uncle Buck and Miss Sophonsiba of this story as the future parents of Ike McCaslin (who supposedly rehearses the events of 'Was'), because Ike mostly belongs to a different world altogether – the world of agonized, anti-heroic private consciousness. More to the point, the distancing that serves to dilute the human and historical content of the action, and so to make the racial code seem less obscene, also serves to deny the human and historical relevance of that action, and so to make the racial code that dictates it seem all the more absurd. The reader is left, as a result, with a troublingly garbled message.

The tale that follows 'Was', 'The Fire and the Hearth', sustains and complicates the racial preoccupations of its predecessor. Lucas Beauchamp, the direct descendant of the founder of the McCaslin family in Yoknapatawpha County, Lucius Quintus Carothers McCaslin, is a singular and powerful representative of the several repressed stories inherent in the Southern family romance. Lucas, after all, is a descendant by the black, slave line, and as such cannot come into his patrimony. The product of incest and miscegenation, a living token of the almost terminal damage wrought by the racial practices of the South, he is the son who has been dispossessed, the brother who is denied. There are few more memorable moments in *Go Down, Moses* as a whole than the scenes of conflict and denial that Faulkner inserted into 'The Fire and the Hearth' as he crafted it together out of existing material: the scene, that is, in which Roth Edmonds refuses to share his bed with his black childhood companion, Henry Beauchamp, any more – and the one in which Lucas Beauchamp confronts Zack Edmonds and fires a gun at him. That second scene, however, takes us into two crucial problems in this story, which have to do with materials and representation: the way Faulkner chose to construct his investigation of race here, and the particular terms in which he decided to dramatize it. The problem inherent in the materials Faulkner chose has been intimated already: he took three essentially comic and stereotypical tales of moonshining, illicitly distilled liquor, and the search for buried treasure, and used these as the basis on which to build his narrative. In the process, he significantly enhanced the speech and stature of Lucas Beauchamp. Nevertheless, Lucas is never completely extricated from the tricks and fairly mechanical humour of the originals.

Around the episode in which Lucas confronts Zack, for example, another scene is played out involving Lucas and Zack's son, Roth, grown up now and in charge of the plantation. In this, Lucas schemes to get George Wilkins out of the distilling business – and, preferably, out of the arms of Lucas's daughter, Nat – by informing on him to Roth. 'He's running a kettle in that gully behind the Old West field', he tells Roth, 'If you want the whisky too, look under his kitchen floor'. The description of Lucas at this point is symptomatic of some unease about the direction in which the narrative is heading. 'Without changing the inflexion of his voice and apparently without effort or even design', we are told,

> Lucas became not Negro but nigger, not secret so much as impenetrable, not servile and not effacing, but enveloping himself in an aura of timeless and stupid impassivity almost like a smell.[53]

The exigencies of the narrative require Lucas, the betrayed son and brother, to become Lucas, the crafty and inscrutable trickster; and so, making the best of a difficult situation, the narrator attributes the change in the tone and implications of the story to a change in the character. Lucas, so it seems, has put on a new narrative task as if it were a mask: he has obligingly shifted from 'Negro' to 'nigger', as the reader is returned to the original, comic materials. This might just about be swallowed, perhaps, if it were an isolated instance. Unfortunately, it is not. Elsewhere, Lucas plays the country mouse to a town mouse in the shape of a divining machine salesman from Memphis; and his crafty behaviour reduces various white men to impotent rage – including Roth ('Get out of here. Go home. And dont come back', Roth tells him). Like Brer Rabbit, and like the shrewd black characters in so many conventional Southern stories, Lucas is shown using a 'dumb fool' exterior to manipulate those supposedly more experienced and knowledgeable than he is: in terms of sheer narrative space, in fact, his tricks and schemes demand most of our attention. The role of George Wilkins is particularly tricky here. Clearly, George's thicker dialect speech and less imposing manner and status make Lucas look good by comparison, and help to liberate him from black stereotypes. But to the extent that Lucas is involved in the same scrapes and foolery as George is, he is tarred with the same brush and his role as true heir and patriarch is vitiated. And, needless to say, the portrait of George in itself tends further to foreground the idea of black man as trickster, and so works against Faulkner's generalized portrait of racial oppression.

What adds to the complications in 'The Fire and the Hearth' is a second crucial problem to which the confrontation between Lucas and Zack alerts us. Lucas goes to kill Zack because he believes that his pride as a man has been challenged. After the death of Zack's wife in childbirth, we learn, Zack kept Lucas's wife Molly in his house for six months, until Lucas demanded her return. Lucas feels that the offence requires the ultimate punishment; and Zack is only saved from being shot (for that matter, Lucas is only saved from an inevitable lynching) when the gun Lucas is carrying misfires. What we are witnessing here is an essentially male contest. Two men who, we are informed, have known each other from infancy, who have fished, hunted, eaten and slept together in the past and lived 'almost as brothers lived', are now separated across the racial divide, and have been brought into collision because one man has taken the other man's woman. The pathos of this scene is that it is a failed male bonding, the closest 'The Fire and the Hearth' ever gets to a love story (apart, that is, from another failed male bonding, involving these two men's two sons). Its tension, in turn, hinges on the fact that it is a virility contest. 'I'm the man', is one of Lucas's favourite remarks. 'I'm the one to say in my house', he later tells Zack's son Roth, 'like you and your paw and his paw were the ones to say in his.' Lucas's pride in himself is a pride specifically in his prerogatives as a male – and in the fact that he is more directly related than any man living to *the* man, Lucius Quintus Carothers McCaslin. It is this that has been offended by Zack stealing 'his' woman. 'You thought I wouldn't, didn't you?' Lucas says to Zack just before he tries to shoot him,

> You knowed I could beat you, so you thought to beat me with old Carothers, like Cass Edmonds done Isaac: used old Carothers to make Isaac give up the land that was his because Cass Edmonds was the woman-made McCaslin, the woman-branch, the sister, and old Carothers would have told Isaac to give in to the woman-kin that couldn't fend for herself.[54]

Lucas's contempt for the 'woman-branch' of the family, the Edmondses, is in fact equalled by his contempt for someone like Ike McCaslin who, although descended by a male line, allows himself to fall victim to 'woman-kin' by repudiating his inheritance – and so, in Lucas's eyes, turning 'apostate to his name and lineage'. Lucas is a proud black man, as the narrative presents him, not so much because of pride in his blackness as on account of his white, male status: the fact that he is descended 'not only by a male line but in only two generations' from the original founding father.

'*Even a nigger McCaslin is a better man, better than all of us*', Roth observes, as he rehearses to himself the episode of conflict between his father and Lucas. Elsewhere, he speculates that Lucas is somehow '*both heir and prototype simultaneously of all the geography and climate and biology which sired old Carothers and all the rest of us*'. Roth is perhaps the closest there is to an autobiographical character in 'The Fire and the Hearth', if only because his relationship with Molly Beauchamp replicates that of Faulkner with Caroline Barr, who died two years before *Go Down, Moses* was published.

It is not necessary to rely on this autobiographical connection, however, to see just how much Roth confirms a structure of feeling characteristic of Lucas, the man he is constantly watching and thinking about, and just how much that structure also inheres in the narrative as a whole. By an elaborate circuit of argument in this story, the main representative of the black race becomes attached to the history of white males. At one point, the narrative even identifies the face of Lucas Beauchamp, as Roth re-members and imagines it, with the 'composite' face 'of a whole generation of fierce and undefeated young Confederate soldiers'. Lucas, it seems, is connected up not only to the founding father but to the defenders of the faith. At the very least, this muddies the waters as far as representation of racial conflict is concerned. Far from being as, say, Joe Christmas is, a site of racial and ideological struggle, Lucas appears to be more of a McCaslin than any of the McCaslins and more white, even, than the whites. Somehow, conflict has been bleached or driven out of him. 'Instead of being at once the battleground and victim of the two strains', as the narrator puts it, 'he was a vessel, durable, ancestryless, non-conductive, in which the toxin and its anti stalemated one another.'[55] He has, in short, fulfilled the male desire for transcendence. On the one hand, he seems to be soaked in the passage of time, a mobile emblem of the McCaslin story. On the other, he exists in pure self-containment. Either way, he functions purely within a white verbal economy, a white framework of reference. Other characters may call him 'nigger', but it seems to be the dearest wish of the narrative to deny him all black memories and status – and to drain his moments of supreme personal authority of anything approaching a racial coloration.

Lucas has no specifically black memories. Nor does he have the memory of any mother-figure to rival his preoccupation with his grandfather. For that matter, most of his emotional energy is invested in males. There is no moment in his relationship with Molly to match that time when he and Zack wrestle each other 'over the centre of the bed' in the founding father's house, locked in an embrace that speaks equally of love and death. Lucas's response to women, and indeed that of the narrative, is registered in a passage that immediately follows the confrontation between him and Zack. 'She went on, neither answering nor looking back', the narrator says of Molly as her husband observes her,

> impervious, tranquil, somehow serene. Nor was he any longer watching her. He breathed slow and quiet. *Women*, he thought. *Women. I wont never know. I dont want to. I ruther never to know than to find out later I have been fooled.*[56]

Women exist outside the parameters of understanding: that is not an uncommon theme in Faulkner's work. What is new is that it does not seem to matter. Here and elsewhere in *Go Down, Moses* the real story is the male one. So women characters, when they appear at all, tend to remain anony-mous, as in 'Delta Autumn' and even 'Pantaloon in Black'. Or they are fragmented into a series of physical and verbal gestures, like Miss

Sophonsiba in 'Was' with her lace cap, her fan, her perfume, her roan tooth and her genteel, pretentious diction. Or alternatively, like Molly Beauchamp they disappear into cliché: a stock reading of female mystery ('*I wont never know. I dont want to*') and tranquillity ('impervious, tranquil, somehow serene') for which the narrator scarcely bothers to invent a single new phrase. Lucas has the patriarchal figure of Lucius Quintus Carothers McCaslin to commemorate and invoke. Ike McCaslin has almost too many fathers, educating him by instruction and example: Uncle Buck, Uncle Buddy, Cass McCaslin and Sam Fathers. Even to rehearse the question of a maternal presence in Lucas's life, however, is to realize just how irrelevant women are to his concerns and to those of the narrative. Similarly, just to remember the grotesque fact that Miss Sophonsiba is Ike's mother is to expose the irrelevance of females and female descent to these stories: apart, that is, from when violation, matters of incest and miscegenation are also involved. Strictly speaking, Ike has no mother and does not seem to need one.

This is a point, in fact, at which the central stories of *Go Down, Moses* overlap: a place, or area, where the concerns and assumptions of 'The Fire and the Hearth' coincide, are shared, with the hunting stories, 'The Old People', 'Delta Autumn', and above all 'The Bear'. In 'The Fire and the Hearth', Faulkner's representation of racial relationships, racial oppression and its bitter harvest, is complicated and even, to an extent, undermined not only by the original comic material and the preoccupation with white genealogy but also by the concentration on an exclusively male story. A similar reliance on male narrative is at work in a powerful tale like 'The Bear': making its reading of the South and its history, at the very least, problematic. As almost everybody who has discussed 'The Bear' has pointed out, it is not so much one narrative as two, linked together. One operates mostly in the realm of myth and concerns the annual hunt for a bear called Old Ben: an animal that is seen as 'a phantom, epitome, and apotheosis of the old wild life which the little puny humans swarmed and hacked'.[57] The other concerns Ike McCaslin's discovery of family guilt: the fact that the founding father, involved as he was in fathering a child on his own, slave daughter, was implicated in the dreadful burden of Southern history. Taking them separately, there can be no doubt about the power of these two stories. In the narrative of the hunt, the verbal devices of repetition and incantation link up with ritual gestures – such as Ike's surrendering of his gun, compass and watch, the implements of civilization, the first time he sees the bear – to give everything a quality of legend: the feeling that, like the cycle of the seasons, this is a primal tale, told many times. And, in order to stop things becoming too portentous, the intimations of myth do not elbow out a sense of the sweat and smell of an ordinary hunting expedition. Faulkner's success here depends, in fact, on making the story of the initiation of Ike into the mysteries of the wilderness seem both apocalyptic and mundane. The bear is an aged, brown grizzly, scarred and maimed and petulant, as well as an emblem of the wild. Sam Fathers is an old man, of very mixed parentage, scraping a living as a scout, as well as 'the chief, the prince' who instructs Ike. And the story that encloses these characters is at once a rite of passage and the kind of tall tale Sam and his friends might tell around the camping fire, about the one that got away. If the hunting narrative in 'The Bear' is full of old tales and talking, then the other story, about Ike's uncovering of the ghosts in the family closet, is similarly packed – in this case, with old signs and signifying. Ike has to learn to read the cryptic clues contained in the family ledger, in order to piece together the family secret. In turn, the reader is forced into a similar activity: moving back and forth in time, collecting the scraps of information and trying to understand them. In effect, the reader shares Ike's experience as inheritor and interpreter: we participate in his curiosity, his occasional feelings of frustration and, not least, in his eventual sense of shock.

The problem comes when Faulkner tries to connect these two stories up. The link is an apparently simple one: the values that Ike has learned in the wilderness require him to reject his inheritance. What he has come to understand through the annual ritual of the hunt militates against any tolerance, let alone acceptance, of a racial history of violence and oppression. This sounds perfectly straightforward; the difficulty comes when the details are investigated. The illusions of power over nature and ownership are clearly being dismissed: Ike has come to learn that nobody owns the land. Now he is casting aside a past and a patrimony that claimed to possess both land and people, and that still seems to proclaim, 'They're mine!' – in other words, that nature and human nature are available for use and profit. However, it is not easy to see what Ike is putting in the place of the system he rejects; or, even if it is possible to see what this is, it remains pretty difficult to appreciate it. The story of the hunt, Ike's venture into the wilderness, is, after all, a variation on the myth of the American Adam: that narrative, basic to so many American legends, in which the hero (and it has to be a hero, not a heroine) goes into the woods or lights out for the territory to restore lost innocence and uncompromised individuality.[58] To say that this is socially simplistic, given the situation Ike confronts, seems almost superfluous. Ike, in fact, does not so much reject the past as shuffle off responsibility for it, and the system it perpetuates. In practical terms, this means that he hands over the inheritance to someone else, his cousin, who is perfectly happy to exploit the land and the tenants; Ike, meanwhile, lives apart from the plantation but receives a small sum from the proceeds of exploitation to supplement his income. The hunting narrative and the narrative of racial injustice just do not fit together; and Ike can find no satisfactory way of translating the language of the one into the idiom of the other. There is no real bridge, either conceptual or political, for him to cross from myth into history, no way of turning the 'timeless' values absorbed during the hunt into a viable moral practice.

Faulkner as much as admits that the connection between the two narratives is at best wobbly, and that as a result Ike never manages to weld his two series of experiences into a coherent set. The admission is tacitly there, in the first place, in the fact that he allows these narratives to inhabit utterly different genres, using his familiar, dualistic vocabulary of 'nature' and 'culture'. In the woods, it is all endless, cyclical rituals and talking, apparently, while on the plantation it is all account books, reading and deciphering. Not quite so tacit, perhaps, but equally symptomatic of Faulkner's uneasiness is the occasional windiness of the rhetoric. At times, he seems to be using an elaborate verbal camouflage, deployed either through the narrative voice or through the voice of Ike, to conceal the uncertainty or even futility of Ike's gestures: to try to make up in volume for what the argument lacks in terms of focus and fit. Then there are the clues scattered through the narrative that Ike's solutions to his problem are perhaps less than satisfactory: Ike's infinitesimal hesitation, for instance, before daring to suggest that black people are in some ways better than white – or, for that matter, his inability to talk about the simplicities of the heart in anything but the most complexly discursive of terms. This might be interpreted as careful positioning of the protagonist on Faulkner's part: one weapon in an armoury employed to place Ike in a critical context. The only trouble is that, when it comes down to it, the armoury is pretty bare and that, for the most part, Ike and the narrator share one voice – and that voice is clearly meant to be the voice of authority. Such occasional gestures of criticism are probably best seen as further symptoms of Faulkner's uncertainty, his uneasiness about the viability or even the validity of the path Ike has chosen to pursue. The uncertainty is, in any event, evident in his comments on Ike after *Go Down, Moses* was published. In 1955, for instance, he suggested that Ike 'should have been more affirmative instead of shunning people'; in 1957, on the other hand, he was insisting that Ike had 'fulfilled his destiny'; by 1958, however, Faulkner was back to arguing that Ike was one of those people 'in any time and age that cannot face and cope with the problems'.[59]

Faulkner never said it , but a simpler and truer answer to any questions about Ike McCaslin would have been to confess that he was not really sure. He could clearly see the problems inherent in Ike's position but, unfortunately, he could think of no alternative. The problem was an intractable one for Faulkner, and his protagonist. In the wilderness story, after all, ownership of the land is equated with Original Sin. But Faulkner was not about to abjure land ownership altogether; while in his portrait of Ike McCaslin he devised someone who could not live happily inside the system of ownership, nor find a viable space outside it. So, in their different ways, author and character ended up living within the system, even profiting from it, and falling back on occasional irony (on Faulkner's part) or distaste (on Ike's part) to make that position tolerable. The situation was made even more problematical because the Adamic myth Faulkner had chosen to use as his narrative touchstone, and via which Ike received his education, was inadequate to the circumstances – not just because it did not fit the historical issues at stake, but also because it was and is, by any standards, an exclusively male narrative. There is no place for black women here as anything other than mute, characterless victims; and there is no place for white women as anything other than agents of the system. It is not simply the case, as it is in 'The Fire and the Hearth', that women characters are demoted to insignificance in 'The Bear'. It is that on the most important occasion when a white woman does appear in the story, it is in the role of seductress: trying to use her wiles and 'womanflesh' to lure Ike back into the embrace of his guilt-ridden heritage. The woman Ike marries remains resolutely unnamed: she is generic 'woman', or rather 'wife'. And in her generic role, her aim is to make Ike promise to reclaim the McCaslin estate: otherwise, she warns him, she will not share his bed. She speaks in brief, feverish staccato: 'Lock the door', 'Promise', 'And that's all. That's all from me.' Like the snake Ike encounters in the wilderness, '*She already knows more*', Ike thinks, '*than I with all the man-listening in camps . . . ever heard of.*'[60] She is the tempting Eve of the Adamic myth: using her knowledge, her neuroses and her sexuality in an attempt to lure the American Adam into a repudiation of the truth he has learned. Ironically, this is one of the few places in 'The Bear' where the two narratives do seem to connect.

They connect here, of course, because what is occurring is a strategy of displacement. The two narratives are only really at ease with each other when the innocence of the protagonist can be assumed and plausibly maintained: so that, by extension, the problem of just how Ike translates Adamic values into Southern history, and the history of his family, can be quietly suppressed. Something else that works in this direction, although hardly with any great success, is the curiously selective reading of the regional past that Ike and the narrator sometimes share. Of course, the guilty founding father is the core fact of the narrative: incest and miscegenation are seen to be at the heart of the family romance. There is a double edge to the interpretation of the regional past in terms of one family, however. What is gained in intensity of focus can be lost on a more general level: the reader might infer, quite simply, that these are problems peculiar to one family. This difficulty can be evaded if there is enough fictional contextualizing: sufficient links as there are in, say, *Absalom, Absalom!* between the different fields (personal, familial, social) in which historical conflicts occur. But, in 'The Bear', it is noticeable that when the broader dimensions of the Southern past, and not specifically the McCaslin past, are at issue, then the language of a land 'cursed' by its inhabitants is muddied by some fairly tendentious arguments. During the fourth section of the story, for example, Ike manages to intimate that maybe black people were not ready for freedom after the Civil War (but then, perhaps nobody ever is, is the rhetorical escape-route), and that the Northern invaders were responsible for 'rapine and pillage'. Southerners fought the War, Ike suggests, 'not because they were opposed to freedom as freedom', but rather, for the old reasons for which man (not the generals and politicians but man) has always fought . . . : to preserve the status quo or to establish a better future one to endure for his children.[61]

Lynching is mentioned, certainly, but the lynch mobs, we are told, left behind 'the bodies of white and black both': which may be true in an absolute sense (there were, after all, some white victims), but hardly does justice to the true causes and terrible racial consequences of lynch law. There is even space found for a traditional – which is to say, conventionally racist – rehearsal of the horrors of Reconstruction. We learn, for instance, of 'a United States marshal in Jefferson who signed his official papers with a crude cross, an ex-slave called Sickymo'. This character, while still a slave, 'would steal his master's grain alcohol and dilute it with water and peddle it', Ike observes; and he 'attained his high office because his half-white sister was the concubine of the Federal A.P.M.'. The point is not that such excursions into the territory of *Gone With the Wind* are entirely without historical foundation; still less, that they constitute the full reading of Southern history in 'The Bear'. It is simply that they divert attention from the idea of historical guilt: they erect obstacles between the familial dimensions of the story, where the guilt-ridden nature of the past is incontrovertible, and the wider social dimensions, where notions of guilt and innocence become at the very least blurred. To the extent that extenuation of regional guilt, as distinct from familial guilt, is there in the narrative, it makes it easier for Ike to live with the presumption of his innocence: perhaps all he needs to do, after all, is to distance himself from the McCaslin plantation, not the social system of the South. But also to the extent that it is there, it makes it difficult for the reader to take this version of the past as an adequate one: in still another sense, the crossover from myth to history has not been credibly achieved.

It is not hard to see why 'The Bear' became a key text, at the time when Faulkner first enjoyed wide public recognition. The attempt to read history in terms of myth, and Adamic myth at that, Ike's pursuit of disengagement, and his devout belief that he might somehow liberate himself from the agony of the past: all exercised appeal during a period when many people, lured by similar motives, were venturing sometimes along just the same paths. Nor is it much harder to appreciate now that Ike's position begs too many questions, that the Adamic myth carries its own suppressions with it, and that in any case the connection between myth and history is imperfectly made. There is damage here, wrought by Faulkner's materials and his project: the narratives he exploits, and his assumption that to declare a position he has to assume an authoritative voice. The damage does not, however, deprive 'The Bear' of impact. On the contrary, it only adds to it: that is, once we see the story not as Faulkner seems to have intended it, as a declaration of independence from the past, but as a confession of imprisonment – subjection to the worrying, wasting facts of time. A condition of innocence, wholeness and transcendence is the aim of the author/narrator and protagonist: expressed, for example, in the 'peopleless'[62] self-contained and utterly unselfconscious state of being that all three ideal figures in the story – Old Ben, the dog named Lion that eventually brings Old Ben down, and Sam Fathers – happen to share. But it is a condition that lies out of reach: neither Faulkner nor Ike can convincingly link the experience of the wilderness with the 'bitched' (to use Faulkner's word) or 'cursed' (to borrow Ike's term) terrain of their ordinary, social lives. However hard they try, they cannot realize their aim of transfiguring the bleak particulars of history by relocating them in the blinding, universal light of myth. Their failure, though, is what gives 'The Bear' its power and pathos: which comes from dissonance, not the harmony Faulkner evidently intended. In the end, the story memorably enacts its own dilemma, which is also that of its author and its anti-heroic hero; it describes and rehearses the pain of discovering that things do not connect – that the fissure between myth and history has not, after all, been healed.

Sandwiched between 'The Fire and the Hearth' and the first of the wilderness stories in the book, 'The Old People', is 'Pantaloon in Black'. At the end of the volume is the story that gives *Go Down, Moses* its title. Taken together, the two tales can be seen as object lessons in how to tell a tale of race, and how not to. 'Go Down, Moses' is clearly meant to offer a contrast between 'nature' and 'culture', the primal simplicity of black people and the mired complexities of whites. On the one hand, there is the intuitive Molly Beauchamp who can sense that her grandson, whom she has not seen in years, is in trouble. On the other, there is the cerebral Gavin Stevens, who cannot understand how Molly gets her sixth sense, and cannot cope with the emotionally charged wake that concludes the story. One trouble with the narrative, however, is that the terms underpinning it could easily be turned on their heads: at the close, after all, Stevens reacts *instinctively* to what is a *ritualized* expression of grief, marked in a language that is part of the black Southerner's cultural inheritance. Another is that, as a whole, 'Go Down, Moses' remains imprisoned in the idiom and perspectives of the white folk of Yoknapatawpha. Molly Beauchamp and her grandson are stereotypes, figures respectively of unimpatient endurance and impenetrable waywardness; the paternalism of the town worthies, who pay for the transportation of the corpse of the grandson back to Jefferson, puts the racial divide into softer focus; and the voice of Stevens, while not entirely authoritative, tends to overlap with that of the narrator – the both of them rather too inclined to take the black/white division (and, for that matter, the female/male one) as an unalterable fact of life. 'It's our grief', says Miss Worsham, the old white woman who grew up with Molly 'as sisters would'; and we are obviously meant to read this and approve. The voice of Miss Worsham is not heard at the wake, however: it remains unincorporated into a chorus of woe that is resolutely black – speaking of griefs that, in local as well as historical terms, are definitively other, outside the white domain ('Roth Edmonds sold my Benjamin', 'Oh yes, Lord. Sold him in Eygpt'). 'Southern paternalism developed as a way of mediating irreconcilable class and racial conflicts', the historian Eugene Genovese has observed, 'it was an anomaly, even at its moment of greatest apparent strength.'[63] Too often in this story, though, that paternalism is taken at face value: as if the belief that 'we', black and white, are all part of one family could not only soften the edges of racial division – it could also allow some people, like Miss Worsham, to ignore them.

The strength of 'Pantaloon in Black' is that it does not make the same mistakes as 'Go Down, Moses' does. On the contrary, the otherness and also the subjectivity of the central black character, Rider, is freshly caught and fully communicated. Faulkner finds a language – or, rather, languages – to render Rider's human presence; and he then shows how the language of white society, deployed by the deputy who narrates his own version of Rider's last days towards the end of the tale, suppresses that humanity and translates presence into absence. Rider is there for us in the narrative, via his patterns of speech of course, but even more thanks to a complex interplay of sense impressions that enable us both to see him and to see with him:

> He . . . crossed the last field . . . into the lane. It was empty at this hour of Sunday evening – no family in wagon, no rider, no walkers churchward to speak to him . . . – the pale, powder-light, powder-dry dust of August from which the long week's marks of hoof and wheel had been blotted by the strolling and unhurried Sunday shoes, with somewhere beneath them, vanished but not gone, fixed and held in the annealing dust, the narrow, splaytoed prints of his wife's bare feet where on Saturday afternoons she would walk to the commissary . . . he strode on . . . , his body breasting the air her body had vacated, his eyes touching the objects – post and tree and field and house and hill – her eyes had lost.[64]

Loss of life is seen here as a loss of the visible objects of the world, in all their beautiful particularity. And loss of a loved one is felt as a similar loss to the senses: Rider's wife is no longer there to be looked at and touched – to have her body 'breasting the air' with his – even though Rider suspects that she may still be there, hovering beneath the surface of things. The country lane is a kind of palimpsest: Rider can almost read the footprints, the vanished traces of his wife, beneath the accumulating dust. He can sense her elusive presence even in her absence, tantalizingly hidden from view. Faulkner is using a vocabulary here, circulating around the paradoxes of desire, that is familiar from his earliest writing. But he is making it say something fresh and powerful: about the intolerable nature of loss and the unappeasable character of grief – how mourning can become, at one and the same time, a gesture of farewell and a refusal.

What adds to the strength of passages like this one, and others in which the emotional state of Rider is caught for us, is that, while Faulkner never dives down into interior monologue, he requires the reader to contemplate the character's feelings and to share them. The otherness of Rider is respected: there is no pretence that it is easy for white narrator or white readers to know exactly how he feels, that centuries of division and Rider's own personal history of dispossession can simply be circumvented or ignored. But, at the same time, the sheer quality of concentration given to our seeing of Rider, and our seeing of what he sees, means that we are assaulted by the power and perplexity of his emotions. We are forced to look at, and consider, his humanity. Rider aware of the traces left by his wife beneath the dust of a country lane, Rider pursuing her phantom figure glimpsed by the kitchen door, Rider attempting to drown his pain in physical effort: the muscular rhythms of Faulkner's language, rehearsing such times, turn emotion into a sensory experience, a physical force. The racial divide is not minimized, still less suppressed, the particulars of the character's life – as a poor black man living in the South in the first half of this century – are honoured. Nevertheless, white narrator and readers are permitted to participate in his suffering for a while, his bewilderment and uncontrollable rage at his loss. The prose enacts, however briefly, a moment of communion.

The bitter irony of the later part of the story, when an anonymous deputy offers his version of how Rider behaved after the death of his wife – and, in the process, manages to misread just about all Rider's actions – is that it turns the earlier part upside down. The presumption of the deputy is that there is no real barrier between him and the man he describes. He knows black people, he believes. What is more, he knows 'they ain't human'.[65] His language is predicated on a series of assumptions that are precisely the opposite of those on which the language used earlier, by the narrator, was based. He will have no trouble discovering and disclosing the totality of black life, he assumes, there is no serious effort of attention required. Nor will he experience any difficulty plumbing the feelings of someone on the other side of the racial divide: not least because, as the deputy sees it, black people do not have any feelings worth talking about. The language of the deputy, in effect, both performs and defends an act of exclusion. He not only assumes that what he cannot say cannot exist, he argues that: what is not and evidently cannot be spoken of – namely, the inner life of a black person – is, the deputy insists, not actually there. 'Pantaloon in Black' is one of the finest of Faulkner's shorter narratives, perhaps the finest. And it is so because it locates the sources of racial oppression so energetically and clearly, in a social currency that confidently denies the human presence of the oppressed. Not only that, it locates alternative ways of saying and seeing: a sounder currency that enables human subjects to acknowledge their separation and their connection, their status as individual agents in a community. There are more ambitious narratives in *Go Down, Moses*: among them, those that attempt to investigate the tangled relations between black and white in a more specifically historicized way. No story is more effective than this one, however, in fulfilling what seems to have been Faulkner's seminal aim while he was preparing the book – of making a statement, a contribution in a world that seemed terminally divided and (to use Faulkner's own term) 'destruction-bent'. Like all the best moments in *Go Down, Moses*, 'Pantaloon in Black' does not preach or insist but it says something, not so much thanks to what it says as to how it says it: through the interrogation and rehabilitation of systems of speech, the ways we speak of and speak to each other. It subverts old habits of language and perception and it tentatively proposes new ones; and that, in the end, is how it makes a difference.

IV   WATCHING THE DETECTIVES: *INTRUDER IN THE DUST*

After the publication of *Go Down, Moses*, it was six years before Faulkner completed another novel. There were some practical reasons for this delay: in particular, financial pressures forced him to return to Hollywood to work for Warner Brothers. Initially, the contract was for a period of seven years but, after working off and on for the studio from 1942 to 1945, Faulkner managed to get released when a friend interceded on his behalf with Jack Warner. Working in Hollywood had its compensations. Faulkner renewed his friendship with the director Howard Hawks, and assisted him on two of the best films of the period, *To Have and Have Not* and *The Big Sleep*. His contribution was what he was best at, reworking scripts: 'with a script that didn't work', another screenwriter who knew Faulkner observed, 'he would take a key scene and make it go. What Bill did was to make the whole picture better.' Faulkner also began an affair again with Meta Carpenter, who was now divorced. The relationship was less passionate than it had been: 'the great difference', Meta recalled, 'was that he pretended not to need me as impellingly as he once had for companionship'. And it made both Faulkner's wife and his lover feel short-changed: with Estelle bitter and resentful, and Meta complaining that all she got was 'the leavings' while 'his wife and daughter had everything'. But, in purely selfish terms, it offered Faulkner some compensation for what he felt was the failure of his marriage – and also a defence against an environment he claimed to detest. 'They worship death here', he remarked of Hollywood, 'They don't worship money, they worship death.' His dislike of working for what he called 'a hack's motion picture wages', in a place where there seemed to be 'nobody ... with any roots', was aggravated by the suspicion that he might be spoiling his talent. 'I have realised lately', he confided to his publisher, 'how much trash and junk writing for movies corrupted into my writing.'[66] What made matters even worse was that, if he was prostituting himself by writing for the movies as he clearly felt he was, then he was doing so at bargain rates. 'I've got America's best writer for $300 a week', boasted Jack Warner at a Hollywood party; and even at the end of his stint with Warner Brothers Faulkner was earning no more than he had when he first went to work for Metro-Goldwyn-Mayer thirteen years earlier.

'I am 47 now', Faulkner wrote at the end of 1944, 'I have three more books of my own I want to write. I am like an aging mare who has say three more gestations in her before her time is over.' This was one reason for wanting to free himself of the obligation of writing for the movies as soon as he was financially able to do so. Another was more specific: he was already working on what he called 'my epic poem', the book that was eventually to be published as *A Fable*. 'I believe now', he declared in 1946, 'that it's not just my best book but perhaps the best of my time.' But it cost him enormous effort – and not just because he was forced to work on it between screenwriting assignments. 'I feel I'm written out', he would confess mournfully upon occasion. His writing seemed much more a product of the will now. 'I am writing and rewriting', he admitted, 'weighing every word, which I never did before: I used to bang it out like an apprentice paper hanger and never look back.' At the same time as he was plugging away at what seemed like endless revisions of his 'epic poem', other tasks apart from screenwriting preoccupied him: in particular, the preparation of *The Portable Faulkner*. Faulkner could hardly have been gratified to learn from the editor of the volume, Malcolm Cowley, that by 1945 all his books except *Sanctuary* were out of print. Nevertheless, the task of helping Cowley excited him, encouraging him to review his achievement. As part of that review, he prepared a map of Yoknapatawpha for the volume, and he confided to Cowley that he was thinking of compiling what he termed 'a Golden Book of my apocryphal county . . . an alphabetical, rambling genealogy of the people, father to son to son'. As Cowley and Faulkner hoped, the publication of *The Portable Faulkner* in 1946 marked a turning-point in the revival of Faulkner's fortunes and the rehabilitation of his reputation. After it appeared, Faulkner became more and more of a public figure. As he began to move further into the public arena, however, something that had already been discernible in *Go Down, Moses* became more marked. His writing took on a steadily more self-conscious, even polemical edge. Faulkner was later to admit the difference. When he was young, he said, he had written to please himself, an ambition that had kept him 'furiously engaged'. It was only, as he put it, 'after I got old and began to slow down that I became conscious there were people that read the books'.[67] And along with that awareness, evidently, came a renewed sense of responsibility: a sense of the writer as citizen and educator.

This is to put it crudely, of course: but the drift towards a more obviously public resonance is there, in elements of *Go Down, Moses* and then in the novel that eventually followed it in 1948, *Intruder in the Dust*. This new book, initially thought of in 1940 as 'a mystery story, original in that the solver is a negro, himself in jail for the murder', had assumed more clearly social and polemical dimensions by 1948. Faulkner had reached an impasse with his 'epic poem', he felt. So he set it aside, he explained to his editor, to work on a 'short novel set in my apocryphal Jefferson'. The

book was 'a mystery-murder', although 'the theme' was 'more [the] relationship between Negro and white'. 'But it's a story', he insisted, 'nobody
preaches in it.' This was a point he was to repeat later: *Intruder in the Dust*,
he wrote in March, 1948, 'is a good story, not just a document'. Not that
the book he was working on had a title at that time. Even when it was
completed, he was still searching around for the right phrase to introduce the narrative and give the prospective reader some idea of its concerns: unusually for him, he played with many possibilities (among them
'Jugglery in the Dust' and 'Imposture in the Dust') before settling for the
one by which the book is now known. 'As it is now', he said of his new
novel, 'it is a mystery story plus a little sociology, and psychology.' It had
changed again from what he had originally intended. 'It started out to be
a simple quick 150 page whodunit but jumped the traces', he declared,
'strikes me as being a pretty good study of a 16 year old boy who overnight
became a man.'[68] Even after the book was published, Faulkner continued
to play around with it in a peculiarly self-conscious way. Early in 1949, he
sent two pages of new text for inclusion in any new edition of *Intruder in
the Dust*, in which the writer inserted himself in the narrative. In these new
pages, Gavin Stevens – who looms large over the novel – refers to the
ending of *Absalom, Absalom!*, written by what Stevens describes as 'a mild
retiring little man over yonder at Oxford'. Just what Faulkner's reason was
for this addition it is difficult to say: perhaps it was a feeble attempt to
distance himself from Stevens's garrulousness by indicating that, even in
the fictional world of Yoknapatawpha, he and Stevens were not one and
the same. Whatever the reason, though, the publishers wisely never added
this material.

Throughout his career, Faulkner was prone to uncertainty about his
own work. However, as his tinkering with *Intruder in the Dust* indicated, this
tendency became aggravated the older he grew. His estimate of *A Fable*,
for instance, fluctuated wildly as he worked on it: in the course of just one
letter, written in 1947, he first declared, 'now and then I think the stuff
is no good', then added a few paragraphs later, 'there's nothing wrong
with this book; I am just getting older and dont write fast anymore'.[69] The
problems he had even fixing on a title were, perhaps, a symptom of his
uncertainty about just what his priorities were, exactly what he thought he
was doing in his new novel. Beginning with a mystery story, Faulkner had
first oscillated away from this towards the issue of race and then found
himself spending more and more time on the story of Charles Mallison's
initiation into adulthood. There were particular reasons why he was interested in any one of these three strands in the narrative. He had always
been attracted to detective stories, not least because of the task the traditional sleuth had of reconstructing the past; and the theme of the boy
becoming, or failing to become, a man had preoccupied him at least from
the moment when he began writing fiction. The race issue had special
urgency for him at the time too. His growing sense of the public role he
had to perform encouraged him to think about it; so did his previous

experience of writing about race in *Go Down, Moses* (there are even some specific echoes, preoccupations carried over from the earlier novel). And then there was the pressure of contemporary politics. In the year in which *Intruder in the Dust* was published, the breakaway Dixiecrat party contested the presidential election: it had split from the Democratic party specifically over the civil rights element in the Democratic programme, the governor of Mississippi was its vice-presidential candidate, and Mississippi was one of four states in which it carried the electoral college. Of course, the election took place some ten months after Faulkner began work on the novel, but he was well aware of the political impetus building up over the race issue; and this also played its part in complicating his narrative – pushing him towards turning 'a mystery-murder' into a story that was also about (as he put it once) 'white . . . responsibility to the Negro'.

Faulkner's device for bringing these three separate narrative strands together was a simple one: Charles Mallison grows up in the process of proving that Lucas Beauchamp is not guilty, as accused, of murdering a white man. With the help of his black companion, Aleck Sander, and Miss Habersham, a spinster of nearly eighty years 'whose name', we are told, 'was now the oldest which remained in the county',[70] he saves Lucas from a probable lynching; and, in acting with courage and initiative, in defiance of both his father and, for a while at least, his uncle Gavin Stevens, he crosses the threshold (a recurrent image in the novel) from boyhood into manhood. The device is a plausible one, certainly: but unfortunately it does not work. This is not because there is anything inherently and mutually antagonistic about the three elements that Faulkner was working with: it has to do, rather, with his conception of what he was doing. For Faulkner, the 'mystery-murder' was the 'popular' strand in his new novel: his first, probable reference to *Intruder in the Dust* was, after all, to 'a blood-and-thunder mystery which should sell (they usually do)'. And on to this he then superimposed two strands more in keeping with his growing sense of himself as a 'serious' writer, with a responsible role to play and something important to say. As far as its assumptions went, the project was one characteristic of the times: which occupied a midway position between the pursuit of pure seriousness inscribed in high modernism and the cultural relativism characteristic of postmodernist art. Writers of the period still accepted the split between 'popular' and 'serious' announced or accepted by modernism: but, very often, they tried to use 'popular' forms as vehicles for 'serious' themes, in order to break away from what was perceived as the elitism and obscurantism of the great modernist writers. The most notable Southern example of this strategy, prior to *Intruder in the Dust*, was *All the King's Men* by Robert Penn Warren, published in 1946. The task was self-defeating, however, in the sense that the narrative was inevitably broken on the back of its own assumptions, the belief in the existence of an essential division between 'popular' medium and 'serious' message. In terms of practical details, what this usually meant is what it means in *Intruder in the Dust*: the 'popular' form was ruptured by the demands of the 'serious' theme, while the 'serious' theme floated free, unanchored in the story. The plot, being only a pretext in the end, was fractured by the pressures of the message; while the message, having been imposed rather than emerging out of the urgencies of the narrative, never quite slotted into the plot – and, more often than not, slid away into over-insistence and preachiness.

Admittedly, Faulkner does try to make the detective tale that supplies the popular vehicle for the message exciting. A single sentence gives a melodramatic opening to the novel, announcing the arrest of Lucas Beauchamp because, 'as the whole town . . . had known since the night before', 'Lucas had killed a white man'. The false story is told, of how Lucas is supposed to have killed Vinson Gowrie, one of the notorious Gowrie clan from Beat Four. Lucas assigns Charles his mission of inspecting the corpse: 'My pistol is a fawty-one Colt', he tells Charles, 'He wasn't shot with no fawty-one Colt.' And the subsequent episodes then derive some urgency from the constant references to time passing, the impending threat of mob violence – and the device of withheld information characteristic of the detective tale: chapter 4 ends, for instance, with Charles and his two confederates finding the wrong corpse in Vinson Gowrie's grave. To supply some kind of narrative centre for these events, Faulkner uses Jefferson town square. Gatherings there punctuate the plot and chart its gradual progression: the mob gathers, lingers, and disperses when the true murderer turns out to be the victim's own brother, then at the end the normal routines of trading and talking on the square are restored. Even in the earlier part of the novel, however, the plot sometimes creaks. No convincing explanation is given, for instance, why Lucas keeps so quiet when he is arrested: the most compelling reason seems to be one of narrative exigency, because the young initiate has to be assigned the task of unearthing the truth. And that plot is, in any event, interrupted from time to time by a big speech or generalization: about, say, the 'ultimate cosmolined doom' threatening the machine age, the tedious mediocrity of modern culture, the 'fluidity' of women, 'their . . . willingness to abandon with the substanceless promptitude of wind or air itself not only position but principle too'[71] – and, of course, the special nature of the South and its racial problems. The generalization is sometimes put in the mouth of Gavin Stevens, sometimes (rather implausibly, on occasion) in the mind of the sixteen-year-old protagonist; sometimes it simply issues from the anonymous narrator. Whatever, it belongs in the end to one voice that simply flows in and out of those immediate sources (the comments on women, for instance, begin in Charles's mind and finish up a paragraph later in Stevens's mouth); and their net effect is to dissipate tension, to tempt us to lose track of the detective story.

This rupturing of the plot is, it has to be said, only a tendency in the earlier part of *Intruder in the Dust*; for a while, the narrative maintains some kind of momentum. Gradually, however, plot becomes submerged in preaching. The murder is effectively solved three-quarters of the way through the novel: with the discovery that Vinson Gowrie was killed with a German Luger automatic, 'like the one Buddy McCallum brought home from France in 1919 and traded that summer for a pair of foxhounds' – the other participant in the trade being Vinson's brother, Crawford. After this, the mob simply disperses from the square: 'they ran', Gavin Stevens explains, in horror at the crime of fratricide. The capture of Crawford and his subsequent suicide we only hear of by the way, and at several removes from the site of the action. Faulkner hastily disposes of the detective story, with a recapitulation from Gavin Stevens of how and why Vinson was killed and Lucas blamed. Even the corpse is dismissed in a fairly summary fashion: the sheriff, we are told, disposed of what little evidence he had by 'giving it back' to Vinson's father, 'old one-armed pistol Gowrie where even two children and an old woman couldn't get it back this time'.[72]

The stage being cleared, and the bodies shuffled off in this swift fashion, that much more time is left for the voice of the narrative, working mainly through Gavin Stevens, to expatiate on various matters: above all, on the South and what Stevens chooses to call 'Sambo'. There is a perceptible slackening of narrative tension, in fact, even before the true murder weapon and the true murderer are exposed: as Stevens expands on the idea which he feels the adventures of Charles and his confederates illustrates, that the South must be left to implement racial justice without interference from the North. And that slackening is only compounded when the talking goes on after the event – about the need, as it is put at one point,

> to defend not Lucas not even the union of the United States but the United States from the outlanders North East and West who with the highest of motives and intentions (let us say) are essaying to divide it at a time when no people dare risk division by using federal laws and federal police to abolish Lucas's shameful condition.[73]

Faulkner does try to restore some narrative punch to the final pages of the novel, with a piece of serious comedy: Lucas Beauchamp insists on paying Stevens for his services and demands a receipt. Lucas will be in debt to nobody; nor does he expect anything less than the politeness and paperwork that white people believe they owe each other. But this hardly compensates for the sense that the story was over some time ago. And it does not take away from the uneasiness created, not only by the garrulousness of the dominant narrative voice, but also by the tendentious nature of the arguments that have been erected over the tale of detection.

Those arguments revolve around the idea of change through accommodation, the belief that the South can and must solve its own problems. Most contemporary critics and reviewers of *Intruder in the Dust* correctly saw it as a novel with a thesis, developing Faulkner's notions about what to do over the racial issue. As a result, Faulkner found himself attacked, on the one side, by Southern conservatives, who wanted no accommodation of any kind made for black people, and, on the other, by black people and those whites of a more liberal inclination, Northern or Southern, who saw Faulkner's stance as, at best, a form of self-delusion and, at worst, a delaying tactic. The generalized argument about race relations is, in fact, the weakest element in the racial strand of the novel. It is easy to drive a coach and horses through the holes in that argument; and, over the years, many have done so. Quite apart from the simple empirical fact that Stevens admits, that Southerners had not been conspicuous in their pursuit of racial justice up until then, there are some serious conceptual flaws at work here. Stevens, and the narrative voice, dismiss the notion of law as a means of social change and argue vigorously against dissonance and division: to impose racial equity, so the argument goes, using legal instruments or whatever, will divide black from white and Northerner from Southerner. This is clearly to ignore in principle what was proved in practice only a few years after *Intruder in the Dust* was published, by the 1954 Supreme Court decision on the 'separate but equal' defence: that, while the law alone cannot initiate or ensure change, it can serve as an agency or conduit through which change is channelled and promoted. And, even more remarkably perhaps, it is to overlook Faulkner's own ample testimony to the potentially creative nature of division: time and again in his fiction, it is crisis, confrontation and outright opposition that precipitate transformations, personal and social. In all his best work, Faulkner shows that (*pace* Gavin Stevens) to divide may be precisely to change.

That so many commentators on *Intruder in the Dust* have found it easy to extrapolate its social message and then argue for or (more frequently) against it is, in any event, a measure of how casually it sits on top of the plot. It is perfectly possible to talk about Gavin Stevens and his ideas about race without even referring to the story of Lucas Beauchamp, on which those ideas supposedly depend; in fact, more often than not, this is the way it is done. The fit between plot and polemic is, by any standards, an imperfect one: not least, because it is difficult, to the point of impossibility, to connect Lucas to the rhetoric about 'Sambo' that characterizes the later part of the narrative. The character of Lucas to whom we are introduced here is far removed from the notional figure of the black Southerner that Stevens spends so much time discussing. In part this is because, like the Lucas Beauchamp we meet in *Go Down, Moses*, what Lucas emphasizes about his identity is not its racial dimension but the dimensions of gender and family: he is, he insists, a proud descendant by a male line of Lucius Quintus Carothers McCaslin. This could be construed as a strategy on Lucas's part, a calculated way of using genealogy to resist local attempts to (as Gavin Stevens puts it) 'make a nigger out of him'. Certainly, there is an element of this in his behaviour. The subtle game Lucas plays with Charles Mallison, for instance, over the money and presents that the white boy tries to give him, suggests as much – as does the way he reacts to one racial slur (and nearly gets killed as a result) by pointing out that the kind of people who insult him 'aint', as he puts it, 'even Edmondses'. However, the insistence on the patriarchal status of Beauchamp is something shared by the narrative. The reader never sees him in anything other than the terms in which Charles sees him: as a solitary figure ('I aint got no friends') encased in the marks of his patriarchal status, among them a broadcloth suit, a fine raked hat and a heavy watch-chain. Even his toothpick is gold, Charles observes, 'such as his own grandfather had used'.[74] This perception or positioning of Lucas in the novel is a definite advantage as far as its initiation element is concerned. Lucas Beauchamp, still, solitary and laconic, becomes one of those grandfatherly figures in Faulkner's work who are, in fact, the true father-figures. His quiet presence – and, even more, his authoritative voice and the vision of him looming in the young protagonist's consciousness – help initiate Charles into the condition of manhood, what it means to take responsibility for himself. However, it does further problematize the racial strand: because Lucas stands apart both from the generic portrait of black people that Stevens paints and from the other black characters. On top of that, Lucas's immobility strangely absents him from the detective story element. Going against his original plan of having the black character himself solve the murder of which he is accused, Faulkner allows the white boy to do all the running, to provide the active resistance. So, when the novel refers specifically to racial injustice, to black restiveness or collaboration between black and white Southerners, it is not really the figure of Lucas Beauchamp that springs to mind. Lucas is an interesting, problematical character; in many of his little social gestures he is, in his own terms, deeply subversive. But he hardly seems an appropriate figure on whom to build the generalized argument about race. For he is trapped, not in the vocabulary of 'nigger' and 'Sambo', but in a different kind of language, in which he is not so much the actor as the acted upon. He is sprung from jail in the end, but he is never really freed from the prison of determining white actions and judgements.

It is important to make a distinction here about Lucas Beauchamp. In terms of his reported actions, Lucas often challenges the preconceptions of his white neighbours. The most moving example of this is the moment when Charles Mallison realizes that Lucas's failure to recognize him once sprang from grief over the death of his wife: even if that moment does happen to recall 'Pantaloon in Black' in a diminished key (*'He was grieving'*. Charles thinks, *'You dont have to not be a nigger in order to grieve'*). As far as the fundamental representation of him is concerned, however, issuing from the deep structure of the novel (to borrow a term used earlier), Lucas is a less challenging figure: something which even the way he grieves seems to indicate. Lucas is manifestly a gentleman, whose grieving is characteristically quiet and contained, a function of his aristocratic reserve. Violence is foreign to him in a way that it is not to, say, Rider or Joe Christmas; he responds to everything with a patrician dignity. This is not necessarily to wish that Lucas had committed an act of violence, or alternatively reacted with violence of emotion: although if he had it would have made the whole issue of black actions and white perceptions more provocative and potentially enlightening – just as it is in 'Pantaloon in Black' and *Light in August* or, for that matter, Richard Wright's novel *Native Son* (1940). But it is to point out how unlikely, even impossible, the idea of Lucas's guilt is from the first: because, however threatening his mere presence may be to some of the other characters white and black, he does not threaten the dominant discourse of the narrative, which inscribes him as an authoritative, deeply reassuring figure. He is, we are constantly reminded, like Charles Mallison's grandfather, a patriarch full of years and honour. As such he benefits, not only from continual references to his composed manner and air of simple authority, but also (and more significantly) from the patrician tendencies of the novel as a whole: the moral investment *Intruder in the Dust* clearly has in the patriarchal tradition of the South. Violence in this story is the prerogative of those who, in Lucas's words, 'aint even Edmondses'. There is no sense of what is called 'the loud fury of blood and revenge' coming from the privileged classes in general, let alone the plantation gentry: 'doctors and lawyers and ministers'[75] are conspicuous by their absence, we are told, from the mob gathering in the town square. Nor is there any intimation that, if not actively involved, they are nevertheless complicit. On the contrary, members of the patrician class are seen, actually or potentially, as redeemers. Roth Edmonds, we learn, would have been able to contain the threat of lynching, had he not unfortunately been in a Memphis hospital. Gavin Stevens does his sometimes ineffectual best, once he is persuaded to help. Above all, the lady with the oldest surviving name in the county is one of the rescuers who dig up the grave to discover the truth. Not only that, she then sits in front of the jail as a kind of moral defence: the sacrosanct nature of her gender and status will be enough, evidently, to discourage the mob from breaking in to seize Lucas, who they believe is there.

Just how comfortably Lucas fits into the patrician mould is intimated by the description of his home in the opening chapter, when Charles Mallison enters it for the first time. The home and its furnishings are described in reverent detail: as if they measured not only the parameters of Lucas's ordinary environment but also the mental and moral fabric of his life. No attempt is made to romanticize home and belongings in an obvious way: the furniture includes, we are told, 'a battered cheap Grand Rapids dresser' as well as 'a vast shadowy tester bed which had probably come out of old Carothers McCaslin's house'. But what emerges from all this scrupulously careful itemizing of property and possessions is, like the account of the MacCallum family home in *Flags in the Dust/Sartoris*, a portrait conceived in nostalgia. This is not least because the focus is upon objects preserved from, and often commemorative of, the past: such as 'the gold-framed portrait-group on its gold easel', in which Lucas appears (along with his wife) in characteristic, patriarchal uniform, with 'only the toothpick missing'. The references to the relative poverty of the surroundings – to 'a bare worn quite clean paintless rugless floor',[76] for instance – only serve to foreground their intrinsic dignity: they have, we are asked to infer, an authenticity, a nobility not acquired from wealth or show but learned instinctively from the past. This is an environment that stands at the opposite extreme from the grubby random world of those poor whites who constitute most of the lynch mob. For that matter, it is equally far removed from the suburban anonymity of the new South where, as the narrator perceives it, every man assumes 'an inevictable quit-claim on a wife a car a radio and an old-age pension'. The net effect of this loving portrait of hearth and home is to monumentalize their owner: to enable a transformation of Lucas into a figure of whom the narrative can deeply approve, because he is neither of the mob nor of the modern. He is still, quiet and solid, like the objects that define him; he has been given the sanction, the stamp of approval of earlier times. In terms of the more fundamental, patrician values of the book, he is not really represented as other at all. He is not 'one of them', in short, as far as the narrative eye perceives him; quite the contrary, he is 'one of us'.

The wedge that this seminal conception of Lucas Beauchamp drives into the surface arguments of the book is not difficult to see. The black/white division on which those surface arguments concentrate takes a back seat, whenever Lucas is around, to considerations of class, gender and culture. What matters about him, what determines the narrative representation of him, has very little to do with his racial identity: it stems from the fact that he is a patriarchal figure, descended by a male line from one of the earliest settlers in the county. As such, he is an emblem and agent of continuity, and he exposes the hidden agenda of the novel. *Intruder in the Dust* may talk about change through accommodation; as the portrait of Lucas suggests, however, its fundamental investment is in conservation and restitution – the maintenance of the past rather than the management of the future. This is not to accuse Faulkner of disingenuousness, as some early, liberal critics of the novel did. There is no doubt that, however muddled his views on race might have been, he was in regional terms a moderate, who hoped to see the condition of Southern blacks significantly improved over time. Equally, it is clear that he tried to inject those views into *Intruder in the Dust*, using Gavin Stevens to articulate them – and to tell the North, not least, that the South was entitled and needed to solve its own problems. The fact is, though, that the fundamental drift of the novel is towards the pieties and practices of the past. It is from these pieties, after all, that Lucas derives his authority. The language takes flight on those occasions when 'the enduring land' and those few people who still live on it, and with it, are celebrated. One notable passage, for instance, offers this for our veneration as 'the land's living symbol':

> a formal group of ritual almost mystic significance identical and monotonous as milestones tying the county-seat to the county's ultimate rim as milestones would: the beast the plough and the man integrated in one foundationed into the frozen wave of their furrow tremendous with effort yet at the same time vacant of progress, ponderable immovable and immobile like groups of wrestling statuary set against the land's immensity . . .[77]

Conversely, the idiom of *Intruder in the Dust* acquires a harsher edge and a sharper bite whenever the opposite of these 'ponderable and immovable and immobile' forms of life is contemplated: which is to say, the feverish movement and noise of the emerging culture. 'The automobile has become our national sex symbol', Gavin Stevens laments; and, as if to prove his point, the town as Charles perceives it seems to be full of the rust and confusion of machinery. Towards the end of the novel, for instance, Jefferson town square is described in this way:

> the radios had to play louder than ever through their supercharged amplifiers to be heard above the mutter of exhausts and swish of tyres and the grind of gears and the constant horns, so that long before you even reached the Square you not only couldn't tell where one began and the other left off but you didn't even have to try to distinguish what any of them were playing or trying to sell you.[78]

In this narrative, stillness and silence are embraced with a passion, noise and mobility are the enemy. To be 'vacant of progress' is the model prescribed by the book's deep structure; not to move at all, or as little as possible, is its ideal mode – like the land, or the heroic statuary of farmer, beast and plough, or, for that matter, like the monumental figure of Lucas Beauchamp.

Faulkner does try to take account of this fundamentally conservative drift, towards a presciption of immobility, in some of the arguments he gives to Stevens. In particular, he has Stevens distinguish between the kind of 'homogeneous' culture that might come about, from a confederation of Southerners white and black, and what he terms the culture of 'the second best' that characterizes modern America: 'the cheap shoddy music', as Stevens puts it,

> the cheap flash baseless overvalued money, the glittering edifice of publicity foundationed on nothing like a cardhouse over an abyss and all the noisy muddle of political activity . . . – all the spurious uproar produced by men deliberately fostering . . . our national passion for the mediocre.[79]

Quite apart from the unpleasantly racial terms in which this attack on modern culture is sometimes couched, however (there is, for instance, a reference to immigrants as 'the coastal spew of Europe'), there remains the problem of exactly what kind of change is anticipated. All the approval (and detail) is reserved for what survives of the 'homogeneous' cultures, the social practices preserved from the past: such as that 'capacity to wait and endure and survive' which is identified as the principal legacy of black life. It seems superfluous to point out that those cultures were evolved in conditions of racial separation, and so could hardly be sustained or work in a more fluid, interracial climate: that, in other words, they do not in themselves offer a preliminary basis, let alone an adequate model, for change. All that needs to be noted, surely, is what was remarked upon by several critics of the novel when it first appeared – people, as it happens, from different ends of the political spectrum: that, when it comes to critical, determining points in the discussion – such as a consideration of just how change is to come about, and what precisely change will produce – the language tends to become vague and circumlocutory, and the argument is often specious, sophistical or just plain muddled.

When Gavin Stevens, for example, imagines Northerners objecting that Southerners have done little to improve race relations over the previous hundred years because (as the generic Northerner is imagined saying to the Southerner) '*you not only cant you wont*', his reply is a bewildering mixture of historical revisionism, blame, warning and defiance. Northern invaders after the Civil War, he claims, '*did more than even John Brown to stalemate Lucas's freedom*'; a new, moral invasion of the South will promote not only division but '*dissolution*'; and besides, he says, if '*we*' '*cant*' or '*wont*', '*then you shall not*'.[80] By this time, it is difficult to tell where the argument is coming from, let alone what recipe it has for the future. The programme of social transformation of the South by the South seems to have been temporarily dislodged by the need to justify the past – and to make a stand in the present, and possible future, that recalls some of Faulkner's own, more notorious comments about fighting for Mississippi, over the racial issue, if the need arose. The case for change has been supplanted by the case for the South, in scarcely suppressed defence of the proposition 'my home and birthplace right or wrong'. Here and elsewhere, in fact, *Intruder in the Dust* is torn apart by its contradictions, the fissures in and between different layers of narrative. The explicit acceptance of the need for social transformation comes into conflict with a profound attachment to the 'ritual almost mystic significance' of the old ways. The analysis of the division between black and white is complicated, and even disqualified, by the narrative investment in the patriarchal tradition. The talk about progress is overshadowed by the rhythms of commemoration and repetition. And the detective story, the story of Lucas Beauchamp, and the arguments over the South and 'Sambo' not only do not fit together, very often they actively work against each other. Stevens is unable to construct a coherent, plausible case related to the experience of the novel, quite simply, because that task is an impossible one. At its best, *Intruder in the Dust* is a register of the confusions of the time when it was written and the man who wrote it: confusions, that is, of race, region and class. But it does not, and by its nature cannot, offer anything approaching a solution to them.

What emerges relatively unscathed from all of this is the initiation element in the book: the story, intermittently developed, of how the young, white protagonist grows up under the pressure of learning about himself and what is called at one point 'the long tradition of his native land'. One reason for the relative success of this narrative strand is simple: in itself, it is done with economy and considerable skill. At the beginning, Charles Mallison is introduced to the reader in a state of innocent identification with his surroundings. The crisis over Lucas and his supposed murder of

Vinson Gowrie creates rupture. By the end (of the initiation element, that is, not the novel, which goes on for longer than this requires), Charles has re-entered the community on a more knowing, critical basis: he has learned to see his culture as flawed but improvable, and himself as a separate, active citizen. The experience of initiation exercised a particularly strong hold on Faulkner's mind, which was why he rehearsed it so often and, as here, so well. And, this time, it is given a strong ritualistic element as it is in 'The Bear': for instance, the only time in the book when Charles Mallison is named is when Lucas assigns him his task, as if the quest itself has given him identity. Charles must see and learn the truth for himself, Lucas will not tell him; and as he digs up the grave with his two confederates, he seems to be exhuming not only a corpse but the buried past – the repressed myths of his culture and the suppressed self, his own dark twin of knowledge. It is symptomatic of the ritualistic, rather than pychological, approach to the experience of growing up on this occasion that Charles experiences 'shame' over the burden of debt he feels towards Lucas: 'shame', that is, a collective, communal feeling, rather than the more personal, inward-directed emotion of guilt. What Charles learns about, Faulkner is clearly indicating, is 'a part of his heritage': 'the dirt, the earth which had bred his bones and those of his fathers for six generations', as it is put at one point, and that 'was still shaping him into not just a man but a specific man . . . with . . . the specific passions . . . of a specific kind and even race'.[81] His initiation is a personal one, of course, but it is also intended to be one representative of his community. The rituals aspire to a cultural dimension here, as they do in 'The Bear': on some level, at least, Charles is meant to be acting on behalf of his 'kind', as he struggles to renew himself by coming to terms with the past.

Whether this cultural dimension is convincing is very much open to question: the rituals work on a primal level, as they do in 'The Bear', but there is surely insufficient dramatic evidence to link Charles up with the specifics of Southern history. Quite simply, we know too little about Charles's 'fathers for six generations'; there is no equivalent here of the McCaslin family ledger. What is indisputable, though, is that Faulkner manages to give a mythical resonance to the initiation story while staying true to the particulars of a personal case. What also helps, and is another reason for the relative success of this strand in the novel, is that, for once, the different elements do fit together or, if not always that, do not actively conflict. The point has already been made that the representation of Lucas Beauchamp, while it tends to vitiate the racial dimension of *Intruder in the Dust*, does not conflict with the initiation story: on the contrary, it makes Lucas even more convincing as the instigator of the quest and the source of authority. The detective story element works well here too because it enables Faulkner to develop what is, by now, a familiar conceit with him: that is, the sleuth as historian, resurrecting the past and in the process coming to know himself. Even the rhetoric about race, mostly put in the mouth of Gavin Stevens, has a part to play. If Mr Mallison is a false father-figure and Beauchamp a true father-figure then, in this context, Stevens can be construed as something just as interesting: a paternal presence who learns along with the son, and then attempts to turn that learning into words. The translation process is imperfect, by any standards. But that matters less, from the standpoint of Charles growing up, since what is crucial here is the ritual rather than the rhetoric: the quietness and relative simplicity of the young boy's progression towards manhood makes us forget, for a while, about Stevens's liking for ever more convoluted talk.

For a while, that is, but not all the time: the problem is that the initiation element hardly monopolizes the novel. Quite often, it disappears; in particular, like the other dramatic strands it tends to become swamped by the discussions of the South and 'Sambo' towards the end. And, while it does not lose or even gains from the other narrative elements, it cannot resolve their intrinsic confusions, or the contradictions that cut across the detective tale, the representation of Lucas and the talk about race. Charles is eventually restored to the community; and he has clearly been educated, during the period of his alienation from it. As far as the other members of the community are concerned, though, nothing much seems to have been learned. The routines of the town square are reinstated in the final chapter of the novel; after a brief and violent interruption, normal service is resumed. Gavin Stevens insists that this is not what it seems; the people of Jefferson do feel guilty over the way they have treated Lucas, he argues, and will spend the rest of their days performing numerous little acts of contrition. But what they appear to be given over to, at the close of the book, is not so much gestures of compensation as elaborate rituals of forgetting. The restoration of habit, the rehabilitation of the customary, works at the very least to cast doubt on Stevens's claim: it hardly seems likely that the town will make restitution, let alone that significant social alterations are in the pipeline. Apart from his defence of the moral consciousness of his neighbours, Stevens devotes most of his closing remarks to his by now familiar assaults on the consequences of progress. The closing exchange between him and Lucas does, it is true, restore a flagging narrative, with the kind of clipped, punchy dialogue that Faulkner was probably reminded of during his collaboration with Howard Hawks – and it certainly can be read as a subtle piece of power-play on Lucas's part:

'Now what?' his uncle said. 'What are you waiting for now?'
'My receipt,' Lucas said.[82]

However, this exchange only adds to the feeling of closure: a debt is being paid in full, the sense is, and this particular account book can now be closed. *Intruder in the Dust* is a troublingly uneven novel, rife with contradictions: dissonances that issued out of the way it was written and were, in any case, implicit in those positions on race and region that Faulkner felt compelled to embrace. One simple measure of this is that, by the end, the reader knows Charles Mallison has grown up, but does not know for certain what he has grown up into: just what, in other words, are and will be the cultural determinants of his manhood. That subject remains obscured, caught in the crossfire of conflicting claims and speculations – a puzzle, in short, much tougher than the one of who killed Vinson Gowrie, that even the sharpest of detectives might find impossible to solve.

6

The Way Home

Intruder in the Dust marked the beginning of financial security for Faulkner. The film rights to the book were sold to Hollywood for $50,000. And, when filming began in Oxford in 1949, Faulkner found himself, for once, the object of favourable local attention. A full-page advertisement appeared in the town newspaper the *Eagle*, for instance, financed by merchants who wished to announce their pride in the fact that Oxford had been chosen as the setting for the film version of 'Mr. William Faulkner's Great Story, Intruder in the Dust'. Faulkner's relation to fame, particularly in his homeplace, remained ambivalent, however. He was gratified by his new public status in a way, if only because it made local people see him, at least for a while, as a glamorous figure rather than an eccentric one. 'Much excitement here, since they are making a movie of my book in Oxford', he wrote in a letter early in 1949, 'It's too bad I'm no longer young enough to cope with all the local girls who are ready and eager to glide into camera focus on their backs.'[1] But, as a sardonic comment like this one indicated, he was aware just how fleeting and adventitious that status was. One of the problems of his later life and writing, in fact, was that, while he felt compelled sometimes to cut a public figure – to the extent, that is, of making public declarations of principle, even in his fiction – there was a strong undertow of feeling within him that tended to associate the public with the factitious. A deeply private man by instinct and training, his best work had entered the public arena by way of the recognition that public and private are two sides of the same coin, joined together through the currency of language. But as he was nudged, with some reluctance, into a public role – the successful man of letters speaking from the South – that recognition began to falter; and Faulkner oscillated with ever more

11. Faulkner at Notre Dame, Paris, 1925. (Courtesy Brodsky Collection, copy supplied by Center for Faulkner Studies, Southeast Missouri State University)

12. The house Faulkner and his wife Estelle bought in 1929: 'Rowanoak', later spelled 'Rowan Oak'. (Courtesy UPI/Bettman Archives)

13. Meta Carpenter, William Faulkner, Ben Wasson and Dorothy Parker on the patio of playwright Marc Connelly's Hollywood home, 1935. © Brodsky Collection, copy supplied by Center for Faulkner Studies, Southeast Missouri State University.

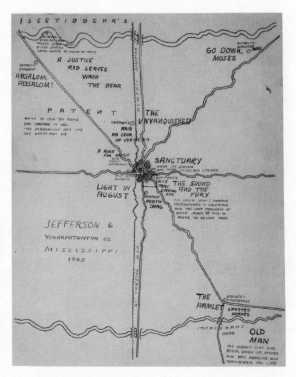

14. Faulkner's 1945 pen-and-ink map of Yoknapatawpha County. (Courtesy Brodsky Collection, copy supplied by Center for Faulkner Studies, Southeast Missouri State University)

15. Faulkner with Joan Williams, whom he met in 1949. (Courtesy of Joan Williams)

16. Faulkner receiving the Nobel Prize for Literature from the King of Sweden, Stockholm, 1950. (Courtesy of Popper-foto)

17. The outline, day by day, of *A Fable* (1954) on the walls of Faulkner's office at Rowan Oak. The small bed was used for rest between periods of writing. (Courtesy UPI/Bettman Archive)

18. 'Thursday', a detail from the outline for *A Fable*. (Courtesy William Faulkner Collection [#6074.41] Special Collections Department, Manuscript Division, University of Virginia Library)

19. Faulkner reading beneath a portrait of his great-grandfather, Rowan Oak, 1955. (Courtesy UPI/Bettman Archive)

20. Faulkner displaying his newly won 'pink' huntsman's coat at a Thanksgiving fox hunt at Farmington Country Club, Virginia, 1960. (Courtesy UPI/Bettman Archive)

21. Faulkner, March 20th, 1962, less than four months before his death. (Courtesy UPI/Bettman Archive, photo by Jack Cofield)

22. The small desk and typewriter that Faulkner used in his office at Rowan Oak. (Courtesy UPI/Bettman Archive)

23. The porch at Rowan Oak, where Faulkner would often sit in the late afternoon looking over the garden and woods surrounding his home. (Courtesy UPI/Bettman Archive)

violence between a public face and a private space that seemed to be definitively separate, mutually exclusive. There was, inevitably, loss on both sides. For if the strength of Faulkner's earlier work had stemmed from his ability to weave private and public together into one seamless web of dialogue, then the weakness of the later, where it occurs, comes from a disentangling of the threads, a rupture between words in the market place and words in the mind. What author and reader alike are left with is, on the one hand, a public address system and, on the other, the gravitation towards solipsism and silence: worlds as far apart, really, as the podia on which Faulkner received his prizes and gave his speeches – and the hotel rooms to which he retired, sometimes, simply to drink.

As many commentators have pointed out, the emergence of Gavin Stevens as a major character in Faulkner's work is symptomatic of this new bias and fissure. Stevens permitted Faulkner to manage two, quite separate things at once: the manufacture of public rhetoric, and the replication of private anxieties. Stevens could act as a mouthpiece: making declarations of principle that were more or less coextensive with his creator's opinions, and which tended to go dramatically untested and unchallenged. And he could also act out deep-rooted fears and fantasies by recalling aspects of Faulkner's own emotional life and realizing Faulkner's instinctive need for imaginative mastery and control. Much of this is evident from the book Faulkner published in 1949. 'I am thinking of a "Gavin Stevens" volume, more or less detective stories', Faulkner wrote to his publisher at the end of 1948. Nearly all of the stories, he explained, were already in print. However, he went on,

> There is one more which no one has bought. The reason is, it is a novel which I tried to compress into short story length. It is a love story, in which Stevens prevents a crime (murder) not for justice but to gain (he is now fifty plus) the childhood sweetheart which he lost 20 years ago. It will probably run to about 150 pages, which should make a volume as big as INTRUDER.[2]

The final story was to give its title to the volume, *Knight's Gambit*, and, in the event, also helped to foreground the intimate relation between character and author – in terms of emotional temperature as well as age. Like Faulkner, it seemed, Stevens had had a childhood sweetheart who had married an older man, had given her husband a boy and a girl, and had lived abroad for years before returning home. And, like Faulkner in terms of dreams rather than destiny, Stevens was now in his early fifties reaching out to recover a youthful love, the lost girl of his earliest, original desires. 'He was a Harvard graduate', the narrator says of Stevens in the first story in *Knight's Gambit*, called simply 'Smoke',

> a loose-jointed man with a mop of untidy iron-gray hair, who could discuss Einstein with college professors and who spent whole afternoons among squatting men against the walls of country stores, talking to them in their idiom.[3]

Faulkner could be cruelly ironic about Stevens at times, and the physical features – which are quite unlike Faulkner's – act as a distancing measure of sorts. Nevertheless, the autobiographical dimension is there, as much in the satisfaction of needs as in the representation of facts. In *Knight's Gambit*, in particular, Stevens not only speaks for the author on occasion, nor even just replicates elements in his life: he also enjoys advantages beyond his creator's reach. At ease equally with professors and simple country folk, enjoying an emotional fulfilment that does not seem to impinge on his bachelor freedom, Stevens in these stories realizes a social fluency, a composure and intellectual control that Faulkner himself could, evidently, only imagine.

One reason, and the major one, why the sense of composure and control is so powerful in *Knight's Gambit* is that all of the stories that go to make up the volume are fairly rudimentary detective tales. Whether or not the detective story as such is a fundamentally conservative form is open to argument. What is far less arguable is the fact that, as Faulkner practises the detective story form here, it acts to manage risk and control danger. The structure of each story in *Knight's Gambit* is basically the same. There is disruption in the community, taking the readily decipherable shape of violence – and violence that emanates, more often than not, from an outsider, an interloper. The detective seeks out, isolates and resolves the disruption. The system, the communal *status quo* then returns to normal working order. In earlier Faulkner narratives, violence, physical or emotional or both, was often an agent of change, seen as unpleasant perhaps but inevitable. In these tales, however, it becomes the means by which the magisterial figure of Gavin Stevens can prove his worth and confirm, eventually, the continuity of communal practices; it enables him, in short, to define himself as a solid citizen in a solid community. The roles that Stevens assumes as detective are, certainly, multiple: the way he goes about solving a mystery and resolving disruption differs, in fact, with each individual story. But the aim remains constant: to isolate the cause of communal disease and instability. And the effect is always the same: to restore the body politic to an apparently sound and pristine health.

In the first story in *Knight's Gambit*, for instance, Stevens is the detective as orator and magician. He uses his courtroom skills and a simple conjuring trick to ensnare the murderer. In the second, 'Monk', he is, by contrast, the detective as artist. 'I will have to try to tell about Monk', says the narrator of the tale, Charles Mallison,

> I mean, actually try – a deliberate attempt to bridge the inconsistencies in his brief and sordid and unoriginal history . . . Because it is only in literature that the paradoxical and even mutually negativing anecdotes in the history of the human heart can be juxtaposed and annealed by art into verisimilitude and credibility.[4]

However, it is not Charles but his Uncle Gavin who works out the logic of Monk's story: using what Charles himself terms 'the nebulous tools of supposition and inference and invention' to 'make something out' of the evidence available to him – and, in the event, turning detection into an interpretive act that depends on finding 'the right ciphers'. If in 'Monk' Stevens 'reads' meaning into his subject and then 'writes' that meaning for us, then in the third tale, 'Hand Upon the Waters', he adventures on discovery. As the abundance of gambling references in this story alert us, he becomes rather obviously the detective as risk-taker, guesser and gambler: who gambles, among other things, that those responsible for a particular murder will return to the scene of their crime, provided the right bait is set.

In the next two stories in the book, 'Tomorrow' and 'An Error in Chemistry', Stevens assumes the masks of, respectively, the detective as narratee or historian and the detective as memorialist, the keeper of communal lore. 'Tomorrow' is easily the more impressive of these two. In it, just for once, Stevens says very little. He wants to find out why one local man forced a mistrial by standing out from his eleven fellow-jurors; and, to do this, he has to learn about that man's life by listening to the stories told by his neighbours. Stevens's words are few, and signify careful attention to the words of others: 'tell' (so he can hear), 'wait' (so he can absorb what he is being told), 'of course' (when he has absorbed and understood). 'Just tell it', Stevens asks his informants, 'I've got to know.' He is told, and knows; and, in the process, he comes to learn – the reader is advised – about the 'lowly and invincible of the earth'. He becomes the guardian of a history that is at once particular and general. 'An Error in Chemistry' is perhaps the feeblest story in the volume. The trick on which it turns is simple: Stevens exposes a supposed master of disguise, who is also the villainous murderer of the piece, because that murderer makes one elementary mistake. Assuming the appearance of an old Southern landowner, one of his victims, the murderer mixes a cold toddy for Stevens and the local sheriff in the wrong way. The outsider reveals his status as outsider through his ignorance of communal practice; the villain discloses who he is simply by not knowing what any upstanding male member of the community would have known from young manhood. 'Even I knew', Charles Mallison, the youthful narrator, observes, 'that to make a cold toddy you do not put the sugar into the whisky' as the murderer has tried to do. 'You first put the water into the glass', he explains, 'and dissolve the sugar into the water in a ritual almost; then you add the whisky.'[5] All that Stevens has to do here, really, is to confirm the self-exposure of the villain. As keeper of the flame, it is up to him to place an error that, as Charles points out, is not just one of chemistry but one of communal custom: he has to see, and to note, that the rites have not been properly observed.

As Faulkner explained to his publisher, the title story in *Knight's Gambit* witnesses Stevens assuming the role of detective as lover. By means of a complicated plot, that mixes the memories and desires of its author into the life of its protagonist, a planned murder is prevented and, in the event, a woman once loved and lost is recovered. Faulkner does not

completely shy away from criticism of his lawyer hero in this tale. For instance, he pokes gentle fun at Stevens's desire to turn 'the Old Testament
back into the classic Greek into which it had been translated from its lost
Hebrew infancy':[6] a task that seems as pointless as it is evidently protracted
(it has already preoccupied him, we are told, for twenty years). But the
major thrust of the narrative is towards identification and closure: authorial identification with the dreams of the lover-detective, that is, and a
conclusion that combines the exiling of villainous influences and outsiders with a marriage union that restores and redeems the past. It is indica-
tive of the wish-fulfilment nature of the story that even the potentially
disruptive elements implicit in the relation between Gavin Stevens and the
woman he eventually marries, Melisandre Harriss, are siphoned off into a
safe – which is to say, controllable – space. Gavin and Melisandre may have
been childhood sweethearts: but there is no hint of regression at work
here, let alone the suggestions of incest inherent in the family romance.
Introversion is the preserve of another relationship: the fierce affection
that Melisandre's son, the would-be murderer Max, feels for his sister and
that helps tempt him towards violence. So it becomes Gavin Stevens's
function not to collude in regressive impulses but to expose and expel
them. In this story, the intimate affection the protagonist feels for a lost
lady is not just unaccompanied by destructive impulses, it is directly opposed to them. The hero manages to reunite with the object of his youthful desires *and* to dismiss the dark twin: sending Max, and his coiled-up,
introjected passions, packing.

'His was indeed a split personality', the narrator observes of Stevens at
one point in 'Knight's Gambit',

> the one, the lawyer, the county attorney who walked and breathed and
> displaced air; the other, the garrulous facile voice so garrulous and facile
> that it seemed to have no connection with reality at all and presently hearing
> it was like listening not even to fiction but to literature.[7]

As a passage like this eloquently testifies, Faulkner could be well aware of
his own inclinations even while he was indulging them. The garrulous
voice that tends to make reality evaporate, the gap between the public face
that 'breathed and displaced air' and the private space that 'seemed to
have no connection with reality at all': in describing the 'split personality'
of his 'county attorney' character, Faulkner is clearly diagnosing his own
case. That diagnosis does not feed into the author's creative practice in
'Knight's Gambit' or any of the other stories in the volume, however: at
least, not in any way that radically alters the narrative. Stevens's voice is
allowed to dominate, to assume authority despite the qualms Faulkner expresses about it here. And the closure towards which every one of the tales
moves is founded on the determining power, the control that the mere
presence of Stevens exerts: using his ratiocinative skills, and his knowledge
of the community and custom, to move things towards a reassuringly stable

conclusion. The dominating images of 'Knight's Gambit', it has been pointed out, are horseflesh and chess. What is worth adding to this, perhaps, is that the imagery of horses is not nearly as definitive a force in the narrative as the references to chess are. Horses connote instinct, destructive, subliminal urges that are, for the most part, conspicuous by their absence from the tale. Love is love remembered; hate is something alluded to; we never really see these or other emotions *at work* in the characters. Chess, on the other hand, goes right to the heart of the moral imperatives of this and the other stories. It describes exactly the representation of the way things are here: a complex puzzle, a game that the astute gamesmaster can not only control but also resolve. The gamesmaster, the detective: these are two expressions of the same impulse, the motive that shapes *Knight's Gambit* and its characterization of Gavin Stevens. Private anxiety can be and is mastered in the public space, the shaping assumption is. Passion becomes a problem that can be solved if only the correct strategies are followed, the vital clues addressed, the right voice or ritual used to displace the real.

As far as the public space of Faulkner's own life was concerned, the next few years were to confirm his eminence. The volume, *Collected Stories of William Faulkner*, was published in 1950 to general critical acclaim. His fiction as a whole began to win sales and earn him money: by the end of 1950, for instance, more than 100,000 copies of his books had been sold in Modern Library editions, nearly two and a half million had been printed in paperback, and another third of a million copies were about to be published. And the prizes and literary awards began to flow in his direction: most notably, he was informed in November 1950 that he had been give the Nobel Prize 'for his powerful and independent artistic contribution in America's new literature of the novel'. Gratified though he was by all this attention, however, Faulkner continued to struggle for some privacy. His first reaction on learning that he had won the Nobel Prize was characteristic. 'I won't be able to come to receive the prize myself', he explained to a reporter, 'It's too far away. I am a farmer down here and I can't get away.'[8] Eventually, he was persuaded to go to Stockholm to accept the award in person; Estelle insisted that, while she herself had no desire to visit Sweden, their daughter Jill wanted to go. Nevertheless, Faulkner went into alcoholic hibernation in the period prior to departure: as if the mere thought of the public spotlight, fame and fortune, were enough to drive him to drink. And, during the trip to Sweden, his behaviour was uncertain and erratic. The speech Faulkner gave after accepting the Nobel Prize has become one of his most famous pieces of prose. Phrases like 'the human heart in conflict with itself', or 'I believe that man will not only endure: he will prevail', taken from that speech, have become crucial in shaping the public persona of Faulkner, the great American artist, the distinguished man of letters. The story of his days just prior to the award ceremony and banquet are, however, the record of a man suffering acute anxiety and discomfort in the public gaze, and, when he delivered the speech, nervous, unshaven, speaking rapidly and too far from the microphone, his words were apparently inaudible. In any case, the first reaction to published versions of that speech, in the United States especially, was surely the right one. It might be splendidly stirring, the response was, but how did all those references to 'the old verities and truths of the heart, the old universal truths' fit in with a book like *The Sound and the Fury*? The fame of the Nobel Prize acceptance speech has, by now, perhaps blinded us to the fact that it is, at best, a glorious piece of windy oratory: that tries to make up in terms of rousing cadences for what it lacks in substance. It is as if Faulkner were trying to hide his fragile, private self here behind the bold periods of public declamation: the contrast between the anxious, unshaven, virtually inaudible speaker and the confident, even strident tones of the speech ('I decline . . . I refuse . . . I believe') is a poignant measure of this. Too often in the later novels, intimacies of character and intensities of feeling are submerged under great waves of rhetoric. This offers something with a piquant difference: a private man wilfully losing himself, for a moment, in the public voice – masking his fears and anxieties behind the specious certainties of the big speech.

Those anxieties were, in any event, propelling Faulkner towards another novel. On his return from Stockholm, Faulkner met Meta Carpenter again by arrangement – or Meta Rebner as she now was, since she had remarried the man from whom she had obtained a divorce and was already coming to realize her mistake. They renewed their sexual relationship when they came together in New York, and then continued it when Faulkner returned for a while to Hollywood in 1951 to work with Howard Hawks. By this point in his life, however, the woman onto whom Faulkner was projecting the most intense of his erotic feelings was not Meta, but someone else entirely: Joan Williams, a student and an admirer of his work, who was more than thirty years his junior. This was the 'new young woman' that he always seemed to need; and, even more than on on other, similar occasions, the relationship was fraught with difficulty. 'You want me to be your father', Faulkner observed to the woman he still addressed as 'Miss Williams', shortly after they first met in the summer of 1949. Which was partly true: Joan Williams, an aspiring writer, wanted to learn from Faulkner. She wanted him as a teacher as well as, probably, a father-figure. Faulkner, as usual, wanted many things: a sister, a confidante, a disciple perhaps but, above all, a lover. There were clandestine meetings. Estelle got wind of the new involvement and tried, unsuccessfully, to stop it. Joan continued to insist that what she wanted was to learn from the master. Faulkner continued to need her as more than just a pupil. Nevertheless, he was astute and desperate enough to realize that one way of maintaining contact was to go along with the idea that he was helping her to write. As long ago as 1933, he had written to his publishers about a new novel that he had in mind. It had, he said, 'a good title, I think: REQUIEM FOR A NUN'. 'It will be about a nigger woman', he added; 'It will be a little on the esoteric side, like AS I LAY DYING.' He had even written a few pages before abandoning it, dominated by the character of Gavin Stevens and the image of a jail. Now he asked Joan to help him with a play he had in mind, with the same title. It would, he explained in a letter written to her early in 1950, be about 'a "nigger" woman, a known drunkard and dope user' who 'one day suddenly and for no reason, . . . murdered a child'.[9] He, the master, would sketch the outlines and she, the pupil, would develop the detail. They would collaborate, meeting and writing to each other, until they got it exactly right.

So *Requiem for a Nun* began to be developed as a play, and as a pretext for sustaining relations with Joan Williams. It offered Faulkner the opportunity to think in terms of the more obviously public arena of the stage; and it afforded him occasions for meeting a young woman who, gratifyingly but also maddeningly, thought of him more as a writer and a teacher than as a man and a potential lover. Even at first, there was probably more to it than that. Faulkner had been told by an actress friend, Ruth Ford – a young woman whom he had first met in 1943, when she was a student at the University of Mississippi – that what she wanted, more than anything, was for him to write her a play. He may have had this in mind as he started work on the project. Certainly, he did end up writing a stage version of the *Requiem for a Nun* story which, he insisted, was 'for Ruth . . . until she herself refuses it'. More as there was, though, or might have been, these two, quite separate impulses were the determining ones in pushing him towards his story of 'a "nigger" woman': his interest in public performance – an interest that had been with him from the first, but never properly realized in his own writing – and his burning personal need to find, or invent, some sort of justification for keeping in touch with Joan Williams. 'I tell you again', he wrote to Joan early in 1950, 'the play is yours too. I would not have thought of writing one if I hadn't known you'.[10] But Joan was not interested in even keeping up the pretence that the project was anything other than his, although he continued to send her samples and accounts of his progress.

From fairly early on, Faulkner began to realize that what he was writing was not only not a collaborative work, it was in addition not really a drama. 'It is not a play', he confided to Joan in May 1950, 'will have to be rewritten as a play. It is now some kind of novel.' 'I realise now more than ever that I cant write a play', he told his editor in the same month. And as he worked on the tale of his ' "nigger" woman', Nancy Mannigoe, and found himself more and more involved in resurrecting the story of Temple Drake, he began to think of what he was doing as 'an interesting experiment in form', consisting of 'play-scenes, inside a novel'. By August, he told Joan he was working on 'the scaffolding stuff that holds my three acts in a book': in other words, the three narrative sections. Less than a year later, in June 1951, he told another correspondent, 'I finished the mss. yesterday. I am really tired of writing . . . I'll probably never quit, though, until I die.' But even though the play was now a novel and the act of collaboration had become all his own work, the old, radically mixed motives persisted. Just nine days after declaring that *Requiem for a Nun* was finished, and only five days after the typescript of the final section was in proof, Faulkner wrote to tell Joan that he was coming to New York 'to produce what I still think of as our play, even though you have repudiated it'.[11] *Requiem for a Nun* was completed, gone to the printers, but the desire for public performance, and the need for private satisfaction, were still there burning away. The thirsts that had helped bring the novel into being remained, evidently unquenched, after its printing and even its publication.

At times, as when he was writing to his publishers about the work in progress, Faulkner chose to think of *Requiem for a Nun* as a formal experiment. At others, he would insist that 'it was not experimentation': the book was written the way it was, he would declare, because 'that was the best way to tell that story'. Nearly always, though, he would intimate or even argue that the structure of *Requiem for a Nun* was a necessary one: that what he was after was, as he put it once, 'the contrapuntal effect which comes in orchestration'. 'The hard give-and-take of the dialogue was played against something that was a little mystical', he observed, and that 'made it sharper, more effective'. For all the talk about technique, however, the structure of the novel is a very simple one: with three acts of a highly stylized drama each preceded by a long narrative section that is related in physical context. Act I is set in Jefferson and is preceded by 'The Courthouse', which focuses on the building of the town jail and courthouse and the establishment of the township. Act II is set in the Governor's Mansion in Jackson, the state capital; and, before it, 'The Golden Dome', as one critic comments, 'encapsulates the entire history . . . of civilisation' itself . . . ending with the . . . description of the Jackson, Mississippi of "A.D. 1950" '. Finally, Act III takes us to the Jefferson jail, where Nancy Mannigoe is awaiting execution; and the section that acts as prologue to this weaves in and out of the history of Jefferson, the South and the United States, but its metaphorical hub is that same jailhouse, past and present. This section contains, and concludes with, what is probably the most memorable image of the novel: of a 'scratching almost depthless in a sheet of old barely transparent glass' in the old jail. Made by the jailer's daughter, and saying simply 'Cecilia Farmer April 16th 1861', it appears to the narrator to announce 'across the vast instantaneous intervention, from the long time ago: *Listen, stranger; this was myself: this was I.*'[12] 'The Jail', as this last prologue or preamble is called, alters in style and momentum several times. And there are similar shifts in language elsewhere. 'The Courthouse', for instance, moves from humour and folktale to a more rigorously empirical mode; while 'The Golden Dome' starts off with some evocative, polysyllabic prose, describing the beginnings of geologic time, then gravitates more towards flat matter-of-fact statement the nearer the narrator comes to the present. But although these shifts are striking, they hardly complicate the basic narrative arrangements. *Requiem for a Nun* is not structurally complex or challenging in the way that, say, *As I Lay Dying* and *Absalom, Absalom!* are: Faulkner has simply solved the problem of whether he was writing a drama or a novel by, in a sense, writing both – interleaving novelistic and dramatic sections on related physical planes.

Whether the connection between the narrative and dramatic sections goes further than related planes of space is, not surprisingly, one of the major problems raised by the novel. So, too, is the meaning of the act that occupies the dramatic centre of *Requiem for a Nun*. At the beginning of the story, Nancy Mannigoe has been sentenced to death for the murder of one of the children of Temple Drake. Under the relentless probing and questioning of Gavin Stevens, it gradually emerges that Nancy killed the child in order to stop Temple running off with the brother of Red, her lover in *Sanctuary*, and so ruining her home and the lives of both her children. As a corollary of this, it also becomes clear that Temple had hired a 'nigger dopefiend whore' as a nursemaid in the first place, not as an act of charity, but because she needed someone to talk to and Nancy was 'the only animal in Jefferson that spoke Temple Drake's language'. Temple had previously insisted that the Temple Drake who had spent six weeks in a Memphis whorehouse 'and loved it' was gone, to be replaced by Mrs Gowan Stevens. Now, it appears, this was not so at all. Nancy killed, so the argument goes, as an act of sacrifice: 'To save my soul – if I have a soul', as Temple herself eventually puts it, 'If there is a God to save it – a God who wants it –.'[13] Nancy's act of apparently casual slaughter was, in fact, an act calculated to redeem Temple – and, not least, intended to remind her that her past was not dead because nobody's ever is. Temple can try to come to terms with all her yesterdays, but she cannot escape them.

'The past is never dead. It's not even past.' This remark, made by Gavin Stevens, is perhaps the most famous in *Requiem for a Nun*; and, if it is taken as authoritative, it bears out the surface argument of the dramatic sections of the novel, just outlined. The trouble lies in that 'if', the question of Stevens's authoritativeness here. One commentator has suggested that any reading of *Requiem for a Nun* must answer the question of whether the 'tendency of the book as a whole is to endorse or undermine the validity' of this memorable statement – and then gone on to argue that the narrative does actively undermine it, because it demonstrates as a whole that the past is in fact dead. This question of the pastness or otherwise of the past is, of course, inseparable from the problem raised by the central, determining act of Nancy's killing of Temple's baby. Is this, as much of the surface argument of the drama invites us to believe, an act of sacrifice and redemption? Or is it a senseless act of slaughter? Is Nancy the 'nun', the saint, saving Temple by forcing her to acknowledge and come to terms with her umbilical attachment to the past? Or is Nancy the sinner, crucifying Temple the 'nun', the true bride of the suffering Christ, because her belief that Temple is doomed to a repetition of all her yesterdays is fundamentally mistaken? The critical commentary here offers us the interpretive equivalent of a hung jury. On the one side are those who see Nancy taking 'upon herself the burden of Temple's sins' and, in the process, 'transmuted into a Christ-figure'. On the other are those who regard the killing of Temple's child as an 'offence . . . worse than Temple's intent had been' – or, even more strongly, as 'the most savage and reprehensible act of violence in all of William Faulkner's fiction, . . . the act of a mad-woman'. In between these poles, in turn, are critics of a kinder, gentler, but intellectually woollier inclination, who praise the intention but deplore the act. As one of them puts it, Nancy is 'the saint' who manages to 'save Temple and her older child', 'but we can't help feeling that she might have saved them without sacrificing a baby that had a right to its own salvation'.[14] Impeccable sentiments, certainly: but quite how this could be done, or what kind of 'salvation' it is that depends on denying 'salvation' to others, remains not at all clear.

Really, the immediate answer to these related questions of the connec-tions between narrative and dramatic sections, between past and present, and between Nancy's act of murder and the idea of sacrifice, is – or should be – very simple. The fact of the matter is that they cannot be answered, at least not in any straightforward or definitive way, because the evidence, the necessary backing or proof, just is not there; it is just not available in the text. *Requiem for a Nun* does not have a complex structure, but it does have a problematical one – and one that, growing out of its complicated genesis, effectively prohibits resolution. There are, first of all, intensely personal feelings at work in the book, circulating around the ideas of love and sacrifice, guilt and responsibility, marriage and family. And these are, nearly all of them, filtered into the dramatic sections of the story. Temple is in many ways a replication, a dark mirror image of her creator. She is caught as Faulkner was, when writing *Requiem for a Nun* (although not for the first time), between the erotic promise of a new young mate – the possibility of repeating earlier sexual adventures – and the more mundane task of struggling to make a marriage survive. There may possibly be an element of authorial guilt at work in the implication that an impulse to deny the marriage vows has to be punished in as terrible a way as the death of a child. Be that as it may, there is certainly a sado-masochistic streak noticeable in Gavin Stevens's treatment of Tem-ple, as he tries to make her face her past and confess her sins. Critics of quite different persuasions have commented on the sheer cruelty of some of his words and behaviour: as he perseveres with the attempt, as one commentator has put it, to 'get' her. 'I'm trying to tell it, enough of it. Can't you see that?', Temple implores the Governor, 'But can't you make him [Stevens] let me alone so I can. Make him, for God's sake, let me alone.'[15] Gavin will not or cannot let her alone, however: he talks inces-santly, whipping her with words, reconstructing what he perceives as the horror of her past and the baseness of her impulses. At one moment, in the heat of reconstruction, he even feels that he has *become* her. 'I am Red now', that is, Temple's former lover, Stevens declares as he rehearses her days in a Memphis brothel. Then, 'Temple now', he claims, as the re-hearsal continues. It is hardly necessary to remind ourselves how often

Stevens permitted Faulkner to play out parts of his own life, or voice his own opinions, to see what is happening here. Gavin Stevens both is and attacks Temple Drake at times in the drama. At even greater length, Faulkner both is and attacks Temple via the garrulous figure of the lawyer. The dramatic sections become, among other things, a form of self-inquisition, a means by which the author can accuse and interrogate himself.

The dramatic sections of *Requiem for a Nun* were, of course, what Faulkner began with when he embarked on his project of a collaboration with Joan Williams. Given this initial history, it is perhaps not so surprising that they offer a secret harbour for some of his innermost feelings. The narrative sections came as he gravitated, reluctantly, towards the idea of a work that was all his own, and are written in a series of much more public modes: not least, because Faulkner seems to be addressing his own public status and achievements here. This is not simply a case of drawing on more public material: although it is worth pointing out the close correlation between parts of the narrative sections and public statements like the Nobel Prize acceptance speech, and his exploitation of more obviously public resources like the tall tale in 'The Courthouse' or a travel guide to Mississippi in 'The Golden Dome'. What is more to the point, and surely more interesting, is that so much of all three narrative prologues appears to be devoted to review and commemmoration. The story of Yoknapatawpha is rehearsed and recapitulated, and the meanings that the distinguished author of that story wants his audience to address are announced and repeated – in particular, the idea of the destruction of individual freedom by the machinery of mass society. This is, in short, a public Faulkner, reviewing his work as a kind of public property. And reviewing it in a public voice: the style of the sections (it has already been noted) shifts continually, but the impulse to give public resonance to what is being said remains a constant. Every voice with which the narrative speaks has this in common with all the others: it announces and enunciates. It invites 'you' the reader – who is assumed to be an 'outlander', an outsider to place and text, and who is first implicitly and then directly addressed – to listen and attend. The apocryphal history of Yoknapatawpha, the names and faces of people like the Sutpens, the Sartorises and the Compsons, are recalled in a kind of public auditing procedure. Fiction as history is then inserted into history as fiction. The past and present of Jefferson and its environs is then wired up to the historical circuits of the American South and the United States – as in these two brief passages recalling the departure, in due course, first of the Native American and then of the covered wagon:

> and now indeed the last mocassin print vanished from that dusty widening, the last toed-in heel-less light soft quick long-striding print pointing west for an instant, then trodden from sight – taking with it (the print) not only the mocassins but the deer-hide leggings . . . because Ikkemotubbe's Chickasaws now wore Eastern factory-made jeans and shoes sold them out of Ratliff's and Compson's general store . . .
>
> . . .

... and the wagon did not vanish slowly and terrifically ... but was swept, hurried, flung not only out of Yoknapatawpha and Mississippi but the United States too ...[16]

The rhetorical splendour of passages like these is vital to Faulkner's evident project of public summation: he seems intent, at such moments, on fulfilling his long-held ambition to write the Golden Book of his county. And just as vital in this respect is the image of the 'print' that is picked up here and reappears throughout the narrative sections: most obviously, in the references to the 'scratchings' of Cecilia Farmer on a jailhouse window. Other commentators have pointed out how the summary of the meanings of Cecilia's inscription ('*Listen, stranger; this was myself: this was I*') recalls Faulkner's description of the artist as someone who wants to leave 'a scratch' on the 'wall of oblivion ... – Kilroy was here – that somebody a hundred, a thousand years later will see'.[17] What is worth adding to this is that the figure of the scratch, mark or print allows Faulkner further to aggrandize his project, to endow it with still more public resonance by linking it up with the westward story of America, the errand into the wilderness. The artist makes his mark on the blank wall. The pioneer leaves his print on the trail, worn away eventually but still somehow present beneath the prints of later settlers and other immigrant groups. Each generation in turn inscribes itself on the page of history: a page that, like that windowpane in the old jailhouse, is at once a substance and an absence, an object and a transparency. Writing, making a mark, functions throughout these three narrative sections as a revelatory figure for how we act out as well as know history: how we 'write' ourselves into time. Not least, it becomes a way for Faulkner to announce that he has written the story of Yoknapatawpha, not as some kind of self-contained, self-evident legend, but as something to be incorporated into the history 'written' by others. It is not, in short, a private property, it is a public one: part of the common stock of historical experience, and knowledge.

Undoubtedly, there are connections to be discovered between the resonant public voices of the narrative sections and the feverish private dialogues that characterize the dramatic episodes: most obviously, both narratives and drama are concerned with the issue of responsibility, the degree to which an individual is accountable for his or her actions. Even here, however, there are differences, even dislocation between the two modes of the novel. The burden of the narratives is that the present is sadly but successfully getting away from the past, with the result that the individual and the notion of individual responsibility are being crushed by the new mass society; while the drama plays obsessively with the idea that past choices have radical present consequences, so that no matter how hard the present tries the past remains powerfully there – not merely to haunt it, but to shape it. Admittedly, this difference is not an absolute one but rather a matter of tendency. The past, after all, leaves its 'print' or 'mark' in the narrative account of writers and pioneers; and Temple does, after all, claim that she is no longer the person she was. But the tendency is still there; and it has a marked, even determining influence on our reception of, respectively, narrative and drama. The past is a trace, an elusive and often vanishing hieroglyph, in the narrative sections; it is buried, like the old jailhouse, beneath 'the tiered symmetric bricks and the white-washed plaster'[18] of present structures. In 'The Jail' (and, for that matter, 'The Courthouse' and 'The Golden Dome'), history is seen fundamentally as an act of dispossession, a rupturing of the past from the present; 'going fast now' is the refrain of the narrator, as he charts how one generation swallows up another. In the drama, however, history involves much more an act of reconstruction, a re-enactment of the past by the present. 'I'm trying to tell it', says Temple as she attempts to speak her yesterdays into being; 'I am Red now', says Gavin Stevens, as he feels he has actually *become* them.

The difference between the primarily public languages of the narratives, and the markedly private idioms of the dramatic episodes, as far as these issues of past and present are conerned, can perhaps be measured by one striking illustration: the different uses to which Faulkner puts his favourite Shakespearean speech, from Act v of *Macbeth*. Both narrative and dramatic sections refer, in particular, to the phrase 'tomorrow and tomorrow and tomorrow' several times. When Temple Drake refers to it, however, it is in terms of the burden of guilt that she feels she must carry with her from the present into the future: the responsibilities from today that will be her yesterdays 'tomorrow' and that she must try, at least, to accept. 'Tomorrow and tomorrow and tomorrow, forever and forever and forever –', she says in Act ii. 'This time tomorrow, you won't be anything at all', she tells Nancy,

> But not me. Because there's tomorrow, and tomorrow, and tomorrow. All you've got to do is, just to die. But let Him tell me what to do. No: that's wrong; I know what to do, what I'm going to do; I found that out . . . But let Him tell me how. How? Tomorrow, and tomorrow, and still tomorrow. How?[19]

Selfish as this sounds, and confused as it is, it nevertheless expresses Temple's central perception: that she cannot escape the *determining* presence of the past – that her yesterdays and todays will feed into her tomorrows 'forever and forever and forever'. 'I'm sunk', Temple declares later, 'We all are. Doomed. Damned.' 'Of course we are', replies Stevens, 'Hasn't He been telling us that for going on two thousand years?' The damnation that is recorded in the narrative sections is rather different, though. When the same phrase, 'tomorrow and tomorrow and tomorrow', is recalled and rehearsed in 'The Jail' it conjures up a sharply contrasting kind of doom:

> tomorrow, and the railroad did run unbroken from Memphis to Carolina . . . tomorrow, and there would be grown men in Jefferson who could not even remember a drunken Indian . . . another tomorrow – so quick, so rapid, so

fast – and not even a highwayman any more of the old true sanguinary girt...[20]

This is time seen as a potentially endless succession of present tenses: a series in which each new term, every fresh day tends to wipe out its predecessor. The past is not authoritative here, and still less determining. It is, at most, a spectre, like the 'lost face' or the 'fragile and workless scratching' of Cecilia Farmer, haunting the present and reminding it of what it has just about lost. 'Tomorrow and tomorrow and tomorrow.' In the mainly public discourses of the narratives that phrase measures out a remorseless process of forgetting, an erasure of today from which, it seems, tomorrow will be only nominally recalled. In the more private languages of the drama, though, the emphasis is much more on the inexorable fact of remembering: today now becomes something that tomorrow will not only be obliged but doomed to re-enact. No wonder, then, that critics of *Requiem for a Nun* have tended to disagree about just what is going on, and, in particular, about what exactly is being said on the subjects of the past and guilt. What is going on here has been profoundly affected by what *was* going on when the book was being written: the several, quite different impulses that shaped, on the one hand, the narrative and, on the other, the dramatic sections. And what is being said here, in turn, is rich with contradiction: the message is, to some extent, a confused one because the medium is the message and the medium is irrevocably mixed.

When, in 1957, the question was put to Faulkner of just who the nun was in *Requiem for a Nun*, his answer was simple. 'The Nun', he declared, 'is Nancy.' However, when he was asked if that was because 'she was very separated from the world as the nun is', he came back with a much more complicated response. 'Well', he explained,

> it was in the – that tragic life of a prostitute which she had to follow simply because she was compelled by her environment, her circumstances, to be it... she was just doomed and damned by circumstances to that life. And, despite that, she was capable within her poor dim lights and reasons of an act which whether it was wrong was of complete almost religious abnegation of the world for the sake of an innocent child. That was it – it was paradoxical, the use of the word *Nun* for her, but I – but to me that added to her tragedy.[21]

Quite apart from his general caveat against accepting the authority of the author, Faulkner's own remarks about his novels were notoriously untrustworhy: this cannot be taken as, in any sense, the definitive word on the matter. Its interest lies, in fact, in its status not as explanation but as symptom, the way it alerts us to Faulkner's basic approach to the novel – after he had written it and, arguably, before that too. What is notable about what he says here is, first of all, his scrupulous avoidance of moral judgement. The dilemma of Nancy is described for us, its causes and consequences are located, but there is no feeling that ethical terms can be applied in anything other than a 'paradoxical' fashion. The vocabulary of 'saint', 'sinner', or 'nun', the thrust is, can only be applied, if at all, in an offkey, aslant way: so as to unravel the tensions inherent in Nancy's situation, and the conflicts implicit in any choice she feels obliged to make. Along with that, what is remarkable is the author's desperate attempt to resolve the tangle in which he finds himself, as he struggles to avoid moralizing, by falling back on transparently emotive phrases and references to tragedy. Nancy, as Faulkner describes her here, is 'doomed and damned', 'compelled by her environment, her circumstances', but she is also somehow 'tragic'. She only enjoys 'poor dim lights and reasons' but she commits an act that, 'whether it was wrong' or not, demonstrates an 'almost religious abnegation' – and this, Faulkner would have us believe, 'added to her tragedy'. The contradiction is acute. Judgement is eschewed but then the tragic dimension is claimed; choices are described, almost simultaneously, as socially determined and noble; Nancy is a 'poor dim' social victim yet somehow a 'religious' figure making a deliberate, heroic stab at renunciation. The use of the phrase 'for the sake of an innocent child', poignantly focuses Faulkner's conceptual difficulties here. Trying, if not to exonerate Nancy, then at least to offer a plea in mitigation, he uses an emotive term that, ironically, only reminds us of the horror of her act. What she has done, after all, 'for the sake of' one 'innocent child' is slaughter another one – even younger and, quite probably, even more innocent.

All of this is not to join some other critics in wagging a moral finger at Faulkner, or at any one or more of the characters in *Requiem for a Nun*. It is, rather, to point out that Faulkner was acutely, intuitively aware of the problematical nature of his book. He knew, or sensed at least, that there were unanswered questions lurking in what he had chosen to call his 'play-scenes, inside a novel'.[22] And this led him, when he was asked about them, into all kinds of responses and strategies: ranging from the studious refusal to rush into moral judgement to rhetorical evasion ('for the sake of an innocent child') and intellectual casuistry (the use of the term 'tragedy' to give the appearance of resolution to patently unresolvable conflicts). This points us towards another way of looking at the problem of the relation between the different sections, narrative and dramatic, of *Requiem for a Nun*: or, to be more accurate, towards a more positive way of looking at the evident lack of any simple, straightforward connection between them. They do not offer any solutions; even in their author's eyes they do not, although occasionally he protested rather too much that they do. They cannot, really, given their radically different emotional origins and rhetorical tendencies. What they can do, however, wonderfully well, is expose a series of problems. They can unravel the sheer difficulty of relating past to present – in, for instance, the process of making a choice and accepting its consequences – through the simple device of juxtaposing alternative versions of that relationship. The device is not a calculated one, of course, but it is no less effective for that. To the question of what yesterday means to today, and what today will mean to tomorrow, the novel offers a plural answer, the product of its own narrative shifts. Those shifts are, in turn, the shifts of the author, as he passes between private and public spaces and voices: which, crucially, he has learned to think of, to experience and represent, as separate and (if at all) only minimally related. In this respect, the interest of *Requiem for a Nun* lies precisely in its multiple character: its conflicting biases of statement, its not entirely premeditated and certainly unmastered mixing of different forms and idioms. The connections are not there, finally, between drama and narrative, although many commentators want them to be; a solution to the problem of history and responsibility is not discovered, although the novel sometimes seems to give the impression that it is. What there is, instead of a resolution ('tragic', or of any other kind), is the unearthing and exhibiting of a dilemma: the revelation that Gavin Stevens may well be right when he claims 'The past is never dead' – and, then again, he may well not be.

The pluralism of *Requiem for a Nun* is not entirely to be identified with the divisions between the narrative and dramatic sections, of course. It has already been observed that, in sections like 'The Jail', the old can be represented as leaving its 'imprint' on the new; while Temple Drake tries at least to unpick today from yesterday. But the main impulse of the narratives *is* to measure what is called, at one point, 'the long invincible arm of Progress'. 'There was no time', 'that fast now', 'that rapid': phrases like this, from 'The Jail', register just how much all three narrative sections – in their different ways – take up and run with the idea of change. Time in 'The Courthouse', for instance, is seen as a process of more or less unplanned obsolescence: with each yesterday seeming to each today, in turn, like 'an anachronism out of an old dead . . . age'. In 'The Golden Dome', similarly, separation and substitution provide the key: as in 'The Courthouse', in fact, the different dimensions of time are so divided one from another that they evidently require different idioms – in both cases, evocation gives way to documentation. Above all, perhaps, in 'The Jail' what we are left with to signify times past is Faulkner's favourite image of absent presence, loss and longing: the recollection of a woman's 'lost and insatiable face drawing the substance – the will and hope and dream and imagination – of all men'.[23] This is the teasing outline of Cecilia Farmer, who is never even seen in any terms other than her trace or mark, and who can as a result appear to be all women – and none. Quite simply, the drive of the narratives is forward, for good ('progress') and ill ('loss'): each section picks up and complicates the visionary elements in many of Faulkner's more public utterances, not least the Nobel Prize acceptance speech. The impetus of the dramatic sections, by contrast, is backward: as Faulkner replicates his own plumbing of some of his innermost fears and anxieties in the investigative strategies of Gavin Stevens. Together, Stevens and Temple Drake reconstruct the past and in the process strip down the personality, depriving it of its more recent accretions: revealing at the heart of, most clearly, Temple herself the isolated, troubled consciousness that links yesterday to today and tomorrow. 'Temple Drake is dead', Temple asserts: but the re-creative strategies of Gavin and Temple, as they probe back into yesterday, and their deconstructive activities, as they push down ever deeper beneath the mask of today, reveal that the old Temple Drake is still very much alive. 'What in God's name do you want?' Temple asks Stevens in Act I. To which Stevens replies, 'I told you. Truth.' And the dramatic sections of the novel urge us to believe that this is precisely what Gavin, Temple herself, and the reader eventually get: a truthful sighting of the terrible marriage between past and present, of which the offspring are suffering and guilt.

Perhaps this was why Faulkner believed that *Requiem for a Nun* was a project that remained resolutely unfinished, even after it had gone to the printers: not just because it never became a collaborative work, and only later appeared on the stage, but because its account of the relations between the different dimensions of time, and its consequent representation of the problem of moral responsibility, were as fractured as the narrative structure. The story which became a play and then a cross between narrative fiction and drama: in its eventual, published form it is as notable for what it does not do, as for what it does – the fracture of narrative shape is also a fracture of meaning. It shuffles between conflicting notions of historical action and knowledge in a way that frustrates those readers seeking coherent communication – and that also resists the author's own burning need, at times, to realize formal closure and intellectual security. Deep personal needs at work in the dramatic sections of the novel help to stimulate messages, circulating around the authoritative presence of the past, that tend to conflict with the more publicly oriented voices of the narrative, announcing a remorseless process of progress and division. Temple Drake, in this context, can be juxtaposed with Cecilia Farmer: the one partly a projection of intimately autobiographical feelings about how old times are indelibly attached to new ones, the other mostly a figure of just how evanescent and elusive those old times are. 'You – everyone – must, or anyway may have to pay for the past', declares Gavin Stevens in one of the more famous statements of the drama; and this, he explains, is because the 'past is something like a promissory note with a trick clause in it which . . . fate or luck or chance can foreclose on you without warning'.[24] As a comment both on individuals and on cultures, however, what Stevens says here remains unproven at the end of *Requiem for a Nun*; evidence is mustered that equally supports and denies his claim. So the reader, too, is left with unfinished business.

II   OF CROWDS, CONTROL AND COURAGE: *A FABLE*

One of the things that marked the next few years of Faulkner's life, following the appearance of *Requiem for a Nun* to a generally lukewarm reception, was the continuing and increasingly radical contrast between public and private faces. After receiving the Nobel Prize, Faulkner's public status was consolidated by further awards and big speeches on public occasions. In 1952, for instance, he was invited to address the Delta council of cotton planters and businessmen. Appearing on the same platform as two state governors, he duly obliged his audience of five thousand by addressing them on the importance of individual freedom and responsibility and the evils of welfare programmes. Work on a theatrical version of *Requiem for a Nun*, television scripts of his stories 'The Brooch' and 'Shall Not Perish', a retrospective and partly autobiographical essay 'Mississippi' in *Holiday* magazine, more frequent trips away from Oxford to New York, France and England: all this, and more, assisted in his transformation into – to adapt the Yeatsian phrase – a fifty-five-year-old, unsmiling public man. At the same time as Faulkner was being reassured about his public reputation, however, his private life seemed to descend into ever deeper turmoil. A fall from a horse exacerbated the back problems that had been with him for much of his life: which encouraged him to drink even more than usual, to the point of collapse. Forced into hospital by his drinking, he was diagnosed on one such occasion as 'an acute and chronic alcoholic'. 'Never in my life have I been so unhappy and depressed', he wrote in 1952; and the depression became so acute, at one time, as to persuade him to see a psychiatrist. The psychiatrist saw Faulkner as 'a man built to suffer', for whom 'the problems of the South . . . were somehow related to his own tensions'. Faulkner's only response to psychiatric treatment, however, was outrage at the bill of $450. He resolved in future to 'stay with . . . a simple doctor' who only charged $85, 'out of which', he added, 'I got one bottle of Seconal capsules.'[25]

'Back not much better', Faulkner wrote in August 1952,

> probably impossible with my nature and occupation – natural nervousness, inability to be still . . . probably the great trouble is unhappiness here, have lost heart for everything . . . have not worked in a year now, stupid existence seeing what remains of life going to support parasites who do not even have the grace to be sycophants. Am tired, I suppose.[26]

Part of the reason why Faulkner felt so 'tired' and depressed, at least in private, was because the relationship with Joan Williams was dwindling away to nothing. Briefly – and mainly at Faulkner's insistence – they had become lovers: but Joan was finally to tell Faulkner, late in 1953, that the physical differences between them were too great. Even before then, the affair continued to be characterized by conflicting motives: with Joan emphasizing the literary dimension of their relationship and Faulkner seeking emotional and sexual satisfaction – although willing to play the role of literary mentor, if that seemed to be the only way of maintaining the connection. Faulkner apparently felt that he was repeating earlier patterns of erotic longing, although in an even more desperate and diminished key. When he talked to Joan of his need for her, for example, he resorted to some of the same phrases he had used with Helen Baird and then later Meta Carpenter. The quotation from *Cyrano de Bergerac* was resurrected, *'ton nom c'est comme une petite sonnette d'or / Pendant dans mon coeur...'*; Faulkner even gave Joan a small piece of jewelry to hang over her heart. He also resorted to his own words from the end of 'Wild Palms'. 'Haven't I been telling you ... that between grief and nothing, I will take grief?' he asked Joan in 1953; and it seemed, in a way, that he did not even have the privilege of *that* choice. As Joan began to distance herself, Faulkner became aware that she did not even want very much of his literary advice any more, perhaps because of the emotional price involved. 'I learned to write from other writers', he declared plaintively, 'Why should you refuse it?' It must have appeared to him, in effect, that he was gravitating from the grief of unsatisfactory companionship simply to nothing. Once again, the lost lady was well and truly lost.

Just as marked during these years, really, as the growing friction between public and private levels of experience was Faulkner's continuing struggle with his 'epic poem'. The struggle was, in any event, not unrelated to that friction, since the story that Faulkner at one time tentatively entitled 'Who?' and ended up calling *A Fable* was, like much of his later work, partly an attempt to give a public resonance to his private beliefs. As more than one commentator has pointed out, the roots of this project reach right back to Faulkner's early emotional involvement in the First World War, signalled not least by his first published novel. As Faulkner himself pointed out, however, in a brief foreword to *A Fable* when it was eventually published in 1954, the 'basic idea' for the book originated with two of his associates in Hollywood, the director Henry Hathaway and the producer William Bacher. Stories had grown up about the Unknown Soldier and Hathaway had been attempting to work the subject into a film script. He had tried the idea on several writers before he and Bacher decided, in 1943, to see if they could interest Faulkner. The proposal was that Faulkner would write a film script based on the idea of the Unknown Soldier being a later version of Christ; Hathaway would direct the film and Bacher would produce it, and Faulkner would be free to make further use of the idea in whatever fictional form he thought appropriate. Explaining all this to his agent in November 1943, Faulkner added that he would like to translate the basic narrative idea first into a story, for a magazine and then a collection, and afterwards a play. 'It is a fable, an indictment of war perhaps', he had already told the same correspondent earlier, in October, when he provided a synopsis. Now, in November, he forwarded fifty-one pages, adding 'this is about half of it'.[27]

The project of the Unknown Soldier never became a film. What is more to the point, Faulkner's narrative gradually mushroomed. By the middle of 1946, he had sent nearly 200 pages to his agent; by early in 1948, this had increased to almost 500 pages of a manuscript so complicated that one page was numbered 120-Z-42. Continually writing, altering and rewriting, Faulkner worked away at what he called 'my big book', punctuating this with other work, including the writing of three other books – and sometimes with no work at all, during periods when he would feel that he was 'written out'. Perhaps the most remarkable aspect of all the thought and labour Faulkner expended on *A Fable*, though, was not the ten years he spent, off and on, preparing it, but the way the whole process of preparation and revision was marked by radical swings of mood: as supreme confidence in his project would give way, sometimes, to despair. It may have been the fact that the work owed its inception to someone else that aggravated his difficulties, making him more than normally uncertain about what he was doing; it may have been that, unusually for him, he began with an idea rather than an image or a character. Whatever the reason, he oscillated throughout the writing of *A Fable* between ebulliently high and depressively low opinions of what on one occasion he termed his 'magnum o'. 'I am doing a thing which I think is pretty good', he wrote of the book in 1945, then added, 'Unless I am wrong about it, have reached that time of an artist's increasing years when he no longer can judge what he is doing.' Eight years later, in 1953, he was playing the same uncertain tune: 'It is either nothing and I am blind in my dotage, or it is the best of my time.' The anxieties about failing artistic powers that characterize these remarks were poignantly developed in a letter he wrote to Joan Williams, also in 1953. 'The work, the mss. is going again', he informed her, 'Not as it should, in a fine ecstatic rush like the orgasm we spoke of at Hal's that night. This is done by simple will power: I doubt if I can keep it up too long.'[28] The linking of artistic and sexual potency here may be rather too obvious to be remarked on: but it is worth recalling, and comparing, Faulkner's description of the erotic tension and excitement that, so he intimated, lay behind the writing of *The Sound and the Fury*. Added to that, it is also worth remembering (especially in the context of just who these words were addressed to) that, for him, the practice of art and male sexual desire always seem to have been connected. This was, of course, sometimes in complex ways, involving mixed ideas of consummation and substitution. Here, however, things are very much simpler: possible degeneration as a writer is lined up with other factors, concerning probable decline as a sexually active man.

The feelings of insecurity that accompanied the preparation of *A Fable* continued after Faulkner wrote 'December 1944 Oxford, New York and Princeton 1953' at the bottom of the final page of the manuscript. 'I love the book', Faulkner wrote to his publishers, 'gave ten good years of my life to it.' Appropriately for a work that he hoped would be 'the greatest of our time', he dedicated *A Fable* to his daughter Jill. But, Jill observed, Faulkner 'was dissatisfied with it when it was finished'. 'This was to be a great work. But it wasn't', she added, 'I think he knew it all along. He knew that he was out of his element ... he had made a big play about dedicating it ... But he never once mentioned it again.' This is a little harsh: almost as if Jill were getting back at her father for his famously cruel remark to her – after she had said to him, 'Think of me', during one of his alcoholic collapses – 'Nobody remembers Shakespeare's children.' Still, it contains an element of truth. *A Fable* is structurally complicated. The germinating story of a Christ-like Corporal, who sets off a mutiny that leads to a three-day cessation of conflict during the First World War, is interleaved with other narratives that similarly explore the problems of war and peace, obedience and rebellion, human rapacity and the human capacity for love. The chronology of that story and the others is disrupted: for instance, although as a modern allegory of Passion Week the narrative is set over seven days (plus a section called 'Tomorrow'), it begins with 'Wednesday' and then cuts back to 'Monday'. And, in a way that often recalls cinematic technique, it uses juxtaposition, cross-cutting between different times and characters, and fadeouts from one scene to another, to propel the action and implement meaning. Complicated as that structure is, however, requiring careful and sometimes pained attention on the part of the reader, much of the actual writing is lumpen and pedestrian. Too often, the narrative strains for effect. The replication of the Trinity, for example, via the constant grouping of things and people in threes, is both clumsy and portentous, while some of the rhetoric is forced to the point of absurdity ('not enormity, but monstrosity', declares the narrator of one supposedly significant event, 'the monstrous incredibility, the incredible monstrosity').[29] The narrative voice, too, is something of a problem. As in much of Faulkner's work from the early 1940s onwards, the different voices of the characters all tend now and then to become one voice – by turns feverishly excited or devoutly solemn – that appears to be substituting 'simple will power' for the 'fine ecstatic rush' of the earlier writing. The aim behind this monolithic tendency seems to be to impose meaning by authorial fiat: but all it does, really, is dissipate the potential power of what is being said – and, quite probably, build up resistance in the obstinate reader.

A paradox at the heart of *A Fable*, in fact, is that it tends towards a denial in practice of what it preaches; it often says one thing, and does another. It celebrates human individuality and variety. But the net effect of the anonymising narratives, with their avoidance of detailed social specification or even proper names, is frequently to turn the individual characters into allegorical ciphers, and to flatten out the fictive landscapes into one, vast emblematic surface. It clearly means to side with the dream of freedom against the forces of authoritarianism; it proclaims liberty. However, arguably the most authoritarian impulse in the book is to be found in the dominant narrative voice: which not only assumes precedence over all the other voices but sometimes takes them over completely, while it dictates meaning to the supposedly compliant reader. The portrait of the varieties of fascism that runs through *A Fable* is frequently powerful. Take the character of General Gragnon, for example. He, we are told, has forfeited 'his birthright in humanity' by allowing himself to become the slave of duty. There is some sympathy for him: but he is seen above all critically, as an honourable man who has allowed himself to lose sight of his own individuality – and, for that matter, the individuality and humanity of others – in the process of dedicating himself to the machinery of war. To this extent, he is like other military leaders in the book: the corps commander, for instance, who sees human beings as a 'malleable mass' that the great leader 'heaps and pounds and stiffens' into something 'cohered and purposeful for a time' – or the group commander, who regards humankind as no more than a machine 'with . . . vents and orifices'.[30] As with so many of the characters in the book, he is an orphan; and his 'unfathered, unmothered' state is quietly linked to his need for authority. Having lost his place not only in his blood family, the intimation is, but in the human one as well, he has found a substitute network of allegiance – another kind of 'family' – in the army and the state. Powerful as this portrait is, though, of the impulse towards absolute command and obedience, its power – and the power of other portraits like it – is dissipated by the presence of similar impulses in the narrative. The insistence on the anonymity of the characters, after all, works against any sense of individual human agency: the feeling that it is people with particularized stories who shape and influence public events. And it is not merely the anonymising strategy that has the effect of stripping history of its personal dimension. Just as crucial is the invention of a collective character in *A Fable*, punctuating the action and propelling it at times, that appears to underwrite the military leaders' idea of humankind as an undifferentiated mass or mechanism. The trenchant critique of fascism and authoritarianism is in effect refracted, in an odd and disconcerting way, through a narrative idiom that attributes a determining influence to 'the crowd': represented, not really as a collection of people, but as a uniform, collective force, possessed of 'one single face' and one voice, 'one stir, one exhalation, one movement'.

Here, however, it is necessary to be careful. To some extent, the representation of the crowd as an impersonal and powerful agency does collude with the general tendency towards anonymity in *A Fable*: it does tend to 'de-individualize' the action. But that representation is more complicated, and subtler than these remarks might suggest. If the weakness of the novel *as a novel* lies in its lack of narrative specification, then that also is where its interest lies. Albeit at a serious price, which makes it less than successful as a fiction and often strained even as a rhetorical *tour de force*, *A Fable* does offer a thoughtful investigation into human possibilities, circulating around a series of dualisms. The most fundamental of these dualisms is suggested by one character, the Reverend Sutterfield, when he declares (resorting to the oratorical mode that characterizes rather too many remarks made in the novel):

> Evil is a part of man, evil and sin and cowardice, the same as repentance and being brave. You got to believe in all of them, or believe in none of them. Believe that man is capable of all of them, or he aint capable of none.[31]

One critic has likened Faulkner's pursuit of a 'pure and intact' style in *A Fable* to his much earlier stab at 'extreme purity and deliberate universality' in his verse: 'qualities', the critic argues, 'that are probably even less compatible with fiction than with poetry'. Others have compared it to the Latin *fabula*, denoting legend or myth, or to Faulkner's own notion of the New Testament – which he said was 'full of ideas' whereas the Old Testament was 'full of people'. Another way of looking at it, perhaps, is as a modern version of a medieval 'debate': in which generalized, allegorical figures discuss the human past, present and, above all, the human future within the framework of a firm structure of belief. In the medieval debate, of course, the interest and direction is teleological: towards theological notions of damnation and salvation. The religious scaffolding that Faulkner uses, however, only serves to emphasize the difference. For him, the debate takes place in history: the vital question is what people are going to do with their beings in time. And a great deal of that debate hovers over what is seen as a prime motor of historical change: the people, as they merge with and occasionally emerge from the crowd.

The crowd is powerfully there right from the beginning of *A Fable*. 'Long before the first bugles sounded from the barracks within the city and the cantonments surrounding it', the narrative begins, 'most of the people in the city were already awake.' Awakened into a sort of brotherhood of the nameless, the people then press forward to find out what is happening on this day when, as we find out soon, the Corporal, his twelve disciples and other mutineers are being brought into town. 'The people', 'the crowd', 'the mass': the terms are interchangeable. And what is remarkable about the portrait of this vast, anonymous force, as it spills out into the streets, pushing back the troops that seek to control it, is the emphasis on its fluid, volatile and (for the moment) uncontrollable nature, registered in the dominant imagery of the flood:

> Even before the bugles' echoes died away, the warrened purlieus were already disgorging them . . . the trickles became streams and the streams became rivers until the whole city seemed to be pouring down the broad boulevards . . .
>
> . . .
>
> They met the first troops here . . . already in position and waiting as though the murmur of the flood's beginning had preceded it . . .
>
> . . .
>
> . . . Accelerating now, the crowd poured into the boulevard. It flung the cavalry aside and poured on, blotting the intersecting streets as it passed them as a river in flood blots up its tributary creeks . . .[32]

Although there has been sound – the signal from the bugle, the murmur of the crowd, a shout of command to the troops – there has been as yet no articulate speech. That happens when an unnamed woman gets trampled underfoot: a woman who, it turns out later, is the wife of the Corporal. The first person to speak is an anonymous sergeant, trying to control the flood: 'pick her up', he declares 'savagely' when he sees the woman lying on the ground, then demands, 'Who does she belong to?' The response comes from a 'voice' in the crowd, which observes of the woman,

'She's hungry.' The 'hand' that belongs to this 'voice' then offers bread. 'Hand' and 'voice' finally become 'a man not so young actually, but rather simply youthful-looking', who asks: 'But now she has eaten bread . . . With that morsel, she should have bought immunity from her anguish, not?'

In a way, this brief opening sequence sums up the major trajectory of the novel. The crowd is a fluid force, full of potential and, when awakened, almost impossible to master and control. It is also, initially and collectively, an *amoral* force: it has no innate moral sense, no more than a literal flood has. This is not because there are no moral energies at work within it but because, as *A Fable* slowly discloses, it represents the human possibility writ large: it is made up of individuals each of whom carries within him or her the human capacity for love and rapacity, resistance and fascism, repentance and evil. Out of this crowd a moral direction comes for a moment. A 'voice' initiates entry into the world of moral action. An individual – albeit an anonymous one – emerges from the crowd, and endows both himself and the collective movement of which he is a part with a temporary, provisional moral identity through the agency of speech. He speaks himself and 'the people' to whom he belongs into moral being by recognizing the needs of another, and then responding to that need. He articulates the positive direction in which the human possibility can go; shortly after that, he sinks back into the flood and *generalized* anonymity. As far as the presentation of the crowd throughout *A Fable* is concerned, this is a recurrent pattern. Mass movements are punctuated by the emergence of a (usually anonymous) figure or voice who acts as a moral catalyst: giving focus, and a clearer sense of direction, to the momentum of which he or she is a part. And what goes for the portrayal of all that, at one point, is called 'the deliberate pour of the crowd'[33] also goes for the general strategies of representation in the book. In this case, it is the tidal wave of the narrative that seems to carry along with it the generalized, irresistible forces of history: to create a sense of fluid potential, historical process. Then out of *this*, in turn, emerge particular – if not always particularly individualized – characters, whose histories are usually told to us in an abbreviated, anonymous way so as to situate and explain their dreams and destinies. They act out their part, steer the narrative in a particular direction: broadly, towards authoritarianism or rebellion, control or release. Then, afterwards, they sink back into the fluent, turbulent idiom that characterizes – or, rather, shapes and dictates – the general momentum of the novel.

Observing the actions of one crowd, close to halfway through *A Fable*, one character – an unnamed lawyer – gives detailed expression to the idea that it is 'the mass . . . moving itself in one direction' that is the prime agent of history. 'Not Genghis' horns, nor Murat's bugles' determine historical change, he reflects,

> let alone the golden voice of Demosthenes or Cicero or the trumpet-blast of Paul or John Brown or Pitt or Calhoun or Daniel Webster, but the children

dying of thirst amid Mesopotamian mirages and the wild men out of the
northern woods who walked into Rome carrying even their houses on their
backs and Moses' forty-year scavengers and the tall men carrying a rifle or
an axe and a bag of beads who changed the colour of the American race . . .[34]

The passage echoes and anticipates other observations scattered through
the narrative; and so too does what the lawyer then goes on to remind
himself. This ability of the ordinary human being 'to move *en masse* at his
own impulse', the lawyer reflects, is only too well understood by 'the lords
proprietors of his massed breathing, the hero-giant precentors of his
seething moil' who have 'used his spendthrift potency in the very act of
curbing and directing it'. They 'ever had', the lawyer thinks, and they
'ever would'. The occasion that prompts these reflections, as it turns out,
illustrates the power of mass movement for good, just as the opening
sequence does: in this case, the crowd, given articulation and direction by
the anonymous owner of a 'calm, irascible voice', liberates the Reverend
Sutterfield from captivity. But the reflections themselves clearly negotiate
a different possibility: in which the fluid mass of the mob is transformed
into a fixed instrument of power, an agent of absolute authority.

There is a fascinating connection here, between Faulkner's representation of crowds and authority and an important account of the vocabulary
of fascism. In his book, *Male Fantasies,* Klaus Theweleit takes a close look
at the language and imagery of German fascism in the period between the
two World Wars. And he generalizes from the specific example of fascist
'soldier males' a European history which is to be understood as the history
of the European body, 'its splitting into child and adult, into genders,
classes, and fragments of itself'. Examining the process by which cultural
prohibitions are absorbed, in particular Theweleit reveals a telling pattern
of language in the novels and autobiographies of fascist soldiers. These
soldiers, as Theweleit puts it, 'freeze up, become icicles in the face of
erotic femininity'. 'It isn't enough simply to view this as a defence against
the threat of castration', he adds, 'by reacting in that way, in fact, the man
holds himself together as an entity, a body with fixed boundaries.' The
mass of the people, as well as women, are seen in terms of floods, streams,
ocean, dirt, slime, pulp, against which the body must be tightened so that
it does not dissolve or explode. The men 'want to avoid swimming at all
costs, no matter what the stream', Theweleit argues, '. . . they want whatever floods may come to rebound against them; they want to stop, and
dam up, those floods'.[35] They regard themselves, in short, as rocks in and
against a raging sea.

What is so remarkable about Faulkner's portraits of the crowd and the
army, really, when they are read in the context of these remarks, is how
insistently he repeats these patterns of language. The people are a 'malleable mass', according to one of the commanders, who must be pounded
and stiffened into an instrument 'coherent and purposeful'. The army, in
turn, is represented conceptually as a vast 'interlocked' machine and

physically as an inflexible, 'impregnable' body – run by men who seem to have become frozen, as here, into fixed postures of attention:

> 'So,' the German general said. 'That is both of you. Three of us.' He sat down . . . and took up the filled brandy glass and sat back and erect again, into that same rigidity of formal attention as when he had been standing to toast his master, so that even sitting the rigidity had a sort of visible inaudibility like a soundless clap of heels, the filled glass at level with the fixed rigid glare of the opaque monocle; again without moving he seemed to glance rapidly at the other glasses. 'Be pleased to fill, gentlemen,' he said. But neither the Briton nor the American moved.[36]

The sense of impregnability and immobility here is overwhelming: from the rigidity of his body and the fixity of his stare right through to the opacity of his monocle, the general is a closed, impermeable figure. And it is under the command of men like this, during the course of *A Fable*, that the crowd becomes the army, either literally or figuratively: that is, it is translated into an agent of authority and rapacity, the will to power. Its fluidity of motion is frozen into a fixed network of communication and destruction: divided off from the rest of humanity and the possibility of change. By means of the dominating, dualistic images of the crowd as flood and the army (or the crowd shaped by the hands of a 'great leader') as a fixed object, *A Fable* links the debate over the possible directions history might take to a whole series of other, dualistic possibilities. The open system inviting participation, contact and change, versus its closed opposite that resists participation or alteration of any kind. The body that embraces otherness, its part in the lives of others, versus the body that withdraws and separates. The 'female' experience of immersion versus the 'male' desire for transcendence. All these dualisms are not just implicit in the figurative structure of the book. They are more or less explicit, thanks to the sheer insistence of the figurative reference – and the arguments of characters like the lawyer.

Fluidity is not just an attribute of the anonymous crowd, as it goes about its business. At crucial moments of rebellion, particular figures assume the same or similar qualities: just as, at crucial moments for the assertion of authority, specific people like the German general become rocklike in their fixity. When, for example, certain characters – an English runner and the Reverend Sutterfield – emulate the example of the Corporal by moving out of the trenches unarmed in a gesture of peace, their action – and the action of the regiment that then follows them – is described in terms of the fixed suddenly become fluid. 'Then the runner was beside' the Reverend Sutterfield, we are told, shouting 'Look at them!': that is, at the regiment rising out of the trenches. 'He did so', the narrative goes on,

> and saw them . . . crawling on their hands and knees . . . faces clothes hands and all stained as though forever one single nameless and identical colour from the mud in which they had lived like animals for four years, then rising to his feet . . . 'Over there too!' the runner cried, turning him again until he

saw that also: the distant German wire one faint moil and pulse of motion . . .
then he heard the the voices too and knew that his was one also – a thin
murmuring sound rising into the incredible silence . . .[37]

The emergence of these figures from the trenches, on both sides of the
front line, is presented as an evolution of men out of primeval slime. It is
the worst nightmare of Theweleit's 'soldier males' come true: mud become motion. These characters have slipped out from under the machinery of authority for a moment. In doing so, the narrator intimates, they
have rediscovered their 'voices too': they can – like the unnamed figure
who offers bread to a needy woman at the beginning of the novel – *speak*
themselves into being.

'War, war, war', declares an old woman at one point in *A Fable*, 'Don't
you ever get tired of it?' She speaks for just about all the women in the
book: who are possessed of the same teasing fluidity as women are in
Faulkner's other work, accompanied now by what is called 'the ancient
limitless mammalian capacity not for suffering but grieving, wailing . . .
without shame or self-consciousness'. A ground bass to the narrative is, in
fact, supplied by the cry of women, as they observe so many of their men
caught up in the paralysing, destructive rituals of war. Sometimes, that cry
is a vast, generalized one: as when the narrator talks about 'the single
voice of all the women in the Western world' heard in opposition to the
sound of battle. At other times, it is more specific. A character named
Levine, for instance, plays out the old Faulknerian theme of the man who
arrives 'too late' for the war; and he blames his delay in enlisting on his
'own inability to say no to a woman's tears' – the tears, that is, of his
mother. Two of the last female figures on whom the story dwells are worth
mentioning here: an anonymous old Frenchwoman and Marthe, one of
the sisters of the Corporal. When a detachment of soldiers is sent after the
war to get a body for the tomb of the Unknown Soldier in Paris, we learn
that they are met by an old lady: still seeking the body of her son – killed,
so she was told, in 1916. She insists that the body the detachment recovers
is that of her son, even though it is unrecognizable. And she pays the
detachment for it: such is the intensity of her grief that she needs the body
with her, to console her – as a physical expression and object of her un-
extinguished love. It becomes necessary to come up with another body, to
replace the one sold to the old woman. What is found in 'the corpse of
the earth' is another unidentifiable corpse, unearthed in the area around
Marthe's farm. The implication is that this is the Corporal, who was
executed by a firing-squad for leading the mutiny and whose body then
disappeared. The Corporal, we already know, 'had been her [Marthe's]
brother but she had been his mother too'; and she has apparently taken
him back to the land she had hoped to restore. 'Restoring the land would
not only palliate the grief', Faulkner has Marthe reflect to herself,

the minuscule integer of the farm would affirm that he [the Corporal] had
not died for nothing and that it was not for an outrage that they grieved, but

for simple grief: the only alternative to which was nothing, and between grief and nothing only the coward takes nothing.[38]

The echoes of earlier Faulknerian remarks about 'grief' and 'nothing' are fairly obvious here, as is the likeness of this figure, who is both sister and mother, to other women in Faulkner's fiction. Like so many of the women in *A Fable*, Marthe combines the motion and mystery of earlier Faulkner females with an evidently inexhaustible ability to endure emotional pain. An icon of suffering, she is as receptive, as pliable and potentially generous, as the earth with which she too is associated – and from which she hopes to gain a kind of redemption.

The army and the crowd, the male and the female – and the father and the son: the final stage in this conflict between the fixed and the fluid, obedience and resistance, control and release, is played out in the debate between the Marshal, sometimes called the Old General, supreme commander of the Allied Forces, and the Corporal – who, it turns out, is the Old General's child. The remarkable thing about this debate, really, is that it *is* a genuine conflict: which is to say, it is dramatic, not simply didactic. The Old General is a not entirely unsympathetic character. What is more, he is given the power of some of Faulkner's own rhetoric, and he articulates needs that Faulkner himself clearly felt. 'We are two articulations', he says of humankind at one point to the Corporal, when he is trying to tempt him to forsake the men who followed him: 'I champion of this mundane earth . . . you champion of man's baseless hopes and his infinite capacity – no: passion – for unfact.' The 'two articulations' are both fully articulated in this scene of temptation. The Corporal certainly speaks – or stays eloquently silent – he is given an adequate voice and dramatic presence: but so also, in his own way, is the Marshal. Some of this sense of a real struggle between the two men comes from the fact that both of them, and especially the Marshal, are not merely permitted the full power of Faulkner's general rhetorical style: they are occasionally allowed to repeat his own actual words. At one point, for instance, as several critics have suggested, the older man, assisted a little by the younger, echoes the Nobel Prize address. 'After the last ding dong of doom has rung and died', the Marshal declares, there will still be man's 'puny and inexhaustible voice, still planning'. 'Because man and his folly –' he goes on. 'Will endure', interrupts the Corporal. 'They will do more', the Marshal continues 'proudly'. 'They will prevail'.[39] The voice of the older man becomes the voice of Faulkner here; and, just for a moment, the voice of the younger man does too. They seem to collaborate in echoing the author. And this is not just because, as elsewhere in *A Fable*, all voices tend to become one voice, that of the 'Sole Owner & Proprietor' of the narrative. It is because the two of them, rebellious son and authoritative father, are replicating the divisions of their creator: they are debating a conflict that is internal and, in its origins, profoundly autobiographical.

Which brings us to the temptations the father offers to the son, the instruments he uses in an attempt to assert his power. They are, inevitably (given the numerical inclinations of this book), three. 'Take my car', the Marshal says first: he offers the Corporal escape. Then, 'Take the world': he offers him wealth and power. Finally, 'Take life': he offers him survival. 'I give you liberty', the Marshal proclaims as he expands on the first temptation. What, more specifically, he is promising, it turns out, is the luxury of withdrawal. 'I have papers to pass you aboard any ship you choose and command its captain', he explains. 'Then South America – Asia – the Pacific islands; close that window fast; lock it forever on that aberrant and futile dream.' Rebellion is to be replaced by retreat into a personal space, the peace and quiet of privacy. 'I will acknowledge you as my son', the Marshal then declares, describing the second temptation. In this instance, in conspicuous contrast to *Absalom, Absalom!*, the father seeks to master the son not by denying him but by announcing the fact of paternity. So announced, the son will enter into the realm of the father: which is a realm of many things but, above all, the realm of the imagination and language. What, in particular, the Marshal ends up promising the Corporal here is what he calls Paris: 'that Paris which only my son can inherit from me', he insists – a place that even more than 'Rome, Cathay and Xanadu' is a hauntingly imaginative domain. 'What can you not – will you not – do with all the world to work on . . . ?' the Marshal asks. 'You will be God.' In effect, the Corporal is offered absolute authority – and, more especially, the absolute authority of the author: who, as Faulkner liked to claim sometimes, may very well be 'like God' not only in his power but also in his prerogatives. 'I am an old man, you a young man', complains the Marshal at last, embarking on the third temptation. 'You become old, you see death then', he goes on. 'Then you realise that nothing – nothing – nothing – . . . is as valuable as simple breathing.'[40] The terrible poignancy of this final bid for the young man by the old one stems from the fact that it is both a celebration and a lament: a hymn to life, certainly, but also a howl of rage against the inexorable fact of growing old 'and the anguish of an irreparable, worn-out body'.

Privacy, authority, survival: it does not take too much imagination to see how intimately these temptations spoke to Faulkner himself, particularly at the time when he was writing *A Fable*. The desire to be, if necessary, 'the last private individual on earth' had been with him a long time. It had only been complicated, and in a way exacerbated, by his experience of fame and his growing awareness of the split between public reputation and private anxieties: in such circumstances, withdrawal must have seemed particularly attractive. The authority of authorship, too, was a notion that sometimes glowed with promise for a man tempted to see himself as owner of land both literal and figurative. It enticed him even more now that other kinds of power, artistic and sexual, seemed to be slipping away from him – and as he cast a retrospective, proprietorial eye over all he had written, the apocryphal county he had invented. The sense of waning power also added a special edge to the linked ideas of youth and life. 'I will be dead in a few years', he could say just as the Marshal does; in the meantime, he felt chained to a body that, if not 'worn-out' exactly, was certainly wearing down. 'Damn it, I did have genius . . .', Faulkner wrote in a letter just twelve months before *A Fable* was published. 'It just took me 55 years to find out. I suppose I was too busy working to notice it before.'[41] Listening to the Marshal arguing, haranguing, talking on and on to the quietly confident Corporal – who seems utterly at ease with *his* genius, secure in himself and his powers of sympathy and persuasion – it is tempting to see, in the contrast between them, a version of the older Faulkner addressing his younger self: trying to take on the younger man's quiet power, or else take it away. Be that as it may, it does seem clear that, on some level or other, Faulkner is talking to Faulkner in this debate between father and son; the dialogue dramatizes a deeply personal conflict. In a strictly practical sense, of course, the Marshal loses the argument because he does not succeed in tempting the Corporal. As for the conceptual framework, however, the dualistic terms on which the entire novel turns: things are much more even-handed there. Dramatizing the 'two articulations' that he obviously recognized within himself, Faulkner manages to keep the debate open, to make the conflict one that requires our attention because both sides are given a full hearing.

The temptation scene is not unique in *A Fable*, but it is exceptional: unfortunately, there are relatively few other moments in the novel that share its dramatic focus and bite, that have the same sense of a contest in which there are strong, plausible arguments on both sides. 'It's getting right now', Faulkner wrote to his agent during one of the early stints of working on his 'big book'. 'It was a tragedy of ideas, morals before; now it's getting to be a tragedy of people.' The trouble was that he should have seen 'ideas' and 'people' as somehow divisible – as if either thought or character had an existence independent of the other – and that he should have, at least, initiated his project with supposedly autonomous 'ideas'. Faulkner was probably closer to the truth when, in 1953, he told Joan Williams that *A Fable* was going to be his 'last, major, ambitious work' because he was 'getting toward the end, the bottom of the barrel'. 'The stuff is still good', he added, 'but I know now there is not very much more of it, a little trash comes up constantly now, which must be sifted out.'[42] *A Fable* may not, in fact, represent Faulkner's last stab at greatness; and 'trash' is certainly too tough a way of describing all that Faulkner sensed he ought to edit out of his work in progress. Still, as Faulkner recognized, there was material there that needed pruning or omitting, as the words multiplied and the pages accumulated over the years. Sadly, the sifting process was never perfect. And when, in November 1953, Faulkner sat down to prepare the vast manuscript for publication, he was suffering from acute depression; as a result, the final stages of editing failed to sift out all that the earlier stages had missed.

Flawed in conception, uneven in execution, *A Fable* was also hampered, then, by its author's reluctance or simple inability to select adequately and to cut. But, for all that, it remains a powerful testament: not least, to Faulkner's understanding of the contending impulses that help to make up history. The strength of the book, really, lies in its monumentalism: its representation of the crowd, the mass of people, as a fluid agent of change or, alternatively, as a repressive instrument of authority; its bold interpretation of human nature and historical process in terms of a warring embrace of opposites; its fashioning of a narrative idiom that, sometimes at least, registers the vital connection between private lives and public events. And there, also, is where the weakness of *A Fable* is to be found: in Faulkner's pursuit of a monumental sweep, his desire to say 'big' things in a 'big' way. The generalizing bias of the story tends to simplify things, to suppress problems and prohibit conflict; the narrative voice is too resonantly monolithic, at times; the tendency towards anonymity and allegory means that much of the grit, the persuasive detail of ordinary human experience is left out. On receiving advance copies of *A Fable*, Faulkner wrote to one of his editors, the man who had helped him prepare the final version of his manuscript. 'The books . . . are very fine', he declared, 'I am as proud as you are.' 'If we are right'. he went on, 'and it is my best and not the bust I had considered it might be, I will ask nothing more.'[43] *A Fable* is certainly not Faulkner's 'best', as he had hoped: but neither is it 'a bust', as he had occasionally feared it would be. It is, rather, poignant testimony to his belief that the quality a writer had to have, above all, was courage – 'courage', as he put it, 'to risk being guilty of bad taste, clumsiness, mawkishness, dullness' – and that, consequently, the worst thing it was possible to say about a book was, 'it isn't ambitious enough'.

III   Distant Voices, Desperate Lives: *The Town*

'I have just started on another novel, the second Snopes volume', Faulkner wrote in December 1955. This news was addressed to the new young woman to whom he had formed an attachment, Jean Stein, almost forty years his junior. 'I feel pretty good over your reaction to the new Snopes stuff', he confessed to her about a month later. 'Does it make you nervous to find out somebody needs you? How vain does it make you?' 'I still feel', he added, 'that perhaps I have written myself out and all that remains is the empty craftsmanship – no fire, force, passion anymore in the words and sentences. But as long as it please you, I will have to go on.' Faulkner was returning to the plan of the Snopes saga he had sketched over ten years previously – and beyond that, of course, to themes and characters that he had first brought into written life in *Father Abraham*. The work proceeded rapidly: in part, because of its long gestation – Faulkner was, after all, exploiting material he had been thinking about for thirty years – and, in part, because he found it possible to incorporate actual published stories: 'Centaur in Brass', which had first appeared in 1932, and

'Mule in the Yard', which had been published two years later. Despite the
speed with which Faulkner worked, however, the quiet confidence that
had accompanied his earlier writing continued to elude him. 'The book
is going too good, I am afraid', he confided to Jean Stein, 'my judgement
may be dead and it is no good.' 'I still cant tell, it may be trash except for
certain parts, though I think not', he told his publisher just two months
before the manuscript was completed, 'I still think it is funny, and at the
end very moving; two women characters I am proud of.' Exploiting elements from the story of the Falkner family – and, in particular, from
Faulkner's memories of his grandfather, the banker John Wesley Thompson
Falkner – the novelist gradually brought the story to the point where
Father Abraham begins: with Flem Snopes triumphant, elevated to the
position of president of one of the two Jefferson banks. 'Just finishing the
book', Faulkner announced to Jean Stein in August 1956. 'It breaks my
heart, I wrote one scene and almost cried. I thought it was just a funny
book but I was wrong.'[44]

The reasons for Faulkner's confusion as he worked on *The Town* (the
title he had first devised for the second volume of the Snopes trilogy in
1939) were the ones familiar to his later years: fears about the possibility
of his waning powers as man and writer, an increasingly anxiety-ridden
romanticism that seemed to make him incapable of finding anyone commensurate to his capacity for wonder, a growing discomfort with the split
between his public eminence and his private distress. 'I know, as you must,
that Bill feels some sort of compulsion to be attached to some young
woman at all times', Estelle wrote to Faulkner's publisher and friend in
1956, 'At long last I am sensible enough to concede him the right to do
as he pleases, and without recrimination.' 'It is not that I do not care', she
added, '. . . but all of a sudden I feel sorry for him – wish he could know
without words between us, that it's not very important after all.' That
confession speaks volumes about the silences that persisted between
Faulkner and his wife, and the quiet desperation that, on one side at least,
was slowly subsiding into resignation. But while Estelle was, so she claimed,
resigning herself to the sad compromises of their marriage, Faulkner himself was, as she perceived, still searching for romantic adventure and the
illusion of erotic renewal. 'He had some young girl with him', one of
Faulkner's first loves, Helen Baird, reported caustically after she had met
him by chance on Pascagoula beach in the late autumn of 1955, 'But you
have to expect that.'[45]

So if the new young women on whom Faulkner projected his romantic
longings were often bewildered by the sheer ferocity of his attentions,
then in turn the women whom he had previously adored could look at
him with pity, as Estelle did, or, as Helen Baird preferred to, with mordant
irony. And what made the pain and pathos of Faulkner's situation at this
time even more painful was that, as he was only too well aware, he was a
prophet without honour in his own country. Honours continued to shower
upon him from abroad: in 1955, for instance, he spent three months

talking, lecturing and generally being fêted in Japan (where he was praised for the inscrutability of his 'Oriental' demeanour!) and Europe. In Mississippi, however, his outspokenness on the race issue was earning him the titles of 'nigger-lover' and 'Weeping Willie Faulkner', as well as what he termed 'threatening fan mail' and 'nut angry telephone calls at 2 and 3 a.m.'. 'I can see the possible time when I shall have to leave my native state', he declared in 1955, 'something as the Jew had to flee from Germany during Hitler.' In fact, one of the minor functions of *The Town* seems to have been to act as a refuge from all this local unrest and hostility. 'Doing a little work on the Snopes book', Faulkner told his publisher some time in the winter of 1955–6, 'Miss. such an unhappy state to live in now, that I need something like a book to get lost in.'[46]

Getting lost seems an appropriate phrase to describe the narrative trajectory of *The Town*. There are two central threads to the story. One concerns the steady rise of Flem Snopes. Exploiting everything – including his wife Eula's long-standing affair with the town mayor and bank president Manfred de Spain – Flem slowly climbs the ladder of success. From superintendent of the town power plant, a position that de Spain creates for him, he moves to the post of vice-president of the bank, then finally becomes president. Along the way, his ambitions subtly alter. As those inveterate Snopes-watchers Gavin Stevens and V.K. Ratliff gradually realize, it is not just power Flem wants now but 'respectability'. 'When it's just money and power a man wants', Ratliff observes,

> there is usually some place where he will stop: there's always one thing at least that ever – every man won't do just for money. But when it's respectability he finds out he wants and has got to have, there ain't nothing he won't do to get it and then keep it.[47]

Manipulating the members of his family and the more powerful figures of the town, Flem gets what he wants: by the time the book closes, he has not only acquired de Spain's job he has also bought his house – to which he has added columns, 'extry big ones' as Ratliff points out, to lend a specious air of antiquity, *inherited* authority. This thread of the story was probably the one Faulkner began with: in Faulkner's mind, and in that earlier, unfinished narrative, *Father Abraham*, Flem was already president of the bank before one word of *The Town* had been written. He was circling back here, to explain the details of an ascent that he had imagined in its broad outline three decades earlier. This material pushed the author towards social comedy of a kind he had hardly ever ventured on before, but with which he was familiar thanks to the work of earlier Southern writers who had tapped a rich vein of small-town satire – notably, Ellen Glasgow in books like *Virginia* (1913) and *The Romantic Comedians* (1926). 'I thought it was just a funny book', Faulkner had said, 'but I was wrong.' And the main reason he felt he was wrong was that a second narrative thread pushed him towards not comedy but pathos: not small-town social satire but small-town tragedy.

The second, central thread in *The Town* is intimated in other remarks made by Faulkner while he was preparing the manuscript, about the 'two women characters' he claimed to be 'proud of' and 'one scene' during the composition of which he 'almost cried'. This thread concerns Eula Varner Snopes and her daughter Linda, the product of a brief but passionate coupling with a character named Hoake McCarron in *The Hamlet*. Whatever else may be said about Eula in this second novel in the Snopes saga, one thing is clear: she is trapped. She is trapped, first of all, in the claustrophobic atmosphere and rituals of a small town that is secretly 'accessory' to her affair with de Spain but would never openly admit the fact of adultery – and would punish the adulterers if that fact were made a matter of public revelation or admission. 'You simply cannot go against a community', Gavin Stevens observes, in connection with Eula and the dangerous dividing line she treads between public complicity and public knowledge, hidden and open secrets. And as Gavin senses, both in her liaison with the mayor and in the rumours she trails with her about the true father of her daughter, Eula pushes the town's capacity for hypocrisy – its willingness to countenance the illicit, as long as the right game of social subterfuge is played – just about as far as it can go. Nowhere else in Faulkner's work does the community of Jefferson seem so irretrievably bourgeois: so paralysed in the rituals of the dinner table or the society ball, and so enmeshed in conversations that skirt around a controversial fact without ever quite alighting upon it. This leads into the second way Eula is trapped: in her house and family, the thin air of suburban living and the stifling conventions of marriage to a man she has never loved. 'Suddenly I knew where I had seen the room and hallway before', says Gavin Stevens, when he goes to visit Eula at the house she shares with Flem and Linda,

> In a photograph, the photograph from say *Town and Country* labelled *American Interior*, reproduced in colour in a wholesale furniture catalogue, with the added legend: *This is neither a Copy nor a Reproduction. It is our own Model scaled to your Individual Requirements.*[48]

Trapped in this bourgeois doll's house by her sense of obligation to Linda, Eula is willing to sacrifice anything to save her daughter from what, in terms of this narrative and setting, appears to be the ultimate horror: the loss of reputation, 'respectability' or 'civic virtue'. Eventually, she is even willing to sacrifice her life. She kills herself, evidently preferring Linda to know her mother to be a suicide rather than an adulteress. Eula's motive for destroying herself may seem implausible if it is taken as many critics have taken it: as something issuing from her personal determination, her own feelings as a singular human subject. But it just about survives inspection if it is seen, as it surely must be, as one further, pathetic symptom of Eula's entrapment: she is imprisoned, her suicide tells us, not just in the material world of 'respectable' Jefferson but in its mental and moral chains. Her determining fear of the scarlet letter that might be pinned on her, as a public inscribing of her private life, shows just how much her manacles are mind-forged.[49]

Here, however, we are beginning to enter into the problem of the narrative getting lost, disappearing in the thickets of its own complications. There is no reason why small-town social satire and small-town tragedy should not inhabit the same story. One of Faulkner's earliest mentors, Sherwood Anderson, had demonstrated how it could be done, in books like *Winesburg, Ohio* (1919); and, in fact, some of the best moments in *The Town* recall that earlier Mid-Western narrative. Certain episodes, for instance, recollect Anderson's capacity for stretching social satire to the point where it edges into the comedy of the grotesque, or where it starts to float off into the surreal. The whole business of I.O. Snopes having mules placed on a sharp curve on the railroad track, so that he can collect compensation from the train company, brings the old and the new into collision in a way that is at once macabre and comic; while the elaborate means by which Montgomery Ward Snopes and his small-time pornography business are eliminated, without the fact of a trade in pornography ever being publicly admitted, plays a sardonic variation on Anderson's own exposures of provincial hypocrisy. In turn, the account of Eula's suicide repeats similar episodes not just in Anderson's fiction but in the poetry of Edwin Arlington Robinson or Edgar Lee Masters. In poems like, say, Robinson's 'Richard Cory' ('And Richard Cory, one calm summer night, / Went home and put a bullet through his head') or some of the pieces in Masters's *Spoon River Anthology* (1915), the comic futility of small-town life assumes a tragic dimension, just as it does in the story of the trapped life and sudden death of Eula Varner Snopes. At such moments, the horror of repressed feeling spills out over the humdrum of the everyday – and Faulkner signals his own revolt from the village with a seriousness that does not undermine the satire to be found elsewhere but, on the contrary, serves to underwrite it. Reciting the absurdities of social practice that the small town compels, and the moments of violence it initiates: the problem does not *necessarily* lie here, in Faulkner's use of two, time-honoured strategies for registering American provincial life – its elaborate rituals and, for that matter, its steady erosion by what is called at one point 'the motor age'.[50] It lies, rather, in the additional complications that issue from the author's own apparent uncertainty of motive: his failure to explain – not least, to his own satisfaction – just what he was doing with this material that had been with him for so long. Some of this uncertainty can be inferred from the trio of characters who act as narrators, Charles Mallison, V.K. Ratliff and Gavin Stevens, as they struggle to work out why the people they talk about behave the way they do. And even more of it is clearly evident in the representation of another trio – the characters who are mostly responsible for propelling the narrative, keeping the action going: Gavin Stevens again and, of course, Flem Snopes and his wife Eula.

As far as the presentation of the three main agents of plot in *The Town* is concerned, there is a curious lack of focus. All three come to us disconcertingly blurred, via a narrative idiom that seems neither certain nor, alternatively, aware of its lack of certainty and able, in some way, to come to terms with it. Eula, for instance, may belong in some ways to a narrative tradition that Faulkner had scarcely exploited up until this time: a tradition that uses scenes from provincial life, local colour and social realism, to register the experience of specifically social forms of entrapment. Like Edna Pontellier, for instance, the heroine of Kate Chopin's 1899 novel, *The Awakening*, Eula is a desperate woman denied her desires, ground in the mill of the conventional, and seeing no way out except in suicide. Like Kate Swift, the sexually frustrated schoolteacher in *Winesburg, Ohio*, she tries to reach out to men of her acquaintance who only minimally meet her needs and really only exacerbate her discontent. Like Carol Kennicott, the central character in Sinclair Lewis's *Main Street* (1920), she finds herself the victim of the emotional and imaginative poverty of her neighbours: Gavin Stevens even suggests that the real reason for her suicide was boredom. 'She was bored. She loved, had a capacity ... to give and accept love', Stevens declares, 'Only she tried twice and failed twice to find somebody not just strong enough to deserve, earn it, match it, but even brave enough to accept it.' Whatever the immediate motive, it is credible that such a character would kill herself if that seemed to be the only way to escape bourgeois convention; since in death as in life she is seen, on one level, as a Southern variation on the Madame Bovary figure, driven into a corner by small-town morality. The only trouble is that this is not the only level on which she is seen. Especially towards the beginning of the novel, she comes to us trailing the mythic associations that surrounded her in *The Hamlet*. She is, Stevens suggests,

> that Frenchman's Bend Helen, Semiramis – no: not Helen nor Semiramis: Lilith: the one before Eve herself whom earth's Creator had perforce in desperate and amazed alarm in person to efface, remove, obliterate, that Adam might create a progeny to populate it.[51]

This might be dismissed as Stevens's romanticism elevating a bored suburban housewife into a mythic version of the female principle, telling us more about the narrator than it does about the subject. The fact is, though, that all the narrators share the tendency to translate Eula into an earth goddess, and to see her in terms of desire and absence: to identify her, in short, with a familiar Faulknerian vocabulary that spells out the legendary name, 'Woman'. What is perhaps more to the point, it is Eula herself who is given remarks like the following (this one is addressed to Stevens, when she is offering herself to him):

> You spend too much time expecting. Don't expect. You just are, and you need, and you must, and you do. That's all. Don't waste time expecting.[52]

This fits in perfectly with the preternatural creature of Stevens's and other people's occasional imaginings, but it hardly belongs with the frustrated woman who eventually kills herself rather than be branded a whore. The two versions of Eula, Lilith and Bovary, the 'incandescent shape' 'too much . . . for any one human female package to contain' and the pathetic victim of the boredom of provincial life: these do not go together, any more than the narrative idioms to which they belong do. We are left, as a result, with a character who is neither clear nor clearly represented as an enigma: someone about whom the author seems to have changed his mind, in the course of writing the book.

'This was not the first time I ever thought how apparently all Snopeses are male', Stevens observes at one moment in *The Town*, 'as if the mere and simple incident of woman's divinity precluded Snopesishness and made it paradox.' Stevens goes on to qualify this: '*Snopes*', he suggests, is 'some profound and hermaphroditic principle . . . vested always physically in the male'. But the qualification does little to alter the determining conception: if, on one level, Eula Varner Snopes is the female principle incarnate, then, on that same level, Flem Snopes is its male equivalent – or, rather, opposite. 'Woman . . . just by breathing, just by the mere presence of that fragile and delicate flesh', as the narrative puts it, 'warps and wrenches milieu itself to those soft unangled rounds and curves and planes.' Man, on the contrary, drives onward and upward: striving like Flem to penetrate new territories, to climb up the ladder of wealth and power, to erect monuments to himself and, indeed, to turn himself into a monument, a testament to his fixed purpose. Woman is fluidity, man is fixity; woman is all curves and rounds, man is all straight lines and rigorous angles; woman is all feeling, and man is all force. These are all, by now, recognizable Faulknerian equations, and the relationship between Flem and them is obvious: he is the male will to power made flesh. He is also, on a less primal level, the character the reader encountered in *The Hamlet*: who has followed through on the logic of capitalism, so that for him material profit and personal advancement are not just the main considerations, they are the only ones. Faulkner complicates the message by emphasizing how impeccably bourgeois Flem's specific ambitions are – he wants, after all, to be 'respectable' – and by making little secret of the link between Flem and his neighbours: Manfred de Spain, for instance, uses his office as mayor to invent a position for the husband of his mistress – an action that says as much about him as it does about Flem. There are, however, no serious contradictions here. Flem as the male will incarnate, Flem as the logic of capitalism, Flem as the absolute bourgeois: these are all perfectly reconcilable, and are made to seem so as the narrative records Flem's apparently unstoppable ascent within the society that comes to seem more and more made in his image. The problem does not lie here. It lies, really, in the same place as it does in the portrait of Eula: in Faulkner's gradual and (during the course of the novel) growing use of a narrative tradition that commemorates the pathos of provincial life – that advises us how sad living is, in a small town certainly and perhaps else-where as well. 'He's impotent', Eula tells Gavin Stevens, talking about Flem towards the end of *The Town*, 'He's always been.' 'You've got to be careful or you'll have to pity him', she warns, 'He ... couldn't bear being pitied ... Like he can live with his impotence, but you mustn't have the chance to help him with pity.'[53] Stevens cannot cope with this information for the time being. The reader, however, has no alternative but to recog-nize Flem's vulnerability: the very fact that he is unable to deal with pity only makes him an even more pathetic figure. To say that this muddies the waters is an understatement: this makes Flem a different creature altogether, someone who seems to have wandered in off the sad streets of Winesburg, Ohio. He, too, appears to be a victim, if not of society then of circumstance. The focus is not just softened, it is once again blurred by the collision between quite different narrative modes.

'Uncle Gavin had lived in Jefferson or in little towns all his life', his nephew Charles Mallison observes; and to the extent that Faulkner per-mits Stevens to be defined by this small-town environment – as a middle-aged Galahad and constant object of town gossip – he slips easily into the scenes from provincial life. An adolescent dreamer heading towards the male menopause, he is the young knight of Faulkner's earlier fiction – Quentin Compson, say, or Horace Benbow – grown old, or at least much older: a man who wants, as he himself puts it, 'not to encounter' the object of his affections but 'continuously just to miss her yet never be caught at it'. Clearly, on Faulkner's part there is an element of self-mockery at work here. As Gavin switches his attentions from Eula to her daughter Linda, plying the sixteen-year-old high-school girl with 'banana splits and ice-cream sodas and books of poetry', it is difficult not to think of the author falling desperately in love with women increasingly younger than himself. A would-be protector of Eula's honour, who recoils in dismay when Eula actually offers herself to him, he is perceived much of the time through a narrative prism which, like the one in *Winesburg, Ohio,* allows room for both pity and irony. And just as Faulkner's earlier dreamers had 'real men' to contend with, by whom to measure their own conspicuous lack of conventional masculinity, so Stevens has his own, rather comic rivals. There is, first, Eula's lover, Manfred de Spain. A 'real man' in the sense that he drives a red sports car and bears a 'long scar' from his military experience in Cuba, his juvenile tactics – which include racing his car, noisily and defiantly, past Gavin's house and sending Gavin a used condom – suggest that he comes from something other than the tradi-tional heroic mould. If he is a hero, then he is a comically contracted one; and so, even more so, is Gavin's second rival, a local garage mechanic named Matt Levitt, the boyfriend of Linda who claims to have 'won the Golden Gloves up in Ohio or somewhere'. 'By Cicero, Gavin', comments Stevens's brother-in-law, as Levitt in turn races his car past the house so as to show just who the 'real man' is,

You're losing ground. Last time you at least picked a Spanish-American War hero with an E.M.F. sportster. Now the best you can do is a Golden Gloves amateur with a home-made racer. Watch yourself, bud, or next you'll have a boy scout defying you to mortal combat with a bicycle.[54]

Comments like these, shared between several townsfolk and the narrators, help situate Stevens as a figure simultaneously pathetic and comic: the village dreamer as he is conceived of in the fiction of Sherwood Anderson or, for that matter, the poems of Edwin Arlington Robinson. 'Miniver sighed for what was not, / And dreamed, and rested from his labours', says Robinson of one such character, 'He dreamed of Thebes and Camelot, / And Priam's neighbours.' The point is, though, that Stevens is not just rendered to us through prisms shaped by others. He is permitted to speak for himself. Being Gavin Stevens, he says a lot ('talking ... I usually am', he himself admits at one point); and a lot of what he says has an intensity, a simple ferocity of purpose that cuts across irony and pity and immerses the reader in some familiar Faulknerian obsessions. 'And then I heard the door', Stevens confides as he describes Eula leaving him, shortly before she commits suicide,

and it was as if she had not been. No, not that; not *not been*, but rather no more *is*, since *was* remains always and forever, inexplicable and immune, which is its grief. That's what I mean: a dimension less, a substance less, then the sound of a door and then, not *never been* but simply *no more is* since always and forever that *was* remains, as if what is going to happen to one tomorrow already gleams faintly visible now if the watcher were only wise enough to discern it or maybe just brave enough.[55]

This, and other passages in *The Town* like it, have a power and persuasiveness that issue out of two things: the author's evident identification with what is being said and, related to this, its repetition and revision of some of the old ineradicable rhythms and familiar phrases from books like *The Sound and the Fury*, *As I Lay Dying* and *Absalom, Absalom!* Faulkner is no longer making wry fun of Stevens, he is caught up in his passion and, in the process, replaying old obsessions: about, for instance, the elusive nature of desire and its objects, the interpenetration of past and present, or the slippery nature of the relationship between language, human presence and absence. This is moving into an imaginative terrain utterly separate from the one inhabited by the middle-aged Galahad, that actively prohibits comedy and pathos. It is not really that we are being presented with a new dimension of character – as we are in, say, Faulkner's earlier books, when the narrative dips down below the surfaces of social behaviour. Rather, we are being offered a new character altogether: someone who is as separate from the village knight approaching menopause that we encounter elsewhere as Eula as Lilith is from Eula as Bovary – or as Flem as male will incarnate or seamless capitalist is from Flem the vulnerable creature of circumstance. In short, we seem somehow to have entered another novel.

This is the crucial point. Passages like the one just quoted work well in isolation. The trouble is, when we read them in context they appear simply to contradict other moments in the story: we are left in a confusion that is considerably less than fruitful, as a character slips from one narrative identity into another one, utterly different. When Faulkner's major novels were first published, a number of reviewers (among them, F.R. Leavis) claimed that the author was using different narrative techniques because he did not really know what he was doing.[56] Unfair though this criticism surely was and is, as far as the major novels are concerned, it does perhaps have some point, some relevance here. In *The Town*, at least, Faulkner does appear to be oscillating between different kinds of narration because he is unsure about his subject. He is unclear about just how to take his characters and the stories they enact and so, as a result, are we. Nor is this lack of certainty simply a matter of character representation and slippage between conflicting narrative modes: one of the most remarkable features of the second book in the Snopes trilogy is the tendency of the three narrators to replicate their creator's own difficulties. Faulkner seems, albeit instinctively, to be pushing the device of the unreliable narrator to new extremes here, as Charles Mallison, V.K. Ratliff and Gavin Stevens all, in turn, admit their ignorance – and, for that matter, the ignorance of the other two narrators – confess the problems they have experienced in investigating motive, unravelling the reason why certain events have occurred: in effect, disclose the difficulty, or perhaps the impossibility, of ever properly working things out.

The preoccupation with language is one symptom of this tendency to foreground the impediments to explanation. Mallison comments several times on his uncle's habit of slipping between two voices, that of the former student of Harvard and Heidelberg and that of the country lawyer; while Ratliff is constantly trying to 'correct' his dialect speech, and even has conversations with Stevens and Mallison about whether he is right to do so or not. These doubts about the way things should be said are, of course, inseparable from uneasiness over what should be said. Here as elsewhere in Faulkner's work, consciousness is predicated in speech; and so not to know precisely how to speak is, to an extent, not to know where one stands or the way things are. The entire inclination of the book, towards uncertainty of speech and instability of explanation, is in fact succinctly caught in its shortest narrative section, the ninth, which consists of eight words in two sentences. It is given to V.K. Ratliff, who is commenting on Gavin Stevens. 'Because he missed it', Ratliff says, 'He missed it completely.'[57] The particular reference here is to Stevens's failure to understand that it is respectability that Flem Snopes is really after: but it does not take a great deal of ingenuity to see that the remark can have a more general application. Characters, especially narrators, are constantly 'missing it' in *The Town*. Like their creator, they can neither believe nor be comfortable in their unbelief: they can neither subscribe wholly to one explanation, one speech system or type of narrative representation, nor admit the need for a shifting, plural view.

This is one difference between the narrative plurality of *The Town* and that of Faulkner's earlier work: a technique of subversion has now become a symptom of uncertainty. Faulkner clearly wants to pin his story down to a particular way of telling it. The trouble is, he cannot; the lens slips, while he tries to hold it steady, and the focus is blurred. So what was a creative use of confusion in the earlier writing, or at least some of it, becomes, simply, confusion. That is one difference. Another one is signalled by what is probably the most famous passage in the book, where Gavin Stevens describes the view from a ridge 'on beyond Seminary Hill' – from which, he says, 'you see all Yoknapatawpha in the dying last of day beneath you'. Taken in isolation, as it usually is, it is a powerful and moving piece of prose: not least, because it appears to express Faulkner's desire, which grew with him as the years passed, to write some final testament, a farewell tribute to his apocryphal county before he abjured the rough magic of his craft. 'And you stand suzerain and solitary above the whole sum of your life', Stevens declares, towards the beginning of this passage,

> First is Jefferson, the centre, . . . beyond it, spreads the County, . . . yourself detached as God Himself for this moment above the cradle of your nativity and of the men and women who made you . . . you to preside unanguished and immune above this miniature of man's passions and and hopes and disasters . . .[58]

Gavin Stevens is not Faulkner, of course, but – as most critics have recognized – the passage as a whole has a resonance that stems from its autobiographical origins. Faulkner seems to be trying to fulfil a need here, to stake a final claim to his county. Seen in this light, what is most remarkable about the comments just quoted is, surely, their detachment: the speaker stands 'suzerain and solitary', 'unanguished and immune' above a panorama that derives a strange, calm beauty precisely from its separateness. There is simple, elegiac feeling, there is sympathy perhaps: but there is above all a sense of being apart, an impulse of absence and departure. Nothing could be further removed from the emotions generated by the earlier, major novels: which are major, not least, because of the ferocity of the author's involvement. In books like *The Sound and the Fury* and *Absalom, Absalom!*, Faulkner is in there investigating his own case and, in the process, producing work that acts as both symptom and evidence: drawing a map of Yoknapatawpha that is, he instinctively knows, also a chart of himself, *his* place and *his* past. In *The Town*, precisely the opposite is the case. Now Faulkner is at times insisting on, and at others assuming, his separateness from the fictional space he describes. So intent is he upon this that he does not seem to realize just how implicated he is in his characters', and especially his narrators', confusions. The temptation to take on the role of 'God himself' in his fiction was always there for Faulkner. In the best of his earlier work, though, that temptation was resisted or at least challenged, as indeed were any claims to authority: here in *The Town*, by comparison, he seems to long for the safety and security of a God-like view. Unlike Gavin Stevens standing on the ridge, he cannot get it; and so he slips between different narrative forms, all presumed to be authoritative for a while, and various perspectives, every one of which is marked by a quality of aloofness. 'A man has got to know his – himself', comments V.K. Ratliff during the course of the story, '. . . Because what somebody else jest tells you, you jest half believe, unless it was something you already wanted to hear.'[59] Telling, however, and telling from a distance, is what much of the second volume in the Snopes saga is about. The result is a narrative in which the reader can only 'jest half believe', because he or she has to look at everything in miniature, as it were – and, not only that, as though through a blurred glass, darkly.

IV   THEN THE LETTING GO: *THE MANSION*

Faulkner began the third volume of the Snopes saga, *The Mansion*, just nine months after *The Town* was published. He had been disappointed with the unenthusiastic reviews for *The Town*. 'You shouldn't put off too long writing something you think is worth writing', he said when someone mentioned the poor reviews to him, and in particular one reviewer's comment that he seemed tired of the Yoknapatawpha chronicle. And the Snopes story, he confessed, 'I have had in mind for thirty years now. So maybe it could be a little stale to me, though I don't think that's true, either.'[60] 'Stale' or not, Faulkner set to work on *The Mansion* with what was for him, at this late stage in his career, unusual energy and enthusiasm. Incorporating stories already written, 'By the People' and 'Hog Pawn', he had completed the first draft of the book by the beginning of 1959: concluding with the passage, quoted earlier in this study, that incorporated imagery which first excited his imagination some three decades earlier when he set out to become a writer. A major key to the writing process now, in fact, was recapitulation. As Faulkner continued with the book that he described as 'the last of my planned labours', he felt compelled more than ever to repeat and reinvent familiar stories from the history of Yoknapatawpha: ranging from the comic tall tale of the visit made by Virgil and Fonzo Snopes to a Memphis brothel, first told in *Sanctuary*, to the fierce melodrama of the life and death of Bayard Sartoris III, recollected from *Flags in the Dust/Sartoris*. In this sense, the story of Mink Snopes returning to Jefferson after thirty-eight years in prison to kill his brother Flem, takes on a peculiarly autobiographical dimension. It is as if Faulkner is dramatizing his own return – perhaps for the last time, perhaps for the penultimate one – to the country of his imagination, in this story of a poor, bare, forked animal who goes back to his homeplace with just one more job to do.

'Where you been the last five years, dad?' asks a young man who gives Mink a lift, when he realizes that Mink knows nothing about the Second World War, 'Asleep?' To which Mink replies, 'I been away.'[61] The assault of the strange new world of America at mid-century on the consciousness of a man who has been 'away' in prison for nearly four decades is powerfully rendered. Disoriented by the omnipresence of automobiles, the urban sprawl, the simple, physical discomfort of walking on concrete rather than dirt roads, this Rip Van Winkle figure not only gave his creator the chance to return and recapitulate. He offered him the opportunity for elegy. By means of the figure of Mink, Faulkner could dramatize the shock of the new (which had come to him in a more protracted fashion than to Mink, but was no less painful for that); and he could also commemorate the older, more provincial and quieter world both author and character had lost – in which, for instance, the only cars in town belonged to one or two local dignitaries. The impulse towards recapitulation created problems for Faulkner, particularly when this involved recollecting narrative details from the two earlier volumes in the Snopes saga. Eventually, he had to have help resolving some of the more serious discrepancies between what he wrote in 1958–9 and what he had written earlier for *The Hamlet* and *The Town*. Even then, he thought it wise and right to insert a prefatory note to *The Mansion* to the effect that, as he put it, 'there will be found discrepancies and contradictions in the thirty-four-year progress of this particular chronicle' because ' "living" is motion and "motion" is change and alteration and therefore the only alternative to motion is un-motion, stasis, death'. If repetition produced technical problems about consistency for Faulkner, though, then the elegaic impulse created something more complicated. The chance to recall a life that was lost was opened up, of course, to measure the harshness of the collision between old and new and the dimensions of the psychological crisis created by material change. But so too was the opportunity for accepting the inevitability of alteration, for making peace with a different world and perhaps diminished hopes as well: regret could, and was, accompanied by feelings of reconciliation.

'Pappy really changed', Faulkner's daughter Jill recalled of him during these final years, 'He became so much easier to live with . . . he was a different man . . . He was enjoying life.' This may be a little too simple. Faulkner could still claim sardonically, at about this time, that perhaps peace and happiness occur only in retrospect. 'I'm inclined to think', he told one of his classes at the University of Virginia, 'that the only peace a man knows is – he says, Why good gracious yesterday I was happy.' 'Maybe peace is not is', he added, 'but was.'[62] He could also drink himself into what a friend called a 'near-state of catalepsy', or put himself in situations that seemed calculated to test him and, in particular, his idea of manhood. Taking up foxhunting in Virginia, for example, he was described as being 'all nerve' as a rider and hunter. 'I love the thrill of danger', he confessed, 'I'm scared to death of horses, that's why I can't leave them alone.' In some ways, then, Faulkner was still the restless, even self-destructive figure of his youth: intensely private, interested in disguise ('What more do you want from me, an American farmer?' he asked a European journalist in 1957), haunted by models of male courage that he both longed and feared to imitate. But, as his daughter recognized, he was more capable of an even mood now: he could, within his own terms, be mellow even without the help of alcohol, and sociable. Some of this probably had to do with material security. 'I just can't stand that Hollywood shit', he declared in 1957; and he did not have to stand it any more. He could sell the film rights to his books for tidy sums now, but he no longer had to write for the movies. When the film version of *The Sound and the Fury* appeared in 1959, he even refused to help with the publicity, pointing out that the contract specifically stated that he did not have to read the screenplay or see the picture. 'I have got a belly full of Oxford', he also told a friend in 1957. And he did not need to put up with his Mississippi homeplace any more either, if he did not want to. Travel was an alternative: to Europe, perhaps, as an honoured guest, to New York City or Princeton University. And another, more preferable one as far as Faulkner was concerned was what was by now his second home in Charlottesville, Virginia: where he first gave class conferences at the university and then acted as consultant to the college library – and where, in 1959, he bought himself a house.

Along with this relative material security, and the greater flexibility and freedom of choice it facilitated, there was the sense of an ending, of things being brought to a satisfactory – or, at least, acceptable – conclusion. Faulkner's fame as a writer was one sign or certificate of this: as 'man working' (to use his own phrase) he could feel, at last, that he had done more than reasonably well. Another sign, perhaps still more satisfying to him, was offered by such moments as those in 1958: when he gave away his brother Dean's daughter in marriage (so completing payment of a debt that he felt he had incurred as a result of Dean's untimely death) and then, towards the end of the year, when he was presented with a second grandson, named after him. Even the marriage to Estelle seems to have settled down at this stage, if not into complete contentment then into a *modus vivendi* based on mutual acceptance and shared memories – and, not least, on Faulkner's recognition of his own ageing. That process of settling down is registered, among other ways, in the fate of Gavin Stevens in *The Mansion*. Perpetual romantic though he is, doomed to pursue Eula Varner Snopes and then her daughter Linda, he ends up by making his own gesture of acceptance. As we have already learned from *Knight's Gambit*, he marries the widow Melisandre Harriss, whom in their shared youth Stevens had loved and lost. She is a mother of two, as Estelle was when she married Faulkner. She is also wealthy, thanks to her first husband; and Stevens goes to live with her in her refurbished and remodelled ancestral home, where they become (as Charles Mallison wryly puts it) 'the squire and his dame among his new ancestral white fences and electric-lit stables'.[63] It is difficult not to suspect an autobiographical touch here, as Stevens replicates his own creator's sinking back into the resignation, and relative peace, of advancing age. There is a touch of irony, of course, but it is an irony that colludes with feelings of sad acceptance: a gentle, quietly humorous shrug of the shoulders to accompany the sense of defeat – and the vision of steadily diminishing horizons.

The feeling of sinking away, dissolving back into mixed feelings of peace, resignation and a kind of muted contentment with the human lot, is perhaps most notable in the closing pages of *The Mansion*. 'So this is what it all come down to', observes V.K. Ratliff, after Flem has been killed and the house Flem took over from Manfred de Spain has been returned to what remains of the de Spain family, 'the only sister of Major de Spain, Manfred's father, and her only child':

> All the ramshacking and foreclosing and grabbling and snatching, doing it by gentle underhand when he could but by honest hard trompling when he had to ... And now all that's left of it is a bedrode old lady and her retired old-maid schoolteacher daughter ...[64]

'Maybe there's even a moral to it somewhere', Ratliff adds, 'if you jest knowed where to look.' To which Stevens replies, 'There aren't any morals. People just do the best they can.' 'The pore sons of bitches', Ratliff observes, turning his own summary of Flem's career into a plaint for humanity – which Stevens himself then takes up and echoes: 'The poor sons of bitches.' Everything is distanced, dissolved into a gesture of regret for the vanity of human wishes, a philosophical quietism that levels all the activities of 'the long human recording' by placing them between the stars and the earth. 'Overhead', the narrator comments in the final chapter, 'celestial and hierarchate, the constellations wheeled through the zodiacal pastures': reducing all the activities of the world, including those tiny parts of it called Frenchman's Bend and Jefferson, to a futile tale, briefly told. Beneath is the earth, that earth above which Flem had tried to erect his monuments: Flem, we are told, has three monuments to himself and the story of his enterprise – the water-tower, the mansion he has had remodelled, and the gravestone, 'the outrageous marble lie' he has had made in memory of Eula.

Mink Snopes, the man who propels the action in these closing pages, resists the pull of the earth at first. 'The very moment you were born out of your mother's body', he remembers, '... right away the earth started in to draw you back down into it.' And 'as soon as you could move', he reminds himself, 'you would raise your head even though that was all, trying ... to pull erect ... to get away from the earth, to save yourself.' He will not lie down on the earth, without something between himself and it, because, dangerously seductive, it offers the promise of release: something he cannot afford to contemplate until he has fufilled his mission of revenge

– a mission which requires him, as he constantly reminds himself, to 'be a man'. Once Flem is killed, however, once the job is done, Mink feels that he can relax and allow himself to be absorbed back into the quiet dust. 'He could risk it', he believes; he lies down with no impediment or guard between the earth and him. Lying there, the reader is told,

> he could feel the Mink Snopes that had had to spend so much of his life just having unnecessary bother and trouble, beginning to creep, seep, flow easy as sleeping; he could almost watch it, following all the little grass blades and tiny roots, the little holes the worms made, down and down into the ground already full of the folks that had the trouble but were free now . . .[65]

Not literally dead like Flem, he can nevertheless allow himself to die away; he can resign himself to the luxury of letting go. It is a gesture of farewell to the iron laws of necessity and history – to the compulsion to 'be a man' and pursue projects that (as Ratliff puts it at one point) enable a man to feel 'completely complete'. '*I'm free now*', Mink tells himself, as he slips away from a realm of struggle that is conceived of as male into a dimension of gentleness, peace, and the abolition of consciousness that is seen as definitively female, identified with the body of the other.

There are two points that perhaps need to be emphasized about this gravitation towards calm of mind, all passion spent at the end of *The Mansion*, this gradual unclenching of the narrative. The first is that the primary terms in which this is all imagined replay a duality familiar in Faulkner's work between active male principle and passive female. On the one hand, there is the world of law in which men talk of contracts, make bargains and pursue justice or revenge. On the other, there is a world 'immured, inviolate in silence, invulnerable, serene', identified with the mother earth, and the mother as earth, where communication seems neither possible nor necessary. 'Maybe to live outside human sound is to live outside human time too', thinks Gavin Stevens, 'Maybe . . . the entire dilemma of man's condition is because of the ceaseless gabble with which he has surrounded himself.' The silent earth offers a refuge from all this. So, in its own way, does the silence of Linda Snopes. She returns to Jefferson, having been deafened by an exploding shell during the Spanish Civil War; and she seems, as a result, to have become 'the bride of quietude and silence' – to have assumed the quietness and permanence of the earth, just as her mother Eula appears to have taken on its patience and plenty. For Stevens, she remains inviolable. '*We are the 2 in all the world who can love each other without having to*'[66] make physical love, he writes to her: writes to her, because that is the main way they communicate, even when they are together. There is clearly an autobiographical element at work here. Faulkner is thinking of the young women with whom a physical relationship is now no longer likely; and he is inventing a young woman with whom his sole point of contact is also his fictional *alter ego*'s main one – the sign, the duplicities of the written word. Perhaps more important than this, though, is how this imagining of women in *The Mansion*, and in particular the book's main woman character, facilitates its dying fall. Playing upon dreams of the female as earth and the earth as female that had been with him from the beginning of his career, Faulkner has one male character, Flem, return to the bosom of the earth, another one, Mink, allow himself to be absorbed back into the peace and quiet of mother earth, and a third, Gavin Stevens, accept that he cannot possess someone who, like the earth, exists apart from all claims of desire and ownership. All three, in their different ways, give up the pursuit of mastery, the assertion of self and power, in recognition of a world 'forever safe from change and alteration'. They fall back from the pursuit of projects and the erection of monuments into what is termed at one point, in connection with Eula Varner Snopes, the simple willingness 'jest to be, like the ground in the field'.

The second point about this dying away at the end of *The Mansion* is a much larger and more problematical one; and it has to do with the extent to which the mood of calm, and even resignation, with which Faulkner concludes the stories of his three main male protagonists is anticipated, prepared for by the rest of the novel. A careful, or at least suspicious, reader might well be unsurprised by the way Flem, Mink and Gavin all sink back into quiescence, if only because of certain narrative clues scattered earlier on, and particular tendencies in the narrative. There is a constant tendency towards resolution, for instance: a continuing inclination to dissolve threats and resolve particularly disruptive elements in the story, which is compounded by the habit of distancing carried over from *The Town* (here, as in the second novel in the Snopes saga, all the narrators are disposed to 'gabble' – to use Stevens's word – to talk about events in a detached way rather than re-create them). The story of Clarence Snopes, which occupies chapter 13 of *The Mansion*, is a case in point. The account of Clarence Snopes's rise to power is, in many ways, a superb illustration of Faulkner's capacity for analysing the political in terms of the personal. Clarence began, we learn, as the leader of a 'gang of cousins and toadies who fought and drank and gambled and beat up Negroes and terrified women . . . around Frenchman's Bend'. He was then made constable on the orders of Will Varner, who wanted to bring his casual violence under control. This appointment, apparently, 'was where and when Clarence's whole life . . . seemed at last to find itself like a rocket does at the first touch of fire'. Translating his racism into the rhetoric of law and order, first joining the Ku Klux Klan and then attacking it when it suited his political purposes, using every trick and every appeal to 'human baseness' that he could manage, he became a state senator. He was transmogrified, in fact, into:

Senator Clarence Egglestone Snopes, pronounced 'Cla'-nce' by every free white Yoknapatawpha American whose right and duty it was to go to the polls and mark his X each time old man Will Varner told him to.[67]

Quietly, Faulkner links this account of Clarence's ascent of the political ladder to figures like Huey Long and the whole history of Southern white populism. Revealing just how much Clarence is a weathercock of political fashion, Faulkner also describes the dilemma of white liberals: 'the doomed handful of literate liberal underpaid white-collar illusionees', as the narrator puts it, 'who had elected' Clarence Snopes '. . . because they thought he had destroyed the Ku Klux Klan' – together with 'the other lesser handful of other illusionees', like Stevens and Ratliff, 'who had voted for Clarence as the lesser of two evils'.

The crunch comes when Clarence runs for Congress. He is up against a war hero, a white man who led black troops; and, in order to win, the senator plays the race card, intimating that his opponent is a secret 'nigger-lover'. Until now, the story of Clarence has been a brilliantly satirical and deeply serious analysis of the darker side of Southern politics: a world in which race can outweigh all other considerations, where victory can go to those 'with a little brass . . . and no inhibitions', and where 'agencies created in the dream or hope that people should not suffer or . . . at least suffer equally' become a a source of corruption. The logic of the story says that this malign emblem of the will to political power should win, so moving from 'the . . . minor-league hog trough at Jackson' to 'that vast and limitless one in Washington'. However, Faulkner will not allow it. Here as elsewhere in *The Mansion*, the threat is suddenly dissipated, the disruptive agent is firmly dismissed – and the device used on this occasion is a more than usually implausible one. Clarence, we are asked to believe, is the victim of a trick, by which a group of dogs at an election picnic are made to mistake his trousers for a nearby dog-thicket and urinate on his leg. The humiliation forces him to withdraw, not only from the race for Congress, but from politics in general. Ratliff instigated the trick; and, when he tells Stevens what he has done, Stevens perhaps speaks for the reader – and, surely, for the author's own uneasiness over the narrative device he has used – when he says, 'Well I'll be damned. It's too simple. I don't believe it.' Will Varner is brought in, in an attempt to bolster the credibility of this resolution. It is he, we are told, who insisted on Clarence withdrawing from political life because he did not want Frenchman's Bend represented by someone who, as he puts it, 'ere a son-a-bitching dog that happens by can't tell from a fence post'.[68] In itself, the episode at the election picnic is a fine tall tale, a robust and enjoyable piece of comic business. But as a conclusion to what had been, up until then, a trenchant account of Southern politics – and, in particular, its complex corruptions – it is both anomalous and unsatisfactory: really no more than a symptom of the authors's evident need to resolve narrative tensions whenever they arise – to translate potential crisis into calm.

Apart from this tendency to dissipate tension, there are other clues that indicate which way the narrative is tending. Notable among these is the steadily increasing use of that telling phrase, 'the poor son of a bitch'. Fairly early on in *The Mansion*, the phrase is universalized. Miss Reba, the proprietor of a Memphis brothel who was first encountered in *Sanctuary*, applies it to all of suffering humanity: 'All of us. Every one of us', as she voices it, 'The poor son of a bitches.' The refrain is taken up in a prayer spoken by the Reverend Goodhay, a preacher with whom Mink stays on his way to Jefferson: 'Save us Christ, the poor sons of bitches.'[69] And the gradual alteration of perspective on the Snopeses as a clan is pinpointed by the substitution of a single letter: from 'pure sons of bitches' the Snopeses are transformed into 'pore sons of bitches'. What this alteration signals, of course, is what is confirmed in the closing pages of the story: the slow but steady shift from social and historical analysis to a kind of metaphysical quietism. From a perspective in which characters are seen as socially and historically responsible for their actions and the world they inhabit – and in which, therefore, some can be defined as corrupt or callous, 'pure sons of bitches' – Faulkner gravitates towards a quite different one: a perspective in which all are seen as victims, dwarfed by the stars, dominated by the earth, ultimately impotent and deserving of our pity.

The portrait of Flem is, unsurprisingly, a clear measure of this change. There were moments in *The Town* when Flem seemed to become a creature of pathos. Now, those moments multiply: not least because, as Ratliff observes, he seems 'to be satisfied' with all he has acquired and has nowhere further up he needs to go. He has apparently no more ambitions or desires left to fulfil. Certainly, the old Flem, the seamless capitalist, returns from time to time. There is, for instance, the episode in which he buys the 'ancestral acres' of the Compson family from Jason Compson at what turns out to be a bargain price – after he has had the land turned into 'a subdivision of standardised Veterans' Housing matchboxes' called Eula Acres. More often than not, though, he comes across as a sad and lonely figure. Sitting in the house to which no visitor ever comes, he seems now to have nothing to do: 'then something happened' is no longer a phrase associated with him, because he has become the victim rather than the agent of plot. And with his feet propped up on a 'little wooden ledge, not even painted, nailed to the front' of his 'hand-carved, hand-painted Mount Vernon mantelpiece', he somehow does not seem to belong to his surroundings; there is a barrier, and a not entirely invisible one at that, between himself and the places he nominally owns. Even Flem's legendary caginess tends to excite pity. 'He didn't dare', his cousin Montgomery Ward Snopes observes of him, 'He didn't dare at his age to find out that all you need to handle nine people out of ten is just to trust them.'[70] So what was a sign of his power in *The Hamlet* is now seen as a mark of his vulnerability. 'A virgin', really, as far as human contact of any kind is concerned, he is portrayed as someone who does not have the *courage* or the *confidence* to give credit. Or, to put it in Montgomery Ward's more cynical terms, Flem has evidently been imprisoned so long in his own self-defences he cannot see that to trust people can be a way of getting them to trust you – and so a very useful form of manipulation, an easy kind of people-management.

Given this translation of Flem from seamless capitalist into another
instance of suffering humanity, it is hardly surprising that he is described
as a 'poor son of a bitch' too: 'the pore son of a bitch over yonder in that
bank vault counting his money', as Ratliff puts it – seeking safety in his
safe and, equally, safety in numbers, the dogged counting of his cash. Not
that Flem tries to hide from Mink, or to protect himself when Mink comes
looking for him. On the contrary, he simply waits for Mink; and when
Mink finally shoots Flem the words used to describe Flem are telling – he
is, the narrator confides, 'immobile' and 'detached'. No longer man in
motion, he seems already, before the gun is fired, to have given up. 'What
do you reckon Flem's reason was for setting there in that chair', Ratliff
asks, 'letting Mink snap them two shells at him until one of them went off
and killed him?' 'Maybe he was jest bored too', Ratliff then says, answering
his own question, 'Like Eula . . . the pore son of a bitch.' 'He was impotent', Stevens responds, '. . . When he got in bed with a woman all he
could do was go to sleep.' 'The poor sons of bitches', the lawyer adds,
'that have to cause all the grief and anguish they have to cause.'[71] The
transformation of Flem is now complete. An isolated figure, who had, we
are told, 'no auspices . . . fraternal, civic, nor military: only finance' and no
property to speak of, 'belonging simply to Money', he seems as much of
a poor, bare, forked animal as the man who kills him. A victim, simultaneously, of the abstractions of the balance sheet and the absurdities of
existence, he is perceived as, at worst, someone who had to do what he
did, only to sense in the end the futility of the enterprise and, at best, as
part of a level moral playing-field: no different, finally, from all the other
'poor sons of bitches' who strut and fret their hour upon the stage and
then are gone. There is no real bitterness in this perception, either on
Faulkner's part or that of his characters: the detachment Flem shows, at
the moment of his death, is shared by everyone else. So is the passivity. 'All
he could do was go to sleep' seems, in fact, an appropriate epitaph for
most of the characters in the novel: as they subside from action into
anonymity, allowing themselves to unwind from 'all the grief and anguish',
the anxiety of having to desire and act.

What works against this general process of dissolution, and arguably
makes the quietism of the closing pages of *The Mansion* a surprise for many
readers, can be summed up in two works: Mink Snopes. Mink is the main
agent of plot. He is, by far, the most dynamic, the most wilful and purposeful
character in the novel. More to the point: despite all the clues, the references to 'poor sons of bitches' and early attempts at narrative resolution,
he it is who, more than anyone else, tempts the reader to read and think
in terms of social and historical action – and to share in the specific drama
of a singular life. Admittedly, Mink is, in some ways, a minimalist creature.
Tiny, 'almost as small as a child', his conversational speech is clipped and
spare; and sometimes what he has to say he never gets around to saying
at all. He finds no time, for instance, 'between the roar of the gun and the
impact of the shot', to tell Houston why he is killing him. All the reader

gets is what Mink would have said, if he had had the opportunity, and that is sparse enough, as much a stoic repression of his sense of outrage as an expression of it:

> I ain't shooting you because of them thirty-seven and a half four-bit days. That's all right; I done long ago forgot and forgive that. Likely Will Varner couldn't do nothing else, being a rich man too and all you rich folks has got to stick together or else maybe some day the ones that ain't rich might take a notion to raise up and take hit away from you. That ain't why I shot you. I killed you because of that-ere extry one-dollar pound fee.[72]

Nor are Mink's conscious thought processes especially expansive, although like the passage just quoted they have their own rough poetry. Equating thinking with talking, he tends towards the formulaic, the set-piece that, for instance, he repeats to himself when still labouring under the delusion that Flem will come and save him from the consequences of killing Houston – or, later, when he recalls exactly what he must do in order to get out of jail at the earliest possible opportunity. '*To do whatever they tell me to do*', he recites silently to himself,

> *Not to talk back to nobody. Not to get into no fights. That's all I got to do for jest twenty-five or maybe even jest twenty years. But mainly not to try to escape.*[73]

Even his decision to kill Flem, when eventually he is released from Parchman prison, is announced baldly: as if it has erupted out of a process that barely approaches an analysis of causes and possible choices. On this level, perhaps, he does seem like just another instrument of fate, whose only defence against the inevitable is his proud conviction that, as he tells himself early on in the novel, 'he would not be, would never be, reconciled to it'.

But this is not all there is to the representation of Mink, by any means. What there is besides is suggested right from the first, in the opening chapter of the *The Mansion*. Weaving in and out of Mink's consciousness, the narrative combines the vernacular rhythms of his speech with the ritualistic, formulaic patterns of his thought processes – then, in a manner reminiscent of *As I Lay Dying* or *The Hamlet*, it dips down below that to a more apocalyptic idiom that responds and corresponds to the turmoil of his emotions, that speaks in a way *for* him rather than from him. This third level of language is fired into activity particularly at those moments when Mink is driven to curse his existence and the conditions that govern it: the circumstances, often personified as a perverse 'they' or a powerful, sometimes unpredictable deity called 'Old Moster', that make his life in jail to some extent no different from his life outside – and ensure that, as far as he and 'people of his kind' are concerned, it is (as Mink rehearses it) not they who 'owned even temporarily the land' but 'the land itself which owned them'. At this level, the ebb-and-flow of Mink's instinctive meditations sometimes assumes a generalized intonation: as if what is being said,

is being said for him still certainly, but also for all those like him with
'their doomed indigence and poverty'. The personal edge, the harsh poetry
of individual pain remains in place, but it is made all the sharper, the
harsher by a sense of *typicality*, of a broader social dimension – as in this
brief passage in which Mink is considering what he will no longer have to
do, now that he is in prison:

> No more now to go to a commissary store every Saturday morning to battle
> with the landlord for every gram of cheap bad meat and meal and molasses
> and the tumbler of snuff which was his and his wife's one spendthrift orgy.
> No more to battle with the landlord for every niggard sack of fertiliser, then
> gather the poor crop which suffered that niggard lack and still have to battle
> the landlord for his niggard insufficient share of it.[74]

In effect, the power of Mink as an agent of plot resides in two things:
a narrative idiom that uses different levels of speech to register the different dimensions of his being, and a narrative representation that makes a
painful particular case (in whose pain the reader is required to share) into
the tale of a tribe, a revelation of social injustice. The account of Mink
Snopes works to draw us into him, yet also understand him for the frail,
slightly ridiculous but also fiercely proud creature he is. On top of that,
it helps us to recognize him as a significant historical instance, a paradigm
of tenant life in the South. Mink fights desperately against material circumstances that he often describes as a supernatural agent, but which we
are compelled to see as a specific social system in which, as usual, 'the rich
folks . . . stick together'. Through him, in turn, Faulkner constructs a reading of public history that draws the strength of its analysis precisely from
its personal origins, its complexly layered re-creation of an individual life.
The complexity of the speech idioms does not cease as the novel continues: right up until the end, the gravitation between different vocabularies
catches the mixed nature of Mink's world, the plain facts and the heroic
dreams that compel his attention and take hold of his consciousness. But
the perception of Mink as the incarnation of a particular historical conflict: that does begin to fade, or at least take second place to the gestures
of farewell, peace and dissolution, with which Faulkner clearly wants to
conclude the novel. There is an argument to be made in favour of all this,
which is simultaneously personal and formal. Mink, we could say, is simply
succumbing to the temptations of the earth that he has resisted for so
long: like his creator, if in a more dramatic way, he is beginning to wind
down. And as the narrative describes this movement towards relaxation
and rest, it falls back on the verbal equivalent of a tried and tested cinematic strategy: gliding from close-up into long-shot, the prose immerses
the story that has been told in a vaster panorama – a landscape in which
the individual life suddenly assumes anonymity. But this argument does
not affect the fact that something that is, quite probably, unexpected is
happening here. The gentle propelling of Mink towards the status of just
one more 'poor son of a bitch', a metaphysical victim, is not so easy to

anticipate because, for most of the novel, the social edge, the idea of economic struggle, is just as crucial. There is a difference of dramatic intonation, a relative thinning out of the terms in which Mink exists for us in the rest of the story. As a result, we the readers – or, at least, some of us – are likely to be surprised.

Surprised, that is, until we return to the conditions in which *The Mansion* was written: which is to say, until we remember the long period of gestation it shared with *The Town*, and the gathering mood of equanimity – the sense of coming to terms with life and reaching towards the completion of labours – in which Faulkner prepared the manuscript. 'So this is what it all come down to': that remark could be made in sorrow or in bitterness but, equally, it could be uttered in a rueful, philosophical way. And, given in particular that Ratliff is the speaker here, the last option seems to be the safest bet. Faulkner did not break his creative staff when he came to the end of this novel, although he seems to have believed for a while that he was about to. This was not, after all, to be his finale. But he was, he knew, moving towards the end; and this helps to explain the mood that colours *The Mansion*, especially near its conclusion – the tendency to recapitulate and reconcile, to offer some formal gestures of farewell and at least the possibility of letting go. There are moments in the third book in the Snopes saga that simply do not work; there are others that, while moving and persuasive in themselves, do not quite accommodate or do full justice to the tensions the narrative has disclosed. There is a slackening here, which means that this novel cannot equal the excitement of much of the earlier work: the sustained pitch of intense personal feeling and ferocious historical analysis that characterizes, above all, most of the fiction written between 1929 and 1940. Nevertheless, there is the story of Mink Snopes, with its vivid mix of idioms and its powerful reading of public experience in terms of private emotion. And there is also the pleasure of return and recovery: familiar tales told and embellished, the elusive object of desire negotiated one more time, Stevens and Ratliff swapping stories again – and, in the process, replicating two sides of their creator, the cosmopolitan man of letters and the provincial teller of tall tales. '*I'm free now*': that is just about Mink's last comment to himself, as he prepares to lie down on the earth. It seems to have been Faulkner's comment to himself too, as he embarked on what he once called 'the . . . way home':[75] contemplating death after life in terms of rest after work, and something very closely resembling peace.

Postscript: Back to Earth

I THE ROMANCE OF THE FAMILY: *THE REIVERS*

'It's been two months now since I've done anything much but ride and hunt foxes', Faulkner wrote in February 1961. A month later he declared in another letter, 'since I ran dry three years ago, I am not even interested in writing anymore: only in reading for pleasure in old books I discovered when I was 18 years old'.[1] Faulkner found comfort in returning to and dipping into stories that were old friends by now, recalling dialogues that he had had with them for more than four decades. As he himself indicated, however, much more of his time was devoted to foxhunting: quite often, he would go hunting four or five times a week. Foxhunting supplied him with the last of his several public poses, the personae that throughout his adult life had enabled him both to express his needs and to keep some ultimate part of himself intact and inviolate. Playing the part of the foxhunter, Faulkner could indulge his love of the woods and the rituals of the hunt; and he could also sustain all those ideas about male courage and conquest, virile power and liberty, that for him had frequently circulated around the figure of the man on horseback. Not only that: foxhunting offered a refuge from a bewildering contemporary world that seemed committed to the idea of radical social change. The conflicts over civil rights, the new frontier announced by the new President, above all that paradigm of modern times, the car – which Faulkner, in his last book, was to call 'the mechanised, the mobilised, the inescapable destiny of America': all this could be forgotten, exorcized by immemorial rites and by the sheer physical pleasure of galloping through the woods and hills of Virginia. There was a certain amount of wilful myopia in all of this: Faulkner did not have, or care, to remind himself that many of his fellow-hunters could afford the leisure of the hunt precisely because of their lucrative involvement in the new world of fluid capital and apparently unlimited consumption. But there was also an element of commemoration:

in the last stage of his life, the novelist was returning, after his own fashion, to the places of childhood and memory – to his father's livery-stable, the sounds and smell of horses, and to the resplendent, cavalier figure of Colonel William Clark Falkner who, as his great-grandson had once said, 'rode through the country like a living force'.

Return and restoration are, in fact, the distinguishing characteristics of these final years. Faulkner was circling back. Not least, he was reversing the journey of his predecessors. Members of the Falkner clan had moved from the eastern seaboard, North Carolina and then Virginia, to Tennesseee and Missouri before settling in Mississippi. Now Faulkner was returning eastward, spending more and more of his time in his new haunts in and around Charlottesville. The split from Oxford became all the more definite with the death of Faulkner's mother Maud, in October 1960. She remained tough and laconic to the end, telling Falkner that she did not wish to be embalmed because 'I want to get back to earth as fast as I can.' Nursing his mother, telling her stories or just sitting with her had been a major occupation, or to be more exact an act of devotion: with her gone, Faulkner had even more reason for spending most of his time with *his* descendants in Virginia. 'I live up to my arse in delightful family', he confessed in the autumn of 1961: when he was not foxhunting, very often he was enjoying the company and comforts of his three grandsons. Journeying between Oxford, where Maud had died, and Charlottesville, where Jill and her sons lived, was now, in any event, just about the only travel that Faulkner was willing to contemplate. Early in 1962, for instance, he was to refuse an invitation from President Kennedy to dine at the White House, with other American Nobel Laureates and prize winners, on the grounds that, as he put it, 'I'm too old at my age to travel that far to eat with strangers.' The gruff hauteur of this refusal was typical of Faulkner's last persona: as the stiff-backed horseman, immersed in country ways and family matters, he could repel all outlanders, any invasion of his privacy – from however eminent a source – if he felt so inclined. 'Even while I was still writing', Faulkner insisted, 'I was merely a writer and never a literary man',[2] and now that he was hardly writing at all he felt less tempted than ever to talk about books, or pay much explicit attention to his own achievement. As foxhunter as well as grandfather, he could enjoy a kind of anonymity, a convenient refuge from the demands of the larger, public world.

'The mind has slowed down a little', Faulkner admitted in 1962, 'and it don't like new things. It likes the old things just like the old man wants his old shoes, his old pipe.' Already, when he said this, that preference for 'old things' had sent him back to the subject of his final novel, *The Reivers: A Reminiscence*, which he began active work on early in 1961 and had completed by the autumn of that year. The backward glance, the impulse to return that determines the nature of this book is apparent in its title. And even before the title was chosen or the book was written, it was evident in Faulkner's choice of material: which took him back to the idea of a story about 'a sort of Huck Finn' that he had first broached to his publisher in 1940. As Faulkner had first outlined what he called 'the Huck Finn novel' some two decades before he wrote it, it incorporated elements that were later to be used in *A Fable*. Nevertheless, the animating conception and central characters were there. His idea, Faulkner explained, was to show a boy growing up fast to become 'a man, and a good man'. The agency of change was to be a trip to Memphis, and in particular a horse-race; the main agent of change was to be a prostitute 'with a good deal of character and generosity and common sense'. The boy's companions on the trip were to be a black 'family servant' and 'a big, warmhearted, courageous, honest, utterly unreliable white man with the mentality of a child'; and, during the trip, the boy was to go through 'in miniature all the experiences of youth which mold the man's character'. When Faulkner finally set to work on this idea in 1961, there were inevitably changes: both the black character and the prostitute were made much younger, for instance, than was originally planned. But the basic constellation of figures remained the same: Lucius Priest, the boy, Boon Hogganbeck, the 'big warmhearted, courageous, honest, utterly unreliable white man', Ned McCaslin, the Priest family coachman, and Everbe Corinthia or 'Corrie' the prostitute. The journey to Memphis remained a determining structural feature of the narrative, as did the interest in horses and horse-racing. And the idea that the boy should learn 'courage and honour and generosity and pride and pity' as a result of experiences that 'in his middle class parents' eyes stand for debauchery and degeneracy and actual criminality':[3] that, too, sustained the writer as he attempted to give a more cutting edge to the mellow tale he was rehearsing – to turn an act of imaginative return, in short, into a story of initiation.

Two of the last adjustments Faulkner made to the manuscript of his last novel before it was published were to decide on the title and to alter the first page – so that the first two words, 'Grandfather said', were removed from the opening sentence and placed alone, in capital letters, to supply a frame for the entire telling of the tale. Both were clues to the writer's impulse and intentions. 'The Reivers', Faulkner explained to his publisher, was 'the old Scottish spelling' of a word meaning stealers or plunderers. In broad terms, the title refers of course to Lucius, Boon and Ned who steal the car belonging to 'Boss' Priest, Lucius's grandfather, and take it to Memphis – where, in turn, Ned steals it in order to exchange it for a horse (which he plans to race and with which, eventually, he hopes to win back the car). In this form, however, with the archaic spelling, it alludes to something else as well: the author's sense of his own origins. 'My ancestors came from Inverness, Scotland',[4] Faulkner once claimed, insisting that the principal family lines were Falconer, Murray, McAlpine and Cameron. In using this word, still more than in subtitling the book 'a reminiscence', Faulkner was in effect signalling his act of return and recovery, the feeling that he was looking back, not just to his immediate family or his American ancestors, but to all those anonymous men and women who had preceded him by centuries – and who were still there, he believed, present in his own blood. The foregrounding of 'Grandfather said' was, in turn, a more personal and poignant signal: Lucius Priest, the 'grandfather' who tells the story, is an old man recalling in the 1960s events that occurred to him in 1905, when he was eleven. The point was underlined by the fact that Faulkner dedicated *The Reivers* to his own grandchildren: this novel, the author is alerting us, is a journey into reminiscence for him too, a man only three years younger than his narrator – an imaginative, if not literal, adventure in commemoration.

The impulse to commemorate is actually so powerful in *The Reivers* that one commentator has described it as 'a family portrait album'. Faulkner himself is there, of course: as the young man recollected and the old man recollecting. His great-grandfather is recalled, as 'the actual colonel, C.S.A. – soldier, statesman, politician, duellist' who 'built his railroad in the mid-seventies' ('and destroyed it' is the only fictional addition here). So is his grandfather: as the banker who, like John Wesley Thompson Falkner, enjoys the 'courtesy title' of 'Colonel', 'acquired partly by inheritance and partly by propinquity'. As the Sartorises, these two figures hover on the periphery of the action, recalling some of the specific details of Falkner family lore. But no less telling, as far as this process of recollection is concerned, is the more central character of 'Boss' Priest, Lucius's grandfather, remembered now in tranquillity. An imposing, hieratic presence, whose power is evident from his nickname, 'the Boss' instructs his grandson in the mysteries of what it means to be a gentleman – by what he does and, no less, by what he says. 'A gentleman can live through anything', he tells Lucius near the end of the story,

> He faces anything. A gentleman accepts the responsibility of his actions and bears the burden of their consequences, even when he did not himself instigate them but only acquiesced in them, didn't say No though he knew he should.[5]

Kneeling to his grandfather at this moment, Lucius admits his authority, and the knowledge of paternalist responsibility that – in the time present of the narrative – Lucius is now trying to pass on to *his* grandsons. Reading this episode, it is not difficult to see Faulkner's sense of his own place in the family line at work here. Like Lucius, the author seems to be recollecting lessons in patriarchal power and obligation: lessons learned, in this instance, from a character who incorporates elements of both his own great-grandfather and his grandfather. Like Lucius, too, he appears intent on transmitting these lessons to the future keepers of the flame, the young people to whom, in fact as well as fiction, this tale is initially addressed.

The representation of the immediate, and literal, father-figure in *The Reivers* is an illustration of the degree to which this book is an act, not only of recovery, but of reconciliation. In conspicuous contrast to what occurred over thirty years before, when Faulkner was writing *Flags in the Dust/*

Sartoris, his father is now given a place in the story, with only a slight change of name: from Murry to Maury. Admittedly, Maury Priest, Lucius's father, is not the real figure of authority here. There is, perhaps, no more revealing evidence of that than in the final pages: when, just before 'Boss' Priest instructs Lucius in the ways and means of a gentleman, he stops his son from administering a beating to his grandson. 'This is what you would have done to me twenty years ago', Maury protests, falling back from the role of punishing father into that of protesting son. To which 'the Boss' replies, 'Maybe I have more sense now',[6] before dismissing Maury to deal with the women while *he* does the right thing: that is, teaches Lucius his lesson and so seals the experience of the narrative. Nevertheless, while the ultimate impotence of Maury Priest is hardly denied, and he is not permitted to be the the keeper of the patriarchal flame, he is granted his own business and the title of 'gentleman'. Faulkner makes his peace with his father, not by attributing to him a paternal power that – in his oldest son's eyes, at least – he never possessed, but by seeing him as an honourable man, a son and a father who did his best. He is granted a presence; and there is perhaps even a gesture towards filial affection, or at least understanding, implicit in the fact that this fictional shadow of Murry Falkner is allowed to inhabit the world that Murry loved best – the world, that is, of men, horses and stables.

Other participants in the Faulkner family romance are there, recalled with almost universal affection: including Caroline Barr, 'Mammy Callie', who appears as 'Aunt Callie that nursed us in turn'. But just as revealing, really, of the mellow mood in which *The Reivers* reminisces, and reinvents the familial past of its author, is what it does not say, or include. Lucius's mother is a shadowy figure. This is perhaps because Faulkner's own mother had only just died, and the memories of the loss were too recent and painful. Or perhaps it was because Faulkner was, he sensed, far better at dramatizing the failure of maternal love, or the loss of the mother-figure, than he was at depicting the good mother. Either way, to play down the part of Mrs Priest was to make things easier for the author, and to avoid anxiety. Besides that, it was to go along with the predominantly male emphasis of the narrative. Powerful female figures are normally there in Faulkner's stories for the same reason powerful black figures are: to disrupt the equilibrium, to threaten the assumptions or even the identities of the primarily white, male protagonists. So to avoid a powerful female figure of any kind was arguably one among several ways to ensure that as little as possible spoiled the sense of things being brought to a smooth conclusion. The only significant women characters in *The Reivers* are the whores with hearts of gold, Corrie and Miss Reba, who play a motherly role without enjoying motherly power or mystery: who have some of the maternal obligations but little or no maternal authority, and so never even begin to endanger the focus on the male line the narrative maintains – or its preoccupation with the prerogatives of 'a gentleman'. Avoiding conflict between the sexes and the races, the novel also studiously avoids serious conflict *within* the male world. The other significant omission in *The Reivers* is of sibling rivalry. Lucius, like his creator, is the oldest of four brothers. However, the other three, all 'younger and therefore smaller'[7] than he is, are hardly mentioned except as household appendages, mute members of the clan. They are there to swell the numbers, to convey a sense of the warmth and plenitude of a decent-sized family group: but there is never any question of rivalry. Unlike Bayard Sartoris III in *Flags in the Dust/ Sartoris* or Henry Sutpen in *Absalom, Absalom!*, Lucius does not have a dark twin to haunt him; nor, like Quentin Compson in *The Sound and the Fury* or Darl Bundren in *As I Lay Dying*, do the demands of his brothers put his own needs in jeopardy. In emotional terms, at least, he takes unchallenged pride of place: he is the lone, and privileged, star of his generation.

At one critical moment in *The Reivers*, Lucius recollects something that, he says, 'Father and Grandfather must have been teaching me before I could remember because I don't know when it began, I just know it was so.' It was, he explains, 'that no gentleman ever referred to anyone by his race or religion'.[8] The lesson is recalled just when one character, Corrie's odious young cousin Otis, calls Ned McCaslin a 'nigger'; and it touches on something at the heart of the novel. The world commemorated by Lucius – and, through him, by Faulkner – is one of instinctive deference and division: where everything operates on what is called, early on in the book, 'some unspoken gentleman's ground' and there is therefore no need to insist, to be offensive or defensive – no need, in short, to use a word like 'nigger'. It is not that the Yoknapatawpha County *circa* 1905 recollected here is not racist. It clearly is. This is a world of Jim Crow cars and 'the ancient mystic solidarity of race': in which black people are expected to address every white man using the prefix 'Mr', and there is assumed to be some innate, unanalysable connection between, on the one hand, black adults and, on the other, white children and animals. This Yoknapatawpha, revered in memory, is racist but it does not have to call attention to its racial categories. White people do not have to threaten or curse to get their way here; they have got it already. A complex network of inherited assumptions, an insidious and almost imperceptible process of cultural training – everything that prevents Lucius from remembering if he has ever actively learned from his predecessors: all this has made racial separation automatic, part of the mental and material fabric, and made racism itself into an apparently 'natural' response, something so fully absorbed that it does not require thought.

All this goes, of course, for the society the narrator and author recollect; and, unfortunately, most of the time it goes for the method, the manner of recollection. For the most part, the black characters in *The Reivers* are black stereotypes: conceived *by the novel*, as well as by the society the novel describes, as creatures existing beyond some definitive racial line, their personalities determined by race. Ned McCaslin, for instance, gravitates towards the convention of the wily, crafty black man, who conceals his cunning behind a deferential manner: a disguise that is only broken by

the occasional 'Hee hee hee' of wicked glee. He has an instinctive knowledge of horseflesh, the ways and needs of animals, an eye for the women
and a smooth tongue to match: 'When I sugars up a woman', he boasts,
'it ain't just empty talk. They can buy something with it too –.' He is also,
as the story makes only too apparent, elusive and unreliable, lazy and
loquacious, and by no means entirely honest. Another, older black man,
Uncle Parsham, with whom Lucius stays for a while, is a more dignified
figure. A person of relatively few words, 'in a white suit . . . and a planter's
hat, with perfectly white moustaches', his every move is slow and deliberate. In his case, though, the narrative is clearly flirting with another stere-
otype: Uncle Tom, the old 'black patrician' (to give the character the title
accorded to him in this book) who is benevolent and courteous, devout
and ethical – and, above all, kind to a white child. The portrait of McWillie,
in turn, the black boy against whom Lucius competes in his horse-races,
invokes a simpler convention, familiar to any reader of plantation romance or, for that matter, to anyone who has come across early film
portraits of African-Americans:

> Then he turned, jerked his whole head around to look back and I remem-
> ber still the whites of his eyes and his open mouth . . . I sincerely believe I
> even heard him yell back at me: 'Goddammit, white boy, if you gonter race,
> race!'[9]

This is the 'Step "n" Fetchit' character translated to a Southern racetrack
and deposited on a horse: eyes bulging, jaw hanging slack in simple dis-
belief and fright at the mysterious ways of white folk. Admittedly, there are
occasional hints to the contrary of all this, an intimation or two that black
masks are just that: masks, assumed for convenience or survival. 'He was
not Uncle Remus now', Lucius observes of Ned on one occasion, 'But
then, he never was when it was just me and members of his own race
around.' The occasions, however, are few and far between. In fact, apart
from another, later reference to Ned not 'being Uncle Remus or smart or
cute or anything now', they hardly exist at all: not even when Ned *is* just
with Lucius and other black people, despite what Lucius himself may
claim. The main thrust of the novel is not away from stereotypes but
towards them: nearly all of the time, black characters are identified with
– rather than distinguished from – their black masks. Apart from one or
two momentary notes of reservation, or guilt, the narrative colludes with
the culture it commemorates by seeing race as a determinant, not just of
status, but of identity, the way a person thinks and is.

Here, in effect, we are faced with another side to the act of reminiscence, that impulse to return and restore a lost world that animates *The
Reivers*. Like the setting of 'Was', the first story in *Go Down, Moses*, this is
a place of ritual, operating according to agreements that never need to be
spoken, relying on games like a horse-race and codes of behaviour to
settle things and solve problems. And, whatever may be said about 'Was',

in this case *this* is a place conceived in nostalgia: seen as innocent, precisely because the assumptions on which it operates are never questioned and never need to be defended. If racism is acknowledged in the text, in fact, it is so only in marginal characters like Otis, or a redneck deputy sheriff called Butch who turns up in Parsham: people who are not 'gentlemen' in any sense of the word, and whose racist inclinations are located as one, telling symptom of their blindness to paternalist values. Faulkner has circled back in this novel to a healing notion of his family, which is all to the good – or, at least, all to his personal benefit. But he has also reverted, through the reminiscences of his narrator, to an idyllic vision of patriarchy: a dream of the good old days, already on the cusp of change, the goodness of which stems directly from the fact that the divisions are still there and go almost entirely unchallenged. There is no Lucas Beauchamp here, still less is there a Joe Christmas, threatening to cross over the colour line, that barrier between black and white that is as invisible but also as powerful as breath. On the contrary, there is Ned McCaslin telling a trio of white gentlemen, 'If you could just be a nigger one Saturday night, you wouldn't never want to be a white man again as long as you live.'[10] In this environment, blacks as well as whites are happy with a pattern of community founded on strict rules of separation and subordination. That, at any rate, is how the world of 1905 looks to an old man in the 1960s, as he recollects the world of his youth – and as he recollects, and regrets a time when both that world and he were gradually beginning to alter.

'Women are wonderful', Lucius observes at one point in the story, 'They can bear anything.' That echoes a remark made by Faulkner himself, during one of his class conferences at the University of Virginia: 'women are marvellous, they're wonderful, and I know very little about them'. Not entirely by coincidence, it also offers a clue to the way women characters are treated in *The Reivers*. After their own fashion, they are just as subordinated as the black characters are, governed by a gentleman's agreement that gives them their allotted space; and, once again, that act of subordination is exercised by the narrative as well as by the culture it describes. They are subjected to a narrative gaze that sets them clearly apart, within their own closely defined boundaries. Situated there, they can become the beneficiaries of male honour, the object of protective rituals that are in effect forms of domination, while all the while remaining patient, devoted, selfless and self-sacrificing – in a word, 'wonderful'. This quiet and unquestioned positioning of women is seen as peculiar, of course, to the society that both Lucius and Faulkner commemorate. The society in which, in the time present of the novel, narrator and author find themselves stranded is marked by just the opposite: a breaking down of barriers, an edging away from the traditional dispositions of gender. One topic, in fact, over which several nostalgic tears are shed is female 'freedom', the eruption into the social world since 1905 of women who are evidently not content with the role of 'lady'. 'We – they – went to the ladies' parlour', Lucius says, describing his arrival with his companions at a hotel in Parsham,

In those days females didn't run in and out of gentlemen's rooms in hotels as, I am told, they do now, even wearing, I am told, what the advertisements call the shorts or scanties capable of giving women the freedom they need in their fight for freedom; in fact, I had never seen a woman alone in a hotel before (Mother would not have been here without Father) and I remember how I wondered how Everbe without a wedding ring even could have got in. They – the hotels – had what were known as ladies' parlours, like this one where we now were . . .[11]

This lament for the loss of the traditional lines of demarcation could perhaps be treated as something that is intended to place Lucius for us: rather, that is, than as something with which we are meant to nod and smile in rueful agreement. But whether recalling the good old days of deference and division, or talking more bluntly about 'a hysteria of women', the voice of Lucius is singular and authoritative. It is, we are clearly asked to believe, the voice of wisdom describing the getting of wisdom: even, or rather especially, on the subject of women.

The portrait of Everbe Corinthia, or Corrie, the prostitute, is revealing in this respect. Boon Hogganbeck, her boyfriend, harbours a need 'to shield a woman, even a whore': to protect her from danger and calumny. Lucius does too. So when Corrie's cousin Otis tells Lucius in some detail about what Corrie does for a living, Lucius feels obliged to defend her honour, by using physical violence against the creature who would impugn it. He fights Otis. 'I knew nothing about boxing and not too much about fighting', Lucius confesses. 'But I knew exactly what I wanted to do: not just hurt him but destroy him.' Lucius is injured, but he reaps his reward. Corrie is so touched by what he has done that she resolves to reform: 'You fought because of me', she exclaims, with a mixture of amazement and gratitude. Reverting to her respectable given name of Everbe Corinthia, she now acts as a mother to Lucius, washing his clothes and generally seeing after his welfare. She also gets a job – a particularly noble one, looking after an invalid. 'She ain't just reformed from the temptation business', her former madam Miss Reba comments, 'she's reformed from temptation too.'[12] Eventually, she marries Boon, by whom she then has a child. The last line of *The Reivers* is, in fact, the announcement of the new baby's name: ' "His name is Lucius Priest Hogganbeck," she said.' Corrie has been 'saved': translated from whore, if not to virgin exactly, then to lady, by the courtly action of an eleven-year-old boy. In turn, Lucius has proved his worth, not just as a man but as a gentleman – by saving her, performing the right protective rituals. As a result, he has entered into nominal if not literal paternity: he has already earned the patriarchal right to pass on his name to the next generation, to take his proper place in the male line.

The regressive impulse is acute and powerful in *The Reivers*, then: driving author and narrator back into a golden age, coincident with their youth, when social divisions were not insisted upon because they were instinctively accepted – and when personal or familial division (the pain of separation and self-consciousness, say, or filial and fraternal conflicts) were apparently never a problem. 'Nobody in Jefferson locked mere homes in those innocent days',[13] Lucius remarks in passing; and that remark somehow encapsulates the narrative tendency to portray northern Mississippi, at the turn of the century, as a site of peace, prosperity and contentment. If there are threats here – and there have to be, really, to keep the story going – they are comic ones, to do for instance with the trials and tribulations of a jaunt in a borrowed car to Memphis, or horse-racing and wagers: all of which are safely framed in narrative reminiscence, with both narrator and reader knowing they will eventually be resolved. Or if they seem to be more serious, even for a moment, then those threats come from outside: outside the family, that is, and mostly from outside the cocooned space of Jefferson as well – from creatures like Otis and the redneck deputy sheriff Butch, both of whom are finally sent packing. There is none of that feeling of internal combustion that makes reading the novels of the period 1929 to 1940 such a disturbing experience: little or no sense of those disruptive forces, lurking *within* the psyche and *within* family and social groups, that make living such a risky project for so many of Faulkner's major characters – and speaking, saying things properly, a difficult, even impossible one.

One threat that definitely comes from outside is 'progress, industry, commerce': which is seen throughout *The Reivers* as a rough beast about to be born. What is called, at one moment, 'the . . . nightmare vision of our nation's vast and boundless future' is certainly there in the novel, but there only on the margins: making the 'innocent' world of old Jefferson seem all the more precious because it is, we are reminded, on the point of vanishing. Not for the first time in his fiction, Faulkner chooses to identify the shock of the new with the automobile, 'a small mass-produced cubicle containing four wheels and an engine' that is (the narrative explains) 'the basic unit' of modern America's 'economy and prosperity'. Here, however, this portent of 'the machine age' is subdued by the nostalgic element it moves in; it gets caught up in the conciliatory undertow of the story, the impulse to heal and reconcile. Of course, the narrative directs our attention to what later times will bring, all that will happen long after Lucius and his friends return from Memphis. Two cars 'commingling' their dust on a dirt road, for instance, are said to produce 'one giant cloud like a pillar, a signpost raised and set to cover the land with the adumbration of the future'.[14] But that is the news for later. As far as 1905 is concerned, the car is seen as a far more comforting, quaint, and even familiar phenomenon, woven somehow into the fabric of humorous exchange. So, if Ike Snopes in *The Hamlet* has 'his' cow to fall in love with, then Boon Hogganbeck has 'his' automobile: which is no more 'his' in law than Ike's cow is, naturally, only 'his' by right of affection. 'Boss' Priest's car, 'a Winton Flyer', becomes Boon's 'soul's lily maid, the virgin love of his innocent heart'. He lavishes his attention on it, spends hours gazing

at it, washes it sometimes four or five times a day; and then, in the manner
of many a heartsick lover, whisks it away for a few days in the big city.

Even in normal times, the Winton Flyer comes across as an endearingly
absurd arrangement. 'You cranked it by hand', Lucius explains,

> while standing in front of it, with no more risk (provided you had remembered
> to take it out of gear) than a bone or two in your forearm; it had kerosene
> lamps for night driving and when rain threatened five or six people could
> readily put up the top and and curtains in ten or fifteen minutes...[15]

And the trip to Memphis is definitely not normal times, allowing author
and narrator to exploit the further humorous possibilities of this 'expen-
sive useless mechanical toy'. On the way there, the car gets stuck in Hell
Creek bottom. 'Held helpless and impotent' in a 'primeval setting of ooze
and slime and jungle growth', it has to be dragged out of the mud by a
pair of very capable mules. Arriving there, it then disappears, thanks to
the shenanigans of Ned McCaslin; and our attention is focused on the old-
time adventures in horse-racing that are meant to lead to its recovery. The
portent of things to come is, in effect, a comic tool: the object of a misplaced infatuation, for a while the bargaining counter in a bizarre exchange, a forlorn toy that has to be rescued from danger by mules and
horses. In the times past of *The Reivers*, the new does not threaten the old,
it has to be saved by it. Only Boon Hogganbeck, a man with 'the mentality
of a child', is inclined to prefer abstract horsepower to good solid horseflesh. Nobody else takes the Winton Flyer seriously: not even its owner,
'Boss' Priest, who bought it to spite Colonel Sartoris and would prefer to
keep it locked away in the carriage house.

So the positioning of the new on the comic edge of a world of escapades and dreams tends to defuse any threat it poses. The movement into
the future marked by the eruption of the car into this remembered landscape is denied by the emotional trajectory of the novel: emotionally and
imaginatively, *The Reivers* drives back into the past, bathing even the few
signs of modern times that are allowed entry into the Jefferson of 1905 in
the sepia colours, and soft focus, of nostalgia. A regressive impulse, the
need to return and recuperate, is even at work in the experience of initiation that Faulkner began by seeing as the key to the novel. 'The Huck
Finn novel' he had called the book that later became *The Reivers*, when he
first began thinking about it in 1940. And the narrator keeps reminding
us about this element, the idea of learning and growing up, by referring
to his 'education' or 'fall', his entry into a 'foreign country' of 'unillusion',
or by talking about an 'innocence and childhood ... forever lost'. For that
matter, he reminds us in a lengthier, more discursive way, in passages like
the following, which occurs almost exactly half-way through the story:

> I was just eleven, remember. There are things, circumstances, conditions in
> the world which should not be there but are, and ... you would not escape

them even if you had the choice, since they too are a part of Motion, of participating in life, being alive. But . . . I was having to learn too much too fast, unassisted; I had nowhere to put it, no receptacle, no pigeonhole prepared yet to accept it without pain and lacerations.[16]

This represents the novel at its best: with its subtle weaving between Lucius old and young, its gentle mix of perspectives, and its air of intimate address – talk directed in fictive terms at Lucius's grandchildren but in fact, of course, at us, the readers. It also locks neatly into those moments in the story which seek to persuade us that Lucius is undergoing a radical transformation: moments that usually involve choice and travel. As 'the road to McCaslin forked away from the Memphis road', for instance, Lucius tells us us that he faced an 'irrevocable decision', whether to go and stay with his cousins or set off for the city. And as the road to Memphis takes him closer and closer to the downtown area, he appears to see his own experience of alteration replicated in the historical alterations of the landscape, the change in his surroundings from rural to suburban to urban. 'The die was cast now', Lucius declares, as he recalls the moment when he and his companions crossed the creek out of their own country into what Boon termed 'civilization', 'we looked not back to remorse or regret or might-have-been'. And those brave words seem to find confirmation in some equally brave actions: defending Corrie against Otis, and riding a few horse races in the belief that his fate, and that of his friends, depend on him winning.

For all the bravado of some of his words, however, and even the bravery of many of his actions, Lucius often longs to return. 'What I wanted was to be back home', he admits at one point, 'I wanted my mother.' 'I was anguished with homesickness', he confesses elsewhere,

wrenched and wrung and agonized with it: to be home, not just to retrace but to retract, obliterate: make Ned take the horse back to wherever . . . he had got it and get Grandfather's automobile and take it back to Jefferson, in reverse if necessary, travelling backward to unwind, ravel back into No-being, Never-being . . .[17]

Lucius feels repeatedly that, as he puts it in his old age, 'I . . . didn't want to have to make any more choices, decisions.' Which is an understandable feeling for an eleven-year-old boy, confronted with strange experiences and new challenges. The fact of the matter is, however, that in the end his wish comes true: he does not have to make any. The conclusion of *The Reivers* circles back, if not into 'No-being, Never-being' exactly, then into the world of settled pieties with which it began. The crisis initiated by the adventures of Lucius and his companions is resolved, not by them, but by a version in triplicate of the *deus ex machina*, a trio of patriarchs: 'Boss' Priest, of course, Colonel Linscomb, the owner of the horse against which Lucius races, and Mr van Tosch, the true owner of the horse Lucius rides. 'I had quit', Lucius exclaims, 'I wasn't making decisions any more.' He is conveyed to the patriarchal homeplace of Colonel Linscomb, where he almost goes to sleep at the dinner table in mingled exhaustion and relief. After that, he is restored to his own patriarchal homeplace in Jefferson, where he is taught his lesson about the ways of a gentleman.

Immediately before the return to Jefferson, the three patriarchs sort things out among themselves so that, after one more horse race, the *status quo ante* is restored: property and power return to their rightful owners. The talk between the three gentlemen is markedly authoritative: not just because it settles problems, but because it declares its own power. As the three agree between themselves about how to create concord out of discord, to clean up the mess that the young folks and the lower orders have created, much of what they say is a quiet reminder of the degree to which they are in charge, and everything is subordinated to them. 'I'm the boss in my house', declares Colonel Linscomb. 'You don't know my man Hogganbeck', 'Boss' Priest tells him. 'So I'll either have to buy Ned, or sell you Coppermine', says Mr van Tosch, neatly identifying power and possession, control of horses and people with ownership of them. It is not that Lucius has learned nothing. On the contrary, he has learned a lot. 'You learned a considerable about folks on that trip',[18] Ned tells him, and he is right. It is that what Lucius has learned merely entitles him to a more considered place in that elaborate system of deference and division to which 'the Boss' holds the key. He does not light out for the Territory ahead of the rest, as Huckleberry Finn intends to do at the end of Twain's novel: he goes home to his family, more prepared than before to enter into his inheritance and become a gentleman, like his grandfather.

The slippage between the 'grandfather' who tells the tale and the 'grandfather' about whom the tale is told in effect alerts us to what is happening in *The Reivers*: Lucius departs from his patrimony but only so that he can return to it eventually, fit and ready to become 'the Boss' when his time arrives. He is restored as Faulkner had been when he wrote this final novel, to 'delightful family'; and, by the time he comes to recall his trip to Memphis in the Winton Flyer, he will have arisen as Faulkner had to the grandfatherly role that seems to confirm the benevolence of the old ways and the survival, somehow, of patriarchal culture. There is an implicit contradiction here: between the benign figure of the narrator, dispensing wisdom to his grandchildren just as 'Boss' Priest did once to him, and the regretful references to the coming of the machine age and the new woman that run like a subdued bass note through the book. The sense of continuity created by the narrative pattern of regression and recovery, and by the narrative frame of a 'grandfather' echoing the wisdom of *his* 'grandfather', is at odds with the remarks that punctuate the story recording terrible and apparently irreversible change. Those remarks, though, occupy the edges of the story. By the end of *The Reivers*, they more or less disappear, are rescued from our attention. Like the more dangerous, disruptive characters, Buck and Otis, they are shuffled offstage, so as not to spoil the prevailing sense of harmony. Nothing is allowed to compromise the final closing of the family circle: which is enlarged now to embrace Everbe Corinthia, the whore become wife and mother, Boon Hogganbeck, the childlike dependant become responsible husband and father, and Lucius Priest Hogganbeck, the sign and seal of Lucius's own assumption of paternalist duty. The move towards return and restoration that marks this book, as it does the last few years of Faulkner's life, ends by colouring the narrative present as well as the narrative past in gentle, autumnal shades, the sepias and soft focus of a dream world. The 'innocent days' of 1905 are the main beneficiaries of Faulkner's quiet surrender to the temptations of memory, the imaginative equivalent of an ebb tide. But the new days of the 1960s, as they are represented in the warm narrative presence of Lucius – rather, that is, than in the parenthetical remarks about social transformation: these, too seem bathed in the securities of an old order, the comforts of hearth and home. They invite us to think, or at least hope, that, despite everything else that has happened over the last sixty years or so, within the family nothing much may have changed.

II 'I WAS HERE'

Faulkner had a chance to read some of *The Reivers* to an audience in April 1962, less than two months before it was published and less than three months before he died. He began his reading by saying that he was going to 'skip about a little to read about a horse race which to me is one of the funniest horse races I ever heard of'. That remark resurrected the old familiar Faulkner who had denied the authority of authorship, and insisted that his books could and did speak for themselves – in a multitude of voices. He had changed, certainly, as the honours accumulated and he gravitated from the role of son to that of father and then grandfather. For instance, as he approached what nearly forty years earlier he had called 'the back door' of death, his passionate commitment to memory assumed a different hue, tinged as it was by feelings of dispossession and regret – and by rage about the dying of the light. Attending a talk the novelist gave in May 1962, his old friend Malcolm Cowley even observed that Faulkner's words 'had a tone of retrospection' about them, 'of lament for the dignity and freedom of the past, that was not exactly new for him, but that seemed to have a new resonance'. Faulkner had changed then, as the yesterdays accumulated and the body grew weaker, but certain fundamentals remained the same. Sometimes, the old ferocity of feeling would return: bouts of drinking or episodes of reckless horseriding that would lead Faulkner himself to admit that he was 'being a damn fool and acting like a forty-five-year-old'. And there survived in the old Faulkner, just as much as in the young one, a fierce need for privacy, together with respect for the privacy of others: impulses that compelled him to listen to what the voices said inside and around him, to put down what the voices said in his narratives – and then treat those narratives as if they spoke their own identities into being, and so had separate, complex lives of their own. Privacy, subjectivity, the idea of the individual human agent struggling into identity through words: just how total his investment still was in those principles was suggested by a short piece he wrote in 1961. It was composed as a tribute to Albert Camus, who had recently been killed in a car accident, and concluded with these words:

> When the door shut for him, he had written on this side of it that which every artist who also carries with him that one same foreknowledge and hatred of death, is hoping to do: *I was here.* He was doing that, and perhaps in that bright second he even knew he had succeeded . . . What more could he want?[19]

Faulkner had said as much as this many times before. The writer, he had insisted, wants to make his or her mark, to inscribe 'Kilroy was here' on the door or wall of oblivion before passing through. And not just the writer: to make a mark, to realize an identity in words and speech, was an impulse he saw all human beings as sharing, including (as his own fiction had disclosed)[20] someone as humble as the daughter of a small-town jailer. To inscribe presence in this way was not, of course, a narcissistic process for him: the three words, '*I was here*', carried equal emphasis, and they defined '*I*' as someone who belonged '*here*', in a local habitation – apart from, but also a part of, the community. In personal terms, this meant that, while Faulkner's work bore the indelible marks of his own life, it was, he hoped, attached to the works and lives of others. It bore the weight, and was borne on the voices, of many other people caught up in similar problems and enmeshed in just the same conflicts and debates. There is no need to fall back on some specious notion of a vast, anonymised universality here, in order to explain the generalizing power of Faulkner's fiction (although, admittedly, Faulkner himself was sometimes tempted in this direction in his later years). On the contrary, all that is required is to follow the writer's own intuitions, his understanding that speech and so identity belong to a specific culture – and then to acknowledge that it is the specificity, the historicity of his writing that links it up to our own lives. Reading a Faulkner story, attending to its voices and arguing with them (as one would with a friend, to use Faulkner's own analogy), we are involved in an activity that is vitally connected to what Faulkner was doing when writing it. We are engaging with other voices, other lives – including, above all, the voices and life of the author – in terms of how we speak and who we are. We are being invited into a debate, a dialogue that requires a recognition of the living tissue of language that binds and separates us, as readers, characters and narrators: that asks us to assert, and also to honour, privacy. Autobiography *is* history, Faulkner realized. He wrote out of tensions that were his precisely because they were those of his special place and time. His books say, '*I was here*', certainly. But they say it for others besides himself: others, that is, including the reader.

Faulkner Family Trees

I THE FALKNERS

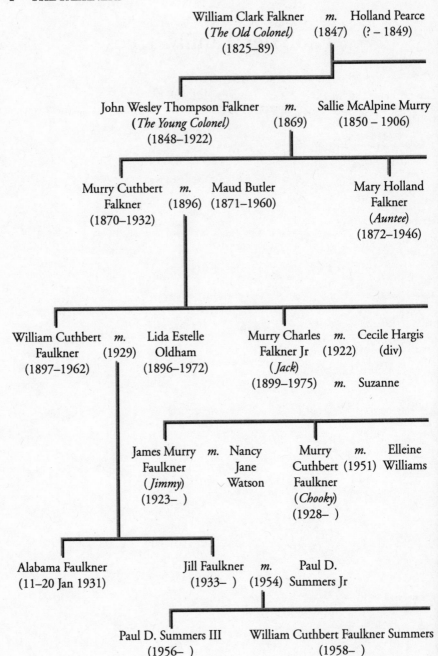

William Clark Falkner *m.* Holland Pearce
(*The Old Colonel*) (1847) (? – 1849)
(1825–89)

John Wesley Thompson Falkner *m.* Sallie McAlpine Murry
(*The Young Colonel*) (1869) (1850 – 1906)
(1848–1922)

Murry Cuthbert *m.* Maud Butler Mary Holland
Falkner (1896) (1871–1960) Falkner
(1870–1932) (*Auntee*)
(1872–1946)

William Cuthbert *m.* Lida Estelle Murry Charles *m.* Cecile Hargis
Faulkner (1929) Oldham Falkner Jr (1922) (div)
(1897–1962) (1896–1972) (*Jack*)
(1899–1975) *m.* Suzanne

James Murry *m.* Nancy Murry *m.* Elleine
Faulkner Jane Cuthbert (1951) Williams
(*Jimmy*) Watson Faulkner
(1923–) (*Chooky*)
(1928–)

Alabama Faulkner Jill Faulkner *m.* Paul D.
(11–20 Jan 1931) (1933–) (1954) Summers Jr

Paul D. Summers III William Cuthbert Faulkner Summers
(1956–) (1958–)

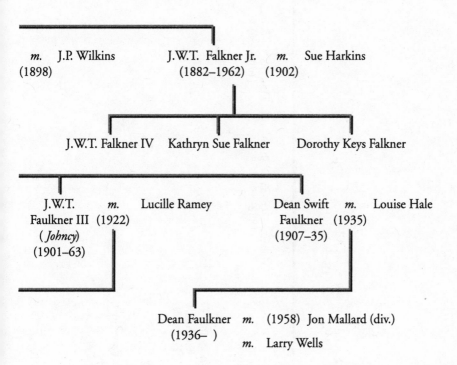

─── *m.* (1851) Lizzie Vance (**see chart III**)

m. J.P. Wilkins
(1898)

J.W.T. Falkner Jr.
(1882–1962)

m. Sue Harkins
(1902)

J.W.T. Falkner IV   Kathryn Sue Falkner   Dorothy Keys Falkner

J.W.T.
Faulkner III
(*Johncy*)
(1901–63)

m.
(1922)

Lucille Ramey

Dean Swift
Faulkner
(1907–35)

m.
(1935)

Louise Hale

Dean Faulkner
(1936–)

m. (1958) Jon Mallard (div.)

m. Larry Wells

A. Burks Summers
(1961–)

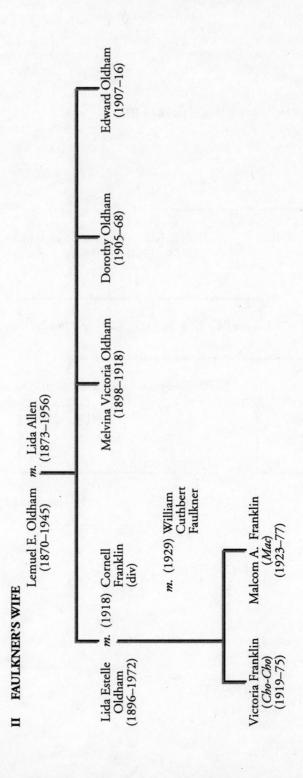

II   FAULKNER'S WIFE

Lemuel E. Oldham   *m.*   Lida Allen
(1870–1945)   (1873–1956)

Melvina Victoria Oldham
(1898–1918)

Dorothy Oldham
(1905–68)

Edward Oldham
(1907–16)

Lida Estelle Oldham   *m.* (1918) Cornell Franklin
(1896–1972)   (div)

                        m. (1929) William
                                    Cuthbert
                                    Faulkner

Victoria Franklin
(*Cho-Cho*)
(1919–75)

Malcom A.   Franklin
(*Mac*)
(1923–77)

III   THE OLD COLONEL'S SECOND WIFE AND FAMILY

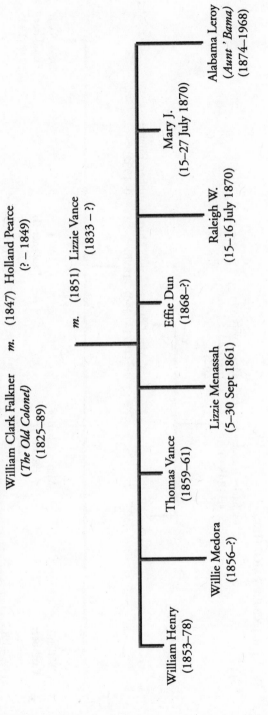

William Clark Falkner   *m.*   (1847)   Holland Pearce
(*The Old Colonel*)   (? – 1849)
(1825–89)

m.   (1851)   Lizzie Vance
(1833 – ?)

William Henry
(1853–78)

Willie Medora
(1856–?)

Thomas Vance
(1859–61)

Lizzie Menassah
(5–30 Sept 1861)

Effie Dun
(1868–?)

Raleigh W.
(15–16 July 1870)

Mary J.
(15–27 July 1870)

Alabama Leroy
(*Aunt 'Bama*)
(1874–1968)

IV FAULKNER'S MOTHER

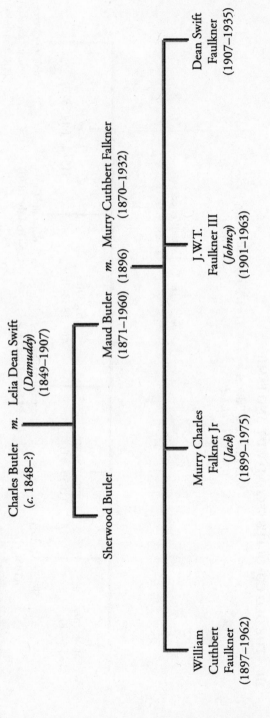

Charles Butler *m.* Lelia Dean Swift
(*c.* 1848–?) (*Damuddy*)
(1849–1907)

Sherwood Butler

Maud Butler *m.* Murry Cuthbert Falkner
(1871–1960) (1896) (1870–1932)

William
Cuthbert
Faulkner
(1897–1962)

Murry Charles
Falkner Jr
(*Jack*)
(1899–1975)

J.W.T.
Faulkner III
(*Johncy*)
(1901–1963)

Dean Swift
Faulkner
(1907–1935)

Chronology

1825	6 July	William Clark Faulkner (hereinafter 'William Clark Falkner'), later known as 'The Old Colonel' and the future great-grandfather of William Faulkner, is born in Tennessee.
1840		William Clark Falkner sets off from Missouri, where the family is now settled, travelling first to Tennessee and then to Mississippi.
1845		William Clark Falkner is identified in local records as a resident of Ripley, Mississippi.
1846–7		William Clark Falkner serves in the Mexican War.
1847	9 July	William Clark Falkner marries Holland Pearce.
1848	2 Sept.	John Wesley Thompson Falkner, later known as 'The Young Colonel', is born in Ripley, the only child of William Clark Falkner and Holland Pearce Falkner; future grandfather of William Faulkner.
1849		William Clark Falkner kills Robert Hindman, and is tried and acquitted.
	31 May	Holland Pearce Falkner dies.
1851		William Clark Falkner kills Erasmus Morris, and is tried and acquitted.
	12 Oct.	William Clark Falkner marries Elizabeth Houston Vance, with whom he has eight children. William Clark Falkner publishes *The Siege of Monterrey*, an autobiographical poem, and *The Spanish Heroine*, a novel.

1861		William Clark Falkner is elected colonel of the Magnolia Rifles, after Mississippi secedes from the Union.
1862		Ousted as colonel, William Clark Falkner returns to Ripley.
1863		William Clark Falkner forms the Partisan Rangers, re-enters the Civil War conflict and participates in the Battle of Manassas.
1869	2 Sept.	John Wesley Thompson Falkner marries Sallie McAlpine Murry. They settle in Ripley.
1870	17 Aug.	Murry Cuthbert Falkner is born, the first child of John Wesley Thompson Falkner and Sallie Murry Falkner; the future father of William Faulkner.
1871	27 Nov.	Maud Butler is born, the daughter of Charles Butler and Lelia Dean Swift Butler ('Damuddy'); the future mother of William Faulkner.
1871–2		William Clark Falkner, Richard Thurmond and others set up a company to build a railroad.
1881		William Clark Falkner publishes *The White Rose of Memphis*, a novel that becomes very popular.
1885		John Wesley Thompson and his family move to Oxford, Mississippi.
1889	5 Nov.	After being elected to the state legislature, William Clark Falkner is shot by Richard Thurmond in Ripley and dies the next day.
1896	19 Feb.	Lida Estelle Oldham is born in Bonham, Texas, the daughter of Lemuel and Lida Oldham; the future wife of William Faulkner.
	9 Nov.	Murry Cuthbert Falkner marries Maud Butler. They settle in New Albany, Mississippi.
1897	25 Sept.	William Cuthbert Falkner (hereinafter 'Faulkner') is born in New Albany, the first child of Murry Cuthbert Falkner and Maud Butler Falkner.
1898		Murry Cuthbert Falkner is appointed treasurer of the of the railroad built by his grandfather's company. The family moves to Ripley.
1899	26 June	Murry C. Falkner ('Jack') is born, the second son of of Murry and Maud Falkner.
1901	24 Sept.	John Wesley Thompson Falkner III ('Johncy') is born, the third son of Murry and Maud Falkner.

1902		John Wesley Thompson Falkner sells the railroad. Murry Cuthbert Falkner and family move to Oxford, where Murry begins shifting between a series of jobs.
1903		Lemuel and Lida Oldham, and their daughters Estelle and Victoria, move to Oxford.
1905		Faulkner enters first grade, Oxford Graded School.
1907	1 June	Lelia Swift Butler ('Damuddy') dies.
	15 Aug.	Dean Swift Falkner is born, the fourth son of Murry and Maud Falkner.
1909		Faulkner works in his father's livery stable.
1910		John Wesley Thompson Falkner establishes the First National Bank of Oxford.
1911		Faulkner enters eighth grade. Increasingly playing truant, he spends much of his time sketching and writing stories and poems.
1914		In June, Faulkner takes his poetry to Phil Stone, which marks the beginning of their friendship. He enters the eleventh grade in September, only to drop out in December.
1915		Faulkner and Estelle Oldham begin a close relationship. In September, Faulkner returns to school to play football, suffers a broken nose, and drops out again. He goes bear-hunting at 'General' James Stones's camp in November.
1916		Faulkner works briefly at his grandfather's bank. He visits the University of Mississippi campus at Oxford frequently and continues to write poetry, showing some of it to Estelle Oldham.
1917		Faulkner's first published work appears, a drawing in *Ole Miss*, the University of Mississippi yearbook.
1918		Estelle Oldham announces her engagement to Cornell Franklin. Faulkner tries to enlist in the United States Army, and is rejected. He leaves for New Haven, Connecticut, where he stays with Phil Stone and works for the Winchester Repeating Arms Company. In April, Estelle Oldham and Cornell Franklin are married. Three months later, in July, Faulkner reports to the Recruits' Depot, Toronto, as a recruit in the Royal Air Force. He is posted to the Cadet Wing, Long Branch, and then to the School of Military Aeronautics, Toronto. His brother,

Marine Private Jack Faulkner is wounded near Argonne Forest in November. With the end of the First World War in November, Faulkner is discharged and returns to Oxford in early December. Also in December, Murry Falkner is appointed assistant secretary at the University of Mississippi.

1919 Victoria Franklin is born in February, the daughter of Estelle Oldham Franklin and Cornell Franklin. Estelle Franklin visits her parents in Oxford. Faulkner works on poems that will appear in *The Marble Faun*.

6 Aug. Faulkner's first published poem, 'L'Apres-Midi d'un Faune', appears in the *New Republic*. In September, Faulkner enrols as a special student at the University of Mississippi. He begins publishing poems, and one prose sketch, in the student newspaper, *The Mississippian* and in the Oxford *Eagle*.

1920 Faulkner wins a poetry prize offered by Professor Calvin Brown of the University of Mississippi. He helps with the Boy Scout troop over the summer. In September, he joins the Marionettes, a student drama group. In November, he withdraws from the university. He hand-letters six copies of *The Marionettes*, a verse play written for the drama group.

1921 Faulkner completes *Vision in Spring*, a collection of love poems, and presents Estelle Franklin with a gift volume during one of her visits to her parents. In the autumn, he moves to New York at the invitation of Stark Young and is hired as a bookshop clerk by Elizabeth Prall. He rents a room in Greenwich Village. Returning to Oxford in December, he becomes postmaster at the university post office.

1922 13 March John Wesley Thompson Falkner dies.
Faulkner publishes 'Portrait', a poem, in *The Double Dealer* in June. In the late summer, he is appointed scoutmaster.

1923 Malcolm A. Franklin is born in December, the son of Estelle and Cornell Franklin.

1924 In May, the Four Seas Company of Boston agrees to publish *The Marble Faun*, sent in by Phil Stone, for a fee of $400. Faulkner transcribes a gift booklet, *Mississippi Poems*, in October. In the same month, he is dismissed from the post of scoutmaster because of his drinking; and he resigns from the position of

		postmaster, under the threat of legal proceedings, following a visit from the postal inspector. He visits Elizabeth Prall in New Orleans during the autumn, and meets her husband, the writer Sherwood Anderson.
	15 Dec.	*The Marble Faun* is published, dedicated to Maud Faulkner and with a preface by Phil Stone.

1925   In January, Faulkner travels to New Orleans, with the intention of sailing to Europe. He stays there, becoming friends with several writers and artists. He publishes in *The Double Dealer* and the New Orleans *Times-Picayune*, and begins work on *Soldier's Pay*. Alternating between New Orleans and Oxford and visiting the Mississippi coastal resort of Pascagoula, he meets and falls in love with Helen Baird. He also writes poems which he will later complete and collect as *Helen: A Courtship*. Then, early in July, Faulkner sails from New Orleans to Europe, with William Spratling. He travels in Italy and Switzerland. He takes a room on the Left Bank in Paris and spends a week in England. He works on a novel, *Elmer*, which is never completed. In December, he returns to the United States and to Oxford.

1926   Moving in with William Spratling in New Orleans, Faulkner dedicates a hand-lettered tale, *Mayday*, to Helen Baird.

    25 Feb.   *Soldier's Pay* is published. In the summer, Faulkner stays in Pascagoula and dedicates the hand-lettered gift book of poems, *Helen: A Courtship*, to Helen Baird. He also works on *Mosquitoes*, which is completed in September. Living first in Oxford and then in New Orleans, he collaborates with William Spratling on *Sherwood Anderson and Other Famous Creoles*, caricatures of New Orleans figures that include a Faulknerian parody of Anderson.

1927   Faulkner works on *Father Abraham* and *Flags in the Dust*, then concentrates on the latter. He also writes a fairy tale for the daughter of Estelle Franklin, Victoria, *The Wishing Tree*, which will be published after his death.

    30 April   *Mosquitoes* is published. Faulkner returns to Pascagoula in the summer. In November, *Flags in the Dust* is rejected by Boni & Liveright, the publishers of Faulkner's first two novels.

1928		Faulkner writes *The Sound and the Fury*, in Oxford and then in New York. *Flags in the Dust* is accepted by Harcourt, Brace & Company, provided cuts are made.
1929	31 Jan.	*Sartoris*, the revised version of *Flags in the Dust*, is published. In April, Estelle and Cornell Franklin are divorced. With *The Sound and the Fury* completed but rejected by Harcourt, Brace & Company, Faulkner finishes the typescript of *Sanctuary*.
	20 June	Faulkner marries Estelle Oldham Franklin in Oxford. They spend their honeymoon in Pascagoula, where Estelle attempts to drown herself. In the autumn, Faulkner takes a job at the university power plant.
	7 Oct.	*The Sound and the Fury* is published by Jonathan Cape & Harrison Smith. Faulkner begins work on *As I Lay Dying* towards the end of October, finishing the manuscript early in December.
1930		In January, Faulkner completes the typescript of *As I Lay Dying* and begins his 'sending schedule', a listing of short stories and the dates when they were sent to magazines and then either accepted or rejected. Then in April Faulkner and his wife buy a house in Oxford dating back to 1844, and name it 'Rowan Oak'. They move in during June.
	30 April	Faulkner's first story in a national magazine is published: 'A Rose for Emily' in *Forum*.
	6 Oct.	*As I Lay Dying* is published. Faulkner meanwhile works on *Sanctuary* in order to make it suitable for publication.
1931	11 Jan.	Alabama Faulkner is born, the daughter of William Cuthbert Faulkner and Estelle Oldham Faulkner. She lives for only nine days.
	9 Feb.	*Sanctuary*, now revised, is published. In the summer, Faulkner begins work on *Light in August*.
	21 Sept.	*These 13*, Faulkner's first collection of short stories, is published. In October, Faulkner attends the Southern Writers' Conference in Charlottesville, Virginia, and then goes to New York, staying there until December, when Random House publishes a limited edition of his story, *Idyll in the Desert*.
1932		In February, Faulkner finishes *Light in August*; the next month, the Modern Library publishes an edition of *Sanctuary* with an introduction by the author describing his revisions. Faulkner arrives in Culver City, California, in May as a contract writer for MGM.

7 Aug.	Murry Falkner dies. Faulkner returns to Oxford; then, in October, he goes back to MGM for three weeks.
6 Oct.	*Light in August* is published by Harrison Smith & Robert Haas.

1933

	In February, Faulkner begins taking flying lessons; later in the year, he buys a plane.
20 April	*A Green Bough* is published. *Today We Live,* a film based on a Faulkner story 'Turn About', goes on general release at the end of April; Faulkner is given a screen credit. Faulkner meanwhile goes to New Orleans for several weeks of screenwriting on location.
24 June	Jill Faulkner is born, the only surviving child of William and Estelle Faulkner.

1934

	Early in the year, Faulkner begins writing the work that later becomes *Absalom, Absalom!* In February, he flies to New Orleans for the dedication of Shushan Airport, which will provide material for *Pylon.*
16 April	*Doctor Martino and Other Stories* is published. Faulkner starts work on several stories that are later used in *The Unvanquished.* In July, he goes to work at Universal Studios for three weeks at $1000 a week; he then returns to Oxford to write *Pylon.*

1935

25 March	*Pylon* is published. Faulkner continues writing *Absalom, Absalom!*
10 Nov.	Dean Faulkner dies in a plane crash. Faulkner assumes responsibility for Dean's pregnant widow. The following month, Faulkner returns to Hollywood, to work at Twentieth Century-Fox. Acting as a screenwriter for the director Howard Hawks, he meets Hawks's script clerk, Meta Carpenter. He later begins an intimate relationship with her that lasts intermittently for fifteen years.

1936

	Faulkner completes the manuscript of *Absalom, Absalom!* at the end of January. A breakdown leads to a stay in a nursing home in Byhalia, Mississippi. From February to May, he works at Twentieth Century-Fox, continuing his affair with Meta Carpenter. Returning to Oxford in June, he then goes back to Hollywood in July with Estelle and Jill, expecting to stay a year.
26 Oct.	*Absalom, Absalom!* is published by Random House, of which Harrison Smith & Robert Haas is now a part.

1937

	Meta Carpenter marries Wolfgang Rebner. Estelle and Jill return to Oxford in May; Faulkner follows in

August. He begins work on *The Wild Palms* in the following month. Then in October he goes to New York: there, he meets Meta Rebner, and suffers a severe back injury from a steam pipe, while drunk.

1938	15 Feb.	*The Unvanquished* is published. Faulkner continues writing *The Wild Palms*, and buys land which he names Greenfield Farm. In November, he begins the first book in a projected trilogy, later to be called *The Hamlet*.
1939	19 Jan.	*The Wild Palms* is published. The day before this, Faulkner is elected to the National Institute of Arts and Letters.
1940	31 Jan.	Caroline Barr ('Mammy Callie'), the African-American woman who helped to raise Faulkner, dies.
	1 April	*The Hamlet* is published. Faulkner is now writing the stories that are later used in *Go Down, Moses*.
1941		Faulkner continues work on the stories for *Go Down, Moses*, including the shorter version of 'The Bear'.
1942	11 May	*Go Down, Moses* is published, in the first edition as *Go Down, Moses, and Other Stories*. In July, Faulkner goes to work for Warner Brothers for five months as part of a long-term contract, at only $300 a week. He resumes his affair with Meta Carpenter.
1943		In January, Faulkner returns to Hollywood for seven months. Eventually, he is assigned to work with Howard Hawks on *To Have and Have Not*, for which he receives a screen credit. In October, he starts work on the story that is later to become *A Fable*.
1944		In February, Faulkner reports back to Hollywood again. Estelle and Jill join him in June. After spending two months on *To Have and and Have Not*, he continues working with Howard Hawks, on *The Big Sleep*, then returns to Oxford in December.
1945		Faulkner is back at Warner Brothers, for what will turn out to be his last stint for the studio, from June to September. He resumes work on *A Fable*.
1946		In March, Faulkner is released from his contract with Warner Brothers. *The Portable Faulkner* is published in April, which helps to revive interest in his work. In December, the one-volume Modern Library edition of *The Sound and the Fury* and *As I Lay Dying*

appears with the 'Compson Appendix', which supplies details about the history of the Compson family.

1947   Faulkner continues work on *A Fable*, submitting a portion of it, 'Notes on a Horsethief', to the *Partisan Review*, which rejects it. In April, Faulkner meets a series of six classes at the University of Mississippi.

1948   27 Sept.   *Intruder in the Dust* is published. MGM pays $50,000 for the film rights. In November, Faulkner is elected to the American Academy of Arts and Letters: at the time of his election, he is away hunting deer.

1949   In February, Faulkner helps with the filming of *Intruder in the Dust* in Oxford. He meets Joan Williams in August.

   27 Nov.   *Knight's Gambit* is published.

1950   In February, Faulkner is in New York, seeing Joan Williams. He begins work on *Requiem for a Nun*, which he regards as a collaboration with her. He receives the Howells Medal for distinguished fiction in May, from the American Academy of Arts and Letters.

   21 Aug.   *Collected Stories* is published. In November, Faulkner is awarded the 1949 Nobel Prize for literature. He travels with his daughter Jill to Sweden in December, to receive the prize and deliver an acceptance speech.

1951   10 Feb.   *Notes on a Horsethief*, a section of *A Fable*, is published. Faulkner returns to Hollywood in February, to work with Howard Hawks, at $2000 a week. He renews his relationship with Meta Carpenter, who is now separated from her husband. In March, he receives the National Book Award for *Collected Stories*; and the next month he spends three weeks in France and England. He goes to New York in July for one week, to work on the stage version of *Requiem for a Nun*.

   27 Sept.   *Requiem for a Nun* is published. Faulkner spends two weeks in October and one week in November in Cambridge, Massachusetts, working on the stage version of the story. In October, he receives the Legion of Honour from the French Consul in New Orleans.

1952   In May, Faulkner addresses the Delta Council in Cleveland, Mississippi, and then leaves for a one-month trip to France, England and Norway. He addresses the French Congress for the Liberty of Culture. During the summer, he and Joan Williams become lovers. In November, he stays in New York and Princeton, working on *A Fable* and seeing Joan Williams. In the same month, he also undergoes a series of electroshock treatments.

1953   Faulkner alternates between New York and Oxford from January until October. He is hospitalized for alcoholism and neurological disorders, and briefly has psychiatric treatment. He completes *A Fable* in November, dedicating it to his daughter Jill. In the same month, he leaves for Paris, to work on the film *Land of the Pharoahs* with Howard Hawks, then on to Stresa and St Moritz. On Christmas Eve, he meets Jean Stein, a young American, in St Moritz and begins an intimate relationship with her.

1954   Faulkner moves between England, France, Italy and Switzerland during January and early February, before joining Hawks on location in Cairo, where he has to be nursed. He spends three weeks in France in late March and early April, and then returns to New York and, finally, Oxford. *The Faulkner Reader* is published in April.

2 Aug.   *A Fable* is published. In August, Faulkner makes his first trip for the State Department, to the International Writers' Conference in São Paulo.

21 Aug.   Jill Faulkner marries Paul D. Summers Jr. In September, Faulkner goes to New York to see Jean Stein.

1955   In January, Faulkner receives the National Book Award for Fiction for *A Fable*, and in April *A Fable* also wins him a Pulitzer Prize. A series of letters to the Memphis *Commercial Appeal* on racial injustice, beginning in late March, earn Faulkner criticism from segregationists, white liberals and black activists. Faulkner leaves for a three-week trip to Japan in July, organized by the State Department. He spends two days with his stepdaughter Victoria and her husband in Manila, and also visits Europe.

14 Oct.   *Big Woods*, consisting of four hunting stories already in print, is published. In December, Faulkner takes Jean Stein to New York and Pascagoula.

1956   Faulkner divides his time between New York and Oxford, and also visits his daughter Jill in Charlottesville, Virginia. He continues writing articles on racial issues, and works on *The Town*.

15 April	Paul D. Summers III is born, the first child of Jill Faulkner Summers and Paul Summers Jr. In September, Faulkner becomes involved in the 'People-to-People Programme', an attempt by the Eisenhower administration to promote American culture in Eastern Europe.
1957	Faulkner is writer-in-residence at the University of Virginia, Charlottesville, between February and June. In March, he spends two weeks in Greece on a trip organized by the State Department; while there, he receives the Silver Medal of the Athens Academy.
1 May	*The Town* is published. From May until August, Princeton University Library presents an exhibition, 'The Literary Career of William Faulkner'.
1958	Faulkner returns to the University of Virginia in January as writer-in-residence. He is refused a permanent position by the President of the University, evidently because of his moderate racial opinions. In March, he spends two weeks at Princeton University for the Council on Humanities, then alternates between Charlottesville (subsequently, Albemarle County) and Oxford. He works on *The Mansion*.
2 Dec.	William Cuthbert Faulkner Summers is born, the second son of Jill and Paul Summers.
1959	In January, the play *Requiem for a Nun* has its American première in New York. Faulkner fractures a collarbone, when he falls from a horse in Charlottesville, in March. He and his wife buy a house in Charlottesville in August. During September, Faulkner attends a UNESCO conference in Denver, Colorado.
13 Nov.	*The Mansion* is published.
1960	In August, Faulkner accepts a position at the University of Virginia, Charlottesville, that has few duties attached to it. In the autumn, he is asked to wear the colours of the Farmington (Va) Hunt Club.
16 Nov.	Maud Butler Falkner dies. In December, Faulkner wills all his manuscripts to the William Faulkner Foundation.
1961	Faulkner visits Venezuela in April, on a trip sponsored by the State Department. He works on *The Reivers*.
30 May	A. Burks Summers is born, the third son of Jill and Paul Summers.

1962   In January, Faulkner is injured in another fall from a horse in Charlottesville. He visits the US Military Academy for two days in May, where he reads a passage from *The Reivers*, now completed. In May, he receives the Gold Medal for Fiction, awarded by the American Academy of Arts and Letters, in New York.

4 June   *The Reivers* is published.

17 June   Faulkner is injured in a fall from a horse in Oxford.

5 July   Faulkner is admitted to Wright's Sanitarium in Byhalia, Mississippi.

6 July   Faulkner dies of a heart attack.

7 July   Faulkner is buried in St Peter's Cemetery, Oxford.

Notes

Notes to Chapter 1: Fictions of History

1 Malcolm Cowley, *The Faulkner–Cowley File: Letters and Memories 1944–1962* (New York, 1966), p. 126. See also *Selected Letters of William Faulkner*, ed. Joseph Blotner (New York, 1977), p. 276; J.M. Huizinga, *The Waning of the Middle Ages* (New York, 1954), pp. 39, 41. I am indebted to Maggie Brown, Minnie Ruth Little, Bessie Summers and others for comments on Faulkner's family, and other information given to me, during my visits to Oxford, Mississippi, in the summers of 1988 and 1992. An earlier version of part of this opening section was offered as a paper at the Faulkner and Ideology conference in Oxford, Mississippi in 1992. Due acknowledgements are made to the conference organizers and to all those who commented on the paper and offered suggestions for revision.

2 'On Privacy (The American Dream: What Happened To It?)', in *Essays, Speeches, and Public Letters*, ed. James Meriwether (London, 1966), pp. 70, 71. See also Frederick R. Karl, *William Faulkner: American Writer* (London, 1989), pp. 17–18.

3 The equivocal nature of Faulkner's relation to his homeplace has been the subject of a good deal of comment: not least, from Faulkner himself. On this, see the summary of Faulkner's attitude by the writer of this study, in Richard Gray, *The Literature of Memory: Modern Writers of the American South* (London, 1977), p. 201.

4 *Lion in the Garden: Interviews with William Faulkner 1926–1962* ed. James B. Meriwether and Michael Millgate (New York, 1968), p. 216. See also pp. 9, 219, 229, 248, 273.

5 Ibid., p. 9. See also pp. 217, 243.

6 *Faulkner–Cowley File*, p. 82. See also pp. 74, 77; *Mosquitoes* (New York, 1927), p. 209. For details of Faulkner's service record and his subsequent stories about it, see Joseph Blotner, *Faulkner: A Biography*, 2 vols (New York, 1974), pp. 205ff; David Minter, *William Faulkner: His Life and Work* (Baltimore, Md, 1980), pp. 30ff; Judith Wittenberg, *Faulkner: The Transfiguration of Biography* (Lincoln, Neb., 1979), pp. 32ff.

7 *Lion in the Garden*, p. 32. See also pp. 57, 131; *Faulkner in the University: Class Conferences at the University of Virginia 1957–1958*, ed. Frederick L. Gwynn and Joseph L. Blotner (Charlottesville, Va, 1959), pp. 248, 268; *Faulkner–Cowley*

File, p. 114; 'An Introduction to *The Sound and the Fury,*' *Mississippi Quarterly,* xxxvi (1973), 412.

8   *Faulkner in the University,* p. 79. See also pp. 109, 131, 136, 238; *Selected Letters,* pp. 41, 232, 296.

9   *Lion in the Garden,* p. 18. See also pp. 128, 174, 251.

10 Mikhail Bakhtin, *Problems of Dostoevsky's Poetics,* ed. and trans. Caryl Emerson (Manchester, 1984), p. 7. See also *Lion in the Garden,* p. 19; *Selected Letters,* p. 413; Mikhail Bakhtin, *The Dialogic Imagination,* ed. and trans. Caryl Emerson and Michael Holquist (Austin, Texas, 1981), p. 332.

11 Bakhtin, *Problems of Dostoevsky's Poetics,* p. 131. This quotation is from the translation by W.W. Rorsel. (Ann Arbor, Mich., 1973). All other quotations from *Problems of Dostoevsky's Poetics* are from the Caryl Emerson translation, previously cited, unless otherwise stated. See also *Problems of Dostoevsky's Poetics* (Emerson translation), pp. 195, 202, 282, 287; *Dialogic Imagination,* pp. 252, 294, 337, 378; *The Formal Method in Literary Scholarship,* trans. Albert J. Wehrle (Baltimore, Md, 1978), p. 8; *Marxism and the Philosophy of Language,* trans. Ladislav Matejka and I.R. Titunik (Cambridge, Mass., 1986), pp. 86, 93; *Speech Genres and Other Late Essays,* trans. Vern W. McGee (Austin, Texas, 1986), p. 84; *Lion in the Garden,* p. 116; *The Sound and the Fury* (1929; London, 1954 edition), p. 52. For the sake of convenience, I have attributed the works associated with Bakhtin's name to him. However, I am aware of the problems involved here and, in particular, of the probability that Medvedev and Volosinov were, at least, partly responsible for, respectively, *The Formal Method in Literary Scholarship* and *Marxism and the Philosophy of Language.* Since my aim is simply to enter into a dialogue with the ideas developed in these books, I can only refer the reader interested in the problems of their authorship to the relevant introductions to the translations already cited and to chapter 1 of Tzvetan Todorov, *Mikhail Bakhtin: The Dialogical Principle,* trans. Wlad Goldzich (Manchester, 1984).

12 Bakhtin, *Problems of Dostoevsky's Poetics,* p. 265. See also pp. 75, 251; *Dialogic Imagination,* p. 279; *Marxism and the Philosophy of Language,* p. 96; *Speech Genres,* pp. 69, 71, 91, 93, 94, 95, 99.

13 Mikhail Bakhtin, *Freudianism: A Marxist Critique,* trans. I.R. Titunik (New York, 1976), p. 128. See also *Dialogic Imagination,* pp. 337, 356; *Problems of Dostoevsky's Poetics,* p. 276; Todorov, *Bakhtin,* p. 24.

14 *Faulkner–Cowley File,* p. 78. See also p. 74; 'Mississippi', in *Essays, Speeches, and Public Letters,* pp. 36, 39; 'Letter to a Northern Editor', in *Essays, Speeches, and Public Letters,* p. 87.

15 Bakhtin, *Problems of Dostoevsky's Poetics,* p. 287. See also *Selected Letters,* pp. 234, 251–2, 263, 424.

16 *Essays, Speeches, and Public Letters,* pp. 120, 124.

17 Ibid., p. 167. This passage is from 'Address to the U.S. National Commission for U.N.E.S.C.O.', given in 1959. The passage previously quoted is from 'Address upon Receiving the Nobel Prize for Literature', given in 1950.

18 Bakhtin, *Dialogic Imagination,* p. 276.

19 *Absalom, Absalom!* (1936; London, 1937 edition), p. 127.

20 *Faulkner–Cowley File,* p. 14. See also Mikhail Bakhtin, *Rabelais and His World,* trans. Helene Iswolsky (Cambridge, Mass., 1968), p. 367.

21 *Absalom, Absalom!,* p. 9. See also p. 378; James Meriwether, 'Faulkner's "Mississippi"', *Mississippi Quarterly,* xxv (1972), 16.

22 'An Introduction to *The Sound and the Fury*', ed. James B. Meriwether, *Mississippi Quarterly*, XXVI (Summer 1973), 412.

23 Blotner, *Faulkner*, pp. 531–2. See also *Selected Letters*, p. 235; *The Town* (1957; London, 1958 edition), p. 272.

24 Hayden White, 'Getting Out of History', in *Tropics of Discourse: Essays in Cultural Criticism* (Baltimore, Md, 1978). See also Fredric Jameson, *The Political Unconscious: Narrative as a Socially Symbolic Act* (Ithaca, N.Y., 1981); Raymond Williams, *Marxism and Literature* (New York, 1977), p. 126.

25 Lucien Goldmann, *The Hidden God*, trans. Philip Thody (London, 1956), p. 49. See also *Faulkner in the University*, p. 3; *Faulkner at West Point*, ed. Joseph L. Fant and Robert Ashley (New York, 1961), p. 90.

26 *Faulkner in the University*, p. 3. See also *Lion in the Garden*, p. 255; frontispiece to *Absalom, Absalom!*

27 Allen Tate, *Essays of Four Decades* (New York, 1968), p. 545. See also Karl, *Faulkner*, p. 68.

28 *Requiem for a Nun* (1951; London, 1953 edition), pp. 199–200. See also Francis B. Simkins and Charles R. Roland, *A History of the South* (1953; rev. edn, New York, 1972), pp. 114–15; John Ray Skates, *Mississippi* (New York, 1979), p. 73; Noel Polk, *Faulkner's 'Requiem for a Nun': A Critical Study* (Bloomington, Ind., 1981), pp. 19–20.

29 Matthew B. Hammond, *The Cotton Industry: An Essay in American Economic History* (New York, 1897), p. 149. See also Alex M. Arnett, *The Populist Movement in Georgia* (New York, 1922); John D. Hicks, *The Populist Revolt: A History of the Farmer's Alliance and the People's Party* (Minneapolis, Minn., 1931); Wayne Mixon, *Southern Writers and the New South Movement 1865–1913* (Chapel Hill, N.C., 1980); Frederick A. Shannon, *The Farmer's Last Frontier: Agriculture 1860–1897* (New York, 1945); Comer Vann Woodward, *The Origins of the New South 1877–1913* (1951), vol. IX of *A History of the South*, ed. Wendell H. Stephenson and E. Merton Coulter, 10 vols (Baton Rouge, La, 1947–67).

30 *The Mansion* (1959; London, 1961 edition), p. 92. See also Skates, *Mississippi*, pp. 133–5.

31 *Mansion*, p. 91.

32 Ibid. See also p. 92.

33 'Shall Not Perish', in *Collected Stories* (1950; New York, 1977 edition), p. 102. See also Skates, *Mississippi*, p. 120.

34 Daniel J. Singal, *The War Within: From Victorian to Modernist Thought in the South, 1919–1945* (Chapel Hill, N.C., 1982), p. xii. See also Skates, *Mississippi*, p. 134; Vann Woodward, *Origins of the New South*, p. 111.

35 John Faulkner, *Men Working* (New York, 1941), p. 63. See also Jack Temple Kirby, *Media-Made Dixie: The South in the American Imagination* (Baton Rouge, La, 1978), p. 159; John C. McKinney and Linda B. Bourque, 'The Changing South: National Incorporation of a Region', *American Sociological Review*, XXXVI (June 1971), 399.

36 *The Hamlet* (London, 1940), p. 65.

37 Ibid., p. 63.

38 Ibid., p. 66.

39 Walter Hines Page, *The Life and Letters of Walter Hines Page*, 2 vols (New York, 1922), vol. I, p. 91. See also *Absalom, Absalom!*, p. 303.

40 *Intruder in the Dust* (1948; London, 1949 edition), pp. 187–8. See also *Requiem for a Nun*, p. 85.

41 Bakhtin, *Dialogic Imagination*, p. 342.

42 Robert Somers, *The Southern States Since the War, 1870–1871* (London, 1871), p. 114. See also Sidney Andrews, *The South Since the War: As Shown by Fourteen Weeks of Observation and Travel in Georgia and the Carolinas* (Boston, Mass., 1866), p. 1; Edward King, *The Southern States of North America* (London, 1875), p. 451.

43 Francis Hopkinson Smith, *Colonel Carter of Cartersville* (London, 1891), pp. 61–2. See also Thomas Nelson Page, *On Newfound River* (London, 1891), p. 2; Preface to *Red Rock: A Chronicle of Reconstruction* (London, 1898).

44 *The Town* (1957; London, 1958 edition), p. 302. See also *Knight's Gambit* (1949; London, 1951 edition), p. 117; Bakhtin, *Dialogic Imagination*, p. 250; Fredric Jameson, 'Postmodernism, or The Cultural Logic of Late Capitalism', *New Left Review*, 146 (July–Aug. 1984), 66.

45 'Mississippi', p. 11. See also Skates, *Mississippi*, pp. 4, 5, 7, 66.

46 Huizinga, *Waning of the Middle Ages*, pp. 39, 41. See also Michael O'Brien, *The Idea of the American South, 1920–1941* (Baltimore, Md, 1979), p. 113.

47 For a fuller discussion of some of the events and issues mentioned here, see Monroe Lee Billington, *The American South: A Brief History* (New York. 1971), pp. 96ff; Avery O. Craven, *The Growth of Southern Nationalism 1846–1861* (1953), vol. VI of *History of the South*, ed. Stephenson and Coulter, *The Coming of the Civil War* (Chicago, 1957), pp. 36–66, and *Civil War in the Making, 1815–1860* (Baton Rouge, La, 1961), pp. 50ff; William and Bruce Catton, *Two Roads to Sumter* (New York, 1963), p. 70; Simkins and Roland, *History of the South*, pp. 167–78.

48 James Henry Hammond, 'Hammond's Letters on Slavery', in *The Pro-Slavery Argument: As Maintained by the Most Distinguished Writers of the Southern States* (Charleston, S.C., 1852), pp. 162–3.

49 Henry Hughes, *A Treatise on Sociology, Theoretical and Practical* (Philadelphia, Pa, 1854), p. 292. See also William J. Grayson, 'The Hireling and the Slave', in *The Hireling and the Slave, Chicora, and Other Poems* (Charleston, S.C., 1856), pp. 50ff.

50 Richard H. King, *A Southern Renaissance: The Cultural Awakening of the American South, 1930–1955* (New York, 1980), pp. 26–7. See also Bertram Wyatt-Brown, *Southern Honor: Ethics and Behavior in the Old South* (New York, 1982), pp. 251–2.

51 *Sound and the Fury*, p. 154. See also pp. 81–2.; Darwin T. Turner, 'Faulkner and Slavery', in *The South and Faulkner's Yoknapatawpha*, ed. Evans Harrington and Ann Abadie (Jackson, Miss., 1977), p. 64.

52 Louis Althusser, 'Ideology and the State', in *Lenin and Philosophy, and Other Essays*, trans. Ben Brewster (London, 1977), p. 154. See also 'Mississippi', p. 37.

53 Raymond D. Gastil, 'Homicide and a Regional Culture of Violence', *American Sociological Review*, XXXVI (June 1971), 416. See also Althusser, 'Ideology and the State', pp. 138, 160; Vann Woodward, *Origins of the New South*, p. 159; *U.S.A. Bureau of Census: Historical Statistics of the United States, Colonial Times to 1957* (Washington, D.C., 1960), p. 12; Blotner, *Faulkner*, pp. 54–5.

54 Blotner, *Faulkner*, p. 114. See also C. Vann Woodward, *The Strange Career of Jim Crow* (New York, 1955), p. 66; Walter White, *Rope and Faggot: A Biography of Judge Lynch* (New York, 1929), pp. 19–20, 234, 237, 268, 331.

55 *Lion in the Garden*, p. 262. See also p. 260; *Essays, Speeches, and Public Letters*, p. 223; Blotner, *Faulkner*, pp. 15, 89–91.

56 *Essays, Speeches, and Public Letters*, pp. 155–6. See also pp. 108, 149, 151, 157;

Lion in the Garden, pp. 143, 144, 161, 183; Joseph Blotner, *Faulkner: A Biography* (New York, 1984, one-volume edition), pp. 618, 656; Karl, *Faulkner*, p. 640.

57 Arthur Mizener, *The Far Side of Paradise: A Biography of F. Scott Fitzgerald* (1949; New York, 1959 edition), p. 65.

58 *Go Down, Moses* (1942; London, 1960 edition), p. 91. See also *Sanctuary* (1931; London, 1953 edition), p. 176. Two useful books on this subject are Charles H. Nilon, *Faulkner and the Negro* (New York, 1965) and Thadious M. Davis, *Faulkner's 'Negro': Art and the Southern Context* (Baton Rouge, La, 1983). Of related interest are Lee Jenkins, *Faulkner and Black–White Relationships* (New York, 1981) and *Faulkner and Race*, ed. Doreen Fowler and Ann Abadie (Jackson, Miss., 1987). For other, recent discussions of black characters in Faulkner's work, see note 40 to chapter 2 of this book.

59 *Intruder in the Dust*, p. 13. See also *Soldier's Pay* (1926; London, 1964 edition), p. 119; *Flags in the Dust* (1973; New York, 1974 edition), p. 127; *The Unvanquished* (1938; London, 1955 edition), p. 60; Jean-Paul Sartre, *Baudelaire* (Paris, 1947), p. 201 (my translation). There is an excellent discussion of the function and importance of scent in Faulkner's work in André Bleikasten, *The Most Splendid Failure: Faulkner's 'The Sound and the Fury'* (Bloomington, Ind., 1976).

60 *Intruder in the Dust*, p. 84. See also p. 236.

61 Althusser, 'Ideology and the State', p. 169. See also William L. Andrews, *The Literary Career of Charles W. Chesnutt* (Baton Rouge, La, 1980), p. 276.

62 Wilbur J. Cash, *The Mind of the South* (New York, 1941), p. 89. It is perhaps worth pointing out that this elevation of *white* women, or at least *some* white women, together with the division of women into virgins or whores that accompanied it, introduced a fairly obvious contradiction into the Old South's image of itself. This contradiction was at its most pressing when it came to the position of black women. As mentioned earlier in this chapter, the idea that the Old South was an extended family, incorporating black and white, meant that women of both races could be regarded as 'sisters'. To this extent, the fear of incest and the fear of miscegenation were not only linked but inseparable. However, the tendency discussed here, to differentiate between different 'kinds' of women, and in particular to assign the sexual function to black women (along with some white women), broke the link between incestuous and inter-racial sex. In the belief systems of the Old South, these two contradictory ideas coexisted, the one commonly given priority over the other according to the needs of the particular situation or argument. The Old South was not torn apart by this contradiction: there were other, rather more brutal and material factors at work. Needless to say, though, it did not help spokesmen for the *status quo* to construct a coherent case. It was one symptom, among many, of the generally makeshift, patchwork nature of the story the Old South devised to protect its position: the degree to which conflicting arguments could be and were summoned to defend or even celebrate the idea of patriarchy and the feudal dream.

63 *Sanctuary*, p. 17. See also p. 133; *Sound and the Fury*, pp. 80, 118; *Light in August* (1932; London, 1960 edition), pp. 93, 143; *Town*, p. 45; *Go Down, Moses*, p. 240; Herbert Marcuse, *Eros and Civilization: A Philosophical Inquiry into Freud* (1955; Boston, Mass., 1966 edition), pp. xiv–xv. Two discussions of Faulkner's treatment of women characters that reach different conclusions are Sally R. Page, *Faulkner's Women: Characterization and Meaning* (Deland, Fla, 1972) and

David Williams, *Faulkner's Women: The Myth and the Muse* (Montreal, 1977). Of related interest are Ann Firor Scott, 'Women in the South: History as Fiction, Fiction as History', and Susan Donaldson, 'Gender and the Profession of Letters in the South', in *Rewriting the South: History and Fiction*, ed. Lothar Hönnighausen and Valeria Lerda (Tubingen, 1993). For other, recent discussions of women characters in Faulkner's work, see note 40 to chapter 2 of this book.

64 *Absalom, Absalom!*, p. 109. See also p. 114. On Mr Compson, see *Faulkner in the University*, p. 3; Bleikasten, *Most Splendid Failure*, pp. 109–14; Michael Millgate, *The Achievement of William Faulkner* (London, 1966).

65 *Sound and the Fury*, p. 86.

66 *Sanctuary*, pp. 177–8. See also p. 73, 133; *Sanctuary: The Original Text*, ed. Noel Polk (London, 1981), p. 16. For discussions of *Sanctuary* that see it in terms of a vision of evil, see, e.g., Cleanth Brooks, *William Faulkner: The Yoknapatawpha Country* (New Haven, Conn., 1963); Olga Vickery, *The Novels of William Faulkner* (Baton Rouge, La, 1964). See also, Albert Guerard Jr, 'The Misogynous Vision as High Art: Faulkner's *Sanctuary*', *Southern Review*, XII (1976), 215–31.

67 *As I Lay Dying* (1930; London, 1963 edition), p. 38. See also 'Dry September', in *Collected Stories*, p. 169; *Requiem for a Nun*, pp. 202, 231; *Intruder in the Dust*, p. 50; *Absalom, Absalom!*, p. 361; Brooks, *Yoknapatawpha Country*, p. 30; Cash, *Mind of the South*, pp. 46–8.

68 *Hamlet*, pp. 305–8.

69 Ibid, p. 306. See also Millgate, *Achievement of Faulkner*, p. 190; Bakhtin, *Dialogic Imagination*, p. 261.

70 *Absalom, Absalom!*, p. 303. See also Estella Schoenberg, *Old Tales and Talking: Quentin Compson in William Faulkner's 'Absalom, Absalom!' and Related Works* (Jackson, Miss., 1975).

71 Augustus Baldwin Longstreet, *Georgia Scenes: Characters, Incidents, etc., in the First Half-Century of the Republic* (New York, 1835), pp. 20–1. For folk versions of the 'horse-swapping' theme, see Richard M. Dawson, *Jonathan Draws a Long Bow* (Cambridge, Mass., 1946), pp. 83ff, and *American Folklore* (Chicago, 1954), pp. 71ff.

72 *Unvanquished*, p. 36.

73 Skates, *Mississippi*, pp. 80–1. See also pp. 83, 87–9; *Faulkner in the University*, p. 43.

74 'Red Leaves', in *Collected Stories*, p. 315. See also pp. 320, 324.

75 Ibid., p. 330.

76 Jameson, *Political Unconscious*, p. 17.

77 'A Justice', in *Collected Stories*, p. 359–60. See also John Faulkner, *My Brother Bill: An Affectionate Reminiscence* (New York, 1963), p. 65.

78 *Absalom, Absalom!*, p. 387. See also p. 12.

79 *Sound and the Fury*, p. 110. See also Bakhtin, *Marxism and the Philosophy of Language*, p. 39.

80 'A Justice', p. 343.

81 Ibid., p. 344. See also 'A Courtship', in *Collected Stories*, p. 361.

82 Jameson, *Political Unconscious*, p. 17.

83 *Lion in the Garden*, pp. 30–1.

84 See A.J. Bezzerides, *William Faulkner: A Life on Paper* (Jackson, Miss., 1980), pp. 23, 53, 92, 122.

85   *Lion in the Garden*, p. 177. See also *Faulkner and the Southern Renaissance*, ed. Doreen Fowler and Ann Abadie (Jackson, Mississippi, 1982), p. 201.

86   *Lion in the Garden*, p. 255. For a fascinating reinterpretation of the life of William Faulkner's great-grandfather, see Joel Williamson, *William Faulkner and Southern History* (New York, 1993), pp. 41–64.

87   Blotner, *Faulkner* (one-volume edition), p. 22.

88   Robert Cantwell, 'The Faulkners: Recollections of a Gifted Family', in *William Faulkner: Three Decades of Criticism*, ed. Frederick J. Hoffman and Olga Vickery (New York, 1963), p. 56.

89   Blotner, *Faulkner* (one-volume edition), p. 23.

90   Michael O'Brien, *Rethinking the South: Essays in Intellectual History* (Baltimore, Md, 1988), p. 22. See also Ben Wasson, *Count No 'Count: Flashbacks to Faulkner* (Jackson, Miss., 1983), p. 25.

91   *Faulkner–Cowley File*, p. 66. See also Blotner, *Faulkner* (one-volume edition), p. 569; Meta Carpenter Wilde and Orin Borsten, *A Loving Gentleman: The Love Story of Meta Carpenter and William Faulkner* (New York, 1976), p. 79; Wittenberg, *Faulkner*, p. 7.

92   Blotner, *Faulkner* (one-volume edition), p. 34. See also John Faulkner, *My Brother Bill*, p. 73.

93   John Faulkner, *My Brother Bill*, p. 11. See also Blotner, *Faulkner*, pp. 53, 68; Karl, *Faulkner*, p. 96.

94   *Faulkner in the University*, p. 251. See also *Light in August*, p. 359; *Sartoris* (1929; London, 1964 edition), p. 374.

95   Blotner, *Faulkner* (one-volume edition), p. 350. See also pp. 18–19; Dean Faulkner Wells, 'Dean Swift Faulkner: A Biographical Study' (MA thesis, University of Mississippi), 1975, p. 4.

96   Elizabeth Wright, *Psychoanalytic Criticism: Theory in Practice* (London, 1984), p. 113. See also Jacques Lacan, 'The Mirror Stage as Formative of the Function of the I as Revealed in Psychoanalytic Experience', in *Ecrits: A Selection*, trans. Alan Sheridan (London, 1977), pp. 1–7; Blotner, *Faulkner* (one-volume edition), p. 31; Karl, *Faulkner*, pp. 28, 31; Wittenberg, *Faulkner*, pp. 24–5.

97   Martin Kreisworth, *William Faulkner: The Making of a Novelist* (Athens, Ga, 1983), p. 144. See also John T. Irwin, *Doubling and Incest/Repetition and Revenge: A Speculative Reading of Faulkner* (Baltimore, Md, 1978); John T. Matthews, *The Play of Faulkner's Language* (Ithaca, N.Y., 1982).

98   Blotner, *Faulkner* (one-volume edition), p. 240. See also pp. 237, 459; Carpenter Wilde, *Loving Gentleman*, p. 52.

99   *Faulkner: A Comprehensive Guide to the Brodsky Collection*, ed. Louis D. Brodsky and Robert W. Hamblin (Jackson, Miss., 1982–5), p. 258. See also Carpenter Wilde, *Loving Gentleman*, pp. 77, 127.

100 Carpenter Wilde, *Loving Gentleman*, p. 279.

101 'Verse Old and Nascent', in *William Faulkner: Early Prose and Poetry*, ed. Carvel Collins (Boston, Mass., 1962), p. 115. See also Carpenter Wilde, *Loving Gentleman*, p. 200.

102 'Introduction to *The Sound and the Fury*,' *Mississippi Quarterly*, p. 415. See also 'Verse Old and Nascent', p. 115.

103 *Mansion*, pp. 22, 192. See also 'An Introduction to *The Sound and the Fury*', ed. James B. Meriwether, *Southern Review*, VIII (Autumn 1972), 710; *Soldier's Pay*, p. 207; *Mosquitoes*, p. 96.

104 'Nympholepsy', in *Uncollected Stories of William Faulkner*, ed. Joseph Blotner

(London, 1980), p. 335. See also pp. 332, 333, 334, 336. For 'L'Apres-Midi d'un Faune' and 'The Hill', see *Early Prose and Poetry*, pp. 39–40, 90–2.
105 *Town*, p. 9.
106 *Soldier's Pay*, p. 175.
107 *Mosquitoes*, p. 265. See also pp. 23, 89, 137, 138, 253.
108 *Flags in the Dust*, pp. 190–1. See also *Go Down, Moses*, p. 226; *Mansion*, p. 216. In *Sartoris*, 'quietness' is substituted for 'quietude': see pp. 134, 261.
109 *Lion in the Garden*, p. 239.
110 Bakhtin, *Dialogic Imagination*, p. 237. See also Julia Kristeva, *La Révolution du langage poétique* (Paris, 1984).
111 *Essays, Speeches, and Public Letters*, p. 117.
112 Blotner, *Faulkner* (one-volume edition), p. 45.
113 Ibid., p. 46. See also pp. 44, 102.
114 Ibid., p. 45.
115 Wells, 'Dean Swift Faulkner', p. 7. See also John Faulkner, *My Brother Bill*, p. 70; Murry Falkner, *The Falkners of Mississippi* (Baton Rouge, La, 1967), p. 7; Blotner, *Faulkner*, p. 79.
116 Blotner, *Faulkner* (one-volume edition), p. 357. See also pp. 355–6; Carpenter Wilde, *Loving Gentleman*, p. 33.
117 Carpenter Wilde, *Loving Gentleman*, p. 33. See also *Sartoris*, pp. 43, 311, 356; Wells, 'Dean Swift Faulkner', p. 20.
118 Blotner, *Faulkner*, p. 1044. See also Blotner, *Faulkner* (one-volume edition), pp. 324, 417, 438.

Notes to Chapter 2: Faulkner the Apprentice

1 *Thinking of Home: William Faulkner's Letters to His Mother and Father 1918–1925*, ed. James G. Watson (New York, 1992), p. 118. Among the many discussions of early Faulkner that I have found helpful, apart from the works cited in the following notes, are Max Putzel, *Genius of Place: William Faulkner's Triumphant Beginnings* (Baton Rouge, La, 1985); Lothar Hönnighausen, *William Faulkner: The Art of Stylization in Early Graphic and Literary Work* (Cambridge, 1986); Michel Gresset, *Fascination: Faulkner's Fiction, 1919–1936*, adapted from the French by Thomas West (Durham, N.C., 1989).
2 *Thinking of Home*, p. 149. See also pp. 15–16, 47, 48, 50, 110, 188; Ben Wasson, *Count No 'Count: Flashbacks to Faulkner* (Jackson, Miss., 1983), p. 156.
3 *William Faulkner: Early Prose and Poetry*, ed. Carvel Collins (Boston, Mass., 1962), pp. 55–6. See also pp. 62, 102.
4 Ibid., p. 115. See also p. 117.
5 'Books and Things. American Drama: Eugene O'Neill', in *Early Prose and Poetry*, p. 89. See also pp. 87, 94, 95, 96, 116. On the importance of Southern speech and rhetoric to Faulkner, see, in particular, Stephen B. Ross, *Fiction's Inexhaustible Voice: Speech and Writing in Faulkner* (Athens, Ga, 1989).
6 *The Marionettes: A Play in One Act*, ed. Noel Polk (Charlotttesville, Va, 1971), pp. 13–14. See also pp. ix–x; James B. Meriwether, *The Literary Career of William Faulkner* (1961; Columbia, S.C., 1971 edition), pp. 8–9; Michael Millgate, *The Achievement of William Faulkner*, (London, 1966), p. 8; Ilse D. Lind, 'The Effect of Painting on Faulkner's Poetic Form', in *Faulkner, Modernism and Film*, ed. Evans Harrington and Ann Abadie (Jackson, Miss., 1978), pp. 113–14.

7   *Marionettes*, p. 7. See also p. 10.
8   Ibid., p. 22. See also pp. 42, 47–8, 54.
9   *Vision in Spring*, ed. Judith L. Sensibar (Austin, Texas, 1984), p. 17. See also Judith L. Sensibar, *The Origins of Faulkner's Art* (Austin, Texas, 1984), esp. ch. 10.
10 *Vision in Spring*, p. 25.
11 Ibid., p. 38. See also p. 48; Cleanth Brooks, *William Faulkner: Toward Yoknapatawpha and Beyond* (New Haven, Conn., 1978), pp. 11–15.
12 Ibid., p. 55. See also p. 83.
13 Judith L. Sensibar, 'Introduction' to *Vision in Spring*, p. ix. See also *Origins of Faulkner's Art*.
14 *The Marble Faun, and A Green Bough* (New York, 1965), p. 11. See also Brooks, *Faulkner: Toward Yoknapatawpha and Beyond*, p. 25.
15 *The Marble Faun, and A Green Bough*, p. 12.
16 Ibid., p. 50. See also p. 13.
17 Ibid., p. 14.
18 *Lion in the Garden: Interviews with William Faulkner, 1926–1962*, ed. James B. Meriwether and Michael Millgate (New York, 1968), p. 253. On the relationship between writer and reader in Faulkner, see Warwick Wadlington, *Reading Faulknerian Tragedy* (Ithaca, N.Y., 1987).
19 *Helen: A Courtship, and Mississippi Poems*, ed. Carvel Collins and Joseph Blotner (New Orleans, La, and Oxford, Miss., 1981), p. 156. See also *A Faulkner Miscellany*, ed. James B. Meriwether (Jackson, Miss., 1974), pp. 70–97; Brooks, *Faulkner: Toward Yoknapatawpha and Beyond*, pp. 8–11, 143.
20 *The Marble Faun, and A Green Bough*, p. 7. See also pp. 7, 11, 20, 29, 44, 64.
21 Ibid., p. 16. See also p. 60.
22 *Mansion*, p. 399.
23 *New Orleans Sketches*, ed. Carvel Collins (New York, 1968), pp. 33–4. See also pp. 41, 46, 47.
24 Ibid., pp. 55–6. See also p. 54, 57; Brooks, *Faulkner: Toward Yoknapatawpha and Beyond*, p. 114; Richard Gray, *Writing the South: Ideas of an American Region* (Cambridge, 1986), p. 111.
25 *New Orleans Sketches*, p. 134. See also p. 131.
26 *Father Abraham*, ed. James B. Meriwether (New York, 1983), p. 16. See also pp. 13, 16, 19; Meriwether, *Literary Career of Faulkner*, pp. 40–4, 69–73; Millgate, *Achievement of Faulkner*, pp. 24, 180–3; Joseph Blotner, *Faulkner: A Biography*, 2 vols (New York, 1974), pp. 526–31; David Minter: *William Faulkner: His Life and Work* (Baltimore, Md, 1980), pp. 78–9.
27 *Uncollected Stories of William Faulkner*, ed. Joseph Blotner (London, 1980), p. 504. See also pp. 514, 519, 523; Joseph Blotner, *Faulkner: A Biography* (one-volume edition, New York, 1984), p. 177.
28 *Elmer*, p. 346. See also pp. 353, 354, 383. See also Blotner, *Faulkner* (one-volume edition), p. 164. There are two longer fragments and several shorter versions of this story in the William Faulkner collection, Alderman Library, University of Virginia, Charlottesville. The Elmer papers have been published as part of the *William Faulkner Manuscripts*, under the general editorship of Joseph Blotner, Thomas L. McHaney, Michael Millgate and Noel Polk (New York, 1987), in volume I, ed. Thomas L. McHaney. All page references here, however, are to the version edited by Dianne L. Cox. published in *Mississippi Quarterly*, XXXVI (Summer 1983), 337–460. See also Thomas L. McHaney, 'The

Elmer Papers: Faulkner's Comic Portraits of the Artist', *Mississippi Quarterly*, XXVI (Summer 1973), 281–311.

29 *Elmer*, p. 345. See also pp. 365, 370, 374, 376.

30 Ibid., p. 435. See also p. 388.

31 Ibid., p. 400. See also Blotner, *Faulkner* (one-volume edition), p. 162.

32 *Mayday*, ed. Carvel Collins (Notre Dame, Ind., 1976), p. 87. See also pp. 49. 50, 82, 84; *New Orleans Sketches*, p. 167; James G. Watson, 'Literary Self-criticism: Faulkner in Fiction on Fiction', *Southern Quarterly*, XX (Fall 1981), 51.

33 *Helen: A Courtship, and Mississippi Poems*, p. 112. See also pp. 111, 114, 123.

34 Ibid., p. 112.

35 Ibid., p. 113. See also p. 119; Lewis P. Simpson, 'Sex & History: Origins of Faulkner's Apocrypha', in *The Maker and the Myth: Faulkner and Yoknapatawpha*, ed. Evans Harrington and Ann Abadie (Jackson, Miss., 1977), pp. 45–6.

36 Judith Wittenberg, *William Faulkner: The Transfiguration of Biography* (Lincoln, Neb., 1979), p. 47. See also *Soldier's Pay*, p. 128; Blotner, *Faulkner* (one-volume edition), pp. 144–5, and 'Introduction' to vol. III of *William Faulkner Manuscripts*.

37 *Soldier's Pay*, p. 38. See also pp. 7, 22, 43, 97. On flight in general, see Clive Hart, *The Dream of Flight* (London, 1972); on the particular attidudes of people in the 1920s to flight, see John William Ward, 'The Meaning of Lindbergh's Flight', in *The Shaping of Twentieth-century America*, ed. Robert Abrams and Lawrence L. Levine (Boston, Mass., 1971).

38 *Soldier's Pay*, p. 256. See also pp. 49, 56, 107, 162, 175, 186; Blotner, *Faulkner* (one-volume edition), p. 182; Brooks, *Faulkner: Toward Yoknapatawpha and Beyond*, pp. 67–99.

39 *Soldier's Pay*, p. 223. See also pp. 49, 102, 111, 246, 247.

40 Ibid., pp. 28, 224. See also pp. 96, 125. Among the more useful recent discussions of black characters, relating to what is being argued here, are Eric J. Sundquist, *Faulkner: The House Divided* (Baltimore, Md, 1983) and Michael Grimwood, *Heart in Conflict: Faulkner's Struggles with Vocation* (Athens, Ga, 1987). Recent discussions of the female in Faulkner, equally relevant here, include *Faulkner and Women*, ed. Doreen Fowler and Ann Abadie (Jackson, Miss., 1985); Judith B. Wittenberg, 'William Faulkner: a Feminist Consideration', in *Modern Critical Views: William Faulkner*, ed. Harold Bloom (New York, 1986), pp. 233–46; Minrose Gwin, *The Feminine and Faulkner* (Knoxville, Tenn., 1989). A number of the essays in *Faulkner's Discourse: An International Symposium*, ed. Lothar Hönnighausen (Tübingen, 1989) are also worth looking at in this connection, as is much of the discussion and analysis in André Bleikasten, *The Ink of Melancholy: Faulkner's Novels from 'The Sound and the Fury' to 'Light in August'* (Bloomington, Ind., 1990).

41 *Soldier's Pay*, pp. 92–3. See also pp. 20, 142; *Flags in the Dust*, p. 127; *Sanctuary*, p. 89.

42 *Soldier's Pay*, p. 128. See also p. 144.

43 Ibid., pp. 126, 136, 141, 265, 266. See also Gail Mortimer, *Faulkner's Rhetoric of Loss* (Austin, Texas, 1983).

44 *Soldier's Pay*, p. 218. See also pp. 30, 217, 241, 262.

45 Ibid., p. 74.

46 Ibid., p. 266. See also pp. 189, 256, 257, 259.

47 *Mosquitoes*, p. .109. See also pp. 72, 156, 209, 210, 261, 262; Blotner, *Faulkner* (one-volume edition), pp. 182–4, 186–8; and 'Introduction' to vol. IV of *William Faulkner Manuscripts*; John T. Irwin, *Doubling and Incest/Repetition and Revenge: A Speculative Reading of Faulkner* (Baltimore, Md, 1978), pp. 106ff.

48 *Mosquitoes*, p. 202. See also pp. 16, 28, 49, 80, 154, 207.
49 Ibid., pp. 122–3. See also pp. 227, 265; Blotner, *Faulkner* (one-volume edition), p. 189; Sensibar, 'Introduction' to *Vision in Spring*, p. xxviii.
50 *Mosquitoes*, p. 86. See also pp. 66, 122, 152, 209, 210, 224, 280.
51 Ibid., p. 158. See also pp. 89, 108, 227.
52 Ibid., p. 175. For further discussion of variations on this image see ch. 1 of this study.
53 Ibid., p. 156.
54 Ibid., p. 64.
55 Ibid., p. 172. See also p. 149.
56 Ibid., p. 142. See also pp. 152, 253, 288.
57 Pierre Bourdieu, *Outline of a Theory of Practice*, trans. Richard Nice (Cambridge, 1977), pp. 15, 81. See also Louis Althusser, 'Ideology and the State', in *Lenin and Philosophy, and Other Essays*, trans. Ben Brewster (London, 1977); Julia Kristeva, 'Stabat Mater', in *The Female Body in Western Culture: Contemporary Perspectives*, ed. Susan R. Suleiman (Cambridge, Mass., 1986), pp. 99–118. Although I make rather different use of this material, I am indebted to Philip M. Weinstein, *Faulkner's Subject: A Cosmos No One Owns* (Cambridge, 1992), for drawing my attention to it. For the quotation from *Absalom, Absalom!*, see p. 139.

Notes to Chapter 3: Rewriting the Homeplace

1 'A Note on Sherwood Anderson', in *Essays, Speeches and Public Letters*, ed. James B. Meriwether (New York, 1966), p. 8. See also Joseph Blotner, *Faulkner: A Biography*, 2 vols (New York, 1974), pp. 531–2; *Lion in the Garden: Interviews with William Faulkner, 1926–1962*, ed. James B. Meriwther and Michael Millgate (New York, 1968), p. 255.
2 Malcolm Cowley, 'Introduction' to *The Portable Faulkner* (New York, 1946), p. 5. See also *Lion in the Garden*, pp. 107, 255; John Pilkington, *The Heart of Yoknapatawpha* (Jackson, Miss., 1981), p. 9.
3 Blotner, *Faulkner*, pp. 559–60. See also *William Faulkner of Oxford*, ed. James W. Webb and A. Wigfall Green (Baton Rouge, La, 1965), p. 52; *Faulkner in the University: Class Conferences at the University of Virginia 1957–1959*, ed. Frederick Gwynn and Joseph Blotner (Charlottesville, Va, 1959), p. 285. On the revision of *Flags in the Dust*, see, e.g., Joseph Blotner (ed.), 'William Faulkner's Essay on the Composition of *Sartoris*', *Yale University Library Gazette*, XL (Jan. 1973), 123–4, and 'Introduction' to vol. v of *William Faulkner Manuscripts*, ed. Joseph Blotner *et al.* (New York, 1987).
4 *Sartoris*, p. 32. See also p. 214.
5 Ibid., p. 261. See also p. 136; *Flags in the Dust*, p. 406. On the plantation Hotspur and Hamlet figures, see William R. Taylor, *Cavalier and Yankee: The Old South and the American National Character* (London, 1963).
6 *Sartoris*, p. 1. See also Mikhail Bakhtin, *The Dialogic Imagination*, ed. and trans. Caryl Emerson and Michael Holquist (Austin, Texas, 1981), pp. 15–17; Jean-Paul Sartre, 'Time in Faulkner: *The Sound and the Fury*', in *William Faulkner: Three Decades of Criticism*, ed. F.J. Hoffman and O. Vickery (New York, 1963), p. 228; Joseph Blotner, *Faulkner: A Biography* (one-volume edition, New York, 1984), p. 194.

7 *Sartoris*, p. 3. See also pp. 42, 143.
8 On the theory of displacement as Sigmund Freud uses it, see *Introductory Lectures on Psychoanalysis*, trans. and ed. James Strachey (New York, 1966), p. 144.
9 *Sartoris*, p. 281. A very short conversation, and a few more lines in a similar vein, follow the passage quoted here.
10 Ibid., p. 229. See also pp. 228, 237.
11 Dorothy Tuck, *A Handbook of Faulkner* (London, 1965), p. 16. See also Blotner, *Faulkner* (one-volume edition), p. 205.
12 *Faulkner in the University*, p. 61. See also p. 77; 'Introduction' to the Modern Library Edition of *Sanctuary*, in *Essays, Speeches and Public Letters*, p. 176; *Faulkner at Nagano*, ed. Robert A. Jelliffe (Tokyo, 1956), p. 106; Blotner, *Faulkner*, p. 1522. On the dating of the stories about the Compson family, see Norman Holmes Pearson, 'Faulkner's Three Evening Suns', *Yale University Library Gazette*, 29 Oct. 1954, 61–70; Michael Millgate, *The Achievement of William Faulkner* (London, 1966), p. 90; Blotner, *Faulkner*, pp. 565–7. David Minter, *William Faulkner: His Life and Work* (Baltimore, Md, 1980), points out that 'although there is no conclusive evidence for dating the stories earlier than *The Sound and the Fury*... there is good circumstantial evidence – that Quentin is older in "That Evening Sun" than he lives to be in *The Sound and the Fury*; and that Benjy does not appear in the stories' (p. 283). On the revisions to the manuscript, see Noel Polk, 'Introduction' to vol. VI of *William Faulkner Manuscripts*.
13 Maurice Coindreau, 'Preface' to *Le bruit et la fureur* (1938), p. 14, trans. George M. Reeves, in 'Preface to *The Sound and the Fury*', *Mississippi Quarterly*, XIX (Summer 1966), 107–15. For further discussion of the tangled relationship of *The Sound and the Fury* to Faulkner's own life, see Blotner, *Faulkner*, pp. 550–663; Judith B. Wittenberg, *William Faulkner: The Transfiguration of Biography* (Lincoln, Neb., 1979), pp. 75–87; Minter, *Faulkner*, pp. 91–107.
14 Cited in Minter, *Faulkner*, p. 95.
15 *Lion in the Garden*, p. 245. Cf. p. 222; *Faulkner in the University*, p. 71. For an account of the book's genesis that is slightly different in its emphases, see *Faulkner at Nagano*, pp. 103–5.
16 *Faulkner in the University*, p. 6.
17 'An Introduction to *The Sound and the Fury*', ed. James B. Meriwether, *Southern Review*, VII (Autumn 1972), 709. See also, *Mosquitoes*, p. 208; 'An Introduction to *The Sound and The Fury*', ed. James B. Meriwether, *Mississippi: Quarterly*, XXVI (Summer 1973), 415.
18 'Caddy... is first and foremost an image' (Andrè Bleikasten, *The Most Splendid Failure: Faulkner's 'The Sound and the Fury'* (Bloomington, Ind., 1976), p. 65. Caddy is not, however, unique. Although Addie Bundren in *As I Lay Dying* is a very different figure, or rather a very different kind of absent presence, she is just as complex and paradoxical: as fierce in her demands as Drusilla Hawk, as committed to motion as Faulkner's nymphs, and as close to the earth, 'clinging to it', as Eula Varner or Lena Grove. See also *Mosquitoes*, p. 89.
19 *Sound and the Fury*, pp. 52–3. For a rather different notion of the language of this section, see Cecil C. Moffitt, 'A Rhetoric for Benjy', *Southern Literary Journal*, II (Fall 1970), 32–46.
20 Wesley Morris and Barbara Alverson Morris, *Reading Faulkner* (Madison, Wis., 1989), p. 119. See also *Sound and the Fury*, pp. 49, 50.
21 *Sound and the Fury*, p. 159. See also p. 82; Henry James, *The Art of the Novel*, ed. R.P. Blackmur (New York, 1942), p. 42.

22 *Sound and the Fury*, p. 109. See also pp. 142, 143; Bakhtin, *Dialogic Imagination*, p. 342.

23 *Sound and the Fury*, p. 82. See also pp. 91, 113, 151. For a discussion of the possible link between Quentin's aristocratic pose, the declining culture to which he tries to attach himself, and his preoccupation with incest, see Bleikasten, *The Most Splendid Failure*, pp. 115, 127. Walter R. Taylor, *Faulkner's Search for a South* (Urbana, Ill., 1983), argues that Faulkner never completely disengaged himself from the patrician values of the South. Stephen B. Ross, *Fiction's Inexhaustible Voice: Speech and Writing in Faulkner* (Athens, Ga, 1989), emphasizes Quentin's passive absorption of 'others' words' (p. 181).

24 *Sound and the Fury*, pp. 163, 174. See also Bleikasten, *The Most Splendid Failure*, p. 147; Stephen B. Ross, 'Jason Compson and Sut Lovingood: Southwestern Humor as Stream of Consciousness', *Studies in the Novel*, VIII (1976), 278–90; Blotner, *Faulkner* (one-volume edition), p. 217. The full title of *Sut Livingood's Yarns* is *Sut Lovingood: Yarns Spun by a 'Natural Born Durn'd Fool'* (New York, 1867). Faulkner numbered Sut Livingood among his favourite characters: see *Lion in the Garden*, p. 251. On Harris and his contribution to Southwestern humour see, e.g., Kenneth Lynn, *Mark Twain and Southwestern Humor* (Boston, Mass., 1960); Tony Tanner, *The Reign of Wonder* (Cambridge, 1956), pp. 100–3; Richard Gray, *The Literature of Memory: Modern Writers of the American South* (London, 1977), pp. 115–8.

25 This phrase is borrowed from Mikhail Bakhtin, *Problems of Dostoevsky's Poetics*, ed. and trans. Caryl Emerson (Manchester, 1984), p. 101.

26 *Sound and the Fury*, p. 261. The phrase 'implied author' is, of course, taken from Wayne Booth, *The Rhetoric of Fiction* (Chicago, 1961).

27 *Sound and the Fury*, p. 284. See also p. 264; Edmond L. Volpe, *A Reader's Guide to William Faulkner* (London, 1964), p. 125. For a detailed examination of the book's ending, see Beverley Gross, 'Form and Fulfillment in *The Sound and the Fury*', *Modern Language Quarterly* (December 1968), 439–49.

28 *Sound and the Fury*, p. 35. See also p. 245.

29 See Thadious M. Davis, *Faulkner's 'Negro': Art and the Southern Context* (Baton Rouge, La, 1983), pp. 99ff; Blotner, *Faulkner* (one-volume edition), p. 219.

30 'Introduction' to *Sanctuary*, p. 177. See also *Faulkner in the University*, pp. 90–1; Blotner, *Faulkner* (one-volume edition), pp. 234, 235; *Lion in the Garden*, p. 226. On the manuscript of *As I Lay Dying*, see Thomas L. McHaney, 'Introduction' to vol. VII of *William Faulkner Manuscripts*.

31 *As I Lay Dying*, p. 189.

32 Ibid., pp. 190–1. The problems some critics have with *As I Lay Dying* are perhaps suggested by their reluctance either to acknowledge that it is one of Faulkner's major novels or, in certain cases, to give it detailed consideration. For two otherwise very perceptive (and very different) books that, respectively, take the first and the second of these positions, see John Pikoulis, *The Art of William Faulkner* (London, 1982) and Philip M. Weinstein, *Faulkner's Subject: A Cosmos No One Owns* (Cambridge, 1992) (Weinstein says that he omits *As I Lay Dying* from scrutiny 'because so much of its representative quality is shared with *The Sound and the Fury*' (p. 3n): but this is surely to beg a very large number of questions).

33 *As I Lay Dying*, p. 86.

34 Mikhail Bakhtin, *Rabelais and His World*, trans. Helene Iswolsky (Cambridge, Mass., 1968) p. 371. See also p. 94; *Dialogic Imagination*, p. 24.

35 *As I Lay Dying*, p. 167.
36 Ibid., p. 192.
37 Ibid., p. 24.
38 Ibid., p. 93.
39 Ibid., p. 53.
40 Ibid., p. 202. See also pp. 7, 40, 58, 144, 164.
41 Ibid., p. 55. See also pp. 13, 79.
42 Ibid., p. 92. See also pp. 39, 47, 66, 75, 127. On interpellation see Louis Althusser, 'Ideology and the State', in *Lenin and Philosophy, and Other Essays*, trans. Ben Brewster (London, 1977): 'ideology "acts" or "functions" in such a way that it "recruits" subjects among the individuals (it recruits them all), or "transforms" the individuals into subjects (it transforms them all) by that very precise operation which I have called *interpellation* or hailing, and which can be imagined along the lines of the most commonplace everyday police (or other) hailing: "Hey, you there".' See also ch. 1 of this study.
43 *As I Lay Dying*, p. 64.
44 Ibid., p. 137. See also p. 44.
45 Ibid., pp. 136–7.
46 Ibid., p. 140.
47 Ibid., p. 208. See also p. 161.
48 *Faulkner in the University*, p. 273. See also Blotner, *Faulkner* (one-volume edition), p. 69.
49 'Introduction' to *Sanctuary*, p. 178. See also *Lion in the Garden*, p. 123. For an account of Faulkner's revisions, see Noel Polk, 'Afterword' to *Sanctuary: The Original Text*, and 'Introduction' to vol. VIII of *William Faulkner Manuscripts*.
50 *Sanctuary*, p. 16. See also Luce Irigaray, *Ce sexe qui n'en est pas un* (Paris, 1977), p. 181 (my translation). On the personal pressures at work at the time Faulkner wrote *Sanctuary*, see Blotner, *Faulkner*, pp. 619ff; Wittenberg, *Faulkner*, 91ff, Minter, *Faulkner*, 108ff; Frederick R. Karl, *William Faulkner: American Writer* (London, 1989), pp. 355ff.
51 Julia Kristeva, 'Il n'y a pas de maître à langage', *Nouvelle revue de psychoanalyse*, xx (Autumn), 135 (my translation). See also *Revolution in the Poetic Language* (New York, 1984).
52 *Sanctuary: The Original Text*, p. 74. See also *Sanctuary*, p. 85. For a different reading of the letters episode, see James G. Watson, *William Faulkner, Letters and Fictions* (Austin, Texas, 1987), p. 108.
53 *Sanctuary: The Original Text*, p. 16. See also *Sanctuary*, pp. 22, 51.
54 *Sanctuary*, p. 190. See also pp. 25, 253. The corrected text of *Sanctuary*, edited by Noel Polk (New York, 1987), has the words 'as she writhed her loins against him' at the end of this passage: which underlines Temple's role here of sexual predator. On the vision that Horace experiences while vomiting, see Noel Polk, 'The Space Between *Sanctuary*', in *Intertextuality in Faulkner*, ed. Michel Gresset and Noel Polk (Jackson, Miss., 1986). For a different reading of the incestuous pattern, see John T. Matthews, *The Play of Faulkner's Language* (Ithaca, N.Y., 1982), p. 257.
55 *Sanctuary*, p. 237. See also pp. 15, 60, 138, 143, 226, 234. The corrected text has the additional remark, 'Jeez – I wouldn't have used no cob', after the words quoted in brackets: emphasizing the hypocrisy at work here. On the binary oppositions (nature/progress, grape arbour/mirror) that Horace gives

voice to here, see Hélène Cixous and Cathérine Clément, *La jeune née* (Paris, 1975), pp. 116–18. On the comments of the local men on Temple, see Joseph R. Urgo, 'Temple Drake's Truthful Perjury: Rethinking Faulkner's *Sanctuary*', *American Literature*, LV (1983), 238.

56 *Sanctuary*, p. 202. See also p. 148.

57 Ibid., pp. 47, 50, 'Temple invited the assault', says Lawrence Kubie, in 'William Faulkner's *Sanctuary*', *Faulkner: A Collection of Critical Essays*, ed. Robert Penn Warren (Englewood Cliffs, N.J., 1966), p. 141. Similar remarks are made by (e.g.) Olga Vickery, *The Novels of William Faulkner* (Baton Rouge, La, 1964), p. 113; James R. Cypher, 'The Tangled Sexuality of Temple Drake,' *American Imago*, XIX (1962), 246; David Miller, 'Faulkner's Women', *Modern Fiction Studies* (1967), 11–12; Fredrick T. Keefer, 'William Faulkner's *Sanctuary*: a Myth Examined', *Twentieth Century Literature*, XV (1969), 102; Calvin Brown, 'Sanctuary: From Confrontation to Peaceful Void', *Mosaic*, VII (1973), 444. For one of the more recent revisionary views, see Robert Dale Parker, *Faulkner and the Novelistic Imagination* (Urbana, Ill., 1985), p. 63.

58 *Sanctuary*, p. 57. See also pp. 6, 7, 103, 203, 252.

59 See Carolyn Porter's discussion of visual and vocal fields in *Absalom, Absalom!*, in *Seeing and Being: The Plight of the Participant Observer in Emerson, James, Adams, and Faulkner* (Middletown, Conn., 1981), p. 60.

60 *Sanctuary*, p. 175. See also pp. 7, 240; *Sanctuary: The Original Text*, p. 3.

61 *Sanctuary*, p. 5. See also pp. 82, 249.

62 Ibid., p. 184. See also pp. 5, 25, 49, 87, 113, 249, 253.

63 Ibid., p. 231. See also pp. 16, 44, 188. For a different reading of the incestuous patterns at work here, which argues that *Sanctuary* is a 'radical novel' calling into question 'the structures of community', see John N. Duvall, *Faulkner's Marginal Couple: Invisible, Outlaw, and Unspeakable Communities* (Austin, Texas, 1990), pp. 60ff.

64 *Sanctuary*, p. 241. See also pp. 18, 93, 97. Polk, 'Afterword', p. 304, emphasizes the connections between the two men.

65 An interesting variation on the Temple Drake figure is offered by a character called Mary Lee in 'The College Widow', one of the story outlines Faulkner wrote for MGM. Mary Lee is involved with three men: the ineffectual young man whom she marries (and who eventually divorces her), a dark 'stranger' to whom she is attracted but fears, and her professor father. Aspects of her relationships with these three recall Temple's relations with Benbow, Popeye and Judge Drake; just as aspects of her personality, febrile, apprehensive, excitable, recall the central female figure in *Sanctuary*. The outline was described as 'an evil, slimy thing' by a reader for MGM, and never went into production. See *Faulkner's MGM Screenplays*, ed. Bruce F. Kawin (Knoxville, Tenn., 1982), pp. 29–53.

66 *Sanctuary*, p. 64. See also p. 176. Wittenberg, *Faulkner*, points out the resemblances between the author and the male protagonists, also drawing attention to the fact that 'little black man' and 'little runt', two terms used to describe Popeye, are 'almost word-for-word, Faulkner's self-portrayal in *Mosquitoes*' (p. 99). My attention was drawn to the quotation from *The Sound and the Fury* by Noel Polk, 'The Dungeon Was Mother Herself: William Faulkner, 1927–1931', in *New Directions in Faulkner Studies*, ed. Doreen Fowler and Ann Abadie (Jackson, Mass., 1984), pp. 61–93.

Notes to Chapter 4: Of Past and Present Conflicts

1 James Meriwether, 'Faulkner, Lost and Found', *New York Times Book Review*, 5 Nov. 1972, p. 72. See also Joseph Blotner, *Faulkner: A Biography* (one-volume edition, New York, 1984), pp. 276, 309; *Faulkner in the University: Class Conferences at the University of Virginia, 1957–1959*, ed. Frederick Gwynn and Joseph Blotner (Charlottesville, Va, 1959), p. 74. On the preparation of the manuscript of *Light in August*, see Carl Fisher, *A Critical and Textual Study of William Faulkner's 'Light in August'* (Michigan: University Microfilms International, 1972); Joseph Blotner, 'Introduction' to vol. x of *William Faulkner Manuscripts* ed. Joseph Blotner *et al.* (New York, 1987); Michael Millgate, 'Introduction' to *New Essays on 'Light in August'*, ed. Michael Millgate (Cambridge, 1987).

2 'An Introduction to *The Sound and the Fury*', ed. James B. Meriwether, *Southern Review* (Autumn 1972), 709. See also *Light in August*, pp. 98, 101, 238, 339, 359. On some of the autobiographical elements here, see Judith B. Wittenberg, *William Faulkner: The Transfiguration of Biography* (Lincoln, Neb., 1979), pp. 117ff; Frederick R. Karl, *William Faulkner: American Writer* (London, 1989), p. 467.

3 On the condition of the South during this period, see George B. Tindall, *The Emergence of the New South, 1913–1943* (1967), vol. x of *A History of the South*, ed. Wendell H. Stephenson and E. Merton Coulter (Baton Rouge, La, 1947–67).

4 Mary Douglas, *Purity and Danger: An Analysis of the Concepts of Pollution and Taboo* (1966; London, 1984 edition), p. 64. See also p. 62, and 'Couvade and Menstruation', in *Implicit Meanings* (London, 1975), p. 61; *Light in August*, p. 80; Fredric Jameson, 'Metacommentary', PMLA, LXXXVI (Spring 1971), 15.

5 *Light in August*, pp. 262–3. See also pp. 64, 83. For two rather different readings of 'community' in *Light in August*, see John N. Duvall, *Faulkner's Marginal Couple: Invisible, Outlaw, and Unspeakable Communities* (Austin, Texas, 1990), pp. 19–36; André Bleikasten, '*Light in August*: the Closed Society and its Subjects', in *New Essays on 'Light in August'*, ed. Millgate, pp. 81–102. For the problematical nature of the evidence regarding the killing of Joanna Burden, see Stephen Meats, 'Who Killed Joanna Burden?', *Mississippi Quarterly*, XXIV (1971), 271–7.

6 *Light in August*, p. 55. See also pp. 5, 37, 333. On the ubiquitous nature of talk in this novel, see Stephen B. Ross, *Fiction's Inexhaustible Voice: Speech and Writing in Faulkner* (Athens, Ga, 1989), p. 52.

7 *Light in August*, p. 190.

8 Pierre Macherey, *A Theory of Literary Production*, trans. Geoffrey Wall (London, 1978), pp. 85, 86.

9 Malcolm X with the assistance of Alex Haley, *The Autobiography of Malcolm X* (1965; London, 1968 edition), p. 107. Richard Godden argues the crucial importance of the word 'nigger' to the life and fate of Joe Christmas in 'Call Me Nigger! Race and Speech in *Light in August*', *Journal of American Studies*, XIX (1980), 235–48: an essay to which I am indebted. On the controversy surrounding *Huckleberry Finn* see, e.g., the notes on contributors in *Satire or Evasion? Black Perspectives on 'Huckleberry Finn'*, ed. James S. Leonard, Thomas A. Tenney and Thadious Davis (Durham, N.C., 1992). Here, John H. Wallace is described as opposing *Huckleberry Finn* 'largely on the grounds of improper language'. Wallace has, in fact, produced his own edition of *The Adventures of*

Huckleberry Finn with the word 'nigger' removed from the text. This, I think, involves a misunderstanding of Twain's aims and a misreading of the text – which, like *Light in August*, surely forces the reader to *place* that word and its ideological underpinnings. Nevertheless, it shows how contentious that word has become and how unwelcome its use is in all but the most openly and viciously racist of environments.

10 *Autobiography of Malcolm X*, p. 107.

11 Georg Lukács, *The Historical Novel*, trans. Hannah and Stanley Mitchell (1962; London, 1969 edition), p. 36. See also *Light in August*, pp. 191, 288; Cleanth Brooks, *William Faulkner: First Encounters* (New Haven, Conn., 1983), pp. 174–5. It is perhaps worth noting that the manuscript version of the fifth chapter of *Light in August* contains references to 'black blood' and 'Negro smell' which were then removed from the published text. Along with this, Faulkner also altered the manuscript so that where Joe, talking about his parents, claims 'one of them was a nigger' he says instead 'one of them was part nigger': so making the question of racial status even more fractional and speculative. On the first point, see Regina K. Fadiman, *Faulkner's 'Light in August': A Description and Interpretation of the Revisions* (Charlottesville, Va, 1975), pp. 42–3. On the second, see Karl, *Faulkner*, p. 479.

12 *Light in August*, p. 80. See also p. 263; James A. Snead, *Figures of Division: William Faulkner's Major Novels* (New York, 1986), p. 88.

13 *Light in August*, p. 263.

14 Ibid., pp. 349–50. See also Roland Barthes, *Mythologies*, selected and trans. Annette Lavers (London, 1972), p. 110.

15 *Light in August*, p. 143. See also pp. 83, 88, 96, 119, 127, 179, 280, 283, 290. Of the voluminous material on the treatment of women in this novel, I have found the following particularly helpful: Doreen Fowler, 'Joe Christmas and "Womanshenegro"', in *Faulkner and Women*, ed. Doreen Fowler and Ann Abadie (Jackson, Miss., 1987), pp. 144–61; Judith Wittenberg, 'The Women of *Light in August*', in *New Essays on 'Light in August'*, ed. Millgate, pp. 103–22; André Bleitiasten, *The Ink of Melancholy: Faulkner's Novels from 'The Sound and the Fury' to 'Light in August'* (Bloomington, Ind., 1990); Philip M. Weinstein, *Faulkner's Subject: A Cosmos No One Owns* (Cambridge, 1992).

16 Douglas, 'Couvade and Menstruation', p. 62; see also *Purity and Danger*, pp. 40, 121; *Light in August*, pp. 173, 302; Lyce, Irigiray, 'La mécanique des fluides', in *Ce sexe qui n'en pas un* (Paris, 1977) and Jane Gallop, *The Daughter's Seduction* (Ithaca, N.Y., 1982) for discussions of male hostility to female 'fluidity' and, in particular, to menstrual flow (which, according to Gallop, 'ignores the distinction virgin/deflowered' and so offers a challenge to 'phallic fantasy' (p. 83)).

17 *Light in August*, p. 378. Weinstein contrasts the abundance of male talk and 'male scenes of camaraderie' with the relative silence and the loneliness of Lena Grove (*Faulkner's Subject*, pp. 18–20).

18 *Light in August*, p. 195. See also pp. 177, 190, 196.

19 Ibid., p. 8.

20 Barthes, *Mythologies*, p. 142. See also Jacques Lacan, *Ecrits*, trans. Alan Sheridan (London, 1977), p. 6. Also, on the general problem of language and power, see Michel Foucault, *Discipline and Punish*, trans. Alan Sheridan (New York, 1979): 'Power produces . . . reality; it produces domains of objects and rituals of truth. The individual and the knowledge that may be gained of him belong to this production' (p. 194).

21 Blotner, *Faulkner*, p. 782. See also *Selected Letters of William Faulkner*, ed. Joseph Blotner (New York, 1977), p. 75; James B. Meriwether, 'The Novel Faulkner Never Wrote: His *Golden Book* or *Doomsday Book*', *American Literature*, XLII (1970), 93–6.

22 *Faulkner's M.G.M. Screenplays*, ed. Bruce F. Kawin (Knoxville, Tonn., 1982), p. 173. See also *Faulkner in the University*, p. 36.

23 Clive Hart, *The Prehistory of Flight* (Berkeley, Cal., 1985), p. 1. See also p. 4.

24 F. Scott Fitzgerald, 'Echoes of the Jazz Age', in *The Crack-up*, ed. Edmund Wilson (New York, 1956), p. 20. See also John William Ward, 'The Meaning of Lindbergh's Flight', in *The Shaping of Twentieth-Century America*, ed. Robert Abrams and Lawrence L. Levine (Boston, Mass., 1971); Jacqueline Fear and Helen McNeil, 'The Twenties', in *Introduction to American Studies*, ed. Malcolm Bradbury and Howard Temperley (London, 1981), pp. 206–7.

25 Robert S. Lynd and Helen M. Lynd, *Middletown: A Study of American Culture* (New York, 1929), p. 22. See also Fear and McNeil, 'The Twenties', p. 207.

26 *Faulkner in the University*, p. 36. See also Lawrence W. Levine, 'Progress and Nostalgia: the Self Image of the Nineteen Twenties', in *The American Novel and the Nineteen Twenties*, ed. Malcolm Bradbury and David Palmer (London, 1971).

27 *Pylon* (1935; London, 1955 edition), p. 57. See also pp. 81, 91, 152. On the background to and preparation of *Pylon*, see Noel Polk, 'Introduction' to vol. XII of *William Faulkner Manuscripts*. On discontinuous landscapes in fiction, see Marshall McLuhan, 'John Dos Passos: Technique vs. Sensibility', in *Fifty Years of the American Novel: A Christian Appraisal*, ed. Harold C. Gardiner (New York, 1968), pp. 162ff.

28 *Pylon*, p. 121. See also pp. 19, 143, 171, 211.

29 Ibid., p. 35. See also pp. 10, 16, 106, 112, 115. The uncertainty of Faulkner's representation of these characters has led to considerable disagreement among critics about whether his attitude towards them is 'positive' or 'negative'. Among those favouring a 'negative' reading are John R. Marvin, 'Pylon: the Definition of Sacrifice', *Faulkner Studies*, I (1952), 20–3; James L. Baker, 'The Symbolic Extension of Yoknapatawpha County', *Arizona Quarterly*, VIII (1952), 227; W.T. Lhamon, '*Pylon*: the Ylimaf of New Valois', *Western Humanities Review*, XXIV (1970), 274–8. Those who emphasize what they see as the 'positive' aspects of Faulkner's representation include: Donald M. Torchiana, 'Faulkner's "Pylon" and the Structure of Modernity', *Modern Fiction Studies*, III (1957–8), 291–308; Olga Vickery, *The Novels of William Faulkner* (Baton Rouge, La, 1964), p. 152; Duvall, *Faulkner's Marginal Couple*, pp. 81–98. All these readings are more or less based on the – in my view, mistaken – assumption that Faulkner is in control of his material.

30 *Pylon*, p. 14. See also pp. 28, 39, 64, 168.

31 Ibid., p. 172. See also p. 15.

32 Ibid., p. 162.

33 Ibid., p. 230. See also p. 229. It is perhaps superfluous to point out that much of what purports to be fact in the second document is pure distortion and misinformation: which adds a further ironic twist to these final attempts to write the life of the pilot.

34 Manuscript titled 'Dark House', Rowan Oak Papers, Special Collections Department, University of Mississippi Library, Oxford. See also *Faulkner in the University*, p. 36; *Selected Letters*, p. 84. For an account of the writing of *Absalom, Absalom!*, see Elizabeth Muhlenfeld, 'Introduction' to *William Faulkner's 'Absalom,*

Absalom!': A *Critical Casebook* (New York, 1984); Noel Polk, 'Introduction' to vol. XIII of *William Faulkner Manuscripts.* See also *Absalom, Absalom!: The Corrected Text* (New York, 1987).

35 Meta Carpenter Wilde and Orin Borsten, *A Loving Gentleman: The Love Story of Meta Carpenter and William Faulkner* (New York, 1976), p. 62. See also Blotner, *Faulkner* (one-volume edition), pp. 347, 356, 364; *Absalom, Absalom!*, p. 127; Fredric Jameson, *The Political Unconscious: Narrative as a Socially Symbolic Act* (Ithaca, N.Y., 1981), p. 102.

36 *Absalom, Absalom!*, p. 261. The critical material available on *Absalom, Absalom!* is now vast. Among the more recent critiques that I have found particularly interesting and provocative are: John T. Irwin, *Doubling and Incest/Repetition and Revenge: A Speculative Reading of Faulkner* (Baltimore, Md, 1978), and the relevant chapters in Eric J. Sundquist, *Faulkner: The House Divided* (Baltimore, Md, 1983); John T. Matthews, *The Play of Faulkner's Language* (Ithaca, N.Y., 1982); Peter Brooks, *Reading for the Plot* (New York, 1984); Snead, *Figures of Division*; Bleikasten, *Ink of Melancholy*; Duvall, *Faulkner's Marginal Couple*; Richard C. Moreland, *Faulkner and Modernism: Rereading and Rewriting* (Madison, Wis., 1990).

37 *Absalom, Absalom!*, p. 247. See also pp. 30, 45, 49, 79, 254, 303.

38 Cited in Tony Tanner, *City of Words: American Fiction 1950–1970* (London, 1971), p. 34.

39 R.G. Collingwood, *The Idea of History* (1946; New York, 1962 edition) p. 243. See also *Absalom, Absalom!*, p. 303.

40 Collingwood, *Idea of History*, p. 215. See also p. 242; *Absalom, Absalom!*, pp. 100–1.

41 *Absalom, Absalom!*, p. 303. See also Collingwood, *Idea of History*, p. 242; Estella Schoenberg, *Old Tales and Talking: Quentin Compson in William Faulkner's 'Absalom, Absalom!' and Related Works* (Jackson, Miss., 1975), p. 135.

42 Jameson, *Political Unconscious*, p. 35. See also pp. 19–20, 102.

43 Hayden White, 'Getting Out of History', in *Tropics of Discourse: Essays in Cultural Criticism* (Baltimore, Md, 1978), p. 6. On the question of the possible relationship between demystification of the past and the breakdown of narrativity in Faulkner's work see, André Bleikasten, 'For/Against an Ideological Reading', in *Faulkner and Idealism: Perspectives from Paris*, ed. Michel Gresset and Patrick Samway (Jackson, Miss., 1983), p. 47.

44 *Absalom, Absalom!*, p. 263. See also pp. 57, 221, 244, 246, 261.

45 Ibid., p. 61. See also pp. 8, 12, 31, 67, 114, 214, 250.

46 Ibid., pp. 357–8. See also p. 174.

47 Ibid., p. 162. See also pp. 15, 20, 43, 60, 117; Mikhail Bakhtin, *The Dialogic Imagination*, ed. and trans. Caryl Emerson and Michael Holmquist (Austin, Texas, 1981), p. 366.

48 Nathaniel Beverley Tucker, *The Partisan Leader: A Tale of the Future* (1836; Richmond, Va, 1862 edition), p. 69. See also *Absalom, Absalom!*, pp. 9, 21, 23, 162, 171. On Northern attitudes towards the South, and Northern rhetoric relating to the South, see Lorenzo Dow Turner, *Anti-slavery Sentiment in American Literature Prior to 1865* (Washington, D.C., 1929) (see, especially, pp. 71, 196): Howard R. Floan, *The South in Northern Eyes, 1831–1861* (New York, 1958) (see, especially, pp. 24–5, 40, 57). On the 'male'/'female' equation in the South/North debate, see Richard Gray, *Writing the South: Ideas of an American Region* (Cambridge, 1986), pp. 60–1; Ann Firor Scott, *The Southern*

Lady: From Pedestal to Politics (Chicago, 1970). That Faulkner knew more than most about the Old South and the Civil War, and conflicting ways of interpreting them, is indicated (among other ways) by his reading: of the 1200 volumes in his library, over a hundred were devoted to these topics. See *William Faulkner's Library: A Catalogue*, ed. Joseph Blotner (Charlottesville, Va, 1964).

49 *Absalom, Absalom!*, p. 20. See also pp. 21, 23, 27, 136, 138, 139, 142, 149, 172. For a different reading of Rosa Coldfield's act of narration, see Wesley Morris and Barbara Alverson Morris, *Reading Faulkner* (Madison, Wis., 1989), pp. 176ff.

50 *Absalom, Absalom!*, pp. 72–3. See also p. 102.

51 Ibid., p. 108. See also pp. 46, 53, 69, 95, 96, 193.

52 Ibid., p. 101. See also Wilbur J. Cash, *The Mind of the South* (New York, 1941), pp. 88–9. On questions of paternity in *Absalom, Absalom!* see, e.g., Irwin, *Doubling and Incest*; Brooks, *Reading for Plot*; Duvall, *Faulkner's Marginal Couple*. Many people have commented on the fact that *Absalom, Absalom!* and Margaret Mitchell's *Gone With the Wind* were published in the same year. For an interesting comparison of the two novels, see Louis D. Rubin, 'Scarlett O'Hara and the Two Quentin Compsons', in *A Gallery of Southerners* (Baton Rouge, La, 1982), pp. 26–48.

53 *Absalom, Absalom!*, pp. 212–13. See also p. 207. On the errors of identity and difference in historical knowledge, as defined by Fredric Jameson, see ch. 1 of this book.

54 Ibid., p. 378. See also pp. 177, 217, 310.

55 Ibid., p. 351. See also pp. 96, 207, 305, 331, 345. Also Irwin, *Doubling and Incest*, for a more detailed discussion of the relationship between Quentin Compson on the one hand and, on the other, Henry Sutpen and Charles Bon.

56 *Absalom, Absalom!*, p. 342. See also p. 317.

57 Ibid., p. 366. On the link between the fear of incest and the fear of miscegenation, see ch. 1 of this book. On the contradictions latent, on this point, in the belief systems of the Old South, see in particular note 62 to ch. 1. In (instinctively) accepting the distinction between incestuous and inter-racial sex, Quentin is responding to the very personal pressures outlined here. And perhaps he is also recalling his father's characterization of the traditional Southern division of females into 'ladies or whores or slaves' (*Absalom, Absalom!*, p. 114): a division that, interestingly enough, Mr Compson attributes to Quentin's dark twin, Henry Sutpen.

58 Ibid., p. 373. See also pp. 100, 370.

59 Ibid, p. 373. See also p. 366. Also Bakhtin, *Dialogic Imagination*: 'the chronotope of threshold ... its most fundamental instance is as the chronotope of *crisis* and *break* in a life' (p. 248). It is perhaps worth pointing out that virtually nobody in *Absalom, Absalom!* crosses the threshold as and when they want to. Even Quentin, as the passages quoted here indicate, has to break in by an alternative entrance. The phrase 'Nevermore Nevermore Nevermore' of course echoes the refrain in Edgar Allan Poe's poem, 'The Raven' ('Quoth the Raven "Nevermore" '): which Poe saw as vital to creating a melancholy atmosphere (see his essay, 'The Philosophy of Composition'). Such was (and perhaps still is) the impact of Poe on Southern writers of this century that one of them, Allen Tate, referred to him as 'our cousin, Mr. Poe'; and the author of 'The Fall of the House of Usher' seems to hover, in a particularly haunting way, behind many of the pages of *Absalom, Absalom!*

60 *Absalom, Absalom!*, p. 139.
61 Ibid., p. 373. For readings of this passage that are different (in turn) from each other and from this one, see Matthews, *Play of Faulkner's Language*, p. 161; Morris and Morris, *Reading Faulkner*, pp. 195–6.
62 Blotner, *Faulkner*, p. 951; on Faulkner's alterations and additions to the stories, see pp. 958ff.
63 *Selected Letters*, p. 84. For positive assessments of *The Unvanquished* see, e.g., Edmond L. Volpe, *A Reader's Guide to William Faulkner* (London, 1964), p. 86; Wittenberg, *Faulkner*, pp. 159–60.
64 *Unvanquished*, p. 16. See also pp. 7, 14, 22, 23.
65 Ibid., p. 28. A good example of the sacrificial woman character who nevertheless remains a 'lady' is Cynthia Blake in the Ellen Glasgow novel, *The Deliverance* (London, 1904). She is described as 'the stuff of martyrs' – a woman whose 'high resolve', we are told, did not diminish her 'outward grace' (p. 97).
66 *Unvanquished*, p. 11. See also p. 13. Also Wittenberg, *Faulkner*, pp. 158–9, for the demythologizing argument.
67 *Unvanquished*, p. 20. See also p. 16. For an example of the faithful black retainer character who, like Joby, follows his 'master' to war, see Thomas Nelson Page, 'Marse Chan: a Tale of Old Virginia', in *In Ole Virginia; or, Marse Chan and Other Stories* (London, 1889). The point is, of course, not that actual, historical prototypes for such characters did not exist, but that the fictional presentations of them excluded any serious discussion of *why* they accompanied their 'masters' to war.
68 *Unvanquished*, p. 107. See also pp. 64, 77, 81. I am indebted, here and elsewhere in this discussion of the representation of women in the book, to Diane Roberts, 'A Precarious Pedestal: the Confederate Woman in Faulkner's *Unvanquished*', *Journal of American Studies*, XXVI (1992), 233–46.
69 *Unvanquished*, p. 132.
70 For an example of the Confederate lady as tomboy, see the portrait of a character called Betty Ambler in Ellen Glasgow, *The Battle-ground* (London, 1902). Francis Pendleton Gaines discusses the stereotypical nature of this character in *The Southern Plantation: A Study in the Development and Accuracy of a Tradition* (New York, 1924).
71 *Unvanquished*, p. 72. See also Jean E. Howard, 'Crossdressing: the Theatre and Gender Struggle in Early Modern England', *Shakespeare Quarterly* (Sept. 1988), 422.
72 *Unvanquished*, p. 156. See also pp. 133, 144, 145.
73 Ibid., p. 163. See also pp. 164, 165.
74 Ibid., p. 159. See also pp. 148, 149.
75 Ibid., p. 172. See also p. 165.
76 Drusilla, we have been told earlier, was in the habit of gathering sprigs of verbena to wear in her hair, 'because she said verbena was the only scent you could smell above the smell of horses and courage, and so it was the only one worth the wearing' (ibid., p. 152). At the time of offering Bayard the duelling pistols, she 'removed the two verbena sprigs from her hair', Bayard tells us, giving one to him to put in his lapel – and casting the other aside, declaring, 'I abjure verbena forever more; I have smelled it above the odour of courage; that was all I wanted' (pp. 163–4). There are two ways of reading this last act of Drusilla's, in which she leaves Bayard her emblem of what it means to be brave – just what the odour of courage and honour is. One way of reading it

is to say, as here, that Faulkner is asking us to believe that Drusilla recognizes the consensus even while she cannot participate in it. The other is to say that Faulkner is so intent on underlining the act of closure at the end of this story that he has Drusilla do two contradictory things: leave, and so confirm her aberrant status, but leave a token that suggests she is somehow a part of the consensus – to the extent, that is, of subscribing to what is now both Bayard's and the community's definition of courage. Either way, closure is secured and Drusilla remains torn, conflicted and outside.

Notes to Chapter 5: Public Faces and Private Places

1 *Selected Letters of William Faulkner*, ed. Joseph Blotner (New York, 1977), p. 106. See also p. 105; Meta Carpenter Wilde and Orin Borsten, *A Loving Gentleman: The Love Story of William Faulkner and Meta Carpenter* (New York, 1976), pp. 62, 78.

2 Carpenter Wilde, *Loving Gentleman*, p. 173. See also pp. 67, 140; Ben Wasson, *Count No 'Count: Flashbacks to Faulkner* (Jackson, Miss., 1983), pp. 144, 149.

3 Carpenter Wilde, *Loving Gentleman*, p. 230. See also pp. 191, 195.

4 *Selected Letters*, p. 338. On the autobiographical aspects of the book, and in particular its relationship to the women in Faulkner's life, see, e.g., Joseph Blotner, *Faulkner: A Biography*, 2 vols (New York, 1974), pp. 981–2; Thomas L. McHaney, *William Faulkner's 'The Wild Palms'* (Jackson, Miss., 1975), pp. 54ff, and 'Introduction' to vol. XIV of *William Faulkner Manuscripts*, ed. Joseph Blotner *et al.* (New York, 1987); Carvel Collins, 'Introduction' to *Helen: A Courtship* (New Orleans, La, and Oxford, Miss., 1981), pp. 86–98; Frederick R. Karl, *William Faulkner: American Writer* (London, 1989), pp. 599–600.

5 *Lion in the Garden: Interviews with William Faulkner 1926–1962*, ed. James B. Meriwether and Michael Millgate (New York, 1968), p. 54. See also Carpenter Wilde, *Loving Gentleman*, p. 91.

6 *Lion in the Garden*, pp. 247. 248. See also *Faulkner in the University: Class Conferences at the University of Virginia 1957–1959*, ed. Frederick Gwynn and Joseph Blotner (Charlottesville, Va, 1959), pp. 171, 176.

7 *The Wild Palms* (1939; London, 1961 edition), p. 19. See also pp. 5, 8, 17; Walter Benjamin, 'The Author as Producer', in *The Essential Frankfurt School Reader*, ed. A. Arato and E. Gebhardt (New York, 1978), p. 265. The most extensive account of the connections between the two stories is in McHaney, *Faulkner's 'The Wild Palms'*. Other discussions of these connections are to be found in, e.g., Blotner, *Faulkner*, p. 983; Cleanth Brooks, *William Faulkner: Toward Yoknapatawpha and Beyond* (New Haven, Conn., 1978), pp. 220–1; Judith B. Wittenberg, *William Faulkner: The Transfiguration of Biography* (Lincoln, Neb., 1979), pp. 174–6; David Minter, *William Faulkner: His Life and Work* (Baltimore, Md, 1980), pp. 171–2; Pamela Rhodes and Richard Godden, '*The Wild Palms*: Faulkner's Hollywood Novel', *Essays in Poetics*, x (1985), 24; John Duvall, *Faulkner's Marginal Couple: Invisible, Outlaw, and Unspeakable Communities* (Austin, Texas, 1990), pp. 42–3; Gary Harrington, *Faulkner's Fables of Creativity: The Non-Yoknapatawpha Novels* (London, 1990), pp. 67–8. On the possible impact of Hollywood on this novel see, e.g., Tom Dardis, *Some Time in the Sun* (New York, 1976), pp. 101, 103; Bruce F. Kawin, *Faulkner and Film* (New York, 1978), and

'The Montage Element in Faulkner's Film' and 'Faulkner's Film Career: the Years with Hawks', in *Faulkner, Modernism and Film*, ed. Evans Harrington and Ann Abadie (Jackson, Miss., 1978), pp. 103–26, 163–81.

8   *Wild Palms*, p. 88. The most extensive account of intertextuality in the novel is (again) in McHaney, *Faulkner's 'The Wild Palms'*. See, e.g., the discussion of the allusions to Hemingway, pp. 13–7; and cf. Brooks, *Faulkner: Toward Yoknapatawpha and Beyond*, pp. 407–8.

9   *Wild Palms*, p. 39. See also McHaney, *Faulkner's 'The Wild Palms'*, p. 55; Brooks, *Faulkner: Toward Yoknapatawpha and Beyond*, p. 212.

10 *Wild Palms*, p. 238. See also p. 19.

11 Ibid., p. 37.

12 Ibid., p. 145. It should be superfluous to add that this is, in no sense, to lay the blame for what occurs on Charlotte. The moralistic attitude adopted by several critics is surely totally inappropriate here. For examples of this attitude, see Michael Millgate, *The Achievement of William Faulkner* (London, 1966), p. 172; Sally R. Page, *Faulkner's Women: Characterization and Meaning* (Deland, Fla, 1972), p. 134; Lewis A. Richards, 'Sex under *The Wild Palms* and a Moral Question', *Arizona Quarterly*, XXVIII (1972), 329, 332. The book is concerned with forms of cultural entrapment shared by all the major characters; although this is, as we shall see, complicated by the author's implicit response to his women characters, which is not so much a matter of moral attitudes as of fundamental (and unacknowledged) narrative positioning.

13 *Wild Palms*, p. 148. See also pp. 31, 106, 145, 147; *Selected Letters*, p. 96; Fredric Jameson, *Marxism and Form* (Princeton, N.J., 1971), p. 96.

14 *Wild Palms*, p. 95. See also Brooks, *Faulkner: Toward Yoknapatawpha and Beyond*, p. 220.

15 On the male positioning of women, see the earlier chapters of this study and the works by Hélène Cixous, Luce Irigiray, and Julia Kristeva already cited. See, in particular, Cixous and Cathérine Clément, *La jeune née* (Paris, 1975). Also Luce Irigiray, *Spéculum de l'autre femme* (Paris, 1974).

16 *Wild Palms*, p. 114. See also pp. 5, 27, 28, 41, 96, 214.

17 Ibid., p. 60. See also pp. 34, 61, 64, 130.

18 Ibid., p. 100.

19 Ibid. See also pp. 81, 97, 210, 239.

20 Ibid., p. 227. See also p. 228. While McHaney sees the ending of 'Wild Palms' in far more affirmative terms, he draws attention to the masturbatory references here: see *Faulkner's 'The Wild Palms'*, pp. 172–4.

21 *Selected Letters*, pp. 107–8. See also pp. 114, 197. On the preparation and writing of *The Hamlet*, see Blotner. *Faulkner*, pp. 1006–34; Thomas L. McHaney, 'Introduction' to vol. XV of *William Faulkner Manuscripts*.

22 *Hamlet*, p. 79. For examples of traditionalist readings of this novel, see Warren Beck, *Man in Motion* (Madison, Wis., 1961); Cleanth Brooks, *William Faulkner: The Yoknapatawpha Country* (New Haven, Conn., 1963). Among the more challenging of the recent discussions are those to be found in Wesley Morris and Barbara Alverson Morris, *Reading Faulkner* (Madison, Wis., 1989); Richard C. Moreland, *Faulkner and Modernism: Rereading and Rewriting* (Madison, Wis., 1990).

23 Mary Douglas, 'Couvade and Menstruation', in *Implicit Meanings* (London, 1975), pp. 60–1. See also *Hamlet*, p. 95.

24 *Selected Letters*, p. 115. See also *Hamlet*, pp. 3–5. Note also Bakhtin's comments on what he calls 'the ideological environment'. 'The ideological environment',

he says, 'is constantly in the process of generation. Contradictions are always present, constantly being overcome and reborn. But for each given collective in each given epoch of its historical development this environment is a unique and concrete whole . . .' (Mikhail Bakhtin, *The Formal Method in Literary Scholarship*, trans. Albert J. Wehrle (Baltimore, Md, 1978), p. 14).

25 *Hamlet*, p. 57. See also p. 58.

26 Ibid., p. 110. See also pp. 106, 322.

27 Ibid., p. 68.

28 Ibid., p. 95. See also p. 121.

29 Ibid., p. 100. See also pp. 95, 114, 147.

30 Ibid., p. 83. See also pp. 113, 118, 149, 192, 259.

31 Ibid., p. 119. See also p. 118.

32 Ibid., p. 140.

33 Ibid., p. 186. See also pp. 165, 166. For 'Afternoon of a Cow', see *Uncollected Stories of William Faulkner*, ed. Joseph Blotner (London, 1980), pp. 424–34; Blotner, *Faulkner*, pp. 961–3.

34 *Hamlet*, p. 190. See also p. 165.

35 Ibid., p. 99. See also pp. 175, 181.

36 On the forms of writing referred to here see, William Stott, *Documentary Expression in Thirties America* (New York, 1973; rev. edn, Chicago, 1986); Sylvia Jenkins Cook, *From Tobacco Road to Route 66: The Southern Poor White in Fiction* (Chapel Hill, N.C., 1976).

37 *Hamlet*, pp. 191–2. See also pp. 216–7, 231.

38 Ibid., p. 214. See also pp. 206, 208, 211, 213, 238.

39 Ibid., p. 205. See also p. 214.

40 Ibid., pp. 331–2.

41 Ibid., p. 305.

42 On this issue of continuity and difference in the relationship between past and present (or, in this case, between present and future), see the discussion of 'Red Leaves' in the first chapter, and the discussion of *Absalom, Absalom!* in the fourth chapter, of this study.

43 *Hamlet*, p. 57. See, e.g., the adverse comments of Tony Hilfer on the final episode in what is otherwise an illuminating reading of this novel, in *American Fiction Since 1940* (London, 1992), p. 64.

44 *Hamlet*, p. 365. See also p. 366.

45 *Selected Letters*, p. 122. See also p. 121.

46 Ibid., pp. 148, 153, 155. See also pp. 125, 139.

47 Ibid., p. 146. On the preparation and writing of *Go Down, Moses*, see James Early, *The Making of 'Go Down, Moses'* (Dallas, Texas, 1972); Blotner, *Faulkner*, pp. 1072–3, 1075–94; Thomas L. McHaney, 'Introduction' to vol. xvi of *William Faulkner Manuscripts*.

48 *Lion in the Garden*, p. 52; *Faulkner in the University*, p. 4. See also *Selected Letters*, pp. 124, 126, 135, 139, 284.

49 *Selected Letters*, p. 152. See also pp. 136, 148, 157; R.B. Nye and J.E. Morpurgo, *A History of the United States* (London, 1964), p. 676.

50 *Go Down, Moses*, pp. 262–3. See also pp. 226. 255.

51 See Lawrence H. Schwartz, *Creating Faulkner's Reputation: The Politics of Modern Literary Criticism* (Knoxville, Tenn., 1989). Schwartz has some powerful points to make about the making of Faulkner's literary reputation, and he marshals some impressive documentation. However, in this reader's opinion, his general critical model is too implicitly conspiratorial, and carries along with it some

fairly questionable assumptions about ideology as false consciousness and the reading public as passive consumers. Useful exemplifications of the direction of thought in the fifties include: Theodor Adorno, *The Authoritarian Personality* (1950); David Riesman, *The Lonely Crowd* (1950); Hannah Arendt, *The Origins of Totalitarianism* (1951); William Whyte, *The Organization Man* (1956); Daniel Bell, *The End of Ideology* (1960). See also Douglas Tallack, *Twentieth-century America: The Intellectual and Cultural Context* (London, 1991), ch. 6.

52 *Go Down, Moses*, p. 15. For a provocative reading of 'Was', see Morris and Morris, *Reading Faulkner*, pp. 123–4.

53 *Go Down, Moses*, p. 52. See also p. 81. For particularly useful readings of 'The Fire and the Hearth' and its relationship to the originating stories, see Michael Grimwood, *Heart in Conflict: Faulkner's Struggles with Vocation* (Athens, Ga, 1987); Philip M. Weinstein, *Faulkner's Subject: A Cosmos No One Owns* (Cambridge, 1992).

54 *Go Down, Moses*, p. 49. See also pp. 36, 98.

55 Ibid., p. 86. See also pp. 94, 96.

56 Ibid., p. 51. See also p. 50.

57 Ibid., p. 147. See also p. 169. The iconic status of 'The Bear' in traditionalist Faulkner criticism is such that no attempt could be made to summarize the extent of that criticism here. The classic traditionalist reading is R.W.B. Lewis, 'The Hero in the New World: William Faulkner's "The Bear" ', *Kenyon Review*, XIII (Autumn 1951), 641–60. For a provocative recent reading, see Michael J. Toolan, *The Stylistics of Fiction: A Literary-Linguistic Approach* (London, 1990), esp. pp. 168–76.

58 See, e.g., R.W.B. Lewis, *The American Adam: Innocence, Tragedy, and Tradition in the Nineteenth Century* (Chicago, 1955).

59 *Lion in the Garden*, p. 225; *Faulkner in the University*, pp. 54, 245.

60 *Go Down, Moses*, p. 240. See also p. 239.

61 Ibid., p. 221. See also p. 222. For a powerful and often persuasive reading of Faulkner's rewriting of history in terms of family, see the chapter on *Go Down, Moses* in Grimwood, *Heart in Conflict*.

62 Ibid, p. 187. See the descriptions of Old Ben (p. 160), Sam Fathers (p. 163), and Lion (p. 181), and compare the description of Lucas Beauchamp in 'The Fire and the Hearth' (p. 86). Whatever the empirical details of their different backgrounds, all four are described as if they existed in a state of absolute self-sufficiency, purity and power. On the male desire for transcendence, see Simone de Beauvoir, *The Second Sex*, trans. H.M. Parshley (New York, 1968). See, e.g., p. xxix, where de Beauvoir talks about woman being compelled to 'accept the status of the Other'. Stabilized 'as object', her immanence is doomed, de Beauvoir argues, 'since her transcendence is to be overshadowed and forever transcended by another ego', that of the male, 'which is essential and sovereign'.

63 Eugene Genovese, *Roll, Jordan, Roll: The World the Slaves Made* (1974; New York, 1976 edition), p. 6. See also, *Go Down, Moses*, pp. 281, 286.

64 *Go Down, Moses*, p. 108. For some particularly penetrating comments on the quality of attention given to Rider's physical presence, to which I am indebted, see Weinstein, *Faulkner's Subject*, pp. 57–9.

65 *Go Down, Moses*, p. 121.

66 *Selected Letters*, p. 248. See also Joseph Blotner, *Faulkner: A Biography* (one-volume edition, New York, 1984), pp. 444, 447, 456, 467; Carpenter Wilde, *Loving Gentleman*, pp. 284, 301.

67 *Faulkner at Nagano*, ed. Robert A. Jelliffe (Tokyo, 1956), p. 68. See also *Selected Letters*, pp. 187, 188, 191, 197, 237; *Lion in the Garden*, p. 54.

68 *Selected Letters*, p. 266. See also pp. 128, 262, 264, 265. On the preparation and writing of *Intruder in the Dust*, see Blotner, *Faulkner*, pp. 1244–54; Noel Polk, 'Introduction' to vol. xvii of *William Faulkner Manuscripts*. On the additional pages for the novel, see Patrick Samway, 'New Material for Faulkner's *Intruder in the Dust*', in *A Faulkner Miscellany*, ed. James B. Meriwether (Jackson, Miss., 1974), pp. 107–12.

69 *Selected Letters*, p. 256. See also p. 262.

70 *Intruder in the Dust*, p. 74. See also *Selected Letters*, p. 122.

71 *Intruder in the Dust*, p. 102. See also pp. 5, 64, 68.

72 Ibid., p. 190. See also pp. 172–3, 183. Faulkner was inconsistent in his spelling of the MacCallum/McCallum family name. In *Intruder in the Dust* (and, for that matter, in the short story, 'The Tall Men', *Collected Stories*, pp. 45–62), the name is spelled McCallum, as the passage quoted in this paragraph indicates. In *Flags in the Dust/Sartoris*, however, it is spelled MacCallum.

73 Ibid., pp. 207–8. For criticism of the argument here in general, and Faulkner's use of the term 'Sambo' in particular, see, e.g., Edmund Wilson, *Classics and Commercials* (New York, 1950), pp. 460–9; Lee Jenkins, *Faulkner and Black–White Relationships* (New York, 1981), pp. 272–4; Walter R. Taylor, *Faulkner's Search for a South* (Urbana, Ill., 1983), pp. 146–65. For more positive comments, and an interesting interpretation of the novel's verbal dynamics, see Morris and Morris, *Reading Faulkner*, pp. 222–38.

74 *Intruder in the Dust*, p. 14. See also pp. 20, 32, 63.

75 Ibid., p. 174. See also pp. 156, 205.

76 Ibid., p. 11. See also p. 195.

77 Ibid., p. 143.

78 Ibid., p. 228. See also p. 231.

79 Ibid., pp. 150–1. See also p. 149.

80 Ibid., p. 209.

81 Ibid., p. 146. See also pp. 17, 94.

82 Ibid., p. 238. Whatever the dramatic merits of this exchange, the 1949 film version of *Intruder in the Dust*, directed by Clarence Brown, ends, not with this, but with a brief conversation between Gavin Stevens and Charles Mallison that emphasizes the moral of the story.

Notes to Chapter 6: The Way Home

1 *Selected Letters of William Faulkner*, ed. Joseph Blotner (New York, 1977), p. 286. See also Joseph Blotner, *Faulkner: A Biography*, 2 vols (New York, 1974), p. 1277.

2 *Selected Letters*, p. 280. On the preparation of *Knight's Gambit*, see Thomas L. McHaney, 'Introduction' to vol. xviii of *William Faulkner Manuscripts*, ed. Joseph Blotner *et al.* (New York, 1987). On the gravitation towards public rhetoric that the character of Gavin Stevens encouraged, see, e.g., Hodding Carter, 'Faulkner and His Folk', *Princeton University Library Chronicle*, xviii (Spring 1957), 95–107; Dayton Kohler, 'William Faulkner and His Social Conscience', *College English*, xi (Dec. 1949), 119–27.

3   *Knight's Gambit*, p. 21. On the autobiographical opportunities offered by the character of Gavin Stevens, see, e.g., Blotner, *Faulkner*, pp. 1285–6; Judith B. Wittenberg, *William Faulkner: The Transfiguration of Biography* (Lincoln, Neb., 1979), pp. 229–30; David Minter, *William Faulkner: His Life and Work* (Baltimore, Md, 1980), pp. 214–15. Karl, rather cruelly but by no means inaccurately, calls Stevens 'the town bore' (Frederick R. Karl, *William Faulkner: American Writer* (London, 1989), p. 830).

4   *Knight's Gambit*, p. 40. See also p. 50. Also Minter, *Faulkner*, p. 215.

5   *Knight's Gambit*, p. 112. See also pp. 81, 85, 88, 95.

6   Ibid., p. 182.

7   Ibid., p. 123. On the dominant imagery in this story, see Karl, *Faulkner*, p. 784.

8   Blotner, *Faulkner*, p. 1338. See also *Essays, Speeches, and Public Letters*, ed. James B. Meriwether (New York, 1966), pp. 119–20.

9   *Selected Letters*, p. 298. See also p. 75; Joseph Blotner, *Faulkner: A Biography* (one-volume edition, New York, 1984), p. 511. On the preparation of *Requiem for a Nun*, see Noel Polk, 'Introduction' to vol. XIX of *William Faulkner Manuscripts* and 'Appendix' to *Faulkner's 'Requiem for a Nun': A Critical Study* (Bloomington, Ind., 1981).

10   *Selected Letters*, p. 300. See also p. 324.

11   Ibid., p. 317. See also pp. 304, 305, 315. For Joan Williams's own fictional account of her relationship with Faulkner, see *The Wintering* (New York, 1971).

12   *Requiem for a Nun*, pp. 230–1. See also *Faulkner in the University: Class Conferences at the University or Virginia 1957–1959*, ed. Frederick Gwynn and Joseph Blotner (Charlottesville, Va, 1959), p. 122; Polk, *Faulkner's 'Requiem for a Nun'*, p. 98. For a study of the narrative style that adopts a different approach, see Hugh Ruppersburg, 'The Narrative Structure of Faulkner's *Requiem for a Nun'*, *Mississippi Quarterly*, XXXI (Summer 1978), 387–406.

13   *Requiem for a Nun*, p. 181. See also pp. 109, 110.

14   Malcolm Cowley, 'In Which Mr. Faulkner Translates Past into Present', *New York Herald Tribune Book Review*, 30 September 1951, 1. See also Michael Millgate, ' "The Firmament of Man's History": Faulkner's Treatment of the Past', in *'Faulkner and History': Papers of the Quarterly's 1971 SMCLA Symposium*, Supplement to *Mississippi Quarterly*, XXV (Spring 1972), 31; William R. Brown, 'Faulkner's Paradox in Pathology and Salvation: *Sanctuary, Light in August, Requiem for a Nun'*, *Texas Studies in Literature and Language*, IX (Autumn 1967), 446; Robert R. Heilman, 'Schools for Girls', *Sewanee Review*, LX (Spring 1952), 306; Warren Beck, *Faulkner* (Madison, Wis., 1976), p. 625; Polk, *Faulkner's 'Requiem for a Nun'*, p. xiii. Also *Requiem for a Nun*, p. 85, for the remark, 'The past is never dead.'

15   *Requiem for a Nun*, p. 132. See also p. 151; Polk, *Faulkner's 'Requiem for a Nun'*, p. 125.

16   *Requiem for a Nun*, pp. 193, 195. On Faulkner's use of a guide to the state, see Thomas L. McHaney, 'Faulkner Borrows from the Mississippi Guide', *Mississippi Quarterly*, XIX (Summer 1966), 117.

17   *Faulkner in the University*, p. 61. See also Michael Millgate, *The Achievement of William Faulkner* (London, 1966), p. 225.

18   *Requiem for a Nun*, p. 197. See also p. 139.

19   Ibid., pp. 241–2. See also p. 184.

20   Ibid., pp. 198–9. See also p. 250.

21   *Faulkner in the University*, p. 196.

22   *Selected Letters*, p. 305. For more information on the dramatic versions of *Requiem for a Nun*, see Nancy Drew Taylor, 'The Dramatic Productions of *Requiem for a Nun*', *Mississippi Quarterly*, xx (Summer 1967), 123–34.

23   *Requiem for a Nun*, p. 229. See also pp. 42, 82, 86, 195, 198, 199.

24   Ibid., pp. 144–5.

25   Blotner, *Faulkner*, p. 1455. See also p. 1454.

26   *Selected Letters*, p. 339. See also p. 350; Blotner, *Faulkner* (one-volume edition), p. 570, and *Faulkner*, p. 1431.

27   *Selected Letters*, p. 179. See also p. 178. On the long genesis of *A Fable*, see Michael Millgate, 'Introduction' to vol. xx of *William Faulkner Manuscripts*. See also A. Keen Butterworth, *A Critical and Textual Study of Faulkner's 'A Fable'* (Ann Arbor, Mich., 1983).

28   *Selected Letters*, p. 344. See also pp. 188, 328, 352; *William Faulkner of Oxford*, ed. James W. Webb and A. Wigfall Green (Baton Rouge, La, 1965), p. 37; Blotner, *Faulkner* (one-volume edition), pp. 473, 588–9.

29   *A Fable* (New York, 1954), p. 128. See also *Selected Letters*, p. 361; Blotner, *Faulkner*, p. 1465, and *Faulkner* (one-volume edition), pp. 473, 588–9.

30   *Fable*, pp. 30, 51. See also pp. 38, 135, 185, 188. On the orphaned state of Gragnon and other characters, see Noel Polk, 'Woman and the Feminine in *A Fable*', in *Faulkner and Women*, ed. Doreen Fowler and Ann Abadie (Jackson, Miss., 1985).

31   *Fable*, p. 203. See also Minter, *Faulkner*, p. 206; Gary Harrington, *Faulkner's Fables of Creativity: The Non-Yoknapatawpha Novels* (London, 1990), p. 97; Wittenberg, *Faulkner*, p. 228. Brooks criticizes the book for its 'unsuccessful mingling of fabulous and realistic elements' (Cleanth Brooks, *William Faulkner: Toward Yoknapatawpha and Beyond* (New Haven, Conn., 1978), p. 230).

32   *Fable*, pp. 4–6. See also pp. 3, 7, 8. 9.

33   Ibid., p. 186.

34   Ibid. See also pp. 187, 188.

35   Klaus Theweleit, *Male Fantasies*, trans. Stephen Conway in collaboration with Erica Carter and Chris Turner, 2 vols (Cambridge, 1987), p. 230.

36   *Fable*, p. 308. See also Mikhail Bakhtin, *Rabelais and His World* trans. Helene Iswolsky (Cambridge, Mass., 1968), pp. 317–22.

37   *Fable*, pp. 320–1.

38   Ibid., p. 399. See also pp. 88, 118, 222, 273, 399, 406.

39   Ibid., p. 354. See also pp. 347–8.

40   Ibid., p. 350. See also pp. 345, 348–9.

41   *Selected Letters*, p. 352. See also *Fable*, p. 350.

42   *Selected Letters*, p. 348. See also p. 250. On the depressed state Faulkner was in during the final stages of preparing *A Fable* for publication, and the consequent imperfections of the final editing process, see Millgate, 'Introduction' to vol. xx of *William Faulkner Manuscripts*. Millgate also offers an excellent account of the perennial fascination that the subject-matter of *A Fable* held for Faulkner in 'Faulkner on the Literature of the First World War', *Mississippi Quarterly*, xxvi (1973), see esp. p. 392.

43   *Selected Letters*, p. 365. See also p. 251; Blotner, *Faulkner*, p. 1213. On the early reviews of *A Fable*, see Sylvan Schendler, 'William Faulkner's *A Fable*' (Northwestern University dissertation), pp. 1–39.

44   *Selected Letters*, p. 402. See also pp. 393, 399–400; Blotner, *Faulkner*, pp. 1586, 1587. On the preparation of *The Town*, see Michael Millgate, 'Introduction' to vol. xxi of *William Faulkner Manuscripts*.

45 Blotner, *Faulkner*, p. 1586. The 'young girl' Faulkner had with him on this occasion was Jean Stein. See also *Faulkner: A Comprehensive Guide to the Brodsky Collection*, ed. Louis D. Brodsky and Robert W. Hamblin (Jackson, Miss., 1982–5), p. 258.

46 *Selected Letters*, p. 390. See also pp. 382, 388; Blotner, *Faulkner*, pp. 1532, 1566, 1597. On Faulkner and race, see also ch. 1 of this study.

47 *Town*, p. 225. See also p. 302. Useful discussions of this novel include those to be found in Warren Beck, *Man in Motion* (Madison, Wis., 1961); Joseph J. Arpad, 'William Faulkner's Legendary Novels: the Snopes Trilogy', *Mississippi Quarterly*, xxii (Summer 1969), 214ff; Joseph W. Reed, *Faulkner's Narrative* (New Haven, Conn., 1973); Eileen Gregory, 'Faulkner's Typescript of *The Town*', *Mississippi Quarterly*, xxvi (Summer 1973), 361–87. On Ellen Glasgow and a regional tradition Faulkner is following in this novel, see, e.g., Anne Goodwyn Jones, *Tomorrow is Another Day: The Woman Writer in the South 1859–1936* (Baton Rouge, La, 1981), esp. pp. 225–70; Elizabeth Jane Harrison, *Female Pastoral: Women Writers Re-visioning the American South* (Knoxville, Tenn., 1992), esp. pp. 17–42.

48 *Town*, p. 192. See also pp. 17, 269. Karl sees Eula Varner Snopes as 'a tragic figure' (*Faulkner*, p. 961).

49 For a trenchant summary of some of the general critical objections to Eula's actions, see Edmond L. Volpe, *A Reader's Guide to William Faulkner* (London, 1964), p. 326.

50 *Town*, p. 6. A useful reminder of what the 'revolt from the village' entailed is to be found in Alfred Kazin, *On Native Grounds* (New York, 1942); Frederick J. Hoffman, *The Twenties: American Writing in the Postwar Decade* (New York, 1949).

51 *Town*, pp. 41–2. See also p. 308.

52 Ibid., p. 85. See also pp. 7, 119.

53 Ibid., p. 285. See also pp. 121, 245.

54 Ibid., p. 164. See also pp. 158, 183.

55 Ibid., p. 288. See also p. 189; Edwin Arlington Robinson, 'Miniver Cheevy', lines 9–12.

56 F.R. Leavis made the comment in a review of *Light in August*. For this and other contemporary reviews, see *William Faulkner: The Critical Heritage*, ed. John Bassett (London, 1975).

57 *Town*, p. 135.

58 Ibid., p. 272.

59 Ibid., p. 224.

60 *Faulkner in the University*, p. 107. See also *Selected Letters*, p. 433.

61 *Mansion*, p. 105. An account of Faulkner's approach to the inconsistencies in the Snopes trilogy, as well as of the preparation of *The Mansion*, is to be found in Michael Millgate, 'Introduction' to vol. xxii of *William Faulkner Manuscripts*.

62 *Faulkner in the University*, p. 67. See also Blotner, *Faulkner* (one-volume edition), p. 671 and *Faulkner*, pp. 1646, 1688, 1708–9; *Faulkner: A Guide to the Brodsky Collection*, ed. Brodsky and Hamblin, p. 264; *Selected Letters*, p. 415.

63 *Mansion*, p. 240. Karl calls *The Mansion* 'a deeply personal book' (*Faulkner*, p. 1001); Minter talks about the damage wrought on it 'by long deferral and mounting weariness' (*Faulkner*, p. 243); while Wittenberg draws attention to the parallels between Stevens and Faulkner here (*Faulkner*, p. 233). For accounts of the novel that see it in more energetic and dramatic terms, see Beck, *Man in Motion*; Volpe, *Reader's Guide to Faulkner*; Cleanth Brooks, *William Faulkner: The Yoknapatawpha Country* (New Haven, Conn., 1963).

64   *Mansion*, p. 393. See also pp. 192, 387, 397, 399.
65   Ibid., p. 399. See also pp. 246, 269, 398.
66   Ibid., p. 225. See also pp. 119, 192, 216, 222.
67   Ibid., p. 274. See also pp. 277, 282, 288.
68   Ibid., p. 295. See also pp. 283, 294.
69   Ibid., p. 254. See also pp. 83, 87, 393.
70   Ibid., p. 73. See also pp. 146, 150, 305, 307.
71   Ibid., p. 394. See also pp. 344, 381, 385.
72   Ibid., p. 45. See also pp. 44, 264.
73   Ibid., p. 54. See also p. 26.
74   Ibid., p. 92. See also pp. 34, 374, 380.
75   'I don't like a man that takes the short way home' was Faulkner's comment
     on Hemingway's suicide. See Blotner, *Faulkner* (one-volume edition), p. 690.

Notes to Postscript: Back to Earth

1   *Selected Letters of William Faulkner* ed. Joseph Blotner (New York, 1977), p. 452.
    See also p. 45; *The Reivers: A Reminiscence* (1962; London, 1970 edition), p. 80.
2   *Selected Letters*, p. 452. See also p. 458; Joseph Blotner, *Faulkner: A Biography*,
    2 vols (New York, 1974), pp. 1765, 1821.
3   *Selected Letters*, pp. 123–4. See also *Faulkner at West Point*, ed. Joseph L. Fant
    and Robert Ashley (New York, 1964), p. 66.
4   Blotner, *Faulkner*, p. 3. See also *Selected Letters*, p. 456. On the preparation of
    The Reivers, see Michael Millgate, 'Introduction' to vol. XXIII of *William Faulkner
    Manuscripts*, ed. Joseph Blotner *et al.* (New York, 1987).
5   *Reivers*, p. 252. See also p. 64; Judith B. Wittenberg, *William Faulkner: The
    Transfiguration of Biography* (Lincoln, Neb., 1979), p. 241. Volpe's tentative
    prophecy that 'though a minor work, *The Reivers* may be of importance in
    future studies of Faulkner' has yet to be fulfilled, even though it was made
    thirty years ago (Edmond L. Volpe, *A Reader's Guide to William Faulkner* (London,
    1964), p. 349). The most useful studies of Faulkner's last novel remain those
    offered in such early accounts of the writer as Cleanth Brooks, *William Faulkner:
    The Yoknapatawpha Country* (New Haven, Conn., 1963); Olga Vickery, *The Novels
    of William Faulkner* (Baton Rouge, La, 1964); Michael Millgate, *The Achievement
    of William Faulkner* (London, 1966).
6   *Reivers*, p. 251.
7   Ibid., p. 7. See also pp. 33–4.
8   Ibid., p. 122. See also pp. 34, 99. 'The nostalgia implies his [Faulkner's] desire
    to return not only to a pastoral idyll, but to a racial idyll when house servants
    and field workers were stratified in the community' (Frederick R. Karl, *William
    Faulkner: American Writer* (London, 1989), p. 1035).
9   *Reivers*, p. 221. See also pp. 61, 141, 153, 183, 218.
10 Ibid., p. 243.
11 Ibid., p. 164. See also pp. 94, 96; *Faulkner in the University: Class Conferences at
    the University of Virginia 1957–1959*, ed. Frederick Gwynn and Joseph Blotner
    (Charlottesville, Va, 1959), p. 45. Faulkner's remark has been used to support
    the argument that his women characters are as fully and richly developed as
    his men: see Cleanth Brooks, 'Introduction' to Sally R. Page, *Faulkner's Women:*

Characterization and Meaning (Deland, Fla, 1972), pp. xi–xii. Whatever the truth or otherwise of this highly arguable general proposition, this particular remark hardly helps to support it. After all, as Weinstein points out, 'What male author would speak of men as "marvellous . . . wonderful . . . I know very little about them"?' (Philip M. Weinstein, *Faulkner's Subject: A Cosmos No One Owns* (Cambridge, 1992), p. 12).

12 *Reivers*, p. 234. See also pp. 133, 135, 148, 254.
13 Ibid., p. 58.
14 Ibid., p. 80. See also pp. 27, 125.
15 Ibid, p. 27. See also pp. 19, 75.
16 Ibid., pp. 131–2. See also pp. 45, 59, 79, 80, 92, 191.
17 Ibid., p. 147. See also pp. 131, 236, 237.
18 Ibid., p. 254. Ned has his own self-interested motives for saying this: but his remark underlines all the references to education and initiation in the novel. See also pp. 232, 239.
19 *Essays, Speeches, and Public Letters*, ed. James B. Meriwether (New York, 1966), p. 114. See also *Faulkner at West Point*, p. 5; *The Faulkner–Cowley File: Letters and Memories, 1944–1962*, ed. Malcolm Cowley (New York, 1966), p. 149; Blotner, *Faulkner*, p. 1810.
20 The reference here is to Cecilia Farmer and the episode of the scratched windowpane. E.O. Hawkins Jr in 'Jane Cook and Cecilia Farmer', *Mississippi Quarterly*, xviii (1965), 248–51, argues that the episode is based on an actual event in the history of Faulkner's homeplace. Faulkner uses the episode in *The Unvanquished* and *Intruder in the Dust*: but, as indicated in chapter 6 of this study, it is in *Requiem for a Nun* that it is given its fullest treatment and explanation.

Bibliography

The Bibliography is divided into the following sections:
I   Books by William Faulkner Published During his Lifetime
II   Books by William Faulkner Published Posthumously
III   Other Published Writings and Significant Editions
IV   Bibliographical Guides to the Works of William Faulkner
V   Memoirs Written by Relatives, Friends or Acquaintances of William Faulkner
VI   William Faulkner: Manuscript Collections
VII   Other Works Cited

I Books by William Faulkner Published During his Lifetime

The Marble Faun (Boston, 1924) (reissued with *A Green Bough*, New York, 1965).
Soldier's Pay (New York, 1926).
Mosquitoes (New York, 1927).
Sartoris (New York, 1929).
The Sound and the Fury (New York, 1929).
As I Lay Dying (New York, 1930).
Sanctuary (New York, 1931).
Idyll in the Desert (New York, 1931).
These 13 (New York, 1931).
Miss Zilphia Gant (Dallas, Texas, 1932).
Light in August (New York, 1932).
A Green Bough (New York, 1933).
Doctor Martino and Other Stories (New York, 1934).
Pylon (New York, 1935).
Absalom, Absalom! (New York, 1936).
The Unvanquished (New York, 1938).
The Wild Palms (New York, 1939).
The Hamlet (New York, 1940).
Go Down, Moses (New York, 1942).
Intruder in the Dust (New York, 1948).

Knight's Gambit (New York, 1949).
Collected Stories (New York, 1950).
Notes on a Horsethief (Greenville, Miss., 1950).
Requiem for a Nun (New York, 1951).
A Fable (New York, 1954).
The Faulkner Reader (New York, 1954).
Big Woods (New York, 1955).
The Town (New York, 1957).
The Mansion (New York, 1959).
The Reivers (New York, 1962).

II BOOKS BY WILLIAM FAULKNER PUBLISHED POSTHUMOUSLY

The Wishing Tree (1927; New York, 1966).
Flags in the Dust (1927–9; New York, 1973).
The Marionettes: A Play in One Act (1920; Charlottesville, Va, 1977).
Mayday (1926; South Bend, Ind., 1977).
Uncollected Stories of William Faulkner (New York, 1980).
Helen: A Courtship (1925–6) and *Mississippi Poems* (1924) (Oxford, Miss. and New Orleans, La, 1981).
Father Abraham (1926; New York, 1983).
Vision in Spring (1921; Austin, Tex., 1984).
Elmer (1925; New York, 1987).

III OTHER PUBLISHED WRITINGS AND SIGNIFICANT EDITIONS

Beck, Warren (ed.), 'Faulkner: a Preface and a Letter', *Yale Review,* LII (October 1962), 157–60.
Blotner, Joseph (ed.), *Selected Letters of William Faulkner* (New York, 1977).
——, 'William Faulkner's Essay on the Composition of *Sartoris'*, *Yale University Library Gazette,* XL (January 1973), 123–4.
——, McHaney, Thomas L., Millgate, Michael and Polk, Noel (general eds) with Meriwether, James B. (senior consulting ed.), *William Faulkner Manuscripts,* 25 vols (New York, 1987).
Brodsky, Louis D. and Hamblin, Robert W. (eds), *Faulkner: A Comprehensive Guide to the Brodsky Collection* (Jackson, Miss.): vol. II: *The Letters* (1984); vol. III: *The de Gaulle Story* (1984); vol. IV: *The Battle Cry* (1985). (For vol. I, see 'Bibliographical Guides', below.)
Collins, Carvel (ed.), 'A Fourth Book Review by Faulkner', *Mississippi Quarterly,* XXVIII (Summer 1975), 399–402.
——, *William Faulkner: Early Prose and Poetry* (Boston, Mass., 1962).
——, *William Faulkner: New Orleans Sketches* (New York, 1968).
Cowley, Malcolm (ed.), *The Faulkner–Cowley File: Letters and Memories, 1944–1962* (New York, 1966).
Cox, Dianne L. (ed.), *Elmer, Mississippi Quarterly,* XXXVI (Summer 1983), 337–460.
Fant, Joseph L. and Ashley, Robert (eds), *Faulkner at West Point* (New York, 1964).

Gwynn, Frederick and Blotner, Joseph (eds), *Faulkner in the University: Class Conferences at the University of Virginia 1957–1959* (Charlottesville, Va, 1959).
Jelliffe, Robert A. (ed.), *Faulkner at Nagano* (Tokyo, 1956).
Kawin, Bruce F. (ed.), *Faulkner's M.G.M. Screenplays* (Knoxville, Tenn., 1982).
Meriwether, James B. (ed.), *A Faulkner Miscellany* (Jackson, Miss., 1974).
——, 'A Note on *A Fable*', *Mississippi Quarterly*, XXVI (Summer 1973), 416–20.
——, 'An Introduction to *The Sound and the Fury*', *Southern Review*, VII (Autumn 1972), 705–10.
——, 'An Introduction to *The Sound and the Fury*', *Mississippi Quarterly*, XXVI (Summer 1973), 410–15.
——, 'And Now What's To Do', *Mississippi Quarterly*, XXVI (Summer 1973), 399–402.
——, *Essays, Speeches and Public Letters* (New York, 1966).
——, 'Faulkner's Correspondence with the *Saturday Evening Post*', *Mississippi Quarterly*, XXX (Summer 1977), 461–75.
——, 'Faulkner's Correspondence with *Scribner's Magazine*', *Proof*, III (1973), 253–82.
——, 'Nympholepsy', *Mississippi Quarterly*, XXVI (Summer 1976), 403–9.
——, 'The Priest', *Mississippi Quarterly*, XXIX (Summer 1976), 445–50.
——, and Millgate, Michael (eds), *Lion in the Garden: Interviews with William Faulkner, 1926–1962* (New York, 1968).
Polk, Noel (ed.), *Absalom, Absalom!: The Corrected Text* (New York, 1986).
——, *As I Lay Dying: The Corrected Text* (New York, 1987).
——, *Faulkner: Novels 1930–1935 (As I Lay Dying, Sanctuary, Light in August, Pylon)* (New York, 1986).
——, *Sanctuary: The Corrected Text* (New York, 1987).
——, *Sanctuary: The Original Text* (New York, 1981).
——, *The Sound and the Fury: The Corrected Text* (New York, 1987).
Samway, Patrick (ed.), 'New Material for Faulkner's *Intruder in the Dust*', in *A Faulkner Miscellany*, ed. James B. Meriwether (Jackson, Miss., 1974), pp. 107–12.
Watson, James G. (ed.), *Thinking of Home: William Faulkner's Letters to his Mother and Father, 1918–1925* (New York, 1992).
Wells, Dean Faulkner and Lawrence (eds), 'Music – Sweeter than the Angels Sing', *Southern Review*, XII (Autumn 1976), 864–71.
Yellin, David G. and Connors, Marie (eds), *Tomorrow & Tomorrow & Tomorrow* (New York, 1985).

IV BIBLIOGRAPHICAL GUIDES TO THE WORKS OF WILLIAM FAULKNER

Blotner, Joseph, *William Faulkner's Library: A Catalogue* (Charlottesville, Va, 1964).
Brodsky, Louis D. and Hamblin, Robert W. (eds), *Faulkner: A Comprehensive Guide to the Brodsky Collection* (Jackson, Miss.): vol. I: *Bibliography* (1982). (For vols II–IV see 'Other Published Writings', above.)
Butterworth, Keen, 'A Census of Manuscripts and Typescripts of William Faulkner's Poetry', *Mississippi Quarterly*, XXVI (Summer 1973), 333–60.
Hayhoe, George F., 'Faulkner in Hollywood: a Checklist of his Film Scripts at the University of Virginia', *Mississippi Quarterly*, XXXI (Summer 1978), 407–19.
Massey, Linton R., *'Man Working', 1919–1962. William Faulkner: A Catalogue of the William Faulkner Collection at the University of Virginia* (Charlottesville, Va, 1968).

Meriwether, James B., *The Literary Career of William Faulkner: A Bibliographical Study* (Princeton, N.J., 1961).
——, 'The Short Fiction of William Faulkner: a Bibliography', *Proof*, I (1971), 293–329.
——, 'William Faulkner: a Checklist', *Princeton University Library Chronicle*, XVIII (Spring 1957), 136–58.
——, *William Faulkner: An Exhibit of Manuscripts* (Austin, Texas, 1959).
Peterson, Carl, *Each in its Ordered Place: A Faulkner Collector's Notebook* (New York, 1975).

V MEMOIRS WRITTEN BY RELATIVES, FRIENDS OR ACQUAINTANCES OF WILLIAM FAULKNER

Cantwell, Robert, 'The Faulkners: Recollections of a Gifted Family', *New World Writing*, II (November 1952), 300–15; reprinted in Frederick J. Hoffman and Olga Vickery (eds), *William Faulkner: Three Decades of Criticism* (New York, 1963), pp. 51–66.
Cochran, Louis, 'William Faulkner: a Personal Sketch', Memphis *Commercial Appeal*, 6 November 1932; reprinted in James B. Meriwether, 'Early Notices of Faulkner by Phil Stone and Louis Cochran', *Mississippi Quarterly*, XVII (Summer 1964), 136–64.
Cullen, John B. with Watkins, Floyd C., *Old Times in the Faulkner Country* (Chapel Hill, N.C., 1961).
Falkner, Murry C., *The Falkners of Mississippi: A Memoir* (Baton Rouge, La, 1967).
Faulkner, Jim, 'Auntee Owned Two', *Southern Review*, VIII (October 1972), 836–44.
Faulkner, John, *My Brother Bill: An Affectionate Reminiscence* (New York, 1963).
Franklin, Malcolm A., 'A Christmas in Columbus', *Mississippi Quarterly*, XXVII (Summer 1974), 319–22.
——, *Bitterweeds: Life with William Faulkner at Rowan Oak* (Irving, Texas, 1977).
Green, A. Wigfall, 'William Faulkner at Home', *Sewanee Review*, XL (Summer 1932), 294–306.
Stone, Phil, 'William Faulkner: the Man and his Work', *Oxford Magazine*, I (1934); reprinted in James B. Meriwether, 'Early Notices of Faulkner by Phil Stone and Louis Cochran', *Mississippi Quarterly*, XVII (Summer 1964), 136–64.
Wasson, Ben, *Count No 'Count: Flashbacks to Faulkner* (Jackson, Miss., 1983).
Webb, James W. and Green, A. Wigfall, *William Faulkner of Oxford* (Baton Rouge, La, 1965).
Wells, Dean Faulkner and Lawrence, 'The Trains Belonged to Everybody: Faulkner as Ghost Writer', *Southern Review*, XII (Autumn 1976), 864–71.
Wilde, Meta Carpenter and Borsten, Orin, *A Loving Gentleman: The Love Story of William Faulkner and Meta Carpenter* (New York, 1976).

VI WILLIAM FAULKNER: MANUSCRIPT COLLECTIONS

William Faulkner Foundation Collection, Special Collections, Alderman Library, University of Virginia, Charlottesville.

Louis Daniel Brodsky Collection, Kent Library, Southeastern Missouri State University, Cape Girardeau.
Humanities Research Centre, University of Texas, Austin.
William B. Wisdom Collection, Howard-Tilton Memorial Library, Tulane University, New Orleans, Louisiana.
Rowan Oak Papers, Special Collections Department, John Davis Williams Library, University of Mississippi, Oxford.
Berg Collection, New York Public Library.
Beinecke Rare Books and Manuscript Library, Yale University, New Haven, Connecticut.
Princeton University Library.

Material relating to the Falkner family and local history is also to be found in:
Special Collections Department, John Davis Williams Library, University of Mississippi, Oxford
Ripley Public Library, Ripley, Mississippi
Mississippi Department of Archives and History, Jackson
Lafayette County Courthouse, Oxford, Mississippi
Tippah County Courthouse, Ripley, Mississippi

VII   Other Works Cited

Abrams, Robert and Levine, Lawrence L. (eds), *The Shaping of Twentieth-century America* (Boston Mass., 1971).
Althusser, Louis, *Lenin and Philosophy, and Other Essays*, trans. Ben Brewster (London, 1977).
Andrews, Sidney, *The South Since the War: As Shown by Fourteen Weeks of Observation and Travel in Georgia and the Carolinas* (Boston, Mass., 1866).
Andrews, William L., *The Literary Career of Charles W. Chesnutt* (Baton Rouge, La, 1980).
Arato, A. and Gebhardt, E. (eds), *The Essential Frankfurt School Reader* (New York, 1978).
Arnett, Alex M., *The Populist Movement in Georgia* (New York, 1922).
Arpad, Joseph J., 'William Faulkner's Legendary Novels: the Snopes Trilogy', *Mississippi Quarterly*, XXI (Summer 1969).
Baker, James L., 'The Symbolic Extension of Yoknapatawpha County', *Arizona Quarterly*, VIII (1952).
Bakhtin, Mikhail, *The Dialogic Imagination*, ed. and trans. Caryl Emerson and Michael Holquist (Austin, Texas, 1981).
——, *Problems of Dostoevsky's Poetics*, ed. and trans. Caryl Emerson (Manchester, 1984).
——, *Problems of Dostoevsky's Poetics*, trans. W.W. Rotsel (Ann Arbor, Mich., 1973).
——, *Rabelais and His World*, trans. Helene Iswolsky (Cambridge, Mass., 1968).
——, *Speech Genres and Other Late Essays*, trans. Vern W. McGee (Austin, Texas, 1986).
——/ Medvedev, P.N., *The Formal Method in Literary Scholarship*, trans. Albert J. Wehrle (Baltimore, Md, 1978).
——/ Volosinov, V.N., *Freudianism: A Marxist Critique*, trans. I.R. Titunik (New York, 1976).
——/——, *Marxism and the Philosophy of Language*, trans. Ladislaw Matejka and I.R. Titunik (Cambridge, Mass., 1986).

Barthes, Roland, *Mythologies*, sel. and trans. Annette Lavers (London, 1977).

Bassett, John (ed.), *William Faulkner: The Critical Heritage* (London, 1975).

Beauvoir, Simone de, *The Second Sex*, trans. H.M. Parshley (New York, 1968).

Beck, Warren, *Faulkner* (Madison, Wis., 1976).

——, *Man in Motion* (Madison, Wis., 1961).

Benjamin, Walter, 'The Author as Producer', in A. Arato and E. Gebhardt (eds), *The Essential Frankfurt School Reader* (New York, 1978).

Bezzerides, A.J., *William Faulkner: A Life on Paper* (Jackson, Miss., 1980).

Billington, Monroe Lee, *The American South: A Brief History* (New York, 1971).

Bleikasten André, 'For/Against an Ideological Reading', in Michel Gresset and Patrick Samway (eds), *Faulkner and Idealism: Perspectives from Paris* (Jackson, Miss., 1983).

——, *The Ink of Melancholy: Faulkner's Novels from 'The Sound and the Fury' to 'Light in August'* (Bloomington, Ind., 1990).

——, '*Light in August*: the Closed Society and its Subjects', in Michael Millgate (ed.), *New Essays on 'Light in August'* (Cambridge, 1987).

——, *The Most Splendid Failure: Faulkner's 'The Sound and the Fury'* (Bloomington, Ind., 1976).

Bloom, Harold (ed.), *Modern Critical Views: William Faulkner* (New York, 1986).

Blotner, Joseph, *Faulkner: A Biography*, 2 vols (New York, 1974).

——, *Faulkner: A Biography*, one-volume edn (New York, 1984).

Booth, Wayne, *The Rhetoric of Fiction* (Chicago, Ill., 1961).

Bourdieu, Pierre, *Outline of a Theory of a Practice*, trans. Richard Nice (Cambridge, 1977).

Bradbury, Malcolm and Temperley, Howard (eds), *An Introduction to American Studies* (London, 1981).

Brooks, Cleanth, *William Faulkner: First Encounters* (New Haven, Conn., 1983).

——, *William Faulkner: Toward Yoknapatawpha and Beyond* (New Haven, Conn., 1978).

——, *William Faulkner: The Yoknapatawpha Country* (New Haven, Conn., 1963).

Brooks, Peter, *Reading for the Plot* (New York, 1984).

Brown, Calvin, 'Sanctuary: from Confrontation to Peaceful Void', *Mosaic*, VII (Spring 1977).

Brown, William R., 'Faulkner's Paradox in Pathology and Salvation: *Sanctuary, Light in August, Requiem for a Nun*', *Texas Studies in Literature and Language*, IX (Autumn 1967).

Butterworth, A. Keen, *A Critical and Textual Study of Faulkner's 'A Fable'* (Ann Arbor, Mich., 1983).

Carter, Hodding, 'Faulkner and his Folk', *Princeton University Library Chronicle*, XVIII (Spring 1957).

Cash, Wilbur J., *The Mind of the South* (New York, 1941).

Catton, William and Bruce, *Two Roads to Sumter* (New York, 1963).

Cixous, Hélène, and Clément, Cathérine, *La jeune née* (Paris, 1975).

Coindreau, Maurice, 'Préface', *Le bruit et la fureur* (1938); trans. George M. Reeves, 'Preface to *The Sound and the Fury*', *Mississippi Quarterly*, XIX (Summer 1966).

Collingwood, R.G., *The Idea of History* (1946; New York, 1962).

Cook, Sylvia Jenkins, *From Tobacco Road to Route 66: The Southern Poor White in Fiction* (Chapel Hill, N.C., 1976).

Cowley, Malcolm, 'In Which Mr. Faulkner Translates Past into Present', *New York Herald Tribune Book Review*, 30 September 1951.

Craven, Avery O., *Civil War in the Making, 1815–1860* (Baton Rouge, La, 1961).

——, *The Coming of the Civil War* (Chicago, Ill., 1957).

——, *The Growth of Southern Nationalism 1846–1861* (1953), vol. VI of Wendell H. Stephenson and E. Merton Coulter (eds), *A History of the South*, 10 vols (Baton Rouge, La, 1947–67).

Cypher, James R., 'The Tangled Sexuality of Temple Drake', *American Imago*, XIX (1962).

Dardis, Tom, *Some Time in the Sun* (New York, 1976).

Davis, Thadious M., *Faulkner's 'Negro': Art and the Southern Context* (Baton Rouge, La, 1983).

Dawson, Richard M., *American Folklore* (Chicago, Ill., 1954).

——, *Jonathan Draws a Long Bow* (Cambridge, Mass., 1946).

Donaldson, Susan, 'Gender and the Profession of Letters in the South', in Lothar Hönnighausen and Valeria Lerda (eds), *Rewriting the South: History and Fiction* (Tübingen, 1993).

Douglas, Mary, *Implicit Meanings* (London, 1975).

——, *Purity and Danger: An Analysis of the Concepts of Pollution and Taboo* (1966; London, 1984).

Duvall, John N., *Faulkner's Marginal Couple: Invisible, Outlaw, and Unspeakable Communities* (Austin, Texas, 1990).

Early, James, *The Making of 'Go Down, Moses'* (Dallas, Texas, 1972).

Fadiman, Regina K., *Faulkner's 'Light in August': A Description and Interpretation of the Revisions* (Charlottesville, Va, 1975).

Faulkner, John, *Men Working* (New York, 1941).

Fear, Jacqueline and McNeil, Helen, 'The Twenties', in Malcolm Bradbury and Howard Temperley (eds), *An Introduction to American Studies* (London, 1981).

Fisher, Carl, *A Critical and Textual Study of William Faulkner's 'Light in August'* (Michigan University Microfilms International, 1972).

Fitzgerald, F. Scott, 'Echoes of the Jazz Age', in *The Crack-up*, ed. Edmund Wilson (New York, 1956).

Floan, Howard R., *The South in Northern Eyes, 1831–1861* (New York, 1958).

Foucault, Michel, *Discipline and Punish*, trans. Alan Sheridan (New York, 1979).

Fowler, Doreen, 'Joe Christmas and "Womanshenegro"', in Doreen Fowler and Ann Abadie (eds), *Faulkner and Women* (Jackson, Miss., 1985).

——and Abadie, Ann (eds), *Faulkner and Race* (Jackson, Miss., 1987).

——, *Faulkner and the Southern Renaissance* (Jackson, Miss., 1982).

——, *Faulkner and Women* (Jackson, Miss., 1985).

Freud, Sigmund, *Introductory Lectures on Psychoanalysis*, trans. and ed. James Strachey (New York, 1966).

Gaines, Francis Pendleton, *The Southern Plantation: A Study in the Development and Accuracy of a Tradition* (New York, 1924).

Gallop, Jane, *The Daughter's Seduction* (Ithaca, N.Y., 1982).

Gardiner, Harold C. (ed.), *Fifty Years of the American Novel: A Christian Appraisal* (New York, 1968).

Gastil, Raymond, 'Homicide and a Regional Culture of Violence', *American Sociological Review*, XXXVI (June 1971).

Genovese, Eugene, *Roll, Jordan, Roll: The World the Slaves Made* (1974; New York, 1976).

Godden, Richard, 'Call Me Nigger! Race and Speech in *Light in August*', *Journal of American Studies*, XIX (Summer 1980).

Goldmann, Lucien, *The Hidden God*, trans. Philip Thody (London, 1956).

Gray, Richard, *The Literature of Memory: Modern Writers of the American South* (London, 1977).

——, *Writing the South: Ideas of an American Region* (Cambridge, 1986).

Grayson, William J., *The Hireling and the Slave, Chicora, and Other Poems* (Charleston, S.C., 1856).

Gregory, Eileen, 'Faulkner's Typescript of *The Town*', *Mississippi Quarterly*, XXVI (Summer 1973).

Gresset, Michel, *Fascination: Faulkner's Fiction, 1919–1936*, adapted from the French by Thomas West (Durham, N.C., 1989).

—— and Samway, Patrick (eds), *Faulkner and Idealism: Perspectives from Paris* (Jackson, Miss., 1983).

Grimwood, Michael, *Heart in Conflict: Faulkner's Struggles with Vocation* (Athens, Ga, 1987).

Gross, Beverley, 'Form and Fulfillment in *The Sound and the Fury*', *Modern Language Quarterly*, XXIX (December 1968).

Guerard, Albert Jr, 'The Misogynous Vision as High Art: Faulkner's *Sanctuary*', *Southern Review*, XII (Winter 1976).

Gwin, Minrose, *The Feminine and Faulkner* (Knoxville, Tenn., 1989).

Hammond, James Henry, 'Hammond's Letters on Slavery', in *The Pro-slavery Argument: As Maintained by the Most Distinguished Writers of the Southern States* (Charleston, S.C., 1852).

Hammond, Matthew B., *The Cotton Industry: An Essay on American Economic History* (New York, 1897).

Harrington, Evans and Abadie, Ann (eds), *Faulkner, Modernism and Film* (Jackson, Miss., 1978).

——, *The Maker and the Myth: Faulkner and Yoknapatawpha* (Jackson, Miss., 1975).

——, *The South and Faulkner's Yoknapatawpha: The Actual and the Apocryphal* (Jackson, Miss., 1977).

Harrington, Gary, *Faulkner's Fables of Creativity: The Non-Yoknapatawpha Novels* (London, 1990).

Harris, George Washington, *Sut Lovingood: Yarns Spun by a 'Natural Born Durn'd Fool'* (New York, 1867).

Hart, Clive, *The Dream of Flight* (London, 1972).

——, *The Prehistory of Flight* (Berkeley, Cal., 1985).

Hawkins, E.O. Jr, 'Jane Cook and Cecilia Farmer', *Mississippi Quarterly*, XVIII (Summer 1965).

Heilman, Robert, 'Schools for Girls', *Sewanee Review*, LX (Spring 1952).

Hoffman, Frederick J., *The Twenties: American Writing in the Postwar Decade* (New York, 1949).

—— and Vickery, Olga (eds), *William Faulkner: Three Decades of Criticism* (New York, 1963).

Hönnighausen, Lothar, *William Faulkner: The Art of Stylization in Early Graphic and Literary Work* (Cambridge, 1986).

——(ed.), *Faulkner's Discourse: An International Symposium* (Tübingen, 1989).

—— and Lerda, Valeria (eds), *Rewriting the South: History and Fiction* (Tübingen, 1993).

Howard, Jean E., 'Crossdressing, the Theatre and Gender Struggle in Early Modern England', *Shakespeare Quarterly*, XXXIX (Summer 1988).

Hughes, Henry, *A Treatise on Sociology, Theoretical and Practical* (Philadelphia, Penn., 1854).

Huizinga, J.M., *The Waning of the Middle Ages* (New York, 1954).

Irigiray, Luce, *Ce sexe qui n'en est pas un* (Paris, 1977).

——, *Spéculum de l'autre femme* (Paris, 1974).

Irwin, John, T., *Doubling and Incest/Repetition and Revenge: A Speculative Reading of Faulkner* (Baltimore, Md, 1978).

James, Henry, *The Art of the Novel*, ed. R.P. Blackmur (New York, 1942).

Jameson, Fredric, *Marxism and Form* (Princeton, N.J., 1971).

——, 'Metacommentary', *PMLA*, LXXXVI (Spring 1971).

——, *The Political Unconscious: Narrative as a Socially Symbolic Act* (Ithaca, N.Y., 1981).

——, 'Postmodernism, or the Cultural Logic of Late Capitalism', *New Left Review*, CXLVI (July–August 1984).

Jenkins, Lee, *Faulkner and Black–White Relationships* (New York, 1981).

Jones, Anne Goodwyn, *Tomorrow is Another Day: The Woman Writer in the South 1859–1936* (Baton Rouge, La, 1981).

Karl, Frederick R., *William Faulkner: American Writer* (London, 1989).

Kawin, Bruce F., *Faulkner and Film* (New York, 1978).

——, 'Faulkner's Film Career: the Years with Hawks', in Evans Harrington and Ann Abadie (eds), *Faulkner, Modernism and Film* (Jackson, Miss., 1978).

——, 'The Montage Element in Faulkner's Film', in Evans Harrington and Ann Abadie (eds), *Faulkner, Modernism and Film* (Jackson, Miss., 1978).

Kazin, Alfred, *On Native Grounds: An Interpretation of American Prose Literature* (New York, 1942).

Keefer, Fredrick T., 'William Faulkner's *Sanctuary*: a Myth Examined', *Twentieth Century Literature*, XV (Spring 1969).

King, Edward, *The Southern States of North America* (London, 1875).

King, Richard, *A Southern Renaissance: The Cultural Awakening of the American South, 1930–1955* (New York, 1980).

Kirby, Jack Temple, *Media-made Dixie: The South in the American Imagination* (Baton Rouge, La, 1978).

Kohler, Dayton, 'William Faulkner and his Social Conscience', *College English*, XI (December 1949).

Kreisworth, Martin, *William Faulkner: The Making of a Novelist* (Athens, Ga, 1983).

Kristeva, Julia, 'Il n'y a pas de maître à langage', *Nouvelle revue de pyschoanalyse*, XX (Autumn 1979).

——, *La révolution du langage poétique* (Paris, 1984).

——, 'Stabat Mater', in Susan Suleiman (ed.), *The Female Body in Western Culture: Contemporary Perspectives* (Cambridge, Mass., 1984).

Kubie, Lawrence, 'William Faulkner's *Sanctuary*', in Robert Penn Warren (ed.), *Faulkner: A Collection of Critical Essays* (Englewood Cliffs, N.J., 1966).

Lacan, Jacques, *Ecrits: A Selection*, trans. Alan Sheridan (London, 1977).

Leonard, James S., Tenney, Thomas A. and Davis, Thadious (eds), *Satire or Evasion? Black Perspectives on 'Huckleberry Finn'* (Durham, N.C., 1992).

Lewis, R.W.B., *The American Adam: Innocence, Tragedy, and Tradition in the Nineteenth Century* (Chicago, Ill., 1955).

——, 'The Hero in the New World: William Faulkner's "The Bear"', *Kenyon Review*, XIII (Autumn 1951).

Lhamon, W.T., '*Pylon*: the Ylimaf of New Valois', *Western Humanities Review*, XXIV (Summer 1970).

Lind, Ilse D., 'The Effect of Painting on Faulkner's Poetic Form', in Evans Harrington and Ann Abadie (eds), *Faulkner, Modernism and Film* (Jackson, Miss., 1978).

Longstreet, Augustus Baldwin, *Georgia Scenes: Characters, Incidents etc., in the First Half-Century of the Republic* (New York, 1835).

Lukács, Georg, *The Historical Novel,* trans. Hannah and Stanley Mitchell (1962; London, 1969).

Lynn, Kenneth, *Mark Twain and Southwestern Humor* (Boston, Mass., 1966).

Macherey, Pierre, *A Theory of Literary Production,* trans. Geoffrey Wall (London, 1978).

Marcuse, Herbert, *Eros and Civilization: A Philosophical Inquiry into Freud* (1955; Boston, Mass., 1966).

Marvin, John R., 'Pylon: the Definition of Sacrifice', *Faulkner Studies,* I (Spring 1952).

Matthews, John T., *The Play of Faulkner's Language* (Ithaca, N.Y., 1982).

McHaney, Thomas L., 'The Elmer Papers: Faulkner's Comic Portraits of the Artist', *Mississippi Quarterly,* XXVI (Summer 1973).

——, 'Faulkner Borrows from the Mississippi Guide', *Mississippi Quarterly,* XIX (Summer 1966).

——, *William Faulkner's 'The Wild Palms'* (Jackson, Miss., 1975).

Mc Kinney, John C. and Bourque, Linda B., 'The Changing South: National Incorporation of a Region', *American Sociological Review,* XXXVI (June 1971).

McLuhan, Marshall, 'John Dos Passos: Technique vs. Sensibility', in Harold C. Gardiner, (ed.), *Fifty Years of the American Novel: A Christian Appraisal* (New York, 1968).

Meats, Stephen, 'Who Killed Joanna Burden?', *Mississippi Quarterly,* XXIV (Summer 1971).

Meriwether, James B., 'Faulkner, Lost and Found', *New York Times Book Review,* 5 November 1972.

——, 'Faulkner's "Mississippi"', *Mississippi Quarterly,* XXV (Spring 1972).

——, 'The Novel Faulkner Never Wrote: His *Golden Book* or *Doomsday Book*', *American Literature,* XLII (Spring 1970).

Miller, David, 'Faulkner's Women', *Modern Fiction Studies,* X (Summer 1967).

Millgate, Michael, *The Achievement of William Faulkner* (London, 1966).

——, 'Faulkner on the Literature of the First World War', *Mississippi Quarterly,* XXVI (Summer 1972).

——, ' "The Firmament of Man's History": Faulkner's Treatment of the Past', in *'Faulkner and History': Papers of the Quarterly's 1971 S.M.C.L.A. Symposium,* Supplement to *Mississippi Quarterly,* XXV (Spring 1972).

——(ed.), *New Essays on 'Light in August'* (Cambridge, 1987).

Minter, David, *William Faulkner: His Life and Work* (Baltimore, Md, 1980).

Mixon, Wayne, *Southern Writers and the New South Movement 1865–1913* (Chapel Hill, N.C., 1980).

Moreland, Richard C., *Faulkner and Modernism: Rereading and Rewriting* (Madison, Wis., 1990).

Morris, Wesley and Barbara Alverson, *Reading Faulkner* (Madison, Wis., 1989).

Mortimer, Gail, *Faulkner's Rhetoric of Loss* (Austin, Texas, 1983).

Muhlenfeld, Elizabeth (ed.), *William Faulkner's 'Absalom, Absalom!': A Critical Casebook* (New York, 1984).

Nilon, Charles H., *Faulkner and the Negro* (New York, 1965).

Nye, R.B. and Morpurgo, J.E., *A History of the United States* (London, 1964).

O'Brien, Michael, *The Idea of the American South, 1920–1941* (Baltimore, Md, 1979).

——, *Rethinking the South: Essays in Intellectual History* (Baltimore, Md, 1988).

Page, Sally R., *Faulkner's Women: Characterization and Meaning* (Deland, Fla, 1972).

Page, Thomas Nelson, *In Ole Virginia; or, Marse Chan and Other Stories* (London, 1899).

——, *On Newfound River* (London, 1891).

——, *Red Rock: A Chronicle of Reconstruction* (London, 1898).

Page, Walter Hines, *The Life and Letters of Walter Hines Page*, 2 vols (New York, 1922).

Parker, Robert Dale, *Faulkner and the Novelistic Imagination* (Urbana, Ill., 1985).

Pearson, Norman Holmes, 'Faulkner's Three Evening Suns', *Yale University Library Gazette*, xxi (October 1954).

Pikoulis, John, *The Art of William Faulkner* (London, 1982).

Pilkington, John, *The Heart of Yoknapatawpha* (Jackson, Miss., 1981).

Polk, Noel, 'The Dungeon Was Mother Herself: William Faulkner: 1927–1931', in Doreen Fowler and Ann Abadie (eds), *New Directions in Faulkner Studies* (Jackson, Miss., 1984).

——, *Faulkner's 'Requiem for a Nun': A Critical Study* (Bloomington, Ind., 1981).

——, 'The Space between "*Sanctuary*"', in Michel Gresset and Noel Polk (eds), *Intertextuality in Faulkner* (Jackson, Miss., 1986).

——, 'Woman and the Feminine in *A Fable*', in Doreen Fowler and Ann Abadie (eds), *Faulkner and Women* (Jackson, Miss., 1985).

Porter, Carolyn, *Seeing and Being: The Plight of the Participant Observer in Emerson, James, Adams, and Faulkner* (Middletown, Conn., 1981).

Pro-slavery Argument: As Maintained by the Most Distinguished Writers of the Southern States (Charleston, S.C., 1852).

Putzel, Max, *Genius of Place: William Faulkner's Triumphant Beginnings* (Baton Rouge, La, 1985).

Reed, Joseph W., *Faulkner's Narrative* (New Haven, Conn., 1973).

Rhodes, Pamela and Godden, Richard, '*The Wild Palms*: Faulkner's Hollywood Novel', *Essays in Poetics*, x (Summer 1985).

Richards, Lewis A., 'Sex under *The Wild Palms* and a Moral Question', *Arizona Quarterly*, xxviii (Spring 1972).

Roberts, Diane, 'A Precarious Pedestal: the Confederate Woman in Faulkner's *The Unvanquished*', *Journal of American Studies*, xxvi (Summer 1992).

Ross, Stephen B., *Fiction's Inexhaustible Voice: Speech and Writing in Faulkner* (Athens, Ga, 1989).

——, 'Jason Compson and Sut Lovingood: Southwestern Humor as Stream of Consciousness', *Studies in the Novel*, viii (Summer 1976).

Rubin, Louis. D. Jr, *A Gallery of Southerners* (Baton Rouge, La, 1982).

Ruppersburg, Hugh, 'The Narrative Structure of Faulkner's *Requiem for a Nun*', *Mississippi Quarterly*, xxx (Summer 1978).

Sartre, Jean-Paul, *Baudelaire* (Paris, 1947).

——, 'Time in Faulkner: *The Sound and the Fury*', in Frederick Hoffman and Olga Vickery (eds), *William Faulkner: Three Decades of Criticism* (New York, 1963).

Schendler, Sylvan, 'William Faulkner's *A Fable*' (Northwestern University dissertation, 1974).

Schoenberg, Estella, *Old Tales and Talking: Quentin Compson in William Faulkner's 'Absalom, Absalom!' and Related Works* (Jackson, Miss., 1975).

Schwartz, Lawrence H., *Creating Faulkner's Reputation: The Politics of Modern Literary Criticism* (Knoxville, Tenn., 1989).

Scott, Ann Firor, *The Southern Lady: From Pedestal to Politics* (Chicago, Ill., 1970).

——, 'Women in the South: History as Fiction, Fiction as History', in Lothar Hönnighausen and Valeria Lerda (eds), *Rewriting the South: History and Fiction* (Tübingen, 1993).

Sensibar, Judith L., *The Origins of Faulkner's Art* (Austin, Texas, 1984).

Shannon, Frederick A., *The Farmer's Last Frontier: Agriculture 1866–1897* (New York, 1945).

Simkins, Francis B. and Roland, Charles R., *A History of the South* (1953; rev. edn, New York, 1972).

Simpson, Lewis P., 'Sex and History: Origins of Faulkner's Apocrypha', in Evans Harrington and Ann Abadie (eds), *The Maker and the Myth: Faulkner and Yoknapatawpha* (Jackson, Miss., 1975).

Skates, John Ray, *Mississippi* (New York, 1979).

Smith, Francis Hopkinson, *Colonel Carter of Cartersville* (London, 1891).

Snead, James A., *Figures of Division: William Faulkner's Major Novels* (New York, 1986).

Somers, Robert, *The Southern States since the War, 1870–1871* (London, 1871).

Stephenson, Wendell H. and Coulter, E. Merton (eds), *A History of the South*, 10 vols (Baton Rouge, La, 1947–67).

Stott, William, *Documentary Expression in Thirties America* (1973; rev. edn, Chicago, Ill., 1986).

Suleiman, Susan R. (ed.), *The Female Body in Western Culture: Contemporary Perspectives* (Cambridge, Mass., 1986).

Sundquist, Eric J., *Faulkner: The House Divided* (Baltimore, Md, 1983).

Tallack, Douglas, *Twentieth-century America: The Intellectual and Cultural Context* (London, 1991).

Tanner, Tony, *City of Words: American Fiction 1950–1970* (London, 1971).

——, *The Reign of Wonder: Naivety and Reality in American Literature* (Cambridge, 1956).

Tate, Allen, *Essays of Four Decades* (New York, 1969).

Taylor, Nancy Drew, 'The Dramatic Productions of *Requiem for a Nun*', *Mississippi Quarterly*, xx (Summer 1967).

Taylor, Walter R., *Faulkner's Search for a South* (Urbana, Ill., 1983).

Taylor, William R., *Cavalier and Yankee: The Old South and American National Character* (London, 1967).

Theweleit, Klaus, *Male Fantasies*, trans. Stephen Conway with Erica Carter and Chris Turner (Cambridge, 1987).

Tindall, George B., *The Emergence of the New South, 1913–1943* (1967), vol. x of Wendell H. Stephenson and E. Merton Coulter (eds), *A History of the South*, 10 vols (Baton Rouge, La, 1947–67).

Todorov, Tzvetan, *Mikhail Bakhtin: The Dialogical Principle* (Manchester, 1984).

Toolan, Michael J., *The Stylistics of Fiction: A Literary-Linguistic Approach* (London, 1990).

Torchiana, Donald M., 'Faulkner's "Pylon" and the Structure of Modernity', *Modern Fiction Studies*, iii (Winter 1957–8).

Tuck, Dorothy, *A Handbook of Faulkner* (London, 1965).

Tucker, Nathaniel Beverley, *The Partisan Leader: A Tale of the Future* (1836; Richmond, Va, 1862).

Turner, Lorenzo Dow, *Anti-slavery Sentiment in American Literature Prior to 1865* (Washington, 1929).

Urgo, Joseph R., 'Temple Drake's Truthful Perjury: Rethinking Faulkner's *Sanctuary*', *American Literature*, lv (Spring 1983).

USA Bureau of Census, *Historical Statistics of the United States, Colonial Times to 1957* (Washington, D.C., 1960).

Vickery, Olga, *The Novels of William Faulkner* (Baton Rouge, La, 1964).

Volpe, Edmond, L., *A Reader's Guide to William Faulkner* (London, 1964).

Wadlington, Warwick, *Reading Faulknerian Tragedy* (Ithaca, N.Y., 1987).

Ward, John William, 'The Meaning of Lindbergh's Flight', in Robert Abrams and Lawrence Levine (eds), *The Shaping of Twentieth-century America* (Boston, Mass., 1971).

Warren, Robert Penn (ed.), *Faulkner: A Collection of Critical Essays* (Englewood Cliffs, N.J., 1966).

Watson, James G., 'Literary Self-criticism: Faulkner in Fiction on Fiction', *Southern Quarterly*, xx (Fall 1981).

——, *William Faulkner, Letters and Fictions* (Austin, Texas, 1987).

Weinstein, Philip M., *Faulkner's Subject: A Cosmos No One Owns* (Cambridge, 1992).

Wells, Dean Faulkner, 'Dean Swift Faulkner: a Biographical Study' (University of Mississippi MA thesis, 1975).

White, Hayden, *Tropics of Discourse: Essays in Cultural Criticism* (Baltimore, Md, 1978).

White, Walter, *Rope and Faggot: A Biography of Judge Lynch* (New York, 1929).

Williams, David, *Faulkner's Women: The Myth and the Muse* (Montreal, 1977).

Williams, Raymond, *Marxism and Literature* (New York, 1977).

Williamson, Joel, *William Faulkner and Southern History* (New York, 1993).

Wilson, Edmund, *Classics and Commercials* (New York, 1950).

Wittenberg, Judith B., 'William Faulkner: a Feminist Consideration', in Harold Bloom (ed.), *Modern Critical Views: William Faulkner* (New York, 1986).

——, *William Faulkner: The Transfiguration of Biography* (Lincoln, Neb., 1979).

——, 'The Women of *Light in August*', in Michael Millgate (ed.), *New Essays on 'Light in August'* (Cambridge, 1987).

Woodward, Comer Vann, *The Origins of the New South 1872–1913* (1951), vol. IX of Wendell H. Stephenson and E. Merton Coulter (eds), *A History of the South*, 10 vols (Baton Rouge, La, 1947–67).

——, *The Strange Career of Jim Crow* (New York, 1955).

Wright, Elizabeth, *Psychoanalytic Criticism: Theory in Practice* (London, 1984).

Wyatt-Brown, Bertram, *Southern Honor: Ethics and Behavior in the Old South* (New York, 1982).

X, Malcolm, with the assistance of Haley, Alex, *The Autobiography of Malcolm X* (1965; London, 1968).

Index